SITUATION SELECTION REGIME AT THE INTERNATIONAL CRIMINAL COURT

School of Human Rights Research Series, Volume 82.

The titles published in this series are listed at the end of this volume.

SITUATION SELECTION REGIME AT THE INTERNATIONAL CRIMINAL COURT

Law, Policy, Practice

Mohammad Hadi Zakerhossein

intersentia
Cambridge – Antwerp – Portland

Intersentia Ltd
Sheraton House | Castle Park
Cambridge | CB3 0AX | United Kingdom
Tel.: +44 1223 370 170 | Fax: +44 1223 370 169
Email: mail@intersentia.co.uk
www.intersentia.com | www.intersentia.co.uk

Distribution for the UK and Ireland:
NBN International
Airport Business Centre, 10 Thornbury Road
Plymouth, PL6 7 PP
United Kingdom
Tel.: +44 1752 202 301 | Fax: +44 1752 202 331
Email: orders@nbninternational.com

Distribution for Europe and all other countries:
Intersentia Publishing nv
Groenstraat 31
2640 Mortsel
Belgium
Tel.: +32 3 680 15 50 | Fax: +32 3 658 71 21
Email: mail@intersentia.be

Distribution for the USA and Canada:
International Specialized Book Services
920 NE 58th Ave. Suite 300
Portland, OR 97213
USA
Tel.: +1 800 944 6190 (toll free) | Fax: +1 503 280 8832
Email: info@isbs.com

ISBN 978-1-78068-618-9
D/2017/7849/133
NUR 828

British Library Cataloguing in Publication Data. A catalogue record for this book is available from the British Library.

CONTENTS

Acknowledgment xi
Abbreviations xiii

General Introduction 1

1. Contextualization of the Problem 1
2. Questions 4
3. Methodology 5
   3.1. Descriptive Part 5
   3.2. Normative Part 6
      3.2.1. Functional Approach to the ICC 7
      3.2.2. In Search of a Theory for the Court 10
      3.2.3. Definition of Expressivism 15
4. Outline 18

PART ONE. FORMULATING THE CONCEPT OF SITUATION IN THE ROME STATUTE SENSE 23

Chapter I
Situation v. Case 27

1. Dichotomy between Situation and Case 27
2. Linkage between Situation and Case 30
3. Reasons behind the Adoption of a Situation-Oriented Procedure 31

Chapter II
Defining Elements of the Notion of a Situation 37

1. The Jurisdictional Element of a Situation 37
2. The Contextual Element of a Situation 38
   2.1. Crisis as the Context of Situations 38
   2.2. Connection between Contextual Element of Crimes and Contextual Element of Situations 40
      2.2.1. Context of War Crimes 40
      2.2.2. Context of Crimes against Humanity 42
      2.2.3. Context of Genocide 45

2.3. Situational Contextual Element in Practice. 47
2.4. Functions of Situational Context. 49

PART TWO. SITUATION SELECTION PROCESS 53

Chapter I
Trigger Mechanism. 57

1. State Referrals. 59
1.1. Making a Referral as a Right for All States Parties. 59
1.2. The Phenomenon of Self-Referral 61
1.2.1. The Emergence of Self-Referrals 62
1.2.2. Benefits of a Self-Referral for the Court's Prosecutor 64
1.2.3. Self-Referrals under Criticism. 66
1.3. Specificity 69
2. The UN Security Council Referral 69
2.1. Legal Basis for UNSC Referrals. 70
2.2. Mutual Benefits 73
2.3. Privileges of the Security Council Referrals 76
2.4. Restrictions on Making a Referral by the UNSC 80
2.5. Security Council Referrals in Practice 82
2.5.1. Situation in Darfur, Sudan. 82
2.5.2. Situation in Libya. 84
2.5.3. Article 16 in Action. 85
3. Communications 86
3.1. Procedural Aspects of Communications 87
3.2. Prosecutor *PROPRIO MOTU* Power. 89
4. Declarations of acceptance under Article 12(3) 91
4.1. Difference between Referrals and Declarations 92
4.2. Declarations in Practice 94

Chapter II
Identification Stage. 97

1. Identification in the Context of Communications. 97
1.1. Forming a Situation from Communications. 97
1.2. ICC and the Situation of ISIS in Iraq and Syria 99
1.3. The End of the Identification Stage. 103
2. Identification in the Context of Referrals 106

Chapter III
Preliminary Examination 111

1. Time Frame 114
2. Information in the Preliminary Examination 117
3. Scope of Preliminary Examination 121
4. Evidentiary Threshold 124

Chapter IV
Making a Decision on the Situation Selection 131

1. Opening an Investigation 131
   1.1. Investigation of Referrals 132
      1.1.1. Announcement of Decision 133
      1.1.2. Article 18 Mechanism 135
         1.1.2.1. Making a Challenge under Article 18 135
         1.1.2.2. Scope of Article 18 138
   1.2. Investigation of Communications 139
      1.2.1. Judicial Authorization 139
      1.2.2. Victims' Participation 142
         1.2.2.1. Participatory Right of Victims 142
            1.2.2.1.1. The Victims' Participation Procedure 145
            1.2.2.1.2. Participation in Situational Phase 147
      1.2.3. Judicial Decision on the Prosecutor's Request 153
2. Decision Not to Open an Investigation 153
   2.1. Rejection of Communications 153
   2.2. Rejection of Referrals 156

PART THREE. SITUATION SELECTION CRITERIA 161

Chapter I
Jurisdiction 165

1. The Court's Jurisdiction Basis 165
2. The Necessity of Jurisdiction's Satisfaction 168
3. Types of Jurisdiction 169
   3.1. Subject-Matter Jurisdiction 170
   3.2. Temporal Jurisdiction 175
   3.3. Territorial Jurisdiction 179
      3.3.1. The Priority of Territorial Jurisdiction 181
      3.3.2. The Scope of Territorial Jurisdiction 182
   3.4. Personal Jurisdiction 184
      3.4.1. The Vital Role of the Nationality Principle in Ending Impunity 185
      3.4.2. Immunities as an Exception to the Personal jurisdiction 187

3.4.2.1. Immunities at the ICC. 187
3.4.2.2. Cooperation Obligation and Immunities 191
3.4.2.3. The ICC Jurisprudence on Immunities 193

Chapter II
Admissibility 201

1. Conceptualization of Admissibility 201
1.1. Distinction between Admissibility and Jurisdiction 201
1.2. Admissibility and the Court's Selectivity. 203
1.3. From Situational Admissibility to Case Admissibility 204
1.4. Components of Admissibility 209
2. Sufficient Gravity Requirement. 211
2.1. Different Functions of Gravity in the Rome Statute. 211
2.2. Gravity as the Admissibility Threshold 214
2.3. Difference between Situational Gravity and Case Gravity 217
2.4. Criteria for Gravity Assessment 218
2.4.1. Scale of crimes 221
2.4.2. Impact of Crimes. 224
2.4.3. Nature of Crimes. 231
2.4.3.1. Thematic Prosecution 231
2.4.3.2. Criminal Themes at the ICC 232
2.4.3.3. Exercising Thematic Prosecution 238
2.4.4. Manner of Crimes' Commission 239
2.5. The Case Study of the Situation of Registered Vessel of the Comoros . . . 240
2.5.1. Description of the Case 241
2.5.2. Analysis of the Situation on Registered Vessel of the Comoros. . . 244
2.6. Big Fish Policy in Light of Gravity 247
3. Complementarity. 253
3.1. Theoretical Pillars of Complementarity. 256
3.2. Complementarity as Admissibility Rule 259
3.2.1. Defining Potential Cases for the Situational Complementarity Assessment 259
3.2.2. The Concept of Case in the Complementarity Assessment 263
3.2.2.1. The Same Conduct Test. 265
3.2.2.1.1. The Conduct Notion at the ICC Case Law. . 265
3.2.2.1.2. Narrow Interpretation of the Same Conduct Test. 274
3.2.2.1.3. Broad Interpretation of the Same Conduct Test. 279
3.2.2.1.4. Sentence-Based Approach Doctrine. 280
3.2.2.2. The Same Person Test 282
3.2.3. Situation of a State's Inaction. 283

3.2.3.1. Arguments Supporting Establishing the Inaction Test . 287
3.2.3.2. Proofs of Being Active 289
3.2.3.2.1. Features of Active National Proceedings . . . 289
3.2.3.2.2. Relevant Evidence to Prove Domestic Activity 293
3.2.3.3. Admissibility of Self-Referrals in light of the Inaction Test 295
3.3. Burden of Proof in the Complementarity Assessment 298
3.4. Genuineness Requirement for the Domestic Proceedings 300
3.5. Situation of State's Unwillingness 305
3.5.1. Due Process Framework in Determining Unwillingness 306
3.5.2. Shielding from Justice 311
3.5.3. Unjustified Delay in Delivering Justice 313
3.5.4. Impartiality and Independence of the Domestic Proceedings . . . 314
3.6. Situation of a State's Inability 315
3.6.1. The situation of Collapse of National Judicial System 316
3.6.2. Situation of Unavailability of the National Judicial System 320
3.6.2.1. Normativity of Unavailability Test 321
3.6.2.2. Legal Characterization: Ordinary Crimes or International Crimes 322
4. Availability of Situations 327

Chapter III
Interests of Justice 333

1. Exceptionality of the Interests of Justice Requirement 334
2. Distinction from the Admissibility Requirement 336
3. Necessity of Examination 338
4. A Concept without Definition 341
5. A Victim-Oriented Notion 342
6. A Context for the Applicability of the Interests of Justice: Justice or Peace 346
6.1. Justice Supporters 348
6.2. Peace Supporters 351
6.3. The Prosecutor Status Quo 354
6.4. Preliminary Examination as a Platform for a Plural Approach 358
6.5. Peace as a Tool for Justice 360
7. Decision Not to Initiate an Investigation 363
8. A Missing Monitoring System 366

PART FOUR. SITUATION SELECTION IN LIGHT OF EXPRESSIVISM....... 369

Chapter I
Conceptualization of Expressivism in the Context of the ICC.................. 371

1. Expressivism and its Beneficial Effects on Victims 372
   1.1. The Emergence of the Victims' Rights in the ICC 373
   1.2. Court's Messages for Victims...................................... 377
2. Expressivism Fosters the Positive Complementarity....................... 379
   2.1. Definition of Positive Complementarity 381
   2.2. Materializing Positive Complementarity............................ 383
      2.2.1. Encouragement 384
      2.2.2. Reverse Cooperation....................................... 385

Chapter II
Implications of Expressivism on the Situation Selection 389

1. Selection of a Situation for Conducting Preliminary Examination as a Platform to Serve Victims 389
2. Lenient Complementarity Assessment.................................. 394

CONCLUSION 401

1. 'Situation' as a Concept with an Ambiguous Definition.................... 401
2. Identification Stage: The Missing Phase at the ICC Architecture 403
3. Selecting a Situation for Highlighting a Forgotten Criminal Theme 403
4. Complementarity as Rule and Complementarity as Principle............... 404
5. No Harm to Victims Principle.. 406
6. A Need for Extending Judicial Review of the Prosecutor's Decisions......... 407
7. An Expressive Situation Selection...................................... 408
8. Implications of Designing an Expressive Situation Selection Regime 410
9. To conclude.. 412

Bibliography 413
ICC Case Tables 429
OTP Documents.. 437
About the Author 439

ACKNOWLEDGMENT

Spending five years at Tilburg Law School, besides visiting University of California Los Angeles, Middlesex University and Galway University, offered me the tremendous opportunity to write this book. In this regard, I have received enthusiastic support of many people, all of whom I owe sincere gratitude.

My supervisors Marc Groenhuijsen and Anne-Marie de Brouwer: I deeply appreciate all your whole-hearted backing and sincere belief in me. I feel fortunate to have had you. Thank you for your invaluable comments and excellent advice you have given me throughout the years and for giving me the space, courage and inspiration I needed to develop my ideas and broaden my knowledge. In addition, I must thank you for all your heartfelt sympathy and support to my personal life.

My colleagues from the Tilburg University's Department of Criminal Law: you made the time I spent working on my thesis enjoyable. Due to your kindness, I looked forward to each day I worked at my offices on the 8th floor in the M building. Thank you for all your companionship.

The reading committee: Professors Kooijmans, you have been a friend rather than a boss for me at Tilburg University before and during my teaching, van Genugten, Smeulers and Dr. Bevers, I always had your great support when I did an internship at the Office of the Prosecutor of the International Criminal Court under your supervision, thank you very much for providing me with your constructive and valuable feedback.

Last but not least, writing this thesis would have been impossible without the support of my parents and family. Fatemeh, you had the more difficult part throughout the years, but I did see nothing except for kind support and great encouragement. I am blessed to have you.

To the next generation, to Zeinab who owns my heart, may the world you grow up is a world without war and suffering and with peace and love. I believe we eventually see such a world.

ABBREVIATIONS

ASP	Assembly of States Parties
CAR	Central African Republic
DRC	Democratic Republic of Congo
HRW	Human Rights Watch
ICC	International Criminal Court
ICD	International Crime Division
ICJ	International Court of Justice
ICTR	International Criminal Tribunal for Rwanda
ICTY	International Criminal Tribunal for the former Yugoslavia
ILC	International Law Commission
IMT	International Military Tribunal
ISIS	Islamic State in Iraq and Syria
JCCD	Jurisdiction and Complementarity and Cooperation Division
LRA	Lord's Resistance Army
NGO	None-Governmental Organization
OTP	Office of the Prosecutor
PTC	Pre-Trial Chamber
RS	Rome Statute
SCSL	Special Court for Sierra Leone
STL	Special Tribunal for Lebanon
TFV	Trust Fund for Victims
TRC	Truth and Reconciliation Commission
UN	United Nations
UNSC	United Nations Security Council
UNSCR	United Nations Security Council Resolution
UNSG	United Nations Secretary-General

GENERAL INTRODUCTION

1. CONTEXTUALIZATION OF THE PROBLEM

In late 2016, the International Criminal Court (ICC, Court) faced a legitimacy crisis: a series of withdrawals by some African States from the Rome Statute surged. These States declared their intentions to terminate their memberships of the ICC. The relationship between the Court and Africa has been fragile over recent years.[1] Calls for mass withdrawals from the Rome Statute were first made by the African Union's Open-Ended Ministerial Committee of Ministers for Foreign Affairs on the ICC. The Committee was established pursuant to the decision of the African Union Assembly during its 25th Ordinary Session, which was held in Johannesburg, South Africa in June 2015.[2] The Open-Ended Committee is composed of Ethiopia, Chad, Burundi, Eritrea, South Sudan, Kenya, Libya, Sudan, Madagascar, Namibia, Zimbabwe and Senegal.[3] In April 2016, the Committee called for the African States Parties to the ICC to collectively withdraw from the Rome Statute, provided that the African demands would not be met.[4] African States had demanded, *inter alia,* recognition for immunity of sitting Heads of State. Two African Presidents have been targeted by the Court, Al Bashir (Sudan) and Kenyatta (Kenya). The Committee first tried to meet the United Nations Security Council (UNSC) to find a solution. However, this effort was not successful. Consequently, Burundi, Gambia and South Africa announced their decisions to leave the ICC. On 12 October 2016, the Parliament of the Republic of Burundi voted to support a plan to withdraw its country from the Rome Statute.[5] Later, Burundi informed the United Nations Secretary-General (UNSG) of its intention to leave the ICC. On 21 October 2016, South Africa announced that it had notified the

1 See: James Nyawo, Selective Enforcement and International Criminal Law, Intersentia, 2017.

2 African Union Assembly, Decision on the Update of the Commission on the Implementation of the Previous Decisions on the International Criminal Court, 2015, available at: www.jfjustice.net/wp-content/uploads/2015/06/Decision-on-the-update-of-the-AU-Commission-on-the-implementation-of-previous-decisions-on-the-International-Criminal-Court.pdf, last accessed at 4 June 2017.

3 All Africa, Africa: The Open-Ended Committee on ICC Meeting Held, 30 September 2015, available at: http://allafrica.com/stories/201510010723.html, last accessed at 4 June 2017.

4 Nyawo, 2017, p. 26, see *supra* note 1.

5 ICC, Press Release, Statement of the President of the Assembly of States Parties on the Process of Withdrawal from the Rome Statute by Burundi, 18 October 2016, available at: www.icc-cpi.int//Pages/item.aspx?name=pr1244, last accessed at 4 June 2017.

UNSG that it was withdrawing from the ICC.[6] Later, Gambia joined this course of withdrawals.[7]

The Fifteenth Session of the ICC Assembly of States Parties (ASP) that was held in November 2016 was considerably affected by the African countries' initiative against the Court. At the time, as the director of a Non-Governmental Organization, I had participated in the Session. I was witnessing how the regular topics in the Session were overshadowed by the African States' decisions. Universality has been one of the core aims of the ICC. In December 2006, the ICC ASP, through Resolution ICC-ASP/5/Res.3, adopted a Plan of Action for achieving universality of the Rome Statute, considering the universality of the Rome Statute is imperative to end impunity. States' withdrawal from the Court was about to hurt the legitimacy of the Court. The Court supporters were sincerely concerned. Nonetheless, the succession of withdrawals interrupted. Among those African States that had declared their intentions of leaving the Court, only Burundi preserved its status. In the meanwhile, Gambia welcomed a new government and President. The new Gambian President, in contrast with his predecessor, adopted a positive and supportive approach to the Court. On 17 February 2017, the new government of Gambia officially notified the UNSG of its decision to rescind the notification of withdrawal with immediate effect.[8] South Africa's decision to withdraw from the ICC was ruled "unconstitutional and invalid" by the High Court of this country.[9] States in the ASP Session largely supported the ICC, and demanded Africa to remain supportive to the Court as always. However, many delegations advised the Court to listen to the African voices and concerns.[10] In this regard, the President of the Court, Judge Fernandez de Gurmendi, at the 2016 ASP session insisted that the Court is committed to listening to the concerns engaged by African nations.[11]

The wave of withdrawals has now fallen, but the probability of another wave is still real.[12] What triggered the first series of withdrawals stemmed from the Court's selectivity. The Court operates in a selective manner. Selectivity is an inescapable feature of the ICC. This institution does not select all situations that include one or

6 HRW, Burundi: ICC Withdrawal Major Loss to Victims-Latest Move Shows Government's Disregard for Victims, 27 October 2016, available at: www.hrw.org/news/2016/10/27/burundi-icc-withdrawal-major-loss-victims.

7 Al-Jazeera, Gambia Withdraws from International Criminal Court, 26 October 2016, available at: www.aljazeera.com/news/2016/10/gambia-withdraws-international-criminal-court-161026041436188.html, last access at 27 June 2017.

8 UN, Gambia: Withdrawal of Notification of Withdrawal, 16 February 2017, available at: https://treaties.un.org/doc/Publication/CN/2017/CN.62.2017-Eng.pdf, last accessed at 4 June 2017.

9 BBC, South Africa's Decision to Leave ICC Ruled 'Invalid', 22 February 2017, available at: www.bbc.com/news/world-africa-39050408, last accessed at 4 June 2017.

10 For instance see the statements made by the Japanese delegation, available at: www.nl.emb-japan.go.jp/itpr_en/20161117_15asp.html, last accessed at 4 June 2017.

11 For instance, see the statements made by the President of the Court, available at: www.geoffreynicefoundation.com/activities_t03.html, last accessed at 4 June 2017.

12 In early 2017, the African Union again advised African States Parties to withdraw from the Rome Statute. See: BBC, African Union Backs Mass Withdrawal from ICC, 1 February 2017, available at: www.bbc.com/news/world-africa-38826073, last accessed at 4 June 2017.

more crimes, which fall within its jurisdiction. Selectivity poses the question of how the Court selects a situation. The Court's selective function should be justifiable and is conducted in a consistent and coherent manner. Otherwise, the Court loses its legitimacy and if the major constituencies, such as States, view the Court as making the wrong choices, "they are likely to withdraw their support from the Court and possibly even seek its destruction".[13] The critical African States believe that the Court is selective in an unacceptable manner. For instance, Bojang, the then Gambian Information Minister, said on State television that the Court had been used "for the persecution of Africans and especially their leaders" while ignoring crimes committed by the West.[14] This argument was the main perception that constituted the African States' attitude to the Court. Some years before the 2016 legitimacy crisis, Jalloh had referred to a "growing perception" that "Africans have become the sacrificial lambs in the ICC's struggle for global legitimation".[15] This perception of the ICC draws an institution that is politics-driven and applies double standards.[16]

As long as the Court is judged from such a perception, its legitimacy remains highly vulnerable. Such a judgment and perception, however, is widespread. This sentiment is not limited to situation countries or States Parties. Such an ambiguity discourages non-member States to join the ICC. For example, in Iran lack of profound and first-hand knowledge of the law, policy and practice of the ICC regarding the situation selection has cast strong suspicion concerning the Court's independence and impartiality.[17]

Nonetheless, one shall ask whether such a perception is accurate or whether if rather is a misperception and misjudgment of the ICC. It seems that the popular judgment about the Court suffers from misinformation and the lack of deep knowledge of the ICC legal system.[18] The Court functions in a selective manner. Selectivity is a built-in and constitutional feature of the Court. However, the selectivity at the Court has a regime. As Krasner defines, a regime is a set of explicit or implicit "principles, norms, rules, and decision making procedures around which actor expectations converge in a given issue-area".[19] Now, it should be assessed to determine whether such a regime is a coherent, transparent and justifiable system.

---

13 Margaret M. de Guzman, 'Choosing to Prosecute at the International Criminal Court', *Michigan Journal of International Law*, 2012, vol. 33, p. 268.

14 The Guardian, Gambia is Latest African Nation to Quit International Criminal Court, 26 October 2016, available at: www.theguardian.com/world/2016/oct/26/gambia-becomes-latest-african-nation-to-quit-international-criminal-court, last accessed at 4 June 2017.

15 Charles Chernor Jalloh, 'Regionalizing International Criminal Law?', *International Criminal Law Review*, 2009, vol. 0, p. 463..

16 See: Wolfgang Kaleck, *Double Standards: International Criminal Law and the West*, Torkel Opsahl Academic Publisher, 2015.

17 For instance, see: Fereydoon Jafari, International Criminal Court and Globalization of Criminal Law: Interaction or Encounter, Shahre Danesh, 2012.

18 For instance, the ICC Outreach Unit in its Outreach Report (2010) refers to its efforts to correct misperceptions and counter misinformation regarding, inter alia, targeting African counties (ICC, Public Information and Documentation Section, Outreach Report 2010).

19 Stephen D. Krasner (ed.), *International Regimes*, Cornell University Press, 1983.

However, the gap in the literature on the situation selection process and criteria has been wide. Over time, some steps were taken to offer a deeper insight into the situation selection regime at the ICC, but they have not been comprehensive. For instance, Guariglia and Rogier, two staff members at the Office of the Prosecutor, dealt with the situation selection at the ICC and referred to good hints, but only in 5 pages.[20] In addition, some scholars, for instance De Guzman, devoted special attention to the gravity concept as one of the main selective factors at the ICC situation selection regime, but these works do not study the whole regime of the situation selection.[21] The widespread perception against the ICC on the one hand, and incompletion of studying the ICC situation selection regime in the body of literature on the other motivated me to gain a profound knowledge of the situation selection at the ICC to see whether, as some presume, the Court has a double-standard situation selection regime or, by contrast, its selectivity is with justification.

2. QUESTIONS

This research revolves around three fundamental questions:

1. What does the situation notion mean? Conceptual questions precede normative inquiries. Without a clear definition of 'situation', no one can respond correctly to the question of how a situation is or should be selected. Ambiguities surrounding the concept of situation extend to the norms ruling its selection.
2. How does the current ICC situation selection regime run? In other words, how *is* a situation selected at the ICC?
   The question of how a situation is selected refers to the process of situation selection. Thus: 1.1. What is the situation selection process? In addition to this procedural query, the how question poses a normative inquiry, namely 1.2. What criteria are applied for selecting a situation?
3. How *should* a situation be selected in light of the normative theory of expressivism?

This book adopts 'expressivism' as a theory that can rationalize the selectivity in the ICC situation selection regime by justifying the exemplary and illustrative function of the Court. Expressivism considers all functions of the Court as instruments that are intended to promote some norms.[22]

---

20 Fabricio Guariglia and Emeric Rogier, 'The Selection of Situations and Cases by the OTP of the ICC', in Carsten Stahn (ed.), *The Law and Practice of the International Criminal Court,* Oxford University Press, 2015, p. 360.

21 Margaret M. De Guzman, 'How Serious are International Crimes? The Gravity Problem in International Criminal Law', *Columbia Journal of Transnational Law,* 2012, vol. 51, p. 58.

22 For more information about expressive theories in general see: Elizabeth S. Anderson and Richard Pildes, 'Expressive Theories of Law: A General Restatement', *University of Pennsylvania Law Review,* 2000, vol. 148.

3. METHODOLOGY

3.1. DESCRIPTIVE PART

This research adopts two approaches in responding to its questions, namely descriptive and analytical. To answer how a situation is selected in terms of process and criteria, this study suggests three sources: law, policy and practice of the ICC. This research aims to, first, clarify how a situation is selected according to the ICC law. According to Article 21 of the Rome Statute, the Court shall apply "in the first place, this Statute, Elements of Crimes and its Rules of Procedure and Evidence." The statutory and legal framework for the situation selection process and criteria consists of two Articles, namely, Article 15 and Article 53 of the Rome Statute. These two Articles draft the main process in which a situation is selected that is known as the preliminary examination stage, and the criteria that should be taken into account for this purpose. In addition to the Rome Statute, the ICC Elements of Crimes, the Rules of Procedure and Evidence, the Regulations of the Court and the Regulations of the Office of the Prosecutor (OTP), provided they are relevant to the situation selection, are taken into account. These accessory legal texts are in place to elaborate what is intended by the Rome Statute.

The relevant provisions at the ICC law regarding the situation selection are legal texts in nature. A text is inherently interpretable. It is primarily the authority and responsibility of the Prosecutor of the Court to select a situation. The ICC law in this regard has outlined the general standards that should be applied by the Prosecutor in selecting situations to prevent an arbitrary selectivity at the ICC. However, those statutory criteria have been left without a precise definition. It is the authority of the Court's Prosecutor to consider and apply them based on her own understanding and interpretation.[23] In this regard, and to promote transparency in her works, the Prosecutor of the Court tends to issue Policy Papers that express her own understanding and interpretation of the statutory requirements and concepts regarding various issues, including situation selection. Those Policies are of immense help in understanding how a situation is selected by the Prosecutor.[24]

In selecting a situation, the Prosecutor shall apply the legal requirements that have been established by the ICC's core legal texts, based on her own understanding of those provisions. Here, the practice of situation selection is a reliable source to understand how the Prosecutor applies the established criteria to select or reject a situation. The practice and jurisprudence of the Court develops the legal system of this judicial institution. The Court is a permanent institution with a concise founding instrument.

---

23 Because this research has been conducted in the reign of Prosecutor Fatou Bensouda, in referring to the Prosecutor of the Court in a general sense, a female pronoun is used.

24 By 2017, the Prosecutor has issued seven Policy Papers as follows: Policy on Children (15 November 2016); Policy paper on case selection and prioritization (15 September 2016); Policy Paper on Sexual and Gender-Based Crimes (20 June 2014); Policy Paper on Preliminary Examinations (1 November 2013); Policy Paper on Victims' Participation (12 April 2010); Policy Paper on the Interests of justice (1 September 2007); Paper on Some Policy Issues before the Office of the Prosecutor (September 2003).

The legal texts of the ICC are developed, understood and fed by its jurisprudence. In practice, many novel questions arise, and answering those questions may change the classical understanding of a notion or function. For this reason, all situations that have been selected by the Prosecutor, have undergone a preliminary examination or have failed to reach the preliminary examination will be taken into account. The practice of the Court in this regard is limited to those instances that have been announced by the OTP.

It should be noted that due to the uniqueness of the situation selection regime at the ICC, there is not any precedence before the Court in this regard. Ad hoc tribunals and national jurisdictions have been primarily case-oriented. Although there is a conceptual distinction between a case and a situation, as will be discussed in detail later, it does not mean that the existing laws, policies and practices as to the case selection at both national or international level are irrelevant to the situation selection regime. Selectivity, as to either a case or a situation, could have some rules in common. For instance, transparency and non-arbitrary selection are applicable to both case and situation selection. In addition, the rules and practices of other tribunals with regard to the case selection can suggest some guidance to select a situation. Taking into account this function, in this thesis, the rules and quotations about the selection of a case has been used in the context of the situation selection regime. This use does not contradict the dichotomy between the notion of case and the concept of situation. However, to keep loyal to the text of a quotation that has been originally stated about the case selection mechanism, the term case used in the original text has been left untouched.

In addition to its descriptive pillar, this research integrates an analytical perspective in all its chapters. In parallel with describing the situation selection regime at the ICC, the law, policy and practice of the Court in this regard are analyzed. The ICC situation selection regime needs further clarification and explanation. The *status quo* leaves some gaps in the regime that need to be identified and filled in. By analyzing the Court's law, practice and policy in this regard, this research seeks to introduce a situation selection regime that is understandable, explanatory, and entirely logical.

3.2. NORMATIVE PART

In addition to its explanatory analysis of the situation selection regime, this research proposes a normative theory that seeks an account of what the situation selection regime ought to be and whether it ought to be at all. The point of departure in this book is the ICC selectivity as an inescapable feature of the Court. Selectivity constitutes a conceptual framework within which the ICC should be seen. All functions of the Court are carried out in a widely selective manner. Although at many domestic legal systems the 'discretionary prosecution' is in place, the selectivity at the ICC has two major differences. First, the discretionary prosecution is applied in the context of specific cases, however, the ICC's selectivity begins with 'situations'. Secondly, contrary to domestic jurisdictions, at the ICC, non-selection of the core crimes is the rule and selection is an exception. In other words, in other jurisdictions, prosecutors exceptionally not select a situation. By contrast, at the ICC, the Prosecutor exceptionally selects a situation or case. Such broad selectivity is rooted in both practical and normative reasons. The Court lacks sufficient resources to deal with all situations and cases that fall within its jurisdiction. In addition to its inability, under the complementarity principle, the Court is not intended to occupy the primary role of States in combating the ICC-identified crimes. In other words, the ICC is only a last resort mechanism, rather than a replacement to national jurisdictions. The permanency of the Court also increases its excessive workload, and makes this organization more selective. The Court's selectivity can hurt the legitimacy of the Court. The Court's legitimacy is a purposive notion that is shaped in light of the Court's effectiveness in realizing its goals and mandates.[25] The extensive selectivity of the Court does not allow the Court to effectively and maximally realize its main constituent objectives referred to in the Preamble of the Rome Statute, namely ending impunity (retribution) and prevention (deterrence).

Setting up some *ex ante* standards that show how the Court selects a situation and making the selection or deselection of a situation transparent and reasoned are necessary steps that should be taken in building a qualified judicial institution with transparency and coherency. Nevertheless, these steps are not sufficient in justifying the Court's bored selectivity.[26] Indeed, the Court's selectivity needs a theory that justifies this feature and is able to justify maintaining a system that functions widely selective. The ICC was founded on what that is called an "incompletely theorized agreement".[27] To fill such a gap, this research theorizes the selectivity and the situation selection regime at the ICC.

This books premises on the expressivism theory. Expressivism as a theory has two aspects and functions. First, it is a descriptive and explanatory theory that justifies the selectivity of the situation selection regime by facilitating the illustrative function of the Court. In addition, this understanding establishes an evaluative framework within which this research reads and interprets the ICC law, and evaluates the policy and practice of the Court as to the situation selection regime. The latter dimension deals with the question of the situation selection regime as it should be.

Adopting the expressivism theory stems from a functional approach to the ICC.

3.2.1. Functional Approach to the ICC

The ICC first and foremost is an international public organization.[28] The most important effect of having such a feature is that the Court is governed by both international law

25 Some argue that the legitimacy of an organization must be "identified with purposes and goals that are consistent with the broader norms and values of its society" (See: Bruce Cronin and Ian Hurd, 'Introduction', in Bruce Cronin and Ian Hurd (eds.), *The UN Security Council and the Politics of International Authority*, Routledge, 2008, p. 6.

26 See: De Guzman, 2012, pp. 289–299, see *supra* note 13.

27 Cass R. Sunstein, 'Incompletely Theorized Agreement', *Harvard Law Review*, 1994, vol. 1733.

28 International Public/Inter-Governmental Organizations are distinct from Private/Non-Governmental Organizations, even if the latter functions internationally. Inter-Governmental organizations are made up by and of sovereign States.

and institutional law.[29] As the ICJ States, "international organizations are subjects of international law and as such are bound by any obligation incumbent upon them under general rules of international law."[30] A precise definition of international organizations is not possible.[31] Article 2 of the draft Articles on Responsibility of International Organizations defines an international organization as "an organization established by a treaty or other instrument governed by international law and possessing its own international legal personality."[32] Inter-governmental organizations like the ICC are creatures of States' will.[33] Such a will is enshrined in a legal instrument, namely the constituent instrument of an organization.

Every organization is a means of realizing specified goals, which are set for that organization by its creators. To see organizations as an instrument is an important element in understanding the role of international organizations in today's world. However, one should bear in mind that an organization is not simply a dead instrument. Conversely, international organizations are an entity of legal personality with a distinctive discretionary power, which allows them to play an active role in achieving their established aims. Indeed, an instrumental approach to organizations only indicates that they serve some specific goals. There are various goals and objectives of varying degrees of importance that persuade States to cooperate with each other in order to realize those aims through the establishment of an institution. The reason behind such cooperation is that States are not able to reach effectively their goals without the cooperation between one another. International relations between States as an inevitable necessity for the contemporary age and the institutionalization of inter-States relations have led to international organizations.[34] The proliferation of international organizations across the world in recent decades demonstrates the efficiency and practical effectiveness of this phenomenon for States in reality. This feature of international organizations leads to the adoption of a functional approach to understanding them.

As Keohane describes, functional explanations are generally *post hoc* in nature, because they account for cause in terms of their effects.[35] In other words, functionalism

---

29 Institutional Law is defined as the law governing the structure and general operations of public international organizations (See: C.F. Amerasinghe, *Principles of the Institutional Law of International Organization*, Cambridge University Press, 2005, p. 13).

30 ICJ, Advisory Opinion, Interpretation of the Agreement of 25 March 1951 between the WHO and Egypt, 20 December 1980, para. 37.

31 Jan Klabbers, *An Introduction to International Institutional Law*, Cambridge University Press, 2002, p. 7.

32 Draft Articles on the Responsibility of International Organizations, Adopted by the International Law Commission at its sixty-third session, 2011.

33 States have an essential quality and that is they have separate will. As Alexander Wendt points out States are intentional or purposive actors and in this sense they are considered as person (See: Alexander Wendt, The State As Person in International Theory, *Review of International Studies*, 2004, vol. 30, p. 291).

34 Amerasinghe, 2005, p. 5, see *supra* note 29.

35 Robert O. Keohane, After Hegemony: Cooperation and Discord in the World Political Economy, p. 80.

is a kind of theory in which effect explains cause.[36] From this viewpoint, international organizations are created by States as instruments to achieve certain goals. This instrumental cooperation between States puts its focus on those goals and objectives, which are sought by States. Functionalism adopts an interpretative approach to the law of organizations. According to this interpretative perspective, the understanding of the law of organizations is not simply about the text of a treaty but also the purposes and functions of organizations.[37] Functionalism promotes the 'functional necessity'. The functional necessity concept asserts that an entity shall be entitled to what is strictly necessary for the exercise of its functions in the fulfillment of its purpose.[38] According to this framework, to identify the powers and authorities of an international organization, its purposes and goals must be considered. In legal terminology, a function is a tool for the accomplishment of purposes.[39]

Functional necessity plays as a standard and yardstick to determine the scope and extent of powers that an organization enjoys to fulfill its mandates. This function has two dimensions. The first one is 'the authoritative aspect', which provides the necessary capacity of an international organization to undertake some activities to realize its primary goals. The second dimension is 'the limitative aspect', which denies any power for an organization behind its functions and purposes. Functional necessity is based on the idea that international law does not automatically grant any substantive rights or obligations to international organizations.[40] Conversely, organizations must be endowed with rights and duties by States and for the purpose of their constituent goals. The extent of powers of an organization shall be limited only to those powers that are necessary for exercising its organizational functions. In other words, whereas States may perform all activities unless their incompetence can be demonstrated, international organizations may not perform any activities unless their competence can be demonstrated.[41] It must be noted that the functional necessity doctrine does not determine the content of powers, which are necessary for each organization. The content of powers may differ from organization to organization.[42]

There are two kinds of powers pertaining to international organizations: implied and attributed. The idea behind attribution is that international organizations can only do those things for which they are empowered.[43] Implied powers are those powers that are not expressly conferred to an organization by its constitutive instrument, but can be derived from the express powers and functions of an organization by the exercise

---

36 Andreas Hasenclever, Peter Mayer and Volker Rittberger, *Theories of International Regimes*, Cambridge University Press, 2004, p. 40.

37 Nigel D. White, *The Law of International Organizations*, Manchester University Press, 2005, p. 9.

38 Peter H. F. Bekker, *The Legal Position of Intergovernmental Organizations: A Functional Necessity Analysis of Their Legal Status and Immunities*, Brill, 1994, p. 39.

39 Ibid., p. 46.

40 Klabbers, 2002, p. 36, see *supra* note 31.

41 Bekker, 1994, p. 76, see *supra* note 38.

42 It is called the 'principle of speciality' (See: Ghasem Zamani, *Law of International Organizations: Personality, Responsibility, Immunity*, The SD Institute of Law Research and Study, 2009, p. 40).

43 Klabbers, 2002, p. 64, see *supra* note 31.

of the necessary implication method. Implied powers are essential to the performance of the organization's duties.[44] The ICJ in the Reparation Case recognized the implied powers doctrine and stipulated that "an organization must be deemed to have those powers which, though not expressly provided in the Charter, are conferred upon it by necessary implication as being essential to the performance of its duties."[45] The main feature of both kinds of powers is that they are based on the intention of constituent States, implied or explicit. Drafters of the constituent instruments of organizations cannot be omniscient, and there may be circumstances in which an organization would need a power not expressly granted in order to function effectively.[46] It is not possible to predict all needs of an organization, because needs are dynamic over time. In such circumstances, the intention of the drafters and founders of a legal treaty should be understood from the eyes of the present readers if an organization is intended to function effectively.

3.2.2. *In Search of a Theory for the Court*

The preamble of the Court explicitly refers to two main objectives of the Court, namely prevention and ending impunity. The OTP's first report of the Prosecutor to UNSC in 2011 stated that "the prosecutors' action will be guided by the object and purpose of the Statute, namely: the prevention of serious crimes of concern to the international community through the ending of impunity."[47] In addition, the judgments of the *ad hoc* tribunals refer to retribution and deterrence as the twin goals of sentencing.[48] These two traditional theories are teleological and deontological respectively.[49] In other words, they are instrumental and moralistic.[50] The former is a forward-looking theory that focuses on the consequences of the punishment. This kind of theory is consequentialist. From this perspective, criminal law is an instrument that can be used to serve various possible ends.[51] The latter is a backward-looking theory, which focuses on the nature of

---

44 Göran Sluiter, International Criminal Adjudication and the Collection of Evidence: Obligations of States, Intersentia, 2002, p. 28.

45 ICJ, Reparation for Injuries Suffered in the Service of the United Nations, Advisory Opinion, 1949, p12. Nonetheless, some authors State that the ICJ adopted a contradictory approach to implied powers doctrine in its judgment in case of Legality of the Threat or Use Of Nuclear Weapons, 1996, with regard to determination of the authorities of the UN agencies (See: Zamani, *2009*, p. 56, see *supra* note 42).

46 Klabbers, 2002, p. 74, see *supra* note 31.

47 Sarah M.H. Nouwen, *Complementarity in the Line of Fire: the Catalyzing Effect of the ICC in Uganda and Sudan,* Cambridge University Press, 2013, p. 409.

48 Robert Sloane, *The Expressive Capacity of International Punishme*nt, Columbia Public Law and Legal Theory Working Papaer, 2006, p. 34.

49 Robert Cryer, Hakan Friman and Darryl Robinson (et al), *An Introduction to International Criminal Law and Procedure,* Cambridge University Press, 2014, p. 29. McGonigle Leyh adopts a different label: consequentialist and non-consequentialist (See: Brianne McGonigle Leyh, *Procedural Justice: Victim Participation in International Criminal Procedure,* Intersentia, 2011, p. 37).

50 Stanford Encyclopedia of Philosophy, Theories of Criminal Law, 14 October 2002, available at: https://plato.stanford.edu/entries/criminal-law, Last accessed at 5 April 2017.

51 Ibid.

crimes and the deserving of criminals to be punished. Although the Court's activities have both retributive and preventive effects and features, these theories do not fit the ICC system well.

The main non-consequentialist criminal theory is retributivism. Retributivists adopt a moralistic approach to criminalization. This theory maintains that punishment is required when moral norms are violated.[52] Retributivism believes that to treat the perpetrators as a means to another end (as utilitarian approaches do) is to fail to respect them as full persons.[53] There is a causal relationship between a crime and punishment. The commission of crimes inherently causes an effect and that is the deserving of the perpetrator of a crime to receive a punishment (principle of causality).[54] Retributivists justify the punishment as an end in itself.[55] The Kantian 'island society about to disband' is a good example showing the absoluteness in retributivism. According to this exemplary situation, if someone commits murder, he deserves to be punished even if he is the last person of a society. Such a perspective results in the absoluteness of punishment. All crimes should be prosecuted and all criminals should be sanctioned. It is in itself the main downside of the retributivism in the context of the international criminal justice system.

This theory is unable to justify the selective justice. Retributivism requires the prosecution of all crimes and criminals. There is no exception and exemption. This theory asserts that punishment should be imposed as the natural effect of the commission of crimes. It is because by committing a crime, the wrongdoer has disturbed the social and moral balance that existed before the crime was committed.[56] Hence, punishment is imposed to restore things to the initial situation. From a deontological perspective, punishment is imposed to negate the wrong and to reassert the right.[57] From a secular perspective, culprits obtain 'unfair advantage' by committing crimes. Therefore, punishment is imposed as "a debt owed to the law-abiding members of one's community; and, once paid, it allows re-entry into the community of good citizens on equal status."[58] Nonetheless, the international criminal justice system is unable to make such a balance between benefits and burdens. This system is intentionally and inevitably selective. The international criminal justice system embraces two kinds

52 Margaret M. De Guzman, 'An Expressive Rationale for the Thematic Prosecution of Sex Crimes', in Morten Bergsmo (ed.), *Thematic Prosecution of International Sex Crimes*, Torkel Opsahl Academic EPublisher, 2012, p. 17.

53 Cryer and Friman and Robinson, 2014, p. 30, see *supra* note 49.

54 Scholars have suggested that desert can be measured either empirically by ascertaining community views, or deontologically by appealing to moral principles (See: De Guzman, 2012, p. 19, see *supra* note 52).

55 McGonigle Leyh, 2011, p. 37, see *supra* note 49.

56 Sharzad Fouladvand, Complementarity and Cultural Sensitivity: Decision-making by the ICC Prosecutor in relation to the Situation in the Darfur Region in Sudan and the Democratic Republic of the Congo, the Degree of Doctor of Philosophy, University of Sussex, 2012, p. 32.

57 Jean Hampton, The Moral Education Theory of Punishment, *Philosophy and Public Affairs*, 1984, vol. 13, p. 215.

58 Sloane, 2006, p. 50, see *supra* note 48.

of selectivity, namely the horizontal and vertical selectivity.[59] Horizontal selectivity means only to deal with some situations among similar situations. Vertical selectivity refers to the selection of only some individuals and cases within a situation and leaving other cases unprosecuted. Retributivism is unable to justify both kinds of selectivity in the international criminal justice system. If the selectivity of the ICC was a matter of inability, there would be a justification to accept retributivism as a theory. Someone would argue that the Court is not able to prosecute all cases, so it shall do whatever it can. Nonetheless, the Court is intended to be selective. Retributivism has been framed in the context of domestic criminal law. However, it is not a perfect theory for the ICC, given the Court's unique features. By prosecuting a handful of crimes, the imbalance created by the commission of crimes is not altered, as requested by retributivism. The ICC as a criminal tribunal has retributive tools at its disposal. Nonetheless, the Court uses punishments as a tool, not as an end, and in an exemplary manner.[60]

Another criminal theory that has some traces in the ICC is deterrence. The deterrence theory lies in the scope of consequentialism.[61] The consequentialist theories are based on the consequences arising from an action. In the eyes of the consequentialists, punishment is not a purpose in itself, but it can only be justified to the extent that it promotes some legitimate purposes, which outweigh the pain inflicted on the wrongdoer.[62] This doctrine utilizes the punishment and criminal intervention to achieve other objectives. The utilitarian theories are forward-looking because they focus on the benefits of criminal justice.[63] This kind of theory is an instrumentalist approach in nature. Criminal law is seen as an instrument that may be used to reach some external goals. The emphasis on deterrence as a goal of international criminal justice

---

59 Kaleck, 2015, pp. 7–8, see *supra* note 16.

60 There are also some other criticisms. Some have questioned the utility of retributivism in the context of the international criminal justice system. On the one hand, it is said that because this theory is based on moral grounds, it is impossible to come to any widespread acceptance of morality. In addition, others argue that retribution therefore is a problematic justification because it presupposes both a coherent community and a relatively stable legal order characterized by shared values. Hobbs in Leviathan asserts that "there is no crime, where no civil society is." These critics tend to believe that the international community has a figurative nature and lacks any capacity to provide some norms. However, these arguments do not seem compelling. There is no objection about the criminal nature of the international crimes. Those values, which are protected by criminalizing the international crimes, are universal. The ending impunity that has been introduced as one of the main constituent goals of the ICC is a notion close to retributivism. Ending impunity aims at preventing the crimes going unpunished. It shows that it put the punishment at the center of its demands. That is why it is said that it is the retributive paradigm that has most influenced international criminal justice responses to mass crimes. In addition, retributivism is a punishment-centered theory. Due to depersonalization as an effect of retributivism, this theory has faced some criticism arguing this it is a kind of blind justice that ignores the interests of victims and the characteristics of the offenders. The only recommendation of retributivism is punishment, while the criminal justice system should be able to provide other responses to the crimes as well.

61 Although deterrence and prevention are often used interchangeably, deterrence is more accurately viewed as a form of prevention (See: De Guzman, 2012, p. 24, see *supra* note 52).

62 Jo Martin Stigen, *The Relationship Between the International Criminal Court and National Jurisdictions: the Principle of Complementarity*, Brill Nijhoff, 2008, p. 12.

63 McGonigle Leyh, 2011, p. 41, see *supra* note 49.

is a recent development.[64] The point of departure in the international criminal justice system was retribution. In the preamble of the UNSC's Resolution establishing the ICTY the importance of deterrence was mentioned: "believing that the establishment of an international tribunal and the prosecution of persons responsible will contribute to ensuring that such violations are halted and effectively redressed."[65] Nowadays, deterrence is usually cited as the principal goal of the ICC.[66]

Deterrence pursues its objectives by issuing a threat of punishment. Threat is a key factor in law. Some define the obligatory part of the law as the threat-backed regulations.[67] Deterrence considers individuals as the rational actors, who act based on the assessment of the benefits-costs of their choices. From a utilitarian perspective, deterrence is simply ineffective, for the person lacks the kind or degree of agency that makes the threat of sanctions an appreciable deterrent.[68] The threat of punishment works if some prerequisites exist. The most important condition is the possibility of imposing the punishment and the probability of carrying out the issued threat. If it is thought that the threat of a punishment is not carried out due to legal or practical obstacles, deterrence loses its effect. In addition, deterrence requires the quality of criminal regulations. The law should be understandable, accessible, and predictable for the public. The citizens of a society should be able to predict the consequences of their conduct.

Moreover, the punishment should be costly if it is imposed on a wrongdoer. There is an assessment between the benefits and costs of the commission of a crime. If the costs do not outweigh the benefits, rationally a sanction does not provide a preventive effect. However, the cost arising from a punishment is not limited to the financial or material costs. Reputation plays a role here. In particular, in the case of the most responsible criminals, economic deterrence analysis is less convincing, but the senior culprits might take into account the reputational effects of international indictment.[69] For this reason, sometimes the mere threat of the criminal intervention, for instance by the issuance of an arrest warrant, works.[70] A leader under an international arrest warrant, even before the execution of the arrest warrant, loses to some degree his or her reputation.

Like other theories, deterrence has not been immune from critics. These objections are not limited to the applicability of this theory in the international sphere, but in

64 Kare Cronin-Furman and Amanda Taub, 'Lions and Tigers and Deterrence. Oh My: Evaluating Expectations of International Criminal Justice', in William A. Schabas, Yvonne McDermott and Niamh Hayes (eds.), *The Ashgate Research Companion to International Criminal Law: Critical Perspectives*, Ashgate, 2013, p. 436.

65 UNSC, Resolution 827, 25 May 1993.

66 De Guzman, 2012, p. 48, see *supra* note 52.

67 Hart refers to two kinds of law: rules of obligation or law as orders backed by threats made by the State (*see:* Hampton, 1984, p. 210, see *supra* note 57).

68 Sloane, 2006, p. 27, see *supra* note 48.

69 Margaret M. De Guzman, 'Giving Priority to Sex Crime Prosecutions: The Philosophical Foundations of a Feminist Agenda', *International Criminal Law Review*, 2011, vol. 11, p. 524.

70 Sloane, 2006, p. 421, see *supra* note 48.

the context of international criminal justice, the critics are louder. Some question the efficiency of deterrence. Bassiouni asserts that the deterrence assumption is one of the most questionable aspects of international criminal justice.[71] It is argued that the international culprits who have power are not affected by the threat of the imposition of international punishments. International punishments are not sufficiently costly. In addition, the punishment of international criminals is an exception rather than a rule. Before the ICTY started its first case, Meron had stated that deterrence would fail to prevent the commission of crimes because "prosecutions for war crimes on both national and international planes are so exceptional that criminals do not believe that they are likely to be prosecuted and punished."[72] This statement still seems to some extent true.

Furthermore, the prospect of apprehending the persons wanted by the ICC is not bright. Rebels in the war-torn societies and the owner of State powers are hardly arrested. The situation of the LRA in Uganda and the Darfur situation are good examples. Briefly, it is doubtful that the international criminals weigh the risk of prosecution against the benefits of their crimes. Here, selectivity matters and affects adversely the effects of deterrence for international criminal justice. If justice is done selectively, it highly reduces the preventive effects of the criminal law. In addition, the severity of the sentence is another factor that causes the strength of the deterrent effect.[73] However, the imprisonment in The Hague is not a terrible situation.[74] In Wippman's words, "the connection between international prosecutions and the actual deterrence of future atrocities is at best a plausible but largely untested assumption."[75] The Court intends to prevent the commission of crimes, however, it seeks this goal in a more flexible and long-term way, instead of immediate solutions. The Court's intervention in on-going conflicts may fail to stop atrocities. The Court is not able to prosecute all crimes even if they fall within its jurisdiction. Deterrence works if it is followed comprehensively. Selectivity reduces the impact of deterrence. As a result, a different theory is needed that is able to explain the selectivity of the Court, besides its deterrent effect.

Retribution and deterrence are all sought by the Court, but they fail to explain the selectivity of the Court. As a criminal tribunal, the Court has inherently retributive functions and aims. Retribution is an inextricable part of the ICC. Nevertheless, the Court needs a theory that is adapted to its selectivity. Classical criminal theories were formed at the domestic level, when a system like the ICC was not in place. The ICC-era needs a new theory. Expressivism seems to have such a capacity.

---

71 M. Cherif Bassiouni, *Introduction to International Criminal Law*, Martinus Nijhoff Publishers, 2013, p. 916.

72 Theodor Meron, 'From Nuremberg to The Hague', *Military Law Review,* 1995, vol. 149, p. 110.

73 Cronin-Furman and Taub, 2013, p. 439, see *supra* note 64.

74 Sloane, 2006, p. 41, see *supra* note 48.

75 David Wippman, 'Atrocities, Deterrence and the Limits of International Justice', *Fordham International law Journal* 1999, vol. 23, p. 474.

3.2.3. *Definition of Expressivism*

Expressivism is one of the theories that have recently come to the center of attention of many scholars. The recent interest in expressivism is very visible in international criminal law. As De Guzman asserts, a growing number of scholars have turned to expressive theories to justify the international criminal justice system.[76] This tendency is detectable in the works of the international tribunals as well. For instance, the first ICTY sentencing judgment declared that it sees "public reprobation and stigmatization by the international community, which would thereby express its indignation over heinous crimes and denounce the perpetrators" as an essential function of punishment.[77]

Expressivism adopts an instrumental approach to punishment and criminal law. The expressivism theory sees criminal punishment as a means for society to express its disapproval of some behaviors.[78] Akhavan refers to the punishment of particular individuals such as Karadzic or Mladic as "an instrument through which respect for the rule of law is instilled into the popular consciousness."[79] For the expressivists, punishment is a purposive phenomenon. It has a function, and that is to convey a message. From such a perspective, law is considered to have 'social meaning' like actions.[80] Law is for both the expression of valued social messages and for altering social norms.[81] For the expressivists, it matters that the public receives the message. In this regard, the understanding of the audience is important.[82] For this reason, international criminal tribunals should ensure the widespread publication and dissemination of judgments to the broadest possible audience.[83] In addition to the dissemination, the Court's products should be explained and clarified well. Once, Moreno-Ocampo asserted that "the preventative impact of the Court will increase if issues are studied at university levels not only in affected communities but worldwide. In order to prevent future violence, politicians and members of the police and the military should be educated about the activities and decisions of the court."[84] Based on this belief, he recommended that primary and high school students should learn about the fate of child soldiers. Publicity and outreach activities are highly advisable from the perspective of expressivism.

---

76 De Guzman, 2011, p. 524, see *supra* note 69.

77 ICTY, Trial Chamber, Drazen Erdemovic case, Sentencing Judgment, 29 November 1996, para. 65.

78 Cronin-Furman and Taub, 2013, p. 439, see *supra* note 64.

79 Payam Akhavan, 'Justice in The Hague, Peace in the Former Yugoslavia? A Commentary on the United Nations War Crimes Tribunal', *Human Rights Quarterly*, 1998, vol. 20, p. 749.

80 Cass. R. Sunstein, 'On the Expressive Function of Law', *University Of Pennsylvania Law Review*, 1996, vol. 144, p. 2022.

81 De Guzman, 2012, p. 32, see *supra* note 52.

82 Diane Marie Amann, 'Group Mentality, Expressivism and Genocide', *International Criminal Law Review*, 2002, vol. 2, p. 118.

83 Sloane, 2006, p. 61, see *supra* note 48.

84 Luis Moreno-Ocampo, 'A Positive Approach to Complementarity: The Impact of the Office of the Prosecutor', in Carsten Stahn and Mohamed M. El Zeidy (eds.), *The International Criminal Court and Complementarity: From Theory to Practice*, Cambridge University Press, 2011, p. 30.

The message-oriented function of criminal law gives an important role to education. Expressivism seeks the prevention of crimes through education. This educational function of punishment is based on the idea that the most effective form of law enforcement is not the imposition of external sanctions, but the inculcation of internal obedience.[85] Expressivism can result in deterrence, but over the long term. This theory focuses less on the immediate instrumental value of punishment and more on the long-term normative values.[86] This attitude is consistent with the permanency of the Court. It makes the ICC a suitable forum for pursuing long-term objectives and effects. In light of expressivism, an expressive perspective has been incorporated in the deterrence theory. The threat-oriented deterrence is based on the imposition of the punishment that is painful. From a moral perspective, it is not consistent with the dignity of human beings. Hegel asserts that if we aimed to prevent wrongdoing only by deterring its commission, we would be treating human beings in the same way that we treat dogs.[87] To overcome such a shortcoming, the 'expressive deterrence' emerged. Expressive deterrence believes that criminal punishment deters crime not because criminals fear the punishment, but because they fear the broader social consequences of a criminal conviction.[88]

Punishment should carry a message, and serve a communicative purpose. It should show the norms of a society and the prohibition of the violation of those norms. An ICTY Chamber in the Nikolic case asserts "the Tribunal and other international courts are bringing about the development of a culture of respect for the rule of law and not simply the fear of the consequences of breaking the law, and thereby deterring the commission of crimes."[89] The theory of expressive deterrence argues that international criminal tribunals deter future atrocities by stigmatizing potential perpetrators as war criminals. In other words, trials must be seen as an effective means of stigmatizing.[90] Other criminal measures such as investigations and arrest warrants should be seen from such a perspective too. Here, the education through criminal measures occurs. The mere expression of norms in books does not suffice. As some authors have maintained, sometimes the commission of international crimes is not prevented, since "there is no legal framework to prevent their commission or to prosecute them *ex postis*. This is not a consequence of the absence of substantive criminal law but rather the absence of criminal procedure."[91] Expressivism adds an educational function and vision to criminal law. Pre-trial, trial and post-trial measures such as investigations, prosecutions and punishments for the expressivists are tools for the norm projection. Such a function is more important where specific crimes reflect a relatively recent

85 Sloane, 2006, p. 44, see *supra* note 48.
86 Ibid., p. 39.
87 Georg W. Hegel, The Elements of the Philosophy of Right (1820).
88 Cronin-Furman and Taub, 2013, p. 440, see *supra* note 64.
89 ICTY Trial Chamber I, Momir Nikolic case, Sentencing Judgment, 2 December 2003, paras. 89–90.
90 Cronin-Furman and Taub, 2013, p. 447, see *supra* note 64.
91 Göran Sluiter, Hakan Friman and Susannah Linton (eds.), *International Criminal Procedure: Principles and Rules*, Oxford University Press, 2013, p. 67.

moral consensus on point, like the prohibition of child soldiering.[92] In this regard, the thematic prosecution has surfaced as a guiding doctrine for the case selection at the ICC.

Expressivism puts its emphasis on education because it believes that international crimes, in contrast with their appearance, are committed as normal behaviors. Tallgren contends that "contrary to most national criminality which is understood to constitute social deviation, acts addressed as international crimes can, in some circumstances, be constituted as conforming to a norm."[93] Given these considerations, one can say that guarantees of non-repetition need a wider range of measures including measures to strengthen the rule of law.[94] If a culture of accountability is created and all actors play their part in prosecuting international crimes, then the critics against deterrence may become blunt over time.[95] The expressivists fulfil their mandates when criminal law is seen as a rule and as a normal reaction to crimes.[96] Impunity is a culture in which the punishment and the criminal intervention are not imaginable and understandable because nobody feels it is a necessary and proper reaction. The Court's expressive function tries to break this culture of impunity. Indeed, it is the moral presence of the Court within a situation of crisis, "which will shape perspectives and strengthen resolve on the need for accountability", through "its own exemplary and standard-setting proceedings."[97]

Expressivism is a good possible way of justifying the selective nature of the Court. To convey a message, the Court does not have to prosecute all cases and crimes. The Court's wide restrictions cause the Court's jurisdiction to be exemplary.[98] Selectivity and the exemplary function of the Court are two sides of a coin. According to the OTP, due to the restrictions "priority will be given to building strong cases over pursuing all plausible cases."[99] It means that the Court focuses on a couple of cases instead of a large number of cases in order to preserve the quality of its prosecutions. It paves the way for the exemplary function of the Court. One may assert that such an exemplary and selective function is not valuable due to its imperfection. Cryer provides an example showing that there is, at least, one important function that is fulfilled by an exemplary criminal system. He mentions that the Stockholm International Peace Research Institute has estimated that in 1993 there were at least 13 conflicts with many casualties, but they are not spoken about in the same way now as Bosnia. Why? His answer to this

---

92 Cryer and Friman and Robinson, 2014, p. 36, see *supra* note 64.

93 Immi Tallgren, The Sensibility and Sense of International Criminal Law, *European Journal of International Law*, 2002, vol. 13, p. 575.

94 McGonigle Leyh, 2011, p. 50, see *supra* note 49.

95 Cryer and Friman and Robinson, 2014, p. 34, see *supra* note 49.

96 Ibid., p. 37.

97 ICC, OTP, Informal Expert Paper: The Principle of Complementarity in Practice, 2003, para. 6.

98 Mauro Politi, 'Reflections on Complementarity at the Rome Conference and Beyond', in Carsten Stahn and Mohamed M. El Zeidy (eds.), *The International Criminal Court and Complementarity: From Theory to Practice*, Cambridge University Press, 2011, p. 144.

99 ICC, OTP, Strategic Plan (2016–2018), para. 47.

important question is interesting; "because there was not a tribunal... there was not something which established the facts."[100]

Recognition and acknowledgement are the point of departure in a criminal system, and they are of great importance from an expressive perspective. It is accepted that one of the effects and functions of the Court is to draw the attention of the world towards a specific crisis. The first Prosecutor of the Court mentioning the background of the situation in CAR I Stated "it is hoped the involvement of the International Criminal Court will also contribute to focusing international attention on the needs of victims and on the risks of continued violence and crimes in the CAR and the region."[101] One of the most important goals of the Court is to serve the interests of victims. The first need and interest of victims is to be heard. The exemplary intervention of the Court can realize such a goal. Taking into account the exemplary intervention of the Court, expressivism sounds like the most consistent theory with the selective nature of the Court. Adopting expressivism as the ruling theory for the ICC forms a guide for the situation and case selection. The Court should select some situations and cases in an exemplary manner. However, this does not mean that the Prosecutor of the Court is free to exercise her discretionary power to select a situation or case in an unfettered way. The gravity requirement is a criterion that directs the Prosecutor in the situation and case selection. Those cases and situations should be selected that serve the expressive mandates of the Court better.

Expressivism is a normative and evaluative framework that has been adopted by this research to analyze the situation selection regime at the ICC. From such a perspective, the law, practice and policy of the Court regarding situation selection are analyzed and evaluated. Reading the situation selection process and criteria in light of expressivism may have some implications that are offered by this research as some recommendations that should be taken into account in selecting a situation. These recommendations premise on the idea that the side effects of selectivity that is harmful for the Court's legitimacy should be lessons.

4. OUTLINE

This research consists of four Parts. Part One addresses the conceptual question of this research. What does a situation mean in light of the Rome Statute? The situation selection is unique at the ICC's architecture, and the ICC law is silent about its definition. To clarify the meaning of the situation notion, first a dividing line between the notion of 'case' and the 'situation' concept is drawn. Although cases stem from situations, the latter is distinct from the former. Preserving the impartiality of the Court in combating the crimes under its jurisdiction has been the main reason behind

100 ICTY, *20 Years of the ICTY: Anniversary Event and Legacy Conference Proceedings*, Grafika Saran, 2014, p. 42.

101 ICC, OTP, Background Situation in the Central African Republic, 22 May 2007.

incorporating the notion of situation at the ICC legal system (Chapter I). Upon stressing that a situation is not a case, the constituent elements of a situation are studied. Each situation in the Rome Statute is composed of two elements: the contextual element and jurisdictional parameters (Chapter II).

Part Two deals with the situation selection process. In this Part, the procedural aspect of situation selection at the ICC is studied. Selecting situations is conducted within a process. At the ICC's architecture, the situation selection process commences with an external mechanism, namely, the trigger mechanism (Chapter I). The trigger mechanism, as established by the founders of the Court, is a mechanism that brings a situation to the attention of the Court. Referrals made by States Parties to the Rome Statute or the UNSC and communications that are sent, mainly, by non-State actors or non-member States are those triggers that grab the attention of the Prosecutor. The Chapter deals with, *inter alia,* the phenomenon of self-referrals that has been somewhat controversial due to its potential effects on the Court's impartiality. Moreover, 'declarations of acceptance' referred to in Article 12(3) of the Rome Statute are also dealt with to highlight the distinction between them and referrals. Upon offering a situation to the Prosecutor, a stage commences that is missing from the ICC legal texts, namely the identification stage. Chapter II explains the functions of this untouched stage, and argues in favor of the necessity of defining this phase as an independent stage.

The central part of the situation selection process is the preliminary examination stage that is studied in Chapter III. The preliminary examination is a filtering process through which the Prosecutor of the Court decides to select or to reject a situation. In Chapter III, procedure, time frame, scope, evidentiary threshold and functions of the preliminary examination are dealt with. Upon conducting a preliminary examination, the Prosecutor should make a decision whether to initiate an investigation into the situation that has already undergone the preliminary examination. Chapter IV deals with the Prosecutor's determination and the extent to which her decisions are under judicial scrutiny. The extent of judicial review of the Prosecutor's decision to or not to pursue with a situation depends on the trigger that activates the Court's jurisdiction. The Rome Statute has made the Prosecutor more responsive to the Court's Judges about her decisions about referrals, compared to her decision on communications.

Part Three addresses the situation selection criteria. Jurisdiction, admissibility, interests of justice and availability are those factors that determine whether a situation should be selected. Chapter I addresses the issue of the Court's jurisdiction. The subject-matter jurisdiction of the Court refers to those crimes that are prosecutable by the Court, namely war crimes, crimes against humanity, genocide and the crime of aggression. Temporal jurisdiction of the Court is open ended thanks to the permanency of the Court. However, its commencement is limited to the date when the Rome Statute entered into force, namely 1 July 2002. The Court lacks universal jurisdiction. Its jurisdiction that is delegated by States Parties is limited to either territory (territorial jurisdiction) or nationals of its States Parties (personal jurisdiction). These two jurisdictional parameters are alternative to each other. In the relevant Chapter, it is discussed that when the Court can intervene in a situation of crisis based on the personal jurisdiction, the Prosecutor should refrain from being inactive. In addition, the controversial issue of immunities before the Court and the Court's jurisprudence in this regard are discussed. The arrest warrants against sitting President Al Bashir of Sudan have provoked hot debates on immunities before the Court and States Parties.

Chapter II studies the issue of admissibility of a situation. Admissibility differs from jurisdiction. It means exercising the Court's jurisdiction. First, the need for the admissibility requirement is explained. The Court is not able and is not intended to prosecute all cases and situations under its jurisdiction. Therefore, it has to make a selection. The admissibility requirement directs and regulates the case and situation selection at the ICC. Admissibility consists of two elements, namely gravity and complementarity. The relevant section of the Chapter clarifies that from a logical perspective, the gravity assessment should proceed the complementarity examination. The gravity assessment is not only a matter of selection and deselection, but it includes prioritizing the selected situations. The gravity factor has not been defined by the ICC law. However, the Prosecutor of the Court has proposed factors that should be taken into account in the gravity assessment, namely scale, nature, impact and manner of crimes. The Chapter sheds insight into these factors, in particular nature and impact factors. The nature factor directs to the 'thematic prosecution' doctrine. According to this doctrine, the Prosecutor should give priority to those situations that are under-prosecuted. This prioritization is justifiable based on the expressive mandates of the Court. Regarding the impact factor, the situation of Registered Vessels of the Comoros is studied in order to explain how the situational gravity is assessed in practice. Impact of crimes is not only victim-oriented, but if the international community is shocked by a situation, the Court should intervene even if the scale of the situation is not high in comparison to other situations.

If a situation is selected and prioritized based on its gravity, then the complementarity rule enshrined in Article 17 of the Rome Statute should be assessed. The Court is intended to be a last resort mechanism. Chapter II studies all dimensions of the complementarity notion too. Complementarity as a rule regulates the relationship between the Court and States in terms of a concurrent jurisdiction over a specific situation or case. However, this rule should be understood in light of complementarity as a principle, which determines the role of the Court in the general context of the international criminal justice system. Prosecuting ICC crimes is primarily the responsibility of States. Only in the case of inaction or inability or unwillingness of States, the Court can intervene. The relevant sections delve into these preconditions for declaring a case admissible before the Court.

To give space to States to fulfill their obligations, a positive approach to complementarity could be adopted aiming at promoting and assisting States to prosecute ICC crimes at the domestic level. Moreover, in the complementarity assessment, a flexible and State-friendly approach should be adopted. The complementarity rule requires assessing of a case. A case, including potential cases in the situational phase, consists of two elements: person and conduct. To define the conduct notion in the situational phase two approaches could be adopted: narrow and broad. One approach is incident-oriented that requires the domestic jurisdiction to mirror exactly the same conduct before the Court. Contrary to this narrow approach, the broad approach is context-oriented, and gives the national jurisdictions a margin of discretion to select different incidents. The relevant section clarifies differences between these two approaches by studying the case law of the Court regarding the situations in Libya and Côte d'Ivoire. At the end, complementarity as it should be, will be discussed. Expressive mandates of the Court in addition to its complementary role in the international criminal justice system, as will be discussed, require adopting a broad approach that is more flexible towards the national initiatives.

Jurisdiction, admissibility and the interests of justice are the statutory requirements that should be taken into account. However, the OTP in 2016, by publishing its Policy Paper on Case Selection, has introduced a new factor that should not only be taken into account in the situation and case selection, but has the final word in this regard, namely operational factors. It is the availability of a situation given operational factors that ultimately determine which situation should be prioritized. Chapter IV addresses operational factors such as the availability of State cooperation or evidence that are necessary to assure an effective prosecution.

The interests of justice presumption constitutes the last Chapter of Part Three. This notion creates a context in which the dilemma between peace and justice may occur. The interests of justice notion has been untouched because there is no jurisdiction at the ICC case law about it. This Chapter enhances the idea that if the interests of victims require the suspension of the Court's intervention into a situation, the Prosecutor should avoid pursuing a situation due to the primacy of the interests of victims at the ICC's architecture. However, to make a compromise with the ending impunity mandate, in such exceptional circumstances, materializing alternatives or traditional mechanisms is recommended. In addition, although the Prosecutor is exempted from proving that an investigation or a prosecution would serve the interests of justice, she has to show that the circumstances have been examined to determine whether there were not substantial reasons to believe that the interests of justice would not be served.

Part Four studies the situation selection regime in light of expressivism. First, it is discussed that expressivism fosters two ideas: victim protection and the positive complementarity. In addition, Part Four addresses the question of implications that are carried by adopting an expressive approach to the situation selection process. In other words, this Part advises to integrate expressivism into the situation selection regime. Such integration comes up with an innovative design that will be discussed in the concluding Part of this thesis.

The research ends with a conclusion and some recommendations. The situation selection regime at the ICC is selective and selectivity has some side effects even if there is a justification to have such a selective regime. This research by introducing expressivism as the most appropriate theory that fits the situation selection regime at the ICC suggests measures that reduce the side effects of selectivity at the Court. For instance, from the expressive regime perspective, outreach activities and public diplomacy are recommended. The Court should explain why and how it selects a situation. This introduction started with an exposé on the ICC's so-called legitimacy crisis as several African States from the Rome Statute expressed their plans to withdraw – and one did – from the Rome Statute. However, labeling the Court as an African criminal court to a large extent stems from misunderstanding and misinformation about the Court. Most of the African situations under the investigation have been referred to the OTP, without the intervention of the Court. Selectivity at the ICC is to some extent shaped by external actors and factors. In addition, as this research discusses, in evaluating the selectivity of the Court, all choices should be taken into account, including those situations that have been selected for conducting a preliminary examination. The preliminary examination stage constitutes a part of the Court's system. These facts, however, need to be expressed and explained by the Court.

The manuscript was concluded in August 2017.

PART ONE

FORMULATING THE CONCEPT OF SITUATION IN THE ROME STATUTE SENSE

The Rome Statute has manifested great originality in its procedural structure. The point of departure for the judicial activities of the ICC is a situation. The concept of situation is still something of a novelty. As an unprecedented notion, the concept of situation deserves more attention. The predominant body of literature on the ICC dealing with the situational issues hardly discusses to elaborate on the notion of situation. However, logically speaking, a conceptual question should precede normative inquiries. Indeed, the latter is affected by the understanding of the former. Situation in the Rome Statute is a construction that forms a procedural stage at the ICC's architecture, namely the situational phase. Moreover, to determine how a situation is and should be selected, we need to clarify the meaning of 'situation' first.

The concept of situation is not defined by the Rome Statute. In addition, the introduction of this notion was based on no precedent. Against the backdrop of the absence of a conventional definition and consensus understanding, the beginning part of this thesis aims at providing some insights into the concept of situation. At first, it shows that there is a distinction between the concept of 'case' which is a classical conception in criminal law and the notion of situation (chapter I.1), though there is still a nexus between them (chapter I.2). Then, the reasons for framing a new notion in the Rome Statute are set out (chapter I.3). The constituent elements of the concept of situation in the Rome Statute sense are uncovered in the final chapter of this part, namely the jurisdictional element (chapter II.1) and the factual component (chapter II.2).

CHAPTER I
SITUATION v. CASE

One method of defining a concept is to define it in an indirect manner by distinguishing the notion at hand from its parallel concepts. From such a perspective, situations might be defined by making a distinction between them and cases. The concept of case is well-known in criminal law. Domestic legal proceedings revolve around cases. The Rome Statute preserves the notion of case, but it introduces a complementary concept, namely situation. Reading the concept of situation through the lens of the case concept is misleading. Classical and conventional facts influence the shape of the understanding of new phenomenon. Because of the wide effects of the concept of situation on the work of the Court, some have advised that to ensure a coherent system, a settled view on the understanding of situations and cases is very important.[1] This chapter seeks to draw the crucial distinction between situations and cases to avoid such misunderstanding.

1. DICHOTOMY BETWEEN SITUATION AND CASE

In the Rome Statute, the notion of 'situation' differs from the concept of 'case'. Initially, such a distinction between cases and situations was not recognized for the ICC. The 1994 Draft Statute, which was developed by the International Law Commission (ILC), allowed States Parties to lodge complaints with respect to specific crimes, rather than entire situations.[2] Draft Article 25(2) asserted, "a State Party which accepts the jurisdiction of the Court under Article 22 with respect to a crime may lodge a complaint with the Prosecutor alleging that such a crime appears to have been committed."[3] It was similar to the national criminal procedures that are triggered by lodging complaints against the accused. Nonetheless, this approach changed later, and complaints against specific cases were replaced with referrals of situations. The main reason behind this change was the concern of some delegations in the preparatory negotiations about the potential for abuse of the State Party's referrals

1 Robert Cryer, Hakan Friman and Darryl Robinson (et al), *An Introduction to International Criminal Law and Procedure*, Cambridge University Press, 2014, p. 446.

2 Philipp Kirsch and Darryl Robinson, 'Referral by States Parties', in Antonio Cassese, Paola Gaeta and John R.W.D. Jones (eds.), *The Rome Statute of the International Criminal Court: A Commentary*, Oxford University Press, 2002, p. 620.

3 Report of the International Law Commission on the Work of its Forty-sixth Session, 2 May – 22 July 1994, Official Records of the General Assembly. p. 45.

for frivolous purposes.[4] In fact, the ability to target specific incidents and persons could direct the Court into one-sided prosecutions and consequently could damage the reputation of the Court due to infamous selective justice. To avoid this undesirable consequence, the possibility of referring specific cases to the ICC for prosecution was rejected. That raised the question: what could serve as a satisfactory substitute for the concept of case? Two proposals were put forward, namely situation and matter. However, most delegations advocated the term 'situation' because of its more general nature and rejected the concept of 'matter' as being too specific for the independent functioning of the Court.[5] The term situation was exactly what was adopted in the final step, namely during the Rome Conference.[6] By doing so, the Rome Statute constitutes an independent stage in its structure based on the notion of situation, namely the situational phase. The situational phase assumes prominent functions in realizing the Court's constituent objectives. Not only its very existence, but also its functions are unique to the Court. The pre-trial phase in the procedural architecture of the Court consists of some levels, namely preliminary examination, investigation and prosecution. A situation is an object for conducting the preliminary examination and investigation, whereas a case is an object for prosecution.

In the absence of a statutory definition, the jurisprudence of the Court has provided a definition of a case. Accordingly, the concept of a case includes "specific incidents during which one or more crimes within the jurisdiction of the Court seem to have been committed by one or more identified suspects."[7] The concept of case encompasses two limbs and components, namely a person and a conduct.[8] On the contrary, a situation is something more than one or some incidents. A situation is a context within which some incidents occur. A situation is broader than a case in the scope. The inherent feature of a case is its specificity, contrary to a situation that is of a general nature. A situation is those parameters within which "the Office conducts its investigative activities."[9] The dividing line between the phase of a situation and the stage of a case is drawn by the issuance of a warrant of arrest or a summons. As Pre-Trial Chamber (PTC) II submits, "the case stage starts with an application by the Prosecutor under Article 58 of the

4 Kirsch and Robinson, 2002, p. 622, see *supra* note 2.

5 Lionel Yee, 'The International Criminal Court and the Security Council: Article 13(b) and 16', in Roy S. Lee, *The International Criminal Court: Making of the Rome Statute*, Kluwer Law International, 1999, p. 148.

6 For instance Article 13(1) of the Rome Statute provides "a situation in which one or more of such crimes appears to have been committed is referred to the Prosecutor by a State Party in accordance with Article 14."

7 For Instance, see: ICC, PTC I, Lubanga case, Decision on the Prosecutor's Application under Article 58, 10 February 2006, para. 21. And ICC, PTC I, Harun and Kushayb case, Decision on the Prosecutor's Application under Article 58(7), 27 April 2007, para. 14. And ICC, PTC III, Warrant of Arrest for Jean-Pierre Bemba Gombo Replacing the Warrant of Arrest Issued on 23 May 2008, 10 June 2008, para. 16.

8 ICC, PTC I, Gaddafi case, Decision on the Admissibility of the Case Against Saif-Al-Islam Gaddafi, 31 May 2013, para. 61.

9 ICC, OTP, Policy Paper on Preliminary Examinations, November 2013, para. 41.

Statute for the issuance of a warrant of arrest or summons to appear."[10] Therefore, once the Prosecutor seeks a warrant, it is her responsibility to identify both a specific conduct, which constitutes a crime, and a person charged with that crime in addition to his/her mode of liability. This identification is made in the context of a situation that has already been under investigation.

The crucial distinction between situations and cases is an established practice in the functioning of the Court.[11] A particular context, for instance, wherein the distinction between the case phase and the situation stage has been observed is the victims' participation at the ICC's proceedings. Article 68(3) of the Rome Statute recognizes a right for the victims to participate in the proceedings before the Court.[12] This right corresponds to an obligation upon the Court to respect such a right by considering the victims' views. The appropriateness of the stage of proceedings in which the victims intend to participate is one condition that should be met for authorizing participation. The Chambers of the Court in many instances have clarified those proceedings that deserve the victims' participation. At first, PTC I, at the ICC's first decision on the application for victim's participation in the proceedings, referred to the separation between the situational stage and the case phase. At the time, the legal representative of some victims submitted their respective requests for participation in the proceedings of the situation in the Democratic Republic of Congo (DRC).[13] In response, PTC I stated that "the Chamber considers that the Statute, the Rules of Procedure and Evidence and the Regulations of the Court draw a distinction between situations and cases in terms of the different kinds of proceedings, initiated by any organ of the Court, that they entail."[14] In light of this distinction, the Chamber acknowledged that "during the stage of investigation of a situation" the status of victim is accordable to "applicants who seem to meet the definition of victims set out in rule 85 of the Rules of Procedure and Evidence."[15] It clarifies that the victims of a situation are differentiated from the victims of a case, and they are not necessarily the same.

---

10 ICC, PTC II, Muthaura case, Decision on the Application by the Government of Kenya Challenging the Admissibility of the Case Pursuant to Article 19(2)(b) of the Statute, 20 May 2011, para. 50.

11 Héctor Olásolo and Enrique Carnero Rojo, 'The Application of the Principle of Complementarity to the Decision of Where to Open an Investigation: The Admissibility of Situations', in Carsten Stahn and Mohamed M. El Zeidy (eds.), *The International Criminal Court and Complementarity: From Theory to Practice*, Cambridge University Press, 2011, p. 402.

12 Paragraph 3 of Article 68: "where the personal interests of the victims are affected, the Court shall permit their views and concerns to be presented and considered at stages of the proceedings determined to be appropriate by the Court."

13 ICC, PTC I, Situation in the DRC, Decision on the Applications for Participation in the Proceedings of VPRS 1, VPRS 2, VPRS 3, VPRS 4, VPRS 5 and VPRS 6, 17 January 2006, para. 20.

14 Ibid., para. 65.

15 Ibid., para. 66. Later, the Appeals Chamber of the Court shed much light on the notion of 'stages of the proceedings'. The Appeal Chamber recognized that the situational phase and the case stage are different but clarified that 'proceedings', in Article 68 is a term "denoting a judicial cause pending before a Chamber" and that is in contrast with an investigation. Indeed, the Appeals Chamber confined the victims' participation to judicial proceedings including "proceedings affecting investigations, provided [that victims'] personal interests are affected by the issues arising for resolution" (See: ICC, Appeals Chamber, Situation in the DRC, Judgment on Victim Participation in

2. LINKAGE BETWEEN SITUATION AND CASE

In spite of the divergence between the concepts of case and situation, there is an attachment between these two notions. A situation is the source of one or more cases. A situation has a broader scope than a case, and the latter is a derivative from the former. Indeed, each situation may conceive some cases. As mentioned, situations are objects for investigation before the ICC. The entire purpose of investigations is to identify any cases.[16] Such cases are identified in the context of a situation. The tie between a case and its situation is important in determining the Court's jurisdiction. The Court may exercise its jurisdiction exclusively on those cases that are linked to a situation under its jurisdiction. A case within a territory without any link to the existing situation in the territory may uncover and direct to another situation in the same territory.

What links a case to a situation is the contextual elements of the situation. In other words, the nexus between a case and its situation is the context in which both situation and case arise. PTC III in its authorizing decision to initiate an investigation in the situation in Côte d'Ivoire states that the authorized investigation would cover all crimes committed after the date of authorization, insofar as the contextual element of crimes, i.e., the link between these crimes and the original situation, is the same. In the eyes of the Chamber, to determine such sameness, "they must, at least in a broad sense, involve the same actors and have been committed within the context of either the same attacks (crimes against humanity) or the same conflict (war crimes)."[17]

The strong correlation between a situation and a case implies that the scope of a case must be sufficiently linked to the initiated investigation, and it must not exceed the temporal, territorial and personal parameters defining that situation.[18] It implies that the situation is a framework within which cases are selected. To assure the existence of such a sufficient link between a case and its corresponding situation, besides the Prosecutor, the Chambers also have an authority to explore the existence of such a tie. For this reason, for instance, in the context of the situation in the DRC, PTC I ordered the Prosecutor to submit his observations and to provide much clarification on the link between the events alleged in his application under Article 58 and the situation in Congo. The Chamber noted that it is necessary for the Chamber to determine "whether such events are sufficiently linked to the situation of crisis that triggered

---

the Investigation Stage of the Proceedings in the Appeal of the OPCD Against the Decision of Pre-Trial Chamber I of 7 December 2007 and in the Appeals of the OPCD and the Prosecutor Against the Decision of Pre-Trial Chamber I of 24 December 2007, 19 December 2008, para. 56).

16 Sarah M.H. Nouwen, *Complementarity in the Line of Fire: the Catalyzing Effect of the ICC in Uganda and Sudan,* Cambridge University Press, 2013, p. 72.

17 ICC, PTC III, Côte d'Ivoire Situation, Decision Pursuant to Article 15 of the Rome Statute on the Authorization of an Investigation into the Situation in the Republic of Côte d'Ivoire, 3 October 2011, para. 179.

18 ICC, PTC I, Harun and Kushayb case, 27 April 2007, para. 14, see *supra* note 7.

the DRC investigation, so as to fall within its scope and therefore within the ICC's jurisdiction."[19]

The standard to determine whether there is a sufficient link between cases and a situation is lenient. For instance, it is normal that crimes within a situation are committed in different times and locations by different perpetrators, but what is important is the existence of a sufficient link between those crimes and the relevant situation. From this perspective, for instance, PTC III in its decision to authorize an investigation into the situation in Côte d'Ivoire considered all violent events in the period between 19 September 2002 and 28 November 2010 as a single situation embracing an ongoing crisis, though they had reached "varying levels of intensity at different locations and at different times."[20] Moreover, it is most likely that the Court as a permanent organisation with open mandates intervenes in ongoing conflicts. In these scenarios, cases may arise from the context of a situation after the Court's jurisdiction over the situation is activated. Here, a sufficient link between the consequent cases and the original situation may exist. Therefore, if a sufficient link exists, "it is irrelevant whether particular individuals or events subsequently charged by the Prosecutor could not have been charged at the time of the original referral."[21] The Court is a predominantly future-oriented tribunal with regards to its mandates.

3. REASONS BEHIND THE ADOPTION OF A SITUATION-ORIENTED PROCEDURE

The Court's jurisdiction is activated over a situation instead of a case. Designing situations as the opening parts of the Court's operation is intended to assure the legitimacy of the Court through endorsing the independence of the Prosecutor. The selection of situations and cases falls within the prosecutorial discretion. Article 42 of the Rome Statute obliges the Prosecutor to act independently; otherwise, the reputation of the Court is affected adversely by the decisions made by the Prosecutor. Independence as required by the Rome Statute is not limited to not acting on external instructions; it also means that "decisions shall not be influenced or altered by the presumed or known wishes of any party."[22] The Prosecutor's independence in selecting situations and cases is sustained if she maintains the principle of impartiality. The construction of situation helps the Prosecutor to retain impartiality in her decisions to make a selection. The principle of impartiality requires the Prosecutor to "apply consistent methods and criteria, irrespective of the States or parties involved or the person(s)

---

19 ICC, PTC I, Situation in the DRC, Decision Requesting Clarification on the Prosecutor's Application under Article 58, 6 September 2010, para. 12.

20 ICC, PTC III, Côte d'Ivoire Situation, 3 October 2011, para. 36, see *supra* note 17.

21 ICC, PTC I, Mbarushimana case, Decision on the Defense Challenge to the Jurisdiction of the Court, 26 October 2011, para. 42.

22 ICC, OTP, Policy Paper on Preliminary Examinations, para. 26.

or group(s) concerned."[23] A situation-oriented approach provides the Prosecutor with an opportunity to adopt a holistic and far-reaching approach to a conflict and to conduct a thorough investigation into crimes allegedly committed by each party involved. Indeed, impartiality requires the Prosecutor not to take into account the side on which a person is fighting for purposes of case selection. For this reason, some commentators have considered avoiding politicization of selections as a main rationale of distinction between a case and a situation.[24] Situation is a general context and crisis that includes all crimes and persons involved irrespective of their nature and affiliation respectively. Adopting such a situational and holistic approach is not a discretion and choice, but rather a statutory obligation. It means that even if a State Party or the UNSC refers a one-sided situation to the Prosecutor, she is not bound by the partiality of the referral. On the contrary, the Prosecutor shall accept the referred situation as a whole. On 16 December 2003, the government of Uganda referred the "situation concerning of the Lord's Resistance Army (LRA)."[25] In response, the then Prosecutor of the Court announced that his office "has informed the Ugandan authorities that we must interpret the scope of the referral consistently with the principles of the Rome Statute, and hence we are analyzing crimes within the situation of northern Uganda by whomever committed."[26] Another instance in which the situational approach requires the Prosecutor to preserve the generality feature of a situation is UNSC referrals that exclude some groups of individuals from the Court's jurisdiction. Legally speaking, in these instances, the UNSC does not refer a situation in the Rome Statute sense.[27] In this scenario, the Prosecutor may ask the UNSC to adapt its referral to the statutory requirements.

The forward-looking and non-retroactive jurisdiction of the ICC made instituting the situational phase necessary. In addition, the history of international criminal justice system shows that this measure was necessary to ensure the impartiality of the Prosecutor and consequently the legitimacy of the Court. The International Military Tribunals in Nuremburg and Tokyo (IMTs), marking the birth of the international criminal justice system in the modern world, are ironically described as victor's justice, because they pursued justice in a one-sided manner. Article 6 of the Charter of the Nuremburg Tribunal provided that the Tribunal was established to punish exclusively "the major war criminals of the European Axis countries." From this perspective, some have characterized the IMTs as 'victors' justice', since "only the vanquished were

23 Ibid., para. 28.

24 William A. Schabas, 'The Rise and Fall of Complementarity', in Carsten Stahn and Mohamed M. El Zeidy (eds.), *The International Criminal Court and Complementarity: From Theory to Practice*, Cambridge University Press, 2011, p. 162. And Kirsch and Robinson, 2002, p. 43, see *supra* note 2.

25 ICC, Press Release, President of Uganda Refers Situation Concerning the Lord's Resistance Army to the ICC, 29 January 2004, available at: www.icc-cpi.int/legalAidConsultations?name=president+of+uganda+refers+situation+concerning+the+lord_s+resistance+army+_lra_+to+the+icc, last accessed at 13 June 2017.

26 ICC, Presidency, Situation in Uganda, Decision Assigning the Situation in Uganda to Pre-Trial Chamber II, 5 July 2004, Annexed Letter.

27 Nouwen, 2013, p. 256, *supra* note 16.

charged with violations of international humanitarian law and the defendants were prosecuted and punished for crimes expressly defined in an instrument adopted by the victors at the conclusion of the war."[28] Exclusion of one party to the Second World War has led other scholars to consider the legacy of the Nuremberg Tribunals as flawed, since its legitimacy was tarnished.[29] Even before the Rome Conference, the experience of IMTs had warned the judges in the International Criminal Tribunal for the former Yugoslavia (ICTY) "to avoid some of the flaws noted in the Nuremberg and Tokyo proceedings."[30]

It should be noted that impartiality does not necessarily require an all-inclusive approach in prosecution. Legally speaking, as the first ICC Prosecutor states, "impartiality does not mean that we must necessarily prosecute all groups in a given situation."[31] At the ICC system, the selection of cases is regulated by some legal criteria. Sufficient gravity and availability are the main factors that the Prosecutor takes into account to select and then to prioritize a case. Affiliation does not play a role here. Here, the so-called 'even-handedness' strategies come up. According to the 'balanced prosecution' policy, a number of cases are selected for prosecution merely based on membership of a particular national or ethnic group rather than the gravity of their crimes.[32] For instance, Del Ponte, then ICTY Prosecutor, believed that a lasting peace could only be reached if all parties to the conflict had been investigated. She once stated, "my remaining investigations cover the region and concern all main parties to the conflict. By completing these investigations, ICTY will have proven that it worked impartially towards achieving justice, peace and reconciliation in the former Yugoslavia."[33] Some scholars have advocated this policy too.[34] This policy, however, did not limit only to investigations. Based on this policy, a representative sampling of Croatians and Muslims were tried at the ICTY, despite the view that Serb forces were primarily responsible for the atrocities. In addition, the Special Court for Sierra Leone

---

28 ICTY, Tadić case, Decision on the Prosecutor Motion Requesting Protective Measures for Victims and Witnesses, 10 August 1995, para. 21.

29 Robert Cryer, *Prosecuting International Crimes: Selectivity and the International Criminal Law Regime*, Cambridge University Press, 2005, p. 206.

30 ICTY, Tadić case, August 1995, para. 21, see *supra* note 28. The IMTs have not been criticized for their selective justice, but there have been other human rights errors. However, Schabas argues that "it is unrealistic to assess trials in 1945 and 1946 by human rights standards that prevail six decades later and that have evolved progressively. On balance, the proceedings certainly met the highest standards of the time on a procedural level" (See: William A. Schabas, 'Victor's Justice: Selecting Situations at the International Criminal Court', *Marshall Law Review*, 2010). In addition, others have argued that the victor's justice at the IMTs was justifiable because it was inevitable (See: Kirsten Sellars, 'Imperfect Justice at Nuremberg and Tokyo', *European Journal for International Law*, 2011, vol. 21).

31 ICC, Statement by Luis Moreno-Ocampo at the Informal Meeting of Legal Advisors of Ministers of Foreign Affairs, New York, 24 October 2005 p. 6, available at: www.icc-cpi.int/NR/rdonlyres/9D70039E-4BEC-4F32–9D4A-CEA8B6799E37/143836/LMO_20051024_English.pdf.

32 Frederiek de Vlaming, 'Selection of Defendants', in Luc Reydams and Jan Wouters and Cedric Ryngaret (eds.), *International Prosecutors*, Oxford University Press, 2012, p. 566.

33 Ibid., p. 558.

34 Jo Martin Stigen, *The Relationship Between the International Criminal Court and National Jurisdictions: the Principle of Complementarity*, Brill Nijhoff, 2008, p. 395.

(SCSL) went the furthest in materializing a balanced approach to prosecutions by organizing three trials, each of them focused on one of the warring parties in the civil war.[35]

However, it seems that sticking to such a policy was not entirely successful at the ICTY, because at the end some remained unhappy. The Serbs continued complaining that they bore the brunt of the prosecutions, while the others claimed that they were victims of selective prosecution in which the criminal responsibility was not the only consideration to initiate prosecution. For instance, in the Čelebići case, Esad Landžo alleged that he was the subject of a selective prosecution policy conducted by the Prosecution.[36] He argued that he was the only Bosnian Muslim who was accused without military rank or command responsibility during the war. Landžo asserted that he was singled out for prosecution "simply because he was the only person the Prosecutor's office could find to 'represent' the Bosnian Muslims."[37] However, the ICTY Appeal Chamber rejected this claim because of the appellant's failure to put forward any evidence proving his assertion and declared that he "was not the subject of a discriminatory selective prosecution."[38]

Schabas opposes the necessity of the balanced prosecution by providing a different line of reasoning. He argues that one of the international tribunals' mandates is to establish the 'historical truth'. For this purpose, "the international tribunals necessarily emphasize the atrocities of one side rather than the other." From this perspective, he defends the justice delivered by the IMTs. According to his point of view, the selectivity of the Nuremburg Tribunals was a positive feature because nobody must think that "the historical truth of World War II is of a number of morally equivalent powers fighting for control of territory, because by that reading of history, the Americans and British were just as evil (or as good) as the Nazis."[39] Nonetheless, partial justice produces partial truth if another party to the conflict has committed unimaginable atrocities, too. It is the classical matter of delivering justice by dirty hands.

Both adoption of a prior balanced prosecution and exclusive prosecution have disadvantages. The policy of even-handedness implies that gravity has not always been the guiding principle in selecting defendants.[40] Nonetheless, as will be discussed, the introduction of the gravity requirement by the Rome Statute for selection of cases was intended to preserve the legitimacy and transparency of the Court. There should not be a discrimination in protecting the victims, and one-sided prosecutions amount to discrimination. Interestingly, Schabas refers to this rule as a reason behind adoption

---

35 William A. Schabas, 'International Criminal Tribunals: A Review of 2007', Journal of International Human Rights, 2008, vol. 6, p. 387.

36 ICTY, Appeals Chamber, Čelebići case, Judgment, 20 February 2001, para. 596.

37 Ibid., para. 612.

38 Ibid., para. 615.

39 William A. Schabas, Rwanda Tribunal Symposium and Victors Justice, 16 August 2009, available at: humanrightsdoctorate.blogspot.nl/2009/08/rwanda-tribunal-symposium-and-victors.html, last accessed at 17 February 2017.

40 Frederiek de Vlaming, 2012, p. 567, see *supra* note 32.

of a situation-oriented approach at the ICC prosecutions. He argues that what matters is that there is no difference among the victims of a conflict, and it is not fair if a discriminative protection applies to victims.[41]

At the ICC, the gravity plays a prominent role in the situation and case selection. In selecting a case the gravity requirement is decisive, not geographical or regional balance.[42] The Prosecutor should act on the gravity requirement to maintain the consistency in her functions and selections. In the preliminary examination, that has expressive mandates, the Prosecutor shall express and show the generality of a situation by examining all grave incidents and allegations brought to her attention. During the preliminary examination, the Prosecutor has wide opportunities to prove her office's impartiality by clarifying the reasons behind her decisions. The outreach and communication activities should be seen as indivisible parts of the preliminary examination. They deserve more attention in light of the expressive mandates of this stage, though in light of the Court's budget it is typically regarded as a Registry task. The Prosecutor should be mindful of the legitimacy and the public perception of the Court by enhancing her informative and expressive activities in the preliminary examination. If she can manage the expectations through outreach activities, there is no need to adopt the balanced prosecution policy. It is likely that within a situation, the cases from different groups to a conflict meet the gravity requirement. In this scenario, Stahn recommends that both sides of the conflict be prosecuted simultaneously in order to counter doubts as to the appearance of impartiality.[43] He requests the Prosecutor to alter the policy of 'sequenced approach' to investigations according to which the OTP investigates cases and groups in a conflict in sequence.[44] However, given the wide restrictions of the OTP and its basic-size policy, it seems that such a simultaneous prosecution is mainly unfeasible. Here, the idea of the 'Case Selection Plan' will be of great assistance to manage the expectations and perceptions. The Plan, as will be discussed later, shows all cases that have been targeted by the Prosecutor for prosecution, though they need to wait until the moment operational factors to initiate an investigation are available.

---

41 William A. Schabas, *Unimaginable Atrocities: Justice, Politics and Rights at the War Crimes Tribunals*, Oxford University Press, 2012, p. 81.

42 ICC, OTP, Policy Paper on Preliminary Examinations, para. 11.

43 Carsten Stahn, 'Complementarity: A Tale of Two Notions', *Criminal Law Forum*, 2008, vol. 19, p. 112.

44 Ibid.

CHAPTER II
DEFINING ELEMENTS OF THE NOTION OF A SITUATION

The preceding chapter indicated that the concept of a situation differs from the notion of a case. Thus, a question arises: what is a situation? A situation, as imagined by the Rome Statute, is a multifaceted notion. It embraces two pillars, namely the jurisdictional pillar and the contextual element. This chapter elaborates the constituent elements of the concept of situation.

1. THE JURISDICTIONAL ELEMENT OF A SITUATION

The Court's jurisdiction is not absolute. It has some constraints, including temporal, territorial and personal confines, besides its subject-matter constraint. In addition, the jurisdiction of the ICC is dormant and it is triggered and activated over a specific situation. In the Rome Statute sense, a situation determines the jurisdictional framework within which the Prosecutor may exercise her discretion in the context of a specific crisis. Situation as a jurisdiction-oriented notion is composed of, *inter alia,* those jurisdictional parameters enshrined in the Rome Statute. These statutory parameters are applied to each crisis in which the Court intents to intervene and determine the boundaries of the Court's intervention, particularly in terms of time and location. PTC I in its decision of 17 January 2006 submits that situations "are generally defined in terms of temporal, territorial and in some cases personal parameters."[45] Regulation 49 of the Court's Regulations is helpful here. The provision relates to the Prosecutor's request for an authorization to initiate investigations. However, it is not limited to this instance, since there is no difference between the meanings of a situation either in context of communications or referrals. According to the Regulation, a situation shall indicate as a minimum: "(a) a reference to the crimes, (b) the places of the alleged commission of the crimes, e.g. country, town, as precisely as possible; (c) the time or time period of the alleged commission of the crimes; and (d) the persons involved, if identified, or a description of the persons or groups of persons involved."[46]

---

45 ICC, PTC I, Situation in the DRC, 17 January 2006, para. 65, see *supra* note 13.

46 Regulation 49 (1) and (2) of Regulations of the Court.

It should be noted that a situation must remain distinct from being attributed to specific individuals.[47] It does not mean that it is not imaginable that the ICC-identified crimes are committed by a small group, but a situation should not be defined in a one-sided manner. As mentioned earlier, the generality of the scope of a situation is the main feature of this concept. Nonetheless, the personal jurisdiction constitutes a narrowing parameter of a situation, if the Court's jurisdiction is exercised based on the personal jurisdiction, instead of the territory jurisdiction.

Situations are objects for different stages at the Court. The jurisdictional parameters of a situation are identified and defined within a process, from identification phase to prosecution. Therefore, the legal aspect of a situation is rather dynamic. Over time and by further investigation, those sides are defined specifically. To avoid major changes, the Prosecutor tends to define a situation as broadly as possible in terms of its jurisdictional parameters.

2. THE CONTEXTUAL ELEMENT OF A SITUATION

Apart from the jurisdictional element, a situation is formed by a contextual element. A situation is not merely an abstract concept. By contrast, the jurisdictional parameters of a situation are defined in the context of a concrete crisis. Bassiouni points this aspect out when he states "situation is the overall factual context in which it is believed that a crime within the jurisdiction of the Court has been committed."[48]

2.1. CRISIS AS THE CONTEXT OF SITUATIONS

The context of a situation can be labeled as a 'crisis' or 'situation of crisis'. Such a naming is not of a legal effect, but it is only to distinguish between the different elements of a situation. The term 'situation of crisis' has been used by the Court. For instance, PTC I in the case of Mbarashimana used the term 'situation of crisis' to refer to the situation concept.[49] In addition, the Prosecutor has occasionally referred to the term.[50] Rastan submits that the usage of this term aimed at defining the parameters on the Court's

---

47 Christoph Safferling, *International Criminal Procedure*, Oxford University Press, 2012, p. 93.

48 Mahmoud Cherif Bassiouni, *Introduction to International Criminal Law*, Martinus Nijhoff Publishers, 2013, p. 680.

49 ICC, PTC I, Mbarushimana case, Decision on the Confirmation of Charges, 16 December 2011, para. 33.

50 For instance, in the Article 53(1) Report on the in the Situation in the Central African Republic, the Prosecutor states "following analysis of the jurisdictional parameters regarding the situation in the CAR since September 2012, the Office concluded that these incidents and the serious allegations of crimes potentially falling within the jurisdiction of the ICC constitute a new situation, unrelated to the 'situation of crisis' previously referred to the ICC by the CAR authorities in December 2004" (ICC, OTP, Situation in the CAR, Article 53(1) Report, 24 November 2014, para. 8).

jurisdiction in objective terms.[51] It means the term crisis refers to the concrete aspect and the contextual element of a situation.

To understand the meaning of 'situation of crisis', an analogy with the notion of 'state of emergency' can be made. The latter has promoted considerable debate in international human rights law, namely the derogation in time of emergency. It is worth recalling that human rights law is an applicable law to the Court under Article 21 of the Statute. Article 15(1) of the European Convention on Human Rights provides that "in time of war or other public emergency threatening the life of the nation any High Contracting Party may take measures derogating from its obligations under this Convention to the extent strictly required by the exigencies of the situation, provided that such measures are not inconsistent with its other obligations under international law." The European Court of Human Rights (ECtHR) in its ruling in Lawless v. Ireland examined the permissible scope of derogations of states' obligations during a 'state of emergency'. For this purpose, the Court firstly referred to the gravity or seriousness of the circumstances to define the state of emergency concept. The ECtHR held that public emergency refers to "an exceptional situation of crisis or emergency, which affects the whole population and constitutes a threat to the organized life of the community of which the State is composed."[52] Hence, a crisis could be understood as exceptional circumstances with collective effects. It has been suggested that the public emergency must be construed as tantamount to war or as analogous to the circumstances of war.[53] Crisis refers to those grave and exceptional circumstances that may contribute to incidents that 'form part of the same crisis or sequence of events for which an investigation has already been authorized'.[54] A crisis, however, may be provoked for various reasons. For example, post-election violence is a typical context in which a crisis arises and may lead to the establishment of a situation before the Court. For instance, in both situations in Kenya and Côte d'Ivoire, the post-election violence constituted a crisis. Fighting for land, water and power and opposing ethnic or religious beliefs all can spark a crisis off.

It should be borne in mind that normalcy is the general rule and the state of crisis is the exception. For this reason, the state of emergency is conceived of as a temporary phenomenon and the measures taken to deal with an emergency must function as a means to end the existing crisis.[55] One can benefit from the exceptionality of the state of emergency to clarify the complementarity principle at the ICC. In the normal course of events, prosecution of crimes is a domestic affair but when a crisis emerges, the Court's intervention is warranted.

---

51 Rod Rastan, 'The Jurisdictional Scope of Situations before the International Criminal Court', *Criminal Law Forum*, 2012, vol. 23, p. 9.

52 ECtHR, Lawless v. Ireland case, Judgment, 1 July1961, para. 28.

53 Héctor Olásolo, *The Triggering Procedure of the International Criminal Court,* Martinus Nijhoff Publishers, 2005, p. 251.

54 ICC, PTC III, Situation in Côte d'Ivoire, 3 Octobre 2011, para. 14, see *supra* note 17.

55 Oren Gross and Fionnuala Aolain, *Law in Times of Crisis: Emergency Powers in Theory and Practice,* Cambridge University Press, 2006, p. 341.

Situations are distinct from each other because their constituent crisis (events and their causes) are different. This is in contrast with the viewpoint of Rastan who maintains that the word 'crisis' is not "a threshold qualifier to the exercise of jurisdiction."[56] By contrast, the contextual element of a situation is an important criterion to identify a situation and to determine its relevant cases. A situation is not formed in abstract. Because of the distinction between situations, Bassiouni states that situations should be determined contextually.[57]

2.2. CONNECTION BETWEEN CONTEXTUAL ELEMENT OF CRIMES AND CONTEXTUAL ELEMENT OF SITUATIONS

'Situation of crisis' is not a legal concept, but law can offer assistance to understand this notion better. A concept in the Rome Statute that may help to identify the factual aspect of a situation is the contextual element of crimes. At the ICC legal system, the material element of crimes consists of two components, namely contextual elements and specific elements.[58] Specific elements are those underlying acts that have been predominantly criminalized by domestic jurisdictions too, such as murder, rape and destruction of properties. All crimes falling within the jurisdiction of the Court, i.e. crimes against humanity, war crimes and genocide, are committed in a specific context. As mentioned, a crisis is those exceptional circumstances that denote the seriousness and gravity of a situation. Similarly, the contextual elements of the Court's crimes demonstrate the gravity of the crimes to concern the international community.[59] The contextual element of crimes is a defining feature of the international crime. If ordinary crimes are committed in the context of specific contexts, they amount to the core crimes. Based on such an affinity between the contexts of situation and crime in the Rome Statute, the contextual element of a situation can be characterized in the form of the contextual elements of the crimes. However, it should be recalled that this likeness does not mean that there is no difference between these two notions. The main difference is the evidentiary threshold to determine the contexts. Identification of a situation is the initial stage of the Court's functioning. Therefore, its relevant evidentiary threshold is at the lowest level. However, identifying the contextual element of the crimes in the preliminary examination or in later stages requires a higher threshold.

2.2.1. *Context of War Crimes*

The contextual elements of ICC crimes deserve an independent research. However, for the purposes of this thesis, a brief description shall suffice. The contextual element

56 Rastan, 2012, p. 10, see *supra* note 51.
57 Bassiouni, 2013, p. 681, see *supra* note 48.
58 ICC, PTC I, Lubanga case, 10 February 2006, para. 80, see *supra* note 7.
59 Margaret M. De Guzman, 'Gravity and the Legitimacy of the International Criminal Court', *Fordham International Law Journal*, 2008, vol. 32, p. 1407.

of war crimes is an armed conflict. It means that "the existence of an armed conflict, be it international or non- international, is a fundamental requirement of the charges under Article 8."[60] It is a jurisdictional threshold and qualifier for war crimes. Not all crimes committed during an armed conflict are war crimes, but there must be a nexus between the acts of the accused and the armed conflict.[61] The contextual element of an armed conflict and the nexus with such a conflict are meant to draw the distinction between war crimes and ordinary criminal behavior.[62] The ICTY Appeals Chamber in the Tadić case states that an armed conflict exists "whenever there is a resort to armed force between States or protracted armed violence between governmental authorities and organized armed groups or between such groups within a State."[63] The ICC Elements of Crimes explicitly require that the conduct that forms a war crime be committed "in the context of and associated with" an armed conflict.[64] As some commentators on the Rome Statute assert, this provision of the Elements of Crimes was meant to reflect the case law of the *ad hoc* tribunals, which states a sufficient nexus must be established between crimes and the armed conflict.[65] This nexus is explained as "the alleged crimes were closely related to the hostilities."[66] However, the causality and nexus requirement is not defined narrowly. To constitute a war crime, "the armed conflict need not have been causal to the commission of the crime, but the existence of an armed conflict must, at a minimum, have played a substantial part in the perpetrator's ability to commit it."[67] Adopting this flexible approach to the meaning of the 'nexus requirement' has a positive effect on the effective prosecution of sexual crimes; it prevents the creation of a loophole to be exploited by defendants by labeling sexual crimes as a 'private' affair, instead of a war conduct.[68] In other words, conflicts constitute exceptional circumstances that facilitate criminality, even if those criminal behaviors are not of a military nature.

The nexus requirement is also flexible in terms of location and time. The Prosecutor does not need to prove that the original conflict took place in the location where the underlying offence is alleged to have occurred.[69] In the words of the ICTY's judges,

---

60 ICC, Trial Chamber I, Lubanga case, Judgment Pursuant to Article 74 of the Statute, 14 March 2012, para. 504.

61 William A. Schabas, *The International Criminal Court: A Commentary on the Rome Statute,* Oxford University Press, 2010, p. 207.

62 Knut Dormann. 'Paragraph 2 (a)', in Otto Triffterer (ed.), Commentary on the Rome Statute of the International Criminal Court, C.H. Beck. Hart. Nomos, 2008, p. 303.

63 ICTY, Tadić case, Decision on the Defense Motion for Interlocutory Appeal on Jurisdiction, 2 October 1995, para. 70.

64 ICC Rome Statute Article 8(2)(a).

65 Dormann., 2008, p. 303, see *supra* note 62.

66 ICC, PTC I, Lubanga case, Decision of the Confirmation of Charges, 29 January 2007, para. 288.

67 ICTY, Kovač case, Judgment, 12 June 2002, para. 58.

68 Christine Byron, *War Crimes and Crimes Against Humanity in the Rome Statute of the International Criminal Court,* Manchester University Press, 2009, p. 15.

69 Gideon Boas and James L. Bischoff and Natalie L. Reid, *International Criminal Law Practitioner Library Volume II: Elements of Crimes under International Law,* Cambridge University Press, 2009, p. 239.

"it is sufficient that the alleged crimes were closely related to the hostilities occurring in other parts of the territories controlled by the parties to the conflict."[70] The ICC Elements of Crimes also refer to 'in the context of' an armed conflict. This expression refers to the temporal and geographic context in a broad sense. It means that crimes can be temporally and geographically remote from the actual fighting.[71] As the Kunarac Appeal Judgment explained, "what ultimately distinguishes a war crime from a purely domestic offence is that a war crime is shaped by or dependent upon the environment – the armed conflict – in which it is committed."[72] Such an armed conflict, irrespective of its characteristic as an international or non-international conflict, is those exceptional circumstances or crisis shaping the contextual element of a situation.[73] The nexus requirement is decisive in determining both the commission of war crimes and the borders of a situation. If, for instance, there is a situation that has been framed based on a specific conflict, the potential sequent conflicts in the same region fall within the given situation only if they have a nexus with the original conflict as the constituent context of a situation.

2.2.2. Context of Crimes against Humanity

Crimes against humanity entail any of the specified acts that are listed in Article 7(1) of the Statute (underlying acts), if they are committed as part of a widespread or systematic attack directed against any civilian population (contextual element). When the underlying acts meet the contextual elements requirement, they exceed the 'jurisdictional threshold' of the ICC and would be considered as the most serious international crimes that fall within the jurisdiction of the Court. According to the ruling made by the PTC, there are five contextual elements with respect to crimes against humanity; i) an attack directed against any civilian population; ii) a State or an organizational policy; iii) an attack of a widespread or systematic nature; iv) a nexus existing between individual acts and the attack, and v) knowledge of the attack.[74] It must be noted that, as PTC submits, the requirement of knowledge with respect to the crimes against humanity cannot be addressed in the situational stage, since the individual perpetrators will only be definitively identified after an investigation is initiated.

The first pillar of the contextual element of crimes against humanity is 'attack'. An attack is distinct from an armed conflict.[75] In accordance with the ICC Elements of Crimes, the attack is understood "to mean a course of conduct involving the multiple

---

70 ICTY, Tadić case, 2 October 1995, para. 70, see *supra* note 63.

71 Cryer and Friman and Robinson, 2014, p. 281, see *supra* note 1.

72 ICTY, Tadić Case, 2 October 1995, para. 70, see *supra* note 63.

73 It must be noted that international and non- international conflicts may coexist in the same territory at the same time. *See*: ICC, Trial Chamber I, Lubanga case, 14 March 2012, para. 540, see *supra* note 60.

74 ICC, PTC III, Situation in Côte d'Ivoire, 3 Octobre 2011, para. 29, see *supra* note 17.

75 Boas, Bischoff and Reid, 2009, p. 41, see *supra* note 69.

commission of acts referred to in Article 7, paragraph 1, of the Statute against any civilian population."[76] Such an attack is not necessarily a military operation. The attack does not need to involve military forces, armed hostilities, or any violent force at all.[77] The imposed conditions upon the attack, namely being widespread or systematic, are an alternative to the nexus requirement in case of war crimes. Crimes against humanity embrace crimes committed in the time of peace as well. Schabas considers this feature of the crimes against humanity as an important evolution in international law that has been confirmed by the Rome Statute.[78]

Traditionally, crimes against humanity were conceived only in association with an armed conflict. For instance, Article 5 of the ICTY Statute provides that the Tribunal shall have the power to prosecute persons responsible for crimes against humanity when they are committed "in armed conflict, whether international or internal in character, and directed against any civilian population." The drafters of the ICTY Statute included the Nuremberg Charter's war nexus in the definition of crimes against humanity, which had the effect of protecting sovereignty by excluding crimes unconnected to armed conflict from the tribunal's jurisdiction.[79] Nonetheless, later the link with armed conflict was cut in order to facilitate the prosecution of peace crimes, besides war crimes. Article 3 of the Statute of the International Criminal Tribunal for Rwanda (ICTR) enacted definition of crimes against humanity without the link with armed conflict, if they are committed "as part of a widespread or systematic attack against any civilian population on national, political, ethnic, racial or religious grounds." Even the jurisprudence of the ICTY departed from the drafters' stance. In the Tadić case in 1995, the Appeals Chamber held that the nexus requirement was peculiar to the jurisdiction of the IMT and therefore "there is no logical or legal basis for this requirement [armed conflict nexus] and it has been abandoned in subsequent State practice."[80]

Such a development was a great achievement in protecting the rights of victims. For this reason, it is said that while the war crimes derive from international humanitarian law, crimes against humanity are rooted in international human rights law.[81] It should be noted that the contextual elements of war crimes and crimes against humanity are sometimes intertwined.[82] Armed conflict as the context of war crimes is created between groups and states. In the context of a war, however, it is most likely that the civilian populations are attacked, not opportunistically but in the furtherance of a

---

76 Article 7(3) of ICC Elements of Crimes.

77 Rodney Dixon, 'Article 7 (1)', in Otto Triffterer (ed.), *Commentary on the Rome Statute of the International Criminal Court*, C.H. Beck. Hart. Nomos, 2008, p. 175.

78 Schabas, 2010, p. 144, see *supra* note 61.

79 Margaret M. De Guzman, 'How Serious are International Crimes? The Gravity Problem in International Criminal Law', *Columbia Journal of Transnational Law*, 2012, vol. 51, p. 31.

80 ICTY, Tadić, Case, 2 October 1995, para. 140, see *supra* note 63.

81 Thomas Margueritte, 'International criminal law and human rights', in William A. Schabas and Nadia Bernaz, *Routledge Handbook of International Criminal Law*, Routledge, 2011, p. 437.

82 For studying the history of crimes against humanity see: Hirad Abtahi, Crimes against Humanity and the Armed Conflict Nexus: From Nuremberg to the ICC, 4 December 2013, available at https://ssrn.com/abstract=2363608 or http://dx.doi.org/10.2139/ssrn.2363608.

plan designed by the parties to the conflict. The situation in Uganda is an example. Violence between the LRA and the Ugandan government brought Northern Uganda into a protracted armed conflict not of an international character. It met the contextual element of war crimes. At the same time and in addition to these hostilities between armed groups, "the LRA also engaged in a pattern of deliberate attacks against civilians, in particular against those residing in IDP camps established by the government."[83] It satisfied the contextual element of crimes against humanity.

The conditions of 'widespread' or 'systematic' are disjunctive. PTC II defines the term 'widespread' as "the large scale nature of the attack, as well as to the number of victims."[84] Therefore, the broadness of the attack can be measured in accordance with the affected objects including the extent of affected territories or the number of victims and damaged objects. An attack may be carried out "over a large geographical area or an attack in a small geographical area directed against a large number of civilians."[85] The term 'systematic' refers to "the organized nature of the acts of violence and to the improbability of their random occurrence."[86] In addition, the requirement of 'course of conduct' that is mentioned in the Rome Statute embodies a systemic aspect as it describes a series or overall flow of events as opposed to a mere aggregate of random acts.[87]

The contextual element of the crimes against humanity has a controversial aspect, and that is the 'policy' element. According to the Rome Statute, there must be a nexus or link between the attack and a governmental or organizational policy. As Chambers of the Court have found, "a State policy does not need to have been conceived at the highest level of State machinery but may have been adopted by regional or local organs of the State."[88] The policy element is jurisdictional because it transforms crimes that would otherwise be national crimes into international crimes.[89] In the Rome Statute, war crimes also have a policy element, but with a different function. Article 8(1) provides that the Court has jurisdiction over war crimes "in particular when committed as part of a plan or policy or as part of a large-scale commission of such crimes." This clause is a guiding rule; it is not a contextual element of the war crime.[90] War crimes

83 ICC, PTC II, Decision on the Confirmation of Charges against Dominic Ongwen, 23 March 2016, para. 62.

84 ICC, PTC II, Bemba case, Decision Pursuant to Article 61(7)(a) and (b) of the Rome Statute on the Charges of the Prosecutor against Jean-Pierre Bemba Gombo,15 June 2009, para. 82.

85 ICC, PTC I, Katanga case, Decision on the Confirmation of Charges, 30 September 2008, para. 395.

86 ICC, PTC I, Al Bashir case, Decision on the Prosecution's Application for a Warrant of Arrest against Omar Hassan Ahmad Al Bashir, 4 March 2009, para. 81. And ICC, PTC I, Decision on the Evidence and Information Provided by the Prosecution for the Issuance of a Warrant of Arrest for Germain Katanga, 6 July 2007, para. 33.

87 ICC, PTC I, Laurent Gbagbo case, Decision on the confirmation of charges against Laurent Gbagbo, 12 June 2014, para. 209.

88 ICC, PTC II, Kenya situation, Decision Pursuant to Article 15 of the Rome Statute on the Authorization of an Investigation into the Situation in the Republic of Kenya, 31 March 2010, para. 89. And, ICC, Côte d'Ivoire situation, 3 October 2011, para. 45, see *supra* note 17.

89 Bassiouni, 2013, p. 663, see *supra* note 48.

90 Elies Van Sliedregt, 'International Criminal Law', in Markus D. Dubber and Tatjana Hornle (eds.), *The Oxford Handbook of Criminal Law*, Oxford University Press, 2014, p. 1155.

may be committed against a member of one of the protected groups under international humanitarian law (IHL). It means that war crimes do not involve collective victims as what exists in crimes against humanity (civilian population) or genocide (a group). Nonetheless, international tribunals have prosecuted systematic rather than isolated war crimes.[91] For this reason, the Rome Statute establishes a policy threshold as a factor to determine the gravity of war crimes.

The ICC Elements of Crimes provide a definition of the crimes against humanity policy. It affirms that "policy to commit such attack requires that the State or organization actively promote or encourage such an attack against a civilian population."[92] Such a policy is implemented either by act or, in exceptional circumstances, by omission or "a deliberate failure to take action, which is consciously aimed at encouraging such attack. The existence of such a policy cannot be inferred solely from the absence of governmental or organizational action."[93] The main justification behind adopting a policy threshold was to avoid dealing with random acts of individuals.[94] The occurrence of crimes against humanity requires both quantitative and qualitative conditions. PTC I in the Gbagbo case affirms that a course of conduct must involve multiple acts, but "since the course of conduct requires a certain 'pattern' of behavior, evidence relevant to proving the degree of planning, direction or organization by a group or organization" is also relevant to the existence of a 'course of conduct' within the meaning of Article 7(2)(a) of the Statute.[95] Such a policy gives a feature to crimes against humanity, namely collectively in perpetration. From this perspective, PTC II submits "such a policy may be made by groups of persons who govern a specific territory or by any organization with the capability to commit a widespread or systematic attack against a civilian population."[96]

2.2.3. *Context of Genocide*

Unlike crimes against humanity and war crimes, the special intent (*dolus specialis*) of perpetrators constitutes a component of the crime of genocide, besides its underlying acts. Article 6 of the Rome Statute provides that killing members of a national, ethnical, racial or religious group, or causing serious bodily or mental harm to members of the group, or deliberately inflicting on the group conditions of life calculated to bring about its physical destruction, or imposing measures intended to prevent births within the group and forcibly transferring children of the group to another group constitute the crime of genocide if they are committed with the intent to destroy the group in whole or

---

91 Robert Sloane, *The Expressive Capacity of International Punishment*, Columbia Public Law and Legal Theory Working Paper, 2006, p. 23.

92 Article 7(3) of ICC Elements of Crimes.

93 ICC Elements of Crimes, footnote 6.

94 To see the arguments in favor and against the policy threshold *see:* Cryer and Friman and Robinson, 2014, pp. 236–240, see *supra* note 1.

95 ICC, PTC I, Laurent Gbagbo case, 12 June 2014, para. 210, see *supra* note 87.

96 ICC, PTC II, Bemba case, 15 June 2009, para. 81, see *supra* note 84.

in part. The genocidal intent is the marker of the definition of genocide, because it sets it apart from the other core crimes.[97]

The requirement of a specific intent for genocide was established to assume a preventative function; it allows the intervention of criminal law before the perpetrators achieve the actual destruction of the targeted group.[98] However, it poses a question: how is the intention determined? Intention is not a concrete and objective matter, and nobody is able to read the minds of others. Intents are deduced from conduct. In other words, behaviors are a mirror for the ultimate intents. Genocide is not merely a matter of intent. It requires that the relevant conduct arising from such intent represents a concrete threat to the existence of the targeted group, as opposed to just being latent or hypothetical..[99] In other words, the intent must be realistic.[100] For this purpose, the ICC Elements of Crimes set out a contextual element that contributes to discovering the genocidal intent. Accordingly, each prohibited act should take place "in the context of a manifest pattern of similar conduct directed against that group" or could itself effects such destruction.[101] This context was set out to maintain some threshold of objective scale and gravity.[102] Indeed, such a policy as a tool helps to deduce the intent.[103] The ICTY Appeals Chamber in one of its judgments states that "the existence of a plan or policy is not a legal ingredient of the crime. However, in the context of proving specific intent, the existence of a plan or policy may become an important factor in most cases."[104] Nevertheless, this attitude changed later at the ICTY. The Trial Chamber in Krštic opposed the Trial Chamber's view and argued: "the requirement that the prohibited conduct be part of a widespread or systematic attack does not appear in the Genocide Convention and was not mandated by customary international law. Because the definition adopted by the Elements of Crimes did not reflect customary law as it existed at the time Krštic committed his crimes, it cannot be used to support the Trial Chamber's conclusion."[105]

At the ICC, a majority in a PTC has taken the view that the contextual provision in the Elements is not inconsistent with the ICC Statute, and therefore they applied it in the case against Al Bashir.[106] This approach offers a narrow interpretation of the crime of genocide that rejects the idea of the lone individual seeking to destroy a group.

---

97 Sliedregt, 2014, p. 1152, see *supra* note 90.

98 Paola Gaeta, 'Genocide', in William A. Schabas and Nadia Bernaz, *Routledge Handbook of International Criminal Law*, Routledge, 2011, p. 112.

99 ICC, PTC I, Al Bashir case, 4 March 2009, para. 124, see *supra* note 86.

100 Claus Kreb, 'The Crime of Genocide and Contextual Elements: A Comment on the ICC Pre-Trial Chamber's Decision in the Al Bashir Case', *Journal of International Criminal Justice*, 2009, vol. 7, p. 304.

101 Article 6 of the ICC Elements of Crimes. See: ICC, PTC I, Al Bashir case, 4 March 2009, para. 113, see *supra* note 86.

102 Cryer and Friman and Robinson, 2014, p. 220, see *supra* note 1.

103 Schabas, 2010, p. 127, see *supra* note 61.

104 See: ICTY, Trial Chamber, Judgment on Defense Motions to Acquit, 3 September 2001, para. 62.

105 ICTY, Appeals Chamber, Krštic case, Judgment, 19 April 2004, para. 224.

106 ICC, PTC I, Al Bashir case, 4 March 2009, paras. 117–33, see *supra* note 86. Although this decision was later overturned, but the above-mentioned finding was reaffirmed in the PTC I's second arrest warrant

Indeed, although "an individual perpetrator may act with the realistic intent to destroy the group if his conduct is in itself capable to affect this destruction, in almost all cases, however, this will not be the case."[107]

It is noteworthy that the contextual element of genocide is comparable to the contextual element of crimes against humanity. A pattern of similar conduct almost resembles a course of conduct. PTC I in the Al Bashir warrant arrest case, to determine whether there were reasonable grounds to believe that the contextual element of the counts of genocide included in the Prosecution's Application had been fulfilled, evaluated the attack on the population of Darfur. The Chamber determined that the attack was large in scale, systematic and largely followed a similar pattern. Given these qualifications, that are largely similar to the contextual elements of crimes against humanity, the PTC satisfied that the acts had taken place in the context of a manifest pattern and consequently concluded that there were reasonable grounds to believe that the contextual element of genocide was fulfilled.[108] Now, it can be understandable why Schabas asserts that genocide constitutes the most aggravated form of crimes against humanity.[109]

2.3. SITUATIONAL CONTEXTUAL ELEMENT IN PRACTICE

A situation in the sense of the Rome Statute is a concept that is formed of two pillars: a jurisdictional component and a factual one. The factual dimension of a situation is its contextual element. This element is comprised of two parts, namely event and cause. The event is those exceptional circumstances or crisis that is adoptable with the contextual elements of ICC crimes, namely an armed conflict (war crimes), a widespread or systematic attack directed against civilian population (crimes against humanity) and a pattern of conducts that produces concrete threat against the existence of a group (genocide). These external and concrete contexts will be defined in terms of jurisdictional parameters within which the Court has to function.

Each situation under investigation at the ICC has a specific contextual element. For instance, in the DRC situation, a protracted armed conflict has constituted the contextual element.[110] Human Rights Watch (HRW) has documented that there is a link between the conflict in the DRC and the exploitation of natural resources.[111] The agriculturalist Lendu and pastoralist Hema ethnic groups constitute the major parties to

against Al Bashir (see: ICC, PTC I, Al Bashir case, 12 July 2010, Second Decision on the Prosecution's Application for a Warrant of Arrest, paras. 13–17).

107 Kreb, 2009, p. 305, see *supra* note 100.

108 ICC, PTC I, Al Bashir case, Second Decision on the Prosecution's Application for a Warrant of Arrest, 12 July 2010, paras. 13–17.

109 William A. Schabas, *An Introduction to International Criminal Court*, Cambridge University Press, 2011, p. 100.

110 ICC, Democratic Republic of the Congo, available at: https://www.icc-cpi.int/drc, last accessed at 15 April 2017.

111 Ituri: Covered in Blood Ethnically Targeted Violence in Northeastern Democratic Republic of Congo, July 2003, p. 12, available at: www.hrw.org/sites/default/files/reports/DRC0703.pdf.

the conflict in the DRC.[112] The situation in Uganda is formed in the context of an armed conflict that was caused by rebellion of the LRA against the central government.[113] Since 1986, a civil war in Northern Uganda between the Ugandan government and the LRA, a rebel force infamous for its abduction and enlistment of children, has killed tens of thousands of civilians.[114] It also provoked an attack against the civilian population. The situation in Sudan was formed in the context of a protracted armed conflict "between the Government of the Sudan including combatants from the Sudan People's Armed Forces and the Popular Defense Force along with the Militia/Janjaweed against organized rebel groups, including the Sudanese Liberation Movement/Army and the Justice and Equality Movement in Darfur, Sudan."[115] In Sudan, multiple armed organizations have been involved in the conflict, next to the government forces.[116] In Kenya, crimes against humanity have been prosecuted. A widespread and systematic attack against the Kenyan civilian population was a context that was caused by the post-election violence of 2007–2008.[117] The Libyan situation witnessed crimes against humanity in the context of a widespread and systematic attack against the Libyan civilian population who demonstrated against the Gaddafi regime in 2011 following the emergence of the Arab Spring.[118] War crimes triggered the intervention of the Court in Côte d'Ivoire. The contextual element of the situation was an armed conflict that was started since the coup attempt of 2002.[119] The situation in Mali was also formed in the context of an armed conflict that was launched by rebellion of Arab organizations in the northern part of the country.[120] The second situation in the CAR is rooted in religious tensions; it was formed in the context of attacks against the Muslim minority by some ethnic groups like Selekas. In addition, an armed conflict of a non-international character between Government forces and organized armed groups and between such groups has been recognized as another context of the situation in the CAR II.[121] The Georgia situation came to the agenda of the Prosecutor due to war crimes committed in the context of an international armed conflict between 1 July and 10 October 2008.

---

112 Sharzad Fouladvand, Complementarity and Cultural Sensitivity: Decision-making by the ICC Prosecutor in relation to the Situation in the Darfur Region in Sudan and the Democratic Republic of the Congo, the Degree of Doctor of Philosophy, University of Sussex, 2012, p. 174.

113 ICC, PTC II, Warrant of Arrest for Kony Issued on 8 July 2005 as Amended on 27 September 2005, para. 5.

114 Roger S. Clark, 'Complementarity and the Crime of Aggression', in Carsten Stahn and Mohamed M. El Zeidy (eds.), *The International Criminal Court and Complementarity: From Theory to Practice*, Cambridge University Press, 2011, p. 1197.

115 ICC, PTC I, Warrant of Arrest for Ahmad Harun, 16 April 2007, para. 3.

116 Alette Smeulers and Maartje Weerdesteijn and Barbora Hola, 'The Selection of Situations by the ICC: An Empirically Based Evaluation of the OTP's Performance', *International Criminal Law Review*, 2015, vol. 15, p. 19.

117 ICC, PTC II, Kenya situation, 31 March 2010, para. 100, see *supra* note 88.

118 ICC, PTC I, Warrant of Arrest for Saif Al-Islam Gaddafi, 27 June 2011, p. 5. And also ICC, Libya situation, Application on Behalf of the Government of Libya Pursuant to Article 19 of the ICC Statute, 1 may 2012, para. 6.

119 ICC, PTC III, Côte d'Ivoire situation, 3 October 2011, para. 181, see *supra* note 17.

120 ICC, OTP, Situation in Mali, Article 53(1) Report, 16 January 2013, paras. 3–4.

121 ICC, OTP, Situation in the CAR II, Article 53(1) Report, 24 September 2014, para. 9.

In the same period, crimes against humanity were committed, because the civilian population, in particular ethnic Georgian civilians, was attacked by South Ossetian forces.[122] These facts show that how the contexts of situations are defined in practice, taking into account the contextual element of crimes take place in a situation.

2.4. FUNCTIONS OF SITUATIONAL CONTEXT

The contextual element of a situation functions in different ways. These functions demonstrate the prominent role that is played by this element in the process of situation selection. Firstly, the contextual aspect of a situation is a major factor in the case selection process. As mentioned before, there should be a sufficient nexus between a case and a situation triggering the jurisdiction of the Court. To recognize such a nexus, the similarity between the jurisdictional parameters is not sufficient, but the contextual element should be the same. It is likely that ICC crimes will be committed in the same territory and in the same period but in different contexts. In this scenario, the difference in the factual contexts leads to the formation of different situations. The Central African Republic (the CAR) is an example here; a territory with two different situations before the Court.

Secondly, the contextual element of a situation has a role in the admissibility assessment of a case. The complementarity principle as enshrined in Article 17 of the Rome Statute provides that a case does not undergo the Court's intervention if it is being or has already been investigated or prosecuted by national jurisdictions. In order to determine whether any national proceedings are active, the Court jurisprudence has established a criterion that is known as 'the same person/substantially same conduct'. In accordance with this standard, a State should investigate or prosecute the same person for the commission of substantially the same conduct in order to prevent the Court's intervention. The notion of 'conduct' is open to judicial interpretation. Here, two interpretive approaches exist. The restrictive approach defines the conduct as an incident-oriented notion. Considering the complementarity principle from this angle gives the Court more space to intervene and imposes more obligations upon states. On the contrary, a liberal approach considers the conduct notion as a contextual concept. This definition is largely similar to the element of a situation's context. This interpretation was applied in the situation in Libya. As an illustration, what constituted the relevant conduct in the proceedings against Al-Senussi was killings and acts of persecution "committed directly or through the Security Forces during the repression of the demonstrations taking place in Benghazi from 15 February 2011 until at least 20 February 2011 and as part of a policy designed at the highest level of the Libyan State machinery to deter and quell, by any means, the revolution against the Gaddafi

[122] ICC, PTC I, Georgia situation, Decision on the Prosecutor's Request for Authorization of an Investigation, 27 January 2016.

regime occurring throughout Libya."[123] It is indeed based on the contextual element constituting the situation in Libya, namely a widespread and systematic attack on civilian population. It was contrary to the approach that requires national jurisdictions to cover all 'incidents' mentioned in the Article 58 Arrest Warrant Application specifying location, time, acts and victims. From the liberal perspective, the same conduct test does not "need to cover all of the same material and mental elements of the crimes before the Court and also does not need to include the same acts attributed to an individual under suspicion'.[124] What is required is conducting an investigation into the same context, namely the same crisis that has been brought before the Court.

Thirdly, the contextual element of a situation is a guiding rule for naming a situation. Naming a situation has no legal effects, but it does not mean that it is not important, in particular for the public audience. The title of a situation must represent its general content and main theme. The current practice of the Court to call the situations based on territory is not an accurate approach. The territory is only one pillar of each situation, though it is a main component. To name a situation, the territorial factor should be accompanied by another element of a situation. Each territory can embrace many potential situations. Geographical naming is misleading. It has been reported that some in the OTP acknowledge that if a situation is defined by the scope of the conflict is better than labeling a situation that is based on fixed geographical boundaries.[125] Rastan, as a legal advisor at the OTP, recommends the Court to revisit its reliance on a territorial classification of situations and to move towards a numerical system, i.e. using digits for naming situations.[126]

A numerical naming has a precedence at the ICC. In 2005, the government of the CAR referred the situation of crimes within the jurisdiction of the Court committed anywhere on the territory of the CAR since 1 July 2002. Upon this referral, the Prosecutor decided to open an investigation focusing on crimes allegedly committed in 2002 and 2003. While this situation was under investigation, the Prosecutor identified a new situation, unrelated to the situation previously referred to the ICC by the CAR authorities in December 2004. Consequently, she decided to open the preliminary examination.[127] The new situation was called the situation in CAR II. Nonetheless, it seems that using other jurisdictional parameters in branding a situation, besides the territorial element is a better policy. Naming is to some extent an act of art. By hearing the name of a situation, someone should get the gist of the situation at a glance.

---

123 ICC, PTC I, Al-Senussi case, Decision on the Admissibility of the Case against Abdullah Al-Senussi, 11 October 2013, para. 71.

124 ICC, Gaddafi case, Separate Opinion of Judge Anita Ušacka, Judgment on the Appeal of Libya Against the Decision of Pre-Trial Chamber I of 31 May 2013 Entitled Decision on the Admissibility of the Case Against Saif Al-Islam Gaddafi, 24 July 2014, para. 58.

125 Nouwen, 2013, footnote, 17, see *supra* note 16.

126 Rod Rastan, 'Situations and Case: Defining the Parameters', in Carsten Stahn and Mohamed M. El Zeidy (eds.), *The International Criminal Court and Complementarity: From Theory to Practice*, Cambridge University Press, 2011, p. 428.

127 ICC, Press Release, Statement of the Prosecutor of the International Criminal Court, Fatou Bensouda, on Opening a New Preliminary Examination in Central African Republic, 24 September 2014.

Using digits produces ambiguity. By contrast, contextual elements are clearer. These parameters could be various from the name of an armed conflict to the main party in a conflict. For instance, the current ICC situations can be labeled as the situation of LRA in Uganda, the situation of post-election violence in Kenya and the situation of 'Strong Cliff Operation' in Palestine, the Situation of ISIS in Iraq and Syria. Here, it is worthy of a mention that when Uganda referred the situation related to its territory, it called the situation the 'Situation concerning the Lord's Resistance Army'.[128] In response, the then Prosecutor of the Court changed the name to the Situation in Northern Uganda. By doing so, he wanted to show the generality of the referred situation and to send this message that his activities would cover the crimes committed by Ugandan forces as well. However, the name of a situation has no legal effect to restrict the scope of the referred situation. The 'situation of LRA' label would refer to a crisis in which the LRA was a major part, but not the only party.

Fourthly, understanding the context in which crimes arise may contribute to the prevention of those crimes. Atrocity crimes are avoidable and the ICC contribution to the prevention of future atrocity crimes or ongoing crimes through timely intervention is important.[129] To prevent ICC crimes, the roots and context of such crimes must be considered and dealt with. Based on this understanding, the OTP Policy Paper on Sexual and Gender-based Crimes directs the Prosecutor to "examine the general context within which the alleged sexual and gender-based crimes have occurred."[130] This examination is a result of the commitment of the OTP to integrate a gender analysis into its works. Such a policy is similarly adopted for crimes against children. The OTP Policy Paper on Children insists that the Office examines "the general context within which the alleged crimes against or affecting children have occurred."[131]

128 ICC, Press Release, President of Uganda Refers Situation concerning the Lord's Resistance Army to the ICC, 29 January 2014.

129 *See:* Héctor Olásolo, 'The Role of the International Criminal Court in Preventing Atrocity Crimes', in Héctor Olásolo, *Essays on International Criminal Justice*, Hart Publishing LTD, 2012.

130 ICC, OTP, Policy Paper on Sexual and Gender-Based Crimes, June 2014, para. 39.

131 ICC, OTP, Policy Paper on Children, November 2016, para. 54.

PART TWO

SITUATION SELECTION PROCESS

The situation selection has two main pillars: process and criteria. The first part of this research conceptualized the situation concept in the sense enshrined in the Rome Statute. The current part addresses the question of how a situation is procedurally selected. The process of the situation selection begins with the trigger mechanism and ends when the Prosecutor determines whether to initiate an investigation. Usually, the law of procedure captures little attention. This is not different for the ICC. The procedural aspect of the situation selection has grabbed scant attention in the literature, whereas it deserves more clarification. This section aims at furthering the clarification on the process of the situation selection in the architecture of the Court. The starting point of the situation selection process is the trigger mechanism that is addressed in Chapter I. Chapter II introduces a missing stage in the process of the situation selection, namely the identification phase, which is a bridge between the trigger mechanism and the preliminary examination. This phase has some important functions that are necessary for the functioning of the OTP. The preliminary examination as the heart of the situation selection process is studied in Chapter III. The preliminary examination is the mechanism in which a situation is selected. The final chapter of this part inquires about the determination phase, when the Prosecutor determines whether to initiate an investigation or to leave it. During this stage, the judicial review of the Prosecutor's decisions emerges.

CHAPTER I
TRIGGER MECHANISM

The jurisdiction of the ICC is dormant. The term 'dormant jurisdiction' was branded by Olásolo. He explains that the phenomenon of dormant jurisdiction arises from the fact that the Court has been given jurisdiction by its States Parties through the Rome Statute.[1] The Court operates based on the theory of 'delegated jurisdiction'. It means that States Parties transfer to the ICC their own territorial and personal jurisdictions over international crimes.[2] As soon as a State joins the Court and ratifies its constituent document, it automatically accepts the jurisdiction of the Court. The consent of a State Party for the jurisdiction of the Court is expressed through ratification.[3] In other words, the essence of State Party membership is that a State accepts the exercise of jurisdiction by the Court over any Article 5 crimes committed on its territory or by its nationals from the applicable date of entry into force of the Statute onwards.[4] This approach is called 'automatic jurisdiction', which is at odds with the initial approach adopted by the 1994 draft Statute. The International Law Commission (ICL) Draft Statute had provided an opt-in or consent-oriented approach. According to the proposal, in every case, all the States affected would have to give their consent in order for the Court to be able to proceed.[5] The opt-in proposal was designed to allow States maximum flexibility in accepting the ICC's jurisdiction, a flexibility that might help maximize the number of States Parties.[6]

Nonetheless, that initial approach in the view of many meant 'à la carte' jurisdiction, which was hardly acceptable for the core crimes.[7] If it was the case, the Court would become a tool in the hands of States. Such a result clearly contradicts the constituent objectives of the Court, namely ending impunity and the administration of an

---

1 Héctor Olásolo, *The Triggering Procedure of the International Criminal Court*, Martinus Nijhoff Publishers, 2005, p. 39.

2 David Luban, 'Fairness to Rightness: Jurisdiction, Legality and the Legitimacy of International Criminal Law', in A. Besson and John Tasioulas (eds.), *The Philosophy of International Law*, Oxford University Press, 2010, p. 579.

3 Hans-Peter Kaul, 'Preconditions to the Exercise of Jurisdiction', in Antonio Cassese, Paola Gaeta and John R.W.D. Jones (eds.), *The Rome Statute of the International Criminal Court: A Commentary*, Oxford University Press, 2002, p. 592.

4 Rod Rastan, 'Situations and Case: Defining the Parameters', in Carsten Stahn and Mohamed M. El Zeidy (eds.), *The International Criminal Court and Complementarity: From Theory to Practice*, Cambridge University Press, 2011, p. 425.

5 Kaul, 2002, p. 594, see *supra* note 3.

6 Young Sok Kim, *The ICC: A Commentary of the Rome Statute*, Wisdom House, 2003, p. 205.

7 Kaul, 2002, p. 593, see *supra* note 3.

impartial justice. As some commentators on the Rome Statute assert, the opt-in and case-by-case consent proposals would have resulted in practical terms in a significantly weakened court.[8] Taking into account these adverse effects, the founders of the Court decided to found an organization with automatic jurisdiction. It means that the Court has jurisdiction over all potential and would-be situations, but if it is going to be exercised over a specific situation, it should be initially awakened and alerted. The trigger mechanism is intended to perform this role. Its name is derived from the idea that the mechanism resembles squeezing the trigger of a gun that makes sounds and draws attention. The trigger mechanism at the ICC suggests a potential situation to the Prosecutor and demands his reaction. It merely draws the attention of the Prosecutor for taking further steps in order to initiate an investigation. In the first policy paper issued by the OTP on the issue of referrals and communication, this function of the trigger mechanism is referred to by saying "senders of communications are encouraged to draw the attention of the Prosecutor to situations that they believe may fall within the jurisdiction of the Court."[9]

The term 'trigger mechanism' is not defined by the legal texts of the Court. As some commentators of the Rome Statute have asserted, the term emerged during the development of the Rome Statute in order to refer to the ability to direct the Court's attention to an event in a particular time and place with a view to the exercise of the Court's jurisdiction over the event.[10] However, it should be borne in mind that the trigger mechanism just suggests a situation, including its jurisdictional parameters. As it will be discussed, the identification of a situation and its jurisdictional framework is the responsibility of the Prosecutor.

The trigger mechanism influences the selectivity of the Court. It is a mechanism that is aimed at deciding whether the ICC's dormant jurisdiction should be activated over a given situation.[11] The Prosecutor of the Court is to some extent a hostage in the hands of the external actors. The Prosecutor is the follower of the international community's demands, rather than the leader. Selectivity is not merely limited to what is selected by the Prosecutor but also includes what is selected for the Prosecutor. This restrictive feature of trigger mechanism is understood better by considering the concerns of the drafters about authorizing the Prosecutor with broad powers. The trigger mechanism endows the Court with jurisdiction, but it determines how the dormant jurisdiction of the Court is activated. In other words, the mechanism answers the question who can bring situations to the attention of the ICC Prosecutor.[12]

---

8 Sharon A. Williams and William A. Schabas, 'Article 12', in Otto Triffterer (ed.), *Commentary on the Rome Statute of the International Criminal Court*, C.H. Beck. Hart. Nomos, 2008, p. 554.

9 ICC, OTP, Annex to the Paper on Some Policy Issues before the Office of the Prosecutor: Referrals and Communications, 2003, p. 1.

10 Robert Cryer, Hakan Friman and Darryl Robinson (et al), *An Introduction to International Criminal Law and Procedure*, Cambridge University Press, 2014, p. 619.

11 Olásolo, 2005, p. 42, see *supra* note 1.

12 Kim, 2003, p. 203, see *supra* note 6.

Determining the triggers of the ICC's jurisdiction proved to be highly contentious and of a highly complex nature during the negotiations.[13] Nonetheless, the main elements of the triggering procedure were agreed upon only hours before the end of the Rome conference.[14] The drafters of the Rome Statute set up an exclusive mechanism. Article 13 establishes three triggers: referrals made by States Parties, referrals made by the UN Security Council, and communications made by the individuals or legal persons such as Non-Governmental Organizations (NGO) that trigger the *proprio motu* authority of the Prosecutor to identify a situation.

1. STATE REFERRALS

A referral is a formal written request to the ICC's prosecutor to investigate a situation.[15] Indeed, a referral is an activation request.[16] Each State Party to the Rome Statute enjoys the right to refer a situation to the Court. By such a referral, States draw the attention of the Prosecutor to a potential situation and take the initiative to activate the Court's jurisdiction. The draft version of the Statute used to describe the State who triggered the jurisdiction of the Court as a 'complainant State' that could lodge a 'complaint'.[17] However, the term 'complaint' was changed to 'referral' in order to clarify the fact that States could not submit a specific case or crime to the court.[18] In this case, the jurisdiction of the Court could be exercised over a situation, rather than specific cases.

1.1. MAKING A REFERRAL AS A RIGHT FOR ALL STATES PARTIES

The right of States to make a referral was never questioned during the preparatory process of the Rome Statute.[19] The ICC is a treaty-based international organization. It was established by its founding States as a tool and facility to realize their common goals. Therefore, it is evident that the States Parties enjoy some advantages including directing the Court's activities by making a referral of a specific situation. It must be

---

13 William A. Schabas, 'The Rise and Fall of Complementarity', in Carsten Stahn and Mohamed M. El Zeidy (eds.), *The International Criminal Court and Complementarity: From Theory to Practice*, Cambridge University Press, 2011, p. 141.

14 Olásolo, 2005, p. 35, see *supra* note 1.

15 Gideon Boas and James L. Bischoff and Natalie L. Reid, *International Criminal Law Practitioner Library Volume II: Elements of Crimes under International Law, Cambridge* University Press, 2009, p. 70.

16 Olásolo, 2005, p. 104, see *supra* note 1.

17 William A. Schabas, War crimes and Human Rights Essays on the Death Penalty, Justice and Accountability, Cameron May, 2008, p. 380.

18 William A. Schabas, *An Introduction to International Criminal Court,* Cambridge University Press, 2011, p. 162.

19 Antonio Marchesi, 'Article 14', in Otto Triffterer (ed.), *Commentary on the Rome Statute of the International Criminal Court*, C.H. Beck. Hart. Nomos, 2008, p. 575.

borne in mind that non-member States are deprived of the right to make a referral. However, they have access to the Court and are able to make a report of crimes. In this scenario, those reports or requests made by non-member States are viewed as communications instead of referrals. For instance, in the situation in Georgia, it was announced that Russia, a State not party to the Rome Statute, had sent 3,817 communications.[20]

Initially, the right of making a referral was extended to any State, provided it had custody of the suspect, i.e., the custodial States. In this scenario, a referral was almost case-oriented. It was the initial proposal of the working group on the question of an international criminal jurisdiction set up by the ILC in 1992.[21] However, later, such a right got limited to the States Parties. Two arguments in favor of such a restriction were set. Firstly, necessary cooperation with the Court can be requested only from the States Parties. Secondly, such a limitation could have the effect of encouraging ratification of the Rome Statute.[22] Making a referral is a privilege of ICC membership that may inspire States to join the ICC.

During the preparatory process, a proposal was posed to limit the right of complaining to the 'interested' States Parties, namely the territorial or custodial State or national State of the victim. However, this proposal seemed as a contradiction to the philosophy behind the existence of the Court. It is believed that ICC crimes were of concern to the international community as a whole and not exclusively to the interested States.[23] Therefore, the concept of interested States was dismissed. Nevertheless, making a referral remained an exclusive privilege for States Parties. Under the Rome Statute, all States Parties have a right to refer a situation irrespective of a nexus between their territories or nationals and crimes that are committed. Therefore, State Party A may refer the situation of State Party B to the ICC.

In 1994, the States Parties' right to refer a situation was made subject to another requirement. According to Article 25 of the draft Statute, a State party could lodge a complaint concerning a crime related to other States if it would accept the jurisdiction of the Court over the same crime. Regarding the crime of genocide there was an extra requirement; such a State should also be a contracting party to the Convention of the Prevention and Punishment of the Crime of Genocide (1948). Indeed, this restriction was a form of 'reciprocity' that was modeled after the International Court of Justice (ICJ)'s jurisdictional system.[24] In this system, a State was able to trigger the jurisdiction

---

20 ICC, Statement of the Prosecutor of the International Criminal Court, Fatou Bensouda, following judicial authorization to commence an investigation into the Situation in Georgia, 27 January 2016, available at: www.icc-cpi.int/Pages/item.aspx?name=otp-stat-27–01–2016-georgia, last accessed at 15 April 2017.

21 Report of the International Law Commission on the Work of its Forty-Sixth Session, 2 May- 22 July 1994', para. 21 (a) and (b).

22 Marchesi, 2008, p. 576, see *supra* note 19.

23 Ibid., p. 578.

24 Philipp Kirsch and Darryl Robinson, 'Referral by States Parties', in Antonio Cassese, Paola Gaeta and John R.W.D. Jones (eds.), *The Rome Statute of the International Criminal Court: A Commentary*, Oxford University Press, 2002, p. 620.

of the Court against others if it had already accepted the jurisdiction of the Court over that crime. This procedure was based on the opt-in regime of jurisdiction that finally was dropped in the Rome Statute. When the phenomenon of the situation emerged, as the commentators of the Rome Statute have submitted, the reciprocity restriction became more complicated; because it would be less clear which specific types of crimes had been committed.[25] Such a development resulted in omitting such a restriction from the Rome Statute. Now, in accordance with Article 14 of the Rome Statute, there is no condition for States to make a referral except for the membership of the ICC. It implies that making a referral by States Parties is a mechanism to trigger the existing jurisdiction of the Court and not to confer the jurisdiction to the Court.

The mechanism may be used by a State Party to activate the Court's jurisdiction, not only over other States, but over itself as well.

1.2. THE PHENOMENON OF SELF-REFERRAL

Self-referral means a State Party refers a situation with respect to its own territory or nationals. The phenomenon of self-referrals was not conceived by the drafters of the Rome Statute. Schabas maintains there is no evidence that during the drafting of the Rome Statute the idea that a State might refer a case against itself was ever contemplated.[26] Indeed, governments were presumed to prefer to prosecute the perpetrators of international crimes themselves in order to gain credibility and political legitimacy.[27] The positive complementarity premises on this presumption. It is believed that States' preference to take the initiative may have catalyst effects on the national legal systems.

A self-referral may occur not only when crimes have been committed on the referring State's territory, but also when they are committed by its nationals.[28] However, what is preferred for the Prosecutor is a self-referral made by a territorial State. Exercising the jurisdiction of the Court based on the personal jurisdiction is not an attractive idea for the Court, due to the restrictions it imposed on the jurisdiction of the Court. It has been proved by the practice of the OTP as to the situation of ISIS in Iraq

---

25 Ibid., p. 622.

26 William A. Schabas, *The International Criminal Court: A Commentary on the Rome* Statute, Oxford University Press, 2010, p. 309. On contrary to the opinion of Schabas, some claim that self-referral was discussed during the negotiating process of the establishment of the ICC; however, it is said that NGOs claimed that States would be reluctant to make referrals of situations to the Court and that the prosecutor should therefore be granted *proprio motu* powers to initiate investigations. (See: Sharzad Fouladvand, *Complementarity and Cultural Sensitivity: Decision-making by the ICC Prosecutor in relation to the Situation in the Darfur Region in Sudan and the Democratic Republic of the Congo, the Degree of Doctor of Philosophy*, University of Sussex, 2012, p. 208).

27 Mahnoush H. Arsanjani and W. Michael Reisman, 'The Law-in-Action of the International Criminal Court', *the American Journal of International Law*, 2005, vol. 55, p. 386.

28 Andreas Müller and Ignaz Stegmiller, 'Self-Referrals on Trial from Panacea to Patient', *Journal of International Criminal Justice*, 2010, vol. 8, p. 173.

and Syria. In the situation, the Prosecutor rejected opening a preliminary examination. She argued that there was no territorial jurisdiction, and the jurisdictional basis for conducting the preliminary examination was narrow.[29]

1.2.1. The Emergence of Self-Referrals

During the preparatory process, it turned out that there were two main different concerns about States' referrals. From one side, it was believed that States' referral would be used rarely to activate the Court's jurisdiction. It was speculated that making a referral against another State would most likely be considered as an unfriendly act against the State confronted with the referral.[30] It created the concern of a weak yet-to-be Court with no case in the docket. Such scepticism did not result in the elimination of State referrals, but resulted in the proposal of *ex officio* powers for the initiation of proceedings.[31] To cope with the problem of non-action of States, the drafters empowered non-State actors to trigger the Court's jurisdiction through communications. On the other hand, some delegations had an opposite view. They were concerned that the option of State referral might be abused by States through sending politically motivated referrals against their rivals. To deal with such a concern, Article 18 was set up.[32] The Article 18 mechanism gives other States the opportunity to challenge the jurisdiction of the Court based on the complementarity principle.

In spite of the silence of the Rome Statute, the self-referral phenomenon emerges in the case law of the Court. The OTP has strongly welcomed self-referrals. The OTP prioritizes self-referrals over other triggers. The Prosecutor has adopted "a policy of inviting voluntary referrals from States to increase the likelihood of important cooperation and support on the ground."[33] From the outset, the Prosecutor was advised by some experts who drafted an annex to the Paper on Some Policy Issues to contact agencies of a State in order to receive referrals of situations; the Policy Paper insists "the Prosecutor will carry out his responsibilities in this way without jeopardizing his independence and impartiality."[34] Moreover, in the Policy Paper on Preliminary Examinations, the OTP explicitly submits that upon conducting a preliminary examination, and when it is satisfied that the OTP is ready to request PTC for authorization "it will inform relevant State(s) with jurisdiction of its determination and inquire whether they wish to refer the situation to the Court. If the State(s)

29 ICC, OTP, Statement of the Prosecutor of the International Criminal Court at the Opening of Trial in the Case against Mr Ahmad Al-Mahdi Al Mahdi, 22 August 2016, available at: www.icc-cpi.int/Pages/item.aspx?name=otp-stat-al-mahdi-160822, last accessed at 15 April 2017.

30 Kim, 2003, p. 243, see *supra* note 6.

31 Marchesi, 2008, p. 578, see *supra* note 19.

32 Arsanjani and Reisman, 2005, footnote 9, see *supra* note 27.

33 ICC, OTP, Report on the Activities Performed During the First Three Years (June 2003-June 2006), p. 2.

34 ICC, OTP, Annex to the Paper on Some Policy Issues before the Office of the Prosecutor: Referrals and Communications, 2003.

concerned elect not to refer the situation, the Prosecutor will remain prepared to proceed *proprio motu*."[35]

In furthering such a policy, for instance, in 2003, following receiving several communications from individuals and NGOs[36], the then Prosecutor of the Court in an address to the Second ASP's Session noted: "I stand ready to seek authorization from a PTC to start an investigation under my proprio motu powers. Our role could be facilitated by a referral or active support from the DRC. The Court and the territorial State may agree that a consensual division of labor could be an effective approach."[37] Following the initiative of the Prosecutor, Kabila, the President of the DRC, in a letter of March 2004, referred the situation in the DRC to the Court as regards events occurring after July 1, 2002. Upon this self-referral, the Prosecutor decided to initiate the first investigation of the ICC based on that referral instead of his *proprio motu* action. Here, the role of *proprio motu* power to stimulate States to refer a situation must not be ignored. As it is said, the power at the Prosecutor's disposal was a useful tool in obtaining a State referral in the situation in the DRC.[38]

The story repeated in the situation in Uganda. It has been claimed that the OTP engaged in lengthy discussion with the Presidential Office in Uganda to encourage them to make a self-referral.[39] These dialogues resulted in a self-referral made by Uganda in 2004. Nouwen describes the referral made by the Ugandan authorities as a wedding ring in an arranged marriage of convenience between Uganda and the ICC.[40] Moreover, in the context of the situation in Kenya, the then Prosecutor, upon receiving several communications, initially tried to encourage the government of Kenya to take the initiative. He sent a letter to Kenyan authorities explaining that 'there were two options for initiating an investigation, namely a referral from the Kenyan Government or an independent decision of the Prosecutor to request authorization from the PTC to start an investigation'.[41] Eventually, it was Kenya's

---

35 ICC, OTP, Policy Paper on Preliminary Examinations, 2 November 2013, para. 98.

36 ICC, Press Release, Communications Received by the Office of the Prosecutor, 16 July 2003.

37 ICC, ASP, Second Assembly of States Parties to the Rome Statute of the International Criminal Court Report of the Prosecutor of the ICC, Mr Luis Moreno-Ocampo, 8 September 2003, available at: www.icc-cpi.int/NR/rdonlyres/C073586C-7D46-4CBE-B901-0672908E8639/143656/LMO_20030908_En.pdf.

38 Jan Wouters and ten Verhoeven and Bruno Demeyere, 'The International Criminal Court's office of the Prosecutor: Navigating between Independence and Accountability?', in Doria and Gasser and Bassiouni (eds), *The Legal Regime of the International Criminal Court*, Martinus Nijhoff Publisher, 2009, p. 349.

39 Roger S. Clark, 'Complementarity and the Crime of Aggression', in Carsten Stahn and Mohamed M. El Zeidy (eds.), *The International Criminal Court and Complementarity: From Theory to Practice*, Cambridge University Press, 2011, p. 1188. However, Nouwen mentions that the Ugandan officials and lawyers involved in the referral whom she had an interview with them denied that there was any such discussion (See: Sarah M.H. Nouwen, *Complementarity in the Line of Fire: the Catalyzing Effect of the ICC in Uganda and Sudan*, Cambridge University Press, 2013, p. 112, footnote 9).

40 Nouwen, 2013, p. 113, see *supra* note 39.

41 ICC, PTC II, Kenya situation, Decision Pursuant to Article 15 of the Rome Statute on the Authorization of an Investigation into the Situation in the Republic of Kenya, 31 March 2010, para. 20.

failure to initiate an investigation that forced the Prosecutor to take the initiative based on the communications.[42]

Stahn argues that a systematic prioritization of self-referrals over *proprio motu* proceedings poses a problem, because it introduces a hierarchy among the trigger mechanisms available to the Prosecutor, which is not foreseen in the Statute.[43] It per se may result in delayed justice. In other words, it may encourage the Prosecutor to wait until a self-referral is obtained. However, it is not a major concern, in particular because of the absence of judicial permission, self-referral processes are faster than *proprio motu* proceedings. There is no legal barrier to give priority to self-referrals. The dependency of the Court on State cooperation makes such a preference inevitable. However, such prioritization must not play as a legal threshold. If there is no prospect for a self-referral, the Prosecutor should activate the jurisdiction of the Court through other triggers, if she has identified one or more ICC crimes in the given situation. The Prosecutor may encourage the State concerned to refer a situation by expressing her intention to intervene in the situation. It falls within her Prosecutorial discretion and is desirable if it helps the Prosecutor to fulfil her obligations by guaranteeing State cooperation. However, the history of the Court has shown that the Prosecutor exercises the *proprio motu* power when States are hesitant to refer a situation. The number of situations under preliminary examination through the choice of the prosecutor has increased.

1.2.2. Benefits of a Self-Referral for the Court's Prosecutor

Self-referrals are appealing for the Prosecutor due to their advantages. Firstly, it is presumed that they secure the cooperation of the referring State. The dependency of the Court on State cooperation is beyond any doubt. In the words of Cassese, an international tribunal resembles "a giant without arms and legs – it needs artificial limbs to walk and work, and these artificial limbs are State authorities. If the cooperation of States is not forthcoming, they cannot fulfil their functions."[44] A State that refers a situation to the ICC reveals its willingness to bring suspects of international crimes to justice[45]; at least, such an assumption can be made. The 2003 Policy Paper of the OTP affirms that in the context of self-referrals, "the Prosecutor can be confident that the national authorities will assist the investigation, will accord the privileges and

---

42 Christine Alai and Njonjo Mue, 'Complementarity and the impact of the Rome Statute and the International Criminal Court in Kenya', in Carsten Stahn and Mohamed M. El Zeidy (eds.), *The International Criminal Court and Complementarity: From Theory to Practice*, Cambridge University Press, 2011, pp. 1226–7.

43 Carsten Stahn, 'Complementarity: A Tale of Two Notions', *Criminal Law Forum*, 2008, vol. 19, p. 111.

44 Antonio Cassese, 'On the Current Trends towards Criminal Prosecution and Punishment of Breaches of International Humanitarian Law', *European Journal of International Law*, 1998, vol. 9, p. 13.

45 Nouwen, 2013, p. 113, see *supra* note 39. And, Harmen van der Wilt, 'States' Obligations to Investigate and Prosecute Perpetrators of International Crimes: The Perspective of the European Court of Human Rights', in Carsten Stahn and Mohamed M. El Zeidy (eds.), *The International Criminal Court and Complementarity: From Theory to Practice*, Cambridge University Press, 2011, p. 687.

immunities necessary for the investigation, and will be anxious to provide if possible and appropriate the necessary level of protection to investigators and witnesses."[46]

Secondly, the Prosecutor sees self-referrals as a secure mechanism that enhances the prospect of success and thus the efficiency of her office. The institution is still in its infancy.[47] Effective and comprehensive cooperation and assistance by States Parties are important to enable the Court to fulfil its mandate.[48] The lack of State assistance is a major challenge for the Court. In December 2014, for instance, as a result of the lack of cooperation, the Prosecutor first dropped all charges against the Kenyan president.[49] Later, she shelved the Darfur investigations because of the non-cooperation of relevant States.[50] In April 2016, the case against Ruto and Arap Sang was terminated by the judges of the Trial Chamber, again, due to the lack of cooperation from Kenya.[51] These cases prove the great need of the Court when it comes down to cooperation of States. The Court's failures seriously hurt the credibility of the Court. To avoid this undesirable destiny, the OTP prefers to intervene in those situations with a bright prospect of success. Nouwen explains that the Prosecutor prefers to "exercise its jurisdiction in situations of relative unwillingness or relative inability, namely, where States are unwilling or unable to conduct domestic proceedings but are not opposed to international investigations and prosecutions."[52] The Prosecutor had initially accepted that the feasibility of prosecution and the prospect of cooperation is a guiding factor in the situation selection. According to the 2003 Policy Paper, the OTP would consider "the availability of evidence, the security of victims, witnesses and staff, the feasibility of conducting an effective investigation in a particular territory and whether the necessary assistance from the international community will be available, including on matters such as the arrest of suspects."[53]

Later, nonetheless, the OTP strongly denied that the feasibility is placed among the selection criteria. In the Policy Paper on Preliminary Examinations, the Prosecutor asserted "feasibility is not a separate factor under the Statute as such when determining whether to open an investigation."[54] However, in practice, taking into account the

---

46 ICC, OTP, Annex to the Paper on Some Policy Issues before the Office of the Prosecutor: Referrals and Communications, September 2003, p. 5.

47 Elies Van Sliedregt, 'International Criminal Law', in Markus D. Dubber and Tatjana Hornle (eds.), *The Oxford Handbook of Criminal Law*, Oxford University Press, 2014, p. 1147.

48 ICC, ASP, Resolution on Cooperation, 21 November 2012.

49 The Guardian, ICC Drops Murder and Rape charges against Kenyan President, 5 December 2014, available at: www.theguardian.com/world/2014/dec/05/crimes-humanity-charges-kenya-president-dropped-uhuru-kenyatta, last accessed at 17 February 2017.

50 The Guardian, ICC Chief Prosecutor Shelves Darfur War Crimes Probe, 14 December 2014, available at: www.theguardian.com/world/2014/dec/14/icc-darfur-war-crimes-fatou-bensouda-sudan, last accessed at 17 February 2017.

51 ICC, Press Release, Ruto and Sang case: ICC Trial Chamber V(A) Terminates the Case without Prejudice to Re-Prosecution in Future, 5 April 2016, available at: www.icc-cpi.int/Pages/item.aspx?name=pr1205andln=en, last accessed at 17 February 2017.

52 Nouwen, 2013, p. 400 see *supra* note 39.

53 ICC, OTP, Paper on Some Policy Issues before the Office of the Prosecutor, September 2003, para. 2.

54 ICC, OTP, Policy Paper on Preliminary Examinations, para. 70.

feasibility in combination with the need for investigation was inevitable. Ultimately, the Prosecutor in her office Policy Paper on Case Selection and Prioritization admitted again that operational factors play a role in prioritization of cases.[55] The recent Policy Paper that was issued focuses on the case selection, but its findings are, largely, applicable to the situation selection too. The Policy Paper on Preliminary Examinations should be revised in light of the Policy Paper on Case Selection due to the great findings and achievements of the latter.

The third advantage of a self-referral for the Prosecutor is that it exempts the Prosecutor from seeking an authorization of PTC. If the Prosecutor decides to initiate an investigation based on her *proprio motu* power, she has to apply for the PTC authorization. However, self-referrals make the Prosecutor free from the judicial review arising from the authorization process.[56]

In the context of the first years of the activity of the Court, another consideration encouraged the Prosecutor to welcome self-referrals. By making a self-referral, fears of an ICC trampling on State sovereignty could be calmed.[57] Indeed, acting on self-referral signaled a message out that the Court would not predominantly act by the Prosecutor's initiatives and discretions.

1.2.3. Self-Referrals under Criticism

Despite the support for self-referrals by the Court, the emergence of this phenomenon sparked some criticism from the outset. The Rome Statute does not explicitly refer to self-referrals. For some scholars, the silence in law rejects the legality of self-referrals. Schabas, for instance, holds that the self-referral that emerged in the situation in Uganda was an invention of the OTP, rather than the result of creative interpretation of the Rome Statute.[58] However, the silence of the Rome Statute is not a convincing argument. In the preparatory process, it was assumed that States would resist the Court's involvement, arguing the merits of their own justice systems.[59] However, the reality showed something different. The States started referring their own situations to seek the ICC intervention.

This shift in States' behavior showed that the constructive ambiguity and the intentional silence in the Rome Statute is rational. The Rome Statute as the ruling text of a permanent organization should be open to interpretation if the effectiveness of the Court matters. The Rome Statute is a living legal document.[60] It requires some

55 "The Office will also take into consideration the following operational case prioritization criteria, to ensure that the Office focuses on cases in which it appears that it can conduct an effective and successful investigation leading to a prosecution with a reasonable prospect of conviction" (ICC, OTP, Policy Paper on Case Selection and Prioritization, 15 September 2016, para. 51).

56 Pavel Caban, 'Preliminary Examinations by the Office of the Prosecutor of the International Criminal Court', *Czech Yearbook of Public and Private International Law,* 2011, vol. 2, p. 203.

57 Nouwen, 2013, p. 119, see *supra* note 39.

58 Schabas, 2010, p. 309, see *supra* note 26.

59 Schabas, 2011, p. 192. see *supra* note 13.

60 ICC, Trial Chamber V(b), Kenyatta case, Decision on Defense Request for Conditional Excusal from Continuous Presence at Trial, 18 October 2013, Para. 77.

degree of openness to interpretation; otherwise, the Court is disarmed and impotent concerning new circumstances. The drafters of the Rome Statute were maybe of an opinion persuading them to leave an issue silent. However, the initial intentions of the founders of the ICC may evolve overtime.[61] Therefore, the insistence should be put on the typical undersigning of the time of implementation instead of the time of drafting. Self-referral is an instance where the Rome Statute leaves a considerable degree of ambiguity and space for creative interpretation.[62] One scenario that was not imagined by the drafters of the Statute was the victimhood of States; when a State is itself under attack and consequently gets weak and incapable of combating international crimes. Akhavan submits that sometimes States may be the victims and their strengthening is required to protect civilian populations against atrocities by non-State actors. He labels the emergence of non-State actor criminals as a feature of the modern world that results in failed States, "due to the proliferation of powerful insurgencies, terrorist groups that have challenged the primacy of the once untouchable State in the global order."[63] In addition, Van der Wilt refers to non-State terrorists who make a State unable to combat international crimes. He argues in favor of self-referrals, because it "may reflect the waning of State power, incapable of reining in non-State actors that constitute new menaces to human rights."[64] Akhavan adds other circumstances warrant self-referrals, such as where a State is unable to afford a costly and complex trial.[65] Apart from the practical circumstances that warrant the Court's intervention, transitional justice may advocate self-referrals. In the context of a society affected by a conflict, groups divided by the conflict may oppose prosecutions at each other's hands.[66] Here, maybe a State prefers to refer its situation to the Court in order to end impunity without adding petrol to the fire.

In conclusion, it is true that the Rome Statute does not explicitly address the issue of self-referrals, but it does not exclude such a possibility either. Article 13 and Article 14 of the Statute merely refer to referrals made by States Parties. The wording of the article in a general and absolute manner makes it open to accepting self-referrals, because self-referrals are a kind of referral. As Robinson stresses, "a failure by the drafters to foresee an eventuality would not by itself constitute an interpretive argument sufficient to overcome the text; a stronger form of claim is required."[67] The suitable interpretative

---

61 Ibid., para. 78.

62 Carsten Stahn, 'Introduction', in Carsten Stahn and Mohamed M. El Zeidy (eds.), *The International Criminal Court and Complementarity: From Theory to Practice*, Cambridge University Press, 2011, p. 3.

63 Payam Akhavan, 'International Criminal Justice in the Era of Failed States: The ICC and the Self-Referral Debate', in Carsten Stahn and Mohamed M. El Zeidy (eds.), *The International Criminal Court and Complementarity: From Theory to Practice*, Cambridge University Press, 2011, pp. 292–295.

64 Harmen van der Wilt, 'Self-Referrals As an Indication of the Inability of States to Cope with Non-State Actors', in Carsten Stahn (eds.), *The Law and Practice of the International Criminal Court*, Oxford University Press, 2014, p. 226.

65 Akhavan, 2011, pp. 292–295, see *supra* note 63.

66 ICC, OTP, Informal Expert Paper: The Principle of Complementarity in Practice, 2003, para. 61.

67 Darryl Robinson, 'Territorial State Referrals and Reflections on ICL Discourse', *Journal of International Criminal Justice*, 2011, vol. 9, p. 362.

approach to the Rome Statute should be adopted taking into account the main feature of the Court, namely its permanency.

The second argument against self-referrals is that this mechanism makes the Court a servant for the referring States' interests. In other words, self-referrals allow States to seek the Court's intervention as a means of driving their rebel enemies into hiding.[68] The practice of the Court has worsened such a concern. Cassese mentions that the striking feature in all the self-referrals is that in each case the referring State asked the Prosecutor to investigate crimes allegedly committed by rebels fighting against the central authorities.[69] Nonetheless, the scenario of the instrumentalization of the Court by auto-referring States, in the words of Kleffner[70], does not seem to be a compelling argument. It is most likely that States Parties try to use the Court in order to realize their own interests, but it is not a necessary implication and consequence of self-referrals. The ICJ has already ruled in the Advisory Opinion on the Legality of the Threat or Use of Nuclear Weapons that the motives of a State in triggering a legal process are legally irrelevant.[71] It does not matter why a State prefers the Court's intervention, because the Prosecutor can control and manage it.

As Stahn submits, a policy of welcoming self-referral must be managed in compliance with the principle of objectivity and the OTP must demonstrate objectivity in its investigations and selection process.[72] It means that the Court is not obliged to accept a self-referral, but it acts on such a mechanism if it meets the statutory requirements. From this perspective, for instance, the Appeals Chamber of the Court states "the Court, acting under the relevant provisions of the Statute and depending on the circumstances of each case, may decide not to act upon a State's relinquishment of jurisdiction in favor of the Court."[73] Hence, the argument that a State may abuse a right it possesses is hardly a conclusive reasoning against having that right.[74] The situation in Uganda is an example in the history of the Court that indicates that the Court can observe its impartiality if the referring State has an intention to misuse its right.

---

68 Boas and Bischoff and Reid, 2009, p. 94, see *supra* note 15.

69 Antonio Cassese, 'Is the ICC Still Having Teething Problems?', *Journal of International Criminal Justice*, 2006, vol. 4, p. 436.

70 Jann K. Kleffner, *Complementarity in the Rome Statute and National Criminal Jurisdiction*, Oxford University Press, 2008, p. 216.

71 ICJ, Advisory Opinion, Legality of the Threat or Use of Nuclear Weapons, 8 July 1996, p. 234.

72 Carsten Stahn, 'Taking Complementarity Seriously: On the Sense and Sensibility of 'Classical', 'Positive' and 'Negative' Complementarity', in Carsten Stahn and Mohamed M. El Zeidy (eds.), *The International Criminal Court and Complementarity: From Theory to Practice*, Cambridge University Press, 2011, p. 275.

73 ICC, Appeals Chamber, Katanga case, Judgment on the Appeal of Mr. Germain Katanga against the Oral Decision of Trial Chamber II of 12 June 2009 on the Admissibility of the Case, 25 September 2009, para. 85.

74 Alejandro Chehtman, 'Jurisdiction', in Markus D. Dubber and Tatjana Hornle (eds.), *The Oxford Handbook of Criminal Law*, Oxford University Press, 2014, p. 405.

1.3. SPECIFICITY

States' referrals, according to Article 14(2) of the Statute, shall as far as possible "specify the relevant circumstances and be accompanied by such supporting documentations as is available to the State referring the situations." This part of Article 14 was not the object of change in the preparatory process.[75] The fulfillment of the obligation under Article 14(2) provides the Prosecutor with considerable contributions for further actions. In addition, it is a safeguard against those concerns about making politically motivated referrals. In this case, a referral is something more than making some general allegations against other States. However, as Schabas recalls, the requirement of specifying should not become the basis for declaring that the Court lacks jurisdiction because the referral did not submit all the information that the referring State could have done with the situation at hand.[76] Indeed, the degree of specificity of a situation cannot be too narrowly construed.[77] In accordance with the Rome Statute, the Prosecutor is authorized to seek as much information as necessary and the requested State is under an obligation to cooperate with the Court in this regard. It is evident that if the referring State truly intends to trigger the jurisdiction of the Court it will do its best to provide the Prosecutor with the necessary information.

In the Rome Statute there is a distinction between communications and referrals made by States regarding the specification requirement. In contrast with the latter, communications do not necessarily need to be informative and determinative with respect to the jurisdictional parameters. Such an exemption is reasonable because the individuals normally do not have access to enough information and lack related knowledge of the procedure of the Court. Therefore, it is not reasonable to require her to provide a report, containing legal arguments and enough information and evidence.

In addition, contrary to the explicit duty imposed on the referring State Party to attach supporting documents to its referral, the Rome Statute is silent about the referrals made by the SC. However, Article 17(1) of the Negotiated Relationship Agreement between the International Criminal Court and the United Nations (UN) just requests the UNSC to immediately transmit the referral of the Security Council to the Prosecutor together with "documents and other materials that may be pertinent to the decision of the Council."

2. THE UN SECURITY COUNCIL REFERRAL

One of the triggers that is set by the Rome Statute is a referral of a situation made by the UNSC. There is a profound relationship between these two institutions, though they function independently. This convergence can be understood in light of the words

75 Marchesi, 2008, p. 579, see *supra* note 19.

76 Ibid., p. 579.

77 ICC, OTP, Informal Expert Paper, 2003, p. 9, footnote 10, see *supra* note 66.

of the ICC President noting that the Rome Statute expresses purposes "which overlap with the goals of the UN... To achieve our collective aims, our institutions must work together. ... Cooperation is important because the Court and the UN are part of an interdependent system of international law and justice."[78] The linking point between the UNSC and the ICC lies in the fact that international crimes, as considered by the Rome Statute's Preamble, threaten "the peace, security and well-being of the world."

The UNSC occupies a decisive and dominant role in maintaining international peace and security. The Charter of the UN, in particular Article 24 and Chapters VI and VII, assigns the UNSC with the exclusive responsibility for maintaining international peace and security.[79] According to Article 24(1) of the Charter, "in order to ensure prompt and effective action by the UN, its Members confer on the Security Council primary responsibility for the maintenance of international peace and security, and agree that in carrying out its duties under this responsibility the Security Council acts on their behalf." In furthering these duties, the UNSC has dealt with the situations of crisis bringing about the occurrence of atrocities and international crimes.

2.1. LEGAL BASIS FOR UNSC REFERRALS

The intervention of the UNSC in the situations wherein international crimes are committed has developed this organization into a leading actor in the field of international criminal justice. The establishment of *ad hoc* tribunals in the 1990s marked the starting point for this new period in the life of the UNSC. By founding the *ad hoc* tribunals, the UNSC has played a direct role in developing international criminal justice through institutionalizing individual accountability for breaches of humanitarian norms.[80] However, from the outset, it should be noted that the UNSC has not been an ideal and perfect mechanism to deliver international justice. The history of the UNSC proves that the Council is inactive when the strategic interests of a permanent member or the behavior of the permanent member itself is threatened in some way.[81] Kaleck sheds some light into the dark history of the selectivity before the UNSC and powerful States with respect to international criminal justice.[82] Nonetheless, selective justice arising from the Council is maybe better than nothing.

---

78 ICC Presidency, Statements to the United Nations General Assembly by Philipp Kirsch the President of the ICC, 8 November 2005, pp. 3–4, available at: www.icc-cpi.int/NR/rdonlyres/CC2EE876-18C6-4182-8A08-C5155B85802A/146328/PK_20051108_English1.pdf, last accessed at 17 February 2017.

79 Max Hilaire, *United Nations Law and the Security Council*, Ashgate Publishing limited, 2005, p. 6.

80 Martin J. Burke and Thomas G. Weiss, 'The Security Council and Ad Hoc Tribunals: Law and Politics; Peace and Justice', in Vesselin Popovski and Trudy Fraser (eds.), *The Security Council as Global Legislator*, Routledge, 2014, p. 242.

81 William A. Schabas, *Unimaginable Atrocities: Justice, Politics and Rights at the War Crimes Tribunals*, Oxford University Press, 2012, p. 80.

82 Wolfgang Kaleck, *Double Standards: International Criminal Law and the West*, Torkel Opsahl Academic Publisher, 2015.

The UNSC established the *ad hoc* tribunals by invoking its authorities under chapter VII of the UN Charter; it was the only way to make the tribunals' mandates and orders binding and effective.[83] From the beginning, the legality of the establishment of the *ad hoc* tribunals was challenging. The ICTY was established by Resolution 827, adopted by the Security Council on 25 May 1993. In the meeting that led to the passing of the Resolution, Brazil and China both questioned the authority of the Council to set up an international criminal tribunal under Chapter VII, but neither considered their reservations enough to vote against the Resolution.[84] Eventually, the constituent Resolution was adopted and thereby the ICTY was established, but it was not an ending point to challenges.

At the first proceeding before the ICTY, namely the Tadić case, the defendant challenged the legitimacy of the ICTY and questioned the legality of the SC's authority to set up the tribunal. This challenge was strongly rejected by the tribunal. As the Appeals Chamber of the tribunal asserted "once the Security Council determines that a particular situation poses a threat to the peace or that there exists a breach of the peace or an act of aggression, it enjoys a wide margin of discretion in choosing the course of action."[85] The Chamber added that nothing in Article 41 of the UN Charter "suggests the limitation of the measures to those implemented by States. The Article only prescribes what these measures cannot be", namely military actions, however, "beyond that it does not say or suggest what they have to be."[86] Therefore, the adoption of a judicial approach to the situations threatening international security and peace may lie among those measures at the UNSC's disposal to reduce the threats. The end of the Cold War brought about a greater willingness to interpret internal conflicts as a threat to international peace and security.[87] When such threats were recognized by the UNSC in the 1990s, it established *ad hoc* tribunals as non-coercive measures falling within the authorities of the UNSC under Chapter VII. According to Article 41 of the UN Charter, "the Security Council may decide what measures not involving the use of armed force are to be employed to give effect to its decisions, and it may call upon the Members of the UN to apply such measures. These may include complete or partial interruption of economic relations and of rail, sea, air, postal, telegraphic, radio, and other means of communication, and the severance of diplomatic relations." The list of the measures at the SC's disposal, mentioned in this article, is illustrative and not exhaustive. The ICTR in one of its decisions refers to this feature of the article and points out that the establishment of judicial bodies falls within the ambit of measures to satisfy the goals

---

83 Vesselin Popovski, 'The Security Council and the International Criminal Court', in Vesselin Popovski and Trudy Fraser (eds.), *The Security Council as Global Legislator*, Routledge, 2014, p. 269.

84 Robert Cryer, *Prosecuting International Crimes: Selectivity and the International Criminal Law Regime, Cambridge* University Press, 2005, p. 53.

85 ICTY, Tadić case, Decision on the Defense Motion for Interlocutory Appeal on Jurisdiction, 2 October 1995, para. 31.

86 Ibid., para. 35.

87 Burke and Weiss, 2014, p. 246, see *supra* note 80.

behind Article 41.[88] The Tadić judgment was rather an ending point for the challenges against the validity of the UNSC's authority to set up judicial tribunals. As Schabas submits, since then the issue of the authority of the UNSC to found criminal tribunals has not been seriously contested.[89]

Legally speaking, the establishment of the *ad hoc* tribunals based on the UN Charter implied that the orders and decisions of the tribunals were equal to the orders of the UNSC. This fact was explicitly supported by the then UN General-Secretary: "an order by a trial chamber shall be considered to be the application of an enforcement measure under Chapter VII of the Charter of the UN."[90] The ad hoc tribunals are a subsidiary organ to the UNSC. All UN members have a duty to obey the decisions rendered by the UNSC under Article 25 of the Charter.[91] The ICJ in the Namibia Advisory opinion underlined that Article 25 of the Charter obliges all member States to comply with the UNSC decisions. In accordance with the ICJ, this obligation goes beyond those members of the UNSC that voted against them and those members who are not members of the Council.[92]

The establishment of the *ad hoc* tribunals was a valuable experience for the international community. This experience paved the way for the founding of the ICC. It is conceived that it is hard to imagine the creation of the ICC without the prior creation of the *ad hoc* tribunals.[93] Indeed, the creation of the *ad hoc* tribunals demonstrated that international criminal justice was possible.[94] The influence of the UNSC was not limited to providing inspiration for the establishment of the ICC. The role of the UNSC in promoting international criminal justice was welcomed by the drafters of the Rome Statute, and a special relationship between these two international organizations was designed.

In the preparatory process, granting the UNSC with vast authorities was under question. The provisions concerning the relationship between the UNSC and the Prosecutor were the most contentious of the entire negotiations.[95] Some delegations argued that the recognition of the UNSC's role at the ICC would reduce the credibility and moral authority of the Court and would limit the Court's role and its independence and impartiality. They argue that it would impose political influence and would

---

88 ICTR, Kanyabash case, Decision on the Defense Motion On jurisdiction, 18 June 1997, para. 27.

89 Schabas, 2010, p. 294, see *supra* note 26.

90 United Nations, Report of the Secretary General pursuant to Paragraph 2 of Security Council Resolution 808, 3 May 1993, available at: www.icty.org/x/file/Legal%20Library/Statute/Statute_re808_1993_en.pdf, last accessed at 17 February 2017.

91 Article 25 of the UN Charter: "the Members of the United Nations agree to accept and carry out the decisions of the Security Council in accordance with the present Charter."

92 ICJ, Advisory Opinion, Legal Consequences for States if the Continued Presence of South Africa in Namibia notwithstanding Security Council Resolution 276 (1970), 21 June1971, para. 116.

93 Vesselin Popovski, 'The Legislative Role of the Security Council's Thematic Resolutions', in Vesselin Popovski and Trudy Fraser (eds.), *The Security Council as Global Legislator*, Routledge, 2014, p. 6.

94 Michail Vagias, *The Territorial Jurisdiction of the International Criminal Court*, Cambridge University Press, 2014, p. 1.

95 Schabas, 2012, p. 90, see *supra* note 81.

confer additional powers to the SC.[96] In addition, some delegations, including Iran and Morocco, were not categorically against the role of the UNSC, but they argued that the UNSC should not refer a situation other than one of aggression to the Court.[97]

Nonetheless, these voices did not draw the attention of the majority. Eventually, a special relationship between the ICC and the UNSC emerged in the Rome Statute. In the architecture of the ICC, the UNSC occupies a high and influential position. The UNSC is authorized to refer a situation to the Prosecutor of the Court, even by ignoring the territorial and national jurisdictions of the Court. The authority of the UNSC to refer a situation under Chapter VII of the Charter indicates that peace and justice can be substantiated simultaneously.[98] In addition to this triggering function, the UNSC, under Article 16 of the Statute, is empowered to stay the Court's investigation or prosecution.

At the time that the Rome Statute was drafted, the ILC reported why the UNSC was granted vast powers: "the Commission felt that such a provision was necessary in order to enable the Council to make use of the court, as an alternative to establishing *ad hoc* tribunals and as a response to crimes which affront the conscience of mankind."[99] Legally speaking, there was no bar for the UNSC to found other *ad hoc* tribunals parallel to the ICC. So, it was necessary to provide the Council with a mechanism that would enable it to fulfill its interest in promoting the investigations, if the intent was for the UNSC not to resort to alternative mechanisms.[100]

2.2. MUTUAL BENEFITS

The designed relationship between the UNSC and the Court has mutual benefits for both organizations. As to the UNSC, by the establishment of the ICC the Council does not need to establish *ad hoc* tribunals any more, which would put an enormous burden on the UN budget.[101] Given the benefits arising from the Court for the UNSC, it has been said that designing such a relation between the UNSC and the Court was a gift to the UNSC from the States in the Rome Conference.[102] By making a referral, the Council imposes a responsibility upon the Court and simultaneously preserves its credibility without paying any cost and doing any action. As it will be mentioned, the Security

96 Schabas, 2010, pp. 294–5, see *supra* note 26.

97 Kim, 2003, p. 239, see *supra* note 6.

98 Juliet Okoth, 'Africa, the United Nations Security Council and the International Criminal Court: the Question of Deferrals', in Gerhard Werle and Moritz Vombaum (eds.), *Africa, the UN Security Council and the International Criminal Court: The Question of Deferrals in Africa and the International Criminal Court*, TMC Asser Press, 2013, p. 203.

99 Report of the International Law Commission on the Work of its forty-sixth Session, Commentaries on draft Statute for the International Criminal Court, p. 44.

100 Olásolo, 2005, p. 91, see *supra* note 1.

101 Christoph Safferling, *International Criminal Procedure*, Oxford University Press, 2012, p. 89.

102 Luigi Condorelli and Santiago Villapando, 'Referral and Deferral by the Security Council', in Antonio Cassese, Paola Gaeta and John R.W.D. Jones (eds.), *The Rome Statute of the International Criminal Court: A Commentary*, Vol(I), Oxford University Press, 2002, p. 572.

Council did not hide the fact that it had taken into account the financial benefits of using the ICC when it made its referral in Sudan.

There are also some advantages for the Court that persuaded its founders to accept the role of the UNSC. At first, by avoiding establishing *ad hoc* tribunals and giving a mandate to the ICC, the UNSC affirms the legitimacy of the Court. When the UNSC does not set up a parallel mechanism, indeed, it recognizes the existence of the Court and its roles in the world order. It was an important consideration, in particular for the beginning years of the Court's operation. When the Court was established, the UNSC was the single global power managing international criminal justice. The Court needed the support and recognition from the UNSC to be able to play a role in the new world order at the ICC era.

Secondly, through UNSC referrals the reach of the Court extends to non-member States. It is a contribution to the universality of the Court. It also facilitates the cooperation of these States. According to the *pacta tertiis* rule, non-member States are not obliged to cooperate with the Court. The UNSC Resolutions referring a situation under Chapter VII of the UN Charter provide for States an additional, or for some States even an exclusive, basis for the duty to cooperate with the Court.[103] In this regard, in case of non-cooperation, the Court may benefit from the powers of the UNSC, too. According to Article 87(7) of the Rome Statute, upon a UNSC referral, if the Court makes a finding of non-compliance of the State concerned, it refers the matter to the Security Council. In this scenario, the UNSC enjoys more authorities than the Court to oblige a disobedient State to cooperate. These authorities include those referred to in Chapter VII of the UN Charter. UNSC Resolution 1267 demanded that the Taliban authorities in Afghanistan "turn over Usama bin Laden without further delay to appropriate authorities in a country where he has been indicted...and effectively brought to justice." Following therefrom, Resolution 1333 (2000) determined that the failure of the Taliban authorities to comply with the Council's demand constituted a threat to international peace and security.[104] The determination demonstrates that in the viewpoint of the UNSC, a failure to cooperate to fulfil the tasks arising from Chapter VII measures is a threat to international peace and security. This ruling is applicable to the situation of non-cooperation with the Court when UNSC referrals trigger the Court's jurisdiction.

It should be noted, however, that in spite of the expectation of benefitting from the Council's support, the Council has failed to provide sufficient support for the ICC in reality.[105] The drafters of the Statute agreed with the intervention of the Council in view of taking advantage of its backing. Without such an advantage, the intervention of the Council is not valuable. This is a fact that has been echoed by the Court. As the Judges of the Court have Stated, if "there is no follow-up action on the part of the Security

103 Göran Sluiter, International Criminal Adjudication and the Collection of Evidence: Obligations of States, Intersentia, 2002, p. 71.

104 UNSC, Resolution 1333, 19 December 2000, p. 2.

105 Kaleck, 2015, p. 95, see *supra* note 82.

Council, any referral by the Council to the ICC under Chapter VII of the UN Charter would never achieve its ultimate goal, namely, to put an end to impunity. Accordingly, any such referral would become futile."[106] There is also a land-marking instance in the case law of the Court showing the adverse effects of a non-cooperative Council. In December 2014, the Prosecutor of the Court decided to shelve the activities of her office as to the Darfur situation. According to Prosecutor Bensouda, "given this council's lack of foresight on what should happen in Darfur, I am left with no choice but to hibernate investigative activities in Darfur as I shift resources to other urgent cases... What is needed is a dramatic shift in this council's approach to arresting Darfur suspects."[107] Before that, in the context of the situation in Libya, the Prosecutor had raised a warning that "the continuing disparity between resources and expectations, risks systematic underperformance that will not only harm the Court and its mandate, but also the credibility of this Council. This is particularly pertinent for situations that have been referred to the International Criminal Court by the Council."[108]

Apart from playing a role as a trigger, the UNSC have influence on the issue of selectivity at the Court. These effects are not direct, but their importance is no less than making a referral. A legislative behavior in the UNSC has emerged, which represents a significant shift in the Council's strategy to maintain international peace and security. This newly developed practice refers to the adoption of thematic Resolutions addressing global generic threats to peace and security.[109] Indeed, in the new period of the UNSC's life, the country-specific Resolutions have been replaced with the thematic Resolutions that try to encourage international norms. The thematic Resolutions are not considered outside the Charter mandates of the UNSC.[110] The Council pays attention to the areas determined as a threat to international peace and security. These thematic Resolutions are of great importance and assistance for the Prosecutor of the Court in determining the gravity of a situation or case in the situation selection and prioritization. The Court has expressive mandates. Thematic prosecution is a doctrine that directs the Court in the case selection. The findings of the Council help the Court in this regard. The issue of child soldiering is a good example here. The UNSC turned its attention to the rights of child soldiers in the late 1990s.[111] The UNSC adopted some Resolutions with respect to the problem of child soldiering. Resolution 1261 (1999), adopted unanimously, was the

---

106 ICC, PTC II, Darfur situation, Decision on the Prosecutor's Request for a Finding of Non-Compliance against the Republic of the Sudan, 9 March 2015, para. 17.

107 UN News Center, Security Council inaction on Darfur 'can only embolden perpetrators, 12 December 2014, available at: www.un.org/apps/news/story.asp?NewsID=49591#.VY9mm4e4mTc, last accessed at 17 February 2017.

108 UN News Center, Libya: ICC Prosecutor Warns Court's Work Faces 'Deleterious Impact' of Ongoing Instability, 11 November 2014, available at: www.un.org/apps/news/story.asp?NewsID=49311#.WKce51ewbFI, last accessed at 17 February 2017.

109 Popovski, 2014, p. 6, see *supra* note 93.

110 Olivia Bosch, 'A legislative Evolution: UNSC Resolution 1540 Revisited', in Vesselin Popovski and Trudy Fraser (eds.), *The Security Council as Global Legislator*, Routledge, 2014, p. 100.

111 Noelle Quenivet, 'The Security Council as Global Executive but not Global Legislator: the case of Child Soldiers', in Vesselin Popovski and Trudy Fraser (eds.), *The Security Council as Global Legislator*, Routledge, 2014, p. 160.

first Resolution addressing the topic. It strongly condemned the targeting of children in situations of armed conflict including the killing and maiming, sexual violence, abduction and forced displacement, recruitment and use of children in armed forces.[112] In 2004, by its unanimous adoption of Resolution 1539, the Council called upon States to prepare, concrete plans to halt the recruitment and use of children in violation of international obligations.[113] Later, the Council set up the Working Group of Children and Armed Conflict to monitor and report its recommendations about the issue of child soldiers.[114] It is asserted that the systematic engagement of the Council has generated both energy and pressure within the UN system to address the issue of children affected by armed conflict.[115] Even outside of the UN system, such an influence can be traced; this is exactly what happened when the then Prosecutor of the Court decided to charge Lubanga of the recruitment of child soldiers. Sexual violence crimes committed against women in conflicts are another theme warranted by UNSC intervention.[116] The Prosecutor's policy on the prosecution of sexual crimes against women and girls was adopted at the backdrop of UNSC initiatives.

2.3. PRIVILEGES OF THE SECURITY COUNCIL REFERRALS

The authority of the UNSC to refer a situation has two privileges in comparison with States' rights to make a referral. First, the authority of the UNSC is broader than the scope of the authority of the States Parties to refer situations. Unlike States Parties, the UNSC is empowered to refer a situation irrespective of preconditions enshrined in Article 12. It means that the UNSC is able to refer a situation of non-member States. UNSC referrals extend the scope of the ICC's jurisdiction over non-member States. Here, the referral of a situation to the ICC is a decision to confer jurisdiction on the Court.[117] The first Prosecutor of the Court referred to this function of UNSC referring Resolution 1593 that conferred "upon this Court jurisdiction over crimes committed in the Darfur region since 1 July 2002."[118] In addition, the Chambers have rejected challenges against the jurisdiction of the Court over non-member States in the case of UNSC referrals. For instance, in its decision on the Prosecutor's application to issue an arrest warrant against Al Bashir, PTC I asserted that "insofar as the Darfur situation has been referred to the Court by the Security Council, acting pursuant to Article 13(b) of the Statute, the present case falls within the jurisdiction of the Court despite the fact that it refers to the alleged criminal liability of a national of a State that is not a party

112 UNSC, Resolution 1261, 25 August 1999.
113 UNSC, Resolution 1539, 22 April 2004.
114 UNSC, Resolution 1612, 26 July 2005.
115 Quenivet, 2014, p. 175, see *supra* note 111.
116 For instance see: UNSC, Resolution 1325(2000).
117 Dapo Akande, 'The Legal Nature of Security Council Referrals to the ICC and its Impact on Al Bashir's Immunities', *Journal of International Criminal Justice*, 2009, vol. 7, p. 341.
118 ICC, OTP, Public Redacted Version of the Prosecutor's Application under Article 58, Situation in Sudan, 14 July 2008, para. 63.

to the Statute, for crimes which have been allegedly committed in the territory of a State not party to the Statute."[119] It deserves to be noted that the States' obligations to cooperate with the Court under the Rome Statute has a treaty nature. Therefore, non-member States are not obliged to cooperate with the Court, unless the UNSC explicitly obliges these States in its referring Resolution. Both the UNSC Resolutions referring Sudan and Libya do not include a provision obliging non-member States to cooperate with the Court, except for both territorial States. The Resolutions just 'urge' "all States and concerned regional and other international organizations to cooperate fully with the Court."[120]

Secondly, in addition to the power to refer a situation, the Council is authorized to suspend the activated jurisdiction of the Court under Article 16 of the Rome Statute.[121] Such authority has been seen as the primacy of the responsibility of the UNSC to maintain the international peace and security.[122] Article 16 was a compromise between two extreme views in the preparatory process: the idea of an absolute independent prosecutor and the idea of a subordinate prosecutor to the UNSC.[123] Article 16 is usually seen as a preference of peace to criminal justice. When the Council is of the view that the needs of peace require that the question of justice be set aside, at least temporarily, Article 16 allows for a deferral as the best solution in the circumstance.[124] However, it should be recalled that Article 16 is a temporary measure and an exception to the rule.

The suspending authority of the UNSC should be exercised under Chapter VII of the Charter, like its referring authority. It implies that the only situation that justifies a deferral is when such a situation poses a threat to international peace or security. From this perspective, UNSC Resolution 1422 came under fire. On 30 June 2002, the US vetoed a Security Council Resolution that would have extended a UN peacekeeping mission in Bosnia-Herzegovina. The veto occurred due to the concern that US personnel could be subject to prosecutions by the new International Criminal Court. As a condition for extending the peacekeeping mission, the US sought approval of a Resolution that would have permanently barred the ICC from initiating proceedings against peacekeeping personnel from States not parties to its Statute without the Security Council's consent.[125]

---

119 ICC, PTC I, Al Bashir case, Decision on the Prosecution's Application for a Warrant of Arrest against Omar Hassan Ahmad Al Bashir, 4 March 2009, para. 40.

120 UNSC, Resolution 1593, 31 March 2005, para. 2. And UNSC, Resolution 1970, 26 February 2011, para. 5.

121 Article 16 of the Rome Statute: "no investigation or prosecution may be commenced or proceeded with under this Statute for a period of 12 months after the Security Council, in a Resolution adopted under Chapter VII of the Charter of the United Nations, has requested the Court to that effect; that request may be renewed by the Council under the same conditions."

122 Jo Martin Stigen, *The Relationship Between the International Criminal Court and National Jurisdictions: the Principle of Complementarity,* Brill Nijhoff, 2008, p. 237.

123 Sliedregt, 2014, p. 1146, see *supra* note 47.

124 Okoth, 2013, p. 202, see *supra* note 98.

125 Bryan MacPherson Authority of the Security Council to Exempt Peacekeepers from International Criminal Court Proceedings, ASIL Insight, 11 July 2002, available at: www.asil.org/insights/volume/7/issue/9/authority-security-council-exempt-peacekeepers-international-criminal, last accessed at 17 February 2017.

Many States opposed the US effort as an attempt to amend the Rome Statute in excess of the Security Council's authority.[126] As a result, the US proposed a different Resolution that would defer proceedings against peacekeepers for one year. This draft was approved by the Security Council, in July 2002. According to the Resolution, the UNSC, acting under Chapter VII, "requests, consistent with the provisions of Article 16 of the Rome Statute, that the ICC, if a case arises involving current or former officials or personnel from a contributing State not a Party to the Rome Statute over acts or omissions relating to a United Nations established or authorized operation, shall for a twelve-month period starting 1 July 2002 not commence or proceed with investigation or prosecution of any such case, unless the Security Council decides otherwise."[127] The Resolution was renewed just one time more in 2003 through Resolution 1487.[128] In the same year, the Council adopted a Resolution with respect to the conflict in Liberia. The Resolution excluded "current or former officials or personnel from a contributing State, which is not a party to the Rome Statute of the International Criminal Court from the jurisdiction of the Court, unless that State waives its exclusive jurisdiction."[129]

The foregoing Resolution had a positive implication for the Court. By adopting such a Resolution, the Council showed that it had recognized the independence of the Court. The reason is that the Resolution used the term 'request' instead of 'decision', though it was based on Chapter VII of the UN Charter. Such a term complies with the wording in Article 16 of the Rome Statute. The ICC has an independent legal personality, and therefore is not directly bound by Security Council Resolutions.[130] It suggests that the legal obligations of the Court are not based on the determinations of the Security Council, but on the legal framework of the Rome Statute, namely Article 16.[131]

Nonetheless, there was a problem. Resolution 1422 was based on the understanding of the Security Council that a request under Article 16 can be made in general terms.[132] Under Article 39 of the UN Charter, the authorities of the Council under Chapter VII emerge when a threat to peace or security is already recognized. The Resolution raised the question of how the prosecution of those peacekeepers who commit the most serious of international crimes of the concern to the international community as a whole is a threat to international security and peace. Stahn argues that the assertion of the threat to peace is grounded on the inability of the UN to deal with future crises without the support of the US. Such an assumption implies that non-contribution of

126 *See:* UNSC, 4568th meeting Wednesday, 10 July 2002, available at: www.un.org/Docs/pv4568e.pdf, last accessed at 17 February 2017.

127 UNSC, Resolution 1422, para. 1.

128 UNSC, Resolution 1487 (2003) on the United Nations peacekeeping, 12 June 2003.

129 UNSC, Resolution 1497 (2003), para. 7.

130 Carsten Stahn, 'The Ambiguities of Security Council Resolution (1422)', *European Journal of International Law*, 2003, vol. 14, p. 88.

131 Ibid., p. 88.

132 Nina Seider, Jurisdiction over Peacekeeping Forces Before and After the Establishment off the International Criminal Court and the Impacts off Security Council Resolution 1422 and So-Called Article 98 Agreements, Thesis of Masters of Law, University of Cape Town, p. 32.

troops to UN peacekeeping operations is in itself a threat to peace.[133] Indeed, the UN withdrawal from Bosnia would affect the peace and stability. However, what originally constituted a threat to peace and security was the US threat to hamper the operations of the UN, not the ICC's intervention.

In addition, other arguments have been put forward against the Resolution. Bassiouni asserted the Resolution would grant a blanket immunity to all persons involved. Therefore, the Resolution was inconsistent with Article 16 of the Rome Statute, which provided for the UNSC deferrals only on a temporary, case-by-case basis.[134] In addition, the Resolution was not consistent with Article 27 of the Rome Statute. Under Article 27, all persons having any 'official capacity' on the international or the domestic level should be treated equally in the sense that the nature of their capacity is irrelevant with respect to their responsibility. Nonetheless, the Resolution exempted all peacekeepers from non-party States to the Rome Statute from the jurisdiction of the ICC. Some argue that such an exemption should be considered legislative in the sense that it generalizes the rule not to prosecute personnel from member States that are not members of the ICC.[135] However, Resolution 1422 did not exclude all citizens of non-party States from the jurisdiction of the Court, but merely peacekeepers.[136] Therefore, it should be seen as an impunity based on the 'official capacity' as imagined by Article 27. It is interesting to note that under customary international law, criminal jurisdiction for violations committed by members of peacekeeping operations belongs to their sending States.[137] For this reason, the French had proposed the inclusion of a provision in the Statute exempting peacekeepers from international criminal responsibility.[138] However, the proposal failed to grab the approval of other delegations. Stahn argues that the reliance on the jurisdiction of troop-contributing States was justified by the fact that there was not an independent international institution to deal effectively with these abuses.[139] Such a justification is not valid anymore now that there is an international tribunal like the ICC. This issue of international law should be revised in light of the ICC era. The Court's jurisdiction over peacekeepers resembles immunities before the Court. Immunities still bar the national jurisdiction from prosecuting the acting Heads of State, but they are not applicable to the Court. Prosecution of peacekeepers at the domestic level may face legal barricades, but the way for the Court's intervention is open.

The approach adopted by the UNSC had adverse effects on the Court's reputation too, because it directed the Court to deliver justice in a selective manner. When the

---

133 Stahn, 2003, p. 87, see *supra* note 130.

134 Mahmoud Cherif Bassiouni, *Introduction to International Criminal Law*, Martinus Nijhoff Publishers, 2013, p. 703.

135 Bosch, 2014, p. 99, see *supra* note 110.

136 Seider, p. 39, see *supra* note 132.

137 Ilias Bantekas, 'The Need to Amend Article 12 of the ICC Statute: Remedying the Effects of Multilateral Treaties upon Third Parties', *New Criminal Law Review*, 2009, vol. 12, p. 492.

138 Stahn, 2003, p. 95, see *supra* note 130.

139 Ibid., p. 96.

UNSC is selective in its referrals, this creates suspicions of bias and damages the ICC's own integrity.[140]

2.4. RESTRICTIONS ON MAKING A REFERRAL BY THE UNSC

The authority of the UNSC to refer a situation is not unfettered. One major restriction, as mentioned, is that such a referral should be made under Chapter VII of the UN Charter. The source of the authority of the UNSC to seize the Court is to be found in the Charter itself.[141] The UNSC has already exercised that kind of authority with respect to *ad hoc* tribunals. Therefore, the Rome Statute does not add a new power to the Council.[142] The Council should determine whether a situation of crisis constitutes a threat to international peace and security and then finds a referral necessary to maintain peace and security. It enhances the point of view that rendering justice in individual criminal cases contributes to the restoration of international peace and security.[143] The Appeals Chamber of the ICTY States in one of its judgments that there is a common understanding of the membership of the UN at large that "the threat to peace of Article 39 may include, as one of its species, internal conflicts."[144] If the UNSC did not act under chapter VII, it would lose its procedural status as a party to the triggering mechanism and would become a mere informant.[145] In this case, the legal status of a referral made by the UNSC is equal to the value of the communications made by other entities and could not be considered as a different trigger.

Another restriction of the Council's referrals is that they should be in conformity with the jurisdiction of the Court. The Council must live within the parameters of the Rome Statute with respect to such matters as jurisdiction.[146] The PTC of the Court referred in the situation in Sudan to this restriction on UNSC referrals: "by referring the Darfur situation to the Court, pursuant to Article 13(b), the Security Council of the United Nations has also accepted that the investigation into the said situation, as well as any prosecution arising therefrom, will take place in accordance with the statutory framework provided for in the Statute, the Elements of Crimes and the Rules as a whole."[147] Among the jurisdictional parameters, UNSC referrals are exempted from two factors, namely personal and territorial parameters. However, the UNSC shall observe the temporal and subject matter jurisdictions of the Court. The Council is bound to

---

140 Popovski, 2014, p. 282, see *supra* note 83.

141 Condorelli and Villapando, 2002, p. 630, see *supra* note 102.

142 Nonetheless, some author submitted that it has added new power to the SC. For instance, The Rome Statute thereby adds another competence to the UNSC. (*See:* Safferling, 2012, p. 89, see *supra* note 101).

143 Göran Sluiter, Hakan Friman and Suzannah Linton (eds.), *International Criminal Procedure: Principles and Rules*, Oxford University Press, 2013, p. 57.

144 ICTY, Tadić case, 2 October 1995, para. 30, see *supra* note 85.

145 Olásolo, 2005, p. 92, see *supra* note 1.

146 Schabas, 2010, p. 301, see *supra* note 26.

147 ICC, PTC I, Darfur situation, Decision on Application under Rule 103, 4 February 2009, para. 31.

refer those situations including ICC crimes. As mentioned earlier, the UNSC tend to refer a situation to the ICC that is declared as a threat to international security and peace instead of establishing an *ad hoc* tribunal. In this regards, the establishment of the Special Tribunal for Lebanon (STL) should not be seen as an exception to the rule, since the Tribunal was tasked to prosecute terrorism, which was outside the scope of the subject-matter jurisdiction of the Court. Moreover, the UNSC cannot modify the treaty-based bar against the retroactive application of the Statute prior to its entry into force.[148]

Moreover, the UNSC is supposed to refer a situation in the Rome Statute sense, instead of a case. It is considered as a substantive restriction on the SC's referrals.[149] A situation has a gesture of comprehensiveness. The use of situation instead of case in the Rome Conference was to avoid the danger of one-sided referrals.[150] Nonetheless, it was mentioned that the referrals of situations in Sudan and Libya did not meet such a requirement. In both situations, the referring Resolutions exclude some groups of people from the jurisdiction of the Court. For instance, the Resolution referring the situation in Darfur States that the UNSC has decided that "nationals, current or former officials or personnel from a contributing State outside Sudan which is not a party to the Rome Statute of the International Criminal Court shall be subject to the exclusive jurisdiction of that contributing State for all alleged acts or omissions arising out of or related to operations in Sudan established or authorized by the Council or the African Union, unless such exclusive jurisdiction has been expressly waived by that contributing State."[151] The main beneficiaries of inclusion of this exempting clause were American nationals, who usually work in the areas of conflict as peacekeeping forces. The US representatives considered this language in the Resolutions as a 'precedent-setting assurance'.[152] However, criticism against this precedent was initially voiced in the UNSC itself. The Delegation of the Philippines, Mr. Baja, in the session resulting in the adoption of the referring Resolution explicitly said, "operative Paragraph 6 of the Resolution is killing its credibility."[153] In addition, Brazil considered this provision as "a legal exception that is inconsistent in international law."[154] In spite of all errors regarding the referring Resolutions, surprisingly the Prosecutor of the Court did not pay attention to them. The Prosecutor of the Court conducted the preliminary

---

148 Rastan, 2011, p. 424, see *supra* note 4. It should be noted that the reasons behind establishing hybrid tribunals such as STL go beyond what has been referred to in this part. This section just intends to answer the question why the UNSC explored a mechanism outside of the Court if it intended not to make a rival for the ICC.

149 Condorelli and Villapando, 2002, p. 632, see *supra* note 102.

150 Williams and Schabas, 2008, pp. 571–2, see *supra* note 8.

151 UNSC, Resolution 1593, 2005, para. 6.

152 Hyder Corrina, 'The U.N. Security Council's Referral of the Crimes in Darfur to the International Criminal Court in Light of U.S. Opposition to the Court: Implications for the International Criminal Court's Functions and Status', *Berkeley Journal of International Law*, 2006, vol. 24, p. 657.

153 UNSC, 5158th meeting Thursday, 31 March 2005, p. 6, available at: www.un.org/en/ga/search/view_doc.asp?symbol=S/PV.5158, last accessed at 17 February 2017.

154 Ibid., p. 11.

examination in a short time and did not pose any question about the validity of such referrals. Schabas believes that this issue should have been resolved as a preliminary matter before any prosecutions are undertaken, because if that paragraph is illegal the question of severability (salvatorius) arises, which could result in the conclusion that the entire referral is invalid.[155]

2.5. SECURITY COUNCIL REFERRALS IN PRACTICE

Until 2017, the UNSC has referred two situations to the Court, namely the situation in Darfur, Sudan, and the situation in Libya, which will be discussed below to see how referrals are made by the UNSC in practice.

2.5.1. Situation in Darfur, Sudan

In September 2004, US Secretary of State, Colin Powell, called upon the UNSC to take action with regard to what he described as genocide underway in Darfur.[156] Following this request and acting under Chapter VII of the UN Charter, on 18 September 2004 the Security Council adopted Resolution 1564 requesting, *inter alia,* that the UNSG "rapidly establish an international commission of inquiry in order to immediately investigate reports of violations of international humanitarian law and human rights law in Darfur by all parties, to determine also whether or not acts of genocide have occurred, and to identify the perpetrators of such violations with a view to ensuring that those responsible are held accountable."[157]

Upon the UNSC Resolution, the Commission was set up. To fulfil its mandates, the Commission defined four tasks for itself, including, *inter alia*, 'to suggest a means of ensuring that those responsible for such violations are held accountable'.[158] Upon its assessments, the Commission issued a report wherein it recommended that the UNSC refer the situation in Darfur to the ICC. The Commission submitted six major merits for its recommendation. Firstly, it argued that the investigation and prosecution of crimes in Darfur would have an impact on peace and security. Secondly, due to the involvement of the government of Sudan in the commission of crimes, it was thought that trial proceedings in The Hague would ensure a neutral atmosphere. Thirdly, the Court was seen as the best-suited organ for ensuring a fair trial. Fourthly, it was an advantage that the Court was operating and could be activated immediately. Finally, the Commission argued that "the institution of criminal proceedings before the ICC, at

---

155 Schabas, 2010, p. 408, see *supra* note 26.

156 Secretary Colin Powell, Testimony before the Senate Foreign Relations Committee, 9 Sep 2004, available at http://2001-2009.State.gov/secretary/former/powell/remarks/36042.htm, last accessed at 17 February 2017.

157 The International Commission of Inquiry on Darfur, Report to the United Nations Secretary-General, Pursuant to Security Council Resolution 1564 of 18 September 2004, 25 January 2005, para. 2.

158 Ibid., para. 18.

the request of the Security Council, would not necessarily involve a significant financial burden for the international community."[159] In the report, the Commission advanced arguments against alternatives to the Court, too. For instance, as to the possibility of establishing an *ad hoc* tribunal, the Commission put forward two reasons: it would be expensive and slow. Given these two disadvantages, the Commission insisted that "at present no political will appears to exist in the international community to set up yet another *ad hoc* International Criminal Tribunal."[160]

Taking into account the report of the Commission of inquiry, the UNSC on 31 March 2005 adopted Resolution 1593 and referred the situation in Darfur to the Prosecutor of the Court. The Resolution was adopted by vote of 11 in favor and with four abstentions including China and the United States. It is said, however, that the abstention of a permanent member with the power to veto a Resolution is a form of tacit acceptance.[161] The Resolution marked the first time that the jurisdiction of the Court was triggered by UNSC referral. Later, the then Prosecutor of the Court submitted that this referral brought an international, independent and impartial justice component to the collective international and regional efforts to end the violence in Darfur.[162]

The Resolution referring the situation in Darfur includes two provisions that have provoked wide criticisms. The first provision, as discussed earlier, excludes some groups of people from the jurisdiction of the Court. The second problem that emerged in the Resolution is about funding. Acting on the Commission's considerations, it explicitly asserts that "none of the expenses incurred in connection with the referral, including expenses related to investigations or prosecutions in connection with that referral, shall be borne by the United Nations and that such costs shall be borne by the parties to the Rome Statute and those States that wish to contribute voluntarily." This part of the Resolution was considered as an unfriendly attitude by the UNSC towards the Court.[163] That was seen as an injection of some bits of poison into the text by the US.[164] Indeed, the US did not veto the Resolution, but affected it.

The UNSC Resolution activated the Court's jurisdiction over the situation in Darfur. However, since the referral, the situation in Sudan has suffered from a missing factor: the SC's support. The situation in Sudan represents a continued failure in supporting the Court. It resulted in the Prosecutor's decision to hibernate the investigation into the situation in Darfur.[165] The Prosecutor increased this pressure by putting the responsibility of atrocities on the shoulders of UNSC members; "victims of rape are asking themselves how many more women should be brutally attacked for this

159 Ibid., para. 572.
160 Ibid., para. 574.
161 Schabas, 2008, p. 406, see *supra* note 17.
162 ICC, OTP, Statement of the Prosecutor of the ICC to the Security Council Pursuant to UNSCR (1593), 29 June 2005, p. 6.
163 Popovski, 2014, p. 278, see *supra* note 83.
164 Schabas, 2008, p. 406, see *supra* note 17.
165 The Guardian, 5 December 2014, see *supra* note 49.

Council to appreciate the magnitude of their plight."[166] In spite of the hibernation, the Prosecutor had to clarify her decision by saying her message "was addressed to this Council to encourage the exercise of its powers to ensure justice for the long-suffering victims of atrocity crimes in Sudan."[167] She bitterly criticized those people, who, according to her, "have deliberately distorted this call for Security Council action as a victory for Mr. Bashir and other suspects in the Darfur situation."[168] The hibernation tactic is a measure that is used by the Prosecutor in the prioritization of situations and cases. Hibernation is applied when operational factors enforce the Prosecutor to shift its priority to other available courses. The issue will be discussed in detail in the gravity chapter.

2.5.2. Situation in Libya

Despite the fact that the approach adopted by the UNSC in referring the situation in Darfur was heavily criticized, such an approach was again followed by the UNSC when it referred the situation in Libya. On 26 February 2012, the UNSC adopted Resolution 1970 and decided "to refer the situation in the Libyan Arab Jamahiriya since 15 February 2011 to the Prosecutor of the International Criminal Court." The Resolution was passed unanimously owing to the support of the US. Resolution 1970 includes an operative paragraph that excludes "that nationals, current or former officials or personnel from a State outside the Libyan Arab Jamahiriya which is not a party to the Rome Statute of the International Criminal Court" from the jurisdiction of the Court, unless the relevant non-member State waives its exclusive jurisdiction over its nationals.[169] In addition, the Resolution insists "the expenses incurred in connection with the referral" shall be borne "by the parties to the Rome Statute and those States that wish to contribute voluntarily." In the meeting resulting in the adoption of the Resolution, some members were against the exclusion of some people from the jurisdiction of the Court. For instance, the Brazil delegation opposed the exemption from jurisdiction of nationals of those countries not parties to the Rome Statute by arguing that it is not "helpful to advancing the cause of justice and accountability and will not contribute to strengthening the role of the Court."[170] However, this voice was not heard.

Contrary to the situation in Darfur, the UNSC's referral did not follow an inquiry commission. The Darfur's Inquiry Commission was seen as enhancing the legitimacy of the referral.[171] Indeed, the Darfur Inquiry Commission went through the facts and

---

166 UN New Agency, 12 December 2014, see *supra* note 107.

167 ICC, OTP, Statement to the United Nations Security Council on the Situation in Darfur, pursuant to UNSCR 1593 (2005) 29 June 2015, para. 10.

168 Ibid., para. 11.

169 Ibid., para. 6.

170 UNSC, 6491st Meeting, 26 February 2011, p. 7, available at: www.securitycouncilreport.org/atf/cf/%7B65BFCF9B-6D27-4E9C-8CD3-CF6E4FF96FF9%7D/Libya%20S%20PV%206491.pdf, last accessed at 14 June 2017.

171 Luc Coté, 'Independence and Impartiality', in Luc Reydams and Jan Wouters and Cedric Ryngaert (eds.), *International Prosecutors*, Oxford University Press, 2012, p. 406.

analyzed them from a legal perspective, and eventually concluded that such a situation was eligible to be referred to the ICC. In the case of Libya, it did not happen. Instead of the establishment of an independent inquiry commission, the UNSC merely pointed to the Human Rights Council Resolution of 25 February 2011, i.e., one day before the issuance of the SC-referring Resolution. The Resolution demanded to "urgently dispatch an independent international commission of inquiry to investigate all alleged violations of international human rights law in the Libyan Arab Jamahiriya, to establish the facts and circumstances of such violations and of the crimes perpetrated, and where possible identify those responsible."[172] The Commission was established, and it finally issued a report, but after the activation of the Court on the situation in Libya. Taking into account this unprecedented behavior of the Council, some believe that the referral of the situation in Libya was a matter of politics instead of justice.[173]

It must be noted that it seems that there is no prospect and will in the UNSC permanent members for a change. In spite of these arguments against the exclusion clause in UNSC referrals, such a practice followed again in a Resolution regarding Syria. In 2014, the UNSC tried to refer the Situation in Syria to the ICC, but it failed because of the veto exercised by Russia and China. Although the Security Council failed, yet the formulation in paragraph 7 of the draft Resolution was similar to previous excluding provisions. According to the draft paragraph 7, the UNSC "decides that nationals, current or former officials or personnel from a State outside the Syrian Arab Republic which is not a party to the Rome Statute of the International Criminal Court shall be subject to the exclusive jurisdiction of that State for all alleged acts or omissions arising out of or related to operations in the Syrian Arab Republic established or authorized by the Council, unless such exclusive jurisdiction has been expressly waived by the State."[174] At the time of drafting, Argentina expressed its strong objection to the inclusion of the provision and expressed that "the Security Council does not have the power to declare an amendment to the Statute in order to grant immunity to nationals of non-party States who commit crimes under the Statute in a situation referred to the Court."[175]

2.5.3. *Article 16 in Action*

Up until 2017, the UNSC has not exercised its power under Article 16 of the Rome Statute, though it has been requested several times to do so. Upon the challenging issuance of the arrest warrants against the Sudanese President, the African Union (AU), in March 2009, requested for the UNSC to suspend the ICC process with respect to the case against Al Bashir. The request was not responded to affirmatively by the Council. It brought about a strong reaction from the African Union in July 2009 when

172 UNSC, Resolution 1970, 2011, p. 1.
173 Brett D. Schaefer and Steven Groves, 'The Motivation for the Referral of Libya to the ICC: Political Pressure or Justice?', 4 March 2011, available at www.heritage.org/africa/report/the-motivation-the-referral-libya-the-icc-political-pressure-or-justice, last accessed at 17 February 2017.
174 UNSC, UN Doc S/2014/348, 22 May 2014, para. 7.
175 UNSC, 7180th Meeting, 22 May 2014, p. 11.

the Union directed all of its member States not to cooperate with the ICC to arrest or surrender Al Bashir. The Union cited Article 98 of the Rome Statute as the legal basis of its decision.[176]

Upon the issuance of arrest against Muammar Gaddafi, the AU again was concerned that the Gaddafi warrant would undermine its efforts for a peaceful solution. The AU argued that the warrant against Gaddafi "seriously complicates the efforts aimed at finding a negotiated political solution to the crisis in Libya, which will also address, in a mutually reinforcing way, issues relating to impunity and reconciliation." Consequently, it decided that "member States shall not cooperate in the execution of the arrest warrant", and requested the UN Security Council to use its power under Article 16 for deferring the ICC process on Libya.[177] The third time that a request to act under Article 16 was submitted to the UNSC, was in the context of the situation in Kenya. In October 2013, an extraordinary session of Assembly of Heads of State and Government of the African Union on Africa's relationship with the ICC was held in Ethiopia. In the session, the AU members drafted a letter requesting the UNSC to defer the proceedings initiated by the Court against the President and Deputy of Kenya.[178] Moreover, the Permanent Representative of Kenya to the UN addressed the President of the UNSC and notified that his country sought a decision of the UNSC to suspend the investigation and prosecution of the ICC as to its Heads of State.[179] These calls encouraged the UNSC for the first time to consider the issue of a deferral, but the Council failed to adopt a draft Resolution.[180] It seems that the UNSC tends to take the initiative and make a referral and then leave the situation alone. It does not hear the voices neither for support nor for stopping.

3. COMMUNICATIONS

The third trigger that awakens the Court's dormant jurisdiction is communications. The term 'communication' was adopted by the OTP to describe the information provided to her office under Article 15.[181] The primary sources of such communications are individuals and NGOs.[182]

176 Assembly of African Union Thirteenth Ordinary Session 13 July 2009, para. 10.

177 African Union, Decision on the implementation of the assembly decision on the ICC, 30 June 1 July 2011, para. 6, available at: www.au.int/web/sites/default/files/decisions/9647-assembly_au_dec_363–390_xvii_e.pdf, last accessed at 14 June 2017.

178 African Union, Decision on Africa's Relationship with the ICC, October 2013.

179 Identical Letters Dated 21 October 2013 from the Permanent Representative of Kenya to the United Nations Addressed to the Secretary-General and the President of the Security Council, 22 October 2013, available at: www.securitycouncilreport.org/atf/cf/%7B65BFCF9B-6D27–4E9C-8CD3 CF6E4FF96FF9%7D/s_2013_624.pdf.

180 Okoth, 2013, p. 198, see *supra* note 98.

181 ICC, OTP, Annex to the Paper on Some Policy Issues Before the Office of the Prosecutor: Referrals and Communication.

182 Paul de Hert and Mathias Holvoet, 'Art. 15. Prosecutor', in Paul de Hert and Jean Flamme and Mathias Holvoet (et al.)(eds.), *Code of International Criminal Law and Procedure, Annotated,* Larcier, 2013, p. 87.

Defining communications as a trigger that enables the Prosecutor to take action was a major step in the humanization of international criminal law. The humanization has two aspects. Firstly, the ICC Prosecutor as a human being functions to a considerable extent independently from the States' will in the selection of international crimes for prosecution. Making decisions on whether to investigate or to prosecute falls within the scope of the prosecutorial discretion.[183] Such discretion is considered as the embodiment of the Prosecutor's independence.[184] Cryer describes the Prosecutor's power as the "strong element of the structure set up by the Rome Statute, which makes the Rome regime worthy of the name."[185] Secondly, individuals are granted a possibility to access international criminal justice. The personal scope of the right of access to the ICC to report crimes contained in the Rome Statute is universal.[186] It means that all individuals are eligible to make a crime report. It is "a valuable avenue by which concerned individuals and organizations may furnish information to the Prosecutor."[187] Here, in particular, victims play a prominent role. PTC II in one of its decisions submitted that "victims, as well as any other subject, may contact the Court (in particular, the OTP), prior to and irrespective of whether a situation or a case is pending before it, with a view to triggering the exercise of the Prosecutor's *proprio motu* powers."[188] At this early stage, victims may participate actively in the functioning of the Court. The Appeals Chamber of the Court States in one of its decisions, "information that victims can provide to the Prosecutor about the scope of his investigations cannot but be welcome as it could provide nothing other than assistance."[189]

3.1. PROCEDURAL ASPECTS OF COMMUNICATIONS

In contrast to referrals, communications do not necessarily determine a specific situation for the Prosecutor. Communications provide information on crimes within the jurisdiction of the Court. It is the responsibility of the Prosecutor to deduce a situation from the information available. However, communications are a prerequisite for the exercise of *proprio motu* power of the Prosecutor. Schabas submits that the Prosecutor may consider potential situations within the jurisdiction of the Court

183 Fouladvand, 2012, p. 86, see *supra* note 26.
184 Safferling, 2012, p. 91, see *supra* note 101.
185 Cryer, 2005, p. 162, see *supra* note 84.
186 Olásolo, 2005, p. 54, see *supra* note 1.
187 ICC, OTP, Annex to the Paper on Some Policy Issues Before the Office of the Prosecutor: Referrals and Communications.
188 ICC, PTC II, Uganda Situation, Decision on Victims' Applications for Participation a/0010/06, a/0064/06 to a/0070/06, a/0081/06 to a/0104/06 and a/0111/06 to a/0127/06, 10 August 2007, para. 92.
189 Appeals Chamber, Situation in the DRC, Judgment on Victim Participation in the Investigation Stage of the Proceedings in the Appeal of the OPCD Against the Decision of Pre-Trial Chamber I of 7 December 2007 and in the Appeals of the OPCD and the Prosecutor Against the Decision of Pre-Trial Chamber I of 24 December 2007, 19 December 2008, para. 54.

even in the absence of any information provided by a third party.[190] However, the wording of Article 15(2) confines the Prosecutor at this stage to seeking and receiving information.[191] Article 15(2) explicitly refers to the information that has been 'received' by the Prosecutor. In addition, if the drafters of the Rome Statute had an intention to empower the Prosecutor to identify a situation on her motion, they would use such wordings used in the *ad hoc* tribunals' Statutes. Article 18(1) of the ICTY and Article 17(1) of the ICTR read, "the Prosecutor shall initiate investigations ex-officio or on the basis of information obtained from any source. The Prosecutor shall assess the information received or obtained." In the preparatory process, Italy and Trinidad and Tobago suggested Article 15 for the ICC's Statute of the same wording as the *ad hoc* Statutes: "the Prosecutor shall initiate investigation *ex officio* or on the basis of information obtained from any source."[192] Nonetheless, the suggestion was not incorporated into the final version of the Rome Statute. The term *proprio motu* means in one's own motion; in the context of the ICC, it means the Prosecutor may act without any formal referral.[193] The Prosecutor is free from the States' will, but she is not free from the international community's authorization. The Prosecutor functions on behalf of the international community. Communications represent the demand and authorization of international community in the absence of States' request. Understanding communications in this sense has, however, a symbolic value. It is not difficult for the Prosecutor to encourage others to provide her with communications. Nevertheless, the expressive function of this understanding deserves to be preserved.

Communications should be made in writing, but if a person is unable, it is possible to make "such request, application, observation or communication in audio, video or other electronic form."[194] Communications under Article 15 may be submitted to the Court through mail, e-mail or facsimile.[195] According to Regulation 25 of the Regulations of the Court, a communication shall indicate, *inter alia*, the identity of the sender; the situation or case number and the Chamber seized of the matter[196]; the purpose of the communication, and the location, date, and individuals involved in incidents. Although the regulation requires the sender of a communication to indicate his or her identity, it does not mean that anonymous communications are invalid. The PTC in the Gbagbo case submits "anonymous NGO reports may be admitted for the limited purpose that the information contained therein may serve to corroborate other pieces of evidence."[197]

---

190 Schabas, *2010*, p. 319, see *supra* note 26.

191 Jo Martin Stigen, 'The Admissibility Procedures', in Carsten Stahn and Mohamed M. El Zeidy (eds.), *The International Criminal Court and Complementarity: From Theory to Practice*, Cambridge University Press, 2011, p. 507. And Olásolo, 2005, p. 1, see *supra* note 1.

192 Schabas, 2010, p. 316, see *supra* note 26.

193 Morten Bergsmo and Jelena Pejic, 'Article 15', in Otto Triffterer (ed.), *Commentary on the Rome Statute of the International Criminal Court*, C.H. Beck. Hart. Nomos, 2008, p. 586.

194 Rule 102 of the ICC Rules of Procedure and Evidence.

195 See: www.icc-cpi.int/en_menus/icc/contact/Pages/contact.aspx.

196 It should be recalled that communications are made as to a situation, not a case.

197 ICC, PTC I, Laurent Gbagbo case, Decision Adjourning the Hearing on the Confirmation of Charges Pursuant to Article 61(7)(c)(i) of the Rome Statute, 3 June 2013, para. 22.

However, sources that do not provide any details regarding its origins or methodology would be afforded lower weight.[198] It could be less problematic in the situational phase where there is no concrete case.

Upon reciting communications, the OTP shall "send an acknowledgement in respect of all information received on crimes to those who provided the information."[199] In addition, when communications are received, the OTP cannot remain inactive and must carry out some kind of assessment of the reports received.[200] All communications should be taken into account. It is an obligation to maintain the confidence in the OTP.[201]

3.2. PROSECUTOR *PROPRIO MOTU* POWER

Communications give the Prosecutor a power to act on her own motion. The idea of communications was absent from the 1994 ILC draft.[202] At the time, the international community was not yet ready for a prosecutor with independent powers.[203] International relations were traditionally seen as a field exclusively for State actors. The thought that the Prosecutor might launch prosecutions in the absence of a referral began to emerge in the *Ad hoc* Committee in 1995.[204] The commentators of the Rome Statute recall that the issue whether there would be an additional trigger mechanism was one of the most contentious issues throughout the ICC negotiations.[205] There were two lines of argument. Some denied the desirability of the creation of an independent prosecutor, taking into account concerns about politically motivated or frivolous actions against the sovereign States. It was the most prominent concern of the opponents of a powerful prosecutor.[206] In addition, some opposing delegations argued that the absence of a complaint made by States would be "an indication that the crime was not of sufficient gravity or concern to the international community."[207] This point of view arose from the traditional belief that used to define the international community as States. This belief prevented recognizing the individuals as international actors.

On the other hand, NGOs and about 60 States known as like-minded group were aligned from the start of the Rome Conference in pushing for a stronger and more

---

198 Laura-liisa Laving, The Reliability of Open Source Evidence in the International Criminal Court, Master thesis, Lund University, 2014, p. 31.
199 Regulation 28 of the Regulations of OTP.
200 Olásolo, 2005, p. 58, see *supra* note 1.
201 Bergsmo and Pejic, 2008, p. 587, see *supra* note 193.
202 Draft Statute for an International Criminal Court 1994, Article 21(1).
203 Coté, 2012, p. 345, see *supra* note 171.
204 Schabas, 2010), p. 316, see *supra* note 26.
205 Kirsch and Robinson, 2002, p. 582, see *supra* note 24.
206 Ibid., p. 659.
207 UN General Assembly, Report of the Ad hoc Committee on the Establishment of the ICC, 1995, para. 114.

independent prosecutor.[208] They argued that historically States had been reluctant to use existing human rights mechanisms to deal with the violations of human rights. It was believed that if the Prosecutor was not able to take the initiative in the absence of the States' request, the OTP would rarely deal with a situation. At the backdrop of this concern, the authority of the Prosecutor to take initiative based on the communications emerged to avoid making the Court formally subordinate to political institutions.[209]

Due to the divergence between the delegations, the prosecutorial discretion needed a compromise. The system of the Court was largely designed on a compromise between different delegations from different legal traditions. Civil law and common law are two main legal traditions that international criminal law and procedures almost exclusively.[210] In designing the prosecutorial discretion at the ICC, both the common law's adversarial model and the inquisitorial approach adopted by civil law systems were taken into account.[211] Traditionally, in the civil law, as a pure or an ideal type, the prosecutorial discretion is limited and subjected to strict judicial control.[212] In the civil law systems, traditionally, prosecutors used to have less discretion in deciding whom to prosecute.[213] It is called the 'principle of legality' or 'mandatory prosecution'. Moreover, in the inquisitorial model, judges have an have a managerial role too.[214] This approach promotes a system in which the judicial authorities mainly control the investigation and appraisal of evidence.[215] By contrast, in the adversarial tradition, the prosecutor enjoys broad prosecutorial discretion to determine what charges should

---

208 Yvonne Dutton, Rules, Politics and the International Criminal Court: Committing to the Court, Routledge, 2013, p. 14.

209 Fouladvand, 2012, p. 77, see *supra* note 26.

210 Brianne McGonigle Leyh, *Procedural Justice: Victim Participation in International Criminal Procedure*, Intersentia, 2011, p. 66. A legal tradition is defined as "a set of deeply rooted, historically conditioned attitudes about the nature of law, about the role of law in society and the polity, about the proper organization and operation of a legal system and about the way law is or should be made, applied, studied, perfected and taught" (See: John Henry Merryman, *The civil law Tradition: An Introduction to the Legal System of Western Europe and Latin America*, Stanford University Press, 1969).

211 Jingbo Dong, 'Prosecutorial Discretion at the International Criminal Court: A Comparative Study', *Journal of Politics and Law,* 2009, vol. 2, p. 109.

212 It is widely accepted that the distinction between the legal traditions is fading and todays there are not pure adversarial or inquisitorial system within a legal system. (See: Jessica Peake, 'A Spectrum of International Criminal Procedure: Shifting Patterns of Power Distribution in International Courts and Tribunals', *Pace International Law Review,* 2014, vol. 26, p. 184). Civil law and common law systems have been regarded here as ideal types in the meaning provided by Weber (For more information about ideal types see: Maartje Weerdesteijn, *The Rationality of Dictators: Towards a More Effective Implementation of the Responsibility to Protect, Intersentia,* 2016, p. 7).

213 Sluiter and Friman and Linton, 2013, p. 160, see *supra* note 143.

214 Jacobs D., 'A Shifting Scale of Power: Who Is in Charge of the Charges at the International Criminal Court And the Uses of Regulation 55', William A. Schabas, Niamh Hayes and Yvonne McDermott (eds.), *The Ashgate Research Companion to International Criminal Law: Critical Perspectives*, Ashgate, 2013, p. 219.

215 McGonigle Leyh, 2011, p. 71, see *supra* note 210.

be entered against the accused.[216] In this legal tradition, judges are only objective observers and are not responsible to find the truth proactively. Giving considerations to these traditions, a compromise solution was introduced by Argentina and Germany in March 1998.[217] According to their proposal, which finally was enshrined in the Rome Statute with some minor changes, the Prosecutor would be authorized by *proprio motu* power to activate the jurisdiction of the Court but it would undergo judicial review. Indeed, the authorization of the PTC for initiating an investigation was designed as a safeguard against the abuse of prosecutorial discretion. The drafters also provided other safeguards, such as the provisions on qualifications of the Prosecutor[218], and the complementarity principle, that was largely a response to the enhanced powers of the new independent prosecutor.[219]

At the ICC, the prosecutorial discretion in the context of referrals is close to some common-law-oriented systems, where the Prosecutor is free to initiate an investigation without the need to obtain an authorization from judges. However, in *proprio motu* proceedings, the discretion of the Prosecutor approaches the civil law tradition, where the Prosecutor should seek authorization from the judges to initiate an investigation. Kress considers the relationship between the prosecutor and the PTC at this stage as "one of the most striking examples of the uniqueness of the ICC procedural law."[220] It is evident that the influence of judges in international criminal tribunals has increased over time. The evolution of judicial review has moved from an 'abstentionist approach' to a managerial conception.[221] More roles of the judges, less independence of the Prosecutor. Therefore, it has been said that the Prosecutor's independence is much more circumscribed at the ICC than in the ICTY or ICTR, since he or she is subject to considerable supervision by the PTC.[222]

4. DECLARATIONS OF ACCEPTANCE UNDER ARTICLE 12(3)

Paragraph 3 of Article 12 of the Rome Statute reads: "if the acceptance of a State which is not a Party to this Statute is required under paragraph 2, that State may, by declaration lodged with the Registrar, accept the exercise of jurisdiction by the Court with respect to the crime in question. The accepting State shall cooperate with the Court without any delay or exception in accordance with Part 9."

---

216 Peake, 2014, p. 189, see *supra* note 212.
217 Bergsmo and Pejic, 2008, p. 583, see *supra* note 193.
218 Kirsch and Robinson, 2002, p. 661, see *supra* note 24.
219 Schabas, 2011, p. 179, see *supra* note 18.
220 Claus Kress, 'The Procedural Law of the International Criminal Court in Outline: Anatomy of a Unique Compromise', *Journal of International Criminal Justice*, 2003, vol. 1, p. 606.
221 Carsten Stahn, 'Judicial Review of Prosecutorial Discretion: 5 Years on', in Carsten. Stahn and Göran Sluiter, *The Emerging Practice of the International Criminal Court*, Martinus Nijhoff, 2009, p. 255.
222 Boas and Bischoff and Reid, 2009, p. 71, see *supra* note 15.

4.1. DIFFERENCE BETWEEN REFERRALS AND DECLARATIONS

In addition to States Parties, in accordance with Article 12(3) of the Statute, a non-member State can accept the ICC's jurisdiction by lodging a declaration. Such a State is called 'the accepting State', which is distinguished from both member and non-member States. An 'declaration of acceptance' is not equal to a referral. The mechanism of lodging an 'declaration of acceptance' is an alternative to becoming a State party to the ICC in order to expand the jurisdiction of the Court. However, lodging a declaration of acceptance does not automatically trigger the jurisdiction of the Court like a referral. An declaration of acceptance is not an *ad hoc* referral.[223] It is exclusively the power and right of a State Party to make a referral. If a non-member State had the same privilege, there would not be a compelling incentive for joining the Court. In the case of declarations, the Prosecutor may exercise his or her *proprio motu* power under Article 15 of the Statute, if there is any communication requesting her to do so. Therefore, if the accepting State accompanies its declaration by a request from the Prosecutor to initiate investigation over a situation, such a request should be considered as a crime report and communication. Such a declaration does not enjoy more privileges than other communications.

By lodging an declaration of acceptance, the territory and the nationals of the accepting State come under the scope of the jurisdiction of the Court. The jurisdictional function of an declaration of acceptance is confirmed by the OTP in its Policy Paper on Preliminary Examination.[224] The Policy Paper submits "it should be noted that Article 12(3) is a jurisdictional provision, not a trigger mechanism. As such, declarations of the sort should not be equated with referrals, but will require a separate triggering by the Prosecutor *proprio motu* or by a State Party."[225] The difference between referrals and declarations is confirmed in the Côte d'Ivoire situation. According to the PTC, in its decision on the challenge made to its jurisdiction by the defense for president Gbagbo, "a declaration made under Article 12(3) of the Statute cannot be equated with a referral."[226] Surprisingly, Regulation 25(1) of the Regulations of the OTP States the preliminary examination may be initiated based on communications, referrals or "a declaration pursuant to Article 12, Paragraph 3 by a State which is not a Party to the Statute." However, the regulation needs to be amended since it fails to make a distinction between 'communications' and 'declarations of acceptance' in terms of their effects on opening a preliminary examination.

The States Parties do not have any right to make reservations to the Statute. There is a difference between the jurisdictional model that is contained in the Statute of the ICJ and what is adopted by the ICC. According to Article 36(2) of the ICJ Statute, States

---

223 Williams and Schabas, 2008, p. 569, see *supra* note 8.

224 ICC, OTP, Policy Paper on Preliminary Examinations, para. 40.

225 Ibid., footnote 25.

226 ICC, PTC I, Laurent Gbagbo case, Decision on the Corrigendum of the Challenge to the Jurisdiction of the Interactional Criminal Court on the basis of Articles 12(3), 19(2), 21(3), 55 and 59 of the Rome Statute Filed by the Defense for President Gbagbo, 15 August 2012, para. 58.

Parties to the ICJ 'may' recognize the jurisdiction of the Court in all legal disputes concerned. By contrast, at the ICC legal system, becoming a State party to the Court implies that that State accepts the Court's jurisdiction in the future, and there is no need to accept the Court's jurisdiction separately. Nevertheless, the accepting State can limit the temporal scope of the delegated jurisdiction. Indeed, as to declarations, there is an opt-in regime. It means the declaring State consents to the exercise of jurisdiction by the Court with respect to the particular situation concerned.[227] However, the rule is that by lodging a declaration the accepting State accepts the jurisdiction of the Court in general.[228] Rule 44(2) of the Rule of Procedure and Evidence provides: "when a State lodges, or declares to the Registrar its intent to lodge, a declaration with the Registrar pursuant to Article 12, paragraph 3, or when the Registrar acts pursuant to sub-rule 1, the Registrar shall inform the State concerned that the declaration under Article 12, paragraph 3, has as a consequence the acceptance of jurisdiction with respect to the crimes referred to in Article 5 of relevance to the situation and the provisions of Part 9, and any rules thereunder concerning States Parties, shall apply." In the situation of the Côte d'Ivoire, Mr. Gbagbo made a challenge against this effect of the declaration made by the Ivorian government and argued that such a declaration cannot confer jurisdiction over future crimes.[229] The challenge was rejected by the PTC and this rejection was confirmed by the Appeals Chamber. The Appeals Chamber asserts that "unless stipulated in the declaration under Article 12(3) of the Statute, acceptance of jurisdiction is not limited to specific events or a specific situation within the meaning of Article 143 of the Statute. It may also cover crimes under Article 5 of the Statute committed after the declaration has been lodged."[230]

The right of the accepting State to limit the jurisdiction of the Court is limited to the temporal jurisdiction. Article 12(3) States a non-member State can lodge a declaration to the Registrar to "accept the exercise of jurisdiction by the Court with respect to the crime in question." The Appeal Chamber has clarified that the term 'crime in question' in Article 12(3) does not indicate "specific events in the past, in the course of which such crimes were committed."[231] Hence, there is no restriction on the subject-matter jurisdiction of the Court. This interpretation enables the Court to serve "the purposes of deterring the commission of crimes in the future and not only of addressing crimes committed in the past."[232] In the case of a declaration that puts some limits on the Court's jurisdiction, PTC I held that "it will be ultimately for the Court to determine whether

227 Rod Rastan, 'Jurisdiction', in Carsten Stahn (ed.), *The Law and Practice of the International Criminal Court*, Oxford University Press, 2015, p. 145.

228 ICC, Appeals Chamber, Laurent Gbagbo Case, Judgment on the Appeal of Mr Laurent Koudou Gbagbo Against the Decision of Pre-Trial Chamber I on Jurisdiction and Stay of the Proceedings, 12 December 2012, para. 82.

229 On 29 May 2012, Mr. Laurent Koudou Gbagbo filed the Corrigendum of the challenge to the jurisdiction of the International Criminal Court on the basis of Articles 12(3), 19(2), 21(3), 55 and 59 of the Rome Statute.

230 ICC, Appeals Chamber, Laurent Gbagbo Case, 12 December 2012, para. 1, see *supra* note 228.

231 Ibid., para. 80.

232 Ibid., para. 83.

the scope of acceptance, as set out in the declaration, is consistent with the objective parameters of the situation at hand."[233]

4.2. DECLARATIONS IN PRACTICE

The case law of the Court has witnessed some instances of 'declarations of acceptance'. The government of Côte d'Ivoire accepted the exercise of jurisdiction by the Court in accordance with Article 12(3) by lodging the declaration, dated 18 April 2003. The letter states "pursuant to Article 12(3) of the Statute of the International Criminal Court, the Government of Côte d'Ivoire accepts the jurisdiction of the Court for the purposes of identifying, investigating and trying the perpetrators and accomplices of acts committed on Ivorian territory since the events of 19 September 2002. Accordingly, Côte d'Ivoire undertakes to cooperate with the Court without delay or exception in accordance with Part 9 of the Statute. This declaration shall be valid for an unspecified period of time and shall enter into effect on being signed."[234] Moreover, on 17 April 2014, the Government of Ukraine lodged a declaration under Article 12(3) of the Rome Statute accepting the jurisdiction of the ICC. In the letter, Ukraine announced that it "recognizes the jurisdiction of the Court for the purpose of identifying, prosecuting and judging the authors and accomplices of act committed on the territory of Ukraine within the period of 21 November 2013 – 22 February 2014."[235] Upon receipt of this declaration, Prosecutor Bensouda decided to open a preliminary examination into the situation in Ukraine. Later, on 1 January 2015, the Government of Palestine lodged a declaration under Article 12(3) of the Rome Statute accepting the jurisdiction of the International Criminal Court over alleged crimes committed "in the occupied Palestinian territory, including East Jerusalem, since June 13, 2014."[236] Accordingly, on 16 January 2015, the Prosecutor announced the opening of a preliminary examination into the situation in Palestine in order to establish whether the Rome Statute criteria for opening an investigation were met.[237]

Considering these instances, it seems that the Prosecutor of the Court follows Regulation 25 in practice. She opens a preliminary examination upon the receipt

233 ICC, PTC I, Laurent Gbagbo case, 15 August 2012, para. 60, see *supra* note 226.

234 ICC, Côte d'Ivoire situation, Declaration Accepting the Jurisdiction of the International Criminal Court, 18 April 2003, available at: www.icc-cpi.int/NR/rdonlyres/7DA08D8E-FF5E-40C8–92D7-F058D5B032F3/279779/ICDE2.pdf, last accessed at 14 June 2014. Some months later, the government of Uganda in addition to a referral, made a declaration under Article 12 (3) accepting the jurisdiction of the Court as of the entry into force of the Rome Statute.

235 ICC, Press Release, Ukraine Accepts ICC jurisdiction over Alleged Crimes Committed since 20 February 2014, 8 September 2015, available at: www.icc-cpi.int/legalAidConsultations?name =pr1146, last accessed at 14 June 2014.

236 ICC, Press Release, Palestine Declares Acceptance of ICC jurisdiction Since 13 June 2014, 5 January 2015, available at: www.icc-cpi.int//Pages/item.aspx?name=pr1080, last accessed at17 February 2017.

237 ICC, Press Release, he Prosecutor of the International Criminal Court, Fatou Bensouda, opens a preliminary examination of the situation in Palestine, 16 January 2015, available at: www.icc-cpi.int// Pages/item.aspx?name=pr1083, last accessed at17 February 2017.

of declarations of acceptance. The foregoing declarations are worded in general terms. The declarations just express the acceptance of the Court's jurisdiction for the purpose of prosecuting ICC crimes. Referring to this purpose does not mean that they are, necessarily, reporting of crimes or referring a specific situation. It is the common purpose of joining the Court for all States to enable the Court to prosecute the ICC-identified crimes. As the Appeal Chamber of the Court insists, in the case of declarations, "the question of whether a '*situation*' exists becomes relevant only once the Court considers whether it may exercise its jurisdiction pursuant to Article 13 of the Statute."[238]

238 ICC, Appeals Chamber, Laurent Gbagbo case, 12 December 2012, paras. 80–84, see *supra* note 228.

CHAPTER II
IDENTIFICATION STAGE

In the procedural architecture of the ICC, there is a distinct stage between the trigger mechanism and the preliminary examination. Upon the receipt of communications or referrals, the Prosecutor shall identify a situation before opening the preliminary examination. The responsibility of the Prosecutor to identify a situation primarily relates to communications, but it is not limited to them. The identification stage marks the first time in the situation selection process when the Prosecutor makes a selection in the context of communications and referrals.

In the literature on the ICC's procedure, this stage is mainly ignored. However, for instance, Ambos has briefly referred to the identification of a situation stage.[239] However, this untouched stage deserves more attention. The Prosecutor has an authority to design situations.[240] In the context of this stage of the situation selection process, this authority is exercised. This chapter provides insight into the functions of identification stage as to both communications (1) and referrals (2).

1. IDENTIFICATION IN THE CONTEXT OF COMMUNICATIONS

Contrary to the referring entities, those who send communications to the OTP do not report a situation. Communications just provide the Prosecutor with information that may lead to the identification of a situation.

1.1. FORMING A SITUATION FROM COMMUNICATIONS

The OTP Policy Paper on Preliminary Examinations establishes a 'filtering process' comprising of four phases, "in order to distinguish those situations that warrant

---

239 Ambos describes the process of forming a case at the ICC as follows: 1.Obtains *notitia crimini*, 2. starts pre-investigating, 3. identifies a situation, 4. Checks the criteria, and 5. starts a formal investigation 6. Investigating, 7. Applies for a warrant of arrest, 7. PTC issues a warrant (see: Kai Ambos, 'The Colombian Peace Process (Law 975 of 2005) and the ICC's Principle of Complementarity', in Carsten Stahn and Mohamed M. El Zeidy (eds.), *The International Criminal Court and Complementarity: From Theory to Practice*, Cambridge University Press, 2011, p. 1081).

240 Schabas, 2012, p. 80, see *supra* note 81.

investigation from those that do not, and in order to manage the analysis of the factors set out in Article 53(1)'.[241] Phase 2 examines the jurisdiction of the Court, Phase 3 deals with the admissibility requirement and Phase 4 assesses the interest of the justice requirement. The first phase of this filtering system is an initial assessment the purpose of which is 'to analyze and verify the seriousness of information received, filter out information on crimes that are outside of the jurisdiction of the Court and identify those that appear to fall within the jurisdiction of the Court'.[242] Communications are analyzed by the Information and Evidence Unit at the OTP. The Unit will prepare reports analyzing the communications received.[243] In Phase 1, the Unit categorizes the communications received in four different types. A communication may include a) matters which are manifestly outside of the jurisdiction of the Court, b) a situation that has already been under preliminary examination, c) a situation is already under investigation or d) matters which are neither manifestly outside the jurisdiction of the Court nor related to situations already under preliminary examination or investigation and therefore warrant further analysis.[244] According to this filtering process, as soon as a communication is received, the Prosecutor opens a preliminary examination, regardless of the quality and content of the communication. This procedure is designed based on the common understanding that there is no distance between the trigger mechanism and the preliminary examination. All communications undergo a preliminary examination as a filtering process.

However, this design does not seem workable. The OTP receives a large number of communications regularly. If it wants to open a preliminary examination upon each communication, it has to conduct massive preliminary examinations. The preliminary examination should be conducted about a situation. When there is no situation in the Rome Statute sense, there is no space for preliminary examination. Given this clear fact, the Policy Paper on Preliminary Examinations asserts that Phase 2 of the filtering process is the formal commencement of a preliminary examination.[245] However, it is not logical to design a process of four parts and then consider its Phase 2 as the commencement of the process. It implies that the first phase is not a part of the process. Regulation 25 of the Regulations of the OTP provides that upon receipt of communications or referrals, the preliminary examination 'may' be initiated. The word 'may' implies 'possibility'. To find out if opening a preliminary examination is probable or not, an assessment is required. Logically speaking, such an assessment should be done before the preliminary examination, in the identification stage. This phase has distinct functions from the preliminary examination's.

Communications are raw information. When the Prosecutor receives communications, she assesses the seriousness and relevance of information. If they are manifestly outside of the Court's jurisdiction, the Jurisdiction and Complementarity

241 ICC, OTP, Policy Paper on Preliminary Examinations, para. 77.
242 Ibid., para. 78. And, Regulation 27 of the OTP Regulations.
243 Wouters and Verhoeven and Demeyere, 2008, p. 298, see *supra* note 38.
244 ICC, OTP, Policy Paper on Preliminary Examinations, para. 78.
245 Ibid., para. 80.

and Cooperation Division (JCCD) at the OTP will make a report and submit it to the Prosecutor.[246] The JCCD fulfills its responsibilities through the Situation Selection Analysis that is responsible for the assessment in the identification stage. If the Prosecutor agrees, then those communications are removed from the agenda of the OTP. However, those matters that are manifestly outside of the Court's jurisdiction should be determined very strictly. For instance, if a communication refers to a conflict that is happening in the territory of a non-member State without the involvement of a national of States Parties, it is manifestly outside of the jurisdiction of the Court, if there is no cause to extend the Court's jurisdiction over non-member States. Otherwise, the Prosecutor takes the received information into account to identify a situation. Communications just inform the Prosecution of the commission of one or more crimes. They do not necessarily refer to a situation of crisis. Communications may only describe one or more specific incidents. The main function of the identification stage is to design a situation based on the information received, by defining the constituent elements of a situation, namely jurisdictional parameters and contextual elements.

1.2. ICC AND THE SITUATION OF ISIS IN IRAQ AND SYRIA

There is a case in the history of the Court that shows the disadvantages of non-recognition of the identification stage by the Court: the situation of ISIS in Iraq and Syria. Upon the rise of demand for the ICC's intervention, the Court's Prosecutor issued, on 8 April 2015, a clarifying Statement on the alleged crimes committed by the self-proclaimed Islamic State of Iraq and Syria (ISIS). This clarification was in response to numerous inquiries about the OTP's activities in relation to the allegations against ISIS.[247] The Statement should be seen in light of the policy of transparency "in order to promote a better understanding of the process and to increase predictability", namely the policy of transparency.[248]

In the Statement, the Prosecutor referred to some facts regarding the situation of ISIS. According to the Statement, since the summer of 2014, the OTP has been receiving and reviewing allegations of widespread unspeakable atrocities committed in Syria and Iraq by ISIS. It clarifies that the trigger that had drawn the attention of the Prosecutor to the given situation was 'communications'. The Prosecutor admitted that "the atrocities allegedly committed by ISIS undoubtedly constitute serious crimes of concern to the international community and threaten peace, security and the well-

---

246 According to Regulation 7 (a) of the Regulations of the OTP, JCCD is responsible for "the preliminary examination and evaluation of information Pursuant to Articles 15 and 53, paragraph 1 and Rules 48 and 104 and the preparation of reports and recommendations to assist the Prosecutor in determining whether there is a reasonable basis to proceed with an investigation JCCD is composed of the International Cooperation Section and Situation Analysis Section.

247 ICC, OTP, Statement of the Prosecutor of the International Criminal Court on the Alleged Crimes Committed by ISIS, 8 April 2015.

248 ICC, OTP, Policy Paper on Preliminary Examinations, para. 94.

being of the region, and the world." However, she insisted 'Syria and Iraq are not Parties to the Rome Statute'. The ICC lacks 'universal jurisdiction' and its jurisdiction is mainly limited to crimes committed on the territory or by nationals of a State Party, unless the UNSC refers a situation with respect to a non-member State. The territorial jurisdiction is absent from the context of the situation in question. Nonetheless, the Prosecutor acknowledged that the information gathered indicated that several thousand foreign fighters had joined the ranks of ISIS in the past including some nationals of the States Parties. In the absence of 'territorial jurisdiction', the alternative jurisdictional basis for activation of the Court's jurisdiction is 'personal jurisdiction'. Although the Court has rarely invoked this jurisdictional basis, it is a legal basis enshrined in the Rome Statute. Some State Party nationals are among the perpetrators of ICC crimes. Despite the fact that the Court's jurisdiction may be exercised on the personal jurisdiction basis, the Prosecutor claimed an obstacle in the exercise of the Court's jurisdiction: "the prospects of investigating and prosecuting those most responsible, within the leadership of ISIS, appear limited." Indeed, the Prosecutor referred to the policy of focusing on "investigating and prosecuting those most responsible for the most serious crimes, based on the evidence collected in the course of an investigation."[249] Eventually, given these facts, Prosecutor Bensouda concluded that "the jurisdictional basis for opening a preliminary examination into this situation is too narrow at this stage."

The Prosecutor's conclusion provides a basis for some critical observations.[250] Firstly, what the Prosecutor performed should have been done following the opening of a preliminary examination. As mentioned earlier, in the architecture of the ICC, there is a distinct stage between the 'trigger mechanism' and the 'preliminary examination', namely the identification stage. Contrary to the preliminary examination, in this initial stage, the merits and substance of a situation in terms of the 'statutory selection criteria' are assessed. However, the main objective of this stage is to identify a situation that has already been brought to the attention of the Prosecutor by communications. In other words, the main scheme of this phase is identification, rather than examination. There is only one evaluative function and that is to filter out those communications that are manifestly outside the jurisdiction of the Court. To identify a situation for opening a preliminary examination, the affirmative evidence suffices without considering the probable contradictory evidence.[251]

---

249 Ibid., para. 103.

250 For more details see: Mohammad Hadi Zakerhossein, 'To Bury a Situation Alive: A Critical Reading of the ICC Prosecutor's Statement on the ISIS Situation', *International Criminal Law Review*, 2016, vol. 16.

251 A standard proof similar to *prima facie* test. Both Article 18(4) and 19(1) of ICTY refer to the existence of a '*prima facie* case' as the standard of proof for the preferment of an indictment by the prosecutor and for its confirmation by the reviewing judge. This standard is expressed different terms in rule 47(b) as follows:" there is sufficient evidence to provide reasonable grounds for believing that a suspect has committed a crime." Judge Sidhwa in his review of the indictment in the Rajic case (August 1995) says that reasonable grounds for believing neither raises nor lowers the standard of proof required by the expression '*prima facie*'. (See: Gabrielle Kirk McDonald and Olivia Swaak-Goldman (eds.),

As with the situation of ISIS all of the requirements for identifying a situation had been met. In the words of Stahn, ISIS is "*a priori* an easy target for ICC action."[252] In the context of the situation of ISIS, there has been an ongoing armed conflict witnessing the commission of a wide range of ICC crimes. Although the territorial jurisdiction requirement is absent, there is an alternative, namely personal jurisdiction. Therefore, there was no obstacle in the way of opening the preliminary examination. The preliminary examination begins as soon as a situation is identified. It is in the context of a preliminary examination that the jurisdiction of the Court should be assessed in depth and detail. At the identification stage, it is enough to provide an affirmative answer for this question whether there is a national of a State Party in the conflict. Questions about the position and identity of such an individual should be answered later in the preliminary examination. However, the Prosecutor delved into the jurisdiction issue before opening the preliminary examination.

In addition, the Prosecutor confused the legal notion of jurisdiction with the concept of admissibility. There is a line between the jurisdiction assessment and the examination of the admissibility requirement, though this line is not always easy to discern.[253] The Prosecutor concluded that the jurisdictional basis for opening the preliminary examination is 'narrow'. Prosecutor Bensouda's argument is that the policy of the OTP does not allow her to count the nationality of mid- or low-level perpetrators. According to the policy adopted by the OTP, the focus of the Prosecutor's investigative activities will be directed at the persons bearing the greatest responsibility for the most serious crimes.[254] Nonetheless, this argument is weak. This policy is a matter of the admissibility assessment and not jurisdiction determination. Focusing on the 'big fish' is not a jurisdictional threshold. It is a policy, but not a statutory limit on the 'personal jurisdiction' enshrined in Article 12(2)(b) of the Rome Statute. It is evident that the assessment of admissibility and its components, namely the complementarity and the gravity requirements, is the object for the preliminary examination. Therefore, the Prosecutor's idea that the situation of ISIS lacks the jurisdictional basis for opening the preliminary examination is not accurate. In addition, the adopted policy of focusing on high-level perpetrators should not be read narrowly. On the contrary, the OTP has explicitly affirmed that it implements a "building-upwards strategy by first investigating and prosecuting a limited number of mid- and high-level perpetrators in order to ultimately have a reasonable prospect of conviction for the most responsible."[255] Recently, a shift in the strategies of the OTP has been made. The OTP has moved from its previous

---

Substantive and Procedural Aspects of International Criminal Law: The Experience of International and National Court:. Commentary, Brill, 2000, p. 491.

252 Carsten Stahn, 'Why the ICC Should Be Cautious to Use the Islamic State to Get out of Africa: Part 2', 3 December 2014, available at: www.ejiltalk.org/why-the-icc-should-be-cautious-to-use-the-islamic-State-to-get-out-of-africa-part-2.

253 Schabas, 2011, p. 189, see *supra* note 18.

254 ICC, OTP, Policy Paper on Preliminary Examinations, para. 8. And, ICC, OTP, Kenya situation, Request for Authorization of an Investigation Pursuant to Article 15, Situation in the Republic of Kenya, 26 November 2009, para. 78.

255 ICC, OTP, Strategic Plan (2016–2018), July 2015, para. 34.

'focused' investigative approach to 'open-ended', in-depth investigations. Based on this new approach, the OTO "first focus on a wide range of crimes to properly identify organizations, structures, and individuals allegedly responsible for their commission. It will then consider mid- and high-level perpetrators in its investigations and prosecution strategies to build the evidential foundations for subsection cases against those most responsible."[256] Apart from this institutional approach to the low-level perpetrators, the OTP will deal with this category of criminals in an independent manner "where their conduct was particularly grave and has acquired extensive notoriety."[257] This is what exactly coincides with the ISIS situation.

Another error in the Prosecutor's Statement is that the Prosecutor refers to an unprecedented notion, namely, the narrowness of jurisdiction. The Prosecutor's claim is that the legal basis for opening the preliminary examination is too 'narrow'. This unprecedented notion is meaningless in ICC Law. To select a situation for investigation, the jurisdiction requirement either exists or does not exist, regardless of its narrowness or broadness. Judge Kaul explicitly refers to this dilemma in one of his dissenting opinions; according to him, "the Court either has jurisdiction or does not."[258] There is no third possibility.

It has been submitted that using personal jurisdiction to focus on the accountability of 'foreign fighters' is likely to entail a fundamental shift in prosecutorial policy[259], but the availability of personal jurisdiction does not allow the Prosecutor to make such a shift. Territorial jurisdiction is preferable to personal jurisdiction. Using nationality spreads the risk of one-sided prosecutions and non-cooperation of the territorial States where ICC crimes have been committed. Nonetheless, it does not imply that the Court lacks the 'personal jurisdiction'. Personal jurisdiction, with all of its negative effects, is a statutory factor that should be observed by the Prosecutor. The choice of the territorial jurisdiction is merely a matter of preference, priority and policy. However, when there is no basis for the territorial jurisdiction, using nationality is inevitable. Irrespective of its downsides, if the drafters of the Rome Statute intended to deprive the Court of invoking such a jurisdictional principle, they would not confer on the Court the nationality principle. This authorization should be understood in light of ending impunity as the main goal of the Court's functioning. The bottom line is that if the personal jurisdiction exists, the Prosecutor is obliged to proceed in accordance with the Rome Statute.

The Prosecutor made some clarifications on the identification stage in her report on the OTP's preliminary examination activities in 2016. The Prosecutor acknowledged that "in practice, the Office may occasionally encounter situations where alleged crimes are not manifestly outside the jurisdiction of the Court, but do not clearly appear to fall within its subject-matter jurisdiction."[260] To tackle such situations, according to the

256 Ibid.

257 Ibid.

258 ICC, PTC II, Dissenting Opinion by Judge Hans-Peter Kaul in Decision on the Confirmation of Charges Pursuant to Article 61(7)(a) and (b) of the Rome Statute, 23 January 2012, para. 26.

259 Stahn, 2014, see *supra* note 252.

260 ICC, OTP, Report on the Preliminary Examination Activities (2016), para. 15.

report, "the Office will first consider whether the lack of clarity applies to most or a limited set of allegations and in case of the latter, whether they were nevertheless of such gravity to justify further analysis." Still, more factors are taken into account by the Prosecutor in such a situation: "the Office will then consider whether the exercise of the Court's jurisdiction may be restricted due to factors such as a narrow geographic and/or personal scope of the jurisdiction and/or the existence of national proceedings relating to the relevant conduct." Given all of these factors, in addition to the prosecutorial strategy of focusing on those most responsible for the most serious crimes, the Prosecutor "as a general rule, will follow a conservative approach in terms of deciding whether to open a preliminary examination." However, the Prosecutor insists that in such a situation, her office endeavors "to give a more detailed response to the senders of such communications outlining the Office's reasoning for such decisions." The above-mentioned explanations just enhance the arguments set forth against the Prosecutor's decision.

1.3. THE END OF THE IDENTIFICATION STAGE

Upon identification of a situation, the opening of a preliminary examination is of an obligatory nature. Article 15(2) of the Rome Statute provides that the Prosecutor 'shall' analyze the seriousness of information. One can establish a presumption here: identified situations fall within the ICC's jurisdiction, unless they are manifestly outside of this scope. However, if the Prosecutor decides not to open a preliminary examination into a situation proposed by communications, there is no mechanism to challenge such a decision. It is a shortcoming in the architecture of the Court. The Prosecutor should be brought under judicial review as much as possible in order to be prevented from abuse of her authorities.

The case law of the Court shows that there have been some efforts to overcome such a shortcoming. On 23 May 2014, Morsi and the Freedom and Justice Party of Egypt filed an Application to request that a PTC be constituted in order to review the Prosecutor's decision not to open a preliminary examination of international crimes committed in Egypt.[261] According to Regulation 46(3) of the Regulations of the Court, "any matter, request or information not arising out of a situation assigned to a PTC in accordance with Sub-Regulation 2, shall be directed by the President of the Pre-Trial Division to a PTC according to a roster established by the President of that Division."

In the application it was correctly mentioned that "this is the first application of its kind to request the appointment of a Chamber to review a decision of the Prosecutor not to conduct a preliminary examination."[262] The applicant argued that "if the

261 ICC, Egypt situation, Request for Review of the Prosecutor's Decision of 23 April 2014 not to Open a Preliminary Examination Concerning Alleged Crimes Committed in the Arab Republic of Egypt and the Registrar's Decision of 25 April 2014, 23 May 2014.

262 Ibid., para. 3.

Prosecution has made a decision about the binding effect of a Declaration which could be wrong in law, the interests of justice require that there must be a procedure before the ICC to review this decision and to guarantee adherence to the law."[263] Apart from this argument, the applicant put forward a reasoning that the Chambers on the basis of the 'implied powers doctrine' have such authority to scrutinize the Prosecutor's decisions. To prove such a claim, the applicants referred to some precedents of other international tribunals. For instance, the ICTY in the Tadić case stated, "the constitutive instrument of an international tribunal can limit some of its jurisdictional powers, but only to the extent to which such limitation does not jeopardize its 'judicial character', as shall be discussed later on."[264]

On 6 June 2014, the applicant was informed via an email from the Registry that the Presidency decided, "this submission cannot be entertained by the Presidency."[265] The applicant claimed that the Presidency's decision relied solely on Regulation 46(2) and failed to consider and mention Regulation 46(3).[266] According to Regulation 46(2), "the Presidency shall assign a situation to a PTC as soon as the Prosecutor has informed the Presidency in accordance with Regulation 45." Regulation 45, in turn, refers to the trigger mechanisms of Article 13 of the Rome Statute. From the perspective of the Presidency, the situation in question did not fall within the scope of Regulation 45. For this reason, the applicant decided to refile their request before the president of the Pre-trial Division in order to apply Regulation 46(2).[267] Under this application, the Applicant requested the President of the Pre-Trial Division "to assign a PTC to consider the Applicant's request to review the decisions of the Prosecutor and Registrar respectively on the grounds set out in the Request for Review, having received full submissions from the parties. The Chamber would first have to consider its powers of review under the Statute and those that arise from its inherent powers. Thereafter, the Chamber would need to address the specific grounds of judicial review relied on by the Applicant, as outlined in the Request for Review."[268] This time, apart from the argument of implied power, the applicant reasoned that the judicial review of the Prosecutor's decisions was justified in light of the right to access justice.[269] Such a right was already considered by the STL as a right of *jus cogens* feature. In accordance with the STL: "the right of access to justice is regarded by the whole international community as essential and indeed crucial to any democratic society. It is therefore warranted to hold that the customary rule prescribing it has acquired the status of a peremptory norm (*jus cogens*)."[270] Based

263 Ibid., para. 17.

264 ICTY, Tadić case, 2 October 1995, para. 11, see *supra* note 85.

265 ICC, Egypt situation, Re-filing before the President of the Pre-Trial Division of the Request for Review of the Prosecutor's Decision of 23 April 2014 not to Open a Preliminary Examination Concerning Alleged Crimes Committed in the Arab Republic of Egypt and the Registrar's Decision of 25 April 2014, 1 September 2014, para. 6.

266 Ibid., para. 9.

267 Ibid.

268 Ibid., para. 17.

269 Ibid., para. 21.

270 STL, Order Assigning Matter to Pre-Trial Judge, 15 April 2010, para. 29.

on these arguments, the applicant requested the constitution of a PTC in order to deal with the Prosecutor's decision not to open a preliminary examination into the situation in Egypt.

In the context of the situation in Kenya, the PTC had held that "if the document is not linked to a situation of which a PTC is seized, the Registry has to transmit it without undue delay to the President of the Pre-Trial Division in accordance with Regulation 46(3) of the Regulations."[271] The applicant also referred to this precedent in order to demand a prompt reaction. In response, Judge Van den Wyngaert, acting as President of the Pre-Trial Division of the ICC, rendered her decision, and assigned the submitted request to PTC II.[272] Judge Van den Wyngaert argued that the Regulation concerned leaves the President of the Pre-Trial Division with little discretion. "As long as the subject-matter referred to in the Request pertains to an issue that does not appear (a) to fall outside the competence of the PTC, or (b) to be manifestly frivolous, the President of the Pre-Trial Division shall direct it to a PTC, based on a pre-established roster."[273] Once this decision was made, the PTC II started its inquiry into the request submitted by Morsi and his lawyers. After two days, the Chamber dismissed the request and declared that it would not have the authority to review the Prosecutor's decision during this stage. The Chamber stated that its judicial review powers are exhaustively mentioned in Article 53. In accordance with the Chamber, with respect to the communications, "the Chamber may exercise this power only if the Prosecutor has taken her decision on the basis of the criterion of Article 53(l)(c) of the Statute, i.e., if an investigation "would not serve the interests of justice."[274] This decision did not put an end to the efforts of the applicants. Some days later, the applicant requested a leave to appeal from the PTC.[275] Again, the applicant argued that the Chamber did not consider its arguments and reasoning, stating that Chambers enjoy implied and inherent powers to review the Prosecutor's decisions.[276] This request was also rejected by the Chamber. According to the Chamber, the right to lodge an interlocutory appeal under Article 82(l)(d) of the Statute is confined to parties to the relevant proceedings. However, in the eyes of the Chamber, the Applicant cannot be considered as a party to the present proceedings within the meaning of Article 82(l)(d) of the Statute.[277]

The PTC's decision put an end to the Egyptians' efforts. It also may carry an implied message for others who want to use the mechanism of Regulation 46 in the future: there is no way to expand the judicial review over the Prosecutor's decision not to open a preliminary examination. However, it seems that such a decision should be revised.

---

271 ICC, Kenya situation, Decision on a Request for Leave to Appeal, 11 February 2011, para. 14.

272 ICC, PTC II, Egypt situation, Decision Assigning the Request for Review of the Prosecution's decision of 23 April 2014 not to Open a Preliminary Examination concerning Alleged Crimes Committed in the Arab Republic of Egypt and the Registrar's decision of 25 April 2014,12 September 2014.

273 Ibid., para. 3.

274 Ibid., para. 8.

275 Ibid.

276 Ibid., para. 11.

277 Ibid., para. 8.

Regulation 46 is a mechanism recognized by the Regulations of the Court. If it is only a matter of procedure without any practical consequence, it leaves such a mechanism as a redundant one. Maybe, the drafters of the Regulations imagined such a mechanism to assume some practical functions. If it is derived from the judicial review authority, it does not have any other function. A principled approach here should be adopted under light of which the scope of Regulation 46(3) should be interpreted. The judicial review is necessary and it should be applied as much as possible.

2. IDENTIFICATION IN THE CONTEXT OF REFERRALS

The authority of the Prosecutor to identify a situation is not limited to communications. In the case of referrals, there are also some authorities for the Prosecutor, though their scope is narrower. The identification stage assumes some functions. The first and foremost matter that should be identified by the Prosecutor during this stage is the validity of the sending entity. Referrals are made only by a State Party or the UNSC. In the context of State's referrals, the issue of Statehood can be controversial. The identification stage is the moment this issue should be determined as a precondition to take further steps.

There are two major instances in the history of the Court when the Prosecutor has dealt with the issue of the validity of a sending entity. The first one is the first Palestine's attempt to trigger the jurisdiction of the Court. On 22 January 2009, pursuant to Article 12(3) of the Rome Statute, Khashan acting as the then Minister of Justice of the Government of Palestine lodged a declaration accepting the exercise of jurisdiction by the ICC for acts committed on the territory of Palestine since 1 July 2002.[278] The then Prosecutor of the Court, consequently, opened a preliminary examination and after three years declared the lodged declaration invalid. The reason behind such a determination was that the Prosecutor believed that the Statehood of the Palestine was not a clear issue at the time. According to him, competence for determining the term 'State' within the meaning of Article 12 rests, in the first instance, with the UNSG who, in case of doubt, will defer to the guidance of General Assembly.[279] However, such an assessment should have been done before opening the preliminary examination and in the context of the identification phase. The content and function of the preliminary examination are enshrined in the Rome Statute in an exhaustive manner. The assessment of the validity of the sending entity is outside of this scope. This assessment is inevitable and is a precondition for opening a preliminary examination. The validity of referral makers is not a jurisdictional matter that undergoes a preliminary examination. Rather, it is a matter relevant to the trigger mechanism that warrants assessment. It

[278] The declaration can be accessed at: www.icc-cpi.int/NR/rdonlyres/74EEE201-0FED-4481-95D4- C807 1087102C/279777/20090122PalestinianDeclaration2.pdf, last accessed at 17 February 2017.

[279] ICC, OTP, Situation in Palestine, 3 April 2012, para. 5.

shows that there should be a distinct phase between the trigger mechanism and the preliminary examination.

The foregoing situation in Egypt is another example. Once the Registry received the communication, it verified with the Egyptian authorities whether such a communication was transmitted on behalf of the State of Egypt. The Registrar did not receive a positive confirmation.[280] Consequently, on 25 April 2013, the Registrar issued a decision on the Declaration and the Complaint stating that the "communication cannot be treated as a declaration pursuant to Article 12(3) of the Rome Statute." The Registrar's decision Stated that "upon receiving your communication, and as per the established internal procedure, the Registry consulted with the Egyptian authorities on whether or not such communication was transmitted on behalf of the State of Egypt, as a result of which, we did not receive a positive confirmation."[281] On the same day, the Prosecutor dismissed the declaration. The Prosecutor determined that "the applicants lacked *locus standi* to seize the Court's jurisdiction pursuant to Article 12(3) of the Rome Statute."[282] This instance shows that the Court needs a stage in which the validity of sending entities is examined.

The second issue that should be considered in the identification phase of a referral is the question of conformity with the 'situation' notion. The Prosecutor should determine whether a situation has been referred in a neutral manner or in a one-sided way. In case of UNSC referrals, if the Prosecutor has an intention to do its responsibility by challenging the selective nature of the referrals made by the UNSC thereby excluding some nationals from the jurisdiction of the Court, she should deal with this issue at this stage. The authority of the referring States to determine the jurisdictional parameters of a situation is not without limitation. The referring entity should comply with the legal framework of the Court. To assure such a compliance, the final word is for the Court. It is the authority of the Court to determine the jurisdictional boundary of a referred situation.

The argument in favor of such authority has been expressed in the case law of the Court. In the case of Mbarushimana, the PTC, in its decision requesting the clarification on the Prosecutor's application to issue an arrest warrant, held that it is a necessary component of its supervisory functions to identify the scope of a situation.[283] The Chamber noted that the need for such identification is rooted in "the principle of complementarity as the paramount principle governing the relationship between the Court and national jurisdictions, according to which the Court is meant to complement, rather than replace, national jurisdictions, hence, the purest of cases without situational

280 ICC, Weekly Update, April 2014, available at: www.icc-cpi.int/iccdocs/PIDS/wu/ED208_ENG.pdf, last accessed at 17 February 2017.

281 ICC, PTC II, Egypt situation, 23 May 2014, para. 11, see *supra* note 261.

282 ICC, Press Release, The Determination of the Office of the Prosecutor on the Communication Received in relation to Egypt, 8 May 2014, available at www.icc-cpi.int/en_menus/icc/press%20and%20media/press%20releases/Pages/pr1003.aspx, last accessed at 17 February 2017.

283 ICC, PTC I, Situation in the DRC, Decision Requesting Clarification on the Prosecutor's Application under Article 58, 6 September 2010, paras. 6–8.

delimitations might be inconsistent with the principle of complementarity."[284] Therefore, a referral cannot be interpreted as permitting a State to abdicate permanently its responsibility by referring a wholesale of present and future criminal activities without any limitation whether in context or duration.[285] In fact, identifying a crisis fulfills a two-edge limitative function: from one side, it limits the Prosecutorial investigative powers by establishing a framework for the Prosecutor, and from the other side it restricts the States' authority to delegate their jurisdiction.

The third question that should be addressed in the identification stage is whether the referred situation is manifestly outside of the Court's jurisdiction. Indeed, there is no difference between a referral and a communication if they are manifestly outside of the jurisdiction of the Court. In such a case, it is not reasonable to open the preliminary examination. It is unlikely that States refer such situations because it is costly for States to make a referral, so this prevents them from making fruitless referrals. However, it is not impossible. If such a situation is referred, the Prosecutor should have a power to suspend or reject it before opening a preliminary examination. A situation is manifestly outside of the Court's jurisdiction if it is outside of the temporal or territorial/personal jurisdiction of the Court. The subject-matter jurisdiction needs further assessment that should be done during preliminary examination.

Lastly, in this phase the Prosecutor should be satisfied that the constituent elements of the referred situation are explicitly defined and determined in compliance with the Rome Statute, including the jurisdictional parameters and the factual context. This stage is only an identification phase, without an evaluating function. What should be done is limited to identifying the confines of a situation and to adjusting them to the legal system of the Court, if necessary. The main point is that the Prosecutor is, in principle, bound to the parameters determined by the referring entity, unless the referral is not consistent with the legal criteria applicable to the Court. If there is a deficiency or inconsistency, the Prosecutor can demand the referring entity to amend its referral and suspend the identification process or he may do it on his own. In the latter case, the Prosecutor must exercise its *proprio motu* power.

After identifying a situation, according to Regulation 45 of the Regulations of the Court, the Prosecutor 'shall' inform the Presidency of the Court. Right after this notification, the Presidency shall assign the situation to a PTC.[286] As to communications, Regulation 45 provides that the Prosecutor shall provide the Presidency with "the intention of the Prosecutor to submit a request under Article 15, Paragraph 3." It must be noted that the assignment of a PTC should be made prior to submission of a request under Article 15. Therefore, the term 'intention' of the Prosecutor, mentioned in Regulation 45, must be interpreted to mean that the Prosecutor intends to submit a request if upon conducting a preliminary examination of the identified situation he or she decides to do so. It is possible that the Prosecutor, following the preliminary

284 Ibid., para. 9.
285 Ibid., para. 2.
286 Regulation 46(2) of the Regulations of the Court.

examination, decides that there is no basis to initiate an investigation. Such a decision is reviewable by the PTC to the extent that has been foreseen in Article 53(3). Thus, a PTC must exist in all cases to undertake such a function.

The assignment of a PTC is the ending point of the identification of a situation. The identification stage makes an object for conducting the main stage of the situation selection process, namely the preliminary examination.

CHAPTER III
PRELIMINARY EXAMINATION

Preliminary examination constitutes the first step in the core activities of the OTP.[287] In the identification phase, the Prosecutor distinguishes a situation from non-situations. In the current stage, the Prosecutor shall select a situation for investigation among those situations that have already been identified and brought to her attention. The situation selection is made through the preliminary examination. By operating the preliminary examination, the Prosecutor seeks to make a determination whether or not there is a reasonable basis to initiate an investigation. In the preliminary examination, it is determined whether the given situation meets the legal criteria established by the Rome Statute to warrant an investigation.[288] The examination is preliminary because the Prosecutor's decision could be subject to change if the relevant circumstances adjust in later stages. In other words, the findings of the Prosecutor in the preliminary examination are preliminary in nature, and are not "binding for future admissibility assessment."[289] In spite of its preliminary nature, this stage is a prominent structure at the ICC's architecture that helps to realize the Court's expressive functions. The establishment of the preliminary examination has arisen from the specific needs and features of the ICC.

The ICC has a unique and distinct feature in comparison with other international criminal tribunals, namely, its permanency. The permanency of the Court makes it a future-oriented organization with open mandates. It means that there are not predefined situations for conducting an investigation ahead of the ICC. It is the Court in itself that ultimately determines when and where to intervene.[290] The Court's jurisdiction may be activated over all territories and nationals of its States Parties, if they are involved at ICC crimes. The founders of the Court did not limit the jurisdiction of this judicial institution to one or more specific crises. On the contrary, they authorized the Court to deal with all situations of crisis under its jurisdiction. Nonetheless, because the Court lacks sufficient resources to address all situations and cases falling within its jurisdiction, and as a result of its complementary role in combating international crimes, the Court needs to select a small number of situations and cases. The Court functions selectively. It is an organization of a wide range of

---

287 ICC, OTP, Strategic Plan (June 2012–2015), 11 October 2013, para. 38.

288 Caban, 2011, p. 199, see *supra* note 56.

289 ICC, PTC II, Kenya situation, 31 March 2010, para. 50, see *supra* note 41.

290 ICC, OTP, Policy Paper on Preliminary Examinations, para. 24.

restrictions and limitations, both legal and practical. The Court has been marked as much for its constraints as for its ambitions.[291] As the OTP admits, "the office still faces a gap between needs and demands."[292] Once, the ICTY Appeals Chamber indicated that "in many criminal justice systems, the entity responsible for prosecutions has finite financial and human resources and cannot realistically be expected to prosecute every offender which may fall within the strict terms of its jurisdiction."[293] Hence, the Court has to select a situation among many candidates. A selective prosecution is not unjust if its selectivity is justified. The question is not "whether selective prosecution should occur, as it is essentially impossible that it does not, but when selective prosecution is unacceptable."[294] The selectivity of the Court is shaped and managed through the preliminary examination stage. The importance of the situation selection at the ICC has resulted in forming an independent stage has been assigned for this purpose.

Preliminary examination is a process with starting and ending points. During this stage, the ICC receives information pertaining to a situation, and then the input is processed to finally result in an output, namely a decision to or not to initiate an investigation. Through the process of preliminary examination, it should be determined whether a situation falls within the jurisdictional scope of the Court. If the given situation is under the jurisdiction of the Court, then it should be determined whether the given situation is admissible and available to activate the Court's jurisdiction. At the end, if the admissibility and availability of the situation are satisfied, the Prosecutor shall examine the existing circumstances to determine if there are no substantial reasons to believe that an investigation would not serve the interests of justice. The examination of all these factors is conducted based on the available information within an evidentiary framework, namely the reasonableness.

From an institutional perspective, the selection of situations is the responsibility of the Prosecutor. The Prosecutor has discretion to choose from the options available in a criminal issue, namely prosecuting or not prosecuting and plea-bargaining.[295] The discretion of the Prosecutor is a result of her independence.[296] One commentator on the Rome Statute submits that "at the core of the general notion of prosecutorial discretion lies the power to decide whether or not to investigate and prosecute a case."[297] This aspect of the Prosecutor discretion applies in the situation selection too. It means that the Prosecutor's discretion is exercised not only to select a situation but also to reject other situations. Given her broad authorities, the Prosecutor plays a

291 Aka Greenawalt, 'Justice without Politics: Prosecutorial Discretion and the International Criminal Court', *New York University Journal of International Law and Politics*, 2007, vol. 39, p. 621.

292 ICC, OTP, Strategic Plan (2016–2018), para. 44.

293 ICTY, Appeals Chamber, Delalic, Delic and Landzo case, Judgment, 20 February 2001, para. 602.

294 Fabricio Guariglia, 'The Selection of Cases by the Office of the Prosecutor of the International Criminal Court', in Carsten Stahn and Göran Sluiter, *The Emerging Practice Of The International Criminal Court*, Martinus Nijhoff Publishers, 2009, p. 211.

295 Dong, 2009, p. 109, see *supra* note 211.

296 Coté, 2012, p. 352, see *supra* note 171.

297 Morten Bergsmo and Pieter Kruger, 'Article 53', in Otto Triffterer (ed.), *Commentary on the Rome Statute of the International Criminal Court*, C.H. Beck. Hart. Nomos, 2008, p. 1066.

unique role in shaping the scope of the ICC's reach, and consequently in forming the public perception of the Court. It is the Prosecutor who shall manage the selectivity of the Court to prevent hurting the reputation of the ICC. The prosecutor is entitled to carry on the preliminary examination until she feels sufficiently confident about the actual existence of the reasonable basis to initiate an investigation.[298] As PTC asserts, it is up to the Prosecutor to determine "the breadth and scope of this preliminary assessment."[299] Each situation requires a distinct assessment. In the words of the ICC PTC, "the breadth and scope of an examination is situation-specific and depends on the particular features of each situation, including, *inter alia*, the availability of information, the nature and scale of the crimes, and the existence of national responses in respect of alleged crime."[300] For this reason, the case law of the ICC regarding the preliminary examinations has spotted considerable differences in terms of duration. For instance, the preliminary examination with regards to Libya lasted only 5 days[301], whereas the examination of the situation in Colombia, which started in 2004 is still ongoing.

In spite of the prosecutorial discretion in the situation selection, the OTP has adopted a main strategy to serve and promote transparency in its preliminary examination activities. According to the strategy, the Office "intends to further improve the knowledge and understanding of the preliminary examination process by publicly sharing more information about its basis, purpose and method", since this prevents "misperceptions about this aspect of the work of the Office."[302] This strategy preserves the transparency in the OTP. Transparency creates predictability, which increases the legitimacy of the office.[303] This strategy is followed in various ways, including "early interaction with stakeholders, dissemination of relevant statistics on Article 15 communications, public Statements, periodic reports, and information on high level visits to the concerned States."[304] In furthering this strategy, the OTP has adopted the Policy Paper on Preliminary Examinations. The paper "describes the relevant Rome Statute principles, factors and procedures applied by the Office in the conduct of its preliminary examination activities".[305] The Policy Paper is, indeed, the

---

298 Giuliano Turone, 'Powers and Duties of the Prosecutor', in Antonio Cassese, Paola Gaeta and John R.W.D. Jones (eds), *The Rome Statute of the International Criminal Court: A Commentary*, Oxford University Press, 2002, p. 1151.

299 ICC, OTP, Situation in the CAR I, Prosecution's Report Pursuant to Pre-Trial Chamber Ill's 30 November 2006 Decision Requesting Information on the Status of the Preliminary Examination of the Situation in the Central African Republic, 15 December 2006, para. 7.

300 Ibid., para. 8.

301 The situation in Libya was referred to the OTP by the UNSC on 26 February 2011, and on 3 March the Prosecutor determined that that "the statutory criteria for the opening of an investigation into the situation in Libya since 15 February 2011 had been met" (See: ICC, OTP, Report on Preliminary Examination Activities (2011), p. 7).

302 ICC, OTP, Strategic Plan (2012 – 2015), 11 October 2013, para. 38.

303 ICC, OTP, Strategic Plan (2016–2018), para. 32.

304 ICC, OTP, Policy Paper on Preliminary Examinations, para. 95.

305 Ibid., para. 3.

Prosecutor's understanding of the Rome Statute and the relevant rules in order to fulfil her obligations in relation to conducting the preliminary examination.[306]

In addition to transparency, the main result of publishing a policy paper is keeping the consistency in the Prosecutor's choices. The Policy Paper is intended to direct and guide the Prosecutor to select situations within the same framework. Besides the foregoing Policy Paper, the OTP has issued the Policy Paper on Case Selection and Prioritization, which clarifies how the Office decides which cases to be pursued in the context of a situation.[307] Although the recent Paper deals predominantly with the case selection, its findings are of great help for the situation selection too.[308] In addition, in order to promote a better understanding of the situation selection process, the OTP regularly reports on its preliminary examination activities. These outreach activities enable the Office to carry out its mandates without raising undue expectations.[309] In making such reports, however, the Office shall be guided "by considerations for the safety, well-being, and privacy of those who provided the information or others who are at risk on account of such information".[310] The safety protection of those who are involved at the ICC's activities is a major concern of the Court.

In spite of all these activities conducted by the Prosecutor, the Prosecutor's discretion as to the preliminary examination needs more judicial scrutiny. The objectives and aims of the preliminary examination prove the importance of this stage, and it per se indicates the necessity of designating a mechanism in which the Court's Prosecutor are more responsible in terms of her decisions on the preliminary examination. Preliminary examination assumes major expressive mandates that have not drawn sufficient attention. These expressive functions of the preliminary examination make this stage unique at the ICC's architecture.

1. TIME FRAME

The law of the Court is silent about the timeframe of the preliminary examination. It is up to the Prosecutor to spend necessary time examining a situation. There is no time limit for deciding whether to open an investigation.[311] In practice, there is a variety in the period spent for conducting a preliminary examination respecting different situations. For instance, the preliminary examination with regard to the situation in Colombia was opened in June 2004.[312] However, more than one decade,

306 ICC, OTP, Policy Paper on Sexual and Gender-Based Crimes, June 2014, p. 3.

307 ICC, OTP, Policy Paper on Case Selection and Prioritization, 15 September 2016.

308 Mohammad Hadi Zakerhossein, *Comments on the ICC OTP's Draft Policy Paper on Case Selection and Prioritization*, JusticeHub, 29 March 2016, available at: https://justicehub.org/article/comments-icc-otps-draft-policy-paper-case-selection-and-prioritisation, last accessed at on 5 April 2017.

309 ICC, OTP, Policy Paper on Preliminary Examinations, para. 94.

310 Regulation 28(2) of the OTP Regulations.

311 Nouwen, 2013, p. 94, see *supra* note 39.

312 *ICC, OTP, Situation in Columbia, Interim Report, November 2012.*

the examination has continued without resulting in a determination. In contrast with this long period, the preliminary examination as to the situation in Libya lasted only some days. On 26 February 2011, the situation in Libya was referred by the UNSC to the OTP. Later, on 3 March 2011, the Prosecutor initiated an investigation.[313] It is interesting because Colombia can be qualified as a conflict-ridden country for over 50 years[314], whereas the crisis in Libya was newborn, which could warrant more pre-investigative initiatives by the Prosecutor, in particular, where the Court's intervention would precede the works of the United Nations Human Rights Council Commission of Inquiry in Libya.

In the situation of the CAR I, the duration of the preliminary examination had carried on for nearly two years. It was objected to by the government of the CAR. The CAR government requested, *inter alia,* that the Prosecutor provide information on the alleged failure to decide, within a reasonable time, whether to initiate an investigation.[315] Upon this request, PTC III dealt with this issue and announced that the preliminary examination of a situation must be completed within a 'reasonable time' from the reception of a referral.[316] Thus, the PTC requested the Prosecutor to submit a report on the status of the preliminary examination. In fact, the PTC argued that in light of some statutory provisions, namely Article 18(1) and Rule 105(1), the State referring a situation has a right to be informed by the Prosecutor if he declines to initiate an investigating. At the PTC's request, the Prosecutor issued a report on the status of preliminary examination, but he asserted that there is not any judicial review and control over the Prosecutor before rendering a decision by him; the Prosecutor added that only in the interests of transparency did the OTP decide to make this report to the chamber.[317] The report made by the Prosecutor was seen as a "sort of mutual cooperation between the organs of the Court."[318]

So far, a stance that there is not any legal obligation upon to the Prosecutor to submit this type of information has not been dismissed by the Chambers. Article 15(6) only enforces the Prosecutor to notify information-provider after the preliminary examination. However, it does not recognize any role for the PTC to exercise any judicial review before reaching to this level. As it is said by Stahn, this appears to imply that a Chamber has virtually no power of control and no information on the activities of the Prosecutor, unless a request for authorization under Article 15 is made.[319] In his report, the Prosecutor reasoned that the silence of the Statute on the timeframe of

---

313 *ICC, Libya situation, Case information Sheet, available at: www.icc-cpi.int/iccdocs/PIDS/publications/GaddafiEng.pdf.*

314 Smeulers and Weerdesteijn and Hola, 2015, p. 34, see *supra* note 116.

315 ICC, OTP, Situation in the CAR I, 15 December 2006, para. 5, see *supra* note 299.

316 ICC, PTC I, Situation in CAR I, Decision Requesting Information on the Status of the Preliminary Examination of the Situation in the Central African Republic, 30 November 2006, p. 4.

317 ICC, OTP, Situation in the CAR I, Prosecution's Report, 15 December 2006, para. 11, see *supra* note 299.

318 Mohammad M. El Zeidy, 'The Gravity Threshold under the Statute of the International Criminal Court', *Criminal Law Forum*, 2008, vol. 19, p. 54.

319 Stahn, 2009, p. 265, see *supra* note 221.

the preliminary examination was "a deliberate legislative decision that provides the required flexibility to adjust the parameters of the assessment or analysis phase to the specific features of each particular situation."[320] In the eyes of the Prosecutor, the preliminary examination is situation-specific, depending on the particular features of each situation.[321]

The OTP in the Policy Paper on Preliminary Examinations has put forward an argument in favor of the Prosecutor's freedom regarding the openness of conducting the preliminary examination in terms of timing; it ensures that "analysis is adjusted to the specific features of each particular situation, which may include, *inter alia*, the availability of information, the nature, scale and frequency of the crimes, and the existence of national responses in respect of alleged crimes".[322] In addition, both the complementarity principle and the expressive mandates of the preliminary examination favor some flexibility in conducting the preliminary examination in terms of the timing.

The Court shall encourage the national jurisdictions, and it is a time-consuming effort. The Court shall be positive to the national jurisdictions, and facilitating their intervention may take some time. Moreover, the practical shortcomings may serve as an obstacle in the investigation's way, but the Prosecutor should be able to keep the preliminary examination open in order to benefit from its advantages. It is in particular the case when a situation is selected, but not prioritized; situations listed in the situation selection plan remain open in the preliminary examination stage. In addition, if the interests of justice require non-action by the Court, it is an option that the given situation remains open under preliminary examination as long as the exceptional circumstances hamper the initiation of an investigation. The openness of preliminary examination gives the Prosecutor a chance to monitor the circumstances in order to make a determination about the admissibility and the interests of justice presumption.

Hence, setting a deadline for conducting a preliminary examination has fallen out of the PTC's authority. After this event, in some other status the Chambers have shown that they tend not to exercise the judicial review over the Prosecutor before coming to a conclusion. For instance, in the case of Lubanga, the NGO Women's Initiatives for Gender Justice in its submitted observations under Rule 103 on the 'role of the PTC in supervision prosecutorial discretion' argued in favor of the existence of the judicial review over the Prosecutor's activities and considered such authority as an 'inherent duty'.[323] However, the Chamber rejected this claim and noted "investigations in the Situation of the DRC are ongoing and the Prosecutor has not taken any decision not to investigate or prosecutor. The Chamber therefore deems this issue as not appropriate at the present stage of the Proceedings."[324]

---

320 ICC, Situation in the CARI, 15 December 2006, para. 10, see *supra* note 299.

321 Ibid., para. 8.

322 *ICC, OTP, Policy Paper on Preliminary Examinations, para. 89.*

323 ICC, Request Submitted Pursuant to Rule 103(1) of the Rules of Procedure and Evidence for Leave to Participate as Amicus Curiae with Confidential Annex 2, 10 November 2006, para. 13.

324 ICC, PTC I, Decision on the Request Submitted Pursuant to Rule 103(1) of the Rules of Procedure and Evidence, 17 August 2007, para. 5.

Despite the fact that flexibility is necessary for conducting the preliminary examination, one can say that the Prosecutor is responsible to conduct an effective preliminary examination to be able to initiate an investigation as his statutory obligation. Preliminary examination is not only an authority at the Prosecutor's disposal, but also an obligation. The flexibility of the preliminary examination in terms of timing is justified in light of the 'functional necessity' doctrine. However, this doctrine limits such a flexibility for the purposes of the fulfillment of the preliminary examination's function. It means that the endless timeframe of the preliminary examination should not been seen as an excuse for the non-action of the Prosecutor. On the contrary, such a flexibility is in place to empower the Prosecutor to fulfill her mandates effectively. Therefore, the obligatory nature of the preliminary examination warrants the judicial control to secure an effective conduct of this stage, if its duration exceeds a reasonable time. In other words, the PTC must be sure that the Prosecutor fulfills his obligation in an effective manner and has a right to request the Prosecutor to provide information on his activities in case of *prima facie* inactivity of the Prosecutor.

Preliminary examination is free from a specific time limit but it does not mean that the Prosecutor enjoys an absolute freedom and authority. This famous aphorism that 'justice delayed is justice denied' is a principle that guides the Prosecutor to conduct the preliminary examination. It is not accepted to grant the Prosecutor a carte blanche, which justifies delays in the proceedings. El Zeidy suggests a solution to fill this gap in the architecture of the Rome Statute by invoking the 'inherent and implied power' doctrine. He argues that the supervisory role at an early stage is necessary and proper to carry into effect some expressly granted power under Article 53.[325]

2. INFORMATION IN THE PRELIMINARY EXAMINATION

The preliminary examination as a pre-investigative process revolves around information. Information gathering is one of the duties fulfilled by the Prosecutor in the preliminary examination. The Prosecutor has to seek new information that enables her to make a determination whether or not to initiate an investigation. The passive role of the Prosecutor to receive information in the trigger mechanism develops into an active role in the preliminary examination. The role of the Prosecutor at this stage is a kind of fact-finding entity.[326] From this perspective, it is said that preliminary examination is analogous in some respects to the functions carried out by the UN mandated international commission of inquiry that have been established prior to the constitution of certain other international tribunals.[327]

325 El Zeidy, 2008, p. 56, see *supra* note 318.

326 An interview quoted by Sharzad Fouladvand (See: Fouladvand, 2012, p. 146, see *supra* note 26).

327 Sluiter and Friman and Linton, 2013, p. 181, see *supra* note 143.

The scope and amount of information available to the Prosecutor is a factor that affects the Prosecutor's decision to initiate an investigation. If there is no sufficient information, the Prosecutor is not able to proceed with a situation. The scope of an investigation is determined by the available information. For instance, the then Prosecutor, in his request for authorization to initiate an investigation into Côte d'Ivoire, gave two reasons for his intention to limit the temporal framework of his investigation to a specific timeframe, instead of investigation over the entire period from which the ICC could exercise jurisdiction pursuant to the lodged declaration by the government of Côte d'Ivoire. First, the gravity of the violence, which had reached unprecedented levels during the purposed period. Secondly, the existence of a wealth of information available, helping to establish the reasonable threshold.[328] The prominent role of information is not restricted to the OTP. It is also important for the PTC. For example, the PTC III in its decision to authorize the Prosecutor to initiate an investigation in Kenya requested that the Prosecutor provide the Chamber with any additional information on the relevant crimes committed. The Chamber insisted that information is an essential prerequisite for the Chamber to be able to assess whether there is a reasonable basis to proceed.[329]

The preliminary examination commences with handling the information and evidence presented.[330] The OTP maintains an 'evidence database'. This database assists the OTP with proper registration and storage of all information and evidence collected from different sources. Each item or page of the materials is registered with a unique Evidence Registration Number.[331] The prosecutor has a duty to protect the confidentiality of the available information.[332] Regulation 21 of the Regulations of the OTP establishes a framework in which all correspondence of the Office shall be done in a manner that prevents any danger to the safety, well-being, and privacy of those who provided the information or to the integrity of investigations. The absence of publicity is a principle governing the triggering proceedings, in contrast to the criminal proceedings that are governed by the principle of publicity. This principle is justified by the need to avoid potential suspects absconding, and to protect the life of victims and witnesses and the preservation of evidence and information.[333]

The goal of conducting the preliminary examination is to "collect all relevant information necessary to reach a fully informed determination of whether there is a

---

328 ICC, OTP, Côte d'Ivoire situation, Request for Authorization of an Investigation Pursuant to Article 15, 23 June 2011, para. 41.

329 ICC, PTC III, Côte d'Ivoire Situation, Decision Pursuant to Article 15 of the Rome Statute on the Authorization of an Investigation into the Situation in the Republic of Côte d'Ivoire, 3 October 2011, para. 185.

330 PTC II has called the information and evidence presented collectively as 'the material' (see: ICC, PTC II, Decision on the Prosecutor's Application for Summonses to Appear for Francis Kirimi Muthaura, Uhuru Muigai Kenyatta and Mohammed Hussein Ali, 8 March 2011, para. 17).

331 Regulation 23 (1) and (2) of the Regulation of the OTP.

332 ICC, OTP, Policy Paper on Preliminary Examinations, para. 87.

333 Olásolo, 2005, p. 52, see *supra* note 1.

reasonable basis to proceed with an investigation."[334] The determination that is made by the Prosecutor upon the preliminary examination should be both 'informed' and 'well-reasoned'.[335] These qualifications require the Prosecutor to maximize the available information. The method and manner of this preliminary information gathering is not specified in the Statute or the Rules.[336]

In accordance with Rule 104(2) of the ICC Rules of the Procedure and Evidence, "the Prosecutor may seek additional information from States, organs of the United Nations, intergovernmental and non-governmental organizations, or other reliable sources that he or she deems appropriate, and may receive written or oral testimony at the seat of the Court."[337] Here, the Prosecutor is free to decide whether the additional information should be requested from the source itself of the original information provided or from other sources or both.[338] As some experts have mentioned, an appropriate starting point would likely be to obtain information from the prosecuting State about the proceedings.[339] In addition to State resources, open sources and the media are of great help for the Prosecutor in conducting a preliminary examination. The reason is that during this stage of the pre-trial phase of the Court, contrary to the case-specific stage, the Prosecutor cannot deploy the full range of investigative powers at her disposal for the determination of the truth.[340] The first Court's Prosecutor in his request for authorization to initiate an investigation into the situation in Côte d'Ivoire explicitly refers to this category of information sources, including "reporting from international and local media outlets".[341] In the context of the situation in Venezuela, the Prosecutor again referred to using the open sources in order to conduct the preliminary examination: "we conducted an exhaustive search of all readily-available open source information, including media reports and reports of non-governmental organizations and international organizations".[342]

The only obstacle in the way of using an information source is its lack of reliability.[343] The evaluation of information is carried out based on a specific methodology. Such a methodology, as such described by the Prosecutor, is based on criteria, including

334 ICC, OTP, Policy Paper on Preliminary Examinations, para. 2.

335 ICC, OTP, Situation in the CAR I, 15 December 2006, para. 7, see *supra* note 299.

336 ICC, OTP, Annex to the Paper on some policy issues before the Office of the Prosecutor: Referrals and Communications.

337 Rule 104(2) of Rules of Procedure and Evidence.

338 Turone, 2002, p. 1149, see *supra* note 298.

339 ICC, OTP, Informal Expert Paper, 2003, para. 38, see *supra* note 66.

340 Rastan, 2015, p. 150, see *supra* note 227.

341 ICC, OTP, Côte d'Ivoire situation, 23 June 2011, para. 33, see *supra* note 328.

342 ICC, OTP, Response to Communications Received concerning Venezuela, 9 February 2006.

343 For instance, the first Prosecutor in his request for authorization to initiate an investigation into Kenya mentioned a large number of various NGOs as his information sources. "For the purpose of this application, the Prosecutor has relied on a selected number of reliable and publicly available reports on alleged crimes committed during the post-election violence in Kenya, in particular the reports published by: the Commission of Inquiry into Post-Election Violence; the Kenyan National Commission on Human Rights; the Office of the High Commissioner for Human Rights; UNICEF, UNFPA, UNIFEM and Christian Children's Fund; the UN Special Rapporteur on extrajudicial, summary or arbitrary executions; the Oscar Foundation; the Federation of Women Lawyers; Centre

relevance (usefulness of the information to determine the elements of a possible future case), reliability (refers to the trustworthiness of the provider of the information as such), credibility (refers to the quality of the information in itself, to be evaluated by the criteria of immediacy, internal consistency, and external verification), and completeness (the extent of the source's knowledge or coverage vis-à-vis the whole scope of relevant facts).[344] Even at trial phase the information from anonymous resources is admissible, though its probative value may go down in comparison with other sources.[345] The PTC I, in its decision on the confirmation of charges against Lubanga submits "the Chamber considers that objections pertaining to the use of anonymous hearsay evidence do not go to the admissibility of the evidence, but only, to its probative value."[346]

Inquiry and truth commissions are also of great help in the information-gathering process. The principal distinction between these two types of commission lies in the timing and purposes of their establishment.[347] Inquiry commissions focus on making an immediate assessment with regard to the alleged crimes, while truth commissions try to find out what has happened. The practice of the UNSC shows that this organization widely relies on commissions and investigative bodies as subsidiary organs to fulfil its mandates.[348] The findings of such commissions can be used by the OTP in particular in the preliminary examination.

It is not clear whether, in response to the Prosecutor's request for information, States are obliged to cooperate with the Prosecutor to provide her with the requested information. On the one hand, it is said that even in the context of the preliminary examination such obligations are imposed upon States. It is because States Parties' duty to cooperate with the Court under Article 86 extends to all activities of the court, including the preliminary examination.[349] However, it is argued that the States' obligation to cooperate with the Court does not include the preliminary examination, because according to Article 93 such an obligation is limited to investigation and prosecution before the Court.[350] Article 86 also sets a general legal base for the States' obligation to cooperate fully with the Court, but makes it limited to cooperation in its investigation and prosecution. The preliminary examination stage is not a part of investigation or prosecution. On the contrary, it is a pre-investigative phase. Therefore, a clearer legal base in the Statute is needed to claim the existence of an obligation upon States. However, if a State does not cooperate with the Prosecutor to satisfy its needs of information, it does not hamper the way of investigation. By contrast, it causes

---

for Rights Education and Awareness, HRW; and the International Crisis Group." (See: ICC, OTP, Kenya situation, 26 November 2009, p. 3, see *supra* note 254).

344 ICC, OTP, Côte d'Ivoire situation, 23 June 2011, para. 24, see *supra* note 328.

345 ICC, PTC I, Lubanga case, Decision of the Confirmation of Charges, 29 January 2007, para. 103.

346 Ibid., para. 101.

347 Bassiouni, 2013, p. 942, see *supra* note 134.

348 For more information about the list of the commission established by the UNSC, see: www.un.org/en/sc/repertoire/subsidiary_organs/commissions_and_investigations.shtml.

349 Olásolo, 2005, p. 61, see *supra* note 1.

350 Kleffner, 2008, p. 224, see *supra* note 201. And, ICC, OTP, Informal Expert Paper, 2003, p. 10, see *supra* note 66.

the Prosecutor to initiate an investigation in order to obtain much information. This is exactly the reasoning established by the PTC in the situation of Comor's vessels in which the Chamber argued, "it is precisely the purpose of an investigation to provide clarity. Making the commencement of an investigation contingent on the information available at the pre-investigative stage being already clear, univocal or not contradictory creates a short circuit and deprives the exercise of any purpose."[351]

3. SCOPE OF PRELIMINARY EXAMINATION

The preliminary examination is exhaustive. It means that the Prosecutor is authorized and obliged to conduct the preliminary examination with respect to all situations irrespective of the trigger which has brought them to the Prosecutor's attention. Indeed, 'the selection process is not affected by the triggering procedure'.[352]

With respect to communications, Articles 15 (2) and (3) explicitly refer to the preliminary examination.[353] In addition, Rule 48 of the Rules of Procedure and Evidence requires the Prosecutor to consider criteria of Article 53, i.e. the jurisdiction, admissibility and the interests of justice requirements, when it uses Article 15 respecting the examination of communications. However, it does not exempt referrals from the preliminary examination. Article 53(1) obliges the Prosecutor to evaluate the information in the context of referrals as well. It reads 'The Prosecutor shall, having evaluated the information made available to him or her, initiate an investigation unless he or she determines that there is no reasonable basis to proceed under this Statute'. It is a general provision; it means that the Prosecutor should conduct an examination of all situations irrespective of their triggering source.[354] This idea is also enshrined in the Policy Paper adopted by the OTP where it is mentioned that "preliminary examination activities will be conducted in the

351 ICC, PTC I, Situation on the Registered Vessels of the Comoros, Decision on the Request of the Union of the Comoros to Review the Prosecutor's Decision not to Initiate an Investigation, 16 July 2015, para. 13.

352 Luis Moreno-Ocampo, 'A Positive Approach to Complementarity: The Impact of the Office of the Prosecutor', in Carsten Stahn and Mohamed M. El Zeidy (eds.), *The International Criminal Court and Complementarity: From Theory to Practice*, Cambridge University Press, 2011, p. 22, footnote 2.

353 Article 15 (2): "the Prosecutor shall analyses the seriousness of the information received. For this purpose, he or she may seek additional information from States, organs of the United Nations, intergovernmental or non-governmental organizations, or other reliable sources that he or she deems appropriate and may receive written or oral testimony at the seat of the Court." And, Article 15 (3) of the Rome Statute: "if the Prosecutor concludes that there is a reasonable basis to proceed with an investigation, he or she shall submit to the Pre-Trial Chamber a request for authorization of an investigation, together with any supporting material collected. Victims may make representations to the Pre-Trial Chamber, in accordance with the Rules of Procedure and Evidence."

354 Turone, 2002, p. 1146, see *supra* note 298. And Sluiter and Friman and Linton, 2013, p. 143, see *supra* note 274. And the OTP, Policy Paper on Preliminary Examinations, para. 12. And, Nouwen, 2013, p. 75, see *supra* note 39. And Kleffner, 2008, p. 165, see *supra* note 201. And ICC, Application on Behalf of the Government of Libya Pursuant to Article 19 of the ICC Statute,1 May 2012, para. 77.

same manner, irrespective of whether the Office receives a referral from a State Party or the Security Council, or acts on the basis of information on crimes obtained pursuant to Article 15. In all circumstances, the Office will independently evaluate the information available and analyze the seriousness of the information received."[355] Apart from this textual interpretation, this idea is supported by the fact that it was never suggested by the *ad hoc* Committee or the Preparatory Committee that the criteria should not apply.[356]

Referrals made by the UNSC lack any privileges more than other triggers in respect of conducting a preliminary examination. Some maintain that in case of the Security Council referrals, prosecutorial discretion to make a determination about the initiation of an investigation is inconsistent with the role of the Security Council.[357] However, it is not an accurate argument. The Court is independent from the UNSC and enjoys its special legal system. When the UNSC refers a situation to the Court, it implies that it has already accepted the role of the Court and its independence. One of the Court's Chambers refers to the fact that the UNSC "has also accepted that the investigation into the said situation, as well as any prosecution arising therefrom, will take place in accordance with the statutory framework provided for in the Statute, the Elements of Crimes and the Rules as a whole."[358] In practice, the Prosecutor conducts a preliminary examination into UNSC referrals, too. For instance, as to the situation in Libya, the then Prosecutor of the Court in his first report to the UNSC mentioned that his office "conducts a preliminary examination to evaluate all relevant information and to analyze its seriousness in order to determine whether an investigation should be opened."[359]

The authority of the Prosecutor to assess the statutory requirements in respect of a situation referred by the UNSC is the major manifestation of the independence of the Court before the UNSC. The ICC is a judicial organization. As a judicial body, it enjoys some inherent rights and authorities. From such a perspective, the Court enjoys wide authorities to conduct a review of its jurisdiction over a situation or case, irrespective of its initiate source. The Appeals Chamber of the ICTY in Tadić case refers to these kinds of authorities of a judicial organization. In the words of the Chamber: "the incidental or inherent jurisdiction of any judicial or arbitral tribunal, consist[s] of its 'jurisdiction to determine its own jurisdiction'."[360]

The Prosecutorial independence means that the Prosecutor is not obliged to follow the UNSC instruction and findings. As Bassiouni asserts, UNSC referrals are not in any way to be understood as an obligation on the Prosecutor to proceed with

---

355 ICC, OTP, Policy Paper on Preliminary Examinations, para. 12.

356 Stigen, 2008, p. 239, see *supra* note 122.

357 J.D. Ohlin, 'Peace, Security and Prosecutorial Discretion', in Carsten Stahn and Göran Sluiter, *The Emerging Practice of the International Criminal Court,* Martinus Nijhoff, 2009, p. 189.

358 ICC, PTC I, Al Bashir case, 4 March 2009, para. 45, see *supra* note 119.

359 ICC, OTP, First Report of the Prosecutor of the ICC to the UN Security Council Pursuant to UNSCR 1970 (2011), 4 May 2011, paras. 1 and 2.

360 ICTY, Tadić case, 2 October 1995, para. 18, see *supra* note 85.

a prosecution.[361] Such a prosecutorial independence from the UNSC arises from the distinct natures of these two international organizations. The Court is a judicial institution, and the Rome Statute is a legal text. The assessment of the situation selection criteria is a judicial function exclusively falling within the ICC authority. This feature is supported by the Prosecutor addressing the UNSC as to the situation in Libya when she mentioned her Office "will check the factual situation in accordance with the Statute's requirements that include the intervention of an independent and impartial judiciary. The Security Council may decide to present observations, but this is a judicial issue that will be decided by the Judges of the Pre-Trial Chamber."[362] Schabas accurately asserts that the theory of the independent Prosecutor operated as a kind of Trojan horse for the campaign to weaken the grip of the UNSC.[363] It per se demonstrates the great importance of the Prosecutor's authorities in order to reduce the control of the UNSC over the Court. For this reason, in the context of UNSC referrals 'the normal requirements of the Rome Statute will apply, including independent prosecution'.[364]

Here, some have maintained that there is a discernable difference between communications and referrals and that is a presumption that guides the Prosecutor discretion.[365] Article 53(1) provides that the Prosecutor shall initiate an investigation unless he concludes that there is no reasonable basis, whereas Article 15(3) reads the Prosecutor shall request an authorization if she concludes that there is a reasonable basis. In spite of the difference in the two mentioned articles, the Prosecutor should conduct a preliminary examination to determine if there is or not a reasonable basis to initiate an investigation. As to communications, the Prosecutor should try to establish the existence of a reasonable basis, whereas in the case of referrals he shall examine its non-existence. Regarding referrals, because there is not any other party who is able to challenge the existence of a reasonable basis, it is the responsibility of the Prosecutor to consider this issue as well.

As Article 42(1) provides, the Prosecutor "shall be responsible for receiving referrals and any substantiated information on crimes within the jurisdiction of the Court, for examining them and for conducting investigations and prosecutions before the Court." This provision can provide a legal basis for the generality of the preliminary examination's scope. Nonetheless, it is most likely that the scope of the preliminary examination is more limited with respect to referrals, because States referrals usually provide the Prosecutor with more necessary information than communications.

361 Bassiouni, 2013, p. 681, see *supra* note 134.
362 ICC, OTP, Prosecutor Statement to the United Nations Security Council on the situation in the Libyan Arab Jamahiriya, pursuant to UNSCR 1970 (2011), 16 May 2012, para. 7.
363 Schabas, 2012, p. 91, see *supra* note 81.
364 James Crawford, 'The ILC's Draft Statute for an International Criminal Tribunal', *American Journal of International Law,* 1994, vol. 88, p. 147.
365 Sluiter and Friman and Linton, 2013, p. 182, see *supra* note 143.

4. EVIDENTIARY THRESHOLD

The preliminary examination is an evaluative process in which the available information is evaluated and assessed in order to determine whether there is a basis to proceed with a situation. Such an evaluation is conducted based on an evidentiary threshold. This threshold is 'reasonableness'. To decide whether to initiate an investigation, there should be a reasonable basis justifying such a decision.

The ICC is elaborate in drawing the standards of proof. The Court's legal framework is meant to create more clarity and predictability, as well as more accountability of the Prosecutor before the judges.[366] The determination to initiate an investigation made by the Prosecutor is largely subjective.[367] The subjectivity means that the Prosecutor upon due application of her mind be satisfied with regard to the statutory factors referred to in Article 53.[368] However, the Prosecutor's conclusion could not be arbitrary. On the contrary, it must be reasoned and reasonable.[369] The Prosecutor's determination should be made on objective criteria. It implies that in the same circumstances a reasonable observer must arrive at the same conclusion. The Prosecutor is responsible for her decisions before the judges of the Court. The Prosecutor bears the burden of satisfying the prerequisite threshold, as she is the party asserting the existence of such information.[370] For this reason, the Statute is more specific about the evidentiary thresholds. The broader role given to the judges at the ICC framework explains the more elaborate procedure in relation to the standard and burden of proof.[371] An evidentiary threshold makes the Prosecutor's decision reviewable by the Chambers, and it plays a role in shielding the ICC from politically motivated charges and investigations.[372]

In the architecture of the Court, there are different stages. Each stage functions based on a distinct evidentiary threshold. These thresholds are distinct because they have been established in consistence with the circumstances surrounding each stage. The main reason put forward by the Chambers to justify the variety in the evidentiary thresholds is that each standard serves a different purpose and therefore is consistent with that purpose(s).[373] Therefore, the standards of proof must be interpreted contextually.[374] The law of the Court does not give any definition of these standards. The silence of law triggers the judicial interpretation. As one of the commentators on the Rome Statute had pointed out, the practice of the PTC would become the key source for

366 Ibid., p. 1143.
367 Fouladvand, 2012, p. 83, see *supra* note 26.
368 Bergsmo and Kruger, 2008, p. 1069, see *supra* note 297.
369 Ibid., p. 589.
370 Michael Ramsden and Cecilia Chung, 'Reasonable Grounds to Believe: An Unreasonably Unclear Evidentiary Threshold at the ICC Statute', *Journal of International Criminal Justice,* 2015, vol. 13, p. 557.
371 Sluiter and Friman and Linton, 2013, p. 1130, see *supra* note 143.
372 Ramsden and Chung, 2013, p. 557, see *supra* note 370.
373 Safferling, 2012, para. 28, see *supra* note 101.
374 Nancy Amoury Combs, 'Evidence', in William A. Schabas and Nadia Bernaz, *Routledge Handbook of International Criminal Law,* Routledge, 2011, p. 326.

the determination of the more precise content of reasonable basis.[375] As to the evidentiary threshold of reasonable grounds, for instance, the PTC states: "… since neither the Statute, the Rules, nor the Regulations of the Court define any of these standards, an independent analysis by the Chamber to define reasonable basis to believe standard is warranted."[376] For this reason, the jurisprudence of the Court has a rich literature on the meaning of the reasonable grounds.

The Rome Statute refers to four distinctive evidentiary thresholds, namely 'reasonable basis' (for initiating an investigation), 'reasonable grounds' (for the issuance of warrants of arrest or summons to appear), 'substantial grounds' (for the confirmation of hearing) and 'beyond reasonable doubt' (for conviction).[377] Another threshold that should be added to the list is the 'substantial reasons' referred to in Article 53 that regulates the determination whether an investigation or a prosecution may not serve the interests of justice. In contrast with the reasonable basis and substantial reasons standards, which apply to the situational stage, other standards are applicable to the case phase. Generally speaking, the level of the evidentiary threshold of a situation differs from a case. The main target of the case stage is a person, therefore, a higher evidentiary threshold has been established in order to protect the rights of persons. At the confirmation hearing of charges, in accordance with Article 61(7), the 'substantial grounds' must be established to believe that the suspected has committed each of the crimes charged. The PTC I in its decision to confirm the charges against Lubanga submitted that the substantial grounds should be defined as "strong grounds for believing" and it "must offer concrete and tangible proof demonstrating a clear line of reasoning underpinning its specific allegations."[378] Later and upon trial, in order to convict the accused, "the Court must be convinced of the guilt of the accused beyond reasonable doubt."[379] As it can be seen, there is an increasing threshold at the ICC's proceedings, from the moment of a preliminary examination to the moment of the ultimate judgment; each one is consistent and coherent with the related stage.

In the preliminary examination, the Prosecutor's determination should be reasonable. In English, 'reasonable' means fair and sensible, or within the limits of

---

375 Bergsmo and Pejic, 2008, p. 589, see *supra* note 193.

376 ICC, PTC II, Kenya situation, 31 March 2010, para. 29, see *supra* note 41.

377 PTC in its decision to authorize the Prosecutor to initiate an investigation in situation in Kenya describes these different thresholds in these words: he first of the said evidentiary standards, found in Article 58 of the Statute, governs the issuance of an arrest warrant during the pre-trial phase. According to this standard, the relevant PTC is required to be satisfied that there are "reasonable grounds to believe that the person has committed a crime within the jurisdiction of the Court." The next evidentiary standard, applicable at a later stage, concerns the confirmation of charges under Article 61(7) of the Statute. Based on this standard, the respective PTC must determine whether the evidence available is sufficient to establish "substantial grounds to believe that the person committed each of the crimes charged." The highest evidentiary standard, envisaged by Article 66(3) of the Statute, 'beyond reasonable doubt', is required to prove the guilt of an accused at the trial stage (See: ICC, PTC II, Kenya situation, 31 March 2010, para. 28, see *supra* note 41).

378 ICC, PTC II, Kenya situation, 31 March 2010, paras. 38–39, see *supra* note 41.

379 Article 66(3) of the Rome Statute.

reason.[380] The chapeau of Article 53(1) refers to the Prosecutor's determination that there is no 'reasonable basis to proceed', while Article 53(1)(a) refers to the available information that provides 'reasonable basis to believe' that a crime within the ICC's jurisdiction has been committed. These two standards are subsumed, since the latter is one element of the former. Thus, if upon review of the three elements embodied in Article 53(1)(a)–(c) of the Statute, the Chamber reaches an affirmative finding as to their fulfillment, the 'reasonable basis to proceed' standard will consequently be met.[381] The reasonable basis test is the lowest evidentiary standard provided for in the Statute.[382] It is logical, because it is applied in the preliminary examination stage, when "the information available to the Prosecutor is neither expected to be 'comprehensive' nor 'conclusive', if compared to evidence gathered during the investigation."[383] It means that the reasonableness of basis does not require that "the conclusion reached on the facts be the only possible or reasonable one. Nor does it require that the Prosecutor disproves any other reasonable conclusions. Rather, it is sufficient at this stage to prove that there is a reasonable conclusion alongside others (not necessarily supporting the same finding), which can be supported based on the evidence and information available."[384] Such a test is also applicable in the judicial review of the Prosecutor's decisions in the situational phase, when "the Chamber must be satisfied that there exists a sensible or reasonable justification for a belief that a crime falling within the jurisdiction of the Court has or is being committed."[385]

The meaning of reasonableness is similar in both the situational phase (reasonable basis) and the case stage (reasonable grounds). Article 53(1) refers to 'the reasonable basis' for initiating an investigation, but Article 58(1) uses 'the reasonable grounds' to issue an arrest warrant. In referring to a case, either at the issuance of an arrest warrant stage or at the confirmation hearing of charges, the Rome Statute uses the term 'grounds' (reasonable or substantial) to show that it is a different stage from the situational phase whose evidentiary threshold is marked by the term 'basis'. The reasonable basis test is intended to prevent the Court from unwarranted, frivolous, or politically motivated investigations that could have a negative effect on its credibility.[386] On the contrary, the issuance of a warrant needs the reasonable grounds to protect the right of liberty of persons. In spite of this contextual difference enshrined in the wording of the Statute, it does not mean that the substance of the reasonableness test differs.

The interpretation of the PTC in its decision to authorize the Prosecutor to initiate an investigation in Kenya situation should be understood in light of this fact when it submits "the reasonable basis standard under Article 15 of the Statute is even lower than

380 ICC, PTC II, Kenya situation, 31 March 2010, para. 30, see *supra* note 41.
381 Ibid., para. 26.
382 Ibid., para. 27.
383 Ibid., para. 24.
384 Ibid., para. 32.
385 Ibid., paras.34–5.
386 ICC, PTC III, Côte d'Ivoire situation, 3 October 2011, para. 21, see *supra* note 329. And ICC, PTC II, Kenya situation, 31 March 2010, para. 32, see *supra* note 41.

that provided under Article 58 of the Statute."[387] The main distinction between these two stages lies in the fact that the evidence that 'pins' the crimes to an individual is not required when requesting authorization to commence a *proprio motu* investigation.[388] Hence, applying the same evidentiary standard in both circumstances results in different evidentiary material depending on the absence or inclusion of this element.[389]

Given the similarity between the reasonableness in both the situational and case stages, the relevant jurisprudence of the Court about the case phase is applicable to the situational reasonableness. Reasonable grounds standard referred to in Article 58 is based on those possibilities, which are reasonable. In consistence with this meaning, the PTC submits that under Article 58(1), "the evidence need only establish a reasonable conclusion that the person committed a crime within the jurisdiction of the Court, and it is not required that this be the only reasonable conclusion that can be drawn from the evidence."[390] The notion of probability, which constitutes the grounds for issuing an arrest warrant, opposes the notion of improbability. Probability implies that something is probable while other options remain possible. Probability implies a plurality. Hence, it does not mean that the probable issue at hand is the only possibility, which requires the invalidity of other possibilities. In the situation of Sudan, the Prosecutor of the Court charged Al Bashir with the crime of Genocide and applied for an arrest warrant on the basis of charges including the allegedly commission of Genocide.[391] On 4 March 2009, the PTC rendered its decision in the Prosecutor's application, in which the Chamber decided to issue a warrant of arrest against Al Bashir for his alleged responsibility under Article 25(3)(a) of the Statute for the crimes against humanity and war crimes alleged by the Prosecution. However, the Chamber decided not to include the counts of genocide listed in the Prosecution's Application.[392] Therefore, a warrant of arrest was issued, without the charge of genocide.[393]

At the time, the Chamber asserted that there were no reasonable grounds to believe that genocide had been committed because there were no grounds to believe in the existence of a genocidal intent, i.e. the specific intent to destroy.[394] The Chamber did not accept that there were reasonable grounds, because it had given a narrow and unprecedented interpretation of the notion of reasonable grounds.[395] The chamber submitted that "such a standard would be met only if the materials provided by the

---

387 ICC, PTC II, Kenya situation, 31 March 2010, para. 34, see *supra* note 41.

388 Manuel J. Ventura, 'The Reasonable Basis to Proceed Threshold in the Kenya and Côte d'Ivoire Proprio Motu Investigation Decisions: The International Criminal Court's Lowest Evidentiary Standard?', *The Law and Practice of International Courts and Tribunals*, 2013, vol. 12, p. 49.

389 Ibid.

390 ICC, PTC II, Sylvestre Mudacumura case, Decision on the Prosecutor's Application under Article 58, 13 July 2012, para. 19.

391 ICC, OTP, Al Bashir case, Prosecution Application for a Warrant of Arrest, 14 July 2008.

392 ICC, PTC I, Al Bashir Case, 4 March 2009, see *supra* note 119.

393 ICC, PTC I, Warrant of Arrest for Omar Hassan Ahmad Al Bashir, 4 March 2009.

394 ICC, PTC I, Al Bashir case, 4 March 2009, para. 205, see *supra* note 119.

395 It must be noted that there was a separate and partly dissenting opinion of Tudge Anita Ušacka. Therefore, the word 'Chamber' here means the majority of Chamber.

Prosecution in support of the Prosecution Application show that the only reasonable conclusion to be drawn therefrom is the existence of reasonable grounds to believe in the existence of an intent to destroy."[396] Based on this interpretation, the Chamber did not come to the unique and only conclusion that Al Bashir had a genocidal intent. Given the alleged existence of a strategy to deny crimes allegedly committed in Darfur region, for instance, the majority of the PTC considered that "even if the existence of such a strategy was to be proven, there could be a variety of other plausible reasons for its adoption, such as the intention to commit war crimes and crimes against humanity."[397]

Later, the Prosecutor appealed against this decision. The Prosecutor was of the opinion that the majority had applied the wrong legal test to draw inferences for determining the 'reasonable grounds' under Article 58, and had imposed on the Prosecution an erroneous evidentiary burden at this stage.[398] The Prosecutor argued that, as Judge Ušacka in her dissenting opinion held, an inference alleged by the Prosecutor "must be reasonable and there must be no other evidence which would render the intent unreasonable", but, it does not need to be conclusive or definitive.[399] The Prosecutor believed that the standard that the majority had applied required the Prosecutor to establish a fact 'beyond reasonable doubt'.[400] The Appeals Chamber concurred with the Prosecutor's opinion and submitted that "requiring that the existence of genocidal intent must be the only reasonable conclusion amounts to requiring the Prosecutor to disprove any other reasonable conclusions and to eliminate any reasonable doubt. If the only reasonable conclusion based on the evidence is the existence of genocidal intent, then it cannot be said that such a finding establishes merely 'reasonable grounds to believe'. Rather, it establishes genocidal intent beyond reasonable doubt".[401] Another way to rephrase the Appeals Chamber's interpretation of the reasonable grounds would be to say that it not only allows a conclusion that a crime has been committed, but also allows another reasonable conclusion, that is, that a crime has not been committed.[402] For this reason, the Appeals Chamber reveres the decision of the PTC to the extent that the Chamber decided not to issue an arrest warrant in respect of the crime of genocide. Consequently, the PTC issued the second warrant of arrest for Al Bashir on 12 July 2012 with respect to the alleged commission of the crime of genocide.

Preliminary examination is a preliminary stage, and all decisions during this stage are of a preliminary nature. As the Trial Chamber, in the Katanga case, submits, "the assessment of the admissibility is ongoing based on the underlying facts as they exist

---

396 ICC, Al Bashir case, 4 March 2009, para. 158, see *supra* note 119.

397 Ibid., para. 165.

398 ICC, OTP, Prosecution Document in Support of Appeal Against the Decision on the Prosecution's Application for a Warrant of Arrest against Omar Hassan Ahmad Al Bashir, 6 July 2009, para. 1.

399 Ibid., para. 38.

400 Ibid., para. 39.

401 ICC, Appeals Chamber, Judgment on the Appeal of the Prosecutor Against the Decision on the Prosecution's Application for a Warrant of Arrest against Omar Hassan Ahmad Al Bashir, 3 February 2010, para. 33.

402 Ramsden and Chung, 2013, p. 560, see *supra* note 370.

at the time, but subject to revision based on any change to those facts."[403] It follows that "any finding in this Decision is without prejudice to any later submission to, or finding by, the Chamber in the context of a different stage of the proceedings."[404] It includes the admissibility as evidence as well.[405] Even, for this reason, the PTC in its decision on the confirmation of charges against Lubanga submitted, "the admission of evidence at this stage is without prejudice to the Trial Chamber's exercise of its functions and powers to make a final determination as to the admissibility and probative value of obtained evidence."[406] Therefore, the evidentiary threshold applicable to the findings of the preliminary examination is not equal to the threshold that is applied to the trial phase.

403 ICC, Appeals Chamber, Katanga case, 25 September 2009, para. 56, see *supra* note 73.
404 ICC, Côte d'Ivoire situation, 3 October 2011, para. 25, see *supra* note 329.
405 For this reason, PTC in its decision on the confirmation of charges against Lubanga submitted "the admission of evidence at this stage is without prejudice to the Trial Chamber's exercise of its functions and powers to make a final determination as to the admissibility and probative value "of obtained evidence (See: ICC, PTC I, Lubanga case, 29 January 2007, para. 90, see *supra* note 345).
406 *Ibid., para. 90.*

CHAPTER IV

MAKING A DECISION ON THE SITUATION SELECTION

The final stage in the situation selection process is making a decision by the Prosecutor. Preliminary examination as an evaluation process produces an output, namely the prosecutorial decision to or not to initiate an investigation into a situation undergone the process. This finding marks a new phase at the ICC's architecture in which the judges of the Court may exercise a supervisory role over the Prosecutor's discretion. Hence, this phase is important from an institutional and internal perspective.

The Prosecutor, upon conducting a preliminary examination, may arrive at two different conclusions. She may believe that there is a reasonable basis to open an investigation or, by contrast, she may believe the lack thereof. The former furthers a situation into the case phase, whereas the latter puts an end to a situation examination. However, the preliminary examination's findings are preliminary in nature. It means that, as Article 53(4) provides, "the Prosecutor may, at any time, reconsider a decision whether to initiate an investigation or prosecution based on new facts and information."

The present chapter aims at offering some insight into the latest step that is taken in the situation selection process, namely making a determination whether or not to proceed with a situation by conducting an investigation.

1. OPENING AN INVESTIGATION

Preliminary examination is a filtering mechanism to opt for a proper situation for investigation. If the Prosecutor finds that there is a reasonable basis to believe that a situation meets the statutory criteria to initiate an investigation, then she proceeds with the situation. However, the way ahead of the Prosecutor that should be followed to reach the investigation phase is different in terms of the trigger that brings a situation to the Prosecutor's attention. The ICC trigger mechanism produces two products, namely referrals and communications. Referrals are made by States Parties or the UNSC. On the contrary, communications are predominantly made by non-State actors, including NGOs and individuals. As to referrals, if the Prosecutor determines that the statutory requirements to select a situation are met, she initiates an investigation without any need to get extra permission from the Court's judges, whereas the decision of the Prosecutor to open an investigation into a situation communicated to her under

Article 15 needs judicial approval. This is one of the privileges of referrals that have encouraged the Prosecutor to welcome self-referrals.

1.1. INVESTIGATION OF REFERRALS

All situations should undergo a preliminary examination, regardless of the trigger bringing them to the Prosecutor's attention. It means that both referrals and communications are examined by the Prosecutor to determine if they deserve a full investigation. Referrals made by the UNSC are not an exception here. It is the authority and responsibility of the Prosecutor to examine a situation to find out whether the given situation falls within the jurisdiction of the Court, and if it is admissible for the initiation of an investigation. Being admissible implies that a situation has sufficient gravity to activate the Court's intervention. In addition, the admissibility of a situation means that there is no alternative for the Court's intervention at the national level. To make a decision to proceed with a situation requires the Prosecutor to give considerations to the operational needs and factors for conducting an effective investigation. In order to conduct an effective investigation with a bright prospect of success in prosecution, the Prosecutor shall give priority to those situations and cases that are most available for investigation and prosecution.

In the case of referrals, the Prosecutor's decision to investigate a situation directly leads to the investigation phase. As soon as the Prosecutor, pursuant to having evaluated the information available to her, determines that there is a reasonable basis to initiate an investigation, she initiates an investigation *ex officio*. Structurally speaking, in the scenario of referrals, there is no structural boundary between the preliminary examination and the investigation phase. To initiate an investigation, the Prosecutor does not have to get an authorization from the Court's judges. In this context, the Rome Statute has not limited the prosecutorial discretion by giving space to judicial supervision. A referral that represents the consent and will of States is both triggering and authorizing. In correspondence with such a referral, the Prosecutor's decision to accept the request of the referring State is both declarative and constitutive in nature.[407] It is declarative because it declares that the Court's jurisdiction activation prerequisites have been met, and it is constitutive since it per se activates the Court's dormant jurisdiction, without the need for a judicial authorization.

In the absence of a judicial review mechanism, the temporal distance between opening a preliminary examination and the initiation of an investigation in respect of referrals is often shorter than the period that is usually spent for examining communications. For instance, on 17 June 2004, the Prosecutor opened an investigation into the situation in Congo three months after receiving a referral made by the relevant government. This lapse was around 6 months in the Uganda situation (16 December 2004 – 29 July), 4 months in the CAR II situation (30 May 2014 – 24 September),

407 Olásolo, 2005, p. 94, see *supra* note 1.

5 months in the Mali situation (18 July 2013 – 16 January 2013), 2 months in the situation in Darfur (31 March 2005 – 1 June), and less than 10 days in the Libya situation (26 February 2011 – 3 March). It is also the case when the Prosecutor decides not to initiate an investigation. In the Mavi Marmara situation that had been referred by the Comoros in May 2013, the Prosecutor announced her decision not to open an investigation in November in the same year. The longest preliminary examination about a referral has been for the CAR I situation that was referred in December 2004, but the Prosecutor formally opened an investigation in May 2007. On the contrary, the duration of preliminary examinations is longer as to communications. For instance, the preliminary examinations were opened in the situation in Colombia in 2004, in the Afghanistan situation in 2007, and in Nigeria in 2010, but they all are still in progress, at the time of writing this chapter. The need to persuade the judges from one side and the absence of the States' consent from the other stimulate the Prosecutor to conduct the preliminary examination on the communicated situation with more caution.

1.1.1. Announcement of Decision

The legal framework of the Court does not require the Prosecutor to publicize her decision to open an investigation into a referred situation. In practice, however, the Prosecutor officially announces the commencement of an investigation and specifies a start date. Initially, such a publicity policy was so narrow. The Prosecutor initially used to release his decision to initiate an investigation without spelling out any detail. It was the first Prosecutor's practice concerning the situations in Congo and Uganda. On 23 June 2004, the website of the Court released that the OTP "opens its first investigation", without providing any information about the preliminary examination phase.[408] One month later, a short notice was released, stating "Prosecutor of the International Criminal Court opens an investigation into Northern Uganda." The notice just mentioned, "the decision to open an investigation was taken after thorough analysis of available information in order to ensure that requirements of the Rome Statute are satisfied."[409] In the first two situations referred to the Court, the first Prosecutor of the Court did not shed any light on the preliminary examination process and his decisions were made in darkness. Nonetheless, upon the referral of the situation in Darfur by the UNSC, the tendency of the Prosecutor changed. The UNSC Resolution 1593 referred the Darfur situation to the Court on 31 March 2005. In June, the Prosecutor determined that there would be a reasonable basis to formally open an investigation

---

408 ICC, Press Release, The Office of the Prosecutor of the International Criminal Court Opens Its First Investigation, 23 June 2004, available at: www.icc-cpi.int/pages/item.aspx?name=the+office+of+the+prosecutor+of+the+international+criminal+court+opens+its+first+investigation, last accessed at 10 April 2017.

409 ICC, Press Release, Prosecutor of the International Criminal Court Opens an Investigation into Northern Uganda, 29 July 2004, available at: www.icc-cpi.int/pages/item.aspx?name=prosecutor+of+the+international+criminal+court+opens+an+investigation+into+nothern+uganda, last accessed at 10 April 2017.

without delving into the details. However, since Paragraph 8 of the referring Resolution had invited the Prosecutor to address the UNSC within three months of its adoption, at the end of June 2005, the Prosecutor gave its first report on the Darfur situation to the UNSC. The report Stated what the Prosecutor did during the preliminary examination that led to his decision to open an investigation.[410] Since then, the Prosecutor has issued a Statement explaining the process of the preliminary examination that results in her decision to formally open an investigation into a referred situation. As to the first situation in the CAR I, the Prosecutor issued a 'background'.[411] Later, the OTP determined to issue documents titled 'Article 53(1) Report'. These Reports describe the preliminary examination of a situation in detail, regardless of the final decision of the Prosecutor.[412] Article 53(1) Reports are welcome initiatives taken by the present Prosecutor of the Court.

It deserves to be mentioned that there was a wrong practice in the beginning years of the Court's operation regarding the situations referred to the Prosecutor. Regulation 45 of the Regulations of the Court obliges the Prosecutor to "inform the Presidency in writing as soon as a situation has been referred to the Prosecutor" by a State Party or the Security Council.[413] Based on such a notification, Regulation 46 (b) requests the Presidency to "assign a situation to a PTC as soon as the Prosecutor has informed the Presidency." Such a notification and constitution should be done when the Prosecutor is about to open a preliminary examination. However, the timing required by Regulation 45 was not observed respecting the situations in Uganda and Congo. On 17 March 2004, the then Prosecutor sent a letter to the Presidency of the Court informing both the receipt of referrals and his determination that there was a reasonable basis to open an investigation into situations in Uganda and Congo. Following this letter, the then President of the Court in July 2004 decided that the situation in the DRC be assigned to PTC I and the Uganda Situation to PTC II.[414] However, the Prosecutor had delayed in notifying the presidency of the Court. Such notification, according to the ICC law, should had been done before the Prosecutor decided to open an investigation. The preliminary examination process, as will be discussed later, is to some extent subject to judicial review. For this purpose, a PTC should be in place in advance.

410 ICC, OTP, First Report of the Prosecutor of the International Criminal Court, Mr. Luis Moreno-Ocampo, to the Security Council, 29 June 2005.

411 ICC, OTP, Background: Situation in the Central African Republic, 22 May 2007.

412 ICC, OTP, Situation in Mali Article 53(1) Report, 16 January 2013. And, ICC, OTP, Article 53(1) Report, Situation in the Central African Republic II, 24 September 2014. And, ICC, OTP, Situation on Registered Vessels of Comoros, Greece and Cambodia: Article 53(1) Report, 6 November 2014.

413 Regarding UNSC referrals, there is an extra obligation of notification. Regulation 30 of the Court's Regulations: "when a situation has been referred to the Prosecutor Pursuant to Article 13, paragraph (b), and the Prosecutor has determined that there would be a reasonable basis to initiate an investigation, the Office shall notify the Security Council through the Secretary-General of the United Nations."

414 ICC, Presidency, Decision Assigning the Situation in the Congo to Pre-Trial Chamber I, 5 July 2004. And, ICC, Presidency, Decision Assigning the Situation in Uganda to Per-Trial Chamber II, 5 July 2004.

1.1.2. Article 18 Mechanism

Although the Prosecutor is exempted from asking a judicial authorization to open an investigation into a situation referred to her, this does not mean that the authority of the Prosecutor to proceed with such a situation is unfettered. Article 18 of the Rome Statute establishes a mechanism through which the Prosecutor's decision to proceed with a situation may face a challenge. In the preliminary examination, the Prosecutor is obliged to determine if a situation is admissible or inadmissible. It is exclusively up to the Prosecutor to select the potential cases of sufficient gravity and then to figure out whether there are genuine proceedings at the national level or, alternatively, it is the responsibility of the Court to intervene in the absence of such proceedings. However, the Prosecutor's determination about the admissibility requirement during the preliminary examination does not confront any challenge, since States have no opportunity to object to the Prosecutor's decision in this regard. On the subject of communications, the Prosecutor's determination in this regard is brought to the judicial review when the Prosecutor applies for a judicial authorization to initiate an investigation, but lacks referrals. Article 18 is intended to fill such a gap. This article provides States with a chance to challenge the Prosecutor's determination on the admissibility requirement. For this reason, it is submitted that Article 18 "strengthens the complementarity regime."[415] El Zeidy States Article 18 serves a further procedural filter for the benefit of States' sovereignty.[416] Indeed, this mechanism serves the philosophy behind the principle of complementarity, namely the priority of national jurisdictions. Safeguarding this superior jurisdiction "at an early stage of the investigation process is one of the main aims of Article 18."[417] It should be recalled that the Article 18 mechanism is applicable to communications, too. It is a double check of the complementarity rule, because the admissibility requirement in the normal course of event is not assessed by the Court's Judges in the authorization process.

1.1.2.1. Making a Challenge under Article 18

Upon the Prosecutor's decision to formally open an investigation into a situation, Article 18 puts the Prosecutor under an obligation to "notify all States Parties and those States which, taking into account the information available, would normally exercise jurisdiction over the crimes concerned." The method of notification is determined by the Prosecutor.[418] Such a notification shall "contain information about the acts that may

---

415 Silvana Arbia, 'Proactive Complementarity: A Registrar's Perspective and Plans', in Carsten Stahn and Mohamed M. El Zeidy (eds.), *The International Criminal Court and Complementarity: From Theory to Practice*. Cambridge University Press, 2011, p. 53.

416 Mohamed M. El Zeidy, *The Principle of Complementarity in International Criminal Law: Origin, Development and Practice,* Martinus Nijhoff Publishers, 2008, p. 240.

417 Safferling, 2012, p. 197, see *supra* note 101.

418 Daniel Ntanda Nsereko, 'Article 18', in Otto Triffterer and Kai Ambos, *The Rome Statute of the International Criminal Court: A Commentary,* T.C.H. Beck. Hart. Nomos, 2016, p. 841.

constitute crimes referred to in Article 5."[419] If no State responds to the Prosecutor's notification, it implicitly means that the notified State waived the right provided under Article 18.[420] States Parties are free in their decision whether or not to request deferral.[421] Therefore, if there is no action, the Prosecutor could go ahead with the investigation.

A State that has been notified by the Prosecutor "may request additional information from the Prosecutor to assist it in the application of Article 18, Paragraph 2."[422] Additional information may include the potential cases selected by the Prosecution in the preliminary examination. Deferrals under Article 18 are made as to one or more persons and cases. Therefore, the awareness of those cases and persons are necessary for the State requesting a deferral to prove that its national jurisdiction is in place as to those specific cases. Upon the Prosecutor's notification under Article 18, "within one month of receipt of that notification", a State has a right to inform the Court that its national jurisdiction is active about who has been sought by the Prosecutor. The deferral request shall be made "in writing and provide information concerning its investigation."[423] When the Prosecutor has learnt that there is a concurrent jurisdiction, she has to defer to the requesting State. Even if a State is prompted to take action upon the prosecutorial notification, it still merits requesting the prosecutor to defer if before such a deference the concrete steps have been taken. The spirit of the Statute is "to give due deference to State jurisdiction."[424]

Making a deferral does not terminate the role and authority of the Prosecutor. Paragraph 2 of Article 18 States that if a State requests a deferral, "at the request of that State, the Prosecutor shall defer to the State's investigation of those persons." This Paragraph explicitly refers to the deferral of 'those persons', not a whole situation. The expression 'those persons' in the context of Article 18 refers to those potential cases that the Prosecutor is going to create a case against them before the ICC by requesting the issuance of a warrant against them. Therefore, challenges under Article 18 may not remove the Prosecutor from the scene. Even if a deferral is made, it does not concern the investigation into the situation as a whole, but it is limited to one or more cases. If upon a deferral there are admissible cases in the context of a situation, the Prosecutor still may investigate the given situation with respect to those cases.[425] In other words, a deferral under Article 18 does not terminate a situation before the Court. In addition, in the case of a deferral, the Prosecutor assumes a monitoring role to see that the national proceedings remain ongoing and genuine. Article 18 grants the Prosecutor with two measures to fulfil her supervisory mandate. Firstly, Paragraph 5 of the article States that in the case of deferrals, "the Prosecutor may request that the State concerned

[419] Rule 52(1) of the ICC Rules of the Procedure and Evidence.
[420] El Zeidy, 2008, p. 245, see *supra* note 416.
[421] Safferling, 2012, p. 200, see *supra* note 101.
[422] Rule 52(2) of the ICC Rules of the Procedure and Evidence.
[423] Rule 53 of the ICC Rules of the Procedure and Evidence.
[424] Nsereko, 2016, p. 842, see *supra* note 418.
[425] Nouwen, 2013, p. 77, see *supra* note 39.

periodically inform the Prosecutor of the progress of its investigations and any subsequent prosecutions. States Parties shall respond to such requests without undue delay." Secondly, Paragraph 3 of Article 18 States that the Prosecutor's deferral is "open to review by the Prosecutor six months after the date of deferral or at any time when there has been a significant change of circumstances based on the State's unwillingness or inability genuinely to carry out the investigation." If such a change exists, "the Prosecutor may apply to the PTC for authorization in accordance with Article 18, Paragraph 2."[426]

If a State requests a deferral under Article 18, the Prosecutor shall defer to the requesting State as a rule. However, if the Prosecutor decides to reject the deferral request, it is her responsibility to have a judicial approval for such rejection.[427] Such judicial intervention is meant to "silence allegations of political manipulation and bias on the part of the Prosecutor."[428] Indeed, the emergence of PTC was the price that the advocators of an effective and independence prosecutor had to pay to ensure accountability in the exercise of powers.[429] For this purpose, the Prosecutor shall submit an application in writing that "shall contain the basis for the application."[430] In addition, the Prosecutor should inform the requesting State of her application to the PTC, besides a summary of the basis of the application.[431] A request for deferral is equal to making an admissibility challenge. If a State challenges the admissibility of those potential cases with which the Prosecutor intends to proceed, the final word will be with the PTC. The resolution of conflicts between the Prosecutor and States is a matter of judicial nature that requires the intervention of the Court's Judges. To examine the admissibility challenge under Article 18, the PTC decides "on the procedure to be followed and may take appropriate measures for the proper conduct of the proceedings."[432] To make a decision under Article 18, the PTC "shall consider the factors in Article 17 in deciding whether to authorize an investigation."[433] Whatever the Chamber's decision is, it is challengeable by both the State concerned and the Prosecutor. The appeal "may be heard on an expedited basis."[434]

The Article 18 mechanism has an implication for the assessment of the complementarity requirement in the case stage also. At the ICC, a case is formed when an arrest warrant or a subpoena is issued. A case should be admissible to warrant the issuance of an arrest warrant. The fulfilment of the Article 18 obligation encourages the Judges to see a case admissible for issuing an arrest warrant. For instance, the

---

426 Rule 56(1) of the ICC Rules of the Procedure and Evidence.
427 Article 18 of the Rome Statute: "at the request of that State, the Prosecutor shall defer to the State's investigation of those persons unless the Pre-Trial Chamber, on the application of the Prosecutor, decides to authorize the investigation."
428 Safferling, 2012, p. 197, see *supra* note 101.
429 Nsereko, 2016, p. 843, see *supra* note 418.
430 Rule 54.1 of the ICC Rules of the Procedure and Evidence.
431 Rule 54.2 of the ICC Rules of the Procedure and Evidence.
432 Rule 55.1 of the ICC Rules of the Procedure and Evidence.
433 Rule 55.2 of the ICC Rules of the Procedure and Evidence.
434 Article 18.4 of the Rome Statute.

PTC II in issuing an arrest warrant against Kony noted that "the Prosecutor affirms in Paragraph 3 of the application that letters of notification were distributed to all States Parties under Article 18, Paragraph 1 of the Statute, as well as to other States that would normally exercise jurisdiction", and that the Prosecutor had not received from any State information pursuant to Article 18, Paragraph 2 of the Statute." Based on this affirmation, the Chamber declared the case against Kony admissible.[435]

1.1.2.2. Scope of Article 18

The scope of the Article 18 mechanism needs some clarification. At first, the exemption of the UNSC's referrals from the notification obligation referred to in Article 18 matters. Literally speaking, Article 18 refers to the referrals made by States Parties, in addition to communications, but it does not refer to the UNSC's referrals. At the strength of such silence, some believe that the UNSC's referrals are excluded from the Article 18 mechanism.[436] However, from a teleological perspective, one can say that the Article 18 mechanism embraces the UNSC's referrals as well. The right of States to seek a preliminary admissibility ruling is not limited to *proprio motu* proceedings, since Article 18 "first of all is meant as a safeguard in *proprio motu* situations."[437] In other words, Article 18 was not meant to make a distinction between the States referrals and the UNSC ones, but it was intended to address a different issue, namely the necessity of a check and balance mechanism to control the Prosecutor's power to initiate an investigation, given the complementarity principle.

The spirit of Article 18 is to enhance the complementarity rule, and the exclusion of UNSC referrals contradicts such a spirit. UNSC referrals, like other referrals, should satisfy the admissibility requirement. It stands to reason that the Prosecutor inquiries on the potential cases arising from a UNSC referral to see if there have been parallel proceedings at the national level. The complementarity requirement is applicable to all cases before the Court. The Prosecutor has to prosecute only a handful of cases, because of the limited capacities of the Court. Therefore, when there is a national jurisdiction dealing with a specific case, it is not reasonable to occupy the time and money of the Court for the same case. From such a perspective, it is understandable why a commentator States it is unclear why UNSC referrals were removed from the wording of Article 18.[438] Logically speaking, it should not have been removed, except for the notification part. One can argue that due to the publicity of UNSC referrals there is no need to notify States.

---

435 ICC, PTC II, Kony case, Warrant of Arrest for Joseph Kony Issued on 8th July 2005 as Amended on 27 September 2005, 13 October 2005.

436 Indeed, these scholars believe that the UNSC's Referrals can be challenged only under Article 19 (See: Nouwen, 2013, p. 77, see *supra* note 39. And, Wouters, Verhoeven and Demeyere, 2008, p. 305, see *supra* note 38).

437 Stigen, 2011, p. 512, see *supra* note 191.

438 Nsereko, 2016, p. 837, see *supra* note 418.

Another aspect of the Article 18 mechanism that needs more clarification is its scope regarding those States that need to be notified. Article 18(1) obliges the Prosecutor to notify both States Parties and non-member States. There are two arguments in favor of this inclusive understanding. Firstly, literally, Article 18 uses 'and' rather than 'including'. The article states "the Prosecutor shall notify all States Parties *and* those States which, taking into account the information available, would normally exercise jurisdiction over the crimes concerned." Term 'and' implies a conceptual distinction between the word after and before this conjunction. Secondly, the scope of Article 18 should be determined by taking into account the principle of complementarity. The Court's ultimate objective is not to allow ICC crimes go unpunished. In realizing this anti-impunity policy, the priority is by domestic initiatives. Therefore, when a national Court of a non-member State deals with a situation or a case, there is not reasonable basis to proceed with the given situation or case before the Court. What matters is a genuine prosecution or investigation. It does not matter whether such a prosecution is conducted by a State Party or non-member State, by a reputable State or with a notorious one. Therefore, all States with a legal jurisdiction should be notified, since it is a joint effort to bring perpetrators to justice.[439] The Court as the last resort mechanism is not going to substitute States. By contrast, it is intended to facilitate domestic jurisdictions, and membership to the ICC does not affect this Court's policy.

1.2. INVESTIGATION OF COMMUNICATIONS

Contrary to referrals, if the Prosecutor decides to initiate an investigation *proprio motu* and based on the communications she receives, she "shall submit to the PTC a request for authorization of an investigation, together with any supporting material collected."[440] There is an exception for the crime of aggression in this regard. If the Prosecutor decides to initiate an investigation into the crime of aggression, according to Article 15 bis(8), the authorization for the commencement of the investigation in respect of a crime of aggression must be given by 'the Pre-Trial Division'.

1.2.1. Judicial Authorization

The authority of the Prosecutor to open an investigation without prior consent of States or the UNSC has always been controversial. Even at the time of the establishment of the Court, the dilemma of holding prosecutors accountable while ensuring their independence was at the center of debates.[441] Article 15 establishes the Prosecutor's power to prosecute the international suspects on her discretion.

439 Schabas, 2010, p. 340, see *supra* note 26.

440 Article 15(3) of the Rome Statute.

441 Jenia Turner, 'Accountability of International Prosecutors', in Carsten Stahn (ed.), *The Law and Practice of the International Criminal Court*, Oxford University Press, 2015, p. 382.

"The Prosecutor may initiate investigations *proprio motu* on the basis of information on crimes within the jurisdiction of the Court." The PTC II describes Article 15 as "one of the most delicate provisions of the Statute", and "the product of extensive debates and division of views throughout the drafting process and until the end of the Rome Conference."[442] It is even said that the US's oppositional attitude toward the ICC is rooted in the existence of a Prosecutor with sweeping powers enabling her to take action against the will of States. For example, John Bolton, at the time US Under-Secretary for Arms Control and International Security, wrote: "requiring the United States to be bound by this treaty, with its unaccountable Prosecutor and its unchecked judicial power, is clearly inconsistent with American standards of constitutionalism."[443]

In spite of the loud opposing voice of some delegations, the argument in favor of the Prosecutor's *proprio motu* power appealed the majority of States' delegations. It was argued that both States Parties and the UNSC would be unlikely to lodge complaints for various political reasons, so the Prosecutor should be empowered to investigate *ex officio*.[444] Justice Louise Arbour points out that before the Rome Statute came into existence, "there is more to fear from an impotent than from an overreaching Prosecutor."[445] This fear was overcome by empowering the Prosecutor with an independent power to initiate an investigation. In the case of the States or the UNSC inaction, the Prosecutor has been authorized to take the initiative on her own to investigate a situation. However, it was not the only concern emerged in the drafting process of the Rome Statute. Empowering the Court's Prosecutor with excessive powers was worrying for some. The fear led to making the Prosecutor's power balanced by placing it subject to the judicial review.

The ICC provides great accountability on the part of the Prosecutor.[446] The Prosecutor is not allowed to start an investigation on her own, without the will of States. A referral represents the State's consent to authorize the Prosecutor to proceed with a situation. Regarding communications, such a will and consent has been conferred upon PTCs by States to determine whether an investigation should be initiated or not. Article 15(4) States that the PTC "shall authorize the commencement of the investigation", if upon examination of the available information, it considers that "there is a reasonable basis to proceed with an investigation, and that the case appears to fall within the jurisdiction of the Court." The rule and the role of the PTC in this regard is novel in international level, since in the pre-trial phase, the judiciary often get involved when the investigators seek authorization to use coercive measures such as arrest.[447] Incorporating the situation notion into the Rome Statute resulted in some institutional adaptions such as PTCs.

442 ICC, PTC II, Kenya situation, 31 March 2010, para. 17, see *supra* note 41.
443 Wouters, Verhoeven and Demeyere, 2008, p. 350, see *supra* note 38.
444 Schabas, 2010, p. 316, see *supra* note 26.
445 Justice Louise Arbour, 'The Need for an Independent and Effective Prosecutor in the Permanent International Criminal Court', *Windsor Yearbook of Access to Justice*, 1999, vol. 17, p. 217.
446 Stahn, 2009, p. 255, para. 221.
447 Nsereko, 2016, p. 838, see *supra* note 418.

Against this backdrop, one of the PTCs states that the underlying purpose of the judicial review under Article 15(4) is "to prevent unwarranted, frivolous, or politically motivated investigations."[448] This consideration is called the good administration of justice, which is one of the Court's goals.[449] This goal could be reached more effectively by the judicial scrutiny.

When the Prosecutor *proprio motu* requests the activation of the Court's dormant jurisdiction, the judge(s) of the PTCs analyzes the merits of the request and then decide on the Prosecutor's request. The Prosecutor's request shall be in written.[450] It shall contain both facts and supporting reasons of their reality.[451]

The PTC passes three stages to authorize the Prosecutor to initiate a requested investigation.[452] Firstly, it establishes the criteria for the authorization. Secondly, it examines whether the requisite criteria are satisfied, and the chamber finally determines the jurisdictional scope of the authorized investigation. The standards which should be applied to the authorization process are set out in two articles, namely Article 15(4) and Article 53(1). These parameters are jurisdiction, admissibility (consisting of complementarity and gravity) and the interests of justice presumption. Article 15(4) sets a single criterion and that is "the case appears to fall within the jurisdiction of the Court." This criterion is embodied in Article 53(1) too. This overlap does not require a double-check. As the PTC States "a review of Article 53(l)(a)-(c) of the Statute is sufficient for the purpose of this procedure and there is no need to duplicate its assessment of jurisdiction under Article 15(4) of the Statute."[453]

The examination of the Prosecutor's decision to initiate an investigation is conducted within an evidentiary threshold, and that is the reasonable basis standard referred to in both Article 53(1) and Article 15(4). As PTC II argues, to fulfill the function to supervise the *proprio motu* initiative of the Prosecutor to initiate an investigation, the Chamber "applies the exact standard on the basis of which the Prosecutor arrived at his conclusion. This means that the Chamber must equally consider whether the requirements set out in Article 53(1)(a)-(c) of the Statute are satisfied."[454] The PTC analyzes the request of the Prosecutor within an informative framework. Such a framework is comprised of the request of the Prosecutor, the supporting material and annexes submitted by the Prosecutor as well as the victim's

---

448 ICC, PTC III, Côte d'Ivoire situation, 3 October 2011, para. 21, see *supra* note 329.

449 Sluiter, 2002, p. 1147, see *supra* note 103.

450 Rule 50(2) ICC Rules of the Procedure and Evidence.

451 Regulation 49(2) of the Regulations of the Court provides that the Prosecutor's request for an authorization shall contain: a) a reference to the crimes which the Prosecutor believes have been or are being committed and a Statement of the facts being alleged to provide the reasonable basis to believe that those crimes have been or are being committed; (b) a declaration of the Prosecutor with reasons that the listed crimes fall within the jurisdiction of the Court"; in addition to the indication of (a) the places of the commission of the crimes (b) the time or time period and (c) "the persons involved, if identified, or a description of the person or groups of persons involved."

452 ICC, PTC II, Kenya situation, 31 March 2010, para. 3, see *supra* note 41.

453 Ibid., para. 68.

454 Ibid., para. 24.

representations. Such information can be completed upon a request by the PTC. As Regulation 50(4) provides, the PTC "in deciding on the procedure to be followed, may request additional information from the Prosecutor and from any of the victims who have made representations, and, if it considers it appropriate, may hold a hearing."

1.2.2. Victims' Participation

In the assessment of the Prosecutor's request for an authorization to initiate an investigation, victims are granted a role by the Rome Statute. Paragraph 3 of Article 15 reads: "...victims may make representations to the PTC, in accordance with the Rules of Procedure and Evidence." The representations of the victims form a factor that should be taken into account by the PTC.

1.2.2.1. Participatory Right of Victims

The central right of the victims before the ICC is the right to participation. The concept of victim's participation has been described as victims "having a say, being listened to, or being treated with dignity and respect."[455] Article 68(3) of the Rome Statute puts an obligation upon the Court's Chambers to permit victims to present their views and concerns and to consider those views and concerns at appropriate stages of the proceedings.[456] However, there are three conditions: the personal interests of the victims should be affected and the presentation of concerns and views should not be prejudicial to or inconsistent with the rights of the accused and a fair and impartial trial, and the stage of proceedings in which the victims intend to participate should be appropriate. The victims' views and concerns may be presented by the legal representatives of the victims where "the Court considers it appropriate."[457]

Victims' participation in the criminal proceedings causes many positive effects for the Court. On the side of the Court, victims' participation adds a third perspective on the issues at hand and provides the Court with a clearer image of the events. In addition, victims may be used as the evidentiary sources, by giving them an opportunity to submit the evidence.[458] Making presentation to the PTC "can provide factual and legal elements for the decision to authorize the investigation into the situation within which

455 War Crime Research Office, *Victim Participation before the International Criminal Court*, American University, 2007, p. 8.

456 Art 68 (3): "Where the personal interests of the victims are affected, the Court shall permit their views and concerns to be presented and considered at stages of the proceedings determined to be appropriate by the Court and in a manner which is not prejudicial to or inconsistent with the rights of the accused and a fair and impartial trial. Such views and concerns may be presented by the legal representatives of the victims where the Court considers it appropriate, in accordance with the Rules of Procedure and Evidence."

457 Article 68 (3) of the Rome Statute.

458 For the right of submission of the evidence by the victims at the ICC see: Sergey Vasiliev, 'Victim Participation Revisited: What the ICC is Learning About Itself', in Carsten Stahn (ed), *The Law and Practice of the International Criminal Court*, Oxford University Press, 2015, p. 1169.

the same victims claim to have suffered harm as a result of the commission of crimes within the jurisdiction of the Court."[459] In general, victims' contributions to criminal investigations and judicial processes can enhance the quality of criminal trials.[460] Moreover, the victim's participation may legitimize the role of the Court in affected communities.[461] Justice should be seen to be done by the locals. The distance between The Hague and the situation countries is a problem that may lead to misunderstanding and misjudgment. Representation of the victims' views at the ICC may fill the gap between global and local justice. The International Federation for Human Rights has emphasized this 'global/local divide' to push the Court to improve its engagement with affected communities.[462] The extent to which victims feel they have a voice in the proceedings determines the extent of satisfaction that justice has been done.[463] The opportunity to articulate views and concerns enables victims to "be part of the justice process", and by ensuring that consideration is given to their suffering, "they will have confidence in the justice process and view it as relevant to their day-to-day existence rather than as remote, technical and irrelevant."[464] If victims are not satisfied, the re-victimization or the secondary victimization phenomenon arises. This notion emerges when victims are ignored by the legal systems upon the experience of being victimized by offenders.[465] Preventing such a situation encourages the victims to participate in the proceedings.

The independent role of the victims, however, does not seem to be desirable for some organs and actors within the ICC. The adverse effects on the accused's rights and the efficiency of the Court's functioning are the main arguments in opposing the authorization of victims with wide rights. For instance, Judge Van den Wyngaert has voiced heavy criticism against the current status of victims' role at the ICC. She makes a judgment about the victims' system at the ICC based on her own experience in both the ICC and the ICTY. She almost accepts that the ICTY suffered from some shortcomings respecting the victims, but she is not sure if the remedy adopted by the Court is an appropriate one to prevent the secondary victimization.[466] Judge Van den Wyngaert argues that at the ICC a huge amount of time is spent on victim-related issues, which, "obviously, has an impact on the length of proceedings."[467]

---

459 ICC, PTC II, Uganda situation, 10 August 2007, para. 90, see *supra* note 188.

460 Human Rights Center University of California, The Victims' Court? A Study of 622 Victim Participants at the International Criminal Court, 2015, p. 12.

461 McGonigle Leyh, 2011, p. 498, see *supra* note 210.

462 International Federation for Human Rights, Five Myths about Victim Participation in ICC Proceedings, December 2014, p. 19, available at: www.fidh.org/IMG/pdf/cpi649a.pdf.

463 Human Rights Center University of California, 2015, p. 14, see *supra* note 460. And, War Crime Research Office, 2007, p. 9, see *supra* note 455.

464 ICC, ASP, Report of the Court on the Strategy in relation to Victims, 10 November 2009, para. 44.

465 Ibid., p. 48.

466 Christine Van den Wyngaert Hon, 'Victims before International Criminal Courts: Some Views and Concerns of an ICC Trial Judge', *Case Western Reserve Journal of International Law*, 2011, vol. 44, p. 477.

467 Ibid., p. 494.

This effect per se can result in a kind of frustration, since with slow proceedings the fewer trials can be held that conflicts with the ending impunity too.[468] To avoid such adverse effects, the Judge puts forward an alternative idea; "to transform the Trust Fund for Victims into a Reparation Commission, which would directly deal with victims' reparation claims."[469] In this proposal, the victims would not participate in the proceedings, but just seek reparation before the commission that is not needed to be restricted to convictions. However, this suggestion ignores the expressive mandates and the exemplary function of the Court. The limits of the Court to deliver justice for all victims expeditiously should not result in removing the victims from the agenda of the Court. Such a feature requires expectation management to prevent adverse frustration.

Some other scholars insist on the adverse effects of the victims' scheme on the accused's rights. Zappala grounds his article on the assumption that victim participation in criminal proceedings "necessarily implies some sort of conflict with the rights of defendants."[470] He argues that the victims' participation makes a considerable delay in the proceedings that is a violation of the right to an expeditious trial of the defendants concerned. To resolve the conflict between the victims' rights and accused's rights, she believes that the victims' rights "must be counter-balanced against the primacy of the rights of the accused."[471] The delay argument was once put forward at the ICC. After the PTC confirmed the charges against Lubanga, the decision was appealed. The victims in the case filed a joint application in which they requested that the Appeals Chamber authorize their participation in the appeal proceeding, in particular, by submitting written observations.[472] The application was opposed by the Prosecutor, arguing that, *inter alia,* "participation at this limited procedural step may affect the expeditious conduct of the proceedings."[473] The Appeals Chamber rejected the victims' application, since the judges were not convinced that the personal interests of the victims, as a statutory condition for the participation in the proceedings, would be affected in the case in question. The Appeals Chamber believed that the victims have to submit a Statement "in relation to whether and how their personal interests are affected."[474]

However, in the appeal in question, the Appeals Chamber noted that the victims had not put forward any grounds to substantiate whether their personal interests were affected.[475] Contrary to the majority, Judge Song issued a separate opinion. He argued in favor of the victims' participation, and he considered the delay argument too. The

---

468 Ibid., pp. 494–95.

469 Ibid., p. 495.

470 Salvatore Zappala, 'The Rights of Victims v. the Rights of the Accused', *Journal of International Criminal Justice*, 2010, vol. 8, p. 139.

471 Ibid., p. 144.

472 ICC, Appeals Chamber, Decision of the Appeals Chamber on the Joint Application of Victims a/0001/06 to a/0003/06 and a/0105/06 concerning the Directions and Decision of the Appeals Chamber of 2 February 2007, 13 June 2007, para. 5.

473 Ibid., para. 12.

474 Ibid., para. 23.

475 Ibid., para. 24.

judge was not convinced that the victims' participation "would lead to a delay in the proceedings and therefore would be inconsistent with the right to an expeditious trial." He accepted that giving time to victims to make their submissions makes some delay. Nonetheless, "such delay will arise whenever victims are allowed to participate. Unless special circumstances exist, this delay is not inconsistent with the rights of the accused, but merely a consequence of the fact that the Statute provides for the participation of victims in proceedings before the Court."[476] However, to avoid unjustified delays and to ensure the expeditiousness of the proceedings, the judges have been authorized and obliged "to determine whether and when victims shall be authorized to present their views and concerns in person."[477] The Court respects the accused's rights. However, the accused's rights grew in the period of time when there was no space for the victims' rights. Some are against this point of view, but it is reasonable to say that upon the emergence of the victims' rights, the applicability and scope of the accused's rights should be adapted. The constituent objective of the Court and its role for the victims are comparable to the ultimate goal of international humanitarian law. The spirit of international humanitarian law, in the ICC Trial Chamber's words, is to mitigate the suffering from armed conflict, irrespective of who suffers.[478] In a more general context, the Court intends to mitigate victims' suffering by recognizing their victimhood, and by giving them a voice.

1.2.2.1.1. The Victims' Participation Procedure

The first step in the victims' application process for the participation at the ICC's proceedings is "to conduct an effective outreach mission for the purpose of raising an understanding of the Court's mandate vis-à-vis victims."[479] The victims' participation as a voluntary action necessitates initiative by the victims. To take the initiative, victims need to be aware of such a right and mechanism. Such a mandate should be fulfilled by "the Public Information and Documentation Section of the Court, in light of its neutral role as institutional representative and promoter of the Court."[480]

Rule 89 of the Rules of Procedure and Evidence offers more insight into the procedure of the victims' participation in order to determine if they meet the statutory requirements for the purpose of participation. In order to present their views and concerns, "victims shall make written application to the Registrar, who shall transmit the application to the relevant Chamber." In addition, the Registrar shall "provide a copy of the application to the Prosecutor and the defense, who shall be entitled to reply

---

476 Ibid., para. 27.

477 ICC, Trial Chamber VI, Ntaganda case, Decision on the Request by the Legal Representative of the Victims of the Attacks for Leave to Present Evidence and Victims' Views and Concerns, 15 February 2017, para. 10.

478 See: ICC, Trial Chamber, Second Decision on the Defense's Challenge to the Jurisdiction of the Court in Respect of Counts 6 and 9, 4 January 2017.

479 ICC, PTC II, Ongwen case, Decision Establishing Principles on the Victims' Application Process, 4 March 2015, para. 10.

480 Ibid.

within a time limit to be set by the Chamber." Then, it is the Chamber that specifies "the proceedings and manner in which participation is considered appropriate, which may include making opening and closing Statements." In practice, the Registry assists the Chambers to assess the victims' application. The designation of the Registry to assess the victims' application under the supervision of the Chamber has been seen as "the most efficient and appropriate way to consider the applications."[481] In this modality, "the Chamber would set criteria for assessing victim applications. The Registry would then apply the criteria to each application received."[482] The applications that are incomplete "shall not be transmitted to the Chamber."[483] This wide role of the Registry contributes to the judicial economy of the Court that "expedites the processing of victims' applications and the trial proceedings generally, which is clearly in the interests of the victims and the parties."[484]

If a Chamber considers that the person who applied to present her or his views and concern is not a victim, his or her application would be rejected.[485] The Rome Statute is silent about the meaning of a victim, but Rule 85 of the Rules of Procedure and Evidence provides a definition of victims. The Rule recognizes two main kinds of victims, namely natural persons who "have suffered harm as a result of the commission of any crime within the jurisdiction of the Court", and organizations or institutions that "have sustained direct harm to any of their property which is dedicated to religion, education, art or science or charitable purposes, and to their historic monuments, hospitals and other places and objects for humanitarian purposes."[486]

The jurisprudence of the Court has made it clear that Rule 85 sets four criteria in order to obtain the status of victim: the victim must be a natural person; he or she must have suffered harm; the crime from which the harm ensued must fall within the jurisdiction of the Court; and there must be a causal link between the crime and the harm suffered.[487] The harm in the Rome Statute sense "does not necessarily have to be

481 ICC, Trial Chamber VI, Ntaganda case, Decision on Victims' Participation in Trial Proceedings, 6 February 2015, para. 32.

482 Ibid., para. 8.

483 ICC, Trial Chamber VIII, Al Faqi case, Decision on Victim Participation at Trial and on Common Legal Representation of Victims', 8 June 2016, para. 11.

484 Ibid., para. 33.

485 Rule 89(2) of the Rules of Procedure and Evidence.

486 The definition adopted by the Rules of the Procedure and Evidence stems from the UN Declaration on Basic Principles of Justice for Victims of Crimes and Abuse of Power. Article 1 of the Declaration reads "victims' means persons who, individually or collectively, have suffered harm, including physical or mental injury, emotional suffering, economic loss or substantial impairment of their fundamental rights, through acts or omissions that are in violation of criminal laws operative within Member States."

487 See ICC, PTC I, Situation in the DRC, Decision on the Applications for Participation in the Proceedings of VPRS 1, VPRS 2, VPRS 3, VPRS 4, VPRS 5 and VPRS 6, 17 January 2006, para. 79. And, ICC, Trial Chamber VIII, Al Faqi case, 8 June 2016, para. 17, see *supra* note 483. And, ICC, PTC II, Ongwen case, 4 March 2015, para. 43, see *supra* note 479. And, Pre-Trial Chamber I, Decision on Victims' Participation and Victims' Common Legal Representation at the Confirmation of Charges Hearing and in the Related Proceedings, 4 June 2012, para. 20. And, ICC, PTC II, Decision on Victims' Participation at the Confirmation of Charges Hearing and in the Related Proceedings, 26 August

direct."[488] A victim in the Rome Statute sense could be an indirect victim. Indeed, what is necessary is a personal harm but not necessarily a direct one.[489] Indirect victims "must establish that, as a result of their relationship with the direct victim, the loss, injury, or damage suffered by the latter gives rise to harm to them."[490] A perfect example here is the relatives of a deceased person. "a relative of a deceased person can only submit an application for participation in his or her own name, by invoking any mental and/or material harm suffered personally as a result of the death of said person."[491]

If an organization is going to qualify as victims, the organization will have to establish the following criteria: 1) its quality of organization/institution must be established; 2) the individual acting on behalf of the organization/institution must demonstrate his or her capacity to represent the organization; 3) the individual acting on behalf of the organization/institution must establish his or her identity; The organization/institution has suffered direct harm; and 4) the harm suffered is as a result of an incident falling within the parameters of the confirmed charges.[492]

The burden of proof of victimhood is upon victims. If someone claims that s(he) has suffered harm, it is her or his responsibility to prove it. In the authorization process, "the Applicants must demonstrate that there are grounds to believe that they have suffered harm as a result of a crime within the jurisdiction of the Court, such crime having allegedly been committed within the temporal and territorial limits of the relevant situation."[493] At this stage, the assessment of the conditions to obtain a victim status is rather lenient. For instance, as to the causal link, a Single Judge of the Court refers to the fact that there is no need to analyze the various theories on causality and it is sufficient to adopt "a pragmatic, strictly factual approach, whereby the alleged harm will be held as 'resulting from' the alleged incident when the spatial and temporal circumstances surrounding the appearance of the harm and the occurrence of the incident seem to overlap, or at least to be compatible and not clearly inconsistent."[494]

1.2.2.1.2. Participation in Situational Phase

The first opportunity for the victims to exercise their right to present their views and concerns under Article 63(3) of the Statute is the authorization process under Article 15.

2011, para. 40. ICC, PTC III, Fourth Decision on Victims' Participation, 12 December 2008, para. 30. ICC, Trial Chamber III, Decision on 772 Applications by Victims to Participate in the Proceedings, 18 November 2010, para. 38.

488 ICC, Appeals Chamber, Lubanga case, The Appeals of the Prosecutor and the Defense against Trial Chamber I's Decision on Victims' Participation of 18 January 2008, 11 July 2008, para. 1.

489 ICC, Trial Chamber VIII, Al Faqi case, 8 June 2016, para. 20, see *supra* note 483.

490 ICC, Trial Chamber I, Lubanga case, Decision on Indirect Victims, 8 April 2009, paras. 44–52.

491 ICC, Trial Chamber II, Grounds for the Decision on the 345 Applications for Participation in the Proceedings Submitted by Victims, 23 September 2009, para. 56.

492 ICC, Trial Chamber VIII, Al Faqi case, 8 June 2016, para. 23, see *supra* note 483.

493 ICC, PTC I, Situation in the DRC, 17 January 2006, paras. 99–100, see *supra* note 487.

494 Ibid., para. 14.

During this process, "victims may make representations in writing to the PTC."[495] In this moment, the personal interests of the victims may be affected, since victims' representations "can provide factual and legal elements for the decision to authorize the investigation into the situation within which the same victims claim to have suffered harm as a result of the commission of crimes."[496] The assessment of the personal interests of a victim to determine if are affected or not "requires careful consideration on a case-by-case basis."[497] It is so because the question is 'necessarily fact-dependent'.[498] However, the jurisprudence of the Court shows that the personal interest of the victims flows from: i) the desire to have a declaration of truth by a competent body (right to truth); ii) their wish to have those who victimized them identified and prosecuted (right to justice); and iii) the right to reparation.[499] Here, the right to truth plays a prominent role. The right to truth is to be satisfied if "the outcome of such proceedings: i) bring clarity about what indeed happened; and ii) close possible gaps between the factual findings resulting from the criminal proceedings and the actual truth."[500]

The victims' participatory right at the ICC is limited to the participation in the proceedings. The jurisprudence of the Court defines the proceedings as a stage in which the judges of the Court intervene. Therefore, the ambit of the prosecutorial activities in the preliminary examination is out of the victims' reach, except for the authorization process under Article 15. In January 2006, for the first time in the history of the Court, a PTC allowed individuals claiming to be victims to participate in the proceedings during the investigations phase. In June 2005, the International Federation for Human Rights had submitted a letter to the Registry informing that six victims intended to "to participate in the proceedings, be it at the investigation, trial or sentencing stage."[501] The PTC posed a question as to whether the core legal texts of the Court accord victims the right to participate in the proceedings at the stage of investigation of a situation.[502]

The Prosecutor of the Court had responded to the question negatively. The Prosecutor challenged the applicability of Article 68(3) of the Statute at this stage of proceedings by arguing 1) the word 'proceedings' referred to in Article 86.3 does not encompass the investigation of a situation; 2) participation of victims at the investigation stage is inappropriate; and 3) the personal interests of victims were not affected at the investigation stage.[503] The Chamber rejected all these arguments. The Chamber did not accept that there is a conceptual distinction between the proceedings and investigations

495 Rule 50(3) of the ICC Rules of the Procedure and Evidence.

496 ICC, PTC II, Uganda situation, 10 August 2007, paras. 90–92, see *supra* note 188.

497 ICC, Appeals Chamber, 13 June 2007, para. 28, see *supra* note 472.

498 ICC, Trial Chamber I, Lubanga case, 18 January 2008, para. 102, see *supra* note 488.

499 ICC, Abu Garda case, Decision on the 34 Applications for Participation at the Pre-Trial Stage of the Case, 25 September 2009, para. 3. See also ICC, Katanga and Chui case, Decision on the Set of Procedural Rights Attached to Procedural Status of Victim at the Pre-Trial Stage of the Case, 13 May 2008, paras 31-44.

500 ICC, Pre-Trial Chamber I, Katanga case, 13 May 2008, paras. 34–36, see *supra* note 499.

501 ICC, PTC I, Situation in the DRC, 17 January 2006, para. 19, see *supra* note 487.

502 Ibid., para. 22.

503 Ibid., para. 25.

as proposed by the OTP. Such a distinction is made only in Article 127[504], but "the Chamber considers that a general principle of interpretation of the Statute as a whole cannot be inferred from this single example."[505]

Consequently, the Chamber considered that "the term 'proceedings' does not necessarily exclude the stage of investigation of a situation."[506] Here, the Chamber added a teleological argument and gave considerations to the object and purpose of the victims' participation regime that grant "victims an independent voice and role in proceedings before the Court."[507] Indeed, the Chamber advocated the idea that the victims' voices should be heard independently from the Prosecutor. Regarding the appropriateness, the Chamber was of the opinion that "the participation of victims during the stage of investigation of a situation does not per se jeopardize the appearance of integrity and objectivity of the investigation, nor is it inherently inconsistent with basic considerations of efficiency and security."[508] In point of fact, the Chamber rejected the adverse impact of the victim's participation on investigations.[509]

As to the personal interests that should be met as a criterion to facilitate the victims' participation, the Chamber submitted that at the investigation stage, the personal interests of victims are affected in general, "since the participation of victims at this stage can serve to clarify the facts, to punish the perpetrators of crimes and to request reparation for the harm suffered."[510] Based on these arguments, the PTC accorded the status of victim to six victims allowing them to participate in the proceedings at the stage of investigation of the situation in the DRC. Later, the PTC's interpretation of the victims' participation in the situational phase appealed the Appeals Chamber's intervention. In 2007, in the context of the situation in the Congo, the Office of Public Counsel for the Defense appealed against a decision of PTC I. The appeal targeted "the existence of power, if any, to accord procedural status to victims with a view to participating in the Prosecutor's investigations in a situation."[511] The Single Judge of the PTC I had determined that it is feasible to accord procedural status to victims by treading along the path earlier mapped by the decision of the PTC of 17 January 2006.[512]

The Appeals Chamber examined the appeal and Stated that Article 68(3) that confers power upon a victim to participate in any 'proceedings' implies that "participation can take place only within the context of judicial proceedings."[513]

504 Article 127 (2): "its withdrawal shall not affect any cooperation with the Court in connection with criminal investigations and proceedings in relation to which the withdrawing State had a duty to cooperate…"

505 ICC, PTC I, Situation in the DRC, 17 January 2006, para. 37, see *supra* note 487.

506 Ibid., para. 38.

507 Ibid., para. 51.

508 Ibid., para. 56.

509 Ibid., para. 59.

510 Ibid., para. 63.

511 ICC, Appeals Chamber, Situation in the DRC, 19 December 2008, para. 1, see *supra* note 189.

512 Ibid., para. 2.

513 Ibid., para. 45.

The Appeals Chamber argued that 'proceedings' is a term "denoting a judicial cause pending before a Chamber." In contrast, "an investigation is not a judicial proceeding but an inquiry conducted by the Prosecutor into the commission of a crime with a view to bringing to justice those deemed responsible."[514] In addition, the Appeals Chamber argued that at the ICC legal system the authority for the conduct of investigations vests exclusively in the Prosecutor, and victims' participate in the investigation "would necessarily contravene the Statute by reading into it a power outside its ambit and remit."[515] However, the Appeals Chamber admitted that "victims are not precluded from seeking participation in any judicial proceedings, including proceedings affecting investigations", including presentation of their views and concerns under Article 15.3.[516] The Appeals Chamber, later, in the context of Situation in Darfur reaffirmed this view.[517] It seems that the Appeals Chamber is against the victims' participation in the situational phase. However, reading the PTC decision of 17 January 2006 in consistency with the subsequent decisions of the Appeals Chamber makes a compromise that in the investigation stage, the participation of victims is not granted, except for the process of authorization under Article 15(3), which is a judicial process in nature. The spread of the judicial intervention in the situational phase results in the extension of the victims' participation. Such a development in an institution that devotes special attention to victims is desirable.

For applying for the participation at the ICC's proceedings, the Prosecutor is requested to inform the victims of her intention to seek an authorization from the PTC to initiate an investigation, "unless the Prosecutor decides that doing so would pose a danger to the integrity of the investigation or the life or well-being of victims and witnesses."[518] The method of giving such a notice is determined by the Prosecutor. It could be done by "general means in order to reach groups of victims", if it does not pose any risk to the interests of victims.[519] For instance, in the context of the situation in Georgia, the Prosecutor issued a public notice on the Court's website, thereby informing victims of alleged war crimes and crimes against humanity committed in Georgia that she has requested authorization from PTC I to open an investigation.[520]

Following the Prosecutor's notification, victims have 30 days to present their views and concerns.[521] In order to observe the time limit, the Prosecutor shall notify the PTC

---

514 Ibid.

515 Ibid., para. 52.

516 Ibid., paras. 55–56.

517 ICC, Appeals Chamber, Judgment on Victim Participation in the Investigation Stage of the Proceedings in the Appeal of the OPCD Against the Decision of Pre-Trial Chamber I of 3 December 2007 and in the Appeals of the OPCD and the Prosecutor Against the Decision of Pre-Trial Chamber I of 6 December 2007, 2 February 2009.

518 Rule 50(1) of the ICC Rules of the Procedure and Evidence.

519 Ibid.

520 ICC, OTP, Public Notice of the ICC Prosecutor, 13 October 2015.

521 Regulation 50(1) of the Regulations of the Court.

of the date on which the information was provided.[522] Presenting views is voluntary.[523] It is a right that might be exercised by the victims. The Registry of the Court, its Victims Participation and Reparation Section (VPRS), is responsible to receive the views and concerns of the victims. Sometimes, the VPRS takes the initiative in a proactive manner to receive the victims' concerns. For instance, in the Georgia situation, the VPRS conducted a mission to Georgia "in order to help facilitate the Article 15 victim representation process by explaining, among other things: the role of victims in the process; how to complete and submit the representation form; and the importance of directly consulting victims."[524]

The manner and procedure in which the concerns and views of the victims should be brought to the attention of the PTCs are determined by the relevant Chamber. One factor that is considered in establishing the procedure for victims' representations is to ensure that the proceedings are carried out in an expeditious manner.[525] However, there is no one-size-fits-all procedure. In the Kenya situation, the PTC II requested the VPRS to conduct various functions, including identification of the community leaders of the affected groups to act on behalf of those victims who may wish to make representations, in addition to the receipt of victims' representations, assessment of the conditions set out in Rule 85 and, finally, summarizing victims' representations.[526]

Later, the PTC III, in the situation of Côte d'Ivoire rejected the procedure adopted in the Kenya situation by arguing that the previous approach would disproportionally delay the Chamber in resolving a request for authorization.[527] Therefore, the Chamber asked the VPRS to prepare a report based on the representations that were received and just "to undertake a *prima facie* assessment to ensure that only those representations emanating from sources who are potential victims within the meaning of Rule 85 of the Rules are sent to the Chamber."[528]

Based on the order issued by the Chambers, the VPRS makes a report and submits it to the requesting Chamber. These reports include the main views of victims and the reasons forming them. When the PTC evaluates the Prosecutor's request to issue an

---

522 Regulation 87(1) of the Regulations of the Court. For instance, in the situation of Côte d'Ivoire on 23 June 2011 the Prosecutor filed a request for the authorization. He indicated that he had notified the victims of his intention on 17 June 2011.

523 PTC in the situation of Kenya obliged the VPRS to "clarify in all activities and contacts with community leaders of affected groups or victims as referred to in paragraph 9 the purely voluntary nature of such possible representations in the context of Article 15(3) of the Statute, i.e. whether they wish to express their position on a possible investigation or not" (See: ICC, PTC II, Order to the Victims Participation and Reparation Section Concerning Victims' Representations Pursuant to Article 15(3) of the Statute, 10 December 2009, para. 10).

524 ICC, Registry, Report on the Victims' Representations Received Pursuant to Article 15(3) of the Rome Statute, 4 December 2015, para. 11.

525 ICC, PTC II, Côte d'Ivoire situation, Order to the Victims Participation and Reparation Section Concerning Victims' Representations Pursuant to Article 15(3) of the Statute, 6 July 2011, para. 6.

526 ICC, PTC II, Situation in Kenya, Order to the Victims Participation and Reparation Section Concerning Victims' Representations Pursuant to Article 15(3) of the Statute, 10 December 2009, para. 9.

527 ICC, PTC II, Côte d'Ivoire situation, 6 July 2011, para. 8, see *supra* note 525.

528 Ibid., para. 10.

authorization for opening a formal investigation into a situation, the VPRS's reports on the victims' representations are taken into account. It is not an authority or an accessory means to make a decision, but it is a legal obligation upon the judges to give considerations to the victim's views. PTC I, in its decision to authorize the participation of some victims in the situation in Congo, considered that Article 68(3) "imposes an obligation on the Court vis-à-vis victims... it is quite clear that the victims' guaranteed right of access to the Court entails a positive obligation for the Court to enable them to exercise that right concretely and effectively."[529] The VPRS in its report on the victims in the situation in Georgia, for instance, noted that 99% Of the 6,335 victim representations received wanted the Prosecutor to investigate the violence associated with the August 2008 conflict in the Situation in Georgia, while the 51 Georgian victims did not want the Prosecutor to be authorized to open an investigation.[530] According to the report, the opposing victims "cited security concerns, reluctance to revisit traumatic events, and doubt as to the likelihood of the Court process resulting in a personal benefit as the reasons why they were opposed to the Court intervention."[531]

In the situation of Kenya, the VPRS had issued another report briefing the victim's diverse views on opening an investigation and the reasons underlying those views. It was reported that the significant majority of the victims' representations advocated the authorization (383 persons out of 396 representations received), but nine victims disagreed, and four persons did not express their views in this regard.[532] The most frequently cited reasons to support the Court's investigation were deterrence of future violence, a lack of faith in the Kenyan justice system, and a general desire for justice to be done.[533] For opponents, on the contrary, there was no trust at the ICC.[534] Moreover, the victims' views are taken into account in the assessment of other statutory requirements. For instance, the PTC III, in its decision on the authorization of an investigation into the situation in Côte d'Ivoire, on many occasions documented its decision with the victims' presentations. It was done, for instance, to prove both the underlying acts and contextual elements of the alleged crimes.[535] Moreover, in the assessment of the situational admissibility in Kenya, the Chamber considered a wide range of information, including the report on victims' representations, saying that the victims observing that Kenyan authorities do not appear willing to investigate. Finally, based

529 ICC, PTC I, Situation in the DRC, 17 January 2006, para. 71, see *supra* note 487.

530 ICC, Registrar, Report on the Victims' Representations Received Pursuant to Article 15(3) of the Rome Statute, 4 December 2015, para. 21.

531 Ibid., para. 21.

532 ICC, Registrar, Situation in Kenya, Corrigendum to the Report on Victims' Representations and Annexes 1 and 5, 29 March 2010, para. 3.

533 Ibid., para. 4.

534 Ibid., para. 89.

535 For instance, Paragraph 110 of the decision reads "The Chamber has received representations from victims concerning offences of rape allegedly committed by pro-Ouattara forces during the period of post-election violence. One victim was allegedly raped by pro-Ouattara forces in Yopougon. Another victim reports rapes that allegedly occurred in Abidjan"; and "The Chamber has received representations from victims concerning the existence of an armed conflict in Côte d'Ivoire. Three collective representations refer to fighting in May 2011" (para. 126).

on such considerations, the PTC came to a conclusion that there were no national proceedings.[536]

1.2.3. Judicial Decision on the Prosecutor's Request

Upon examining of the Prosecutor's request and considering the victims' views, if the PTC determines that there is a reasonable basis to proceed with an investigation, "it shall authorize the commencement of the investigation."[537] The mandatory nature of authorizing the Prosecutor to initiate an investigation shows that upon making a determination that the statutory criteria are satisfied, there is no room for any judicial discretion to suspend an investigation. The situation selection is primarily determined by the Prosecutor, and the judges' role is limited to supervision and monitoring.

Parameters defining a situation are determined by the Prosecutor. However, in the authorization process, the Chambers can amend them. The PTC II, in its decision to authorize the Prosecutor to initiate an investigation in the Kenya situation, noticed that the temporal scope defined by the Prosecutor was too broad and thus explicitly asserted, "it is the responsibility of the Chamber to define the temporal scope of the authorization for investigation with respect to the situation under consideration."[538] To examine these parameters, the Chamber is committed to considering victims' views and concerns.

2. DECISION NOT TO OPEN AN INVESTIGATION

2.1. REJECTION OF COMMUNICATIONS

Upon conducting the preliminary examination, the Prosecutor may decide not to initiate an investigation. If the Prosecutor concludes that the information available does not provide a basis to initiate an investigation into a situation, the given situation does not reach the investigation stage. The question of inaction by the Prosecutor was only at the back of the minds of the drafters of the Statute, because they were more concerned about the emergence of an over-active prosecutor.[539] For this reason, the Statute is brief on this scenario.

Regarding communications, the only statutory obligation upon the Prosecutor when she decides not to open an investigation is to notify the communicators.[540] In respect

---

[536] ICC, PTC II, Kenya situation, 31 March 2010, para. 186, see *supra* note 41.

[537] Article 15(4) of the Rome Statute.

[538] ICC, PTC II, Kenya situation, 31 March 2010, para. 203, see *supra* note 41.

[539] Stahn, 2009, p. 270, see *supra* note 221.

[540] Rule 49(1): "where a decision under Article 15, paragraph 6, is taken, the Prosecutor shall promptly ensure that notice is provided, including reasons for his or her decision, in a manner that prevents any danger to the safety, well-being and privacy of those who provided information to his or her under Article 15, paragraphs 1 and 2, or the integrity of investigations or proceedings."

of communications, when the number of reports is considerable, public Statements are provided.[541] In this case, the Prosecutor issues a public Statement or response.[542] The main reason supporting the issuance of responses is to enhance transparency in the prosecutorial functions. Broad discretionary powers of the Prosecutor will be a problem if they are coupled with a non-transparent decision, since it may "distort confidence by individuals affected of communities."[543] The Prosecutor's notification must be given "in a manner that prevents any danger to the safety, well-being, and privacy of those who provided information."[544] The Rules of Procedure and Evidence requests the Prosecutor to refer to the reasons for her conclusion in the notification.[545] Indeed, the decision made upon such an emanation must be informed and well-reasoned.[546]

It is submitted that the purpose of the notification obligation is to empower the informant to hand over new information later that could amount to a reasonable basis to proceed.[547] The preliminary examination is preliminary in nature and, thus, is changeable in the future. It means that, as Article 53(4) provides, the Prosecutor may "at any time, reconsider a decision whether to initiate an investigation or prosecution based on new facts and information." The possibility of reexamination of a situation once happened in the situation in Iraq. In 2006, the then Prosecutor of the Court announced his decision not to initiate an investigation into the situation in Iraq and not to seek an authorization from the PTC for this purpose, due to the lack of gravity requirement that made the situation in Iraq inadmissible. However, later, in January 2014, the European Center for Constitutional and Human Rights together with Public Interest Lawyers provided the Prosecutor with new information on the responsibility of United Kingdom officials for war crimes involving systematic detainee abuse in Iraq from 2003 until 2008.[548] Consequently, the Prosecutor of the Court reopened the preliminary examination of the Situation in Iraq.

In some jurisprudences, victims have to be notified of a Prosecutor's decision not to prosecute in order to enable them to challenge such a decision before a court. This remedy is designed to reduce the risk of arbitrary decision-making.[549] Nevertheless, such an effect of the notification is absent from the Court's legal system. The drafters of the Rome Statute did not predict and establish a mechanism to challenge the Prosecutor's decision not to initiate an investigation. The only concern for the Court's founder was to make the Prosecutor accountable before the States. If the Prosecutor rejects a referral, she is responsive to the Chambers if a referring State makes a challenge. Legally speaking, however, the Prosecutor cannot be challenged by non-State

541 Schabas, 2010, p. 323, see *supra* note 26.
542 The OTP has issued two responses concerning Iraq and Venezuela on 9 February 2006 and one Statement on the situation of ISIS in 2015.
543 Stahn, 2009, p. 243, see *supra* note 221.
544 Rule 49(1) of the ICC Rules of the Procedure and Evidence.
545 Rule 105(3) and Rule 49(1) of the ICC Rules of the Procedure and Evidence.
546 ICC, OTP, Situation in the CAR I, 15 December 2006, para. 7, see *supra* note 299.
547 Olásolo, 2005, p. 62, see *supra* note 1.
548 ICC, OTP, Report on the Preliminary Examination Activities (2014), p. 42.
549 Stahn, 2009, p. 254, see *supra* note 221.

complainants. The Mavi Marmara situation proved that it is possible that the Prosecutor does not follow the demand of the international community even when a situation is referred by a State. In that case, in spite of the widespread reaction of the international community that uncovered the global impact of the situation, the Prosecutor decided not to open an investigation. The Prosecutor's negative decision was challenged and ultimately the PTC requested the Prosecutor to reconsider her decision.[550] It shows that the Prosecutor may make a wrong decision.

The ICTY has also witnessed the similar situations where the Prosecutor's decision sounds wrong, such as the NATO Bombing incident against the former Yugoslavia. While the established Committee recommended an investigation of the incident[551], the prosecutor decided not to open an investigation. However, the Prosecutor's decision was not subject to any judicial review. Therefore, nobody can assure that there is no probability of the abuse of power by the Prosecutor. Nonetheless, the founders of the Court just were concerned about the abuse of power in the form of Prosecutor's action, rather than inaction. The Prosecutor's power to activate the Court's jurisdiction on her own is a great development in the history of international criminal justice, though it is not complete yet. It should be completed by making the Prosecutor more accountable. Under Regulation 46(3) of the Regulations of the Court, there is a potential to extend the judicial review in order to cover the Prosecutor's decision not to initiate an investigation in case of communications. This was tried in the situation in Egypt. However, the Court did not accept this solution in the situation in question. It is evident that the judges of the Court tend to avoid spread their monitoring and supervisory function.[552] However, it is hoped that this negating tendency changes in the future. The ICC as a permanent organization enjoys a live legal system; a system that is open to new interpretations and changes. In the ICTY, prosecutorial discretion was initially considered as a virtue, but

550 See: ICC, PTC I, Situation on Registered Vessels of the Union of the Comoros, Decision on the Request of the Union of the Comoros to review the Prosecutor's Decision not to Initiate an Investigation, 16 July 2015.

551 ICTY, Final Report to the Prosecutor by the Committee Established to Review the NATO Bombing Campaign Against the Federal Republic of Yugoslavia, 13 June 2000, available at: www.icty.org/x/file/About/OTP/otp_report_nato_bombing_en.pdf.

552 In the case of granting 6 victims to participate in the situation in the DRC, the Prosecutor sought the leave of the PTC to appeals its decision. The Prosecutor appealed the decision of the PTC not to let him to make an appeal. In his submission, the Prosecutor argued that "the Appeals Chamber has jurisdiction to review the dismissal of his application for leave, notwithstanding the absence of express provision to that end in the Statute." Indeed, the Prosecutor contended that "the absence of mechanism for review of negative decisions under consideration cannot be regarded as anything other than a lacuna in the law." However, the Appeals Chamber dismissed the Prosecutor's approach to interpretation of the Rome Statute to define the scope of the judicial review. According to the Appeals Chamber, Article 82 "does not in terms confer power or competence on the Appeals Chamber to review a decision not stating a subject for appeal." It added, "Article 82 is included in Part 8 of the Statute dealing with appeals and matters incidental thereto. The decisions that are subject to appeal are enumerated in articles 81 and 82 of the Statute. There is nothing in Part 8 to suggest that a right to appeal arises except as provided thereunder." (See: ICC, Appeals Chamber, Judgment on the Prosecutor's Application for Extraordinary Review of Pre-Trial Chamber I's 31 March 2006 Decision Denying Leave to Appeal, 13 July 2006).

this status changed when it was viewed as an impediment to the expeditiousness of proceedings. Thus, it ultimately triggered the judicial intervention.[553]

In case of the ICC, such a shift in the judicial cautious and minimal supervision may be triggered if it is determined that the current practice may make the international community disappointed. "Transparency and judicial scrutiny do not conflict with prosecutorial independence."[554] On the contrary, they both help to have a stronger OTP by absorbing the trust of the international community.

2.2. REJECTION OF REFERRALS

Contrary to communications, the decision of the Prosecutor not to initiate an investigation regarding referrals is subject to judicial scrutiny. The very reason behind the Prosecutor's decision triggers the judicial review in different ways. If the decision of the Prosecutor is based on the Court's lack of jurisdiction or admissibility, the criteria enshrined in Article 53(1)(a) and (b), a request from the referring entity can trigger the judicial review.[555] The Prosecutor shoulders a notification obligation to enable the relevant States to make such a request.[556] The request, according to Rule 107(2), "shall be made in writing, and be supported with reasons, within 90 days following the notification given."[557] For conducting the review, the PTC "may request for the Prosecutor to transmit the information or documents in his or her possession."[558] The PTC may also seek further observations form the referring entities, the Sates or the UNSC.[559]

Moreover, where the issues of the jurisdiction or the admissibility of a case are raised, the PTC, according to Rule 107(5), considers the representations made by "the victims who have already communicated with the Court in relation to that case or their legal representatives." If the Prosecutor's decision is made solely based on Article 53, paragraph 1(c) i.e. when there is not a reasonable basis to initiate an investigation due to the lack of the interests of justice, the PTC should be promptly notified too.[560] The notification obligation is imposed because considering the victims' views are necessary in order to assess the admissibility requirement. As mentioned, the admissibility requirement consists of two elements, namely complementarity and gravity. The gravity standard encompasses some criteria, including the impact upon victims. Therefore, the views of victims play a prominent role in the judicial review on the Prosecutor's

553 Stahn, 2009, p. 240, see *supra* note 221.
554 Ibid., p. 280.
555 Article 53(3)(a) of the Rome Statute.
556 Article 53 (2)(c) of the Rome Statute.
557 Rule 105 (1): "When the Prosecutor decides not to initiate an investigation under Article 53, paragraph 1, he or she shall promptly inform in writing the State or States that referred a situation under Article 14, or the Security Council in respect of a situation covered by Article 13, paragraph (b)."
558 Rule 107(2) of the ICC Rules of the Procedure and Evidence.
559 Rule 107(4) of the ICC Rules of the Procedure and Evidence.
560 Rule 105(4) of the ICC Rules of the Procedure and Evidence.

decision about the admissibility requirement. The Court is intended to serve the interests of victims. The situation and case selection shall realize such a goal. The judges also have a responsibility to assure that the Prosecutor's discretion has been exercised in a way serving the interests of victims. For this reason, Judge Politi, in his decision on victims' application for participation in the Uganda Situation' says that Article 53 that numerated the legal criteria to select a situation and case is "the most significant scenario in which victims may be called upon to play a role, and possibly an influential one, outside the context of a case. This is in light of the concrete possibility that their personal interests would be affected by the decisions of the Prosecutor referred to in that article."[561]

In addition, Rule 92(2) provides that the victims should be notified "in order to allow victims to apply for participation in the proceedings." The recent notification shall be given to those "who have already participated in the proceedings or, as far as possible, to those who have communicated with the Court in respect of the situation or case in question."[562] Contrary to the admissibility and jurisdiction requirements that activate the judicial review in a passive way, if the decision made by the Prosecutor not to initiate an investigation is made solely on the basis of Article 53(1)(c), i.e. the lack of the interests of justice, the PTC may, on its own initiative, review the decision.[563] Undertaking a review by the PTC is a discretionary authority, given the language used in the Statute, i.e. using the term 'may' from Article 53. It should be noted that the *proprio motu* authority of the PTC to review the Prosecutor's declination does not negate the possibility of the referring entities to request such a review. In other words, the judicial review is an addition here.

It was mentioned that if the preliminary examination is conducted on the basis of communications, there is no provision in the Statute to endow the PTC with a scrutiny power if the Prosecutor decides not to initiate an investigation. However, the generality and absoluteness of Article 53(3)(b), which determines the scope of the PTC's authority to review the Prosecutor's decision not to initiate an investigation due to the lack of the interests of justice may include the non-referral situations as well. This broad interpretation of Article 53(3)(b) is consistent with both textual and teleological interpretive approaches. Textually, the wording of the paragraph is general and without any explicit exception and distinction between referrals and communications.[564] Teleologically, the reasons supporting the judicial review and control over the Prosecutor's discretion about the fate of referred situations support a broad interpretation extending the scope of the judicial review. Providing the PTC

561 ICC, PTC II, Uganda situation, 10 August 2007, para. 95, see *supra* note 188.

562 'Victims having communicated with the Court' means victims that, whilst not having (as yet) been allowed to participate in proceedings, have nevertheless been in contact with the Court (See ICC, PTC II, 10 August 2007, paras. 93–94, see *supra* note 188).

563 Article 53(3)(b) of the Rome Statute.

564 Article reads "the Pre-Trial Chamber may, on its own initiative, review a decision of the Prosecutor not to proceed if it is based solely on paragraph 1 (c) or 2 (c). In such a case, the decision of the Prosecutor shall be effective only if confirmed by the Pre-Trial Chamber."

with the authority to approve OTP-initiated investigations was insisted by the drafters of the Statute because they recognized the extremely strong political impact such investigations could have on international peace and security.[565] However, as Heller submits, "an unfounded refusal to investigate a situation can have a similar impact."[566] Both arbitrary prosecution and feckless and ineffective prosecution must be avoided by the judicial supervision.

If the Prosecutor's decision not to initiate an investigation is made according to Article 53(1)(a) and (b), i.e. given the jurisdiction or the admissibility requirement, the PTC "may request the Prosecutor to reconsider that decision."[567] According to Rule 108(2), the PTC may request the Prosecutor to review her decision partly or wholly and the Prosecutor "shall reconsider that decision as soon as possible." In this scenario, the PTC can request the Prosecutor to reconsider his decision, but it cannot force its decision upon the Prosecutor.[568] In other words, the PTC is not allowed to "substitute its own decision for that of the Prosecutor when it reviews an OTP declination."[569] Such limited authority has been justified in light of the institutional independence of the Prosecutor.[570] Nonetheless, the available remedy when the PTC disagrees with the Prosecutor's decision is completely unclear.[571] One can ask if the judicial determination is not of an obligatory nature, what is the function of designing such a mechanism? It can lengthen the proceedings. The judicial review mechanism realizes its constituent objectives if it operates in an effective manner.

If the Prosecutor's decision not to open a full investigation is made solely based on the lack of the interests of justice "the decision of the Prosecutor shall be effective only if confirmed by the PTC."[572] Only in the case of the PTC's confirmation, the Prosecutor "shall proceed with the investigation or prosecution."[573] In May 2013, the Government of the Union of the Comoros referred the situation with respect to the 31 May 2010 Israeli raid on the Humanitarian Aid Flotilla bound for Gaza Strip to the OTP. On 6 November 2013 the Prosecutor announced her decision that "the requirements for opening an investigation into the situation had not been met, and thus the conclusion of the preliminary examination."[574] The referring State objected the Prosecutor's decision. On 16 July 2015, the PTC I requested the Prosecutor to reconsider her decision. The Prosecutor appealed the decision, but the Appeals Chamber decided by majority to

565 Turone, 2002, p. 1142, see *supra* note 298.
566 Kevin Jon Heller, 'The Shadow Side of Complementarity: The Effect of Article 17 of the Rome Statute on National Due Process', *Criminal Law Forum*, 2006, vol. 17, p. 257.
567 Article 53(3)(a) of the Rome Statute.
568 Notburga K. Calvo-Goller, *The Trial Proceedings of the International Criminal Court*, Martinus Nijhoff Publishers, 2006, p. 160.
569 Bergsmo and Kruger, 2008, p. 1075, see *supra* note 297.
570 Stahn, 2009, p. 255, see *supra* note 221.
571 Schabas, 2010, p. 258, see *supra* note26.
572 Article 53(3)(b).
573 Rule 110(2) of the Rules of Procedure and Evidence.
574 See: ICC, Registered Vessels of Comoros, Greece and Cambodia, available at: www.icc-cpi.int/comoros.

dismiss the appeal, without discussing its merits.[575] At the time of writing this chapter, the situation in question is still awaiting the Prosecutor's revised decision to see if she follows the Chamber's advice or, by contrast, she insists on her initial decision.[576] The Prosecutor has announced that her Office is nearing completion of its review and will issue the Prosecutor's final decision under rule 108(3) in the "near future."[577]

575 ICC, Appeals Chamber, Decision on the admissibility of the Prosecutor's Appeal Against the Decision on the Request of the Union of the Comoros to Review the Prosecutor's Decision not to Initiate an Investigation, 6 November 2015.

576 ICC, OTP, Report on Preliminary Examination Activities 2016, para. 327.

577 Ibid., para. 331.

PART THREE
SITUATION SELECTION CRITERIA

In the previous part, the process of situation selection was studied. The current part addresses the situation selection criteria. Selection is the product of evaluation, and each evaluation is carried out on the basis of one or more criteria, if it is not going to be arbitrary. In the preliminary examination process, the Prosecutor of the Court selects a situation within an evaluative framework. This evaluative framework is composed of the criteria introduced by the Rome Statute. To select a situation, these statutory criteria should be taken into account by the Prosecutor. Article 53 of the Statute numerates the factors that direct the Prosecutor in the situation selection process. According to Article 53(1), the Prosecutor shall examine whether three conditions as follows have been met: jurisdiction, admissibility (which in itself encompasses two elements: complementarity and gravity) and the interests of justice presumption. The *ad hoc* tribunals did not have to select a situation but regarding the selection of a case they lacked such criteria to direct prosecutors to select a case. The tribunals' jurisdictions were limited to specified situations, but their prosecutors were almost free in selecting cases. Article 18 of the ICTY Statute, for instance, provided "the Prosecutor shall initiate investigations ex-officio or on the basis of information obtained from any source, particularly from Governments, UN organs, intergovernmental and non-governmental organizations. The Prosecutor shall assess the information received or obtained and decide whether there is sufficient basis to proceed." However, nowhere in the ICTY Statute was any insight into the notion of 'sufficient basis' offered. It was the prosecutorial discretion that determined if there was such a basis to proceed. Nonetheless, the Court's open mandates warranted the elaboration of the situation selection criteria in order to regulate the Prosecutor's powers. The Court operates selectively. Making a selection in an arbitrary manner and without transparency and consistency hurts the Court's legitimacy. Establishing the situation selection criteria was intended to avoid such an adverse consequence. In addition, preventing the emergence of a prosecutor with unfettered powers was another reason supporting the setting of some criteria for the situation selection.

At the ICC legal system, it is primarily the Prosecutor who decides when and where to intervene. Such independence has been considered as the strength of the Court and the basis for its legitimacy.[1] The long history of inaction and failure of States and the UNSC to take action in various situations of crisis encouraged the drafters of the Rome Statute to empower the Court's Prosecutor with a *proprio motu* power to initiate an investigation on her own. However, this power is not unfettered. The authority of the Prosecutor should be exercised within the ICC's legal framework. Upon conducting the preliminary examination, the Prosecutor shall determine whether the statutory parameters are met. A situation can be selected only if the Prosecutor, on a reasonable basis, believes that one or more crimes within the ICC's jurisdiction have been or are being committed, and the given situation is admissible by taking into account the

1 Luis Moreno-Ocampo, 'A Positive Approach to Complementarity: The Impact of the Office of the Prosecutor', in Carsten Stahn and Mohamed M. El Zeidy (eds.), *The International Criminal Court and Complementarity: From Theory to Practice,* Cambridge University Press, 2011, p. 23.

gravity and complementarity requirements. Finally, the Prosecutor needs to determine whether there is no substantial reason to believe that an investigation would not serve the interests of justice. These factors are cumulative, and the Prosecutor is obliged to consider all of them.[2] The situation selection includes prioritization, too. Practical considerations and operational factors should be taken into account to prioritize an available situation over other situations. In the situation selection process, the availability is a factor besides the admissibility requirement. Apart from these positive prerequisites to initiate an investigation, there are two negative conditions, which must be non-existent in the way of investigations: the substantial reasons that prove the Prosecutor's intervention do not serve the interests of justice, and the UNSC's request to suspend an investigation.[3] Under Article 16 of the Rome Statute, the UNSC is authorized to prevent the initiation of an investigation temporarily. In this scenario, the given situation, however, remains under preliminary examination awaiting the moment there is no bar for proceeding.

It is the authority and responsibility of the Prosecutor to make a determination on the foregoing criteria. This task is not limited to referrals made by the States or the UNSC, but also is applicable to communication sent by non-State actors. Rule 48 of the Rules of Procedure and Evidence provides "in determining whether there is a reasonable basis to proceed with an investigation under Article 15, Paragraph 3, the Prosecutor shall consider the factors set out in Article 53, Paragraph 1 (a) to (c)." According to the OTP Policy Paper on preliminary Examinations, the OTP has established a filtering process of three levels to regulate its mandate to conduct preliminary examination. Each level deals with a criterion. In Phase 2, the Court's jurisdiction is analyzed. Moreover, this phase seeks to identify potential cases of the situation at hand in order to assess the admissibility requirement in the next level.[4] Phase three focuses on the admissibility of potential cases in terms of complementarity and gravity under Article 17.[5] And, the last phase examines the interests of justice requirement.[6] This sequential process implies that each factor must be satisfied as a precondition to the next factor. Therefore, if the Court's jurisdiction over a case is not determined, there is no need to analyze the admissibility of the case. In the situation selection assessment, the point of departure for the selection of situations is the jurisdiction assessment. When there is no jurisdiction, there is no space for the Court's intervention.

---

2 Morten Bergsmo and Pieter Kruger, 'Article 53', in Otto Triffterer (ed.), *Commentary on the Rome Statute of the International Criminal Court*, C.H. Beck. Hart. Nomos, 2008, p. 1070.

3 Héctor Olásolo, *The Triggering Procedure of the International Criminal Court*, Martinus Nijhoff Publishers, 2005, p. 41. ICC, PTC III, Côte d'Ivoire Situation, Decision Pursuant to Article 15 of the Rome Statute on the Authorization of an Investigation into the Situation in the Republic of Côte d'Ivoire, 3 October 2011, para. 14.

4 ICC, OTP, Policy Paper on Preliminary Examinations, para. 81.

5 Ibid., para. 82.

6 Ibid., para. 83.

CHAPTER I
JURISDICTION

The first condition to initiate an investigation into a situation is to have jurisdiction. Articles 15(1) and 53(1) of the Rome Statute refer to the jurisdiction requirement. These articles entail that in order to select a situation for investigation the Prosecutor has to come to the reasonable belief that, at least, one crime within the ICC's jurisdiction has been committed. The law of jurisdiction is one of the most controversial fields in international law.[7] The term 'jurisdiction' has been defined by the ICC Appeals Chamber as denoting "the competence to deal with a criminal cause or matter under the Statute."[8] Jurisdiction is the domain of an entity's powers and authorities. As an international organization, there is no power for the ICC, unless such authority is explicitly or implicitly assigned to this institution. The Court's jurisdiction refers to those powers that have been defined for the Court. Every jurisdiction is based on an ultimate rule of recognition.[9] The mandate of jurisdiction is to recognize the powers of an institution. The jurisdiction notion has both empowering and restrictive aspects. From one side, jurisdiction denotes the extent of the Court's power and the scope of its competence to intervene. From the other, it highlights the domain that remains outside of the Court's power. It is indeed the negative aspect of the functional necessity principle that states beyond the necessary functions, there is no power at an organization's disposal.

1. THE COURT'S JURISDICTION BASIS

The ICC as a judicial institution has jurisdiction over the most serious international crimes. However, the possession of jurisdiction needs a legal basis. Even with the premise that there is no right to commit grave crimes, there is still a need for an

---

7 Cedric Ryngaert, *Jurisdiction in International Criminal Law*, Oxford University Press, 2008, p. 6.

8 ICC, Appeals Chamber, Judgment on the Appeal of Mr. Thomas Lubanga Dyilo Against the Decision on the Defense Challenge to the Court's Jurisdiction Pursuant to Article 19 (2)(a) of the Statute of 3 October 2006, 14 December 2006, para. 24.

9 Marc S. Groenhuisen and Antony Pemberton, 'Genocide, Crimes against Humanity and War Crimes: A Victimological Perspective on International Criminal Justice', in Rianne Letschert and Roelof Haveman and Anne-Marie de Brouwer and Antony Pemberton, *Victimological Approaches to International Crimes: Africa*, Intersentia, 2011, p. 13.

additional justification for outsiders to punish the perpetrators of serious crimes.[10] The seriousness of ICC crimes alone is not sufficient to justify and legitimize the Court's intervention. The Court's jurisdiction originates from the 'delegated jurisdiction theory'. International relations are still working based on the States' consent and will. Sovereign States can empower an organization. Jurisdiction and State sovereignty are intertwined. The authority of States to exercise their jurisdictions rests on their sovereignty.[11] Indeed, exercising jurisdiction is equivalent to exercising sovereignty.[12] The ICC as an international organization lacks any sovereignty. Consequently, it lacks any jurisdiction on its own. Nonetheless, the Court' jurisdiction has been delegated by its States Parties. The Court as a treaty-based judicial organization is empowered with criminal jurisdiction by those States that have agreed to delegate some parts of their sovereignty to this institution. There is no rule of international law prohibiting the territorial State from voluntarily delegating to the ICC their own sovereign ability to prosecute.[13] The ICC's jurisdiction could be portrayed as a delegated jurisdiction grounded both legally and morally in the undisputed jurisdictional authority of States.[14] The complementary jurisdiction of the Court should be understood in light of the delegated jurisdiction theory. States have authorized the Court to take action, but provided that they remain inactive.

To empower the Court through delegation, the delegating State should have jurisdiction first, and then the act of delegation is conducted in a valid way.[15] States can empower the Court with only those powers they enjoy on their own. This issue was mentioned in the Nuremberg Tribunal: "the signatory powers created this Tribunal, defined the law it was to administer and made regulations for the proper conduct of the Trial. In doing so, they have done together what any one of them might have done singly, for it is not to be doubted that any nation has the right thus to set up special courts to administer law."[16] All States have criminal jurisdiction, at least, over their whole territory and nationals. On this ground, they have equipped the Court with both personal and territorial jurisdictions. The act of delegation regarding the ICC is done through the ratification of the Rome Statute. The jurisdiction system at the ICC is

---

10 David Luban, 'Fairness to Rightness: Jurisdiction, Legality and the Legitimacy of International Criminal Law', in A. Besson and John Tasioulas (eds.), *The Philosophy of International Law*, Oxford University Press, 2010, p. 579.

11 Permanent Court of International Justice, The Case of the S.S. Lotus (No. 10), 7 September 1927, Para. 47.

12 Zhou Lulu, 'Brief Analysis of a Few Controversial Issues in Contemporary International Criminal Law', in Morten Bergsmo and Lung Yan (eds.), *State Sovereignty and International Criminal Law*, Torkel Opsahl Academic EPublisher, 2012, p. 43.

13 Sharon A. Williams and William A. Schabas, 'Article 12', in Otto Triffterer (ed.), *Commentary on the Rome Statute of the International Criminal Court*, C.H. Beck. Hart. Nomos, 2008, p. 557.

14 Antony Duff, 'Authority and Responsibility in International Criminal Law', in Samantha Besson and John Tasioulas (ed.), *The Philosophy of International Law*, Oxford University Press, 2010, p. 590.

15 Yuval Shany, 'In Defense of Functional Interpretation of Article 12(3)', in Chantal Meloni and Gianni Tognoni (eds.), *Is There a Court for Gaza? A Test Bench for International*, Asser Press, 2012.

16 Judgment: the Law of Charter, 30 September and 1 October 1946, available at www.avalon.law.yale.edu/imt/judlawch.asp, last accessed at 23 April 2017.

treaty-based.[17] It implies that the Court's jurisdiction does not embrace non-member States. By ratifying the Rome Statute, States agree to grant the Court jurisdiction over their citizens and territories with no further consent from States Parties.[18] This system is called 'automatic jurisdiction' mechanism. The ICC's jurisdiction is compulsory.[19] States are not allowed to reject the Court's jurisdiction over ICC crimes after joining the Rome Statute. Article 12(1) of the Rome Statute provides "a State which becomes a Party to this Statute thereby accepts the Court's jurisdiction with respect to the crimes referred to in Article 5."

The principle of 'automatic acceptance of jurisdiction' was absent from the ICL draft, which had contemplated an opt-in regime.[20] However, the initial draft changed. The current system showed that the 1998 ICC negotiations produced a stronger institution than it was originally anticipated.[21] Under the Rome Statute, there has been an exception to the general automatic jurisdiction mechanism. According to Article 124 of the Statute, a State may choose to opt-out of war crimes for an initial seven-year period on becoming a Party to the Statute.[22] This provision was included during a late stage of negotiations in the Rome Conference to ensure that France would support the Statute.[23] The reason was that France had a large number of soldiers as the peacekeeping forces across the world. In practice, Colombia and France are the only two States Parties that have made a declaration pursuant to Article 124. France withdrew its declaration before the end of the seven-year period and Colombia declaration ended on 31 October 2009.[24] This 'transitional' or 'opting out' clause was reviewed by the ASP in the Review Conference in 2010, since Article 124 had stated that "the provisions of this article shall be reviewed at the Review Conference convened in accordance with

---

17 Rod Rastan, 'Situations and Case: Defining the Parameters', in Carsten Stahn and Mohamed M. El Zeidy (eds.), *The International Criminal Court and Complementarity: From Theory to Practice*, Cambridge University Press, 2011, p. 428.

18 Yvonne Dutton, Rules, Politics and the International Criminal Court: Committing to the Court, Routledge, 2013, p. 12. Sharzad Fouladvand, Complementarity and Cultural Sensitivity: Decision-making by the ICC Prosecutor in relation to the Situation in the Darfur Region in Sudan and the Democratic Republic of the Congo, the Degree of Doctor of Philosophy, University of Sussex, 2012, p. 77.

19 Mohamed M. El Zeidy, 'Origin and Genesis of Complementarity', in Carsten Stahn and Mohamed M. El Zeidy (eds.), *The International Criminal Court and Complementarity: From Theory to Practice*, Cambridge University Press, 2011, p. 134.

20 William A. Schabas, *The International Criminal Court: A Commentary on the Rome* Statute, Oxford University Press, 2010, p. 284.

21 Dutton, 2013, p. 14, see *supra* note 18.

22 Article 124: "Notwithstanding Article 12, paragraphs 1 and 2, a State, on becoming a party to this Statute, may declare that, for a period of seven years after the entry into force of this Statute for the State concerned, it does not accept the Court's jurisdiction with respect to the category of crimes referred to in Article 8 when a crime is alleged to have been committed by its nationals or on its territory. A declaration under this article may be withdrawn at any time."

23 Melissa K. Marler, 'The International Criminal Court: Assessing the Jurisdictional Loopholes in the Rome Statute', *Duke Law Journal*, 1999, vol. 49, p. 834.

24 Christopher Hall, 'Positive Complementarity in Action', in Carsten Stahn and Mohamed M. El Zeidy (eds.), *The International Criminal Court and Complementarity: From Theory to Practice*, Cambridge University Press, 2011, p. 1039.

Article 123, Paragraph 1." The States in the Kampala Conference, having reviewed the provisions of Article 124, decided "to retain Article 124 in its current form", but they decided to "further review the provisions of Article 124 during the fourteenth Session of the ASP to the Rome Statute."[25] In November 2015, and during the plenary meeting of the ASP, the States adopted a Resolution in which Article 124 was deleted from the Rome Statute.[26] However, the amendment will enter into force in accordance with Article 121(4) of the Rome Statute, which provides that the ratification of the amendments by seven-eighths States is necessary.[27]

2. THE NECESSITY OF JURISDICTION'S SATISFACTION

To activate the Court's jurisdiction over a specific situation or case, the Court shall first satisfy that it has jurisdiction over the situation or the case in question.[28] Every international court "has power to determine its own jurisdiction, even when there is no explicit provision to that effect."[29] Such authority is enshrined in the 'competence-competence' doctrine. It is a general principle that a tribunal is empowered to make a determination as to its own jurisdiction to deal with the substantive claims in dispute.[30] According to the ICTR Appeals Chamber, "the International Tribunal can and indeed has to exercise its '*compétence de la compétence*'."[31] In spite of its inherent authority, Article 19 of the constituent instrument of the ICC provides "the Court shall satisfy itself that it has jurisdiction in any case brought before it."

25 ICC, ASP, Official Records of Review Conference of the Rome Statute of the International Criminal Court Kampala (31 May – 11 June 2010), page 76.

26 ICC, ASP, Resolution ICC-ASP/14/Res.2, available at: www.treaties.un.org/pages/ViewDetails.aspx?src=TREATYandmtdsg_no=XVIII-10-candchapter=18andclang=_en, last accessed at 23 April 2017.

27 By 2017, only five States ratified the amendment, including Finland, Netherlands, Norway, Portugal and Slovakia.

28 The PTC II in its Decision on the Prosecutor's Application under Article 58 to issue an arrest warrant against Ntaganda submitted that "an initial determination as to whether the case against Mr. Ntaganda falls within the ICC's jurisdiction is a prerequisite for the issuance of warrant of arrest against him" (See: ICC, PTC II, its Decision on the Prosecutor's Application under Article 58 to Issue an Arrest Warrant against Ntaganda, 13 July 2012, Para. 7).

29 ICC, PTC III, Bemba case, Decision on the Prosecutor's Application for a Warrant of Arrest against Jean-Pierre Bemba Gombo, 10 June 2008, para. 11. And, ICC, Decision on the Prosecutor's Application for Summonses to Appear for Francis Kirimi Muthaura, Uhuru Muigai Kenyatta and Mohammed Hussein Ali, 8 March 2011, para. 8. And, ICC, PTC II, Bemba case, Decision Pursuant to Article 61(7)(a) and (b) of the Rome Statute on the Charges of the Prosecutor against Jean-Pierre Bemba Gombo,15 June 2009, para. 23.

30 Herbert Smith Freehills, The Competence-Competence Doctrine and the Enforcement of Arbitral Awards, January 2011, available at: www.lexology.com/library/detail.aspx?g=70303764-71b7-4352-babb-6c8c8d399190.

31 ICTY, Tadić Case, Decision on the Defense Motion for Interlocutory Appeal on Jurisdiction, 2 October 1995, para. 19.

The Rome Statute obliges the Court to 'satisfy' itself that it has jurisdiction. To get satisfied entails that "the Court must attain the degree of certainty."[32] However, the degree of such certainty differs in each stage. In the situational stage and during the preliminary examination process, determinations are preliminary in nature. It implies that these decisions are subject to a change. Given this fact, in the investigation's authorization and the arrest warrant's decisions, the Chambers have submitted that their satisfaction that the Court has jurisdiction over the case or situation brought before them is without prejudice to a subsequent determination.[33] However, Judge Kaul believes the Court's jurisdiction assessment is not "subject to the progressively higher evidentiary thresholds which apply at the different stages of the proceedings", because "the Court either has jurisdiction or does not."[34] Although it is true that the Court's jurisdiction is a static matter, the jurisdiction's determination is dynamic. The jurisdiction assessment is fact-oriented. In each stage, the available facts and information increase that may result in a change in the initial determinations. In addition, repeating the jurisdiction's examination indicates the importance of having jurisdiction at the ICC's functioning.

3. TYPES OF JURISDICTION

Four categories of jurisdiction have been recognized by the Rome Statute, namely subject matter (the crimes that can be investigated and prosecuted), temporal (time frame for the commission of crimes), territorial (where the crimes are committed) and the active personal jurisdiction (individuals who are accountable before the Court). In other words, the OTP through preliminary examination has to examine (a) whether the alleged crimes are those defined under the Rome Statute (jurisdiction *ratione materiae)*; (b) whether the alleged crimes were committed after the entry into force of the Rome Statute (jurisdiction *ratione temporis)*, and (c) whether the crimes were committed in the territory of a State Party or by a national of a State Party to the Rome Statute.[35] Article 53 refers only to the subject-matter jurisdiction by providing that there must be reasonable basis that a crime within the ICC's jurisdiction has been committed. However, this provision must be interpreted in connection with Article 19(1) that is worded in a general style, and provides: "the Court shall satisfy itself that it has jurisdiction in any case brought before it." Therefore, the Prosecutor and Chambers

32 ICC, Decision on the Prosecutor's Application for Summonses to Appear for Francis Kirimi Muthaura, Uhuru Muigai Kenyatta and Mohammed Hussein Ali, 8 March 2011, para. 9.

33 For instance, see: ICC, PTC II, Warrant of Arrest for Raska Lukwiya, 8 July 2005, para. 26. And, ICC, PTC II, Kenya situation, Decision Pursuant to Article 15 of the Rome Statute on the Authorization of an Investigation into the Situation in the Republic of Kenya, 31 March 2010, para. 74.

34 ICC, PTC II, Dissenting Opinion by Judge Hans-Peter Kaul in Decision on the Confirmation of Charges Pursuant to Article 61(7)(a) and (b) of the Rome Statute, 23 January 2012, para. 26.

35 ICC, PTC III, Bemba case, 10 June 2008, para. 12, see *supra* note 894. And, ICC, PTC II, Decision on the Prosecutor's Application under Article 58 to issue an Arrest Warrant against Ntaganda, 13 July 2012, para. 8.

have to examine not only the subject-matter jurisdiction of the Court, but they should determine other kinds of jurisdiction, too. As PTC II states, limiting the Chamber only to assess the subject-matter jurisdiction "would amount to an absurd conclusion, because it excludes an examination of other jurisdictional requirements, the existence or absence of which would directly impact on the Chamber's determination of whether to authorize the commencement of an investigation."[36]

3.1. SUBJECT-MATTER JURISDICTION

Subject-matter jurisdiction refers to the crimes under the Court's jurisdiction. Initially, crimes fallen within the ICC's jurisdiction were not specified. The first draft Statute for the ICC, submitted in 1951 by the Committee on International Criminal Jurisdiction, merely provided that that '[t]he Court shall apply international law, including international criminal law, and where appropriate, national law'.[37] However, ICC crimes were finally defined. The drafters of the Rome Statute added four crimes to the Court's jurisdiction. These crimes, as referred to in Article 5 of the Statute, are the crime of genocide, crimes against humanity, war crimes and the crime of aggression. The Court's jurisdiction over crimes against humanity, war crimes, and genocide was actual from the beginning of the Court's operation. However, the Court's jurisdiction over the crime of aggression has remained potential. Article 5 of the Rome Statute has numerated the crime of aggression as one of the crimes under the Court's jurisdiction. However, this crime had been left without any definition and effect in the 1998 Statute. Article 5(2), deleted in 2010, had stated "the Court shall exercise jurisdiction over the crime of aggression once a provision is adopted in accordance with articles 121 and 123 defining the crimes and setting out the condition under which the Court shall exercise jurisdiction with respect to this crime." Three provisions were adopted in the Kampala Review Conference in 2010 to define the crime of aggression in the Rome Statute. The definition of aggression is in Article 8*bis*, while the conditions under which the Court may exercise jurisdiction are set out in Articles 15*bis* and 15*ter*. Article 8*bis*, adopted by Resolution RC/RES.6 in June 2010, defines the crime of aggression as "the planning, preparation, initiation or execution, by a person in a position effectively to exercise control over or to direct the political or military action of a State, of an act of aggression which, by its character, gravity and scale, constitutes a manifest violation of the Charter of the United Nations." However, the exercise of the Court's jurisdiction over this crime, according to Article 15*ter* (3), is subject to "a decision to be taken after 1 January 2017"; a decision that has not been made yet. Therefore, at the time of writing this thesis, the crime of aggression is still a potential crime within the ICC's jurisdiction.

---

[36] ICC, PTC II, Kenya situation, 31 March 2010, para. 36, see *supra* note 33.

[37] Article 2 of the Report of the Committee on International Criminal Jurisdiction on its Session Held from 1 to 31 August 1951, Draft Statute for an International Criminal Court, UN Doc A/2136 (1952).

The scope of the ICC subject-matter jurisdiction is not static. The permanency of the Court warrants the possibility of adding new crimes or criminal acts to the Court's jurisdiction as a live institution. The history of the Court has once witnessed such an extension. In the Kampala Review Conference, the use of poisonous gases and bullets causing excessive suffering as a war crime in the context of the international armed conflict provisions was extended to non-international armed conflicts.[38] Legally speaking, such an extension is possible in the future.

The crimes within the ICC's jurisdiction are considered as the most serious crimes of concern to the international community as a whole. ICC crimes share a collective character that distinguishes them from ordinary crimes.[39] This collectivity refers to both perpetrators and victims. International criminality has been aptly referred to as 'system criminality'.[40] It means that international crimes are mainly committed on a system level.[41] It is mainly a criminal State or an armed organization that is responsible for the commission of the core crimes. In addition, the international crimes' victims have a collective nature, too. It means that they are mainly targeted as members of a group, rather than individuals. This collectivity results in massive victimhood. Compared to the conventional crime, there are a larger number of victims of the crimes under the Court's jurisdiction.[42] In addition, the warfare development has resulted in destructive effects. In the modern armed conflicts, for instance, the phenomenon of 'civilization of warfare' has emerged. The notion refers to the sharp increase in the number of civilian and non-combatant victims within the conflicts.[43] The collective nature of victims of international crimes aggravates the culpability of the perpetrators as well.[44] The massiveness of ICC crimes and their unique features have been enshrined in the contextual elements of ICC crimes that distinguish them from ordinary crimes.

ICC crimes are composed of two components, namely contextual and specific elements.[45] Specific element of crimes refers to the underlying acts that constitute the substance of a crime such as killing, rape, and pillage. This part of ICC crimes is almost equal to ordinary crimes that largely exist in national criminal laws. What transforms ordinary crimes into international crimes is the context in which the international crimes are committed. The contextual element "elevates the acts concerned, which otherwise would fall exclusively under the responsibility of national jurisdictions,

---

38 ICC, ASP, Amendment to Article 8, Resolution RC/Res.5 adopted at the 12th Plenary Meeting, 10 June 2010.

39 Robert Sloane, *The Expressive Capacity of International Punishment*, Columbia Public Law and Legal Theory Working Paper, 2006, p. 21.

40 Elies Van Sliedregt, 'International Criminal Law', in Markus D. Dubber and Tatjana Hornle (eds.), *The Oxford Handbook of Criminal Law*, Oxford University Press, 2014, p. 1151.

41 Jann K. Kleffner, *Complementarity in the Rome Statute and National Criminal Jurisdiction*, Oxford University Press, 2008, p. 2.

42 Groenhuisen and Pemberton, 2011, p. 12, see *supra* note 9.

43 Ibid., pp. 9 and 10.

44 Sloane, 2006, p. 3, see *supra* note 39.

45 CC, PTC I, Lubanga case, Decision on the Prosecutor's Application under Article 58, 10 February 2006, para. 80.

to international crimes and sets aside considerations of State sovereignty."[46] The contextual elements of ICC crimes were studied in Part One of this thesis, and this section just addresses the jurisdictional effects of ICC crimes' contexts.[47]

Both specific and contextual elements have a jurisdictional effect on the Court's functioning. In the assessment of the jurisdiction, the Chambers first assess the contextual element of crimes to determine whether there are reasonable grounds to believe that the contextual element of at least one crime within the ICC's jurisdiction is present.[48] Only if this question is answered in the affirmative, the Chamber turns "its attention to the question of whether the specific elements of any such crime have occurred."[49] The absence of the contextual element results in the non-existence of the Court's jurisdiction in whole or in part. It is the factual context of a crisis that confines the temporal, territorial and personal jurisdiction of the Court. Therefore, it is possible that within a territory the Court exercises its jurisdiction but limited to specific groups and areas. For instance, the OTP, upon receiving some communications, decided to open a preliminary examination into the situation in Nigeria in November 2010. The information received had contained a series of allegations against different groups across the various regions of Nigeria, including central and northern parts and in the Niger Delta. Nonetheless, by conducting a preliminary examination, the Prosecutor concluded that there was only the situation related to Boko Haram that embraces one or more crimes falling within the ICC's jurisdiction, including the crimes against humanity, and in particular the crimes of murder and persecution on religious grounds.[50] Although it was evident that there were some criminal behaviors in other parts of Nigeria that were committed by other groups, due to the lack of the relevant contextual element, the Prosecutor concluded that it did not appear that ICC crimes were committed in the central and northern parts.[51] The preliminary examination as to the situation of Boko Haram continued. Upon the new developments monitored by the Court, the OTP updated its subject-matter assessment, and declared that since May 2013, crimes occurring in the context of the conflict between Boko Haram and Nigerian Security forces had amounted to war crimes in internal armed conflicts.[52] Indeed, when the Nigerian Government increased its operations against Boko Haram,

46 ICC, PTC II, Dissenting Opinion by Judge Hans-Peter Kaul in Decision on the Confirmation of Charges Pursuant to Article 61(7)(a) and (b) of the Rome Statute, 23 January 2012, para. 32.

47 See: Part One, Chapter II, Section 2.2.

48 ICC, PTC I, Harun and Kushayb case, Decision on the Prosecutor's Application under Article 58(7), 27 April 2007, para. 29.

49 ICC, PTC I, Decision on the Evidence and Information Provided by the Prosecution for the Issuance of a Warrant of Arrest for Germain Katanga, 6 July 2007, para. 26. And ICC, PTC I, Al Bashir case, Decision on the Prosecution's Application for a Warrant of Arrest against Omar Hassan Ahmad Al Bashir, 4 March 2009, para. 53.

50 ICC, OTP, Report on Preliminary Examination Activities, November 2013, para. 209.

51 Ibid., para. 208.

52 ICC, OTP, Speech of Mrs. Bensouda, Seminar Hosted by the Attorney General of the Federation and Minister of Justice of Nigeria, 24 February 2014 p. 11, available at: www.icc-cpi.int/iccdocs/otp/SpeechProsecutor-AbujaNigeriaFra.pdf). And, OTP Report on Preliminary Examination Activities (2014), para. 192.

an armed conflict between the State forces and Boko Haram as an armed organization was formed. By emerging this new context, the Court extended its jurisdiction to war crimes.[53]

Sometimes, the lack of the subject-matter jurisdiction arises from the absence of one factor of the contextual elements, rather than the lack of the entire context. For instance, an armed group is a component of the contextual element constituting war crimes in a non-international armed conflict. Hence, the absence of such a group bars the occurrence of war crimes in this sense.[54] In this regard, the situation in Colombia is an example. The OTP has recognized that in Colombia there has been 50 years of violent conflict between government forces, paramilitary armed groups and rebel armed groups, as well as amongst those groups that constitutes a non-governmental armed conflict.[55] In the context of this internal war, the OTP determined that there were some armed groups that could be considered parties to the ongoing non-international armed conflict in Colombia, including the Urabenos, the Rastrojos, and the Aguilas Negras. However, the Prosecutor believed that the Court would exercise jurisdiction only over the crimes committed by Urabenoses, because it was the only group that sufficiently organized to meet the war crimes' jurisdictional threshold.[56]

Besides the contextual element of crimes, the specific element of ICC crimes should be in place if the Court intends to exercise its jurisdiction. The absence of specific elements in whole or in part bars the formation of crimes. Without a crime, there is no jurisdiction for the Court to intervene. The jurisprudence of the Court has affirmed that the constitutive elements of ICC crimes can be invoked to challenge the Court's jurisdiction. For instance, in the context of the situation in Kenya, the Defense of Ruto and Sang challenged the Court's jurisdiction. They argued the level of organization and structure in which the defendants had allegedly orchestrated the crimes charged did not reach the requisite level to meet the threshold criteria of crimes against humanity punishable under Article 7 of the Rome Statute.[57] According to the defense, the organizational policy requirement that is requested by the Rome Statute was absent. The PTC dealing with the case in its decision on the confirmation of charges affirmed that the Chamber must first rule on said challenges before proceeding with an examination on the merits of the case.[58] Judge Kaul in his dissenting opinion confirmed that this statement means that the majority appeared to acknowledge that

---

53 For the latest status of the situation of Boko Haram in Nigeria see: ICC, OTP, Report on Preliminary Examination Activities, November 2016.

54 In the Lubanga case, the PTC stated that for the purpose of the Rome Statute, the armed groups should have the ability to plan and carry out military operations for a prolong period of time (See: ICC, PTC I, Lubanga case, Decision of the Confirmation of Charges, 29 January 2007, para. 234).

55 ICC, OTP, Report on Preliminary Examination Activities, November 2015, para. 139.

56 ICC, OTP, Report on Preliminary Examination Activities, November 2013, paras. 124–130.

57 ICC, Rute Case, Defense Challenge to Jurisdiction, 30 August 2011, para. 1.

58 ICC, PTC II, Ruto case, Decision on the Confirmation of Charges Pursuant to Article 61(7)(a) and (b) of the Rome Statute, 23 January 2012, Para. 28.

this issue may qualify as a jurisdictional challenge.[59] According to the dissenting Judge, any issue of interpretation, which may affect the applicability of the contextual elements, falls entirely within the 'jurisdiction test', including the organizational policy requirement.[60]

The most recent instance in this regard is the Ntaganda case. Ntaganda was charged with, *inter alia*, war crimes of rape and sexual slavery of child soldiers fighting in his own forces. The accused challenged the subject-matter jurisdiction of the Court before the Trial Chamber VI with respect to these counts. He argued that Article 8(2)(e)(vi) of the Statute does not foresee the possibility of child soldiers who are members of the same armed group as the accused being victims of the war crimes of rape and sexual slavery.[61] Later, the Trial Chamber rejected Ntaganda's challenge.[62] This decision was appealed by the accused. The Appeals Chamber affirmed that Ntaganda's challenge was jurisdictional, and remanded the matter back to Trial Chamber VI, because "challenges, which would, if successful, eliminate the legal basis for a charge on the facts alleged by the Prosecutor may be considered to be jurisdictional challenges."[63] In January 2017, the Trial Chamber re-examined the challenge and found that it has jurisdiction over alleged war crimes of rape and sexual slavery of child soldiers and rejected the Defense's challenge.[64]

Another instance in which the non-existence of a constituent element of ICC crimes resulted in the rejection of the Court's jurisdiction is the situation in the Republic of Korea. In December 2010, upon receiving a number of communications, the OTP opened a preliminary examination on the situation pertaining to two incidents that occurred in 2010 in the Yellow Sea. These incidents included the sinking of a South Korean warship and the shelling of South Korea's Yeonpyeoong Island.[65] The communications received by the OTP charged South Korea with the commission of war crimes. The OTP, in its assessment determined that the fundamental contextual element needed to establish the commission of a war crime, namely the existence of an armed conflict was met in the situation of the South Korea, because there was an international armed conflict between North Korea and South Korea.[66] However, the

59 ICC, PTC II, Ruto case, Dissenting Opinion by Judge Hans-Peter Kaul in Decision on the Confirmation of Charges Pursuant to Article 61(7)(a) and (b) of the Rome Statute, 23 January 2012, para. 30.

60 Ibid., para. 31.

61 ICC, Ntaganda case, Application on Behalf of Mr Ntaganda Challenging the Court's Jurisdiction in Respect of Counts 6 and 9 of the Document Containing the Charges, 1 September 2015, para. 8–13.

62 ICC, Ntaganda case, Reply on Behalf of Mr Ntaganda to Prosecution Response to the Application on Behalf of Mr Ntaganda Challenging the Court's Jurisdiction in Respect of Counts 6 and 9 of the Documents Containing the Charges, 24 September 2015.

63 ICC, Appeals Chamber, Judgment on the Appeal of Mr. Bosco Ntaganda Against the Decision on the Defense's Challenge to the Court's Jurisdiction in Respect of Counts 6 and 9, 22 March 2016, p. 3.

64 ICC, Press Release, Ntaganda case: ICC Trial Chamber VI Rejects Challenge to Jurisdiction over Two War Crimes Counts, 4 January 2017, available at: www.icc-cpi.int/Pages/item.aspx?name=PR1267, last accessed at 24 April 2017.

65 ICC, OTP, Report on the Preliminary Examination Activities (2013), para. 104.

66 Ibid., para. 111.

OTP did not recognize the commission of war crimes in the context of this war. War crimes are against the protected groups. The Rome Statute permits belligerents to carry out "military operations against military targets, even when it is known that some civilian death or injury will occur."[67] In the South Korea situation, according to the information available to the OTP, the attacks were perpetrated only against the military targets.[68] Because of the lack of this constitutive element of war crimes, in June 2014, the OTP finalized its analysis of whether there would be a reasonable basis to believe that a crime within the ICC's jurisdiction had been committed, and announced that there was not such a basis to believe that either incident constitutes a crime within the ICC's jurisdiction.[69]

3.2. TEMPORAL JURISDICTION

The temporal aspect of the Court's jurisdiction was absent initially from the ILC draft. The 1994 draft only included the principle of legality. Later, in the 1996 Report of the Preparatory Committee on the Establishment of an ICC, it was proposed that the temporal jurisdiction of the ICC should be limited to crimes committed after the entry into force of the Statute.[70] Based on this development, Article 11(1) of the Rome Statute states, "the Court has jurisdiction only with respect to crimes committed after the entry into force of this Statute." Temporal jurisdiction must be distinguished from the legality principle (*Nullum Crimen Sine Lege* principle).[71] The former is a procedural rule that might bar the Court from exercising its jurisdiction over a situation or case, but the latter is a substantive rule that prevents a retroactive criminalization. According to Article 22(1) of the Rome Statute, "a person shall not be criminally responsible under this Statute unless the conduct in question constitutes, at the time it takes place, a crime within the ICC's jurisdiction." Under the Rome Statute, a conduct should be considered a crime, even if it had been a permitted act under the perpetrator's national law.[72]

The legality principle has an important implication, namely the non-retroactivity principle. The principle has enshrined in Article 24(1) of the Rome Statute that states "no person shall be criminally responsible under this Statute for conduct prior to the entry into force of the Statute." Contrary to the predecessors of the Court, which mostly had faced the problem of the legality principle, the ICC has stayed out of this trouble,

---

67 Ibid., para. 112.

68 Ibid., para. 113.

69 ICC, OTP, Report on the Preliminary Examination Activities (2014), para. 244.

70 Stephane Bourgon, 'Jurisdiction Ratione Personae', in Antonio Cassese, Paola Gaeta and John R.W.D. Jones (eds.), *The Rome Statute of the International Criminal Court: A Commentary*, Oxford University Press, 2002, p. 547.

71 Sharon A. Williams, 'Article 11', in Otto Triffterer (ed.), *Commentary on the Rome Statute of the International Criminal Court*, C.H. Beck. Hart. Nomos, 2008, p. 539. And, Schabas, 2010, p. 273, see *supra* note 61.

72 Notburga K. Calvo-Goller, *The Trial Proceedings of the International Criminal Court*, Martinus Nijhoff Publishers, 2006, p. 189.

because the Rome Statute has established a prospective jurisdiction. The ICC is only authorized to prosecute those crimes committed after the Rome Statute came into force. Non-retroactive application of international legal instruments is a recognized principle of international law codified by the 1969 Vienna Convention on the Law of Treaties. According to Article 28 of the Convention, "unless a different intention appears from the treaty or is otherwise established, its provisions do not bind a party in relation to any act or fact which took place or any situation which ceased to exist before the date of the entry into force of the treaty with respect to that party."

Under the Rome Statute, the temporal jurisdiction of the Court is strictly prospective.[73] The entry into force of the Rome Statute is the starting point to exercise the Court's jurisdiction. This date for those states that become a party to the Statute after 2 July 2002 is relative. Article 126(2) that provides: "for each State ratifying, accepting, approving or acceding to this Statute after the deposit of the 60th instrument of ratification, acceptance, approval or accession, the Statute shall enter into force on the first day of the month after the 60th day following the deposit by such State of its instrument of ratification, acceptance, approval, or accession." For instance, On 2 January 2015, the Government of Palestine acceded to the Rome Statute by depositing its instrument of accession with the UNSG. According to Article 126, the Statute entered into force for the State of Palestine on 1 April 2015.[74]

However, the temporal jurisdiction of the Court is extensible with respect to those States Parties joining later to the Court. These states are able to extend the Court's jurisdiction beyond the entry into force of the Statute for them. Article 11(2) provides "if a State becomes a Party to this Statute after its entry into force, the Court may exercise its jurisdiction only with respect to crimes committed after the entry into force of this Statute for that State, unless that State has made a declaration under Article 12, Paragraph 3." This provision was once used by Uganda. The Republic of Uganda ratified the Rome Statute on 14 June 2002. Therefore, the Statute would have entered into force on the following 1 September. However, the Ugandan authorities lodged the 'Declaration on Temporal Jurisdiction' in February 2004.[75] The declaration served the purpose of extending the temporal scope of the Prosecutor's investigation to 1 July 2002. The extending effect of the declaration of acceptance operates even if a State first lodges an declaration of acceptance, and then joins the Court. The Government of Palestine, for instance, first lodged a declaration under Article 12(3) accepting the jurisdiction of ICC over the alleged crimes committed in the occupied Palestinian territory since 13 June 2014, on 1 January 2015. Later, Palestine became a member of the ICC starting on 1 April 2015. However, the Court's jurisdiction over Palestine remained intact, i.e. since 13 June 2014.

---

73 Bourgon, 2002, p. 548, see *supra* note 70.

74 UN, United Nation Treaty Collection, Depositary Notification of Accession to the Rome Statute by the State of Palestine, available at www.treaties.un.org/doc/Publication/CN/2015/CN.13.2015-Eng.pdf, last accessed at 23 April 2017.

75 ICC, PTC II, Ongwen case, Warrant of Arrest for Ongwen, 8 July 2005, para. 20.

In addition to States Parties, non-member States also have the right to accept the Court's jurisdiction by lodging an declaration of acceptance under Article 12(3). The article reads: "if the acceptance of a State which is not a Party to this Statute is required under Paragraph 2, that State may, by declaration lodged with the Registrar, accept the exercise of jurisdiction by the Court with respect to the crime in question." A question may be raised here. Do such declarations possess a retroactive effect? Zimmermann believes that declarations under Article 12(3) do not possess automatically retroactive effect.[76] He supports his idea with some reasons. Firstly, given Article 28 of the Vienna Convention on the Law of Treaties, there is a general presumption of non-retroactivity of treaties. In accordance with this article, "unless a different intention appears from the treaty or is otherwise established, its provisions do not bind a party in relation to any act or fact which took place or any situation which ceased to exist before the date of the entry into force of the treaty with respect to that party."

Secondly, the necessity of the coherency and consistency in the Statute as a whole implies that the declarations of acceptance do not possess retroactive effects. Article 11(2) provides that a State becomes a party to the Statute after its entry into force would be under the Court's jurisdiction after the entry into force of the Statute with respect to that State "unless that State has made a declaration under Article 12, Paragraph 3." Therefore, there must be a consistency between becoming a State Party and lodging an 'declaration of acceptance'. As joining to the Court after 2002 does not possess a retroactive effect automatically, accepting the Court's jurisdiction by lodging a declaration should not possess such a necessary effect. This is the reason that Article 12 of the Rome Statute uses the same wording for both non-member States and States Parties, namely 'acceptance'. This wording implies that the effects of the ratification of the Statute and the declaration of acceptance, mutatis mutandis, are the same. Consequently, the declaration of acceptance necessarily does not have a retroactive effect.

Nonetheless, it is possible that a State endows its declaration of acceptance with a retroactive effect. The acceptance of the Court's jurisdiction is consent-based. It is the right of a State to accept the existing jurisdiction of the Court retroactively. What can be proved from the Zimmermann's arguments is that such a declaration does not retroact automatically, but it can have such an effect. The case law of the ICC proves this possibility. Côte d'Ivoire, for instance, lodged an declaration of acceptance on 18 April 2003, thereby accepting the Court's jurisdiction with regard to acts committed on its territory since events of 19 September 2002. The PTC in its decision on the authorization of an investigation into the situation in Côte d'Ivoire concluded that "the Court has jurisdiction over crimes allegedly committed in Côte d'Ivoire since 19 September 2002."[77]

---

76 See: Andreas Zimmermann, 'Palestine and the International Criminal Court Quo Vadis?', *Journal of International Criminal Justice*, 2013, vol. 11, pp. 303–329.

77 ICC, PTC III, Situation in Côte d'Ivoire, 3 October 2011, para. 15, see *supra* note 3.

The temporal jurisdiction of the Court is compulsory. This is a general rule applicable to all situations irrespective of the trigger which bring them to the attention of the Prosecutor. The principle of non-retroactivity is established by the Rome Statute, and it includes the UNSC's referrals. However, the UNSC's referrals can have an effect like declarations of acceptance, and extend the Court's jurisdiction from the referral's date to the entry into force date of the Rome Statute. In referring the situation in Darfur in 2005, for instance, the UNSC's Resolution referred the situation since 1 July 2002.[78] However, the UNSC is not authorized to change this jurisdictional limitation of the Court.

During the first years of the establishment of the Court, the temporal jurisdiction had an important role in preliminary examination. It was because there was an emerging system for seeking accountability, and many intended to benefit from this opportunity to bring the past atrocities to justice. Nonetheless, the absence of the temporal jurisdiction barred many instances from entering the upper stages at the ICC. For instance, in the situation in Venezuela, the then Prosecutor, upon conducting preliminary examination, decided not to initiate an investigation. He supported his decision with some reasons, including the non-existence of the temporal jurisdiction. According to the Prosecutor, "a considerable number of the allegations referred to incidents that are alleged to have taken place prior to 1 July 2002, in particular in connection with incidents occurring in the context of the short-lived coup in April 2002. These events occurred prior to the temporal jurisdiction of the Court and cannot be considered as the basis for any investigation under the Statute."[79]

Contrary to the statutory confine of the commencement of the Court's jurisdiction, there is no ending point for the Court's operations. The ICC is an institution with open-ended mandates. This unique feature of the Court is the reason for non-applicability of statute of limitation in the Rome Statute.[80] If a crime is committed within the temporal jurisdiction of the Court, it will remain under its jurisdiction as long as the Court is in place. The delay in investigation or prosecution is not a bar in the exercise of the Court's jurisdiction, because the situation and case selection at the ICC depends on a wide range of factors, legal and operational, that may lengthen the process of the initiation of an investigation or prosecution. Perpetrators of international crimes should know that the prospect of prosecution before the ICC will not go down.

The main test to determine the temporal scope of a situation is the relevant crisis that makes a context within which a situation is formed. In its decision on the authorization of an investigation into the Kenya situation, the PTC II stated that the temporal scope of the investigation should be confined to the date of the Prosecutor's request, "since this was the last opportunity for the Prosecutor to assess the information available to him prior to its submission to the Chamber's examination."[81] However, this approach

78 See: UNSC, Resolution 1593, 2005, para 1.

79 ICC, OTP, Response to Communications Received concerning Venezuela, 9 February 2006.

80 Article 29 of the Rome Statute: "The crimes within the ICC's jurisdiction shall not be subject to any statute of limitations."

81 ICC, PTC II, Kenya situation, 31 March 2010, para. 207, see *supra* note 33.

came under criticism. Placing the Prosecutor's request as the end line of a situation may ignore the continuing crimes, which go beyond the Prosecutor's request date.[82] In the situation in Côte d'Ivoire, PTC III adopted a different stance. The Chamber did not see a need for setting an end-date to the temporal scope of the authorised situation, since the Court faced a 'volatile environment', which had the potential to re-escalate.[83] Given the existing circumstances, the Chamber submitted that "crimes that may be committed after the date of the Prosecutor's application will be covered by any authorisation, insofar as the contextual elements of the continuing crimes are the same as for those committed prior to 23 June 2011."[84]

This test is also applied to define the commencement of an investigation. For this reason, while the Prosecutor had requested to open an investigation in the situation of Côte d'Ivoire since 28 November 2010, the Chamber obliged the Prosecutor to revert to the Chamber with any additional information on potentially relevant crimes committed between 2002 (when a crisis emerged in Côte d'Ivoire) to 2010. The Chamber argued that HRW's reports as well as the victims' representations had provided indications of human rights violations committed since 2002.[85] On 3 November 2011, the Prosecutor provided further information regarding potentially relevant crimes committed between 2002 and 2010. Finally, the Chamber expanded its authorization for the investigation in Côte d'Ivoire "to include crimes within the ICC's jurisdiction allegedly committed between 19 September 2002 and 28 November 2010."[86]

3.3. TERRITORIAL JURISDICTION

The ICC has no universal jurisdiction. Universal jurisdiction is an idea arising from the Grotius School. Grotius had asserted that every State has jurisdiction over "gross violations of the law of nature and of nations, done to other states and subjects."[87] According to this principle of jurisdiction, it is permissible for states to exercise jurisdiction over some special crimes without any nexus with those crimes. Traditionally, the only consensus that the international community had reached about the exercise of universal jurisdiction was that any State may exercise its universal jurisdiction over acts of piracy that would occur on the high seas.[88] However, over time, the number of crimes falling within the universal jurisdiction has increased. Recently, legislators as well as theorists have returned to Grotius's 'moralized' rationale, and

82 See: Rod Rastan, 'The Jurisdictional Scope of Situations before the International Criminal Court', *Criminal Law Forum*, 2012, vol. 23, pp. 20–23.

83 ICC, PTC III, Situation in Côte d'Ivoire, 3 October 2011, para. 179, see *supra* note 3.

84 Ibid.

85 Ibid., paras. 182–185.

86 ICC, PTC III, Decision on the Prosecution's Provision of Further Information Regarding Potentially Relevant Crimes Committed Between 2002 and 2010, 22 February 2012, para. 37.

87 Hugo Grotius, The Rights of War and Peace, Including the Law of Nature and of Nations, M. Walter Dunne, 1901, p. 247.

88 Lulu, 2012, p. 42, see *supra* note 12.

have proposed universal jurisdiction over those crimes that are subject to international tribunals, including the ICC.[89] The core crimes are not only against a specific state's interests, but are considered as crimes against humanity as a whole. Therefore, the prosecution of these crimes falls within the interests of all states, and there is a right for them in this regard. Nonetheless, the proposal of empowering the Court with universal jurisdiction was not accepted in the Rome Conference. In the preparatory process, the issue of the Court's jurisdiction proved to be among the most controversial issues.[90] Germany proposed that the ICC should be authorized with universal jurisdiction since all states may exercise universal jurisdiction over genocide, crimes against humanity and war crimes.[91] However, several states, in particular the U.S., rejected the idea, and alternatively insisted on a regime in which the consents of both the State of nationality of the accused as well as the State of the territory wherein an offence occurred would be required.[92]

What was inserted at the end into the Rome Statute as a compromise between various ideas was a kind of jurisdiction that is called by some scholars 'the reasonable jurisdiction'.[93] Reasonable jurisdiction authorizes states to exercise their jurisdiction if a nexus between crimes and the state's territory or nationals is established. At the ICC legal system, territorial and personal jurisdictions are alternative to each other. The Court can exercise either territorial jurisdiction or personal jurisdiction.

A State has jurisdiction over all matters arising in its territory.[94] Such authority is called 'territorial jurisdiction'. This jurisdiction has received universal recognition.[95] Territorial jurisdiction is a manifestation of State sovereignty.[96] It implies that a State has the normative power to prescribe criminal prohibitions, which are binding on every person who is, for whatever reason, on its territory.[97] Based on such authority, the States Parties have delegated their territorial jurisdiction to the Court. Article 12 is the central legal source respecting the territorial jurisdiction in the Rome Statute. According to

---

89 Luban, 2010, p. 571, see *supra* note 10.

90 Michail Vagias, *The Territorial Jurisdiction of the International Criminal Court*, Cambridge University Press, 2014, p. 51.

91 The proposal made by Germany at the United Nations Diplomatic Conference of Plenipotentiaries on the Establishment of an International Criminal Court, 15 June – 17 July 1998, (UN Doc A/AC.249/1998/DP.2).

92 See: Amendments proposed by the United States of America at the United Nations Diplomatic Conference of Plenipotentiaries on the Establishment of an International Criminal Court, 15 June – 17 July 1998, (UN Doc. A/CONF.183/C.1/L.70).

93 Ryngaert, 2008, p. 37, see *supra* note 7.

94 Martin Dixon, *International Law*, Oxford University Press, 2007, p. 146.

95 Christopher Kip and James P. Bair (eds.), *International Due Process and Fair Trial Manual*, ABA Center for Human Rights, 2014, p. 77.

96 Williams and Schabas, 2008, p. 556, see *supra* note 13. And, Malcolm N. Shaw, *International Law*, Cambridge University Press, 2003, p. 579. And, Robert Cryer, *Prosecuting International Crimes: Selectivity and the International Criminal Law Regime*, Cambridge University Press, 2005, p. 75. And, Jo Martin Stigen, *The Relationship Between the International Criminal Court and National Jurisdictions: the Principle of Complementarity*, Brill Nijhoff, 2008, p. 15.

97 Alejandro Chehtman, 'Jurisdiction', in Markus D. Dubber and Tatjana Hornle (eds.), *The Oxford Handbook of Criminal Law*, Oxford University Press, 2014, p. 405.

Article 12(2)(a), "the State on the territory of which the conduct in question occurred or, if the crime was committed on board a vessel or aircraft, the State of registration of that vessel or aircraft" has accepted the Court's jurisdiction.

In the Rome Statute, the territorial jurisdiction is an alternative to universal jurisdiction. Indeed, the inclusion of territoriality in the Rome Statute may be read as an indication that the international enforcement of universal human values remains intertwined with traditional State consent doctrine.[98] In 1958, Birely had asserted that jurisdiction over war crimes 'has no territorial basis'.[99] Many years later, what was adopted by the Rome Statute was a step backwards. Contrary to Birely's belief, the Rome Statute established its jurisdiction mainly on the territorial basis. As one of the commentators of the Rome Statute asserts, "the *ratione loci* jurisdiction of the Court is another example that its establishment is closely linked to a compromise between State sovereignty and the needs of international justice."[100]

3.3.1. *The Priority of Territorial Jurisdiction*

Legally speaking, the satisfaction of one of territorial or personal jurisdictions is sufficient to enable the Court to exercise its jurisdiction. However, in practice, the Court prioritizes the territorial jurisdiction. By 2017, all situations under the Court's investigation were based on the territorial jurisdiction of the Court. So far, only in the situation in Iraq has the nationality of the suspects been the basis for asserting the Court's jurisdiction.[101] In addition, in the jurisdiction assessment, the Chambers examine first the territorial jurisdiction. For instance, in the Kenya situation, the PTC asserted that "an affirmative finding on the basis of jurisdiction *ratione loci* in relation to the crimes allegedly committed on the territory of the Republic of Kenya consequently precludes the need to consider jurisdiction *ratione personae*."[102] Such a chronology is deductible from Article 12(2) when it gives precedence to the territorial jurisdiction by putting it in Paragraph (a). Under the territorial jurisdiction, the ICC has jurisdiction regardless of the nationality of the accused, if a crime is committed by a person in the territory of a State Party.[103]

The territorial principle is often considered as the primary basis of jurisdiction over crimes.[104] Article 8 of European Convention on the Transfer of Proceedings in Criminal Matters reads "territorial jurisdiction is widely held to be the strongest and primary basis for jurisdiction." Legally speaking, there is no hierarchy between the

98 Vagias, 2014, p. 282, see *supra* note 90.
99 James Brierly, 'The Nature of War Crimes', in James Leslie Brierly and Hersch Lauterpacht and Claud Humphrey Meredith Waldock, *The Basis of Obligation in International Law and Other Papers*, Clarendon Press, 1958, p. 304.
100 Bourgon, 2002, p. 560, see *supra* note 70.
101 See: ICC, the Situation in Iraq, available at: www.icc-cpi.int/iraq.
102 ICC, PTC II, Kenya situation, 31 March 2010, para. 65, see *supra* note 33.
103 Bourgon, 2002, p. 562, see *supra* note 70.
104 Ibid., p. 567.

jurisdictional principles. However, as a rule, one can say that the State Party with a weaker nexus to crimes should give way to the exercise of jurisdiction by a State Party with a stronger nexus.[105] There are more practical benefits when the jurisdiction is exercised based on the territorial principle. For instance, the Court may have the advantage of the territorial state's cooperation. The territorial State will almost, due to the proximity to the crime, have the best access to testimonies and evidence.[106] In addition, if the Court exercises its jurisdiction merely based on the nationality of offenders, the Court will face some difficulties to have an equal treatment to all parties involved in the conflict, and it can hurt its impartiality. It is possible that some perpetrators from certain nationalities remain out of the Court's jurisdiction. By contrast, if the territorial jurisdiction is the basis for the Court's jurisdiction, the Court can exercise its jurisdiction in respect of alleged ICC crimes committed by any nationals on the territory involved.

It should be noted that the territorial jurisdiction is merely one parameter in forming a situation in the Rome Statute. When the Court is dealing with a situation it does not necessarily mean that the entire territory of the affected State is under the Court's investigation. A situation is a context-oriented notion. In the situation and case selection processes, only those parts of a territory are brought under investigation that are substantially linked with the context of the situation at hand. The Appeals Chamber of the Court, for instance, in the case of Al-Senussi noted that some incidents had taken place in cities other than Benghazi, but Al-Senussi was "only alleged to be responsible for crimes committed in Benghazi." Therefore, in the complementarity assessment of the case in question, the Appeals Chamber stated that "it is irrelevant to show that the Libyan investigation covers crimes allegedly committed in cities other than Benghazi."[107]

3.3.2. The Scope of Territorial Jurisdiction

The Rome Statute explicitly extends the territorial jurisdiction of the Court to crimes committed on board of a vessel, registered by a flag State that is a State Party to the Court. According to Article 94 of the United Nations Convention on the Law of the Sea, 1982, the flag State (i.e., the State in which the ship is registered) shall generally have jurisdiction over ships.[108] In the case law of the Court, there is an example in this respect. The government of the Union of the Comoros, which is a State Party to the ICC, referred a situation to the Court in 2013, in connection with the crimes allegedly committed by the Israeli Defense Forces in May 2013 on the board of the Mavi Marmara

105 Kleffner, 2008, p. 280, see *supra* note 41.
106 Stigen, 2008, p. 21, see *supra* note 96.
107 ICC, Appeals Chamber, Al-Senussi case, Judgment on the Appeal of Mr Abdullah Al-Senussi Against the Decision of Pre-Trial Chamber I of 11 October 2013 Entitled Decision on the Admissibility of the Case against Abdullah Al-Senussi, 24 July 2014, para. 107.
108 Article 94 (1) of the UN Convention provides that "Every State shall effectively exercise its jurisdiction and control in administrative, technical and social matters over ships flying its flag."

vessel in international waters.[109] Based on this referral, the Prosecutor identified a situation entitled "registered vessels of Comoros, Greece and Cambodia." Following the preliminary examination, on 6 November 2014 the Prosecutor of the Court concluded that "the legal requirements under the Rome Statute to open an investigation have not been met", and the preliminary examination was closed.[110] The Prosecutor's decision was challenged by the Union of Comoros before the PTC I. Eventually, the Chamber requested the ICC Prosecutor to reconsider her decision.[111]

The scope of the territorial jurisdiction is not clearly defined by the Rome Statute either. Article 12(1)(a) refers to 'the State on the territory of which the conduct in question occurred'. However, it is questionable when the conduct in question occurs. There are two approaches to this jurisdictional question. Some believe that the conduct occurs on the territory of a state, if it begins on the same territory (subjective territorial). However, others argue that for the occurrence of the conduct on a territory, it is sufficient that one constituent element of the conduct or its consequences and effects occur on the territory of one state, even if the conduct was started in another State outside of the Court's jurisdiction (objective/ubiquity territorial).[112]

In the Working Group on the Crime of Aggression this jurisdictional question was raised that "given that the conduct of a leader responsible for the crime of aggression would typically occur on the territory of the aggressor state", whether "the crime could also be considered to be committed whether its consequences were felt, namely the territory of the victim state."[113] There were some suggestions to resolve this issue. For instance, it was suggested that Article 12 should be amended in a way that "the notion of conduct in Article 12, Paragraph 2 (a) of the Statute encompasses both the conduct in question and its consequence."[114] In addition, there was a view that the issue was best left for determination by the Court itself.[115] Finally, Article 12 remained untouched and opened for interpretation. Now, it is the Court that should determine "whether Article 12(2)(a) Rome Statute can be interpreted broadly so as to accept the Court's

109 See: ICC, Situation on Registered Vessel on the Comoros, Referral under Articles 14 and 12(2)(a) of the Rome Statute Arising from the 31 May 2010 Gaza Freedom Flotilla Situation, 14 May 2013, available at: www.icc-cpi.int/iccdocs/otp/Referral-from-Comoros.pdf.

110 ICC, OTP, Statement of the Prosecutor of the International Criminal Court, Fatou Bensouda, on Concluding the Preliminary Examination of the Situation Referred by the Union of Comoros: "Rome Statute legal requirements have not been met", available at: www.icc-cpi.int/en_menus/icc/press%20and%20media/press%20releases/Pages/otp-statement-06-11-2014.aspx.

111 ICC, Press Release, Pre-Trial Chamber I Requests Prosecutor to Reconsider Decision not to Investigate Situation referred by Union of Comoros, 16 July 2015, available at: www.icc-cpi.int/en_menus/icc/press%20and%20media/press%20releases/Pages/PR1133.aspx.

112 For more information about the kinds of territorial jurisdiction see: Vagias, 2014, see *supra* note 90.

113 ICC, ASP, Assembly of States Parties, Report of the Special Working Group on the Crime of Aggression, Seventh Session of the Assembly of States Parties.

114 ICC, ASP, Report of the Special Working Group on the Crime of Aggression, 9–13 February 2009, para. 38.

115 Ibid., para. 39.

jurisdiction when a crime is committed in part in State Party territory or has effects there."[116]

Rastan concludes that it has commonly been accepted that it is necessary and sufficient that one constituent element of the act or situation has been consummated in the territory of the State that claims jurisdiction.[117] Indeed, a crime is committed within the territory of a State whether in whole or in part of its territory. A crime is committed 'in whole' within the territory when every essential constituent element is consummated within the territory, and it is committed 'in part within the territory' when any essential constituent element is consummated there.[118] If it is committed either in whole or in part within the territory, there is territorial jurisdiction. According to the ubiquity rule, an offense as a whole may be considered to have been committed in the place where a part of it has been committed.[119]

3.4. PERSONAL JURISDICTION

International law permits a State to exercise jurisdiction over its nationals if they commit a crime outside of the territory of that state. This kind of personal jurisdiction is called 'active personal jurisdiction'. Active personal jurisdiction is a kind of extraterritorial jurisdiction.[120] The main argument in favor of the active personal nationality is its role in ending impunity. It is typical that an offender returns to his home country after committing an offense abroad in order to avoid justice in the territorial state. Since extradition laws in many States prohibit the extradition of nationals, the only way to administer justice is the exercise of personal jurisdiction.[121]

In addition to active personal jurisdiction, there is the 'passive personality'. Under passive personality, a State would have jurisdiction over all crimes where the victim is its national, irrespective of the nationality of the offender and place where the crime is committed. This principle is a further extension of the idea that every national is entitled to the diplomatic protection of his own state.[122] However, in the 1930s, the Harvard Draft Restatement on jurisdiction rejected the lawfulness of the passive personality principle, and it has remained controversial.[123] The Rome Statute recognizes only the active personal jurisdiction. According to Article 12(2)(b), if the person accused of the crime is a national of a State Party to the Rome Statute, the Court's jurisdiction may

116 Vagias, 2014, p. 85 see *supra* note 90.

117 Rod Rastan, 'Jurisdiction', in Carsten Stahn (ed.), *The Law and Practice of the International Criminal Court*, Oxford University Press, 2015, p. 167.

118 Harvard Law School's Research, 'Draft Convention on Jurisdiction with Respect to Crime', *American Journal of International Law*, 1935, vol. 29, p. 495.

119 Council of Europe, European Committee on Crime Problems, 'Extraterritorial Criminal Jurisdiction', *Criminal Law Forum*, 1999, vol. 3, p. 446.

120 Chehtman, 2014, p. 406, see *supra* note 97.

121 Ibid., p. 408.

122 Dixon, 2007, p. 152, see *supra* note 94.

123 Cryer, 2005, p. 78, see *supra* note 96.

be exercised. It is said that creating jurisdiction based on the nationality was the least controversial form of jurisdiction during the Rome Conference.[124]

The ICC has jurisdiction over the nationals of its States Parties. Indeed, the States have delegated their own criminal jurisdiction over their nationals to the Court. It means that the Court lacks jurisdiction over the nationals from non-member States. It stems from the treaty nature of the Rome Statute that in the normal course of events does not apply to the third states. The rejection of the German proposal suggesting universal jurisdiction for the Court has been seen as the first objection to the idea of jurisdiction of the Court over non-States Parties.[125] However, there are some exceptions. First, if non-member States' nationals commit ICC crimes on the territory of a State Party, the territorial jurisdiction of the Court embraces them as well. The US was not in agreement with this exception, because it sought an absolute immunity for the non-member States. The U.S. insisted on a regime, which would require the consent of both the State of nationality of the accused as well as the State of territory where the offence occurred.[126] This proposal was, however, dismissed. Secondly, in the case of UNSC referral or when a State lodges an 'declaration of acceptance' under Article 12(3)(b) of the Rome Statute, the nationals of referred or accepting State will be prosecutable by the Court.

The personal jurisdiction of the Court has a restriction. According to Article 26 of the Rome Statute, the Court has no jurisdiction over any person who was under the age of 18 at the time of alleged commission of a crime. This limitation is jurisdictional in nature, because there is no prohibition and restriction on the criminal responsibility for crimes committed by persons under the age of 18, neither conventional nor customary.[127] In addition, the Court's jurisdiction is limited to natural individuals. Legal persons are outside of the Court's reach.

3.4.1. *The Vital Role of the Nationality Principle in Ending Impunity*

Personal jurisdiction is of great help for the ICC to end impunity in the absence of territorial jurisdiction. When international crimes are committed on the territory of a State that is not a member to the ICC, the personal jurisdiction could be a breach into the given situation that otherwise would be protected from the Court's intervention. It is understandable that a State that is not willing to join the ICC is more likely to commit the most serious crimes. If a State is not subject to the violation of the humanitarian and human rights law, it at least signs the Rome Statute to show its solidarity with the Court's objectives. Here, the Prosecutor is committed to shatter the impunity by all powers at her disposal. Personal jurisdiction is one of these effective and legal instruments that

---

124 Schabas, 2010, p. 286, see *supra* note 20.

125 Kleffner, 2008, p. 275, see *supra* note 41.

126 See: Amendments proposed by the United States of America at the United Nations Diplomatic Conference of Plenipotentiaries on the Establishment of an International Criminal Court (UN Doc. A/CONF.183/C.1/L.70), 15 June – 17 July 1998.

127 ICTY, Trial Chamber II, Orić case, Judgment, 30 June 2006, para. 400.

enables the Court to take action, instead of merely watching atrocities. It is true that if the ICC exercises its personal jurisdiction in the territory of a non-member State, its inquiry would remain highly fragmented and selective if solely based on nationality.[128] It is because the Court lacks jurisdiction over the territory on which crimes are being committed, and its jurisdiction will be limited only to specific parties in the conflict, in a scenario where all parties are not members with State Party nationalities.

Nevertheless, to exercise the Court's jurisdiction based on personal jurisdiction should be understood in light of the expressive mandates of the Court. As Rastan asserts, the meaning of the Court exercising jurisdiction in relation to situations that may otherwise remain subject to impunity cannot be easily dismissed.[129] Selectivity in the international criminal justice system is largely inevitable. What matters is that such a selectivity should be justifiable. There is both good selectivity and bad selectivity. A selective justice that is a further step in ending the culture of impunity is a good selective justice. Selective justice, when inevitable, is better than nothing. Annan has inspiring words in this regard: "the fact that we cannot protect people everywhere is no reason for doing nothing when we can."[130]

It should be borne in mind that even if the personal jurisdiction has disadvantages for the Court, the Prosecutor has no authority to refuse to activate the Court's jurisdiction when such a jurisdictional principle is in place. The drafters of the Rome Statute have discerned that the personal jurisdiction is an alternative to the territorial jurisdiction. The Rome Statute does not allow the nationals of States Parties to consider the territories of non-member States as free zones for the commission of crimes. The personal jurisdiction has preventive effects, in addition to expressive results. There are some major instances showing the necessity of the personal jurisdiction at the ICC legal system. One instance is where the criminal liability is based on financial compliance. The commission of ICC crimes needs financial resources and sponsors. Economic benefits derived from the commission of crimes may be instrumental to exacerbating or fueling conflicts.[131] The first Prosecutor of the Court, once, had asserted that "those who direct mining operations, sell diamonds or gold extracted in these conditions, launder dirty money, or provide weapons could also be the authors of the crimes, even if they are based in other countries."[132]

In the context of the international and organized crimes, it is typical that financial resources that facilitate the commission of crimes are located outside of the field of

128 Carsten Stahn, 'Why the ICC Should Be Cautious to Use the Islamic State to Get out of Africa: Part 2', 3 December 2014, available at: www.ejiltalk.org/why-the-icc-should-be-cautious-to-use-the-islamic-State-to-get-out-of-africa-part-2. And, Rastan, 2011, p. 429, see *supra* note 17.

129 Rastan, 2015, p. 152, see *supra* note 117.

130 Kofi A. Annan, *We the People, United Nations,* 2000, p. 48, available at: www.un.org/en/events/pastevents/pdfs/We_The_Peoples.pdf.

131 Rod Rastan, 'Complementarity: Contest or Collaboration?', in Morten Bergsmo (ed.), *Complementarity and the Exercise of Universal Jurisdiction for Core International* Crimes, Torkel Opsahl Academic EPublisher 2010, p. 130.

132 ICC, OTP, Report of the Prosecutor of the ICC, Mr. Luis Moreno-Ocampo to the Second Assembly of States Parties to the Rome Statute of the International Criminal Court, 8 September 2003.

conflicts. Here, if the State on its territory the financial operations are conducted is not a member to the Rome Statute, and if the objective territorial jurisdiction is not accepted as a legal basis for the activation of the Court's jurisdiction, the personal jurisdiction is an instrument at the Court's disposal to deal with the funders and sponsors of atrocities. The prosecution of the financial supporters of a conflict "will be a key deterrent to the commission of future crimes, if they can curb the source of funding."[133] The Yemen War is an example here. The conflict in Yemen escalated in 2015. The Yemen War involves a Saudi-led coalition of Arab states that has launched an all-out air campaign against the Houthi armed groups. The Coalition's operations have resulted in the commission of alleged massive war crimes.[134] Since Yemen is not a member to the ICC, the Court is unable to intervene in this situation of crisis. However, there is a way that could be followed as what has been done as to the war crimes in Iraq. Britain is allegedly fueling the Yemen Civil War by selling the arms to the Coalition.[135] It can be a narrow basis for the ICC to activate its jurisdiction, but its preventive and expressive effects would be broad.

The second context in which the personal jurisdiction can facilitate the Court's presence is the situation in which foreign fighters exist. Foreign fighters are defined as "non-citizens of conflict states who join insurgencies during civil war."[136] The ISIS situation before the ICC is a good example here. The Court has no jurisdiction over Syria and Iraq, two countries on their territories the ISIS atrocities have been committed. However, the presence of foreign fighters in the ISIS conflict could pave the way for the Court's intervention, though the Prosecutor did not accept it.[137] The intervention of the ICC in the ISIS situation is warranted by the personal jurisdiction. Such an intervention has expressive values that, at least, preserve the legitimacy of the Court. Being inactive in one of the most brutal atrocities in the world hurts the reputation of the Court. The ICC should welcome all available legal capacities for activating its jurisdiction, instead of rejecting them.

3.4.2. *Immunities as an Exception to the Personal jurisdiction*

3.4.2.1. Immunities at the ICC

One of the most controversial issues related to the personal jurisdiction of the Court is the question of immunity. Article 27(2) of the Rome Statute explicitly provides that

---

133 Ibid.

134 HRW, Yemen: No Accountability for War Crimes, 12 January 2017, available at: www.hrw.org/news/2017/01/12/yemen-no-accountability-war-crimes, last accessed at 23 April 2017.

135 Owen Bowcott, UK Fueling Yemen Civil War with Arms Sales to Saudi Arabia Says Amnesty, 17 December 2015, available at: www.theguardian.com/world/2015/dec/17/uk-yemen-civil-war-arms-sales-saudi-arabia.

136 Foreign Fighters under International Law, Academy Briefing, 2014, p. 5, available at: www.geneva-academy.ch/docs/publications/Briefings%20and%20In%20breifs/Foreign%20Fighters%20Under%20International%20Law%20Briefing%20no7.pdf.

137 See: ICC, OTP, Statement of the Prosecutor of the International Criminal Court on the Alleged Crimes Committed by ISIS, 8 April 2015.

"immunities or special procedural rules which may attach to the official capacity of a person, whether under national or international law, shall not bar the Court from exercising its jurisdiction over such a person." This provision implies that having an immunity under national or international law is not an excuse at the hands of the accused before the Court.

Article 27(2) addresses the 'personal immunity'. This kind of immunity stems from the official capacity and status of the person who is under protection of such immunity. Diplomats, foreign ministers and Heads of State are among the beneficiaries of this kind immunity at international level. Personal immunity is a temporary immunity. It is conferred only as long as the official remains in office.[138] Personal immunity, as the ICJ explains, is rooted in the need for State officials to be able to perform their functions without fear of arrest.[139] Keeping international relations on is a necessity, even in wartime. In the words of the ICJ judges, "immunities are granted to high State officials to guarantee the proper functioning of the network of mutual inter-State relations, which is of paramount importance for a well-ordered and harmonious international system."[140] Some argue that the gravity of international crimes is a good justification to abandon the immunities. De Guzman, for instance, asserts that when an official is suspected of committing genocide or other widespread human rights abuses, the value of enabling that person to conduct State business pales in comparison to the need to hold them accountable for their crimes.[141] In theory, it makes sense. No official has immunity to function free of fear when he is committing the international crimes. However, it seems that even in such a situation it is better to continue the connection with the culprits at power. If they become isolated and the peace through negotiation is not given a chance, it is quite likely that the wanted leaders stay within their territorial boundaries and worsen the situation in a bloody way.

De Guzman admits that her argument against the immunities is similar to arguments against amnesties. According to her, "the developing norm that international courts disregard domestic amnesties is justified largely by reference to the gravity of the crimes such courts adjudicate."[142] This is the same reason put forward by some internationalized tribunals against amnesties. For instance, the SCSL has held that there is a "crystallizing international norm that a government cannot grant amnesty for serious violations of crimes under international law."[143] Nonetheless, as to amnesties, the question and dilemma of peace or justice is still unresolved. As it will be discussed,

---

138 Dapo Akande and Sangeeta Shah, 'Immunities of State Officials, International Crimes and Foreign Domestic Courts', *European Journal of International Law*, 2011, vol. 21, p. 818.

139 ICJ, Judgment, Case Concerning the Arrest Warrant of 11 April 2000, 14 February 2002, paras. 54–55.

140 ICJ, Joint Separate Opinion of Judges Higgins, Kooijmans and Buergenthal in Arrest Warrant of 11 April 2000, para. 75.

141 Margaret M. De Guzman, 'How Serious are International Crimes? The Gravity Problem in International Criminal Law', *Columbia Journal of Transnational Law*, 2012, vol. 51, p. 58.

142 Ibid.

143 SCSL, Appeals Chamber, Kallon Case, Decision on Challenge to Jurisdiction: Lome Accord Amnesty, 13 March 2004, para. 82.

what matters is the safety and interests of victims. If immunities and amnesties provide certain and considerable contributions to peace and termination of war and misery of victims, they should be given priority.

Nonetheless, the applicability of the immunity rules under international law has changed over time. Indeed, there has been a change in the balance between the law of immunities and international criminal law, in favor of the latter.[144] Nowadays, the perpetrators of international crimes cannot shelter themselves behind their official position. The very purpose of international criminal law is to attribute responsibility to individuals, including State officials.[145] Individual criminal responsibility is a cornerstone for the functioning of the international criminal justice system, and is an indicator of the humanization of such a system. "Crimes against international law are committed by men, not by abstract entities."[146] Under international criminal law, there is a distinction in the applicability of the personal immunity in the case of international crimes. Before national jurisdictions, personal immunity is still valid. In this context, personal immunities have remained intact in customary law.[147] National jurisdictions are not allowed to exercise their criminal jurisdiction over those people who are under the protection of personal immunity. However, in the case of the commission of international crimes, the immunity holders will lose such a privilege and protection before some international tribunals.

The ICJ in two major cases has affirmed the validity of immunities before national court even in case of international crimes. The first case is the Arrest Warrant Case (2000) and the second one is the case of Germany v. Italy (2012). The former relates to the State immunity and the latter relates to the personal immunity. In December 2008, the Federal Republic of Germany filed an application instituting proceedings against the Italian Republic in respect of a dispute originating from Italy's failure to respect the jurisdictional immunity which Germany enjoys under international law by allowing civil claims to be brought against it in the Italian courts, seeking reparation for injuries caused by violations of international humanitarian law committed by the German Reich during the Second World War. In its judgment, the ICJ confirmed that activities of German generals tried in an Italian domestic court were international crimes, but reaffirmed that the immunity, which is affirmed in customary law, is not affected. According to the ICJ, "no conflict exists between *jus cogens* and immunity of a State. Argument about *jus cogens* displacing State immunity has been rejected by national courts. State immunity not affected by violation of *jus cogens*."[148]

---

144 Liu Daqun, 'Has Non-Immunity for Heads of State Become a Rule of Customary International Law?', in Morten Bergsmo and Lung Yan (eds.), *State Sovereignty and International Criminal Law*, Torkel Opsahl Academic EPublisher, 2012, p. 73.

145 Akande and Shah, 2011, p. 840, see *supra* note 138.

146 The Trial of the Major War Criminals before the International Military Tribunal, Germany, 1947, p. 223.

147 Kleffner, 2008, p. 52, see *supra* note 41.

148 ICJ, Germany v. Italy case, Advisory Opinions and Orders Jurisdictional Immunities of the State, 3 February 2012, p. 6.

Before this moment, the ICJ had addressed the issue of immunities in the Arrest Warrant Case. At the time, the DRC instituted a case against the Kingdom of Belgium, in respect of a dispute concerning an international arrest warrant issued on 11 April 2000 by a Belgian investigating judge against the Minister for Foreign Affairs in office of the Cong. In the case, the ICJ stated that a domestic court of one State must respect the immunity of Heads of another state, unless the second State waives this immunity.[149] In its judgment, the Court asserts that "... it has been unable to deduce from this practice that there exists under customary international law any form of exception to the rule according immunity from criminal jurisdiction and inviolability to incumbent Minister for Foreign Affairs, where they are suspected of having committed war crimes or crimes against humanity."[150] However, the Court added "an incumbent or former Minister for Foreign Affairs may be subject to criminal proceedings before certain international criminal courts, where they have jurisdiction. Examples in the International Criminal Tribunal for the former Yugoslavia, and the International Criminal Tribunal for Rwanda, established pursuant to Security Council Resolutions under Chapter VII of the United Nations Charter, and the future International Criminal Court ..."[151] By this statement, the ICJ affirmed the status had already adopted by Article 27 of the Rome Statute.

It should be borne in mind that, according to the Arrest Warrant case, even the non-applicability of immunities before international tribunals is not absolute, since the Court refers to "certain international criminal courts", rather than all courts. In the Charles Taylor case, the SCSL followed the Arrest Warrant case and asserted that "with respect to national criminal courts the operating principle in general international law is that a serving Head of State is entitled to absolute immunity from the jurisdiction of such courts, unless it has been waived by the State concerned."[152]

Contrary to the domestic courts, immunities are not applicable before some international tribunals. It is believed that international tribunals do not create the sort of interstate tensions that happen when states assert jurisdiction over the immunity holders.[153] Indeed, the immunities have not recognized by the international criminal tribunals from the outset, namely from the Nuremburg tribunal, and before the ICJ's Arrest Warrant Case. Article 7 of the Nuremburg Charter provided the official position of defendants, whether as Heads of State or responsible officials in Government Departments, "shall not be considered as freeing them from responsibility or mitigating

149 ICJ, Judgment, Case concerning the Arrest Warrant of 11 April 2000, 14 February 2002, para. 61. The ICJ's Judgment revolves around the immunity of incumbent Ministers for Foreign Affairs, but as some scholars have suggested a teleological interpretation, this judgment extends to other officials, including the Heads of State, who are also responsible for international relations (See: Akande and Shah, 2011, see *supra* note 138).

150 Ibid., para. 58.

151 Ibid., para. 61.

152 SCSL, Prosecutor v Charles Taylor, Decision on Immunity from Jurisdiction, 31 May 2004, para. 52.

153 Frédéric Mégret, 'Too Much of a Good Thing? Implementation and the Uses of Complementarity', in Carsten Stahn and Mohamed M. El Zeidy (eds.), *The International Criminal Court and Complementarity: From Theory to Practice*, Cambridge University Press, 2011, p. 386.

punishment." Later, the United Nations General Assembly adopted principle of international law recognized by the Charter of the Nuremberg tribunal.[154] Cassese argues that non-applicability of the immunities to international criminal tribunals have reach to the threshold of customary rules.[155] Article 7(2) of the ICTY and 6(2) ICTR, with the identical phrasing assert, "the official position of any accused person, whether as Head of State or Government or as a responsible Government official, shall not relieve such person of criminal responsibility nor mitigate punishment." These articles are indisputably declaratory of customary international law.[156]

Immunities are procedural and not substantive.[157] It means that they are a procedural bar in exercising the criminal jurisdiction but they do not justify the wrongdoings or exempt the offenders from the responsibility. States are obliged to prosecute their nationals who have immunity if they are accused of the commission of international crimes. Granting immunity is not to shield criminals.[158] Since the immunities bar states from initiating a criminal investigation against someone who is under immunity, the ICC can consider such a State as inactive or unable to have a genuine investigation or prosecution, when the complementarity requirement is assessed. Therefore, the applicability of immunities at the national level paves the way for the Court's intervention. The PTC III in the Bemba case declared that "it would appear that the CAR judicial authorities abandoned any attempt to prosecute Mr. Jean-Pierre Bemba for the crimes referred to in the Prosecutor's Application, on the ground that he enjoyed immunity by virtue of his status as Vice-President of the DRC."[159] Based on this determination, the case was declared admissible.

3.4.2.2. Cooperation Obligation and Immunities

Article 27 of the Rome Statute establishes two rules: non-applicability of the defense of official capacity (Paragraph 1) and non-applicability of immunities before the Court. The ICC does not recognize immunities. This stance is in consistency with the ICJ Arrest Warrant decision. Indeed, the Court sees itself among those certain international criminal tribunals that have jurisdiction over all officials. However, a question arises: whether such non-applicability affects the States' obligation to cooperate with the Court in implementing an arrest warrant against the Head of state. This question has two answers. If the warrant is issued against a Head of State of a State Party, the States have to implement the warrant, since the States Parties to the Rome Statute have already agreed that their nationals do not enjoy any immunity before the Court

154 UN, General Assembly, Affirmation of the Principles of International Law recognized by the Charter of the Nuremberg Tribunal General Assembly Resolution 95 (I), 11 December 1946.

155 Antonio Cassese, *International Criminal Law*, Oxford University Press, 2008, p. 305.

156 ICTY, Trial Chamber, Furundžija case, Judgment, 10 December 1998, para. 140.

157 Lulu, 2012, p. 50, see *supra* note 12.

158 Ibid.

159 ICC, PTC III, Bemba case, Warrant of Arrest for Jean-Pierre Bemba Gombo Replacing the Warrant of Arrest Issued on 23 May 2008, 10 June 2008.

even if they are the leaders of their countries. Immunities are privileges for states, and not for the persons who enjoy such a privilege. Heads of State have been seen as the personification of the State and as a result are granted immunity.[160] It is their official capacity that warrants such an immunity. Therefore, such an immunity is waivable by states. Article 31(1) of the Vienna Convention on Diplomatic Relations provides "the immunity from jurisdiction of diplomatic agents and of persons enjoying immunity under Article 37 may be waived by the sending State."

Ratification of the Rome Statute is an implied way to waive such a privilege. All States Parties, by ratifying the Rome Statute, including Article 27, simultaneously waive the immunity of their leaders before the Court. In the PTC's decision on Malawi's failure to implement the arrest warrant against Al Bashir when he had a visit to said country, the PTC refers to this argument. According to the Chamber, "acceptance of Article 27(2) of the Statute, implies waiver of immunities for the purposes of Article 98(1) of the Statute with respect to proceedings conducted by the Court."[161] If Article 27 was applied only to trials before the ICC, and did not imply the ability of national authorities to implement the arrest warrants issued by the Court, the whole structure of the Rome Statute would be meaningless.[162] The Court has no enforcement forces and is highly dependent on the State cooperation. To try the Heads of State, the Court needs the State cooperation to arrest those leaders wanted by the Court. Otherwise, there would not be any case before the ICC. All officials of States Parties are under the Court's jurisdiction, and the ICC can request a State party to arrest and surrender a Head of State without having to worry that this would require the requested State to act inconsistently with obligation under international law.[163] Here, the States Parties are obliged to cooperate with the Court.

However, the issue regarding the Heads of non-member States is problematic. It is evident that the Court is authorized to issue an arrest warrant against all persons regardless of their official position. In the Al Bashir case, PTC I issued an arrest warrant against him, while he was the formal president of Sudan. The Chamber explicitly stated that "the current position of Al Bashir as Head of a State which is not a party to the Statute has no effect on the Court's jurisdiction over the present case."[164] Article 27 of the Rome Statute has authorized the Court to prosecute all persons who are under international immunities. However, it is questionable whether under the Rome Statute the States Parties are obliged to cooperate with the Court to implement the Court's warrants against the leaders of non-member States. The waiver of immunity provided by Article 27 does not include non-member States.

---

160 Daqun, 2012, p. 56, see *supra* note 144.

161 ICC, PTC I, Al Bashir case, Corrigendum to the Decision Pursuant to Article 87(7) of the Rome Statute on the Failure by the Republic of Malawi to Comply with the Cooperation Requests Issued by the Court with Respect to the Arrest and Surrender of Omar Hassan Ahmad Al Bashir, 12 December 2011, para. 18.

162 Daqun, 2012, p. 62, see *supra* note 144.

163 Göran Sluiter, *International Criminal Adjudication and the Collection of Evidence: Obligations of States*, Intersentia, 2002, p. 171.

164 ICC, PTC I, Al Bashir case, 4 March 2009, para. 41, see *supra* note 49.

The ICC is a treaty-based organization, and as such Article 27(2) "only applies to Heads of State of States Parties and cannot be invoked against Heads of State of non-party States."[165] Therefore, Article 27 could not be a basis for States Parties to ignore the immunities of non-member States' nationals. Moreover, Article 98 of the Rome Statute declares that States Parties are not obliged to cooperate with the Court if such cooperation violates their international obligations to respect immunities. From this perspective, Article 98 imposes a limitation on the Court to issue a request to arrest and surrender of a non-member State's national in first place.[166]

Reading Articles 98 and 27 together shows that non-immunity of the Heads of State before the domestic courts is not a rule of customary international law.[167] If it had been so, Article 98 should have not recognized an exception to the general obligation of States to cooperate with the Court.[168] In addition, it is said that this article is the legal basis for States Parties of the Rome Statute to grant officials of non-member States with immunity.[169] As Schabas submits, "it is probably going too far to suggest that Article 27(2) applies to nationals of non-party states, any immunities that they may have as a result of customary or treaty law cannot be removed simply because a group of States have decided, by treaty, that such immunities cannot be invoked before an institution of their creation."[170] Article 27 still has a statutory nature. Hence, the rule *pacta tertiis nec nocent nec prosunt* (Treaties neither harm nor benefit third parties) is applicable to Article 27. Nonetheless, it seems that the Chambers of the ICC have a different point of view in this regard.

3.4.2.3. The ICC Jurisprudence on Immunities

The jurisprudence of the ICC is rich on the issue of immunities, thanks to the Al Bashir case. Since the issuance of two arrest warrants against the Sudanese serving Head of State, a hot debate has tabled about the issue of immunities of wanted individuals by the Court. Al Bashir tends to travel to other African countries, including the States Parties to the Rome Statute. Following each visit, this old debate sparks off. The failure of States Parties to implement the Court's warrants against Al Bashir results in the disobedience that warrant the ASP or the UNSC's reaction, according to Article 87(7)

165 William A. Schabas, Obama, Medvedev and Hu Jintao may be Prosecuted by International Criminal Court, Pre-Trial Chamber Concludes, 15 December 2011, available at: http://humanrightsdoctorate.blogspot.nl/2011/12/obama-medvedev-and-hu-jintao-may-be.html, last accessed at 14 June 2017.

166 Sluiter, 2002, p. 170, see *supra* note 163.

167 Daqun, 2012, p. 66, see *supra* note 144.

168 In this regards, Akande states "if under international law, there can be no immunities when an international court wants someone for prosecution, why did the parties to the Rome Statute insert Article 98?." In his opinion, it is the biggest weakness of the ICC Pre-Trial Chambers' decision failing to provide an answer for this question" (See: Dapo Akande, ICC Issues Detailed Decision on Bashir's Immunity But Gets the Law Wrong, 15 December 2011, available at: www.ejiltalk.org/icc-issues-detailed-decision-on-bashir's-immunity-at-long-last-but-gets-the-law-wrong/).

169 Lulu, 2012, p. 52, see *supra* note 12.

170 William A. Schabas, *An Introduction to International Criminal Court*, Cambridge University Press, 2011, p. 80.

of the Rome Statute.[171] To avoid such a consequence, the African States have tried to prove that in accordance with Article 98(1) of the Rome Statute they are exempted from cooperating with the Court in implementing the arrest warrants against Al Bashir. African states argue that there are some international obligations that prevail over their statutory obligation to cooperate with the Court in arresting Al Bashir. These prevailing obligations arise from the immunity of Al Bashir as the acting Head of State under international law, and the decision of African Union not to implement Al Bashir's arrest warrants, which is obligatory for the member-States to the Union.[172]

The Court's Chambers, however, have dismissed the African States' arguments. The Chambers of the Court have put forward two counter-arguments. Initially, the PTC I, in the case of Al Bashir's visit to Malawi in 2011, argued that under the customary law, personal immunities in case of international crimes are not applicable absolutely.[173] In this case, the PTC advocated non-applicability of personal immunities in the case of international crimes, neither before international tribunals nor before national jurisdictions. According to the PTC, "the international community's commitment to rejecting immunity in circumstances where international courts seek arrest for international crimes has reached a critical mass. If it ever was appropriate to say that customary international law immunity applies in the present context."[174] In a corrigendum to this decision, the PTC I added more proof to this claim. According to the Chamber, the recent increase in the Heads of State prosecutions by international

171 Article 87 (7): "Where a State Party fails to comply with a request to cooperate by the Court contrary to the provisions of this Statute, thereby preventing the Court from exercising its functions and powers under this Statute, the Court may make a finding to that effect and refer the matter to the Assembly of States Parties or, where the Security Council referred the matter to the Court, to the Security Council."

172 For instance, See: ICC, The Observations Submitted by the Democratic Republic of the Congo pursuant to the Decision Requesting Observations on Omar Al-Bashir's visit to the Democratic Republic of Congo' dated 3 March 2014. According to the DRC, "the DRC's status as a State Party of the International Criminal Court, its membership in the African Union whose Resolutions are legally binding on all member-States, including the DRC, and the presence on its territory of a foreign sitting Head of State invited by a regional organization have all combined to create a complex, ambiguous and bothersome situation for DRC authorities. In this sensitive context, characterized by conflicting standards in which the DRC cannot make a determination at short notice, the DRC adopted an approach that is most consistent with its obligations under the Rome Statute while respecting the letter of its commitments to the African Union and to COMESA as well as the requirements of peace and stability for itself and the entire sub-region." As to the South Africa case, the government of South Africa added another obligation contradictory with the Al Bashir arrest warrant. Al Bashir attended a summit of the African Union in Johannesburg in June 2015. South Africa believed that Article VIII(1) of the Host Agreement with the African Union obliges the Host State to respect immunities of participants, including Al Bashir. Nevertheless, the majority of PTC II contested this argument by arguing that the Host Agreement did not apply to Al Bashir because he was not "a staff member of said Commission, or as a delegate or other representative of an inter-governmental organization, but attended the African Union Summit in Johannesburg in his capacity as Head of State of Sudan" (See: ICC, PTC II, Decision under Article 87(7) of the Rome Statute on the non-compliance by South Africa with the request by the Court for the arrest and surrender of Omar Al-Bashir, 6 July 2017, para. 66).

173 The arguments put forward by the PTC in case of Malawi were repeated by the same PTC in the case of Bashir's visit to Chad.

174 ICC, PTC I, Al Bashir case, 12 December 2011, para. 42, see *supra* note 161.

courts in the last decade shows that "initiating international prosecutions against Heads of State has gained widespread recognition as accepted practice."[175]

In addition, the Chamber referred to the large number of States Parties to the Court, "all of whom have accepted having any immunity they had under international law stripped from their top officials", and "have renounced any claim to immunity by ratifying the language of Article 27(2)."[176] Consequently, the Chamber concluded "customary international law creates an exception to the Heads of State immunity when international courts seek a Head of State's arrest for the commission of international crimes."[177] Therefore, according to the Chamber, there was no international obligation that would contradict a request for the arrest and surrender of a requested acting Head of State from a non-member State. Based on this argument, Malawi noncompliance was founded by the PTC. According to the Chamber, "the principle in international law is that immunity of either former or sitting Heads of State cannot be invoked to oppose a prosecution by an international court."[178] However, the Chamber's decision in the Malawi case received strong objections. Schabas called the decision 'a lawyer's brief' that is entirely one-sided, and therefore regrettable.[179] At the time, some predicted that the Chamber's point of view would create a risk of States withdrawing from or no longer co-operating under the terms of the Rome Statute.[180] In 2016, this prediction came true when South Africa announced its intention to leave the Court. The strict interpretation provided by the Court's Chambers about the immunity rule, made South Africa confronted with conflicting obligations when Al Bashir visited this country. To avoid being responsible before the Court, the government of South Africa once decided to terminate its membership at the ICC.[181] This attempt, however, became abortive, because of some internal legal barriers.[182]

Legally speaking, the claim of the Chamber that the non-applicability of personal immunities is absolute needs proof. As long as there is no major change in the fundamental principle of equal sovereignty in the international legal system, the criminal immunity of officials should not be denied.[183] The fact that an individual

175 Ibid., para. 39.

176 Ibid., para. 40.

177 Ibid., para. 43.

178 Ibid., para. 36.

179 William A. Schabas, Obama, Medvedev and Hu Jintao may be Prosecuted by International Criminal Court, Pre-Trial Chamber Concludes, 15 December 2011, available at: http://humanrightsdoctorate.blogspot.nl/2011/12/obama-medvedev-and-hu-jintao-may-be.html, last accessed at 14 June 2017.

180 Asad G. Kiyani, 'Al Bashir and the ICC: The Problem of Head of State Immunity' *Chinese Journal of International Law*, 2013, vol. 12, p. 470.

181 For more information, see the statement of South Africa made in the 15th ASP ICC, available at: www.asp.icc-cpi.int/iccdocs/asp_docs/ASP15/GenDeba/ICC-ASP15-GenDeba-SouthAfrica-ENG.pdf.

182 In February 2017, the South Africa's North Gauteng High Court today ruled that the government's attempt to withdraw from the ICC was unconstitutional and invalid, as the government issued its withdrawal notice without consulting parliament. The Court ordered President Jacob Zuma and the Ministries of Justice and Foreign Affairs to revoke the notice of withdrawal (See: HRW, South African High Court Rejects ICC Withdrawal, 22 February 2017, available at: www.hrw.org/news/2017/02/22/south-african-high-court-rejects-icc-withdrawal, last accessed at 30 April 2017).

183 Lulu, 2012, p. 49, see *supra* note 12.

Head of State cannot evade criminal responsibility does not mean that person no longer has immunity. The conviction that prosecutions against Heads of State have gained widespread recognition suffers from a circular argument, since "all of the accused have been indicted by the ICC itself."[184] In addition, according to him, the African Union Commission reaction in the wake of the PTC's decision negates the PTC's evidence of widespread State practice.[185]

Later, Al Bashir and another wanted Sudanese official visited Chad and Nigeria in 2013. In both instances, the governments of Chad and Nigeria made an excuse to justify their failure to arrest Al Bashir, and expressed their commitment to cooperate with the Court. In response, the PTC II in both instances considered that it was not necessary to refer the situation to the ASP or the UNSC.[186] In these instances, the Chamber did not address the applicability of immunities and its effects on the States' obligation to cooperate with the Court. However, later, in the case of Al Bashir's visit to Congo and later to South Africa in 2014 and 2015, the initial assertion of the PTC I was set aside, and another argument set forward by another Chamber. Upon Al Bashir's visit to Chad, the PTC II dealt with the issue to determine whether Chad had complied with its statutory obligation. In the relevant case, the PTC II accepted that the personal immunity is valid before the national jurisdictions by making clear that "it is not disputed that under international law a sitting Head of State enjoys personal immunities from criminal jurisdiction and inviolability before national courts of foreign States even when suspected of having committed one or more of the crimes that fall within the ICC's jurisdiction."[187] However, the Chamber added that there is a distinction between the national and international jurisdiction in terms of the applicability of personal immunities. According to the Chamber, under Article 27(2) of the Rome Statute "the existence of personal immunities under international law, which generally attach to the official capacity of the person, shall not bar the Court from exercising its jurisdiction over such a person."[188]

In addition, the PTC insisted that, according to Article 98(1), the obligation of States Parties to respect the international immunities prevail over their obligation to cooperate with the Court, because "the Statute cannot impose obligations on third States without their consent. Thus, the exception to the exercise of the Court's jurisdiction provided in Article 27(2) of the Statute should, in principle, be confined to those States Parties who have accepted it."[189] The Judges of the Chamber, however, referred to a solution to cope

---

184 Ibid.

185 Daqun, 2012, pp. 64–22, see *supra* note 144. And, Kiyani, 2013, pp. 482–490, see *supra* note 180.

186 See, ICC, PTC II, Al Bashir case, Decision on the Cooperation of the Federal Republic of Nigeria Regarding Omar Al-Bashir's Arrest and Surrender to the Court, 5 September 2013. And, ICC, PTC II, Al Bashir case, Decision on the Cooperation of the Republic of Chad Regarding Abdel Raheem Muhammad Hussein's Arrest and Surrender to the Court, 13 November 2013.

187 ICC, PTC II, Al Bashir case, Decision on the Cooperation of the Democratic Republic of the Congo Regarding Omar Al Bashir's Arrest and Surrender to the Court, 9 April 2014, para. 25.

188 Ibid.

189 Ibid., para. 26. This argument was later reaffirmed by the PTC II Judges with regard to the South Africa case: "States that are not parties to the Statute in principle have no obligation to cooperate with

with the problem of non-member States. According to them, Article 98(1) of the Statute "directs the Court to secure the cooperation of the third State for the waiver or lifting the immunity of its Head of State. This course of action envisaged by Article 98(1) of the Statute aims at preventing the requested State from acting inconsistently with its international obligations towards the non-State Party with respect to the immunities attached to the latter's Head of State."[190]

In spite of these admissions, the Judges of PTC II, emphasized that in the Al Bashir case, there has not been a legal barrier in the way of implementing the warrants. The Chamber argued that when the African States invoke their obligation arising from the AU's decision "the conflict actually lies between the decision of the African Union to retain the immunity of Al Bashir and the UNSC Resolution 1593(2005) which removed such immunity for the purpose of the proceedings before the Court. However, this conflict is resolved by virtue of Articles 25 and 103 of the UN Charter. According to Article 25 of the UN Charter "the Members of the United Nations agree to accept and carry out the decisions of the Security Council in accordance with the … Charter." In its advisory opinion on the Namibia case, the ICJ stated "when the Security Council adopts a decision under Article 25 in accordance with the Charter, it is for member States to comply with that decision … To hold otherwise would be to deprive this principal organ of its essential functions and powers under the Charter."[191]

In addition, regarding the immunity of Al Bashir under the general international law rules, the Chamber maintained that Sudan had waived the immunity of Al Bashir in an indirect manner and through the UNSC Resolution. According to the Chamber, although "immunities attached to Al Bashir are a procedural bar from prosecution before the Court", the cooperation envisaged in the referring Resolution "was meant to eliminate any impediment to the proceedings before the Court, including the lifting of immunities."[192] Resolution 1593 decides that "the Government of Sudan and all other parties to the conflict in Darfur, shall cooperate fully with and provide any necessary assistance to the Court and the Prosecutor pursuant to this Resolution."[193] The Judges of the PTC believed that any other interpretation would render the full cooperation of Sudan senseless. Consequently, "the cooperation of that third State [Sudan] for the waiver of the immunity, as required under the last sentence of Article 98(1) of the Statute, was already ensured by the language used in Paragraph 2 of the UNSC Resolution 1593(2005). By virtue of said paragraph, the Security Council implicitly

the Court and the irrelevance of immunities based on official capacity as enshrined in Article 27(2) of the Statute has no effect on their rights under international law." (See: ICC, PTC II, Al Bashir case, Decision under Article 87(7) of the Rome Statute on the non-compliance by South Africa with the request by the Court for the arrest and surrender of Omar Al-Bashir, 6 July 2017, para. 82).

190 ICC, PTC II, Al Bashir case, 9 April 2014, para. 27, see *supra* note 187.

191 ICJ, Advisory Opinion, Legal Consequences for States of the Continued Presence of South Africa in Namibia (South West Africa) notwithstanding Security Council Resolution 276 (1970), 21 June 1971, para. 116.

192 ICC, PTC II, Al Bashir case, 9 April 2014, para. 30, see *supra* note 187.

193 UNSC, Resolution 1503, para. 2.

waived the immunities granted to Al Bashir under international law and attached to his position as a Head of State."[194]

This line of argument was later reaffirmed by the PTC II in the case of Al Bashir's visit to South Africa. Following the notice of Al Bashir's visit, the Prosecutor had requested the PTC to issue an order clarifying that the Republic of South Africa is under obligation to immediately arrest and surrender Al Bashir.[195] In response, the Chamber asserted any further reminder or clarification to the Republic of South Africa is unnecessary, because "there exists no ambiguity or uncertainty with respect to the obligation of the Republic of South Africa to immediately arrest and surrender Omar Al Bashir to the Court.".[196] In spite of these events, on 13 June 2015, Al Bashir entered South Africa and left the territory of this country in the morning of 15 June 2015.[197]

Later, in May 2016, Al Bashir travelled to other two African States Parties to the Rome Statute. Upon failing to implement the arrest warrants against Al Bashir, the PTC found the non-compliance by both Uganda and Djibouti in July 2016. Both countries repeated the same arguments, and the PTC provided the same answers.[198] As to South Africa, PTC II, by majority, found the failure of South Africa to cooperate with the Court in arresting Al Bashir, however, declared a referral to the ASP or the UNSC is not appropriate in the present circumstances.[199]

In its submission, South Africa had argued that even if the referring Resolution of Council had such an implication to lift immunities, it should have been referred to explicitly in the Resolution.[200] Making a change in the customary law needs something more than implication and speculation. It is what is explicitly referred by Article 31(2) of the Vienna Convention on Diplomatic Relations, which provides that a "waiver must always be express." The majority of PTC II acknowledged that there is no such

194 ICC, PTC II, Al Bashir case, 9 April 2014, para. 29, see *supra* note 187.

195 ICC, OTP, Al Bashir case, Prosecution's Urgent Request for an Order Clarifying whether Article 97 Consultations with South Africa Have Concluded and that South Africa is Under an Obligation to Immediately Arrest and Surrender Omar Al Bashir, 13 June 2015.

196 ICC, PTC II, Al Bashir case, Decision Following the Prosecutor's Request for an Order Further Clarifying that the Republic of South Africa is under the Obligation to Immediately Arrest and Surrender Omar Al Bashir, 13 June 2015, para. 1. One day before this decision, at the request of South Africa, a meeting took place between the representatives of South Africa and the Presiding Judge of the Chamber, Judge Tarfusser, during which the Presiding Judge pointed out, inter alia, that all of the issues tabled by South Africa had already been decided upon by the Court (See: ICC, PTC II, Al Bashir case, Decision under Article 87(7) of the Rome Statute on the non-compliance by South Africa with the request by the Court for the arrest and surrender of Omar Al-Bashir, 6 July 2017, paras. 9–10).

197 Ibid., paras. 11 and 14.

198 ICC, PTC II, Al Bashir case, Decision on the Non-Compliance by the Republic of Djibouti with the Request to Arrest and Surrender Omar Al-Bashir to the Court and Referring the Matter to the United Nations Security Council and the Assembly of the States Parties to the Rome Statute, 11 July 2016. And, ICC, PTC II, Al Bashir case, Decision on the Non-Compliance by the Republic of Uganda with the Request to Arrest and Surrender Omar Al-Bashir to the Court and Referring the Matter to the United Nations Security Council and the Assembly of States Parties to the Rome Statute, 11 July 2016.

199 See: ICC, PTC II, Al Bashir case, Decision under Article 87(7) of the Rome Statute on the non-compliance by South Africa with the request by the Court for the arrest and surrender of Omar Al-Bashir, 6 July 2017.

200 Ibid., para. 36.

waiver, whether explicit or implicit, in the Resolution, but they believed that no such waiver "would be necessary".[201] PTC II argued that a waiver is imaginable only where immunities apply, however, all immunities had been made inapplicable as a result of the effects of Article 27 and the refereeing Resolution.[202] Indeed, the majority of PTC believed that it is immaterial whether the UNSC intended or anticipated that Al Bashir's immunity would be inapplicable under Article 27 of the Rome Statute, because it this is a necessary, un-severable, effect of the informed choice by the Security Council to trigger the jurisdiction of this Court and impose on Sudan the obligation to cooperate with it.[203]The PTC's Judges were of the opinion that UNSC referral would enable the Court to act in the referred situation within the legal regime of the Court and the Rome Statute that, *inter alia,* does not respect immunities.[204]

In spite of the PTC II's interpretation of the referring Resolution, the idea that the UNSC is authorized to waive the immunity of a serving Head of State is still open to question. The basic flaw with this argument is that the UN Charter only takes precedence over other international treaties, not customary international law rules.[205] Article 103 of the UN Charter refers to 'international agreements', instead of 'all international obligations' to show that the Charter prevails only above treaties. The General Assembly in the 'Declaration on Friendly Relations' distinguishes between 'obligations under the generally recognized principles and rules of international law' and 'obligations under international agreements valid under the generally recognized principles and rules of international law'. Regarding immunities, the limit of the UNSC's referrals is clearer, in particular by taking into account Article 10 of the Rome Statute that asserts: "Nothing in this Part shall be interpreted as limiting or prejudicing in any way existing or developing rules of international law for purposes other than this Statute." As the ICJ in the Arrest Warrant case explicitly maintains "although various international conventions or the prevention and punishment of certain serious crimes impose on States' obligations of prosecution or extraction, thereby requiring them to extend their criminal jurisdiction, such extension of jurisdiction in no way affects immunities under customary international law."[206]

Because of these doubts and questions, Akande suggests another solution: the intervention of the ICJ to provide an answer with the question of immunities before the ICC.[207]

---

201 Ibid., para. 96.
202 Ibid.
203 Ibid., para. 95.
204 Ibid., para. 86.
205 Kiyani, 2013, p. 478, see *supra* note 180.
206 ICJ, Judgment, Case concerning the Arrest Warrant of 11 April 2000, 14 February 2002, para. 59.
207 Dapo Akande, An International Court of Justice Advisory Opinion on the ICC Head of State Immunity Issue, 31 March 2016, available at: www.ejiltalk.org/an-international-court-of-justice-advisory-opinion-on-the-icc-head-of-state-immunity-issue/#more-14178.

CHAPTER II
ADMISSIBILITY

The second statutory requirement that should be met before initiating an investigation into a situation is the admissibility. Article 17 of the Rome Statute is the legal and statutory framework for applying the admissibility test. According to Paragraph 1 of this article, "the Court shall determine whether a case is inadmissible where: a) the case is being investigated or prosecuted by a State which has jurisdiction over it, unless the State is unwilling or unable genuinely to carry out the investigation or prosecution; b) the case has been investigated by a State which has jurisdiction over it and the State has decided not to prosecute the person concerned, unless the decision resulted from the unwillingness or inability of the State genuinely to prosecute; c) the person concerned has already been tried for conduct which is the subject of the complaint, and a trial by the Court is not permitted under Article 20, paragraph 3; d) the case is not of sufficient gravity to justify further action by the Court."

1. CONCEPTUALIZATION OF ADMISSIBILITY

This section seeks the meaning of the admissibility requirement in the Rome Statute. For this purpose, firstly the distinction between admissibility and jurisdiction is clarified. Next, the functions of the admissibility requirement and its components are addressed, in order to clarify the important role of the admissibility requirement in selecting a situation or a case.

1.1. DISTINCTION BETWEEN ADMISSIBILITY AND JURISDICTION

To initiate an investigation or prosecution at the ICC, jurisdiction is a necessary requirement, but it is not sufficient. The Rome Statute distinguishes between jurisdiction and admissibility. The assessment of jurisdiction precedes the admissibility assessment. Admissibility is about the exercise of the Court's jurisdiction rather than its existence.[208] In the PTC's words, "the question of admissibility mainly concerns the scenarios or conditions on the basis of which the Court shall refrain from exercising its

[208] Schabas, 2010, p. 40, see *supra note* 20.

recognized jurisdiction over a given situation or case."[209] Hence, the admissibility is a post-jurisdiction issue.

The difference between admissibility and jurisdiction is better understood by considering the difference between 'jurisdiction to prescribe' and 'jurisdiction to enforce'. At the domestic level, a State has power to legislate for all matters within its territorial domain. Such authority is called 'jurisdiction to prescribe' or 'prescriptive jurisdiction'. However, a State needs the 'jurisdiction to enforce' that empowers the State to exercise its prescribed jurisdictions.[210] Admissibility resembles this jurisdiction to enforce.

In the 1994 draft Statute, for the first time, the distinction between 'jurisdiction' and 'admissibility' was made.[211] In the drafting process, some believed that it was not necessary to include the admissibility requirement "as the relevant factors could be taken into account at the level of jurisdiction."[212] However, others rejected this position by maintaining that "a power such as that contained in Article 35 was necessary if the purposes indicated in the preamble were to be fulfilled."[213] It seems that from the outset it was evident for some drafters of the Statute that the ICC would work selectively. Therefore, they proposed a mechanism to manage the Court's selectivity.

The Court's jurisdiction is a matter of law. It is the Rome Statute that determines the jurisdiction of the Court. Nobody has authority to change the ICC's jurisdictional scope and parameters. The jurisdiction assessment is largely objective. However, the admissibility requirement provides the Prosecutor of the Court with discretion and a task to determine whether a situation or case is admissible before the Court. Indeed, the admissibility assessment creates a legal basis for the prosecutorial discretion in the situation and case selection. Although the Statute has referred to the elements of the admissibility requirement, there is no precise definition for the substance of these components. It implies that the admissibility notion is open for the Prosecutor's interpretation in fulfilling their selection authority. However, it does not mean that the Prosecutor can adopt an interpretation in an arbitrary manner. The admissibility requirement should be understood and interpreted in light of the main objectives of the Court. In this regard, the judicial review mechanism is to some extent in place to assure the Prosecutors' conformity of choice with the Court's objectives.

209 ICC, PTC II, Kenya situation, 31 March 2010, para. 36, see *supra* note 33.

210 Derek W. Bowett, 'Jurisdiction: Changing Patterns of Authority over Activities and Resources', *British Yearbook of International Law,* 1982, vol. 53, p. 1.

211 Article 35 of the draft Statute provided "the Court may, on application by the accused or at the request of an interested State at any time prior to the commencement of the trial, or of its own motion, decide, having regard to the purposes of this Statute set out in the preamble, that a case before it is inadmissible on the ground that the crime in question: a) has been duly investigated by a State with jurisdiction over it, and the decision of that State not to proceed to a prosecution is apparently well-founded; b) Is under investigation by a State which has or may have jurisdiction over it, and there is no reason for the Court to take any further action for the time being with respect to the crime; or c) Is not of such gravity to justify further action by the Court."

212 The International Law Commission, Draft Statute for an International Criminal Court with commentaries, 1994, p. 52.

213 Ibid.

1.2. ADMISSIBILITY AND THE COURT'S SELECTIVITY

By doing the admissibility assessment, the Prosecutor makes a selection among those situations that legally fall within the ICC's jurisdiction. Establishing the admissibility test in the Rome Statute has legalized the selectivity at the ICC. The Court is not intended to deal with all cases and situations that are under its jurisdiction. Selectivity is inevitable for the international tribunal's functioning, and should be seen as a fact for the ICC. Here, "the question is not whether to select, but how to select."[214] Even if a case or situation falls within the ICC's jurisdiction, it does not suffice for the Court's intervention. As Judge Pikis in his dissenting opinion in the Ntaganda case asserts, the admissibility test aims to exclude cases "unworthy of consideration by the Court."[215] It is the admissibility test that determines where the Court should intervene and where it should not. In the words of the Court's Chamber, "the question of admissibility mainly concerns the scenarios or conditions on the basis of which the Court shall refrain from exercising its recognized jurisdiction over a given situation or case."[216]

The admissibility requirement is a threshold for the workload of the Court. El Zeidy refers to this function as the philosophy behind the admissibility requirement. According to him, the admissibility and complementarity requirements have been set up "to avoid flooding the International Criminal Court with cases that it could not accommodate."[217] This threshold has been intentionally established due to the Court's open-ended mandates, besides its highly limited resources. The admissibility threshold is a structural and procedural compromise to make a balance between these apparently irreconcilable features of the Court. For this reason, the admissibility assessment is a sophisticated task. The Prosecutor has described the admissibility assessment enshrined in Article 53 as "the point where many of the philosophical and operational challenges in the pursuit of international criminal justice coincide."[218] It is the Prosecutor's responsibility to maximize the benefit of limited resources of the Court in order to realize the Court's goals as much as possible.

Assessing the admissibility requirement is a judicial task.[219] The Court on many occasions has insisted that the final word in evaluating the admissibility is for the Court. Others can make a challenge against the admissibility, but it is the Court that eventually determines whether a situation or a case is admissible. As PTC II has observed, "once the jurisdiction of the Court is triggered, it is for the latter and not for any national

---

214 Fabricio Guariglia, Those Most Responsible' versus International Sex Crimes: Competing Prosecution Themes?, in Morten Bergsmo (ed.), *Thematic Prosecution of International Sex Crimes*, Torkel Opsahl Academic EPublisher, 2012, p. 46.

215 ICC, Situation in the DRC, Judge Pikis Separate and Partly Dissenting Opinion, Judgment on the Prosecutor's Appeal Against the Decision of Pre-Trial Chamber I Entitled Decision on the Prosecutor's Application for Warrants of Arrest, Article 58, 13 July 2006, para. 39.

216 ICC, PTC II, Kenya situation, 31 March 2010, para. 40, see *supra* note 33.

217 Mohammad M. El Zeidy, 'The Gravity Threshold under the Statute of the International Criminal Court', *Criminal Law Forum*, 2008, vol. 19, p. 62.

218 ICC, OTP, Policy Paper on the Interests of Justice, September 2007, p. 2.

219 Moreno-Ocampo, 2011, p. 23, see *supra* note 1.

judicial authorities to interpret and apply the provisions governing the complementarity regime and to make a binding determination on the admissibility of a given case."[220]

The independent position of the Prosecutor in selecting situations and cases has been seen as one of the most valued features of the ICC.[221] Assigning such a position to the Prosecutor can be seen as an important step in humanizing international law. Under the Rome Statute, the Prosecutor as an individual has been empowered to play a leading role in the international criminal justice system. She has been authorized to make a determination that may be in contrast with the state's consent and will. In the case of States' and the UNSC's inaction, the Prosecutor has authority to seek justice. At the ICC-era, a global system evolves largely around the discretion of one person.[222] International prosecutors may not be the most powerful persons in the world but still they do have a considerable amount of power.[223] However, the Prosecutor's powers are accompanied with their accountability. The authorities of the Prosecutor are not unfettered. Authority and responsibility go hand in hand.[224]

1.3. FROM SITUATIONAL ADMISSIBILITY TO CASE ADMISSIBILITY

The admissibility requirement is a criterion in selecting both situations and cases. A situation should be admissible before the Court for conducting an investigation, and a case should be admissible to be prosecuted. In the Rome Statute, the issue of admissibility arises in several stages: before initiation of an investigation (Article 53(1)(b)); before authorization for an investigation (Article 15); and before issuing an arrest warrant (Article 53(2)(b)). Therefore, the admissibility requirement is applicable to both situational and case phases. According to the Appeals Chamber, "Article 17 applies not only to the determination of the admissibility of a concrete case (Article 19 of the Statute), but also to preliminary admissibility rulings (Article 18 of the Statute)."[225]

---

220 ICC, PTC II, Kony case, Decision on the Admissibility of the Case under Article 19(1) of the Statute, 10 March 2009, para. 45.

221 Alette Smeulers and Maartje Weerdesteijn and Barbora Hola, 'The Selection of Situations by the ICC: An Empirically Based Evaluation of the OTP's Performance', in *International Criminal Law Review*, 2015, vol. 15, p. 1.

222 The Prosecutor benefits from a team work, but she is the ultimate person who makes a decision.

223 Luc Coté, 'Independence and Impartiality', in Luc Reydams and Jan Wouters and Cedric Ryngaert (eds.), *International Prosecutors*, Oxford University Press, 2012, p. 943.

224 Turner describes and analyses different methods of controlling the ICC Prosecutor's discretion established by the ICC legal system, such as internal, judicial an political oversight (See: Jenia I. Turner, 'Accountability of International Prosecutors', in Carten Stahn (ed.), *The Law and Practice of the International Criminal Court*, Oxford University Press 2015.

225 ICC, Appeals Chamber, Kenya situation, Judgment on the Appeal of the Republic of Kenya Against the Decision of Pre-Trial Chamber II of 30 May 2011 Entitled Decision on the Application by the Government of Kenya Challenging the Admissibility of the Case Pursuant to Article 19(2)(b) of the Statute, 30 August 2011, para. 37.

The admissibility assessment is contextual. It implies that the admissibility assessment and the evaluation of the elements of this multifaceted test is dynamic.[226] In each stage, the determination of admissibility is preliminary. An admissible situation does not necessarily result in the admissibility of cases arising from such a situation. Each case requires a separate admissibility assessment. In addition, the content and the scope of the admissibility requirement is to some extent different in the situational phase in comparison with the case stage. Generally speaking, the admissibility assessment is more flexible in the situational phase due to the lack of certainty and specificity during this stage. Such vagueness stems from the fact that "no individual suspects will have been identified at this stage, nor will the exact conduct nor its legal classification be clear."[227] It warrants that the admissibility assessment is conducted on a lower evidentiary threshold. The generality of the situational phase has directed the Court to establish the notion of 'potential cases'. In the situational phase, where the concrete cases are absent, the OTP undertakes "a general examination of whether the cases the Prosecutor might decide to undertake are already being investigated or prosecuted by national authorities."[228] Although determinations in the situations phase are preliminary, it does not affect the necessity of considering the admissibility in the preliminary examination. The Court is unable to investigate all situations, as it is unable to prosecute all cases. Therefore, the admissibility determination is mandatory during the stage of situations.[229]

In the situational phase, when the PTC is requested to authorize the Prosecutor to initiate an investigation, the admissibility requirement is tested by the Court's Judges. In the case phase, to the contrary, when the Judges are requested to issue a warrant, it is discretionary for them to assess the admissibility of the case at issue. Article 19 states that "the Court may, on its own motion, determine the admissibility of a case in accordance with Article 17." The term 'may' implies discretion. It suggests that the Court is not obliged to consider the admissibility in the event that there is no challenge made by neither the accused nor any state.[230] When the first Prosecutor of the Court applied for a warrant of arrest against Lubanga and Ntaganda in January 2006, the PTC I for the first time in the history of the Court actively examined the admissibility of a case. The Chamber was of the opinion that a determination of admissibility was to be a pre-requisite for issuing an arrest warrant.[231] Upon the assessment of the admissibility

---

226 Sarah M.H. Nouwen, *Complementarity in the Line of Fire: the Catalyzing Effect of the ICC in Uganda and Sudan*, Cambridge University Press, 2013, p. 79.

227 ICC, Appeals Chamber, Kenya situation, 30 August 2011, para. 38, see *supra* note 225.

228 William W. Burke-White and Scott Kaplan, 'Shaping the Contours of Domestic Justice: The International Criminal Court and an Admissibility Challenge in the Uganda Situation', in Carsten Stahn and Göran Sluiter (eds.), *The Emerging Practice of the International Criminal Court*, Martinus Nijhoff Publishers, 2009, p. 87.

229 El Zeidy, 2008, p. 134, see *supra* note 19.

230 Nouwen, 2013, p. 81, see *supra* note 226.

231 ICC, PTC I, Lubanga case, 10 February 2006, para. 18, see *supra* note 45.

requirement, the Chamber held that the Ntaganda case, contrary to the Lubanga case, was not admissible due to the lack of sufficient gravity.[232]

The then Prosecutor appealed the decision because he believed that, *inter alia,* a determination of admissibility is not a prerequisite for issuing an arrest warrant. The Appeals Chamber agreed with the Prosecutor. According to the Appeals Chamber, the admissibility assessment of a case is not an integral part of the decision on an application for a warrant, since "Article 58(1) of the Statute lists the substantive prerequisites for the issuance of a warrant of arrest exhaustively."[233] Article 58 stipulates only two substantive conditions: the commission of a crime within the jurisdiction of the Court, and the necessity of arresting the suspect. The Appeals Chamber enhanced its opinion by arguing that Article 58(1) reads that the Pre Trial Chamber 'shall' issue a warrant of arrest. The word 'shall' indicates an obligation if the prerequisites listed in the article are met.[234] According to the Appeals Chamber, the obligatory nature of issuing an arrest warrant by the PTC requires a narrow interpretative approach to its authorities and the conditions for fulfilling such a task. Moreover, the Appeals Chamber asserted that during this stage, the PTC "will not have the necessary factual information to determine the admissibility of the case based on the Prosecutor's application", and consequently, it might "substantially prolong the proceedings in respect of the application for a warrant of arrest."[235]

In addition, the Appeals Chamber argued that the PTC had erred because it did not give sufficient weight to the interests of the accused. The proceedings before the PTC were held *ex parte* and with the Prosecutor only. It meant that "those persons against whom warrants of arrest were sought did not have a right to make submissions to the PTC and did not even know about the proceedings."[236] The PTC in its decision had mentioned that its decision was without prejudice to subsequent determinations in the next stages. However, the Appeals Chamber stated that this assertion did not sufficiently protect the interests of the suspect. The Appeals Chamber argued that if the PTC declares a case inadmissible, it authorizes the Prosecutor to challenge such a decision. Then, "if the Appeals Chamber overturns the PTC's decision and determines that the case is admissible, the suspect would be faced with a decision by the Appeals Chamber that the case is admissible. The weight of the suspect to challenge the admissibility of the case before the Pre-Trial and potentially the Appeals Chamber thus would be seriously impaired."[237] Although in the present case the PTC's initial determination meant that Ntaganda was not subjected to a warrant of arrest, "this advantage is only marginal

232 Ibid., para. 89.
233 ICC, Appeals Chamber, Lubanga case, Judgment on the Prosecutor's appeal Against the Decision of Pre-Trial Chamber I entitled Decision on the Prosecutor's Application for Warrants of Arrest, Article 58, 13 July 2006, para. 42.
234 Ibid., para. 46.
235 Ibid.
236 Ibid., para. 49.
237 Ibid., para. 50.

and could be attained through other procedures" such as the Article 19 mechanism.[238] Based on these arguments, the Appeals Chamber established a guiding rule about the *proprio motu* assessment of a case by the Chambers. The discretion for reviewing the admissibility test should be exercised only "when it is appropriate in the circumstances of the case, bearing in mind the interests of the suspect."[239] This judgment forced the PTC to issue an arrest warrant against Ntaganda on 22 August 2006.[240]

Since the publication of this judgment, the Court's Chambers have refrained from *proprio motu* assessment of admissibility when deciding on arrest warrants. They have grounded their approach on the basis of the Appeals Chamber's arguments.[241] For instance, the PTC III, in its decision on the Prosecutor's application for the issuance of an arrest warrant against Laurent Gbagbo, submitted that "Article 19(1) of the Statute confers upon the Chamber a discretionary power to examine the admissibility of a case when it has received an application filed under Article 58 of the Statute. The exercise of this discretion will depend on the circumstances of the case, with appropriate consideration being given to the interests of those concerned."[242] The Appeals Chamber, in its judgment of 13 July 2006, had shed some light into these exceptional circumstances that warrant *proprio motu* assessment of the admissibility test. According to the Appeals Chamber, "such circumstances may include instances where… an ostensible cause impelling the exercise of *proprio motu* review."[243] Since the issuance of this decision, other chambers of the Court have followed this instruction and avoided assessing the admissibility test when the circumstances do not require so. For instance, the PTC I in the Al-Tuhamy case asserted that "no ostensible cause or self-evident factor impels the Chamber to exercise its discretionary power to determine the admissibility of the case against Al-Tuhamy at this stage."[244]

In spite of the predominant tendency among the case law of the Court, in a few instances the PTCs have exercised their *proprio motu* authority to examine the admissibility of a case. In such cases, where the circumstances warrant such an examination, the Appeals Chamber, however, has upheld the PTC's initiatives. For instance, in the case of the LRA suspects, following some developments within

---

238 Ibid., para. 51.

239 Ibid., para. 2.

240 ICC, PTC I, Ntaganda case, Warrant of Arrest, 22 August 2006.

241 See: ICC, PTC, Al-Tuhamy case, Warrant of Arrest for Al-Tuhamy Mohamed Khaled with under Seal and ex parte Annex, 18 April 2013, para. 4. And, ICC, PTC I, Decision on the Prosecutor's Application under Article 58 relating to Abdel Raheem Muhammad Hussein, 1 March 2012, para. 10. And, ICC, PTC I, Decision on the Prosecutor's Application Pursuant to Article 58 as to Muammar Mohammed Abu Minyar Gaddafi, Saif Al-Islam Gaddafi and Abdullah Al-Senussi, 27 June 2011, para. 4. And, ICC, Decision on the Prosecutor's Application for Summonses to Appear for Francis Kirimi Muthaura, Uhuru Muigai Kenyatta and Mohammed Hussein Ali, 8 March 2011, para. 12. And, ICC, PTC I, Al Bashir case, 4 March 2009, paras. 47–48, see *supra* note 49. And, ICC, PTC I, Harun case, 27 April 2007, para. 18, see *supra* note 48.

242 ICC, PTC III, Laurent Gbagbo case, Decision on the Prosecutor's Application Pursuant to Article 58 for a Warrant of Arrest against Laurent Koudou Gbagbo, 30 November 2011, para. 22.

243 ICC, Appeals Chamber, Lubanga case, 13 July 2006, para. 52, see *supra* note 233.

244 ICC, PTC I, Al-Tuhamy case, 18 April 2013, para. 4, see *supra* note 241.

the Ugandan judicial system and the peace process, the PTC II in October 2008 initiated proceedings *proprio motu* to examine the impact of these developments on the admissibility of the case against Kony.[245] Upon its examination, the Chamber ruled that the case remained admissible, based on the inactivity of the domestic authorities.[246] Afterwards, the Defense counsel appealed this decision. They argued that, *inter alia,* the Chamber had initiated the admissibility proceedings in the first place, while it contradicted the Appeals Chamber's judgment in the Ntaganda case.[247]

Nonetheless, the Appeals Chamber dismissed the Counsel's appeal. The Appeals Chamber emphasized the difference between the circumstances in the present review and the under seal nature of the proceedings in the Ntaganda case. The Appeals Chamber referred to two differences. First, the circumstances and context in which the proceedings were ongoing. In the Ntaganda case, proceedings "were held in camera and in which only the Prosecutor participated", but in the Kony case the proceedings were public, and the appointed Counsel for the Defense was present.[248] Secondly, the PTC's decision was based on the gravity of the case that was static because "the facts underlying the assessment of gravity are unlikely to change", whereas the Kony case in which the complementary requirement had been assessed.[249] In addition to the above-mentioned exceptional circumstances, there is another instance that may lead to the circumstances that warrants the *proprio motu* admissibility review, namely, a case in which the suspect has already been in the custody of the custodial state. This was the circumstance in the Katanga case. Katanga was detained in the DRC before being surrendered to the Court. According to PTC I, these circumstances "warrant an initial determination of the admissibility of the case prior to the issuance of a warrant of arrest."[250] Based on this argument, the PTC examined the admissibility of the Katanga case, and declared the case admissible.

Although the arguments and the cautionary judgment made by the Appeals Chamber sound reasonable in principle, in defining an ostensible cause or appropriate circumstances that warrant the *proprio motu* review of the admissibility, a narrow and strict approach should not be applied. The admissibility threshold has multiple functions. It does not serve only the interest of the accused. States have some interests that should be protected by the admissibility threshold as well. The broad powers of the Prosecutor should be under a check and balance system. The case selection is not only a matter of selection, but it includes prioritization. Therefore, the Judges should

---

245 See: ICC, PTC II, Kony case, Decision Initiating Proceedings under Article 19, Requesting Observations and Appointing Counsel for the Defense, 21 October 2008.

246 ICC, PTC II, Kony case, 10 March 2009, para. 52, see *supra* note 220.

247 ICC, Appeals Chamber, Kony case, Refiled Document in Support of Defense Appeal Against Decision on the Admissibility of the Case under Article 19(1) of the Statute dated 10 March 2009, 15 April 2009, paras. 25–36.

248 Ibid., para. 85.

249 ICC, Appeals Chamber, Kony case, Judgment on the Appeal of the Defense Against the Decision on the Admissibility of the Case under Article 19 (1) of the Statute of 10 March 2009, 16 September 2009, para. 85.

250 ICC, PTC I, Ktanga case, 6 July 2007, para. 19, see *supra* note 49.

be aware of why the Prosecutor selects a case at the cost of rejection of other cases. The Prosecutor's choices directly affect the interests of victims. These interests will be better secured by a judicial review mechanism, in the absence of the victims' right to challenge the Prosecutor's decisions.

1.4. COMPONENTS OF ADMISSIBILITY

The admissibility requirement is composed of several factors. Some assert that the admissibility requirement has three components. According to this group of authors, the admissibility requirement consists of complementarity, gravity, and double jeopardy.[251] The Appeals Chamber of the Court has also characterized the admissibility test as "referable in the first place to complementarity (Article 17(1)(a) to (b)), in the second to *ne bis in idem* (Articles 17(1)(c), 20) and thirdly to the gravity of the offence (Article 17(1)(d))."[252] However, other chambers, in their decisions, have maintained that the admissibility requirement is made up of two elements, namely complementarity and gravity.[253] The OTP Policy Paper on preliminary Examinations has adopted this standpoint as well. According to the Paper, "admissibility comprises complementarity and gravity."[254] It affirms that the recent stance is accurate.

The complementarity test as one of the admissibility components embraces 'the double jeopardy requirement' as well. Double jeopardy, as a factor that makes a case inadmissible, is examined in furtherance of the complementarity test. According to Article 20(3) of the Rome Statute, "no person who has been tried by another court for conduct also proscribed under Articles 6, 7 or 8 shall be tried by the Court with respect to the same conduct." In the words of Bassiouni, the Principle of *ne bis in idem* is a corollary to the principle of complementarity.[255] The double jeopardy requirement prevents the Court from prosecuting because of the prior intervention of States. This issue, however, is assessed under the umbrella of complementarity. The double jeopardy rule aims at protecting the accused rights, while complementarity seeks to protect the States' interests. However, a single assessment can satisfy both goals.

---

251 William A. Schabas, 'The Rise and Fall of Complementarity', in Carsten Stahn and Mohamed M. El Zeidy (eds.), *The International Criminal Court and Complementarity: From Theory to Practice*, Cambridge University Press, 2011, p. 190. And, Schabas, 2010, p. 336, see *supra* note 20. El Zeidy divides the admissibility requirement to four factors: "1. Whether the case is being investigated/ prosecuted 2. Whether state has investigated and concluded that there is no basis on which to prosecute; 3. Whether the person has already been tried for this conduct; 4. The gravity" (See: El Zeidy, 2008, p. 160, see *supra* note 19). However, it is clear that the three first factors are embodied in the concept of complementarity.

252 ICC, Appeals Chamber, Lubanga case, 14 December 2006, para. 23, see *supra* note 8.

253 ICC, PTC II, Ruto case, Decision on the Application by the Government of Kenya Challenging the Admissibility of the Case Pursuant to Article 19(2)(b) of the Statute, 30 May 2011, para. 49.

254 ICC, OTP, Policy Paper on Preliminary Examinations, para. 7.

255 Mahmoud Cherif Bassiouni, *Introduction to International Criminal Law*, Martinus Nijhoff Publishers, 2013, p. 684.

At the ICC case law, sometimes what is meant by the term 'admissibility' is one of its constituent elements, namely the complementarity rule. For instance, the PTC II in one of its decisions asserts that "admissibility is the criterion allowing the Court to identify which cases, among those in respect of which it has jurisdiction concurrently with one or more national judicial systems, it is appropriate for it to investigate and prosecute."[256] The term admissibility in this decision refers to the complementarity rule. Initially, complementarity was seen as the first part of the admissibility requirement.[257] The marginal role of the gravity test in the admissibility requirement resulted in using the admissibility as complementarity. However, over time, the gravity requirement surfaced more and more. Now, the admissibility requirement is understood as a requirement with two distinct elements.

Logically speaking, there is an order in the admissibility assessment process. In both situational and case phases, the gravity assessment precedes the complementarity evaluation. It has been claimed that the Statute does not stipulate a sequence in the consideration of gravity and complementarity.[258] However, the precedence of the gravity assessment over the complementarity examination is a logical necessity. The gravity requirement is a factor that selects one or more objects for investigation or prosecution. In a logical order, the Prosecutor has to determine the object(s) of their investigation or prosecution first, and then determines whether there is any concurrent jurisdiction over those chosen objects. This is meaningless if the complementarity assessment is given priority over the gravity examination. The Court first selects the situation or cases it intends to intervene in. Next, it examines the complementarity rule to determine whether there is an alternative for the Court's initiative. When a situation or a case is not grave, it does not matter whether a State is dealing with the situation or case at issue, because such a case or situation will not be addressed by the Court. The gravity plays a quasi-jurisdictional role here.

In the situation of Iraq, the then Prosecutor of the Court firstly addressed the issue of the gravity, and concluded that the situation at hand lacked the sufficient gravity. Therefore, he stated "in light of the conclusion reached on gravity, it was unnecessary to reach a conclusion on complementarity."[259] However, the Prosecutor often tends to prioritize the complementarity assessment over gravity. This practice is visible in the OTP's Reports on the Preliminary Examination Activities.[260] Nonetheless, as mentioned, the gravity assessment should come first.

---

256 ICC, PTC II, Kony case, 10 March 2009, para. 46, see *supra* note 220.

257 ICC, PTC I, Lubanga case, 10 February 2006, para. 30, see *supra* note 45.

258 Fabricio Guariglia and Emeric Rogier, 'The Selection of Situations and Cases by the OTP of the ICC', in Carsten Stahn (ed.), *The Law and Practice of the International Criminal Court,* Oxford University Press, 2015, p. 360.

259 ICC, OTP, Response to Communications Received concerning Iraq, 9 February 2006, p. 9.

260 For instance see: ICC, OTP, Reports on the Preliminary Examination Activities (2016), paras. 215–216.

2. SUFFICIENT GRAVITY REQUIREMENT

2.1. DIFFERENT FUNCTIONS OF GRAVITY IN THE ROME STATUTE

The term 'gravity' has been referred to in the Rome Statute at four different points. In all instances, 'gravity' is a selective factor that should be satisfied. The first context in which the gravity notion has a role is the subject-matter jurisdiction of the Court. The Preamble of the Rome Statute affirms that "the most serious crimes of concern to the international community as a whole must not go unpunished." This perambulatory phase refers to the gravity and seriousness of the nature of those crimes that fall within the jurisdiction of the Court. Article 5 of the Rome Statute enumerates these crimes as crimes against humanity, war crimes, genocide and the crime of aggression. Indeed, gravity in this sense has already played a prominent role in selecting the crimes identified in the Rome Statute. The drafters of the Court were aware of the fact that the ICC would be an organization with more restrictions than abilities. Given this feature, they tasked the Court to prosecute the most serious and the gravest international crimes. It implies that the crimes identified by the ICC are inherently grave and serious.[261]

The gravity here is a jurisdictional threshold that limits the scope of the Court's intervention to some specific crimes. The seriousness and gravity of the core crimes within the jurisdiction of the Court have been enshrined in the contextual elements of crimes referred to in the Statute. The crimes identified by the ICC consist of two components: underlying acts and a contextual element. The latter is a jurisdictional threshold that distinguishes between ordinary crimes and the core crimes. The contextual component represents the enormity of the ICC-identified crimes in terms of both perpetrators and victims. Crimes against humanity should be considered either widespread or systematic, and war crimes should be considered when committed in the context of an armed conflict. However, the Rome Statute does not require the same contextual element of crimes against humanity as for war crimes. Contrary to crimes against humanity, the underlying acts constituting war crimes do not need to be widespread or systematic. Article 8(1) of the Statute reads "the Court shall have jurisdiction in respect of war crimes in particular when committed as part of a plan or policy or as part of a large-scale commission of such crimes." Indeed, the statutory requirement of "either large-scale commission or part of a policy is not absolute but qualified by the expression 'in particular'."[262] The adverb 'in particular' makes the last

[261] Although the gravity has often played a key role in the crimes selection, De Guzman by referring to the subject-matter jurisdiction of the STL argues that the establishment of this institution with a single crime without typical gravity manifests that " a new understanding that international criminal jurisdiction can be employed even without reference to gravity" (p. 36). She concludes that "international criminal law has expanded since its inception, largely in a direction of diminished gravity" (see: De Guzman, 2012, p. 48, see *supra* note 141).

[262] ICC, Appeals Chamber, Lubanga case, 13 July 2006, para. 70, see *supra* note 233.

part of the article advisory instead of obligatory. It means that, for instance, a single serious act of sexual violence could constitute a war crime.[263]

However, there should be a nexus between such an act and the armed conflict that constitutes the context in which war crimes are committed. The absence of a jurisdictional gravity does not mean that war crimes are not grave. The Rome Statute has not added any extra gravity threshold to war crimes, since international humanitarian law had already considered these behaviors as grave crimes and grave breaches of humanitarian rules. Article 49 of the First Geneva Convention (1949) obliges States Parties to prosecute or to extradite the persons who are responsible for the grave breaches of the Convention.[264] Article 50 of the Convention specifies the breaches that are grave, and consequently should be sanctioned by criminal measures.[265] Article 8 of the Rome Statute defines war crimes as the 'grave breaches' of the Geneva Conventions. Therefore, the jurisdictional gravity is embodied in the nature of war crimes. However, gravity as the admissibility threshold is still applicable to war crimes. Some authors refer to the gravity requirement of war crimes as a 'non-threshold threshold' requirement.[266] The insertion of this 'non-threshold' connects the gravity as the jurisdictional threshold to the gravity as the admissibility rule in connection with war crimes.

The second point in which gravity plays a role pertains to the admissibility requirement. The admissibility requirement under Article 17 consists of two elements, namely gravity and complementarity. Gravity as admissibility is a selective requirement in the situation and case selection process. There is a distinction between the jurisdictional gravity and the gravity as admissibility threshold. All crimes referred to in Article 5 of the Rome Statute are grave and serious. Therefore, the gravity under Article 17 is necessarily something different and separate from the jurisdictional gravity. The PTC II in its decision on authorizing the Prosecutor to initiate an investigation in Kenya states: "all crimes that fall within the subject-matter jurisdiction of the Court are serious, and thus, the reference to the insufficiency of gravity is actually an additional safeguard, which prevents the Court from investigating, prosecuting

263 Roisin Burke, 'UN Military Peacekeeper Complicity in Sexual Abuse: The ICC or a Tri-Hybrid Court', in Morten Bergsmo (ed.), *Thematic Prosecution of International Sex Crimes* Torkel Opsahl Academic EPublisher, 2012, p. 336.

264 "The High Contracting Parties undertake to enact any legislation necessary to provide effective penal sanctions for persons committing, or ordering to be committed, any of the grave breaches of the present Convention defined in the following Article. Each High Contracting Party shall be under the obligation to search for persons alleged to have committed, or to have ordered to be committed, such grave breaches, and shall bring such persons, regardless of their nationality, before its own courts."

265 "Grave breaches to which the preceding Article relates shall be those involving any of the following acts, if committed against persons or property protected by the Convention: willful killing, torture or inhuman treatment, including biological experiments, willfully causing great suffering or serious injury to body or health and extensive destruction and appropriation of property, not justified by military necessity and carried out unlawfully and wantonly."

266 Max du Plessis and Stephen Pete, 'Who Guards the Guards', *African Security Review*, 2004, vol. 13, p. 12.

and trying peripheral cases."[267] In the words of the first Prosecutor, "crimes within our jurisdiction are by definition grave crimes of international concern. But gravity in our Statute is not only a characteristic of the crime, but also an admissibility factor, which seems to reflect the wish of our founders that the ICC should focus on the gravest situations in the world."[268] The gravity under Article 17 is a matter of exercising the Court's jurisdiction. It implies that to declare a case admissible, it is not enough to prove that the crimes identified by the ICC have been committed. To activate the Court's jurisdiction over specific situations or cases, those cases and situations should have sufficient gravity. Adding the adjective 'sufficient' implies that the gravity as the admissibility threshold is an addition to the gravity as jurisdiction. The gravity assessment is a statutory obligation upon the Prosecutor. In accordance to the PTC, "the gravity assessment is a mandatory component for the determination of the question of admissibility."[269]

The third context for the gravity's functioning is the 'interests of justice' requirement. Article 53(c) of the Rome Statute suggests this notion as one of the criteria that should be assessed in the preliminary examination. The interests of justice assessment requires taking into account some factors, including the gravity of crimes. The gravity in this context has a narrower meaning than the gravity as admissibility. The Rome Statute refers to two distinct notions, namely, gravity of crimes (interests of justice) and gravity of cases (admissibility). A case has a broader meaning than crime, because a case consists of, *inter alia,* one or more crimes. As will be discussed, the gravity of crimes under the interests of justice requirements refers to the seriousness and degree of destructive consequences and effects of crimes for victims.

The fourth point in which the Rome Statute refers to the term gravity is in the sentencing phase. Article 78(1) of the Rome Statute reads "in determining the sentence, the Court shall, in accordance with the Rules of Procedure and Evidence, take into account such factors as the gravity of the crime and the individual circumstances of the convicted person." This effect of gravity is not limited to the Rome Statute. The *ad hoc* tribunals took the gravity into account as a major consideration when determining the sentence. For instance, in the Kupreškić case it was said that "the sentences to be imposed must reflect the inherent gravity of the criminal conduct of the accused. The determination of the gravity of the crime requires a consideration of the particular circumstances of the case, as well as the form and degree of the participation of the accused in the crime."[270] What is intended to be addressed in this Chapter is gravity as admissibility under Article 17 of the Rome Statute.

---

267 ICC, PTC II, Kenya situation, 31 March 2010, para. 56, see *supra* note 33. And, ICC, PTC I, Lubanga case, 10 February 2006, para. 45, see *supra* note 45. And, ICC, PTC I, Abu Garda case, Decision on the Confirmation of Charges, 8 February 2010, para. 30.

268 ICC, OTP, Statement by Luis Moreno-Ocampo, Informal Meeting of Legal Advisors of Ministries of Foreign Affairs, 24 October 2005.

269 ICC, PTC II, Kenya situation, 31 March 2010, para. 56, see *supra* note 33.

270 ICTY, Kupreškić case, Judgment, 14 January 2000, para. 852. And, ICTR, Kajelijeli case, Trial Chamber II, Judgment and Sentence, 1 December 2003, para. 946.

2.2. GRAVITY AS THE ADMISSIBILITY THRESHOLD

Gravity is a component of the admissibility requirement, besides the complementarity rule. The idea of gravity as a constituent element of the admissibility requirement was first introduced by the International Law Commission (hereafter referred to as ILC) working group in May 1994.[271] The gravity as admissibility was not taken into account seriously as a major factor in the situation and case selection process during the first years of the Court's activities.[272] This was the same story with regards to the academic literature on the ICC.[273] At the time, the efforts of the Prosecutor were widely devoted to the complementarity assessment instead of the gravity assessment, while it was the gravity that should have played the main role in selecting situations and cases. The concept of gravity constitutes the epicenter of the legal regime of the ICC.[274] Overtime, the marginal role of gravity gradually increased.

In 2005, the first Prosecutor, in connection with the situation in Uganda, referred to the gravity threshold to justify his case selection. The then Prosecutor had decided to focus on the crimes committed by the LRA instead of the crimes committed by the State forces. To justify this selectivity, he argued that "the criteria for selection of the first case was gravity. We analyzed the gravity of all crimes in Northern Uganda committed by the LRA and Ugandan forces. Crimes committed by the LRA were much more numerous and of much higher gravity than the alleged crimes committed by the UPDF. We therefore started with an investigation of the LRA."[275] Yet, the Prosecutor failed to provide more clarification and explanation as to why the LRA's crimes were graver. Contrary to the years after inception, these days the Prosecutor routinely emphasizes the importance of gravity considerations in the situation and case selection.[276] The Rome Statute is a living document that runs a permanent institution. It is understandable that the needs and the understanding of the Court change over time. Realizing the importance of the gravity test is a welcome change in the understanding of the Court.

Gravity determines the agenda of the Court. The original philosophy behind the gravity mechanism was to prevent the Court from facing flooding of cases and

---

271 William A. Schabas and Mohamed M. El Zeidy, 'Article 17', in Otto Triffterer and Ambos (eds), *The Rome Statute of the International Criminal Court: A Commentary*, C.H. Beck. Hart. Nomos, 2016, p. 811.

272 Ignaz Stegmiller, 'Interpretative Gravity under the ICC Statute: Identifying Common Gravity Criteria', in Carsten Stahn and Mohamed M. El Zeidy (eds.), *The International Criminal Court and Complementarity: From Theory to Practice*, Cambridge University Press, 2011, p. 609.

273 William A. Schabas, 'Prosecutorial Discretion and Gravity', in Carsten Stahn and Göran Sluiter (eds.), *The Emerging Practice of the International Criminal Law*, Martinus Nijhoff Publishers, 2005, pp. 230–231.

274 Margaret M. De Guzman, 'Gravity and the Legitimacy of the International Criminal Court', *Fordham International Law Journal*, 2008, vol. 32. p. 1400.

275 ICC, OTP, Statement by Chief Prosecutor Luis Moreno-Ocampo, 14 October 2005, p. 3, available at: www.icc-cpi.int/NR/rdonlyres/9AC37606-6662-448F-8689-7317E341E6D7/277305/Uganda_LMO_Speech_141020091.pdf.

276 De Guzman, 2008, p. 1429, see *supra* note 274.

excessive workload.[277] Judge Kovacs, in his dissenting opinion about the Situation of Registered Vessel of the Comoros states that gravity "should function in such a manner as to achieve the ultimate goal for its inclusion, namely to focus on those situations/ cases which are indisputably grave and deserves the attention of the international community."[278] The Prosecutor should select those situations and cases possessing sufficient gravity. The PTC I has argued in favor of this obligation by providing a literal interpretation. According to the Chamber, Article 17(1) of the Statute uses the term 'shall' that "leaves the Chamber no discretion as to the declaration of the inadmissibility of a case once it is satisfied that the case is not of sufficient gravity."[279] The Rome Statute does not define the contours of the gravity requirement. Hence, it empowers the Prosecutor to apply his own interpretation to determine which cases possesses sufficient gravity.

The situation and case selection at the ICC are not only a matter of selection but they involve prioritization too. The situational gravity assessment has two functions: selection and prioritization. This assessment starts with independently examining a situation to determine whether it has sufficient gravity. This dimension of the situational gravity assessment is a legal threshold representing the minimum necessary gravity. Below this threshold, the Court cannot exercise its jurisdiction.[280] However, this is not the end of the story. If a situation satisfies the minimum gravity requirement, then a comparative assessment should be done to determine whether the situation at hand is not only grave, but is the gravest one. For this purpose, comparison is required.[281]

The OTP Policy Paper on case Selection, contrary to the Policy Paper on preliminary Examination, explicitly refers to selection and prioritization as two functions that should be undertaken by the Prosecutor. The Policy Paper on Case Selection and Prioritization was issued in September 2016. According to Regulation 14(2) of the OTP Regulations, "the Office shall make public Policy Papers that reflect the key principles and criteria of the Prosecutorial Strategy."[282] This Policy Paper was made public "in accordance with the practice of the Office to ensure clarity and transparency."[283] Despite the differences between situation selection and the case selection process,

---

277 El Zeidy, 2008, p. 35, see *supra* note 217.

278 ICC, PTC I, Situation on Registered Vessel of the Comoros, Partly Dissenting Opinion of Judge Peter Kovacs, 16 July 2015, para. 18.

279 ICC, PTC I, Lubanga case, 10 February 2006, para. 43, see *supra* note 45.

280 De Guzman, 2008, p. 1403, see *supra* note 274.

281 ICC, PTC I, Situation on Registered Vessel of the Comoros, Partly Dissenting Opinion of Judge Peter Kovacs, 16 July 2015, para. 20.

282 Kai Ambos and Stegmiller in describing the difference between a policy and a strategy say "the OTP uses the terms 'policy' and 'strategy', indiscriminately. The strategy papers cover certain time periods (2006–2009 and 2009–2012) and clarify the strategic objectives for the OTP, while the Policy papers address particular fundamental issues on which the Office wants to provide more clarity and transparency." (p. 417). However, they recommend the OTP to issue one main document with the overall general or specific goals instead of periodic strategies (See: Kai Ambos and Ignaz Stegmiller, 'Prosecuting International Crimes at the International Criminal Court: Is there a Coherent and Comprehensive Prosecution Strategy?', *Crime Law Social Change*, 2013, vol. 59, p. 418).

283 ICC, OTP, Policy Paper on Case Selection and Prioritization, September 2016, para. 3.

some standards that are set by the Policy Paper on case Selection are applicable to the situation selection as well. Selection of a case is made by taking into account three legal criteria referred to in the Rome Statute, namely jurisdiction, admissibility and the 'interests of justice' requirement. Prioritization, in contrast, is not explicitly mentioned by the Rome Statute. De Guzman asserts that as long as the Prosecutor selects cases above the legal thresholds, she is unlikely to deviate from the Rome Statute, even if the cases and situations selected are not always among the gravest situations.[284]

However, the OTP, by issuing the Case Selection Policy Paper for the first time, officially verified prioritization as a part of the case selection. The absence of an explicit reference to such a mechanism should not be construed as a criticism of the Rome Statute. Prioritization is requested by the rationality in prosecution. Rationality requires the proportionality between means and goals. If the Court lacks sufficient resources to discharge its mandates, the rational prosecution requires that the best means be utilized for the Court's purposes. El Zeidy calls the prioritization aspect of the gravity 'the gravest of the grave' policy.[285] Yet prioritization is not an easy task. Arbour, former Prosecutor of the ICTY, insisted in a statement to the December 1997 session of the Preparatory Committee that "in my experience, based on the work of the two Tribunals to date, I believe that the real challenge posed to a Prosecutor is to choose from many meritorious complaints the appropriate ones for international intervention, rather than to weed out weak or frivolous ones."[286] Indeed, to prove the seriousness and gravity of the selected cases and situations is not difficult, but it is often not easy to explain why those choices are more serious than other cases, which are left aside.[287] Prioritization is more complex than selection. The ICC is not able to prosecute all cases falling within its jurisdiction even if they have sufficient gravity. Therefore, the Prosecutor has to prioritize some cases over other cases.

Prioritization of a case is based on two categories of factors. First, those legal standards that have been already taken into account in choosing a case, namely the scale, impact, nature and manner of crimes. However, for the purpose of prioritization, a higher threshold is applicable. In other words, cases are prioritized and aligned based on the degree of their gravity. For instance, if there are two cases that meet the gravity requirement due to their scales, the case with a larger scale should be prioritized. Such prioritization is inevitably based on a comparative assessment. In prioritizing cases, the Office will take into consideration, *inter alia,* "a comparative assessment across the selected cases, based on the same factors that guide the case selection."[288] Secondly, prioritization is based on operational factors. Operational factors, as will be discussed, refer to those non-legal considerations that should be taken into account in prioritizing

---

284 De Guzman, 2008, pp. 1440–41, see *supra* note 274.

285 El Zeidy, 2008, p. 40, see *supra* note 217.

286 See Schabas, 2011, p. 176, see *supra* note 170.

287 William A. Schabas, 'The Short of Arm of International Criminal Law', in William A. Schabas, Yvonne McDermott and Niamh Hayes (eds.), *The Ashgate Research Companion to International Criminal Law: critical perspectives,* Ashgate, 2013, p. 404.

288 ICC, OTP, Policy Paper on Case Selection and Prioritization, 2016, para. 50.

cases and situation. A situation or case should be both legally admissible and practically available.

2.3. DIFFERENCE BETWEEN SITUATIONAL GRAVITY AND CASE GRAVITY

The gravity requirement is applied to both situations and cases. However, the assessment of gravity in the situational phase comes first. The Court exercises its jurisdiction only over those situations possessing sufficient gravity. Article 53 of the Rome Statute only refers to the admissibility of cases rather than situations. The PTCs, however, have interpreted that the gravity threshold is also applicable in the situational phase. In the Ntaganda case, the Chamber asserted "the gravity threshold provided for in Article 17.1.d of the Statute must be applied at two different stages: i) at the stage of initiation of the investigation of a situation, the relevant situation must meet such a gravity threshold and ii) once a case arises from the investigation of a situation."[289]

In the situational phase, the gravity threshold is assessed against the backdrop of two elements, namely the contextual element of a situation and its potential cases within the situation. To initiate an investigation into a situation, both components should have sufficient gravity. In the gravity assessment, the contextual element of a situation should be assessed first. If the contextual element is sufficiently grave, then the Prosecutor goes further in examining the gravity of the potential cases.

Contrary to the contextual element assessment, the assessment of potential cases has been explicitly referred to by the OTP. The OTP's Policy Paper on preliminary Examinations states that "the Office assesses the gravity of each potential case that would likely arise from an investigation of the situation."[290] Addressing the Security Council on the situation in Darfur, the first Prosecutor affirmed that in examining the situational gravity, the nature of the alleged crimes, as well as information relating to those who may bear the greatest responsibility for such crimes, are taken into account.[291] In addition, the Chambers of the Court have affirmed that in the preliminary examination stage the gravity is examined against the backdrop of the likely set of potential cases.[292] Therefore, the evaluation of gravity includes two objects: "(i) the individuals or groups of persons that are likely to be the object of an investigation, including those who may bear the greatest responsibility for the alleged crimes committed; and (ii) the gravity of crimes committed within the incidents which are

289 ICC, PTC I, Lubanga case, 10 February 2006, para. 44, see *supra* note 45. And, ICC, PTC II, Kenya situation, 31 March 2010, paras. 41–50, see *supra* note 33.

290 ICC, OTP, Policy Paper on Preliminary Examinations, November 2013, para. 57.

291 ICC, OTP, First Report of the Prosecutor of the International Criminal Court, Mr. Luis Moreno-Ocampo, to the Security Council Pursuant to UNSCR 1593(2005), 29 June 2005, p. 3.

292 ICC, OTP, Georgia Situation, Corrected Version of Request for Authorization of an Investigation Pursuant to Article 15, 17 November 2015, para. 325. And, see: ICC, PTC II, Kenya situation, 31 March 2010, para. 58, see *supra* note 33. And, ICC, PTC III, Situation in Côte d'Ivoire, 3 October 2011, paras. 202–204, see *supra* note 3.

likely to be the focus of an investigation."[293] Nonetheless, in the assessment of situational gravity, examining the contextual element is logically necessary too. The contextual element is the main component of a situation, and its gravity is determinative in selecting a situation. Therefore, the gravity assessment requires examining three objects: contextual element, potential crimes and potential suspects.

In some instances, the Court's Judges have referred to the contextual element assessment. For instance, the PTC III asserts that "an evaluation of 'gravity' should be conducted in a general sense, as regards the entire situation, but also against the backdrop of the potential case(s) within the context of a situation."[294] The Chamber adds "the assessment should be general in nature and compatible with the pre-investigative stage of a situation."[295] Moreover, in the authorization for initiating an investigation into the Kenya situation, PTC II maintains that in the connection with the gravity assessment "there is interplay between the crimes and the context in which they were committed."[296] These statements show that the Chamber believes the situational gravity assessment requires some particulars different from the gravity assessment in respect with a case. However, the Chambers have not offered more insight into the gravity assessment of the situational context.

The gravity of the situational context is assessed in order to determine whether a situation in itself is sufficiently grave to warrant an investigation. This gravity may be called 'principle gravity'. Theoretically, the gravity of a situation is examined regardless of its potential cases. If the situational context passes the gravity threshold, then the gravity of potential cases within the given situation is assessed. In the situational stage, potential cases are needed for the complementarity assessment. The complementarity assessment is not done in the abstract. Such an assessment is objective, and requires one or more concrete and tangible objects. For this purpose, the gravity is taken into account in order to choose some potential cases. Therefore, this kind of gravity can be called 'accessory gravity'. Nonetheless, what is the main factor in determining whether or not a situation is sufficiently grave is the contextual gravity.

2.4. CRITERIA FOR GRAVITY ASSESSMENT

The gravity assessment needs one or more criteria as its evaluative framework. The Rome Statute lacks any reference to the standards of the gravity assessment. Gravity

293 ICC, PTC II, Kenya situation, 31 March 2010, paras. 188–189, see *supra* note 33.

294 ICC, PTC III, Côte d'Ivoire situation, 3 October 2011, paras. 202, see *supra* note 3. And, in the Mavi Marmara situation, the PTC says that "a gravity determination involves a generic assessment (general in nature and compatible with the fact that an investigation is yet to be opened)" (ICC, PTC I, Situation on Registered Vessels of the Union of the Comoros, Decision on the Request of the Union of the Comoros to review the Prosecutor's Decision not to Initiate an Investigation, 16 July 2015, para. 21).

295 ICC, PTC III, Côte d'Ivoire situation, 3 October 2011, para. 203, see *supra* note 3. And, ICC, PTC II, Kenya situation, 31 March 2010, para. 60, see *supra* note 33.

296 ICC, PTC II, Kenya situation, 31 March 2010, para. 61, see *supra* note 33.

is considered as the most indeterminate concept of the admissibility regime.[297] The definition of gravity has been left for the Court's interpretation. De Guzman advocates the Statute's failure to elaborate the meaning of gravity. She believes that the silence in law enabled the Court's establishment, since it allowed States to support the Court without having to share a vision of gravity's role.[298]

The first judicial interpretation of the gravity notion was the PTC's decision on the Prosecutor's application to issue arrest warrants against Lubanga and Ntaganda. In that case, the PTC, in contrast with the Prosecutor's determination, was of the opinion that the Ntaganda case lacked sufficient gravity. To prove its claim, the Chamber set a definition of gravity. According to the Chamber, to determine whether a situation or case is of sufficient gravity two factors should be taken into account. First, "the conduct which is the subject of a case must be either systematic (pattern of incidents) or large-scale. Second, in assessing the gravity of the relevant conduct, due consideration must be given to the social alarm such conduct may have caused in the international community."[299] According to the Chamber, "such an additional gravity threshold is a key tool provided by the drafters to maximize the Court's deterrent effect."[300]

Later, the PTC's interpretation for the gravity requirement was rejected by the Appeals Chamber. However, the Appeals Chamber refused to offer its own interpretation.[301] Indeed, as some commenters on the Rome Statute have mentioned "when it comes to the assessment of gravity, there is no hard rule to follow."[302] In such circumstances, the Prosecutor of the Court has proposed her own understanding of the gravity parameters. The Rome Statute obliges the Prosecutor to take into account the gravity of a case or situation, without providing a definition. This silence in law has a necessary implication: the Prosecutor is authorized to fulfill her task based on their own interpretation and understanding.

The first Prosecutor of the Court on several occasions had referred to a number of criteria for the gravity assessment. For instance, in 2005 he referred to 'the number of persons killed', in addition to 'number of victims of other crimes' and 'the impact of the crimes' as factors that should be taken into account in the gravity assessment.[303] Later, this initial scope of the gravity criteria was expanded by taking into account the

---

297 Carsten Stahn, 'Taking Complementarity Seriously: On the Sense and Sensibility of 'Classical', 'Positive' and 'Negative' Complementarity', in Carsten Stahn and Mohamed M. El Zeidy (eds.), *The International Criminal Court and Complementarity: From Theory to Practice*, Cambridge University Press, 2011, p. 242.

298 De Guzman, 2012, p. 34, see *supra* note 141. The ambiguity of the gravity notion, in the eyes of de Guzman, has other effect: "the judges and prosecutors have interpreted their tasks so as to bring more and more kinds of crimes and defendants within the purview of international criminal law. Again, the ambiguity of gravity has been helpful, with judges and prosecutors frequently invoking the concept to justify their actions" (p. 36).

299 ICC, PTC I, Lubanga case, 10 February 2006, para. 46, see *supra* note 45.

300 Ibid., para. 48.

301 See: ICC, Appeals Chamber, Lubanga case, 13 July 2006, see *supra* note 233.

302 Schabas and El Zeidy, 2016, p. 816, see *supra* note 271.

303 ICC, OTP, Statement by Moreno-Ocampo, Prosecutor of the International Criminal Court, Informal Meeting of Legal Advisors of Ministries of Foreign Affairs', 24 October 2005, p. 6.

sentencing factors. According to Rule 145(1) of the Rules of Procedure and Evidence, in the sentencing, the considerations should be given to "the extent of the damage caused, in particular the harm caused to victims and their families, the nature of the unlawful behavior and the means employed to execute the crime; the degree of participation of the convicted person; the degree of intent; the circumstances of manner, time and location; and the age, education, social and economic condition of the convicted person."

In 2009, Regulation 29(2) of the OTP Regulations entered into force and codified the gravity assessment. According to this Regulation, "in order to assess the gravity of the crimes allegedly committed in the situation the Office shall consider various factors including their scale, nature, manner of commission, and impact." Defining formal criteria for mapping and selecting cases was a welcome development. Such normalization prevents biased and unfair selection, and enhances transparency and coherency in the selection process. International prosecutors should justify why an investigation should be initiated to prevent the politicization of the decision-making process.[304] According to the OTP Policy Paper on preliminary Examinations, the gravity criteria include both quantitative and qualitative considerations.[305] In addition to the Prosecutor, the Judges have also acknowledged the applicability of these criteria in the gravity assessment.[306]

In the following sections, the meaning of each criterion will be discussed. It is worth noting that those four criteria arose from the Prosecutor's interpretation and understanding. They are not necessarily permanent, as understanding is dynamic. However, as long as there is no announced change in these criteria, these standards could be used as an evaluative framework to examine the consistency in the Prosecutor's choices.

---

304 Morten Bergsmo and Cheah Wui Ling, 'Towards Rational Thematic Prosecution and the Challenge of International Sex Crimes', in Morten Bergsmo (ed.), *Thematic Prosecution of International Sex Crimes*, Torkel Opsahl Academic EPublisher, 2012, p. 4.

305 ICC, OTP, Policy Paper on Preliminary Examinations, para. 61.

306 For instance, the PTC in authorizing the investigation into the situation in Kenya states "in making its assessment, the Chamber considers that gravity may be examined following a quantitative as well as a qualitative approach. Regarding the qualitative dimension, it is not the number of victims that matter but rather the existence of some aggravating or qualitative factors attached to the commission of crimes, which makes it grave. When considering the gravity of the crime(s), several factors concerning sentencing as reflected in rule 145(l)(c) and (2)(b)(iv) of the Rules, could provide useful guidance in such an examination. These factors could be summarized as: i) the scale of the alleged crimes (including assessment of geographical and temporal intensity); ii) the nature of the unlawful behavior or of the crimes allegedly committed; iii) the employed means for the execution of the crimes {i.e., the manner of their commission); and iv) the impact of the crimes and the harm caused to victims and their families. In this respect, the victims' representations will be of significant guidance for the Chamber's assessment" (ICC, PTC II, Kenya situation, 31 March 2010, para. 61, see *supra* note 33). And, also in the decision confirming the charges against Abu Garda it is said that "in the view of the Chamber, several factors may be taken into account in the assessment of the gravity of a case. In this respect, the Chamber agrees with the Prosecution's view that, in assessing the gravity of a case, "the issues of the nature, manner and impact of the [alleged] attack are critical." Further, the gravity of a given case should not be assessed only from a quantitative perspective, i.e. by considering the number of victims; rather, the qualitative dimension of the crime should also be taken into consideration when assessing the gravity of a given case." (ICC, PTC I, Abu Garda case, 8 February 2010, para. 31, see *supra note* 267.).

2.4.1. *Scale of crimes*

According to the OTP's Policy Paper on preliminary Examinations, the scale of crimes "may be assessed in light of, *inter alia,* the number of direct and indirect victims, the extent of the damage caused by the crimes, in particular the bodily or psychological harm caused to victims and their families, or their geographical or temporal spread (high intensity of the crimes over a brief period or low intensity of crimes over an extended period."[307] The scale of crimes is a harm-oriented factor. Such a factor indicates the important status of victims in the eyes of the Court. The amount of suffering the victims within a situation endure determines the priority of a situation for the Court to intervene upon. The Policy Paper refers to the temporal or geographical intensity of a situation as applicable factors in determining the situational gravity. However, it does not mean that the temporal or geographical spread of crimes is an alternative to harms and casualties. This clause of the Paper intends to state that if a vast number of fatalities occurs, the duration of time does not matter. The situation in Guinea is a good example here. In 2009, the Prosecutor of the Court opened the preliminary examination into the situation in Guinea. The contextual element of this situation is a single event that is known as the '28 September massacre'. The incident happened on 28 September 2009, the Independence Day of Guinea, when an opposition gathering at the national stadium in Conakry was suppressed by security forces. According to the OTP Report in 2016, the situation in Guinea is under the complementarity assessment.[308] In the admissibility assessment of the Guinee situation, the gravity requirement was not considered to hamper the Court's intervention in any way.[309] This situation involves considerable casualties that occurred in an intense and brief period, i.e. almost within one day.[310]

The scale is almost a concrete criterion owing to its quantitative nature. The casualties are the first factor in determining the gravity of a situation. As the most objective and straightforward criterion for an assessment in a comparative mode, the scale factor has some advantages that mark it as the principal factor in the gravity assessment. Moreover, the scale of crimes pertains to harm and suffering experienced

---

307 ICC, OTP, Policy Paper on Preliminary Examinations, para. 62.

308 ICC, OTP, Report on Preliminary Examination Activities (2016), paras. 282, 283.

309 ICC, OTP, Report on Preliminary Examination Activities (2015), paras. 41–43.

310 The 2015 OTP's Report on the Preliminary Examination states that in the Guinea situation, based on a UN report, "at least 156 persons were killed or disappeared, and at least 109 women were victims of rape and other forms of sexual violence, including sexual mutilations and sexual slavery." This casualty rate can satisfy the legal gravity requirement, given the scale of crimes. However, comparing with other situations under preliminary examination referred to in the same report, it seems that this situation should not be given priority, while this issue has not been mentioned and discussed by the report. For instance, in the situation of Afghanistan, according to the OTP report, "over 23,000 civilians have been killed in the conflict in Afghanistan in the period between January 2007 and June 2015." It is clear and evident that this situation is bar far graver than the Guinea situation if the Prosecutor intends to select only one of them (ICC, OTP, Report on Preliminary Examination Activities (2015), para. 267).

by the victims. Harm and damage are the primary elements of victimhood.[311] It connects the scale of crimes to the interests of victims. By choosing a situation with massive numbers of victims, the Court intervenes on behalf of more victims. Although the Prosecutor may, taking into account other factors, give priority to another situation smaller in scale, such prioritization should not lead to rejection of situations with larger scale. A case with a larger scale should always be selected by the Prosecutor, even if it is not given prioritization. Situations and cases that are selected remain at the ICC's agenda until they become available for prosecution or investigation.

To determine the scale of crimes within a situation, the total number of casualties within a situation should be taken into account. It means that if a situation includes murder, rape and destruction of the cultural property, the victims of all crimes must be considered in totality. For instance, in the Georgia situation, the Prosecutor referred to the overall casualties in assessing the situational gravity. According to the Prosecutor, "The crimes allegedly committed by South Ossetian forces caused a high number of direct and indirect victims, with an estimated 51 to 113 persons killed, over 5,000 dwellings deliberately destroyed, and somewhere in the range of 13,400 – 18,500 ethnic Georgians forcibly displaced from South Ossetia and the 'buffer zone'."[312] In the situation on Registered Vessel of the Comoros, PTC I opposed the Prosecutor's opinion about the gravity of the situation in question. The Prosecutor had taken into account the small number of persons killed, but the PTC referred to the overall number of casualties, namely, ten killings, 50–55 injuries, and possibly hundreds of instances of outrage upon personal dignity, torture or inhuman treatment.[313]

There is no quantitative threshold for the extent of crimes in determining the gravity of a situation. In the absence of a definite threshold, comparison with other situations before the Court could be decision-guiding. The necessary casualties in the situational assessment should be determined on a case-by-case basis. However, a very small number of victims (such as 10 or 20 victims in an entire situation) would not satisfy the gravity requirement, given the enormity feature of the ICC-identified crimes. Yet the scale of crimes is not the only factor in determining whether a situation is sufficiently grave. The impact of a situation is an alternative that makes a situation sufficiently grave even if the number of its victims is not high.

The gravity assessment requires both selection and prioritization. Prioritizing requires comparison. In the situational gravity assessment, the gravity of the contextual element of a situation should be compared with the contexts of other situations. Perhaps contra indicatively, to assess the gravity of the potential cases arising from a situation, the comparison should be done only within that single situation. Therefore, for instance, it is imaginable that a case would be selected within a situation while its total scale is

[311] Athanasios Chouliaras, 'The Victimological Concern as the Driving Force in the Quest for Justice for State-Sponsored International Crimes', in Rianne Letschert and Roelof Haveman and Anne-Marie de Brouwer and Antony Pemberton, *Victimological Approaches to International Crimes: Africa*, Intersentia, 2011, p. 40.

[312] ICC, OTP, Georgia Situation, 17 November 2015, para. 300, see *supra* note 292.

[313] ICC, PTC I, Situation on Registered Vessel of the Comoros, 16 July 2015, para. 26, see *supra* note 294.

lower than some cases in other situations rather than across all situations. What matters is that a case should be graver than other cases in the same situation. Notwithstanding this logic, the first Prosecutor of the Court in his decision about the situation in Iraq made an inaccurate comparison. Upon receipt of many communications related to crimes committed by the British troops in Iraq after the collapse of the Saddam's regime, the Prosecutor identified a situation and opened the preliminary examination. The contextual element of the situation was the 2003 invasion of Iraq by, *inter alia*, Britain. Within this context, the Prosecutor determined that war crimes had been committed. According to the Prosecutor, the Court had jurisdiction over allegations concerning willful killing or inhuman treatment of civilians and detainees.[314]

However, he denied that the potential cases were admissible before the Court, owing to lack of gravity. The Prosecutor argued that the number of potential victims of crimes in the Iraq situation, i.e. 4 to 12 victims, was different from the number of victims in other situations under investigation at the time, namely situations in Northern Uganda, the DRC and Darfur. According to him, "each of the three situations under investigation involves thousands of willful killings as well as intentional and large-scale sexual violence and abductions. Collectively, they have resulted in the displacement of more than five million people. Other situations under analysis also feature hundreds or thousands of such crime."[315] Nonetheless, this comparative assessment was logically wrong. The Prosecutor should assess the situational gravity of the situation in Iraq by comparing the total number of victims arising from the international armed conflict in Iraq with the total number of victims in other situations to determine which one is graver. In addition, the scale of a situation should be compared with the scale of other situations separately, not collectively. However, what the Prosecutor did, in Schabas' words, was "comparing apples with oranges."[316] The Prosecutor compared the low number of some specific cases in Iraq situation, i.e. cases revolving around killing and crimes of inhuman treatment, with the total number of victims in a number of other situations. According to a report, for instance, the Iraq war had resulted in more than 500 persons killed a day by 2006.[317] This scale was comparable with other situations under the Court's investigation. The number of victims of those specific cases referred to by the then Prosecutor had to be assessed in order to select cases within the situation in Iraq. If the Iraq situation was considered grave by taking into account the total casualties in the situation, the Prosecutor would have had to compare the available cases within the Iraq situation to prioritize them.

---

314 ICC, OTP, Response to Communications Received Concerning Iraq, 9 February 2006, page 8.

315 Ibid., page 9.

316 Schabas, 2005, p. 240, see *supra* note 273. The invalidity of the Prosecutor's argument to deny the gravity of the situation in Iraq was as such that Schabas in one of his books asserted that "many suspected that Moreno-Ocampo was trying to steer clear of a confrontation with one or two major powers" (See: Schabas, 2013, p. 403, see *supra* note 287).

317 CNN, Study: War blamed for 655,000 Iraqi deaths, 11 October 2006, available at: edition.cnn.com/2006/WORLD/meast/10/11/iraq.deaths/, last accessed at on: 15 May 2017.

Given the above-mentioned argument, the approach adopted by the Policy Paper on case Selection and Prioritizations should be amended. In the Policy Paper, it is mentioned that a case is selected within a situation and across different situations.[318] It seems to imply that the Paper suggests a case should be the gravest, not only within a situation but also across different situations. Nonetheless, as mentioned, a case arising from a situation should be assessed in comparison with one or more cases in the same situation. The gravity of the case A1 in situation A does not affect the gravity of situation B.

The scale of a situation is a sufficient condition, but it is not necessary. It means that it is imaginable that a situation is considered sufficiently grave even if its casualties are lower, if it satisfies another alternative requirement: namely the impact.

2.4.2. Impact of Crimes

Another factor set by the Prosecutor as an evaluative framework for assessing the gravity is the impact of crimes. According to the Policy Paper on preliminary Examinations, such an impact may be assessed in light of "the sufferings endured by the victims and their increased vulnerability; the terror subsequently instilled, or the social, economic and environmental damage inflicted on the affected communities."[319] The impact of crimes is an alternative measure to the scale of crimes. It means if the extent of casualties in a situation or case is modest but its impact is vast, the gravity requirement is met. The Prosecutor of the Court, in her decision regarding the situation of Registered Vessel of the Comoros, admits that "in certain circumstances, a single event of sufficient gravity could warrant investigation by the Office."[320] These circumstances mostly refer to the impact of crimes.

A dividing line should be drawn between the scale of crimes and their impact as two distinct factors in assessing the gravity of a situation or case. Each crime targets one or more specified persons or objects. The direct physical, psychological, or material harms inflicted upon victims falls within the category of the scale. For instance, rape causes both bodily and mental harm. However, its emotional effect should not be considered as an independent factor. The impact factor refers to the suffering arising from a crime that is inflicted upon indirect victims. For instance, the effects of a crime on the family members of the targeted victim should be considered under its impacts. In the Situation of Registered Vessel of the Comoros, the Prosecutor referred to the impact factor by saying "the alleged crimes clearly had a significant impact on victims and their families and other passengers involved, who suffered physical and/or psychological or emotional harm as a result of the alleged crimes."[321] In addition, the PTC I in reviewing this

[318] ICC, OTP, Policy Paper on Case Selection and Prioritization, paras. 1 and 8.

[319] ICC, OTP, Policy Paper on Preliminary Examinations, para. 65.

[320] ICC, OTP, Situation on Registered Vessels of Comoros, Greece and Cambodia: Article 53(1) Report, 6 November 2014, para. 144.

[321] Ibid., para. 141.

Prosecutor's decision repeated the reference to the effects on the limited victims and their families as "an indicator of sufficient gravity."[322]

The impact factor, however, should not be assessed in a narrow domain. There are some other instances at the ICC case law that clarify the meaning of the impact of crimes. Displaced population is an example. Under Article 7 of the Rome Statute, the forced displacement or forcible transfer of population may constitute crimes against humanity. The number of victims of this crime constitutes the scale of a case or situation. However, sometimes the displacement occurs voluntarily. It is imaginable that in the context of a campaign of violence or a war, the civilian population intentionally decides to abandon their residence in order to escape the scenes of war to save their lives. Such a displacement as an incidental effect of a war should be considered as the impact of other crimes. Here, the civilian population is not directly targeted but they are affected. Intentional relocation is not a crime with specific victims. It is a consequence of the commission of other crimes. For instance, in the Georgia situation, as a result of the campaign of violence, "the civilian population of ethnic Georgians in South Ossetia was substantially reduced" by at least 75%.[323] This event represents the impact of crimes within a situation.

However, it is not necessary that the affected people reside within the territory of the country in which the situation occurs. It is imaginable that the impact of crimes committed within a situation spreads to other territories. The situation of Registered Vessel of the Comoros is a good example here. In the given situation, it was claimed that the 2010 Israeli attack on the vessels heading to the Gaza Strip had some adverse effects on the Gaza population. In this regard, it was argued that the population in Gaza was suffering from the blockade of the Gaza Strip that had been in place since 2007. Therefore, it would be of great help to the people of Gaza if the humanitarian aid carried out by the vessels if they could reach Gaza. This argument shows a clear instance of the impact of crimes on those persons who are not the direct victims of the crimes committed in a situation. Nonetheless, the Prosecutor of the Court rejected the alleged impact. Prosecutor Bensouda asserted that "it does not appear that the conduct of the IDF [Israeli Defense Force] during the incident can be considered to have had a significant impact on the civilian population in Gaza", because "the supplies carried by the vessels in the flotilla were ultimately later distributed in Gaza."[324] The Prosecutor's conclusion, however, does not contradict the understanding of the impact of crimes in the foregoing sense. The Prosecutor denied only the occurrence of such an impact in the situation at hand based on a factual assessment. However, if such an impact is proven, then its indirect impact on the Gaza population should be taken into account.

The third situation in which the impact of a situation or case may satisfy the gravity requirement is a context in which the commission of crimes results in the vulnerability

---

322 ICC, PTC I, Situation on Registered Vessel of the Comoros, 16 July 2015, para. 47, see *supra* note 294.

323 ICC, OTP, Georgia Situation, 17 November 2015, para. 332, see *supra* note 292.

324 ICC, OTP, Situation on Registered Vessels of Comoros, 6 November 2014, para. 141, see *supra* note 320.

of a populace in the relevant situation. The case law of the ICC has a typical instance in this regard, namely the attack on the peacekeepers. The first time this issue was brought to the attention of the Court was relative to the case against Abu Garda in the Darfur situation. Abu Garda was accused of the commission of an attack against the African Union peacekeepers forces (AMIS: African Union Mission in Sudan). The attack resulted in only 8 persons killed. Notwithstanding the narrow scale of the case, the first Prosecutor determined that the case would be sufficiently grave, owing to its wide impact. According to the Prosecutor: "Peacekeepers are mandated to protect and attacking them jeopardizes their mandate and puts at risk the very viability and continuation of their operations."[325]

Later in the confirmation hearing decision, the PTC I reaffirmed the Prosecutor's determination and argument. The Chamber, by referring to the Prosecutor's assertion that as a result of the attack on the AMIS "initially suspended and then reduced its activities in the area, and that this left a large number of civilians without AMIS protection", concluded that "the consequences of the attack were grave for the direct victims of the attack, that is, the AMIS personnel, and for their families. In addition; the alleged initial suspension and ultimate reduction of AMIS activities in the area as a result of the attack had a grave impact on the local population."[326] Later, in the context of the situation in Georgia, the attack on the peacekeepers constituted one of the major cases. In the South Ossetia war in 2008, both Russian and Georgian peacekeepers were attacked by other party to the conflict.[327] The Prosecutor, by recalling the argument of the PTC in the Abu Garda case, concluded that "since the JPKF[328] tasks included the implementation of the ceasefire agreement and maintenance of the regime of security in South Ossetia, the alleged attack on their personnel and premises could have had a grave impact both on victims of the attack and their families as well as on the local civilian population of South Ossetia."[329] In its authorization to initiate an investigation into the Georgia situation, PTC I noted that, "beyond the immediate casualties or extent of immediate damage, the impact of such crimes also encompasses the detriment to their ability to execute their mission."[330] Hence the admissibility of the situation was confirmed by the Chamber.

However, it should be added that although the impact of a crime may extend to a larger number of the victims, the existence of such effects should be proved and assessed. Indeed, it does not suffice to claim that the peacekeeping operations are theoretically important, and therefore an attack on them is sufficiently grave. It requires a case-by-case assessment. If in a situation, the activities of the peacekeepers are ineffectual or

325 ICC, Abu Garda case, Summary of the Prosecutor's Application under Article 58, 20 November 2008, para. 7.

326 ICC, PTC I, Abu Garda case, 8 February 2010, para. 33, see *supra* note 267.

327 ICC, OTP, Georgia Situation, 17 November 2015, para. 334, see *supra* note 292.

328 Joint Peace Keeping Forces.

329 ICC, OTP, Georgia Situation, 17 November 2015, para. 336, see *supra* note 292.

330 ICC, PTC I, Georgia Situation, Decision on the Prosecutor's Request for Authorization of an Investigation, 27 January 2016, para. 55.

if they are inactive and massive, then an attack against them does not result in a vast impact even if it terminates their mandates. The mere status of being a peacekeeper is not a privilege in the gravity assessment. As Seils asserts, focusing on peacekeepers does not suggest that "peacekeeper's lives are more valuable than those of local people, but that rather it is the damage that such attacks are likely to do to the local people which might justify the selection of such a case."[331] In some instances the peacekeepers do not contribute to peace and security, but they abuse their powers.[332] Therefore, the positive impact of the peacekeeping activities should be first substantiated. De Guzman states that the Prosecutor indeed believed that "the Court has an important role in supporting and encouraging peacekeeping worldwide that can take precedence over the goal of punishing larger-scale crimes."[333] Yet, such a perception is not acceptable. Supporting the peacekeepers does not fall within the mandates of the Court. Therefore, if the Prosecutor makes an assessment in a vacuum, he does not only compare apples with oranges, but he actually compares apples with nothing.[334] The assessment of the impacts of crimes should be based on the concrete and objective harms and damages arising from crimes.

Apart from the victims-oriented impacts, there is another kind of impact, namely, the impact of crimes on the international community. Two layers for the impact of crimes are identified. A "narrow or victim-oriented notion and a wider and community related notion."[335] The preamble of the Rome Statute affirms that the ICC-identified crimes are the most serious crimes of concern to the international community as a whole. It implies that the impact of the core crimes goes beyond the local and directly affected population, but the international community is also a potential victim of such crimes. The Court operates on behalf of the international community. For this reason, the ICC should be sensitive to the global community. The ICC should take responsibility for how this institution is perceived by others.

If the scale of crimes within a situation does not warrant the Court's intervention, but such a situation has received a wide reaction from the international community, the Prosecutor should not remain indifferent. On the contrary, the Prosecutor should respond to the public demands by, at least, opening a preliminary examination. The preliminary examination is a tool at the Court's disposal to respond to local crisis

---

331 Paul F. Seils, 'The Selection and Prioritization of Cases by the Office of the Prosecutor of the International Criminal Court', in Morten Bergsmo (ed.), *Criteria for Prioritizing and Selecting Core International Crimes Cases*, Torkel Opsahl Academic EPublisher, 2010, p. 76.

332 Joanne Mariner, 'UN Peacekeepers who Rape and Abuse are Criminals -so Treat Them as Such', 20 August 2015, available at: www.theguardian.com/global-development/2015/aug/20/un-peacekeepers-rape-sexual-abuse-criminals-car-ban-ki-moon.

333 De Guzman, 2008, p. 1461, see *supra* note 274.

334 Schabas, 2005, p. 241, see *supra* note 273.

335 Stegmiller, 2011, p. 624, see *supra* note 272. In addition, De Guzman asserts that the social alarm has three potential 'audiences': global society, states and affected populations. She says global society comprises all groups and individuals with an opinion about the legitimacy of the ICC, from NGOs to multinational corporations, social movements and informed individuals (De Guzman, 2008, p. 1444, see *supra* note 274).

with global impacts when the conditions to initiate an investigation are not available. Promoting 'general support towards the mandate and activities of the office' is one of the strategic goals of the OTP.[336] When the international community demands an investigation, and the Court is unable to respond to demands, it should manage expectations. Reaching this goal is accessible through public diplomacy and the outreach activities. Outreach has been hailed as an essential part of any transitional justice process.[337] The ICC ASP in 2006 adopted the Strategic Plan for Outreach of the ICC. The Plan takes as a given that "making judicial proceedings public is a central element of a fair trial and therefore necessary to ensuring the quality of justice."[338] In addition, the outreach program is supported by the belief that the value of justice mechanisms lie within their public impact.[339]

From the strength of this belief, the Outreach Strategic Plan urges the Court to "put in place mechanisms to ensure that affected communities can understand and follow the Court", in order to "increase the confidence of these communities in the international criminal justice system."[340] The Court's outreach activities are intended to serve various goals, including providing accurate and comprehensive information regarding the Court's role and activities, promoting greater understanding of the Court's role, responding to the concerns and expectations expressed in general by affected communities and countering misinformation.[341] The Court's outreach activities targets different groups such as general population, media, NGOs, States, victims, women and academic communities. In carrying out its outreach activities, "the Court must endeavor to use clear and consistent messages tailored to different audiences."[342] For this reason, messages should, for instance, be "developed to maximize understanding and support for the Court, manage expectations, and situate the Court as part of a broader international justice system."[343] The Outreach Strategic Plan offers various communications tools for different groups. Media has a prominent role here. "Media development is therefore a crucial component of the outreach plan."[344] Education is also another effectual tool at the Court's disposal that could be followed through training courses and workshops.[345]

In the Lubanga case, the PTC I, in the assessment of the gravity, referred to "the social alarm such conduct may have caused in the international community."[346]

336 ICC, OTP, Strategic Plan (2016–2018), para. 40.
337 Patrick Vinck and Phuong N. Pham, 'Outreach Evaluation: The International Criminal Court in the Central African Republic', International Journal of Transitional Justice, 2010, vol. 4, p. 2.
338 ICC, ASP, Strategic Plan for Outreach of the International Criminal Court, 29 September 2006, para. 2.
339 Vinck and Pham, 2010, p. 3, see *supra* note 337.
340 ICC, ASP, Strategic Plan for Outreach of the International Criminal Court, para. 3.
341 Ibid., para. 13.
342 Ibid., para. 45.
343 Ibid., para. 46.
344 Ibid., para. 88.
345 Ibid., para. 55.
346 ICC, PTC I, Lubanga case, 10 February 2006, para. 46, see *supra* note 45.

However, the Chamber did not provide more clarification or explanation about the meaning of the notion. The social alarm can be seen as equal to the impact on the international community. A crisis that provokes alarm for the international community has vast impact. The social alarm notion was rejected by the Appeals Chamber. The Appeals Chamber, in response to the Prosecutor's challenge against the PTC's decision on the application for warrants of arrest against Ntaganda provided two arguments against the notion of social alarm. Firstly, it argued that social alarm "is not mentioned in the Statute at all." Secondly, the notion "depends upon subjective and contingent reactions to crimes rather than upon their objective gravity... The subjective criterion of social alarm therefore is not a consideration that is necessarily appropriate for the determination of the admissibility of a case."[347] The opposition of the Appeals Chamber here is questionable. First, the silence in the Rome Statute is not a convincing argument. It is evident that the Statute has not mentioned all needs of the Court. A wide range of issues has been left open for interpretation. Contrary to the Appeals Chamber's point of view, the silence in the Statute warranted a judicial interpretation as done by the PTC or the Prosecutor in connection with the gravity requirement. Secondly, the subjectivity of the notion of social alarm is not an authentic argument neither. It is evident that the assessment of the admissibility requirement is subjective in nature. The situation or case selection is predominantly a prosecutorial choice. A contextual or case-by-case assessment are not a problem. What weakens the validity of a subjective examination is lack of consistency and transparency. However, if these considerations are satisfied, it is not a problem to set a subjective test.

Although the Appeals Chamber denied the applicability of the social alarm, the PTC I accepted the role of the public opinion in the gravity assessment in the context of the situation of Mavi Marmara without calling it 'social alarm'. In the recent situation, the Judges of the PTC did not accept the Prosecutor's arguments against the gravity of the situation. The Chamber requested that the Prosecutor review her decision by providing a wide range of arguments in favor of the gravity of the situation at hand. Among those arguments, the Chamber referred to role of the public opinion of the international community in the gravity assessment. Initially, the Chamber asserted that, in light of the available information, "the Prosecutor should have recognized the possibility that the events at issue had an impact going beyond the suffering of the direct and indirect victims." As one of the indicators of such a broad impact, the Chamber referred to the fact that "the international concern caused by the events at issue, which, *inter alia*, resulted in several fact-finding missions, including by the UN Human Rights Council and the UNSG, is somehow at odds with the Prosecutor's simplistic conclusion that the impact of the identified crimes points towards the insufficient gravity of the potential."[348]

Finally, the Chamber terminated its decision by saying that "the Chamber cannot overlook the discrepancy between, on the one hand, the Prosecutor's conclusion that the identified crimes were so evidently not grave enough to justify action by the Court, of

[347] ICC, Appeals Chamber, Lubanga case, 13 July 2006, para. 72, see *supra* note 233.

[348] ICC, PTC I, Situation on Registered Vessel of the Comoros, 16 July 2015, para. 48, see *supra* note 294.

which the raison d'être is to investigate and prosecute international crimes of concern to the international community, and, on the other hand, the attention and concern that these events attracted from the parties involved, also leading to several fact-finding efforts on behalf of States and the UN in order to shed light on the events. The Chamber is confident that, when reconsidering her decision, the Prosecutor will fully uphold her mandate under the Statute."[349] This statement is a compelling and plausible argument.

Here, one can ask how the public opinion of the international community can be measured. Answering this question goes beyond the limits of this thesis but it suffices to say that there is not a direct way to gauge the public opinion in the international sphere, so a representative approach should be adopted. One of the available methods is considering the activities of international and regional organizations like the UN organs, or major international non-governmental organizations like the HRW, and the communications, and media outlets. The UN Human Rights Council reaction to a crisis can be helpful in discovering the impact of the crisis on the international community. Moreover, the UN Security Council's role is considerable, so as to reflect the international concern regarding a specific situation. The Security Council's Resolutions announcing a crisis as a threat to international peace and security in addition to establishing a mission for the situation are reflective of the international concern.[350] Despite the fact that the initiative of the Security Council warrants the Court's intervention directly (through referrals) or indirectly (through the gravity assessment), it should be mentioned that non-intervention of the Security Council is by no means a reflector of a lack of gravity. It is clear that due to the political nature of the Council's decisions, in many situations the Council is inactive. For instance, some scholars have referred to some situations including Myanmar and Pakistan as one of the gravest situations across the world while the UNSC has paid little attention to them; "it is also notable that the human rights violations committed within Nepal, Myanmar and Pakistan are out of reach of the ICC. In these situations, the UNSC has not even qualified these situations as constituting a threat to international peace and security. Here too the lack of jurisdiction shows a shortcoming in the international criminal justice system, showcasing its selective nature."[351]

Indeed, *proprio motu* investigation was designed to make up this deficiency. Because the UNSC is not always a reliable source to reflect the concerns of the international community, the ASP could assume more roles to project the concerns of the international community. It could be suggested that the States Parties to the Court collectively should be able to refer a situation to the Court, as States are able to do so independently. In this scenario, there is less pressure on the referring State in comparison with the situation where a State refers the situation pertaining to another country independently. Such pressures are evident in that no State has referred a situation of another State so far.

---

349 Ibid., para. 50.

350 For instance, in 2004 the Security Council authorized, acting under Chapter VII, to send troops to Côte d'Ivoire and established the United Nations Operation in Côte d'Ivoire (UNOCI), 2004.

351 Smeulers and Weerdesteijn and Hola, 2015, p. 36, see *supra* note 221.

2.4.3. *Nature of Crimes*

Another factor proposed by the Prosecutor in the gravity assessment is the nature of crimes. According to the prosecutorial Policy Paper on preliminary Examinations, this test refers to "the specific elements of each offence such as killings, rapes and other crimes involving sexual or gender violence and crimes committed against children, persecution, or the imposition of conditions of life on a group calculated to bring about its destruction."[352]

2.4.3.1. Thematic Prosecution

Grounding the case selection on the nature of crimes offers a kind of prosecution that is known as 'thematic prosecution'. Thematic prosecution means to orient cases around particular themes of criminality.[353] A thematic approach to the prosecution of international crimes has been insisted upon by the international prosecutors. For instance, Goldstone says that both the ICTY and ICTR have shown a unique concern for prosecuting sex crimes.[354]

Expressivism is the main justification behind the thematic prosecution. The Court's intervention may shatter "the culture of impunity that frequently surrounds the commission of international crimes."[355] What is sought by the international criminal justice system is a culture in which the ICC-identified crimes such as "rape and other forms of sexual harm are identified as harms, they are prosecuted as crimes, and they result in punishment through years of incarceration for those found guilty."[356] To spread the culture of accountability, the thematic prosecution gives priority to those crimes that are mostly under-prosecuted.[357] The crimes in the center of thematic prosecution's attention are largely under-prosecuted at the domestic level. It is not due to the lack of enforcement conditions, but because they have been traditionally marginalized. The impunity surrounding these themes has a cultural effect because it creates circumstances in which the crimes are tolerated, and feelings of fear and shame prevent their victims from seeking justice.

The ICC 'thematic prosecution', however, seeks to express and project the values that have remained marginal, and to encourage States to take action to protect those values that need special protection. Giving priority to specific criminal themes gives voices to those victims whose voices are not heard, while they are victims of the most

---

352 ICC, OTP, Policy Paper on Preliminary Examinations, para. 63.

353 Margaret M. De Guzman, 'An Expressive Rationale for the Thematic Prosecution of Sex Crimes', in Morten Bergsmo (ed.), *Thematic Prosecution of International Sex Crimes*, Torkel Opsahl Academic EPublisher, 2012, p. 11.

354 Richard J. Goldstone, 'International Crimes against Women: Prosecuting Rape as a War Crime', *Case Western Reserve Journal of International Law,* 2002, vol. 34, p. 278.

355 Guariglia, 2012, p. 58, see *supra* note 214.

356 Doris Buss, 'Performing Legal Order: Some Feminist Thoughts on International Criminal Law', *International Criminal Law Review,* 2011, vol. 11, p. 411.

357 *See*: De Guzman, 2012, *supra* note 353.

serious crimes. The ICC has a worthy capacity for exercising the thematic prosecution. Thanks to the complementarity principle, the Court is able to highlight some types of crimes, and encourages and pushes States to prosecute them. Here, thematic prosecution and norm projection may possibly have a 'knock-on effect' on domestic criminal proceedings.[358] As Rastan asserts, gravity guides national investigations, since domestic authorities will be aware that their own activities must relate to cases focused by the Prosecutor due to their gravity.[359] Thematic prosecution then leads to globalization of some norms.

2.4.3.2. Criminal Themes at the ICC

So far, three categories of crimes have been prioritized in light of the thematic prosecution, namely, sexual and gender-based crimes, crimes against children and crimes against the cultural property.

At the ICC, gender-based crimes have been at the center of the prosecutorial activities. Article 54(b) of the Rome Statute requests that the Prosecutor takes into account "the nature of the crime, in particular where it involves sexual violence, gender violence or violence against children."[360] For a long time international criminal courts and tribunals have tended to focus on prosecuting crimes involving killing rather than on sex crimes.[361] A UN report mentions that these crimes are widely under-reported.[362] In Goldstone's words, "men [wrote] the laws of war in an age when rape was regarded as being no more than an inevitable consequence of war."[363] In dealing with war crimes, sexual crimes used to be seen as 'incidental' or 'opportunistic' in relation to other core crimes. Nonetheless, as the Appeals Chamber of the SCSL concludes that rape in war is "not intended merely for personal satisfaction or a means of sexual gratification for the fighter."[364] Indeed, rape has been used as a weapon in conflicts. However, such crimes remain under-prosecuted, and in the context of conflicts are "often tacitly encouraged or tolerated, even if not officially

---

358 Kai Ambos, 'Thematic Investigations and Prosecution of International Sex Crimes: Some Critical Comments from a Theoretical and Comparative Perspective', in Morten Bergsmo (ed.), *Thematic Prosecution of International Sex Crimes*, Torkel Opsahl Academic EPublisher, 2012, p. 313.

359 Rastan, 2011, p. 459, see *supra* note 17.

360 The issue of sexual crimes is of concern to the international community as a whole. The Resolutions adopted by the UNSC are reflective of this fact. For instance, Resolution 1325 adopted in 2000 calls on all parties to armed conflicts to take special measures to protect women and girls from gender-based violence, particularly rape and other forms of sexual abuse. And, Resolution 1820 noted that rape and other forms of sexual violence could constitute war crime, crime against humanity, or genocide.

361 Margaret M. De Guzman, 'Giving Priority to Sex Crime Prosecutions: The Philosophical Foundations of a Feminist Agenda', *International Criminal Law Review*, 2011, vol. 11, p. 516.

362 Report of an Independent Review on Sexual Exploitation and Abuse by International Peacekeeping Forces in the Central African Republic, 17 December 2015, p. 16.

363 Goldstone, 2002, p. 279, see *supra* note 354.

364 SCSL, Appeals Chamber, Issa Hassan and Sesay Morris Kallon and Gbao case, 26 October 2009, para. 440.

sanctioned."[365] Marginalizing sexual crimes against women at the domestic level uncovers the marginalization of women in themselves. De Guzman mentions that "as long as women's lives remain undervalued, societal evaluations of the seriousness of harm to women will be unreliable."[366] The reluctance to prosecute sexual crimes has a wide range of reasons, but the difficulty in speaking about these crimes plays a key role. Indeed, some societies look down on the sexual crimes' victims as if "they did something wrong, thereby placing the guilt and shame on the victims instead of the perpetrator."[367] These circumstances aggravate the culture of impunity surrounding these crimes.

The victims' silence strengthens the culture in which speaking about sexual violence is difficult. Impunity of the sexual crimes' perpetrators has led to secondary victimization, since it entails "both the lack of recognition of the occurrence of a violation and the denial of attribution to someone of the quality of victim."[368] By contrast, giving priority to sexual crimes encourages "more and more women to talk."[369] Given these facts, since the beginning of her work at the OTP, Prosecutor Bensouda has been pursuant with a clear policy, namely giving priority to the gender-based crimes and sexual violence besides the crimes against children. This policy has occupied one of the key strategic goals of the OTP since 2012. The Strategic Plan for 2016–2018 repeats that the OTP has integrated "a gender perspective in all areas of the Office's work" and has selected implementing the policies in relation to sexual and gender-based crimes and crimes against children as one of its strategic goals.[370] The Prosecutor does not intend to focus largely or exclusively on sexual crimes but to integrate these charges in all cases, if they exist, in order to best explain the cumulative harms faced by victims. Such an inclusive approach helps the Prosecutor to contextualize a situation of crisis in a more comprehensive way.

The OTP issued a Policy Paper on Sexual and Gender-Based Crimes in June 2014. The Prosecutor in the Policy Paper admits that her office is committed "to integrating a gender perspective and analysis into all of its work, being innovative in the investigation and prosecution of these crimes, providing adequate training for staff, adopting a victim-responsive approach in its work, and paying special attention to staff interaction with victims and witnesses and their families."[371] According to the Policy Paper, gender perspective requires "an understanding of differences in status, power roles and needs

365 Susana Sacouto and Katherine Cleary, 'The Importance of Effective Investigation of Sexual Violence and Gender-Based Crimes at the International Criminal Court', *Journal of Gender Social Policy and the Law,* 2009, vol. 17, p. 350.

366 De Guzman, 2011 p. 522, see *supra* note 361.

367 Anne-Marie de Brouwer, 'The Importance of Understanding Sexual Violence in Conflict for Investigation and Prosecution Purposes', *Cornell International Law Journal*, 2015, vol. 48. p. 650.

368 Chouliaras, 2011, p. 40, see *supra* note 311.

369 Flor de Maria Valdez-Arroyo, 'Prospect for Thematic Prosecution of International Sex Crimes in Latin America', in Morten Bergsmo (ed.), *Thematic Prosecution of International Sex Crimes*, Torkel Opsahl Academic EPublisher, 2012, p. 107.

370 ICC, OTP, Strategic Plan (2016–2018), para. 4.

371 ICC, OTP, Policy Paper on Sexual and Gender-Based Crimes, para. 2.

between males and females and the impact of gender on people's opportunities and interactions."[372] Gender analysis, according to the Paper, examines "the underlying differences and inequalities between women and men, and girls and boys, and the power relationships and other dynamics which determine and shape gender roles in a society and give rise to assumption and stereotypes."[373] For the Court's functioning, this involves "a consideration of whether and in what ways, crimes including sexual and gender based crimes are related to gender norm and inequalities."[374] It shows that apart from giving priority to the prosecution of sexual crimes, the Prosecutor has added a criminology vision to her works in order to understand better the reasons and causes of such crimes.[375] The Policy Paper clarifies that this category of crimes occupies the top priority of the Prosecutor from the preliminary examination stage.[376] It means that this prioritization is applied to the situational gravity assessment as well, when the Prosecutor intends to choose the potential cases. To justify such prioritizing, the Prosecutor argues that her office "recognizes that sexual and gender-based crimes are among the gravest under the Statute."[377]

Incorporating the thematic prosecution at the ICC legal system produces some structural and institutional benefits too. The Rome Statute enumerates a broad range of sexual violence and gender-based crimes as war crimes and crimes against humanity. This initiative has been seen as a response to decades of inadequate investigation and prosecution of rape and other forms of sexual violence at the international level.[378] However, the mere inclusion of sexual crimes in the Rome Statute is not enough, the inclusion of special structural mechanisms is needed. Thematic prosecution develops "relevant investigative and prosecutorial expertise and expanding the applicable law."[379] Through thematic prosecution of sexual crimes, the judicial institutions are empowered with sufficient knowledge and experience as to how to deal with these

---

372 Ibid., para. 3.

373 Ibid., para. 4.

374 Ibid.

375 Although the thematic prosecution in some situations is necessary, Benson Chinedu Olugbuo discusses that "the solution to sexual violence may not lie with targeted prosecution of international sex crimes. Rather, efforts should be made to address the underlying factors that result in the stigmatization of victims and survivors of sexual violence" (See: Benson Chinedu Olugbuo, 'Thematic Prosecution of International Sex Crimes and Stigmatization of Victims and Survivors: Two Sides of the Same Coin?', in Morten Bergsmo (ed.), *Thematic Prosecution of International Sex Crimes*, Torkel Opsahl Academic EPublisher, 2012, p. 11). In line with this idea, Susanna Greijer suggests that "the more women's roles in society are strengthened, the rarer the systematic attacks against women that we have seen" (Susanna Greijer, 'Thematic Prosecutions for Crimes against Children', in Morten Bergsmo (ed.), *Thematic Prosecution of International Sex Crimes*, Torkel Opsahl Academic EPublisher, 2012, p. 170).

376 The prosecutorial Policy Paper states: "The office pays particular attention to the commission of sexual and gender-based crimes at all stages of its work: preliminary examination, investigation and prosecution" (ICC, OTP, Policy Paper on Sexual and Gender-Based Crimes, para. 4).

377 ICC, OTP, Policy Paper on Sexual and Gender-Based Crimes, para. 3.

378 Sacouto and Cleary, 2009, p. 341, see *supra* note 365.

379 Karen Engle, 'Feminism and Its (Dis)contents: Criminalizing Wartime Rape in Bosnia and Herzegovina', *The American Journal of International Law*, 2005, vol. 99, pp. 781–782.

crimes. These developments involve some measure like "having female personnel interrogate female victims and ensuring that all personnel working with victims of sex crimes receive training in gender sensitivity and other specifically relevant skills."[380]

For this reason, Article 42(9) of the Rome Statute obliges the Prosecutor to "appoint advisers with legal expertise on specific issues, including, but not limited to, sexual and gender violence and violence against children." The importance of this benefit is understood better if by taking into account that some admit rape prosecutions result in failure due to insufficiently skilled and trained investigators.[381] De Brouwer shows how difficulties in prosecution of sexual violence lead to the reluctance of judicial institutions to address these kind of crimes. She uncovers a tendency among the international judges not to deal with sexual crimes, owing to the existing difficulties, including cultural matters.[382] Thematic prosecution focuses on these kinds of crimes, and struggles to pave the way for prosecuting them. The Court's experience in this regard could be followed by others.

At the beginning, the thematic prosecution of sexual crimes insisted on crimes against women and girls. However, the reality is that sexual crimes are gender-based crimes, and they are committed against both men and women. Based on this new understanding, the attention is gradually being directed to crimes against men.[383] De Brouwer sexual violence in conflict can be committed in many different ways, for many different reasons, by anyone (women, girls, men, and boys) and against anyone (women, girls, men, and boys).[384] Thematic prosecution targets the roots and culture in which crimes grow. If sexual violence against women is under-prosecuted because of being under-reported, crimes against male victims have the same feature. If a man is raped, in the eyes of some societies, his manhood is lost and maybe he cannot continue his life with his wife, beside the problem of facing the charge of homosexuality.[385]

Crimes against children are another important theme in the OTP. In November 2016, the OTP issued its Policy on Children. The Policy grounds two main bases for the OTP's functioning regarding children. First, it adopts "a child-sensitive approach in all aspects of its work involving children."[386] Secondly, the Office will address the various ways that crimes may affect children. This Policy directs the Prosecutor to "include charges for crimes directed specifically against children, as well as crimes that acutely or disproportionately affect children."[387] Based on this policy and in light of the thematic prosecution, the OTP has prioritized prosecuting child soldiering in its functions. Interestingly, the first case at the ICC was formed around child soldiers. In

---

380 Greijer, 2012, p. 162, see *supra* note 375.

381 Ambos, 2012, p. 310, see *supra* note 358.

382 See: De Brouwer, 2015, see *supra* note 367.

383 For instance see: Sandesh Sivakumaran, 'Sexual Violence Against Men in Armed Conflict', *The European Journal of International Law*, 2007, vol. 18. Dennis Altman, 'The Landscape of Silence: Sexual Violence Against Men in War', *Culture, Health and Sexuality*, 2016, vol. 18.

384 De Brouwer, 2015, p. 648, see *supra* note 367.

385 Ibid., p. 646.

386 ICC, OTP, Policy on Children, November 2016, p. 2.

387 Ibid.

the context of the situation in the DRC, Lubanga was accused of the war crimes of using child soldiers in the conflict. By choosing the use of child soldiers in its first case, "the ICC legitimizes the very idea of thematic prosecution at the international and national levels."[388] At the time of issuing Lubanga's arrest warrant, some strongly criticized the Prosecutor's selection, because the accused had already been in a local detention due to more serious charges. For instance, Schabas challenged the approach of the Court to the Lubanga case, since the PTC "never examined the relative gravity of the offence for which Lubanga was in the custody in the DRC at the time and the crime with which he was charged before the International Criminal Court."[389] Schabas argues that although the Prosecutor had reasoned that "forcing children to be killers jeopardizes the future of mankind", "the DRC was doing a better job because it was addressing crimes of greater gravity. Certainly genocide and crimes against humanity might also be said to 'jeopardize the future of mankind'."[390]

However, Schabas's criticism is not correct. It should first be noted that some are of the opinion that in choosing the child soldiering as the only charge against Lubanga, it was not a matter of gravity but it was because of the evidence availability. For instance, Bosco believes that the Prosecutor selected the charge of recruiting child soldiers, because the evidence linking him to murder and rape was weak.[391] The evidence availability is a consideration that is now admitted as an important factor in prioritization and selection of the cases under category of 'operational factors'. However, even if the availability of the child soldiering case was not the reason behind the then Prosecutor's decision, the thematic prosecution could justify this selection. Under this theory, the Court assumes a norm proliferation mandate. When there is a crime that is globally under-prosecuted while it is opted for ICC crimes, the Prosecutor may pick that crime in order to shatter the banality of its commission. As to child soldiering, it has been said that "the recruitment of child soldiers has not always been a crime under international law, and remains legal in some domestic systems."[392] The Court, by opting for this crime, tries to deliver a message to the international community that this common behavior should be condemned.

The last criminal theme that has been put in the center of the OTP's activities is crimes against cultural properties. The case of Al-Mahdi is an example here. In July 2012, the Malian Government referred the Situation in Mali to the ICC. By conducting the preliminary examination, the Prosecutor determined that as of January 2012, an ongoing non-international armed conflict continued in the territory of Mali between the government forces and different organized armed groups.[393] Therefore, the information available persuaded the Prosecutor to believe that there was reasonable

388 Bergsmo and Wui Ling, 2012, p. 2, see *supra* note 304.
389 Schabas, 2005, p. 241, see *supra* note 273.
390 Ibid., p. 242.
391 David Bosco, *Rough Justice*, Oxford University Press, 2014, p. 124.
392 De Guzman, 2008, p. 1461, see *supra* note 274.
393 ICC, OTP, Situation in Mali, Article 53(1) Report, 2013, January 2013, para. 3.

basis to believe that war crimes have been committed in Mali.[394] In her report on the Preliminary Examination on the situation in Mali, the Prosecutor refers to the gravity of crimes committed within the given situation, and highlighted the murder and killing.[395] In spite of the centrality of the killings in the Mali situation, PTC I issued a warrant for Ahmad Al Faqi Al Mahdi's arrest exclusively charging him of the war crime of attacking protected objects in Timbukto under Article 8(2)(e)(iv) of the Statute.[396] The accused was tried, and finally on 27 September 2016 was convicted and sentenced to nine years of imprisonment.[397]

The Prosecutor's decision to pursue the Al-Mahdi case in the Mali situation faced various challenges. As to the selected conduct, namely the destruction of cultural property, some believe that such an exclusive selection was wrong because it ignored other atrocities committed in Mali that are, allegedly, more significant than the destruction of some buildings.[398] However, this critical reading of the Al-Mahdi case lacks precision. The Al-Mahdi case should be understood in light of the thematic prosecution that guides the Prosecutor to prioritize a specific criminal theme and a specific category of crimes in order to promote prosecuting those crimes. Such prioritization is justifiable because those themes are generally under-prosecuted and do not trigger the judicial initiatives at the national level, in particular in the countries and societies affected by those crimes.

The Prosecutor's decision to prosecute the attacks on cultural properties in Timbukto is entirely consistent and compatible with the idea of thematic prosecution, and should be understood and read in light of this notion. In the context of conflicts, the objects and buildings barely draw any attention. They are just considered as objects that do not have anything to do with human victims. However, the recent case raised by the Prosecutor has changed the perspective from which cultural properties used to be seen. The Al-Mahdi case and the Prosecutor's approach to it show that cultural properties are not lifeless buildings but human beings are linked to them with strong spiritual and emotional bonds. In the words of Prosecutor, the attack on the cultural property is "a profound attack on the identity, the memory and, therefore, the future of entire populations."[399] The destruction of cultural heritage is not only the destruction

394 Ibid., para. 7.

395 According to the Report, "depending on the sources reviewed, the number of members of the Malian Armed Forces who have reportedly been summarily executed following the attack on the military basis in Aguelhok on 24 January 2012 range between 70 and 153. 145. Nature: the alleged crime constitutes the war crimes of murder of combatants hors de combat under Article 8(2)(c)(i). The killing of combatants hors de combat is no less grave than the killing of civilians." (Ibid., para. 144–45).

396 ICC, Trial Chamber VIII, Al-Mahdi case, Judgment and Sentence, 27 September 2016, para. 2.

397 Ibid.

398 International Federation for Human Rights, Mali: The Hearing of Al Mahdi before the ICC is a Victory, but Charges must be Expanded, 30 September 2015, available at: www.fidh.org/en/issues/international-justice/international-criminal-court-icc/mali-the-hearing-of-abou-tourab-before-the-icc-is-a-victory-but, last accessed at 9 May 2017.

399 ICC, OTP, Statement of the Prosecutor of the International Criminal Court, Fatou Bensouda, at the Opening of Trial in the Case against Mr Ahmad Al-Mahdi Al Mahdi, 22 August 2016, available at: www.icc-cpi.int/Pages/item.aspx?name=otp-stat-al-mahdi-160822, last accessed at 9 May 2017.

of non-living stones and bricks but it is the elimination of differences in beliefs and identities and, as a result, it is a grave violation of the right to be different. The real victims of the cultural properties are not buildings but are those people who have a close bond with those places. And, when a location is considered as a World Heritage site, the international community as a whole is affected. It is worth saying that the OTP is now working on drafting a policy paper on the cultural properties to formulate its thematic prosecution regarding the crimes against cultural properties.[400]

2.4.3.3. Exercising Thematic Prosecution

Thematic prosecution could be exercised in two ways: exclusive and prioritizing. Prosecuting a theme could be done exclusively by not counting other crimes and charges in a case. This approach draws attention to a criminal theme in a more effective way. The Foča case in the ICTY is a clear example of this approach where the tribunal charged a number of former soldiers with crimes related to the infamous 'rape camps' in that city.[401] However, exclusive thematic prosecution can be criticized. Thematic prosecution is justifiable but it should not be applied at the cost of other serious crimes. Focusing on a theme in an exclusive manner undermines the legitimacy of thematic prioritization.[402] Thematic prosecution prioritizes a theme as the starting point of prosecution, but it adds other charges in furtherance of a case. The OTP Regulations instructed the Office to select "incidents reflective of the most serious crimes and the main types of victimization – including sexual and gender violence and violence against children – and which are the most representative of the scale and impact of the crimes."[403] This Regulation directs the Prosecutor to take into account the nature of crimes in a manner that they reflect the main types of victimization. The selected cases should draw a comprehensive picture of the crisis. If the prosecution does not include different episodes of victimization, some victims do not feel that the case brought by the Prosecutor is their cases. By ensuring that the episodes selected for prosecution are clear and illustrative examples of the type of victimization, the victim "whose individual victimization has not been included in the prosecution's charges, may still feel that her suffering is nonetheless being addressed, even if in an indirect fashion."[404] Therefore, at the ICC a prioritizing thematic prosecution should be followed.

---

400 Sam Sasan Shoamanesh and Gilles Dutertre, The ICC and Cultural Property: Reinforced Legal Enforcement of the Protection of Cultural Property in Armed Conflict, 22 June 2016, available at: www.international-criminal-justice-today.org/arguendo/the-icc-and-cultural-property/, last accessed at 9 May 2017.

401 See: ICTY, Foča case, Judgment, 22 February 2001.

402 Christopher Mahony, 'Prioritising International Sex Crimes before the Special Court for Sierra Leone: One More Instrument of Political Manipulation?', in Morten Bergsmo (ed.), *Thematic Prosecution of International Sex Crimes*, Torkel Opsahl Academic EPublisher, 2012, p. 82.

403 Regulation 34(2) of the OTP Regulations.

404 Guariglia, 2012, p. 55, see *supra* note 214.

Thematic prosecution should be accompanied with another policy adopted by the Prosecutor, namely open-ended investigation. This policy was first adopted in the Strategic plan for 2012–2015 and continued in the last Strategic Plan for 2016–2018. This policy is performing in-depth and open-ended investigations. 'In-depth' refers "to the Office's new approach to increasingly collect diverse forms of evidence to support its cases", and the 'open-ended' aspect means that "the Office first identifies alleged crimes (or incidents) to be investigated within a wide range of incidents. This approach implies the need to consider multiple alternative case hypotheses."[405] It provides the Prosecutor with more time to collect evidence in order to build up a case. The Ongwen case represents well this policy in practice. Ongwen, a former commander of the LRA, initially was accused of seven counts based on his individual criminal responsibility: three counts of crimes against humanity (murder; enslavement; and other inhumane acts) and four counts of war crimes (murder; cruel treatment; attack against the civilian population; and pillaging). However, later and upon his surrender to the Court, the Prosecutor in December 2015, charged the accused with new crimes in addition to those set out in the warrant of arrest: a total of seventy counts.[406] This policy was primarily adopted regarding the availability of a case in term of the supporting evidence. This policy is intended to allow the Prosecutor to begin with the most available charges, and then to complete the initial charges with extra ones, if they obtain the relevant evidence. This policy is also workable for materializing the thematic prosecution. The Prosecutor may begin with one single theme in order to highlight the given charge, then they can add extra charges. Indeed, in this scenario, even if there is sufficient evidence for a wide range of charges, the intended theme is prioritized. Another method to materialize the thematic prosecution in a non-exclusive way is the way that is being followed in the Al-Mahdi case. To represent all victimization within a situation, it is not necessary to build up an inclusive and comprehensive case. It is also acceptable that the Prosecutor selects some cases, each one representing a specific theme. In this scenario, ensuing cases should include other charges.

2.4.4. Manner of Crimes' Commission

The last factor that has been offered by the Prosecutor to determine whether a case is grave is the manner of the commission of crimes. To clarify her understanding of the manner factor, the Prosecutor refers to a long list including "the means employed to execute the crime, the degree of participation and intent of the perpetrator (if discernible at this stage), the extent to which the crimes were systematic or result from a plan or organized policy or otherwise resulted from the abuse of power or official capacity, and elements of particular cruelty, including the vulnerability of the victims, any motives involving discrimination, or the use of rape and sexual violence as a

---

405 ICC, OTP, Strategic Plan (2016–2018), para. 34.

406 ICC, OTP, Ongwen case, Alleged crimes (Non-exhaustive List), available at: www.icc-cpi.int/uganda/ongwen/pages/alleged-crimes.aspx, last accessed at 9 May 2016.

means of destroying groups."[407] Giving priority to the manner as a factor in the case selection is to enhance ending impunity. If the manner of the commission of crimes uncovers a culture of impunity, the expressive mandate of the Court warrants the ICC's intervention. Cruelty in the commission of crimes or showing off the atrocities indicate that the perpetrators do atrocities without fear and shame. Such a situation requires the Court's intervention to shatter the impunity. It is mainly the case when the owners of power and force commit atrocities.

The involvement of State agents in perpetrating crimes should be seen as an indicator of gravity, "since violence is exercised by the same officers in charge of protecting the population and ensuring the free and full exercise of all rights and freedoms by all persons subject to their jurisdiction."[408] States tend to prosecute crimes committed by rebels, but they rarely prosecute crimes committed by their own officials and soldiers.[409] A State that commits atrocities itself is not in a position to deliver justice by prosecuting its leaders. To overcome this impunity gap, the priority should be given to the States crimes. However, it does not deny the necessity of prosecuting the rebels' crimes. If the crimes committed by the rebels are committed in brutality, the priority could be given to them. Cruelty in the commission of crimes is a factor that is taken into account by the Prosecutor to assess the gravity requirement. For instance, in the Mali situation the Prosecutor confirmed the gravity of the situation by referring to, *inter alia*, cruelty of crimes. "Some of the detainees were allegedly mutilated, disemboweled, tortured and/or had their throats slit, while others were allegedly executed by being shot in the head."[410] Or, in the Afghanistan situation, the Prosecutor determined that the crimes allegedly committed by the US forces are sufficiently grave because those crimes were committed with particular cruelty, and "in a manner that debased the basic human dignity of the victims."[411] Another example are the ISIS crimes. This terrorist group tends to show off and exhibit their atrocities by recording and sharing them through the media. Such a manner proves the gravity of a case. Cruelty that shocks feelings of the international community uncover its wide impact too.

2.5. THE CASE STUDY OF THE SITUATION OF REGISTERED VESSEL OF THE COMOROS

The current section aims at studying the situation of Registered Vessel of the Comoros, since it has provided a judicial interpretation for the gravity requirement in the situational phase. Indeed, this situation elaborates the meaning of the gravity requirement as a decisive factor in the ICC situation selection regime. The contradiction

407 ICC, OTP, Policy Paper on Preliminary Examinations, para. 64.
408 Valdez-Arroyo, 2012, p. 92, see *supra* note 369.
409 Kevin Jon Heller, 'Situational Gravity under the Rome Statute', in Carsten Stahn and Larissa Van den Herik (eds.), *Future Perspectives on International Criminal Justice*, T.M.C. Asser Press, 2010, p. 237.
410 ICC, OTP, Situation in Mali, Article 53(1) Report, January 2013, para. 146.
411 ICC, OTP, Report on the Preliminary Examination Activities (2016), para. 224.

between the Prosecutor's interpretation and the judicial interpretation emerged in the context of the situation in question helps with understanding the factors that should be taken into account in gauging the gravity of a situation. The situation of Registered Vessel of Comoros was the first time the Court's Judges did not approve the Prosecutor's approach to the gravity requirement.

2.5.1. Description of the Case

On 14 May 2013, the Union of the Comoros referred a situation to the OTP with respect to the Israeli attack on a humanitarian aid flotilla bound for the Gaza Strip in the Mediterranean Sea on 31 May 2010; an event that is also known as the 'Gaza Flotilla Raid'. On the same day, the Prosecutor opened a preliminary examination. In its referral, the government of Comoros argued in favor of the gravity of the referred situation by expressing two main reasons: the international reaction to the attack, and the context in which the attack occurred, namely the Israel-Palestine conflict.[412] To prove the wide impact of the attack on the international community, Comoros enumerated some measures taken in order to investigate the attack, including a fact-finding mission by the UN Human Rights Council, the appointment of a commission of inquiry by the UNSG, and domestic investigations in Turkey and Israel. In addition, the referral recalled an opinion of the Appeals Chamber that assessment of the gravity of the relevant conduct "depends upon subjective and contingent reactions to crimes rather than upon their objective gravity."[413] Upon the referral, by conducting the preliminary examination, the Prosecutor concluded that the information available provided a reasonable basis to believe that war crimes were committed on board the Mavi Marmara vessel on 31 May 2010, thereby satisfying the jurisdiction requirement.

However, the Prosecutor did not satisfy the requirement that there was a reasonable basis to believe that the situation under consideration was admissible, because of the lack of sufficient gravity.[414] The Prosecutor declared the attack on the vessel as a war crime. She recognized that there was an international armed conflict between Israel and Hamas, and the naval blockade of the Gaza strip was part of this conflict. Since the attack on the vessel related to the blockade, the Prosecutor concluded that "the alleged conduct of the IDF soldiers on board the Mavi Marmara took place in the context of Israel's occupation of the Gaza Strip and the naval blockade pertaining to it. Accordingly, the requisite nexus can be established between this context and the alleged conduct."[415] Upon determining the contextual element of war crimes, the Prosecutor concluded there was a reasonable basis to believe that war crimes were committed

---

412 ICC, Situation on Registered Vessel of the Comoros, Referral, 14 May 2013, see *supra* note 109.

413 ICC, Appeals Chamber, Lubanga case, 13 July 2006, para. 73, see *supra* note 233. However, this reference was clearly wrong. First, contrary to the claim of the Comoros, the mentioned statement had been made by the Prosecutor and not by the Appeals Chamber. In addition, the Appeals Chamber by mentioning the statement made by the Prosecutor had intended to show its unacceptability.

414 ICC, OTP, Situation on Registered Vessels of Comoros, 6 November 2014, para. 3, see *supra* note 320.

415 Ibid., para. 128.

on board the Mavi Marmara during the interception of the flotilla, including willful killing, willfully causing serious injury to body and health, and outrages upon personal dignity.[416] In contrast to the determination of war crimes, owing to lack of a widespread or systematic attack, the Prosecutor declared that "there is no reasonable basis to believe that crimes against humanity under Article 7 were committed within the referred situation."[417]

Upon determining the Court's jurisdiction, the Prosecutor dealt with the admissibility requirement. The assessment was conducted based on the four criteria established by the Prosecutor. As to the scale, the available information had showed that the Mavi Marmara was carrying over 500 civilian passengers in total. Among them, ten passengers were killed by IDF. Besides persons killed, it was known that around 50–55 other passengers were injured. The Prosecutor acknowledged that the number of passengers who were victims of outrages upon personal dignity was unclear. Based on the overall casualties, the Prosecutor concluded "it has to be acknowledged that the total number of victims of the flotilla incident reached relatively limited proportions as compared, generally, to other cases investigated by the Office."[418]

In the absence of the scale factor, the Prosecutors addressed the alternative factors. As to the manner, the Prosecutor did not find satisfactory the requirement that "the alleged crimes were systematic or resulted from a deliberate plan or policy to attack, kill or injure civilians or with particular cruelty."[419] In connection with the impact standard, the Prosecutor admitted that the alleged crimes "had a significant impact on victims and their families and other passengers involved", but it did not have "a significant impact on the civilian population in Gaza." In this regards, the Prosecutor argued that while the flotilla did not reach Gaza, the supplies carried by the vessels were ultimately distributed in Gaza. Given these circumstances, the Prosecutor concluded that "the interception of the flotilla cannot be considered to have resulted in blocking the access of Gazan civilians to any essential humanitarian supplies on board the vessels in the flotilla."[420] Ultimately, given the above-mentioned assessment, the Prosecutor declared that "the Office is of the view that the flotilla incident does not fall within the intended and envisioned scope of the Court's mandate."[421]

It was the first time that the Prosecutor of the Court refused to proceed with a situation that was referred by a State Party. Upon the Prosecutor's decision, the Comoros government challenged the decision before the relevant PTC. Comoros raised, *inter alia*, one ground for reviewing: "the failure to properly address the factors relevant to the determination of gravity under Article 17(1)(d) of the Statute."[422] In reviewing the Prosecutor's decision, the PTC I first criticized the Prosecutor's determination on

416 Ibid., para. 19.
417 Ibid., para. 21.
418 Ibid., para. 138.
419 Ibid., para. 140.
420 Ibid., para. 141.
421 Ibid., para. 142.
422 ICC, PTC I, Situation on Registered Vessel of the Comoros, 16 July 2015, para. 11, see *supra* note 294.

the gravity in terms of the manner factor. According to the Chamber, the Prosecutor had erred in disregarding the information as to the live fire prior to the boarding that could prove that the attack was part of a plan.[423] The Chamber was of the opinion that the available information about the live fire was not clearly false, but the Prosecutor put aside the information because she believed that "the evidence was highly contested."[424] According to the Prosecutor, the 'significantly conflicting accounts' had made it "difficult to establish the exact chain of events."[425] The Chamber, in contrast to the Prosecutor's approach to the apparently contradicting information, asserted that when "the events are unclear and conflicting accounts exist, this fact alone calls for an investigation rather than the opposite."[426] In addition, the Chamber referred to the fact that the IDF forces involved in the attack tried to conceal the crimes, this was ignored by the Prosecutor as an indicator of a plan.[427] Given these arguments, the Chamber declared that there were errors in the conclusion of the Prosecutor about the manner standard.[428]

Moreover, the Chamber went further and rejected the Prosecutor's assessment of both the scale and the impact of the situation. As to the scale, the Chamber stated that ten killings, 50–55 injuries, and possibly hundreds of instances of outrages upon personal dignity, or torture or inhuman treatment, which would be the scale of the crimes prosecuted in the potential case(s) arising from the referred situation are "indicator of sufficient gravity, instead of insufficiency" by arguing that "the factor of scale should have been taken into account by the Prosecutor as militating in favor of sufficient gravity, rather than the opposite."[429] Regarding the impact, the Chamber put forward some arguments against the Prosecutor's decision. Firstly, in the Chamber's opinion, the purely victim-oriented impact of crimes was an indicator of sufficient gravity. According to the Chamber, "the physical, psychological or emotional harm suffered by the direct and indirect victims of the identified crimes must not be undervalued and needs not be complemented by a more general impact of these crimes beyond that suffered by the victims."[430] Secondly, the PTC referred to the impact of crimes on the people of Gaza. The Chamber asserted that the commission of crimes on the Mavi Marmara, which were highly publicized, affected the Gaza's people by sending "a clear and strong message to the people in Gaza (and beyond) that the blockade of Gaza was in full force and that even the delivery of humanitarian aid would be controlled and supervised by the Israeli authorities."[431]

---

423 Ibid., paras. 33–35.
424 Ibid., para. 35.
425 Ibid.
426 Ibid., para. 36.
427 Ibid., para. 41.
428 Ibid., para. 45.
429 Ibid., para. 26.
430 Ibid., para. 47.
431 Ibid., para. 48.

Moreover, the Chamber enhanced its argument by referring to the wide impact of crimes on the international community. The scope of the international reaction may represent the impact of the situation. According to the Chamber, "the international concern caused by the events at issue, which, *inter alia*, resulted in several fact-finding missions, including by the UN Human Rights Council and the UNSG, is somehow at odds with the Prosecutor's simplistic conclusion that the impact of the identified crimes points towards the insufficient gravity of the potential."[432] Based on the above-mentioned arguments, the PTC, by majority, requested "the Prosecutor to reconsider the decision not to initiate an investigation into the situation referred to her by the Union of Comoros."[433] Some days later, the Prosecutor of the Court appealed against the decision of the Chamber. Nonetheless, the Appeals Chamber declared the Prosecutor's appeal inadmissible, without assessing its merits. The Appeals Chamber stated that the Prosecutor's appeal was not made pursuant to Article 82(1) of the Statute, because the impugned decision was made under Article 53 instead of Article 18 or 19. Therefore, it was not a decision with respect to jurisdiction or admissibility as imagined by Article 82(1).[434] The Prosecutor is now "preparing to issue the Prosecutor's final decision under rule 108(3) in the near future."[435]

2.5.2. *Analysis of the Situation on Registered Vessel of the Comoros*

As mentioned, in the situational gravity assessment the total casualties within a situation should be taken into account. There is no need for similarity between the scale of a situation as a whole and the scale of each case arising from the situation. A wide situation in terms of casualties may have small cases, if other alternative factors satisfy the gravity requirement. In the situation of the Registered Vessel of the Comoros, the Prosecutor had focused on the small number of casualties that occurred on the deck of the Mavi Marmara, and consequently concluded the situation lacked sufficient gravity. The Prosecutor's decision was challenged by the government of Comoros. To prove that the scale of crimes in the situation at hand was vast and comparable to other situations, the lawyers of the Comoros government argued that the Prosecutor had to take into account the occupation and the Gaza blockade as a context to determine the gravity of the situation at hand. According to the lawyers, "it is thus perfectly permissible for the Prosecutor to take into consideration the wider context of the blockade and the occupation and all acts committed in this context in order to determine whether there is a reasonable basis to believe that the conduct on the vessels over which the Prosecutor does have jurisdiction is sufficiently grave to proceed with an investigation

432 Ibid.

433 Ibid., para. 26.

434 ICC, Appeals Chamber, Situation on Registered Vessel of the Comoros, Decision on the Admissibility of the Prosecutor's Appeal Against the Decision on the Request of the Union of the Comoros to Review the Prosecutor's Decision not to Initiate an Investigation, 6 November 2015, paras. 37–52.

435 ICC, OTP, Report on the Preliminary Examination Activities (2016), para. 331.

i.e. to meet the gravity threshold and guideline requirements of Article 8(1) at this stage."[436]

Based on this argument, the lawyers, by stating that "there are few who would regard the Israel-Palestine conflict as anything other than one of the most serious conflicts of our time", claimed that "the same 10 murders committed in one of the world's gravest conflicts have the gravity of being a part of something much larger."[437] Indeed, the Comoros's lawyers defined the 2010 attack as a part of the Israel-Palestine situation, not as an independent situation. However, this approach suffers from a misunderstanding of the situation notion. The lack of an understanding of the situation notion led to another incorrect argument put forward by the lawyers. By referring to the situation in Palestine under the OTP's preliminary examination, the Prosecutor was requested to take into account "acts committed in this later period of time to determine whether they are related to the crimes committed by the same forces on the Flotilla in the same occupation and conflict, and whether all of these circumstances taken together establish on a 'reasonable basis to believe' that the Flotilla situation is sufficiently grave to warrant investigation."[438] This argument ignores the dividing line between situations. Later, the PTC in its decision on the application for the review of the situation of the Registered Vessel of the Comoros stated "the rules of jurisdiction do not permit the Court to conduct proceedings in relation to possible crimes which were committed elsewhere than on the three vessels falling into its jurisdiction, but the Court has the authority to consider all necessary information, including as concerns extra-jurisdictional facts for the purpose of establishing crimes within its competence as well as their gravity."[439] This statement also uncovers the misunderstanding of the notion of situation.

A situation has two pillars, namely the contextual element and its jurisdictional parameters. Potential and concrete cases arise from a situation as a whole. The context of a situation is a factual element. To determine such a context, the legal contextual elements of the ICC-indicated crimes are helpful. For instance, an armed conflict, either international or non-international, may constitute the contextual element of a situation. The context of a situation has a broad scope embracing all cases and crimes involved. The Union of the Comoros submitted a referral with respect to "the 31 May 2010 Israel raid on the Humanitarian Aid Flotilla bound for Gaza Strip." Therefore, the concrete and objective crisis that constituted the situation of the Registered Vessel of the Comoros was the single Israeli attack on the vessel. What was referred to by the referring State was not the armed conflict in the occupied territories. The Prosecutor had admitted this narrow context, and due to its narrowness she declared that the scale of the crimes within the situation would not satisfy the gravity requirement. According

---

436 ICC, Situation on Registered Vessels of Comoros, Application for Review Pursuant to Article 53(3)(a) of the Prosecutor's Decision of 6 November 2014 not to Initiate an Investigation in the Situation, 29 January 2015, para. 14.

437 Ibid., para. 25.

438 Ibid., para. 31.

439 ICC, PTC I, Situation on Registered Vessel on of the Comoros, 16 July 2015, para. 17, see *supra* note 294.

to the Prosecutor, "the parameters of the Office's assessment are determined by the limited scope of the situation referred, namely a confined series of events primarily on 31 May 2010. By virtue of Article 12(2)(a) of the Statute, the Court's territorial jurisdiction is further limited to events occurring on three vessels in the flotilla and does not extend to any events that occurred after passengers were taken off those vessels. As such, the potential case(s) that could be pursued is inherently limited to an event encompassing a small number of victims of the alleged ICC crimes, with limited countervailing qualitative considerations."[440] In fact, the Prosecutor had not even considered the consequent incidents outside of the vessel.

However, the Prosecutor's perception of the situation notion is erroneous too. In the situation of the Registered Vessel of the Comoros, the Prosecutor determined that war crimes had been committed. The contextual element of war crimes is an armed conflict. In the situation at hand, the Prosecutor grounded the war crimes on the basis of the Israel-Hamas conflict, as an international armed conflict. However, it was not logical. The contextual element of the situation of the Registered Vessel of the Comoros as understood from the referral and the Prosecutor's report is a single event and attack in addition to its consequences. Nonetheless, the contextual element of the identified war crimes, i.e. the Israel-Hamas conflict, goes beyond the scope of the situational context, namely the single attack. Logically, the contextual element of a situation is, and should be, broader than the contextual element of those crimes falling within the given situation. Crimes and their contexts are components of a situation, and logically a component is narrower than the whole. The necessary implication of determining war crimes is, at least, the equality between the contextual element of war crimes and the contextual element of the situation. If the Prosecutor had determined the Israel-Hamas conflict as the contextual element of the situation, it would have been logical to declare the 2010 attack as a war crime within such a context. However, this was not the case in the situation of the Registered Vessels of Comoros. The context of the situation (the attack on the vessel) was narrower than the context of the crimes arising from it (the international armed conflict). Because the Prosecutor had grounded the subject-matter jurisdiction of the Court on a wider context, she had to note that "the Court does not have jurisdiction over other alleged crimes committed in this context, nor in the broader context of any conflict between Israel and Palestine", because the present assessment "is limited to evaluating the gravity of the crimes allegedly committed by Israeli forces on board the vessels over which the Court has jurisdiction during the interception of the flotilla."[441] Nevertheless, it is a clear inconsistency if the Prosecutor accepts a context to determine the jurisdiction of the Court, but rejects it for the gravity assessment. The attack on the vessels could be seen as a part of the Israel-Palestine conflict. In that scenario, the Mavi Marmara incident was a case rather than an independent situation.

The lawyers of the Comoros government and the PTC referred to a considerable number of the international courts' jurisprudence as to the validity of taking into

440 ICC, OTP, Situation on Registered Vessels of Comoros, 6 November 2014, para. 25, see *supra* note 320.
441 Ibid., para. 26.

account to so-called 'extra-jurisdictional' evidence.[442] In the jurisprudence of the international tribunals, such 'extra-jurisdictional' evidence was relevant to "establishing the plan, policy, pattern, state of mind of the accused, and wider context of the particular crimes with which the accused were charged that fell within the jurisdiction of the court."[443] Article 8(1) of the Rome Statute requires the war crimes to be committed as 'part of' a policy or plan or large-scale pattern. Extra-jurisdictional evidence may be used to prove such a policy referred to in Article 8. The ICTY/R Appeals Chamber, in one of its judgments, refers to the functions of the extra-jurisdictional evidence, including clarifying a given context, establishing by inference the elements (in particular, criminal intent) of criminal conduct and demonstrating a deliberate pattern of conduct.[444] However, this is not the case regarding the situation of the Registered Vessel of the Comoros. In this situation, war crimes are not committed due to the lack of their constituent context. The logical inconsistency arising from narrowly defining the given situation bars accepting the Palestine-Israel conflict as the war crimes' context. When there is no war crime, there is no need to detect a policy.

In the British troops' war crimes in Iraq, the first Prosecutor defined the situation in question in a broad sense. The contextual element of the given situation was based on an existing international armed conflict in Iraq that Britain was involved in. Within this context, the Prosecutor identified some potential cases of war crimes, including the willful killing or inhuman treatment of detainees. If the Prosecutor Bensouda's approach to the Mavi Marmara situation had been followed in the Iraq situation, the then Prosecutor had to defined the Abu Ghraib incident as the context of the Iraq/UK situation, and then had to find some war crimes whose context was broader than the situation context. An approach that would clearly be wrong, given the above-mentioned arguments.

2.6. BIG FISH POLICY IN LIGHT OF GRAVITY

A case, actual or potential, comprises conduct and person. The assessment of gravity of a conduct precedes the assessment of ranking of a person who is responsible for

---

442 For instance, the SCSL in one judgment about the Taylor case asserts that "in many instances during the trial proceedings, the Trial Chamber held that evidence falling outside of the temporal and/or geographical scope of the Indictment and/or the jurisdiction of the court, was admissible pursuant to Rule 89(C), as it was relevant to the context and/or chapeau requirements of the alleged crimes, or as evidence of a consistent pattern of conduct under Rule 93. The Trial Chamber reiterates its previous decisions concerning the admissibility of this evidence. However, insofar as the Defense submissions constitute a request for clarification of the permissible and impermissible uses that may be made of such evidence, the Trial Chamber will consider these submissions in determining the limits to be placed on the use of this evidence" (SCSL, Taylor case, Judgment, 18 may 2012, para. 98).

443 ICC, Situation on Registered Vessels of Comoros, Application for Review Pursuant to Article 53(3) (a) of the Prosecutor's Decision of 6 November 2014 not to Initiate an Investigation in the Situation, 29 January 2015, para. 72.

444 ICTR, Appeals Chamber, Nahimana case, Judgment, 28 November 2007, para. 315.

the conduct. In the situation of the Registered Vessel of the Comoros, the Prosecutor did not pay enough attention to those people who bore the most responsibility for the weight of the crimes within the situation. The PTC considered this approach erroneous. According to the Chamber, "the Prosecutor erred in the Decision not to Investigate by failing to consider whether the persons likely to be the object of the investigation into the situation would include those who bear the greatest responsibility for the identified crimes."[445] However, this judicial assertion was not correct, since the Prosecutor had initially determined that the conduct was not sufficiently grave to warrant the Court's intervention. In the context of the absence of this aspect of the gravity threshold, there was no reason to go further and deal with the other aspect of gravity. Without a crime, there would not be someone responsible. The Judge Kovacs in his dissenting opinion refers to this fact, and disagreed with the majority that the Prosecutor erred in her ignorance. In Judge's words, "conducting an examination as to who bear the greatest responsibility was not, in the context of the Prosecutor's examination, determinative for her final decision. This is so because the Prosecutor already found that the crimes committed within the context of the entire situation (and therefore any potential case) have not reached the required threshold."[446]

International crimes are committed by many perpetrators. While a large number of people are responsible for international crimes, the international criminal tribunals prosecute only a handful of perpetrators. Tribunals at the international sphere suffer from wide and various restrictions. These limitations have directed the criminal tribunals at the international sphere to adopt a policy of focusing on those who have the greatest responsibility. Those who commit serious crimes should be held accountable even if they occupy high office. The spirit and letter of the Rome Statute rejects the idea that power should influence the administration of justice.[447] The Rome Statute has put an end to the era in which, as Annan describes, "powerful men committed crimes against humanity, they knew that as long as they remained powerful no earthly court could judge them."[448] Focusing on the most responsible criminals has been followed in two different ways. Some tribunals have considered this policy as a legal jurisdictional threshold. In this scenario, the jurisdiction of a court is limited to those persons who bear the greatest responsibility.

For instance, the SCSL's jurisdiction is legally limited to those who bear the greatest responsibility. The UNSC, in its Resolution establishing the SCSL, stated that "the special court should have personal jurisdiction over persons who bear the greatest responsibility for the commission of the crimes referred to in paragraph 2, including those leaders who, in committing such crimes, have threatened the establishment of and

445 ICC, PTC I, Situation on Registered Vessel of the Comoros, 16 July 2015, para. 23, see *supra* note 294.

446 ICC, Pre-Trial Chamber I, Situation on Registered Vessel of the Comoros, Partly Dissenting Opinion of Judge Peter Kovacs, 16 July 2015, para. 29.

447 Bosco, 2014, p. 20, see *supra* note 391.

448 UN, Press Release, Secretary General says Establishment of ICC is Major Step in March towards Universal Human Rights, 20 July 1998, available at: www.un.org/press/en/1998/19980720.l2890.html, last accessed at 9 May 2017.

implementation of the peace process in Sierra Leone."[449] As the SCSL Trial Chamber has stated, the SCSL was intended to be the court of prosecuting leaders. According to the Chamber, "the severity of a crime or the massive scale of a particular crime should not be the primary consideration."[450] The Statute of the ICTY did not encompass any provision limiting the jurisdiction of the Court to the most senior members. The ICTY started its operations by dealing with the minor culprits. The first suspect before the ICTY, Tadić, was a low-ranking Bosnian Serb. Goldstone, the then Prosecutor of the ICTY, decided to prosecute this minor case to show that the tribunal was in motion.[451] However, this approach changed. In 2004, the UNSC Resolution 1534 directed the Tribunal's prosecutors to elect only such cases for prosecution that targeted persons of the most senior level.[452] Rule 28(a) of the ICTY Rules of Procedure and Evidence, amended in 2004, establishes a mechanism through which only those indictments against the senior offenders would be processed for prosecution.[453]

In contrast to the former category of tribunals, the ICC has followed a different approach by considering focusing on the senior culprits as a matter of policy instead of law. Here, restricting the activities of the Court to leaders is not a jurisdictional restriction, but it is an adopted policy. The Rome Statute does not have any explicit or implicit reference to the necessity of focusing on the senior perpetrators. The only statutory restriction on the national jurisdiction is the prohibition of prosecuting children under 18. Article 27 of the Rome Statute emphasizes that it surely has jurisdiction over the leaders and those who enjoy diplomatic immunities, but it does not limit the Court's jurisdiction to this category of people. There are some arguments in favor of this statutory standpoint. Firstly, seeing the issue from the eyes of the victims, prosecution of low or mid-level perpetrators is desirable. In many cases, the direct victims of international crimes demand to see that the direct perpetrators face justice. Del Ponte, the former Prosecutor of the ICTY, viewed the necessity of addressing mid-level culprits from such a perspective. She believed that prosecution of middle level perpetrators was important because '[f]or the local people, the victims and the survivors, it was these people who brought their world to an end, not the remote governmental architects of the overall policy of genocide'.[454]

---

449 UNSC, Resolution 1315, 14 August 2000, para. 3.

450 SCSL, Norman and Kondewa case, Decision on the Preliminary Defense Motion on the Lack of Personal Jurisdiction Filed on Behalf of the Accused Fofana, 3 March 2004, para. 40.

451 Bosco, 2014, p. 37, see *supra* note 391.

452 UNSC, Resolution 1534, 26 March 2004.

453 According to the Rule, "on receipt of an indictment for review from the Prosecutor, the Registrar shall consult with the President. The President shall refer the matter to the Bureau which shall determine whether the indictment, *prima facie,* concentrates on one or more of the most senior leaders suspected of being most responsible for crimes within the jurisdiction of the Tribunal. If the Bureau determines that the indictment meets this standard, the President shall designate one of the permanent Trial Chamber Judges for the review under Rule 47. If the Bureau determines that the indictment does not meet this standard, the President shall return the indictment to the Registrar to communicate this finding to the Prosecutor."

454 ICTY, OTP, Statement by the Prosecutor addressed to the UN Security Council, 27 November 2001, available at: www.icty.org/en/press/address-prosecutor-international-criminal-tribunal-former-yugoslavia-carla-del-ponte-un, accessed 23 February 2016.

Secondly, non-limitation to the 'big fish' policy is consistent with one of the Court's goals, namely, ending impunity. The culture of impunity emerges when leaders enjoy immunity from criminal prosecutions, but it is not limited to them. The culture of impunity refers to a situation in which there is no judicial reaction to international crimes, regardless of who perpetrates the crimes. Focusing on big fishes has been recommended to fill the impunity gap. It has been thought that in the normal course of events, States are willing or able to prosecute low or mid-ranking perpetrators. To prevent prominent perpetrators from escaping justice, the Court focuses on this category of perpetrators to overcome the impunity gap. However, if there is absolute impunity, the intervention of the Court is desirable and necessary, even if it initially targets the modest culprits. In some occasions, a 'pyramid prosecution' is necessary in fighting impunity.

The third argument against limiting the jurisdiction of the Court to senior leaders is that such a policy does not serve the prevention of the ICC-identified crimes. The Appeals Chamber of the Court in the Ntaganda case addressed this matter. In January 2006, the Prosecutor of the Court applied for warrants of arrest against Lubanga and Ntaganda. On 10 February 2006, PTC I granted the Prosecutor's application for a warrant of arrest against Lubanga, but it refused to issue a warrant of arrest against Ntaganda, due to the inadmissibility of his case. The Chamber asserted that the *Ntaganda* case lacked sufficient gravity because the accused was not among those perpetrators who bore the greatest responsibility. According to the Chamber, to determine whether a case satisfies the gravity threshold, three factors should be taken into account, namely: whether the suspect is one of the senior leaders; the role played by the suspect when the crimes were committed; and the role of the suspect's organization or State in the overall commission of the crimes.[455] The Chamber believed that persons who meet this threshold "are the ones who can most effectively prevent or stop the commission of those crimes."[456]

To justify this assertion, the PTC argued that "only by concentrating on this type of individual can the deterrent effects of the activities of the Court be maximized because other senior leaders in similar circumstances will know that solely by doing what they can to prevent the systematic or large-scale commission of crimes within the jurisdiction of the Court can they be sure that they will not be prosecuted by the Court."[457] The Prosecutor of the Court appealed the decision. To demonstrate the errors in the impugned decision, the Prosecutor, *inter alia*, rejected the rigid interpretation of the gravity threshold given by the PTC. The Prosecutor argued that limiting the Court in the fashion foreseen by the PTC would not maximize the Court's deterrence effect. Interestingly, the then Prosecutor complained that the PTC's test had inappropriately limited his prosecutorial discretion and would make it impossible to investigate and prosecute perpetrators lower down the chain of command. The Prosecutor went further

455 ICC, PTC I, Lubanga case, 10 February 2006, paras. 52–53, see *supra* note 45.
456 Ibid., para. 54.
457 Ibid., para. 55.

and argued that in certain circumstances, the investigation and prosecution of low and mid-level perpetrators might be necessary to generate evidence.[458] Based on the Prosecutor's challenge, the Appeals Chamber, backing the Prosecutor's point of view, rejected the PTC's stand on the gravity threshold. The Appeals Chamber disagreed with the argument that the deterrent effect would be greatest if the ICC only dealt with the highest-ranking perpetrators. On the contrary, the Appeals Chamber was of the view that "the deterrent effect of the Court is highest if no category of perpetrators is per se excluded form potentially being brought before the Court."[459] The Appeals Chamber argued that the exclusion of many perpetrators by focusing only on leaders would hamper the prevention of crimes.[460]

In spite of its initial status in the Ntaganda case, the Prosecutor of the Court has strictly adopted the 'only leaders' policy. The OTP's Policy Paper on preliminary Examinations states "the Office's policy of focusing investigative efforts on those most responsible for the most serious crimes under the Court's jurisdiction."[461] This policy is also known as 'the focused investigations', because according to this policy the OTP focuses on those bearing the greatest responsibility.[462] Elsewhere in this Policy Paper, it is explicitly asserted that in assessing the admissibility requirement the 'big fish' policy is applied.[463] It means that even if the national proceedings are in progress but in relation to those who do not bear the greatest responsibility, the Court declares a case admissible based on the complementarity rule. For instance, in his application to receive an authority to initiate an investigation into the Kenya situation, the then Prosecutor stated "because no national investigations or proceedings are pending against those bearing the greatest responsibility for the crimes against humanity allegedly committed, the Prosecutor submits that the cases that would arise from its investigation of the situation would be currently admissible."[464]

The above-mentioned prosecutorial policy is based on a 'two-tiered approach'.[465] According to this approach, the Prosecutor would choose to prosecute leaders, whereas national prosecutions would be encouraged for lower-ranking perpetrators. The Prosecutor is not able to prosecute all the accused. Therefore, the Prosecutor gives priority to the 'big fish'. As the Prosecutor has stated, "the Office's prosecutorial strategy is without prejudice to States' obligations to investigate and prosecute

---

458 Ibid., para. 66.

459 ICC, Appeals Chamber, Ntaganda case, Judgment on the Prosecutor's Appeal Against the Decision of Pre-Trial Chamber I Entitled Decision on the Prosecutor's Application for Warrants of Arrest, 13 July 2006, para. 73.

460 Ibid., para. 75.

461 ICC, OTP, Policy Paper on Preliminary Examinations, para. 8.

462 Ambos and Stegmiller, 2013, p. 418, see *supra* note 282.

463 "In line with its prosecutorial strategy, the Office will assess complementarity and gravity in relation to the most serious crimes alleged to have been committed and those most responsible for those crimes" (ICC, OTP, Policy Paper on Preliminary Examinations, para. 42).

464 ICC, OTP, Kenya situation, Request for Authorization of an Investigation Pursuant to Article 15, 26 November 2009, para. 55.

465 Greijer, 2012, p. 146, see *supra* note 375.

international crimes, regardless of the level of responsibility of the perpetrators."[466] The Bureau's Report in the Kampala Conference referred to the relationship between this prosecutorial policy and the selectivity of the Court by stating "since the Court has limited resources and capacity and proceeding from the strategy of the Prosecutor, the Court currently only focuses on those bearing the greatest responsibility."[467]

Based on this policy, in the ISIS situation, the new Prosecutor rejected to open the preliminary examination on the given situation by arguing that there was not a jurisdictional basis for this purpose, since the leaders of ISIS would be out of the Court's reach. However, this assessment is not correct. When it is determined that the contextual element of a situation is sufficiently grave, the assessment of gravity of the potential cases should be done among the available cases within the situation. The absence of leaders from the available cases is not a legal obstacle in proceedings with a situation at the ICC legal systems that permits a pyramid prosecution policy. In addition, the preliminary examination findings are preliminary. PTC II, in its decision to authorize the Prosecutor to initiate an investigation into the Kenya situation, asserted that "the Prosecutor's selection of the incidents or groups of persons that are likely to shape his future case(s) is preliminary in nature and is not binding for future admissibility assessments. This means that the Prosecutor's selection on the basis of these elements for the purposes of defining a potential 'case' for this particular phase may change at a later stage, depending on the development of the investigation."[468] Such a temporary and preliminary nature of the preliminary examination findings requires more flexibility in the Prosecutorial approaches at this stage. One implication of this flexibility, consistent with the nature of the preliminary examination findings, is that there should be an interpretation in favor of investigation. For this reason, in the Mavi Marmara situation, the PTC I stated that "if, as stated by the Prosecutor, the events are unclear and conflicting accounts exist, this fact alone calls for an investigation rather than the opposite. It is only upon investigation that it may be determined how the events unfolded."[469] In this situation, the Chamber went further and asserted that the scale of crimes, as one of the major factors in the situational assessment, should be taken into account by the Prosecutor "as militating in favor of sufficient gravity, rather than the opposite."[470]

Focusing on those individuals located at the highest level of command produces a specific side-effect, namely, it would not meet the victims' expectations. It is imaginable that within a situation there are some so-called 'notorious perpetrator'. Their prosecution is advisable even if they do not occupy high organizational level. This type of micro-analysis has a benefit. Someone is prosecuted whose impunity could seriously

466 ICC, OTP, Policy Paper on Preliminary Examinations, p. 103.

467 ICC, ASP, Report of the Bureau on Stocktaking (Complementarity): Taking Stock of the Principle of Complementarity: Bridging the Impunity Gap, 25 March 2010, para. 15.

468 ICC, PTC II, Kenya situation, 31 March 2010, para. 50, see *supra* note 33.

469 ICC, PTC I, Situation on Registered Vessel of the Comoros, 16 July 2015, para. 36, see *supra* note 294.

470 Ibid., para. 26.

disturb the community.[471] For this reason, recently, the OTP has adjusted its approach to the big fish policy. Since 2012, the OTP has adopted a new strategy to gradually build cases upwards by adopting a bottom-up approach. This approach emerged in light of "limitations in investigative possibilities and/or a lack of cooperation and the required evidentiary standards."[472] According to this strategy, the Prosecutor first prosecutes a limited number of mid- and high-level perpetrators in order to ultimately have a reasonable chance to convict the most responsible.[473] Apart from this pyramid prosecution, the Prosecutor, however, admits that the Office would consider "prosecuting lower level perpetrators where their conduct has been particularly grave and has acquired extensive notoriety", since such a strategy would "in the end be more cost-effective than having unsuccessful or no prosecutions against the highest placed perpetrators."[474]

3. COMPLEMENTARITY

The second element of the admissibility notion referred to in Article 17 of the Rome Statute is the complementarity requirement. Through the gravity assessment, the Prosecutor selects those situations and cases that have sufficient gravity and have more gravity compared to other grave situations and cases. Upon selecting a situation or a case on the basis of its gravity, the Prosecutor needs to assess the second element of the admissibility requirement to determine whether the given situation or case is admissible. For this purpose, the complementarity requirement is evaluated as discussed in this section. If there are parallel genuine proceedings at the domestic level, the Court has to declare the Prosecutor's choices inadmissible. Article 17 commences with a reference to Paragraph 10 of the Preamble and Article 1 of the Rome Statute.[475] These recent provisions refer to complementarity as a framework with purpose. The chapeau implies that the complementarity admissibility rule should be understood within the framework of complementarity as a principle. The latter is broader in scope than the former. According to Dworkin, "rules are applicable in an all-or-nothing fashion… But the principles do not set out legal consequences that follow automatically when the conditions provided are met. They incorporate into the law general goals and values."[476]

Complementarity regulates the relationship between the ICC and States. The complementarity principle shows the role of the Court within the international criminal justice system as a whole. The Court is a complementary actor besides other actors in

---

471 Guariglia, 2012, p. 52, see *supra* note 214.

472 ICC, OTP, Strategic Plan (2016–2018), para. 22.

473 Ibid.

474 Ibid.

475 "Having regard to paragraph 10 of the Preamble and Article 1, the Court shall determine that a case is inadmissible where…"

476 Ronald Dworkin, *Taking Rights Seriously*, Harvard University Press, 1977, pp. 22–24.

the international sphere to deliver criminal justice. In this meaning, complementarity highlights international criminal justice as a system. In this system, the Court has some managerial responsibilities in addition to its classical judicial tasks. In contrast, the complementarity rule as an admissibility requirement refers to the complementary role of the Court to deal with a specific situation or case. The complementarity rule has some degree of specialty and narrowness. PTC II has explained the relationship between these two kinds of complementarity in the following terms: "admissibility can be regarded as the tool allowing the implementation of the principle of complementarity in respect of a specific scenario."[477] The Court functions in an exemplary and expressive manner. It selects a few cases and situations as exemplars to further its objectives in the international criminal justice system. In this regard, however, the Court functions as a last resort. The complementarity rule has been predicated on ensuring that the Court is indeed complementary to national justice systems.[478] If there is any genuine national proceeding, the priority is for others, because the Court intervenes only as a last resort. In this context, complementarity as an admissibility rule has been designed to resolve competition between the ICC and domestic courts.[479]

Grounding the Court on the complementarity principle makes this international court different from its predecessors that functioned on the jurisdictional primacy. The *ad hoc* tribunals had primacy over all national jurisdictions.[480] Otherwise, "there would be a perennial danger of international crimes being characterized as 'ordinary crimes' or proceedings being designed to shield the accused."[481] On the contrary, the Court was established on the premise that the responsibility to combat international crimes is first and foremost upon the national jurisdictions. In the case of concurrent jurisdictions, national criminal systems are accorded, rather than the Court, the primary right to investigate or prosecute crimes.[482] Indeed, in the war on international crimes the first bite of the cherry is for national jurisdiction. It means that the ICC's jurisdiction is complementary and subsidiary.[483] At the ICC legal system, the national jurisdiction enjoys a qualified primacy. The Rome Statute empowers the ICC judges "to review the bone fides of national proceedings and, moreover, empowers the Court to recall cases previously deferred where it deems this appropriate."[484] The national jurisdictions have a priority to prosecute the crimes within the ICC's jurisdiction as far as they do it genuinely. Otherwise, the Court's jurisdiction prevails. In the words of Amnesty International, the overall object of the Court is to ensure accountability

---

477 ICC, PTC II, Kony case, 10 March 2009, para. 34, see *supra* note 220. The Chamber in this statement used the 'admissibility' term in the meaning of complementarity as the admissibility rule.

478 Schabas, 2010, p. 336, see *supra* note 20.

479 Nouwen, 2013, p. 409, see *supra* note 226.

480 El Zeidy, 2008, p. 153, see *supra* note 19.

481 ICTY, Tadić case, 2 October 1995, para. 58, see *supra* note 31.

482 Nouwen, 2013, p. 8, see *supra* note 226.

483 Cedric Ryngaert, 'Horizontal Complementarity', in Carsten Stahn and Mohamed M. El Zeidy (eds.), *The International Criminal Court and Complementarity: From Theory to Practice*, Cambridge University Press, 2011, p. 857.

484 Rastan, 2010, p. 88, see *supra* note 131.

"primarily by States, but, under the underlying principle of complementarity, if they prove unable or unwilling to do so, by the International Criminal Court as a last resort."[485]

The articulation of the principle of complementarity has been seen as one of the greatest achievements of the Rome Statute.[486] The issue of complementarity has been referred to twice in the Rome Statute: in both the preamble and the operative provisions of the Statute. The preamble of the Statute emphasizes that the International Criminal Court established under this Statute shall be complementary to national criminal jurisdiction." In addition, according to Article 1, the ICC "shall be complementary to national criminal jurisdictions." This duplicative reference in itself reflects the fundamental importance that States have attached to it.[487] The complementarity issue has been at the heart of the literature and debates on the ICC. Since the emergence of the Court, many scholars have paid considerable attention to this matter. Some scholars have described the complementarity principle as the cornerstone of the Court.[488] Such a description is reflected in the Chambers' words too: "it is well known that the cornerstone of the Statute and of the functioning of the Court is the principle of complementarity."[489] Complementarity is not a normal principle but it is a foundational principle for the Court.[490]

Complementarity literally means completing and perfecting something else or combining two or more concepts which improve the qualities of the other.[491] The ICC's complementarity is understood in the context of the relationship between the Court and States. Complementarity defines and organizes the relationship between domestic jurisdictions and the ICC.[492] The Court complements national jurisdictions by intervention where States failed (quantitatively), and by providing genuine justice when the national proceedings lack genuineness (qualitatively).[493] However, complementarity draws a mutual relationship between the Court and the national jurisdictions to complete each other. The complementary relationship between States and the Court is aimed at founding and enhancing an international criminal justice system.

---

485 Amnesty International, International Criminal Court: US Efforts to Obtain Impunity for Genocide, Crimes against Humanity and War Crimes, 2 September 2002.

486 Carsten Stahn, 'Complementarity: A Tale of Two Notions', *Criminal Law Forum*, 2008, vol. 19, p. 89.

487 Kleffner, 2008, p. 99, see *supra* note 41.

488 For instance, Holmes maintains that "the complementarity regime is one of the cornerstones on which the future International Criminal Court will be built" (see: John T. Holmes, 'The Principle of Complementarity', in Roy S. Lee (ed.), *The International Criminal Court: The Making of the Rome Statute*, 1999, p. 73); And, "Article 17 dealing with admissibility issues is the cornerstone of the Rome Statute" (Williams and Schabas, 2008, p. 606, see *supra* note 13).

489 ICC, PTC II, Kony case, 10 March 2009, para. 34, see *supra* note 220. And, The Prosecution Response to Application on Behalf of the Government of Libya Pursuant to Article 19 of the ICC Statute, June 2012, para. 4.

490 Nouwen, 2013, p. 17, see *supra* note 226.

491 Kleffner, 2008, p. 100, see *supra* note 41.

492 El Zeidy, 2008, p. 4, see *supra* note 19.

493 Stigen, 2008, p. 188, see *supra* note 96.

3.1. THEORETICAL PILLARS OF COMPLEMENTARITY

Establishing the Court on a complementary function is based on some assumptions. The Court is intended to complement States, not to replace them. The complementary role of the Court is because of its practical inability to deal with all situations and cases. The ICC needs States in the course of ending impunity. However, practical considerations are not the only reason behind complementarity. It is primarily the States' responsibility to prosecute international crimes. The Court is not an alternative to the States' obligation in this regard. Nonetheless, it is possible that States are not able or not willing to fulfil their obligations. In this scenario, it is the Court that should counteract inaction of States.

The OTP, in one of its Policy Papers, states that "the system of complementarity is principally based on the recognition that the exercise of national criminal jurisdiction is not only a right but also a duty of States."[494] The Appeals Chamber in the Katanga admissibility judgment asserts that "States have a duty to exercise their criminal jurisdiction over international crimes."[495] The States' obligation to prosecute the international crimes is reflected in the Preamble of the Rome Statute. The Preamble recalls that "it is the duty of every State to exercise its criminal jurisdiction over those responsible for international crimes."

This provision in the Preamble is open to two alternative meanings: a legal duty to prosecute or a policy prescription in favor of national jurisdiction.[496] Some believe that this provision in the Preamble does not impose any obligation upon the States Parties to the Statute in addition to the traditional obligations that have existed in the international law. It is the official standpoint of the Deputy of the Court's Prosecutor when he mentions that "the duty of States to prosecute war crimes and crimes against humanity existed before the Rome Statute came into being, and this pre-existing duty is recalled in the Statute's preamble."[497] Nouwen claims that the Preamble and other articles of the Statute merely recognize each State right to investigate and grant it primacy, but they do not impose an obligating on sates.[498] The origin of this task is the customary rule of *aut dedere aut judicaire* (either extradite or to prosecute). This concept is the cornerstone of the indirect enforcement system regime.[499] The UN International Law Commission in 2014 issued a Report on this rule expressing its important role in combating

494 ICC, OTP, Paper on Some Policy Issues before the Office of the Prosecutor, September 2003, p. 5.

495 ICC, Appeals Chamber, Katanga case, Judgment on the Appeal of Mr. Germain Katanga against the Oral Decision of Trial Chamber II of 12 June 2009 on the Admissibility of the Case, 25 September 2009, para. 85.

496 Darryl Robinson, 'The Inaction Controversy: Neglected Words and New Opportunities', in Carsten Stahn and Mohamed M. El Zeidy (eds.), The International Criminal Court and Complementarity: From Theory to Practice, Cambridge University Press, 2011, p. 496.

497 ICC, OTP, Statement by Mr. Stewart Deputy Prosecutor of the ICC, 'Transnational Justice in Colombia and the Role of the ICC', 13 May 2015.

498 Nouwen, 2013, p. 37, see *supra* note 226.

499 Bassiouni, 2013, p. 488, see *supra* note 255.

impunity.[500] Nouwen believes that this perambulatory provision is merely declaratory of a pre-existing duty. She provides some arguments in proving her claim. Firstly, the provision "speaks of a duty of 'every state', whereas a treaty can impose obligations only on States Parties." Secondly, it "refers to a duty to prosecute international crimes instead of only the international crimes within the ICC's jurisdiction."[501] Thirdly, this duty is mentioned only in the preamble and not somewhere else in the operative parts of the Statute, so "the recital reflects an aspiration."[502] Finally, she adds that the Court lacks any infrastructure for the enforcement of such norms and obligations.[503]

On the contrary, others argue that this clause of the Preamble refers to an emerging obligation upon the States Parties to the Rome Statute. Indeed, the perambulatory clause does not refer only to a pre-existing task, but it intends to add a new dimension and pillar to the existing obligations. Kleffner, first, establishes an interpretive principle: "preamble provisions can contain legal rules which are legally binding and can possess as much as normativity as any other provision in the operative part of the treaty."[504] Then, he argues "the assumption that identical terms in a treaty have an identical meaning suggests that the duty referred to in Paragraph 6 is not merely of a moral or political nature."[505] Although the broad category of international crimes falls within the jurisdiction of the Court, "certain offences had not been recognized as international crimes under customary international law prior to adoption of the Rome Statute."[506] Hence, the former interpretation would imply that some parts of the Rome Statute are not protected and covered by a provision of its Preamble. Necessarily, this implication is not acceptable. Therefore, Paragraph 6 refers to "obligation to investigate ICC crimes as a treaty obligation flowing from Statute."[507] Obliging States to combat ICC crimes is consistent with the spirit of the Rome Statute too. Under the Rome Statute "States are intended to carry the main burden of investigating and prosecuting."[508] It leads to the final destination imagined by Moreno-Ocampo, where, according to him, "proceedings before the ICC, should remain an exception to the norm."[509]

Complementarity begins with the assumption that it is primarily the state's responsibility to prosecute international crimes. However, it is not the end of the story. Complementarity completes this assumption with an accusation, stating that in many situations States do not fulfill their tasks for a wide range of reasons. The reality is that "national institutions have all too frequently proven unable or unwilling to address international crimes."[510] The preceding assumption is normative but the accusation

500 See: UN, ILC, First Report of the ILC on the Obligation to Extradite or Prosecute, 2014.
501 Nouwen, 2013, p. 38, see *supra* note 226.
502 Ibid., p. 39.
503 Ibid., p. 346.
504 Kleffner, 2008, p. 240, see *supra* note 41.
505 Ibid., p. 241.
506 Ibid., p. 245.
507 Ibid., p. 253.
508 ICC, OTP, Informal Expert Paper: The Principle of Complementarity in Practice, 2003, p. 19. fn. 24.
509 Moreno-Ocampo, 2011, p. 21, see *supra* note 1.
510 ICC, OTP, Informal Expert Paper, 2003, para. 2, see *supra* note 508.

is descriptive. The first element is a base for positive complementarity and the second is a ground for the complementarity rule. Complementarity is a balance between the reality and normativity. It starts with what should be but it functions based on what it is. This idea is reflected in this statement made by the then UN General-Secretory: "domestic justice systems should be the first resort in pursuit of accountability. But where domestic authorities are unwilling or unable to prosecute violators at home, the role of the international community becomes crucial."[511] At the ICC era, the obligation of States to prosecute international crimes are supervised by the Court. As El Zeidy maintains, "the main idea behind the entire system of complementarity is to ensure that States carry out their duties of investigation in a manner that achieves the goals behind the Rome Statute."[512] From this standpoint, as Rastan states "the Rome Statute creates not only a court, but a system for the enforcement of core crime norms between national and international authorities."[513] This is a system in which the Court assumes different tasks in different stages, from supervision and management to intervention.

Complementarity is a collective notion. It embraces some meanings under one term. It is widely said that complementarity has two main dimensions in the architecture of the Court. In Stahn's words, complementarity is a tale of two notions.[514] These two tales may contradict each other. That is why Schabas argues that term 'complementarity' may be somewhat of a misnomer, because "two systems function in opposition and to some extent with hostility with respect to each other."[515] The Court has two roles under the name of complementarity: dialogue and monitoring.[516] The relationship with States should be positive and constructive in order to promote their abilities to prosecute the crimes within the ICC's jurisdiction. Simultaneously, the ICC must diligently carry out its responsibilities to verify that national procedures are carried out genuinely.[517] These dual functions makes complementarity a complex notion.

Complementarity serves sovereignty, but not in an absolute manner. The sovereignty notion has been faced with a paradigm shift. Its content has shifted from authority to responsibility. The sovereign States have a responsibility to combat international crimes and to protect the victims. However, they may fail to discharge their responsibility, due to various reasons. If they fail, it is the Court that should step in. This tale of the story is included in Article 17 as well. Indeed, Article 17 provides exceptions to the primary of a state's jurisdiction.[518] For this reason, "for the admissibility determination, the criteria of the complementarity must be sufficiently broad so as to satisfactorily

511 UN, Report of the Secretary-General on the Rule of Law and Transitional Justice in Conflict and Post-Conflict Societies, 12 October 2011, para. 40.

512 El Zeidy, 2008, p. 164, see *supra* note 19.

513 Rastan, 2010, p. 106, see *supra* note 131.

514 Stahn, 2008, p. 88, see *supra* note 486.

515 Schabas, 2011, p. 191, see *supra* note 170.

516 ICC, OTP, Informal Expert Paper, 2003, para. 14, see *supra* note 508.

517 Ibid., para. 3.

518 ICC, OTP, Annex to the Paper on Some Policy Issues before the Office of the Prosecutor: Referrals and Communications, 2003, p. 4.

cover all lacunas allowing States to shield the perpetrator."[519] Therefore, the complementarity rule embraces contradictive interests and ideas. Nouwen asserts that complementarity earned its cornerstone status by reconciling these different interests, namely international justice with State sovereignty.[520] To keep all interests, the Court should assess the national jurisdictions to determine if there is any necessity for its intervention. However, the ICC should first give sufficient space and opportunity to States to fulfil the tasks.

3.2. COMPLEMENTARITY AS ADMISSIBILITY RULE

The complementarity requirement is a criterion that should be taken into account in the situation selection process. Article 17 of the Rome Statute is the legal framework for the admissibility requirement. This article contains the components of the admissibility requirement, namely gravity (Article 17(1)(d)) and complementarity (Article 17(1)(a) and (b)). Article 17 reflects the heart of complementarity.[521] It describes in detail the elements of the complementarity rule. Article 17 sheds light on the notion of admissibility by laying down some criteria, but it leaves those tests without a clear definition. Enormous efforts were made to reduce the element of subjectivity when the complementarity rule's elements were being defined.[522] At the Rome Conference, delegations intended to prevent the ICC from playing a role as an appellate body to review decisions of domestic courts.[523] However, the interpretability is inherent for legal texts, even if they are worded in an objective way.

3.2.1. Defining Potential Cases for the Situational Complementarity Assessment

Article 17 alone does not seem applicable to the situational phase. Article 17 provides some rules with respect to the admissibility of a 'case', instead of a situation. No explicit or implicit reference to the situational phase is made in this article. However, if Article 17 is seen from a holistic perspective a different conclusion emerges. Article 53(1) and Article 15(4), as the legal basis for selecting a situation, provide that the admissibility of a situation should be examined in accordance with Article 17. Indeed, the recent articles add a situational vision to Article 17. The term 'case' carries a determined meaning. The dividing line between the situational phase and the case stage is the issuance of a warrant. Before this moment, there is no case. According to the treaty interpretation rules, identical terms in a treaty text should be presumed to carry an identical

519 Stigen, 2008, p. 19, see *supra* note 96.
520 Nouwen, 2013, p. 16, see *supra* note 226.
521 El Zeidy, 2011, p. 133, see *supra* note 19.
522 Mohamed M. El Zeidy, *The Principle of Complementarity in International Criminal Law: Origin, Development and Practice*, Martinus Nijhoff Publishers, 2008, p. 236.
523 Holmes, 2002, p. 673, see *supra* note 488.

meaning.[524] Therefore, literally speaking, the statement 'a case should be admissible' does not mean that a 'situation' should be admissible. It means that the complementarity analysis is expected to be case-specific rather than situation-specific.[525]

Contrary to the complementarity principle that draws a general picture of the complementary role of the Court in the international criminal justice system as a whole, the complementarity rule organizes the complementary role of the Court in connection with a specific situation or case. The complementarity rule as an assessment-oriented notion requires a concrete object. As the ICC PTC asserts, the admissibility assessment cannot be conducted in the abstract.[526] The complementarity assessment needs a definite and concrete object, namely, a case. Limiting the Prosecutor to assess one or more cases at the domestic level prevents them from monitoring the entire legal system of a State as an internal affair. Robinson asserts that it was "the intent of the drafters that the Court would not judge national legal systems in the abstract, but rather would only assess their handling of particular cases."[527] National jurisdictions are case-oriented. The domestic legal systems deal with cases rather than situations. The complementarity rule is a matter of concurrent jurisdictions. It requires drawing a comparison between the jurisdiction of the Court and the national jurisdictions. A comparable object is a prerequisite for making such a comparison. This comparable object is a case because in the national context the situation concept in the Rome Statute meaning is absent.

Given the foregoing considerations, a question arises: how should the Prosecutor assess the admissibility of a case in the preliminary examination when there is no concrete and actual case? It proposes an inquiry on what is the meaning of the term case in Article 17 when this article is applied in the situational phase. The Court's jurisprudence has provided an answer for this question: potential cases. The OTP Policy Paper on preliminary Examinations states that the complementarity assessment in the preliminary examination stage "is assessed with respect to potential cases that would likely arise from an investigation into the situation."[528] In his application for the authorization for initiating an investigation into the Situation in Kenya, the then Prosecutor asserted that he had considered admissibility by "taking into account the potential cases that would likely arise from an investigation into the situation."[529] This assertion was repeated in the Prosecutor's application for authorization of investigation into the Georgia situation.[530]

---

524 Kleffner, 2008, p. 197, see *supra* note 41.

525 Mark A. Drumbl, 'Policy Through Complementarity: The Atrocity Trial as Justice', in Carsten Stahn and Mohamed M. El Zeidy (eds.), *The International Criminal Court and Complementarity: From Theory to Practice*, Cambridge University Press, 2011, p. 204.

526 ICC, PTC II, Kenya situation, 31 March 2010, para. 49, see *supra* note 33.

527 Robinson, 2011, p. 465, see *supra* note 296.

528 ICC, OTP, Policy Paper on Preliminary Examinations, para. 46.

529 ICC, OTP, Kenya situation, Request for Authorization of an Investigation Pursuant to Article 15, 29 November 2009, para. 51.

530 "This assessment is carried out in relation to the potential cases that are likely to be the focus of an investigation by the Prosecution" (ICC, OTP, Georgia situation, 17 November 2015, para. 278, see *supra* note 292).

In addition, the Chambers of the Court have referred to the issue of potential cases when they authorize the Prosecutor to initiate an investigation into a situation. For instance, in its authorizing decision in the situation of Kenya, the PTC II initially insists that "the Prosecutor and the PTC operate within the parameters of an entire 'situation', rather than in relation to a specific case", because "the Court's jurisprudence has considered that a 'case' falls within the ambit of the Article 19 stage, and it starts after the issuance of an arrest warrant or a summons to appear pursuant to Article 58 of the Statute."[531] Then, the Chamber provides some explanations to show the meaning of a case in the context of a situation. First, it explains why the drafters of the Rome Statute used the term 'case' instead of the situation if they had intended the latter instead of the former. According to the PTC, the current wording enshrined in Article 17 was drafted by the Preparatory Committee and remained unchanged even at the Rome Conference. As PTC II explains, the chapeau of Article 17 of the Statute, which included the reference to a 'case', "remained throughout the drafting process until it appeared in the current text of Article 17 of the Statute."[532] At the Rome Conference, "there was a prevailing trend inspired by the coordinator to avoid reopening the 'substance' of the admissibility provisions, given the difficulty posed in reaching acceptable compromises at the Preparatory Committee." Consequently, "had the relevant working group on Article 53 changed their terminology from 'case' to 'situation', this would have required revisiting the text of Article 17 which, as discussed above, was an unfavorable idea."[533]

Indeed, as some commentators on the Rome Statute assert, at the Rome Conference, the Coordinator's intention was to resist holding informal consultations for as long as possible.[534] Therefore, the term 'case' remained intact. Nonetheless, the PTC insists that the text of the Rome Statute is not mistaken, but the drafters have left it for the Court "to harmonize the meaning according."[535] Given this fact, the Chamber gives its own interpretation by referring to the notion of 'potential cases'. The PTC admits that it fails to "comprehend how the Prosecutor can determine whether a case 'would be admissible', without preliminarily knowing the type of groups of persons or incidents (involving the commission of crimes falling within the jurisdiction of the Court), or both, likely to shape his future case(s)."[536] For this reason, the Chamber introduced the potential cases notion. The Chamber goes further and sets some criteria to define the scope of the potential cases. Accordingly, the potential cases are identified by determining: "(i) the groups of persons involved that are likely to be the focus of an investigation for the purpose of shaping the future case(s); and (ii) the crimes within the jurisdiction of the Court allegedly committed during the incidents that are likely

531 ICC, PTC II, Kenya situation, 31 March 2010, para. 44, see *supra* note 33.
532 Ibid., para. 46.
533 Ibid., 46.
534 Williams and Schabas, 2008, p. 612, see *supra* note 13.
535 ICC, PTC II, Kenya situation, 31 March 2010, paras. 47–48, see *supra* note 33.
536 Ibid., para. 49.

to be the focus of an investigation for the purpose of shaping the future case(s)."[537] In the admissibility assessment, "an examination as to whether the relevant State(s) is/are conducting or has/have conducted national proceedings in relation to the groups of persons and the crimes allegedly committed during those incidents, which together would likely form the object of the Court's investigations."[538]

A case encompasses two components, namely person and conduct. Therefore, the potential cases compose these two elements. In the application for authorization of investigation into the Georgia situation, the Prosecutor refers to different potential cases relevant to different crimes in a clear manner: "in the light of the indefinite suspension of national proceedings in Georgia, the Prosecution has concluded that the potential case of the forcible transfer of ethnic Georgians identified in this Application would be currently admissible. The potential case relating to the intentional directing of attacks against peacekeepers and peacekeeping facilities would be partially admissible at this stage."[539]

It should be noted that the notion of potential cases implies potentiality and temporality. As the Chambers of the Court assert, "the Prosecution's selection of the incidents or groups of persons that are likely to shape future case(s) is preliminary in nature and is not binding for future admissibility assessments, meaning that the Prosecution's selection on the basis of these elements for the purposes of defining a potential 'case' for this particular phase may change at a later stage, depending on the development of the investigation."[540] Finding final cases needs more investigation that should be done following the preliminary examination. The Prosecutor of the Court in the Report on the Preliminary Examination Activities in 2015 mentions that the selection of the potential cases is "without prejudice to any further findings on subject-matter jurisdiction to be made pursuant to additional information that the office could receive at a later stage of analysis."[541]

The determination of potential cases is based on "the information available and that would likely arise from an investigation into the situation."[542] In practice, the Prosecutor makes a list of the potential suspects and crimes, and encloses the list in their application for an authorization of investigation. For instance, as to the situation of Côte d'Ivoire, the Prosecution had attached two confidential annexes; "Annex 1B presents a preliminary list of persons or groups belonging to or associated with the pro-Gbagbo and pro-Ouattara sides that appear to bear the greatest responsibility for the most serious crimes, with an indication of their specific role. As set out in the Office's

537 Ibid., para. 50.

538 Ibid., para. 52. This conclusion is reaffirmed by the Pre-Trial Chamber in the situation in Côte d'Ivoire (ICC, PTC III, Côte d'Ivoire situation, 3 October 2011, para. 44, see *supra* note 3).

539 ICC, OTP, Georgia situation, 17 November 2015, para. 323, see *supra* note 292. It should be noted that the focus of the Prosecutor in using the term 'potential case' is on potential persons rather than potential conduct.

540 ICC, PTC III, Côte d'Ivoire situation, 3 October 2011, para. 45, see *supra* note 3. And, ICC, PTC II, Kenya situation, 31 March 2010, para. 50, see *supra* note 33.

541 ICC, OTP, Report on Preliminary Examination Activities (2015), para. 194.

542 ICC, OTP, Policy Paper on Preliminary Examinations, para. 43.

Prosecutorial Strategy, the category of persons bearing the greatest responsibility includes those situated at the highest echelons of responsibility, including those who ordered, financed, or otherwise organized the alleged crimes. Annex 1A presents an indicative list of crimes within the jurisdiction of the Court allegedly committed during the most serious incidents within the situation."[543]

3.2.2. *The Concept of Case in the Complementarity Assessment*

Article 17 reads that the Court "shall determine that a case is inadmissible where..." This clause shows that the object of the admissibility assessment enshrined in Article 17 is a 'case', including potential cases in the situational phase or actual cases in the case stage. As PTC I in its decision on the Al-Senussi admissibility case asserts, "in accordance with consistent jurisprudence of the Court, a determination of admissibility is case-specific."[544]

The case notion has not been defined by the ICC legal texts. It has been left to the judiciary to provide an interpretation for the case notion. A definition of case was provided for the first time by the PTC III in the Lubanga case, as the first arrest warrant case at the ICC. At the time of issuing the arrest warrant, Lubanga was in the custody of the DRC.[545] Due to this background, the PTC *proprio motu* reviewed the admissibility of the case at hand when it was considering the Prosecutor's application for an arrest warrant. According to the PTC, "it is a *conditio sine qua non* for a case arising from the investigation of a situation to be inadmissible that national proceedings encompass both the person and the conduct which is the subject of the case before the Court."[546] This decision was the origin of the so-called 'same person/ same conduct' standard in the complementarity assessment. The PTC had already provided a definition of the case for a different purpose, namely the victims' participation in the proceedings. At that moment, the Chamber had stated that the concept of a case includes "specific incidents during which one or more crimes within the jurisdiction of the Court seem to have been committed by one or more identified suspects."[547] The same person/same conduct test arose from this initial definition, but in a different context. The initial definition had adopted an incident-oriented approach to the case notion. In the Lubanga case, the term 'incident' was replaced with the 'conduct' expression. Other Chambers have

---

543 ICC, OTP, Côte d'Ivoire situation, Request for Authorization of an Investigation Pursuant to Article 15, 23 June 2011, para. 46.

544 ICC, PTC I, Al-Senussi case, Decision on the Admissibility of the Case against Abdullah Al-Senussi, 11 October 2013, para. 66.

545 ICC, PTC I, Lubanga case, 10 February 2006, para. 33, see *supra* note 45. Lubanga had been arrested on 19 March 2005 by the DRC authorities.

546 Ibid., para. 31. This test is repeated by other Chambers; for instance see: ICC, PTC I, Harun case, 27 April 2007, para. 24, see *supra* note 48. And, ICC, Appeals Chamber, Kenya situation, 30 August 2011, para. 2, see *supra* note 225.

547 For Instance, *see:* ICC, PTC I, Lubanga case, Decision on the Application for Participation in the Proceedings of VPRS1, VPRS2, VPRS 3, VPRS4, VPRS5, VPRS6, 19 January 2006, para. 65.

also applied the same person/same conduct test.[548] In 2009, the Defense of Katanga challenged the admissibility of his case. Katanga believed that the same conduct test was too strict.[549] Nonetheless, neither the Trial Chamber nor the Appeals Chamber addressed this matter. Trial Chamber had found the case to be admissible on a different basis, namely based on the clear and explicit expression of unwillingness of the DRC to prosecute this case.[550] Therefore, the same conduct test did not find an opportunity to receive more clarity.

Later, and in the context of Kenya's admissibility challenge, the Appeals Chamber confirmed the same person/same conduct test by saying "the defining elements of a concrete case before the Court are the individual and the alleged conduct."[551] However, the Appeals Chamber, like other chambers, did not provide a clear meaning for the term 'conduct'. Instead, it added a qualification to the same conduct standard, i.e. the 'substantially'. According to the Appeals Chamber, "for such a case to be inadmissible under Article 17(1)(a) of the Statute, the national investigation must cover the same individual and substantially the same conduct as alleged in the proceedings before the Court."[552] In the Kenya situation, because the Kenyan government was declared inactive, the opportunity to define the 'substantially the same conduct' did not emerge. In Judge Ušacka's words, "the Appeals Chamber adopted the 'same person/substantially the same conduct' test without explaining why it added the term 'substantially' or what this term means."[553]

In 2014, the admissibility of the case against Simone Gbagbo was challenged. The PTC I, in its decision rejecting the challenge, referred to 'the same conduct' test without qualifying it with the 'substantially' adverb. However, the Chamber did not delve into the test because it had declared the case admissible before the Court due to the inactivity of the national jurisdiction.[554] Therefore, no one can draw an inference from this decision that the PTC has deviated from the precedent of other Chambers by removing the substantially adverb, since the Chamber did not intend to deal with the test in detail. In a different context, the Kenyan government had made a similar inference from the Appeals Chamber's judgment on the admissibility of the Katanga case. At the time, Kenya had claimed that there was no consistency between definitions of case made by the Court's chambers, because the Appeals Chamber in the Katanga case had not addressed the same person/same conduct test applied by the PTC. However, the PTC II rejected such inference. According to the Chamber, "the relevant part of the Appeals Chamber's Judgment must be read and understood in its context.

548 ICC, PTC I, Harun case, 27 April 2007, para. 14, see *supra* note 48.

549 ICC, Defense, Katanga case, Motion Challenging the Admissibility of the Case by Defense of Germain Katanga Pursuant to Article 19 (2) of the Statute, 11 March 2009, para. 42.

550 ICC, Trial Chamber II, Reasons for the Oral Decision on the Motion Challenging the Admissibility of the Case (Article 19 of the Statute),16 June 2009, para. 95.

551 ICC, Appeals Chamber, Kenya situation, 30 August 2011, para. 39, see *supra* note 225.

552 Ibid.

553 Ibid., para. 37.

554 ICC, PTC I, Simone Gbagbo case, Decision on Côte d'Ivoire's Challenge to the Admissibility of the Case against Simone Gbagbo, 11 December 2014, para. 65.

It is true that in paragraph 81 of the Judgment the Appeals Chamber stated that it does not have to address in the present appeal the correctness of the 'same-conduct' test used by the PTCs. Nonetheless, in paragraph 80 it made clear that the reason for making this statement was that there was no indication that there were ongoing investigations or prosecutions of any crime allegedly committed by the Appellant, at Bogoro."[555] In 2015, the Appeals Chamber, in its judgment on the challenge against the admissibility of the Simone Gbagbo case, referred again to the 'substantially the same conduct' test.

The ambiguity around the same conduct test finally broke when the ICC case law witnessed more clarity on the test in question. It was thanks to the challenges made in the context of the situation in Libya. As Judge Ušacka, in her dissenting opinion about the Gaddafi admissibility case, asserts, "since 2006, the 'same person/same conduct' test has been developed in the abstract, mostly on the basis of cases in which the States at issue did not challenge admissibility and did not demonstrate that they had undertaken any steps or activities regarding investigations/prosecutions of the alleged crimes or suspect."[556] However, upon the referral of the situation in Libya, the Court was faced with an opportunity to determine the meaning of the same conduct standard. Indeed, the Libya situation was a starting point for developing the case law of the Court with respect to the complementarity rule. As the then Prosecutor of the Court asserts, "this is the first time in the short history of the ICC that a State is requesting jurisdiction to conduct a national investigation against the same individual and for the same incidents under investigation by the ICC."[557] It alone proves the epistemological effects of challenges and questions.

3.2.2.1. The Same Conduct Test

If a State intends to prevent the Court from prosecuting a case, it should prosecute the same case. A case is the same if the domestic jurisdiction deals with the same person and substantially the same conduct.

3.2.2.1.1. The Conduct Notion at the ICC Case Law

In the situation in Libya, both the Saif al-Islam Gaddafi case and the Al-Senussi case run into a challenge. The Libyan government, firstly, challenged the admissibility of the Gaddafi case. In May 2013, the PTC I of the Court rejected the challenge. The Libyan government appealed this decision. One year later, in May 2014, the Appeals Chamber upheld the PTC's decision on the admissibility of the Gaddafi case. In the Al-Senussi case, the Libya government made a challenge against the admissibility of the case. This time, the PTC accepted the challenge and declared the case inadmissible before the

555 ICC, PTC II, Ruto case, 30 May 2011, para. 52, see *supra* note 253.

556 ICC, Appeals Chamber, Ruto case, Dissenting Opinion of Judge Anita Ušacka, 20 September 2011, para. 8.

557 ICC, OTP, ICC Prosecutor Statement to the United Nations Security Council on the Situation in the Libyan Arab Jamahiriya pursuant to UNSCR 1970, 16 May 2011.

Court. However, it was not the end of the story. The defense was not satisfied with the decision, and appealed the PTC's decision. Nonetheless, the Appeals Chamber upheld the decision and the case remained inadmissible.

The PTC I governing these cases adopted a concrete method to define the conduct notion. The Appeals Chamber of the Court, in one of its judgments, asserts that "to be able to carry out the assessment as to whether the same case is being investigated, it will be necessary for a Chamber to know the contours or parameters of the investigation being carried out both by the Prosecutor and by the State."[558] It is necessary because, in assessing the complementarity test, a comparison between the conduct before the ICC and its counterpart before the national jurisdiction is required. For this reason, in the Al-Senussi case, the PTC tried to identify "(i) the conduct of Mr Al-Senussi that is the subject of the proceedings before the Court; and (ii) the conduct of Mr Al-Senussi that is allegedly subject to Libya's national proceedings, as emerging from the evidence presented by Libya in support of its claim."[559]

A case before the Court is primarily formed and shaped by the Prosecutor. Therefore, in the situational phase and in the context of the preliminary examination, the source in which the conduct before the Court is enshrined is the Prosecutor's application for an authorization for initiating an investigation. The Prosecutor's application under Article 15 includes the list of potential cases that will probably be prosecuted by the Prosecutor. In the case of referrals, there is no concrete source to identify the potential cases before the Court. A State's referral may include potential cases, but it would not be binding for the Prosecutor. Case selection is the Prosecutor's responsibility. The Prosecutor should assess complementarity in all situations, including those that have reached the Court through the channel of referrals. Nonetheless, due to a lack of a judicial review over her decision to initiate an investigation into a situation referred by States, there is no way to be aware of the potential cases in the Prosecutor's mind. It is a deficiency and gap in the procedural law of the Court that should be filled. Putting the Prosecutor under judicial review is the most effective method for this purpose.

In the case phase, the parameters that specify the conduct before the Court "set out in the document that is statutorily envisaged as defining the factual allegations against the person at the phase of the proceedings in question."[560] PTC I in the Gaddafi case mentions that these documents are 'warrant of arrest' issued against the accused by the Chamber, as well as the Chamber's decision on the Prosecutor's application for the warrant of arrest.[561] In other words, in the case phase, the warrant of arrest or summons to appear and their corresponding Article 58 decisions are the factual sources for identifying the conduct before the Court.

558 ICC, Appeals Chamber, Gaddafi case, Judgment on the Appeal of Libya Against the Decision of Pre-Trial Chamber I of 31 May 2013 Entitled Decision on the Admissibility of the Case Against Saif Al-Islam Gaddafi, 21 May 2014, para. 85.

559 ICC, PTC I, Al-Senussi case, 11 October 2013, para. 67, see *supra* note 544.

560 Ibid., para. 66.

561 ICC, PTC I, Gaddafi case, Decision on the Admissibility of the Case Against Saif-Al-Islam Gaddafi, 31 May 2013, para. 78.

In the Saif Al-Islam Gaddafi case, the PTC surveyed both warrant of arrest against the accused and the relevant decision on the Prosecutor's application. In the arrest warrant, the Chamber had found reasonable grounds to believe that "Saif Al-Islam Gaddafi is criminally responsible as an indirect co-perpetrator, under Article 25(3)(a) of the Statute, for the following crimes committed by Security Forces under his control in various localities of the Libyan territory, in particular in Benghazi, Misrata, Tripoli and other neighboring cities, from 15 February 2011 until at least 28 February 2011: i) murder as a crime against humanity, within the meaning of Article 7(1)(a) of the Statute; and ii) Persecution as a crime against humanity."[562] The arrest warrant, however, did not specify the constituent events and incidents of the alleged crimes. The warrant only drew the general context of the criminality of Gaddafi within a jurisdictional framework in terms of time and location. In the warrant, the conduct was a crime-oriented notion instead of incident-oriented. In the words of the PTC, "the Warrant of Arrest does not refer to specific instances of killings and acts of persecution, but rather refers to acts of such a nature resulting from Mr Gaddafi's use of the Libyan Security Forces to target the civilian population which was demonstrating against Gaddafi's regime or those perceived to be dissidents to the regime."[563] The PTC I's Judges in their Article 58 Decision described Gaddafi's conduct similar to what they had already referred to in the arrest warrant.[564]

Contrary to the warrant of arrest, the Article 58 Decision included "a long, non-exhaustive list of alleged acts of murder and persecution committed against an identified category of people within certain temporal and geographical parameters."[565] However, the Chamber brought to light that "the events expressly mentioned in the Article 58 Decision do not represent unique manifestations of the form of criminality alleged against Mr Gaddafi in the proceedings before the Court. They constitute rather samples of a course of conduct of the Security Forces, under Mr Gaddafi's control, that allegedly carried out an attack committed across Libya from 15 February 2011 onwards against the civilians."[566] Indeed, the PTC I acknowledged the exemplary nature of arrest warrants at the ICC's system. The exemplary nature of warrants arises from the selective functioning of the Court. As mentioned, the Court functions in a selective manner consistent with its expressivist mandates. In prosecuting a case, what is more important is grasping the main criminality rather than specific events in the context of which crimes are committed. Based on this understanding, the PTC concluded that "it would not be appropriate to expect Libya's investigation to cover exactly the same acts of murder and persecution mentioned in the Article 58 Decision as constituting instances of Mr Gaddafi's alleged course of conduct."[567] Indeed, the Chamber adopted a realist approach to the complementarity assessment. The ICC-identified crimes are

---

562 ICC, PTC I, Warrant of Arrest for Saif Al-Islam Gaddafi, 27 June 2011, p. 6.
563 ICC, PTC I, Gaddafi case, 31 May 2013, para. 80, see *supra* note 561.
564 Ibid., para. 83.
565 Ibid., para. 81.
566 Ibid., para. 82.
567 Ibid., para. 83.

committed in an intense and broad manner, and include a large number of incidents. They are too widespread to be prosecuted comprehensively even in the national sphere. Therefore, the Chamber admitted that a margin of selectivity is inevitable, both in the international sphere and in the national one. The Court seeks to prosecute the main criminal themes.

The conduct notion in this sense provides a more flexible evaluative standard. Based on this definition, the Chamber initially admitted that "the crimes with which Libya contemplates charging Mr Gaddafi under Libyan legislation, do not cover all aspects of the offences to be brought under the Rome Statute", but affirmed that "these offences together with the provisions under articles 27 and 28 of the Libyan Criminal Code may sufficiently capture Mr Gaddafi's use of his control over the Libyan State apparatus and Security Forces to kill and persecute hundreds of civilian demonstrators or alleged dissidents to Muammar Gaddafi's regime between 15 and at least 28 February 2011, as alleged in the Warrant of Arrest."[568]

Indeed, the PTC acknowledged that the charges brought against Gaddafi in Libya did not cover those incidents underlying the conduct in the proceedings before the Court, but they could represent, substantially, the same conduct. In spite of adopting such a broad approach to the conduct notion, the Chamber finally declared the case admissible before the Court. The admissibility of the case was not because of the difference in the conduct before the Court and Libya in theory, but the situation was declared admissible due to inactivity of the Libyan judicial system in action. In this regard, the Chamber first confirmed that the Libyan authorities had taken some initiatives. According to the Chamber, "the evidence presented satisfactorily demonstrates that a number of progressive steps directed at ascertaining Mr Gaddafi's criminal responsibility have been undertaken by the Libyan authorities, and that an investigation is currently ongoing at the domestic level."[569] Nonetheless, the Chamber believed that such activities were not made as to the case before the Court, even in its broad meaning. Judges concluded that Libya had fallen short of substantiating "by means of evidence of a sufficient degree of specificity and probative value, the submission that the domestic investigation covers the same case that is before the Court."[570]

It is worth saying that the PTC I, at the end of its decision on the Gaddafi case, mentioned that despite the fact that Libya had sufficient opportunities to submit evidence in support of its admissibility challenge, it failed to do so. However, the Chamber added that even if Libya had provided compelling and defining evidence, it would not have affected the ultimate result. In the view of the Chamber, if it happened, serious concerns would remain with respect to "the second limb of the admissibility test, namely Libya's ability genuinely to carry out the investigation or prosecution against Mr Gaddafi."[571] Judge Ušacka in her dissenting opinion claims that this

568 Ibid., para. 113.
569 Ibid., para. 132.
570 Ibid., para. 135.
571 Ibid., para. 137.

statement proves that "the Pre- Trial Chamber was not even itself entirely certain about its finding that Libya was not investigating the same case."[572] Indeed, the flexible test established by the Court resulted in some uncertainty in its evaluation. It is evident that the more loose and flexible a test is, the fewer cases fall outside of its scope. For this reason, the Chamber enhanced its argument in favor of the admissibility of the case by providing other reasoning, besides the inaction scenario. Favoring proceedings at the domestic level, and the broadness in the meaning of the conduct test, favors a liberal approach in assessing the complementarity rule.

Some months later, when the challenge against the admissibility of the Al-Senussi case was made, the same PTC repeated its interpretation about the same conduct test in its previous decision. The judges of the PTC, primarily, determined the accused conduct in the proceedings before the Court. Based on the warrant and its corresponding Article 58 decision, the Chamber concluded that "the present case before the Court concerns the individual criminal responsibility of Mr Al-Senussi for killings and acts of persecution by reason of their (real or perceived) political opposition to the Gaddafi regime carried out on many civilian demonstrators and political dissidents, allegedly committed directly or through the Security Forces during the repression of the demonstrations taking place in Benghazi from 15 February 2011 until at least 20 February 2011 and as part of a policy designed at the highest level of the Libyan State machinery to deter and quell, by any means, the revolution against the Gaddafi regime occurring throughout Libya." According to the Chamber, "this constitutes the relevant conduct alleged in the proceedings before the Court that defines the scope of the criminal case against Mr Al-Senussi."[573]

This time, in its decision, the Chamber referred to the Prosecutor's observation about the meaning of the conduct notion. The Chamber reported that the Prosecutor, while satisfied that Libya was investigating the same case against Al-Senussi, had considered that in all circumstances and in all cases, the 'conduct' term must always be understood as 'incident-specific', and that a warrant of arrest necessarily includes the incidents because it must include reference to time and place of the alleged crimes. According to the Prosecutor, the term 'incidents' identifies "criminal acts that occur in a particular location and at a specific time and in the framework of a course of conduct and series of events."[574] The Chamber insisted that "the identification of the conduct that is alleged in the proceedings before the Court cannot be done in the abstract."[575]

However, the Chamber amended the Prosecutor's interpretation by establishing a rule: "what is in all cases required at every phase of the proceedings before the Court is that the alleged criminal conduct be sufficiently described with reference to precise temporal, geographic and material parameters, but not that such conduct be invariably composed of one or more 'incidents' of a pre-determined breadth."[576] The conduct is

572 ICC, Appeals Chamber, Gaddafi case, Separate Opinion of Judge Anita Ušacka, 21 May 2014, para. 45.
573 ICC, PTC I, Al-Senussi case, 11 October 2013, para. 71, see *supra* note 544.
574 Ibid., para. 72.
575 Ibid., para. 74.
576 Ibid., para. 75.

a general notion consisting of some incidents. However, in the eyes of the Chamber, the incidents selected by the Court do not necessarily need to be equal to the incidents under investigation at the domestic jurisdiction. Nonetheless, those incidents at the domestic proceedings should indicate that the conduct covers the relevant context. The PTC recalled its Article 58 Decision in the Al-Senussi case, and stated that the decision contained a list of particular 'incidents' or 'events' that constituted the factual parameters of the criminal conduct against Al-Senussi before the Court. However, "these 'incidents' or 'events' do not represent unique manifestations of Mr Al-Senussi's alleged criminal conduct, but rather are illustrative and non-exhaustive samples of discrete criminal acts that substantiate the evidentiary threshold of 'reasonable grounds to believe' that Mr Al-Senussi is criminally responsible for the direct and indirect commission of the crimes of murder and persecution perpetrated against civilian demonstrators and political dissidents to the Gaddafi regime."[577]

Finally, the Chamber concluded that "the conduct that is alleged in the criminal proceedings against Mr Al-Senussi is not shaped by the 'incidents' mentioned in the Article 58 Decision, it is not required that domestic proceedings concern each of those 'events' at the national level in order for the Chamber to be satisfied that Libya is investigating or prosecuting Mr Al-Senussi for substantially the same conduct that is alleged in the proceedings before this Court."[578] However, the Chamber completed this assertion by adding that "all or some of the 'incidents' or 'events' referred to in the Article 58 Decision are encompassed in the national proceedings may still constitute a relevant indicator that the case subject to said proceedings is indeed the same as the one before the Court."[579] Consequently, the Chamber declared the case of Al-Senussi inadmissible before the Court. According to the Chamber, "the evidence submitted by Libya is sufficient to conclude that concrete and progressive steps are being undertaken by the domestic authorities in the proceedings against Mr Al-Senussi and to identify the scope and the subject-matter of such proceedings."[580]

Both decisions rendered by the PTC I about the admissibility of cases regarding the situation in Libya were appealed. However, the Appeals Chamber confirmed both decisions. In its judgments, the Appeals Chamber provided more detail on the issue of the sufficient 'sameness' in the conduct test. In the case of Gaddafi, the Appeals Chamber referred to the components of a case as "the suspect under investigation and the conduct that gives rise to criminal liability under the Statute."[581] The Appeals Chamber insisted that "in assessing admissibility, what is required is a judicial assessment of whether the case that the State is investigating sufficiently mirrors the one that the Prosecutor is investigating."[582]

577 Ibid., para. 76.
578 Ibid.
579 Ibid., para. 79.
580 Ibid., para. 160.
581 ICC, Appeals Chamber, Gaddafi case, 21 May 2014, para. 85, see *supra* note 558.
582 Ibid.

The idea of mirroring invited the Appeals Chamber to adopt an incident-oriented approach in defining the conduct notion. The Conduct that defines a case is "described in the incidents under investigation which is imputed to the suspect."[583] In the eyes of the Chamber, an incident "is understood as referring to a historical event, defined in time and place, in the course of which crimes within the jurisdiction of the Court were allegedly committed by one or more direct perpetrators", but the Appeals Chamber added that "the exact scope of an incident cannot be determined in the abstract. What is required is an analysis of all the circumstances of a case, including the context of the crimes and the overall allegations against the suspect."[584] Nevertheless, the Appeals Chamber's definition of conduct seems to be equal to the PTC's definition, but with a different wording. The Appeals Chamber puts its stress on the incident notion as the main constituent element of the conduct. However, in defining the incident it provides a definition-carrying generality. According to the Appeals Chamber, the conduct in the 'same conduct' test should be understood by taking into account the contextual element of crimes and circumstances. Making the conduct dependent on general context and circumstances makes this notion different from the classical meaning of an incident as a specific and single event.

Upon clarifying the meaning of the conduct, the Appeals Chamber, in the Gaddafi case, dealt with the issue of sameness. The Appeals Chamber insisted that the extent to which both conducts at the ICC and the domestic proceedings should overlap depends on the circumstances of each case. The Chamber stipulated that "it is not possible to set down a hard and fast rule to regulate this issue."[585] The Appeals Chamber mentioned that the opposite ends of the spectrum are straightforward. If the underlying incidents under investigation of both the Prosecutor and the State were identical, the case would be inadmissible, and if they were completely different, the case would be declared admissible. However, the problem arises with respect to those instances between these two extremes. Here, the Appeals Chamber was of the view that "if there is a large overlap between the incidents under investigation, it may be clear that the State is investigating substantially the same conduct; if the overlap is smaller, depending upon the precise facts, it may be that the State is still investigating substantially the same conduct or that it is investigating only a very small part of the Prosecutor's case."[586]

In determining the substantial sameness, the Appeals Chamber established a guiding rule. According to the Chamber, "in carrying out this assessment, a Chamber should consider any information provided by the State concerned as to why it is not investigating incidents that are being investigated by the Prosecutor and should take this into account in deciding whether the State in question is investigating substantially the same conduct. In addition, this judicial assessment should include a consideration of the interests of victims and the impact on them of any decision that

583 Ibid., para. 62.
584 Ibid.
585 Ibid., para. 71.
586 Ibid., para. 72.

a case is inadmissible at the Court despite not all of the incidents being investigated domestically."[587] Indeed, the Appeals Chamber refers to one of the major functions of the Court under the positive complementarity theory, namely dialogue with States. The Chamber admits that the complementarity rule needs mutual understanding and cooperation. The Prosecutor of the Court insists on the necessity of taking into account the reasons behind the difference in choices made by the State in assessing the same conduct test as well. According to the Prosecutor, "if the focus of the national investigation or prosecution differs in any respect from the ICC case, the Chamber will need to scrutinize the national efforts closely, including reasons for such divergence, in order to determine whether the national authorities and the ICC are focused on substantially the same conduct."[588] Such inquiry requires interaction and dialogue with the states. The Court selects a case and situation based on operational factors. Such factors may affect the prosecution policies at the domestic level. One or more incidents may be non-feasible for the domestic courts, and consequently will be replaced with other incidents, representing the same crime before the Court.

Following all these arguments, in reviewing the admissibility of the Gaddafi decision, the Appeals Chamber, as did the PTC, left the same conduct test aside, and invoked the inactivity argument to declare the case in issue admissible. The Chamber argued that Libya had stated its intention to investigate Gaddafi fully, even if there was currently only limited investigative activity taking place. Nonetheless, the Chamber dismissed such an understanding of activity in the national jurisdiction. According to the Appeals Chamber, "if it has only been established that 'discrete aspects' of the case before the Court are being investigated domestically, it will most likely not be possible for a Chamber to conclude that the same case is under investigation."[589] Consequently, due to inactivity of the Libyan government, the Appeals Chamber upheld the PTC decision in the Gaddafi case.

The Appeals Chamber, in the case of Gaddafi, failed to reach a consensus. Judge Ušacka dissented from the rigid approach of the majority to the conduct notion. Judge Ušacka argued that such a rigid approach requires States to assume a copy-paste function and mirror the proceedings before the Court to prevent the Court's intervention. In this scenario, "instead of complementing each other, the relationship between the Court and the State would be competitive, requiring the State to do its utmost to fulfill the requirements set by the Court."[590] Judge Ušacka added, "conduct should be understood much more broadly than under the current test. While there should be a nexus between the conduct being investigated and prosecuted domestically and that before the Court, this conduct and any crimes investigated or prosecuted in relation thereto do not need to cover all of the same material and mental elements of the

---

587 Ibid., para. 74.

588 ICC, OTP, Katanga case, Prosecution's Response to Document in Support of Appeal of the Defense for Germain Katanga Against the Decision of the Trial Chamber *Motifs de la décision oral relative à l'exception d'irrecevabilité de l'affaire*, 31 July 2009, para. 65.

589 ICC, Appeals Chamber, Gaddafi case, 21 May 2014, para. 77, see *supra* note 558.

590 ICC, Appeals Chamber, Gaddafi case, Separate Opinion of Judge Anita Ušacka, 21 May 2014, para. 52.

crimes before the Court and also does not need to include the same acts attributed to an individual under suspicion."[591] Usaka referred to the Gaddafi case to make clear her assertion: "the goal of fighting impunity is also achieved, even if not exactly the same conduct as that before the Court is under investigation by Libya, but if the suspect's link to the use of the Security Forces in Libya and their consequences are the subject of the investigation of the Libyan authorities."[592]

Later, when the case of Al-Senussi was presented before the Appeals Chamber, the Chamber reaffirmed its findings in its decision on the Gaddafi case. The Appeals Chamber repeated that "the overlap or sameness would depend upon the facts of the specific case."[593] In this case, the Appeals Chamber brought a part of the PTC's decision under criticism. The PTC I, in its decisions, had not adopted a strict incident-centered approach. The PTC was of the opinion that "the specific incidents alleged against Mr Al-Senussi did not form part of the comparator in deciding on whether Libya is investigating the same case."[594] Nonetheless, the Appeals Chamber disagreed with such an assertion. In accordance with the Appeals Chamber, "this is not in line with the jurisprudence of the Appeals Chamber just cited, which considers such incidents to play a central role in this comparison."[595]

However, the Appeals Chamber confirmed the ultimate conclusion of the PTC. The Appeals Chamber believed that "the PTC indeed relied, at least in part, on the underlying incidents to assess the sameness of the cases being investigated and used them to conclude that Libya was investigating the same case."[596] In other words, the PTC had grounded its evaluation on the assessment of concrete incidents. In sum, the Appeals Chamber found that "while the PTC's findings as to the relevance of the incidents for the question of whether the same case is being investigated diverged from the Appeals Chamber's jurisprudence in the Gaddafi case, it nevertheless considered those incidents when actually assessing whether Libya was investigating the same case as that before the Court."[597] However, the PTC I had not indeed ignored the role of incidents in determination of the same conduct. Nonetheless, the Chamber was of the view that the incidents are merely indicators of a more general context underlying the notion of conduct. The Appeals Chamber was of the same view, though it described the conduct as an incident. Indeed, the difference between the Appeals Chamber and the PTC is a matter of terminology.

As mentioned, the term 'case' within the meaning of Article 17 embraces two components, namely person and conduct. The conduct part of the test "raises issues of interpretation and needs further clarification."[598] If the conduct before the Court is

---

591 Ibid., para. 58.
592 Ibid.
593 ICC, Appeals Chamber, Al-Senussi case, 24 July 2014, para. 100, see *supra* note 107.
594 Ibid., para. 101.
595 Ibid.
596 Ibid., para. 103.
597 Ibid., para. 110.
598 ICC, PTC I, Gaddafi case, 31 May 2013, para. 61, see *supra* note 561.

different from the conduct in the national proceedings, it results in the admissibility of the case before the Court, even though the accused has been prosecuted for other conduct at the national level. For instance, in the case against Mr Gbagbo, Switzerland had opened an investigation against the accused for money laundering. However, the PTC issuing the arrest warrant asserted that "the Swiss enquiry has not led to any charges and it will in any event address crimes that are outwit the subject matter of the present Application."[599] This was the same story with respect to the case against Mrs. Gbagbo. In that case, Gbagbo had already been charged by her country, but for economic crimes.[600] The Court did not consider this background as an obstacle to declaring the case at hand admissible.

3.2.2.1.2. Narrow Interpretation of the Same Conduct Test

The Court's case law has established a yardstick to assess if the conduct before the ICC and the domestic jurisdiction is the same, namely the 'substantially same conduct' test. The 'substantially same conduct' test consists of three components: substantially, conduct and sameness. All of these elements require interpretation and clarification. Two main interpretative approaches can be adopted to the same conduct test: narrow and broad. The former is mainly literal and rigid, and the latter provides more flexibility because it focuses on the context rather than the text. From the narrow perspective, the conduct is an incident-oriented notion. It means that the conduct that constitutes a case is equal with one or more specific incidents. The incident itself is a concrete event with a specific place, time, perpetrators, and in particular, victims. In other words, incidents are those concrete events that form the underlying acts of the ICC-identified crimes.

The number and identity of victims is a distinguishing feature in separating an incident from the others. For instance, in the Katanga case, the PTC I identified a protracted armed conflict, that took place from July 2002 until the end of 2003 in the Ituri, as the context of the case against Katanga. In this context, the Chamber believed that the group under command of Katanga, acting with a common purpose, carried out an attack on the village of Bogoro which started on or around 24th February 2003.[601] According to the Chamber, during the attack and in the aftermath, members of the involved groups committed several criminal acts against civilians, primarily of Hema ethnicity, including the murder of about 200 civilians, pillaging and the sexual enslavement of several women and girls. In this case, murder, pillaging and sexual enslavement as crimes against humanity constitute the conduct before the Court. However, all of these crimes consist of some incidents that have specific victims and took place in a specific time and place. For instance, in the forgoing instance, 200 civilians were killed; some of them on the day of attack and some of them later; some

599 ICC, PTC III, Laurent Gbagbo, 30 November 2011, para. 19, see *supra* note 242.

600 ICC, PTC III, Decision on the Prosecutor's Application Pursuant to Article 58 for a Warrant of Arrest against Simone Gbagbo, 2 March 2012, para. 10.

601 ICC, PTC I, Katanga case, Urgent Warrant of Arrest for Germain Katanga, 2 July 2007.

of them in location A and others in location B. These are incidents forming a context in which the ICC-identified crimes were committed. Also, if the attack on Bogoro village was a part of a larger attack against the Hemas, and there were other villages under attack, the attack on Bogoro would be an incident besides other incidents and events.

Another clarifying example is the Mr Gbagbo case. The conduct in the Gbagbo case was widespread and systematic attacks on political opponents to retain power by all means, including by lethal force that resulted in murder, rape and persecution.[602] This conduct is materialized in four specific incidents, including i) the attacks relating to the RTI demonstrations between 16 and 19 December 2010; ii) the attack on the women's march in Abobo on 3 March 2011; iii) the Abobo market shelling on 17 March 2011; and iv) the Yopougon massacre on 12 April 2011.[603] The case against Simone Gbagbo was also formed around these four specific incidents. In the PTC's opinion, the conduct that constituted the Simone Gbagbo case was her individual responsibility for "the commission, jointly with Laurent Gbagbo and his inner circle and through the Ivorian Defense and Security Forces, who were reinforced by youth militias and mercenaries, of the crimes of murder, rape and other forms of sexual violence, inhuman acts and persecution committed" in the context of four specific incidents.[604] The Côte d'Ivoire Government alleged that the PTC had erred in law, *inter alia,* when it unduly restricted its analysis of the relevant conduct to a comparison of the incidents, and it failed to attach due weight to the circumstances of the case and the context of the crimes.[605] In response, the Appeals Chamber rejected this argument on that point only because the argument "is limited to this general statement. Code d'Ivoire does not explain which circumstances or context the PTC ought to have considered and how such consideration would have affected the PTC's conclusion."[606] This statement implies that there is a space for the domestic jurisdictions to select one or more alternative incidents from what has been selected by the Court as far as it is justified. However, in this case, the Côte d'Ivoire Government did not suggest any alternatives to the Court's choices.

The incident-oriented approach to the conduct test requires that if, for instance, the Court selects some specific victims of the crime of murder, the national jurisdiction should select exactly those incidents including those victims. It is evident that such a narrow interpretation broadens the scope of the Prosecutor's authority to intervene in a situation. The former Prosecutor had adopted such narrow approach to the conduct notion. The then Prosecutor of the Court in the Katanga case once asserted that "the term 'case' should therefore be understood as being constituted by the underlying event, incident and circumstances – i.e. in the criminal context, the conduct of the suspect in

602 ICC, PTC III, Laurent Gbagbo case, 30 November 2011, para. 5, see *supra* note 242.
603 Ibid., para. 55.
604 ICC, PTC I, Simone Gbagbo case, 11 December 2014, para. 44, see *supra* note 554.
605 ICC, Appeals Chamber, Simone Gbagbo case, Judgment on the Appeal of Côte d'Ivoire Against the Decision of Pre-Trial Chamber I of 11 December 2014 Entitled Decision on Côte d'Ivoire's Challenge to the Admissibility of the Case against Simone Gbagbo, 27 May 2015, para. 74.
606 Ibid., para. 79.

relation to a given incident."[607] Somewhere else, he had offered his own interpretation of the 'substantiality' term in a way that it would preserve the incident-oriented feature of the same conduct test: "the term 'substantially' indicates that the national authorities are not necessarily required to charge the suspect under the exact same legal qualification. While the conduct itself must necessarily be the same, meaning the underlying acts and incidents concerned, the legal characterization of such conduct may differ: it must be the same in substance."[608] The next Prosecutor has followed a bit more of a flexible approach: "substantially serves to explain in relation to what 'sameness' attaches, namely, to the substance of the criminal behavior. Thus, a case will be 'substantially the same' if any difference in the underlying facts and circumstances are minor."[609]

The main argument in favor of the narrow approach is its consistency with the literal interpretation of the case notion. The advocators of this approach assert that Articles 17(1) and 20(3) should be read together in order to keep the consistency between these two articles.[610] Literally, such a holistic reading of these provisions ties the conduct notion to the concept of *ne bis in idem*. Article 20(3) deals with the issue of double jeopardy. It provides "no person who has been tried by another court for conduct also proscribed under article 6, 7, 8 or 8 *bis* shall be tried by the Court with respect to the same conduct." In addition, Article 17(1)(c) states that a case is inadmissible if "the person concerned has already been tried for conduct which is the subject of the complaint." It is said that the consistency requires that the conduct in Article 17 is equivalent with the conduct in the meaning of *ne bis in idem*. Idem includes the same date, place, victims and situations.[611] It results in the conclusion made by the Prosecutor that investigations of other similar conduct would not render a case inadmissible.[612]

Despite the literal interpretation of Article 17, it appears that such an interpretation is questionable. A text should be read in light of its corresponding context. The 'double jeopardy' rule has been used by the pro-Prosecutor as a yardstick to prove that the conduct, in the meaning of Article 17, should be as specific as the conduct in the context of the 'double jeopardy' rule. However, the introductory part of this argument, namely the specificity of the conduct in the *ne bis in idem*, can be challenged. The '*ne bis in idem*' rule in the Rome Statute should be read contextually, i.e. in the context of the international criminal justice system, instead of the domestic contexts. When double jeopardy transforms into the international context, it undergoes some changes. It is not

---

607 ICC, OTP, Prosecution Response to Motion Challenging the Admissibility of the 19 the Case by the Defense of Germain Katanga, pursuant to Article 19(2)(a), 30 March 2009, para. 58.

608 ICC, OTP, Prosecution Response to Application on Behalf of the Government of Libya pursuant to Article 19 of the ICC Statute, 5 June 2012, para. 25.

609 ICC, OTP, Prosecution's Response to Application on Behalf of the Government of Libya relating to Abdullah Al-Senussi Pursuant to Article 19 of the ICC Statute, 3 May 2013, para. 67.

610 Rastan, 2011, p. 440, see *supra* note 17.

611 Nouwen, 2013, p. 55, see *supra* note 226.

612 See: ICC, OTP, Katanga case, 31 July 2009, para. 29, see *supra* note 558.

reasonable to ignore the major differences between the contexts in the international and national spheres. Indeed, instead of amending the conduct notion in Article 17, the conduct term in Article 20 should be read and understood in light of the context in which it is going to be applied. The double jeopardy rule in the Rome Statute is broader than its counterpart at some of national legal systems. It means that if a case has already been prosecuted by a national jurisdiction, the Court should stay away even if the domestic Court has dealt with different instances of the same conduct. The same 'conduct' term in Article 20 should be as general as the conduct in Article 17. Nonetheless, upon the Court's intervention, if a State intends to prosecute those crimes, which have not already been addressed by the Court, there is no legal barrier in the way of prosecution at the domestic level. The meaning of the complementarity principle is well represented in this situation. The Court is not intended to deal with all crimes. Therefore, there is a space for States to cover those aspects that have remained outside of the Court's reach. The Katanga case is an example here. It has been reported that the DRC is going to prosecute Katanga for some offences such as his alleged role in the killing some UN peacekeepers, who has been released from the ICC detention upon serving his sentence, due to his conviction before the Court.[613] Such developments in the future should be welcomed.

Moreover, the narrow definition raises some implications that do not seem to be defensible. It hampers the catalyst effect of complementarity. If the same conduct test is incident-oriented, it reduces the effectiveness of complementarity. Article 17 begins with the clause that the complementarity rule should be read given the complementarity principle enshrined in the preamble. The complementarity rule encourages the State to take initiative if it deems a task possible. However, in the case of a narrow approach to the conduct test, "a State is impossible to win an admissibility challenge. The State that wishes to render that case inadmissible must literally copy the ICC case in terms of person, conduct, incidents and mode of liability."[614] A situation embraces a large number of incidents. Neither the Court nor the domestic jurisdictions are able to cover all these incidents.

Nouwen explains that the adoption of such a narrow definition of the conduct test is grounded in a strict anti-impunity policy. "The Court absolute anti-impunity approach persists and all other interest are subjected to the aim of eradicating impunity, the same conduct test in its strictest interpretation may survive."[615] Indeed, the supporters of the narrowness of the conduct test provide the anti-impunity goal as the perambulatory framework within which Article 17 should be read. Nonetheless, it is evident that they only consider one aspect while ignore other dimensions. The Court has to keep a balance between various considerations and interests. It is probably the most difficult

---

613 Yahoo News, DR Congo to Prosecute Militia Leader Katanga, Convicted by ICC, 18 January 2016, available at: http://news.yahoo.com/dr-congo-prosecute-militia-leader-katanga-convicted-icc-085546905.html.

614 Nouwen, 2013, pp. 55–56, see *supra* note 226.

615 Ibid., p. 58.

task of the Court. The complementarity rule is stationed in the middle of different roles: a role as watchdog and its function as gentle motivator of domestic proceedings.[616] In the Laurent Gbagbo case, the Defense invited the Chamber to interpret the conduct notion in a flexible manner. They submitted that "the short-sighted view of complementarity adopted by Trial Chamber II fails to take account of the wider goals of international criminal justice, in particular the need for national jurisdictions to build capacity to try such crimes domestically in order to involve the affected communities as part of the overall process of reconciliation and peace building."[617] This claim had been referred to by the Counsel of Katanga in the motion challenging the admissibility of the case against the accused. According to the Defense, the test adopted by the PTC was wrong because it "could negatively impact on the purposeful design of the State, which was meant to encourage domestic proceedings."[618] The narrow adoption of the conduct test hampers positive complementarity activities. As Stahn submits, it "makes it difficult to accommodate interaction between the Court and domestic jurisdictions or positive complementarity approaches in the context of admissibility challenges."[619]

The narrow approach to the conduct test is such that an approach decreases the scope of the prosecutorial discretion in the national jurisdictions. The Kenyan government, in the context of the Ruto admissibility challenge, refers to the adverse effect of the narrowness of the tests on the independence of the national prosecution. According to the Kenyan government, "the same person test could be seen as compelling State authorities to surrender independence on the 'say-so' of the ICC prosecutor whose mere identification of possible suspects could embarrass a State to adjust its own proper prosecution policy in order to avoid the State humiliation of having authority wrested away to the ICC for those chosen or identified as suspects by the Prosecutor."[620] Although this statement is about the 'same person' test, it can be asserted about the 'same conduct' test as well.

Complementarity does not seek the replacement of the Court to the national jurisdictions. It should not hurt the national prosecutorial independence and discretion. By contrast, under the complementarity principle, the Court aims at enhancing its counterparts in the national sphere. What is intended by complementarity is that a State genuinely deals with international crimes and their perpetrators. This aim does not require that all incidents, including all times, places, and victims are addressed by the national prosecution. As the Prosecutor of the Court who has discretion to make a selection among the incidents, the domestic prosecutors enjoy prosecutorial discretion. Even they, typically,

---

616 Carsten Stahn, 'Admissibility Challenges Before the ICC: From Quasi-Primacy to Qualified Deference', in Carsten Stahn (ed.), *The Law And Practice of the International Criminal Court*, Oxford University Press, 2015, p. 231.

617 ICC, PTC I, Decision on the Requête relative à la recevabilité de l'affaire en vertu des Articles 19 et 17 du Statut, 11 June 2013, para. 12.

618 ICC, Defense, Katanga case, 11 March 2009, para. 43, see *supra* note 549.

619 Stahn, 2015, p. 236, see *supra* note 616.

620 ICC, Kenya situation, Reply on Behalf of the Government of Kenya to the Responses of the Prosecutor, Defense and OPCV to the Government's Application Pursuant to Article 19 of the Rome Statute, 13 May 2011, para. 27.

are in a better position for such a selection as long as they exercise their authority in good faith. It is because the domestic prosecutors are more familiar with the local considerations that should be taken into account in delivering justice. National jurisdiction should be broadly encouraged to pursue the similar conduct, but in a broad sense.

3.2.2.1.3. Broad Interpretation of the Same Conduct Test

Contrary to the narrow approach to the conduct notion, a broader approach can be adopted. From this recent perspective, the conduct before the domestic proceedings should represent the criminality of the accused before the Court. Such criminality embraces the contextual element of the situation at hand, the subject matter or the ICC-identified crimes and the gravest underlying acts forming such crimes in addition with the gravest incidents that constitute the underlying acts. Article 7(2)(a) of the Rome Statute indicates that an attack directed against any civilian population is "a course of conduct involving the multiple commission of acts referred to in paragraph 1 [of Article 7 of the Statute] against any civilian population." The Chambers have defined the term 'course of conduct' as "a series or overall flow of events as opposed to a mere aggregate of random acts."[621] The 'course of conduct' implies multiple commissions of acts.[622] The conduct test also refers to the course of conduct. It embraces a number of incidents and events. It does not matter which operation or incident is presented before the domestic proceedings. It is sufficient if those operations represent the attack underlying the crimes against humanity.

The conduct is formed of incidents but it is not limited to specific incidents. One example clarifies this point of view. In the context of a widespread attack or a prolonged internal war within a definite time and place, the accused commits murder and rape against specific victims in street A, and later he or she repeats his or her conduct in street B. It implies that the victims of each case are different. In this case, the conduct is commission of war crimes or crimes against humanity of rape and killing in a specific temporal and territorial context. Here, it does not matter if the national proceedings are prosecuting event B while the Court is dealing with event A. The conduct before the Court is not incident A or incident B, but it is a general criminality that embraces both incidents. Hence, if the State concerned has dealt with one of these two incidents, the Court assesses the genuineness of the domestic activities. As the Appeals Chamber has stated, Article 17 of the Statute establishes a two-step test: "(i) whether, at the time of the proceedings in respect of an admissibility challenge, there is an ongoing investigation or prosecution of the case at the national level; and, in case the answer to the first question is in the affirmative, (ii) whether the State is unwilling or unable genuinely to carry out such investigation or prosecution."[623]

---

621 ICC, PTC I, Laurent Gbagbo case, Decision on the confirmation of charges against Laurent Gbagbo, 12 June 2014, para. 209.

622 Ibid.

623 ICC, Appeals Chamber, Katanga case, 25 September 2009, paras. 75–79, see *supra* note 495.

When the Prosecutor faces the difference in incidents or crimes, the Court must inquire about reasons behind the choices of the domestic courts. If the domestic jurisdiction is active about the same conduct, even by prosecuting the different incidents, the Prosecutor can still examine the genuineness of the proceedings by taking into account the gravity of the incidents at hand. Indeed, the difference between what has been selected by the Prosecutor and what has been chosen by the State should not be inconsistent with the intent to bring the suspect to justice. These features show that the complementarity rule assessment is highly sensitive to a case-by-case basis. As PTC I, in its decision on Gaddafi admissibility case, asserts, "the determination of what is substantially the same conduct as alleged in the proceedings before the Court will vary according to the concrete facts and circumstances of the case and, therefore, requires a case-by-case analysis."[624]

In a nutshell, the 'conduct' in the meaning of the 'same conduct' test consists of four components, namely: context, subject-matter (crime), underlying acts and incidents. The contextual element refers to the general context in which a situation is defined. The subject matter refers to the ICC-identified crimes of genocide, war crimes and crimes against humanity. Underlying acts refer to those acts that legally constitute the core crimes such as murder and rape for 'crimes against humanity'. The national proceedings should embrace the three first elements. However, they can be different in incident. As to subject matter and underlying acts, the legal characterization does not matter as long as they are same in substance, and embrace the generality inherent in these crimes. It should be borne in mind that in the preliminary examination when the concrete cases have not yet turned up, the flexibility of the assessment is greater. The Prosecutor should preserve her dialectic relationship with the States to understand the reasons behind a State's choice.

3.2.2.1.4. Sentence-Based Approach Doctrine

Both gravity and complementarity assessments are charge-oriented. The charge-oriented approach focuses on charges and the nature of crimes. It does not matter what a crime is called, but the nature should be the same. Simone Gbagbo was sentenced to 20 years in prison in her own country, because of disturbing the peace, forming and organizing armed gangs and undermining State security.[625] However, because they were not those crimes under the Court's jurisdiction, the case against her remained admissible before the Court. Nonetheless, Heller believes that trying Mrs Gbagbo after 20 years would not have benefit for the Court. Heller proposes a sentence-centered approach that puts its focus on sentences in the complementarity assessment. Indeed, Heller proposes an alternative to the charge-based definition of the conduct that

[624] ICC, PTC I, Gaddafi case, 31 May 2013, para. 77, see *supra* note 561.

[625] The Guardian, Ivory Coast Court Sentences Wife of Ex-president to 20 Years in Prison, 10 March 2015, available at: www.theguardian.com/world/2015/mar/10/ivory-coast-court-sentences-wife-of-ex-president-to-20-years-in-prison, last accessed 10 May 2017.

revolves around the gravity of crimes. When there is doubt that the national crimes under prosecution are as grave as those charges presented before the Court, the sentence-centered approach suggests that the amount of sentences should be taken into account. He agrees that most scholars accept that an inadequate sentence can justify the ICC pre-empting a national prosecution of an ordinary crime, but does not "suggest that the ex post imposition of a lengthy sentence can compensate for the *ex ante* decision to charge an ordinary crime that is not serious."[626]

Heller argues that the Court should take into account sentences when determining whether a national prosecution of an ordinary crime is admissible. "As long as a national prosecution results in a sentence no less severe than the defendant would receive at the ICC prosecution, the case should be inadmissible regardless of the gravity of the crime or the same conduct."[627] In the pre-conviction phase, where the quantity of a sentence is not known to be compared, Heller suggests that "the Court would compare the average sentence for the international crime charged by the ICC with the average sentences for the ordinary crime being investigated by the stat. as long as the national average was equal or greater, the case would be inadmissible."[628] This test is applicable in particular in the situational phase, where there are only potential cases without conviction. Heller provides an example: If a defendant charged with the crime against humanity of murder is convicted of assault and sentenced to 30 years prison, an assault conviction does not reflect the gravity of murder, but 30 years in prison is far longer than the defendant would like receive if he were convicted by the ICC of murder as a crime against humanity. In such a scenario, the case should be declared inadmissible before the Court.[629] He argues that if the ICC prosecution for the international crime would result in a sentence that is no more severe than the national prosecution for the ordinary crime, what justifies the Court's intervention? His response is straightforward; "Nothing."[630]

Heller accepts that there may be some gravity deficit in a national prosecution for an ordinary crime, because "the element of collective perpetration or collective victimization that distinguishes international crimes from ordinary ones will necessarily be lacking."[631] Nonetheless, he states that a gravity deficit can be acceptable. According to him, such unacceptability is obvious in some situations where, for instance, genocide is charged as assault, but what about murder and manslaughter, reckless murder or looting and theft?[632] He believes that in such scenarios, the severity of sentence makes up the gravity. Heller notes that the charge-based approach is highly

626 Kevin Jon Heller, 'A Sentence-Based Theory of Complementarity', in William A. Schabas, Yvonne McDermott and Niamh Hayes (eds.), *The Ashgate Research Companion to ICL: Critical Perspectives*, Ashgate, 2013, p. 337.
627 Ibid.
628 Ibid., p. 338.
629 Ibid., p. 340.
630 Ibid., p. 342.
631 Ibid.
632 Ibid., p. 343.

ICC-oriented, contrary to the sentence-based approach that "leads to a more State centric approach to the prosecution of ordinary crimes."[633] Indeed, the sentence-based approach by providing the states with more space and flexibility is more consistent with the principle of complementarity. This approach appears to have some merits.

Nevertheless, the applicability of this approach is questionable in the gravity and complementarity assessment at the ICC. At the ICC, the nature of crimes and the criminal themes matter. If the national jurisdiction prosecutes someone only because of the murder of one person and convicts him of the death penalty while other serious crimes like sexual violence or extermination or child soldiering have been put aside and the victims of those crimes have remained voiceless, such a prosecution does not meet the same case test and the Court can step in due to inactivity of the State in question. In contrast with Heller's point of view, it can be asserted that the Court will gain much with the second trial of the accused. Such a trial gives voice to those victims left voiceless by national proceedings. In international criminal justice trials are important. A more comprehensive trial to cover the enormity of the crimes is more important than a severe sentence that is given for a narrow portion of atrocities.

Heller elsewhere suggests eliminating the substantially same conduct requirement by amending the Rome Statute in order to give more consideration to States.[634] However, as such, the test needs not be eliminated. Adopting a broad interpretation as suggested by this paper could realize the goal that Heller's suggestion intends to realize, namely, giving opportunity to the domestic jurisdiction for action.

3.2.2.2. The Same Person Test

The other constituent limb of a case in the admissibility assessment is 'the same person'. The person who is sought by the Court should be the same as the person who has been or is being prosecuted by the national authorities. Otherwise a case is declared admissible before the Court. For instance, the then Prosecutor of the Court, in his application under Article 58 in the Darfur situation, asserted: "the Prosecution noted carefully all that had been carried out to that point. In particular, a Special Court for Darfur had been established in June 2005. The Prosecution was informed that between June and November 2005 the Special Court had completed six criminal trials. However, none of the trials in question related to either of the individuals mentioned in this application or were in respect of the incidents mentioned in the current application. The trials conducted at that point related to purported low level suspects who were not likely to figure in any case before the Court."[635]

At first glance, it seems that the 'same person' test is straightforward. However, this test in the context of the situational phase needs much attention. The test in the context

633 Ibid., p. 341.

634 See: Kevin Jon Heller, 'Radical Complementarity', *Journal of International Criminal Justice*, 2016, vol. 14.

635 ICC, OTP, Kushayb case, Prosecutor's Application under Article 58(7), 27 February 2007, para. 256.

of a situation has never been dealt with by the Court. On the contrary, in the context of the case phase, this issue was dealt with in one of the Court's PTCs. The reasoning of the Chamber may shed some light upon this issue in the situational phase as well. After issuing summons to appear against Mr Ruto, the Kenyan government made a challenged against this decision under Article 19. The government of Kenya argued that it is sufficient to investigate 'persons at the same level in the hierarchy' rather than the same persons. This challenge relied on the test established by the Chamber in the 31 March 2010 authorization decision for investigation into the situation in Kenya, which had referred to "the groups of persons that are likely to be the object of an investigation by the ICC", and concluded that it was not necessary to investigate the same specific persons.[636] The Chamber rejected this assertion. According to the Chamber, this interpretation was misleading.[637] The Chamber explained that the criteria established by the Chamber in its authorization decision pertained to the situational phase, not the case stage. According to the Chamber, "at that stage, the reference to the groups of persons is mainly to broaden the test, because at the preliminary stage of an investigation into the situation it is unlikely to have an identified suspect. The test is more specific when it comes to an admissibility determination at the 'case' stage."[638] Therefore, it can be asserted that in the case phase the same person requires the absolute 'sameness', i.e. identity. Upon the initiation of the investigation, the Prosecutor selects a suspect for prosecution. Only if a State conducts the proceedings against the same person, does the Court have to defer the case to the domestic jurisdiction. On the other hand, in the situational phase, it appears that the same person test is applied with flexibility. During this stage, one can assert that the applicable standard is 'the same person at the same level and hierarchy'.

In the situational phase, nothing is final. The Prosecutor identifies merely the potential cases. At this stage, it is sufficient that the Prosecutor determines that the national jurisdiction is dealing with the persons within those levels and hierarchies that the Prosecutor has already selected. For instance, if a brigade is responsible for the commission of an ICC-identified crime and the national jurisdiction is dealing with one of the commanders of the brigade, the Prosecutor cannot declare the case admissible unless they prove that the non-prosecution of that specific person is inconsistent with the intention to bring the accused to justice. Here, the Prosecutor should adopt an inquisitorial approach based on the dialogue with States concerned. Differences in cases selected by the Court and those selected by States could be justifiable. To determine the validity of such a difference, the State's considerations should be taken into account.

3.2.3. *Situation of a State's Inaction*

To declare a case admissible before the Court, Article 17 sets some requirements, including unwillingness and inability of States. If a State that has jurisdiction is

636 ICC, PTC II, Ruto case, 30 May 2011, para. 53, see *supra* note 253.
637 Ibid., para. 54.
638 Ibid.

unwilling or unable to prosecute the ICC-identified crimes, the Court may step in. However, there is another status for declaring a case admissible before the Court, namely, 'inactivity'. The Appeals Chamber in the Katanga case asserts that "according to the clear wording of Article 17(1)(a) and (b) of the Statute, the question of unwillingness or inability of a State having jurisdiction over the case becomes relevant only where, due to ongoing or past investigations or prosecutions in that State, the case appears to be inadmissible."[639] Article 17(1) shows that the point of departure in the complementarity assessment is not the question of willingness or ability of the State concerned, but it is the consideration of activity or inactivity of the State in question. The inaction test reduces the tasks of the Court under the complementarity rule. In the absence of any acting state, "the Chamber need not make any analysis of unwillingness and inability."[640] Here, a prong test has been established. Firstly, the OTP considers whether there is or has been any domestic investigation or prosecution in relation to the case at hand. Then, and only if the first requirement is met, the Office shall examine whether "such national proceedings are vitiated by an unwillingness or inability to genuinely carry out the proceedings."[641] A considerable part of the ICC case law has dealt with the inactivity issue, because the majority of cases have been declared admissible before the Court due to the simple absence of domestic proceedings.[642]

It is worth noting that the assessment of inactivity is not conducted in the abstract. There should be concrete objects for such an assessment. For this reason, the same person and the same conduct test have been established to ensure the specificity of the complementarity assessment. Under Article 17, in the complementarity assessment process, "the question is not merely a question of investigation in the abstract, but is whether the same case is being investigated by both the Court and a national jurisdiction."[643] It means that it does not simply suffice that the domestic courts are dealing with a case, but "it must be the same case (substantially the same conduct) that is being investigated domestically."[644]

One question about the complementarity assessment is whether the proceedings conducted by non-State actors make a case inadmissible before the Court. Article 17 revolves around the notion of States' proceedings. It does not refer to the proceedings conducted by other entities. There are two categories of non-State actors, namely, international or hybrid tribunals and non-State organizations and groups. As to international or hybrid tribunals, in spite of the silence in the Rome Statute, one can assert that their proceedings are a legal obstacle in the way of the Court's intervention. Du Plessis, on the contrary, maintains that the prosecution of a case before a regional court, such as the African Court, would not bar the ICC from prosecution on the basis

---

639 ICC, Appeals Chamber, Katanga case, 25 September 2009, para. 75, see *supra* note 495.
640 ICC, PTC I, Lubanga case, 10 February 2006, para. 40, see *supra* note 45.
641 ICC, OTP, Policy Paper on preliminary Examinations, para. 49.
642 Nouwen, 2013, p. 45, see *supra* note 226.
643 ICC, Appeals Chamber, Kenya situation, 30 August 2011, para. 36, see *supra* note 225.
644 ICC, PTC I, Gaddafi case, 31 May 2013, para. 83, see *supra* note 561.

that Article 17 specifically refers to 'states'.[645] Nonetheless, regional or international tribunals are States' collective responses to international crimes. States may choose to exercise their jurisdiction by the delegations of powers to a regional tribunal.[646] They did the same regarding the ICC. Indeed, the choice of a collective response is to exercise State sovereignty.[647] Therefore, as Akande suggests, it is not coherent if the rule permitting prosecution of crimes by individual states, simultaneously, prevents them from acting collectively.[648]

In addition, the Court has a complementary role in the international criminal justice system as a whole. It aims at ending impunity by cooperation of all actors. Therefore, a genuine prosecution by a regional tribunal should be seen as prosecution by a State such that the case is inadmissible before the ICC.[649] The Court lacks enough resources to invest in those situations where the Court's intervention is not necessary. So, there is no justification to activate the Court's jurisdiction over a situation or case that has already been dealt with by others. Given these considerations, some experts assert that "while Article 17 requires ICC deference to investigations and prosecutions carried out genuinely by a 'State', the OTP should as a policy matter be prepared to adopt a similar approach in respect of the ICTY, the ICTR, hybrid tribunals such as the Sierra Leone Special Court, courts and tribunals of UN administered territories, and other such courts."[650] Nowadays, a tendency among the international community towards the hybrid and regional courts is visible. The African Court of Justice and Human Rights is an example.

Proliferation of mixed courts should not be seen as a negative development, but "rather a necessity in the current situation of international relations, aimed at strengthening the incipient international system of criminal jurisdiction."[651] The term 'hybrid' or 'internationalized' may refer to the applicable law or to the nationality of judges ruling these tribunals.[652] A hybrid court has a large number of advantages in comparison with a mere international court or national tribunal. From a financial perspective, hybrid courts are desirable because they have proven themselves to be much cheaper.[653] Cassese, in his report on the efficiency of the SCSL as a mixed tribunal, states that this judicial body is "designed to avoid the pitfalls of two *ad hoc* international

---

645 Max Du Plessis, Implications of the AU Decision to Give the African Court Jurisdiction over International Crimes, Institute for Security Studies Paper, June 2012, p. 11.

646 Miles Jackson, 'Regional Complementarity', *Journal of International Criminal Justice*, 2016, vol. 14, p. 1069.

647 Dan Sarooshi, I*nternational Organizations and Their Exercise of Sovereign Powers*, Oxford University Press, 2005 p. 18.

648 Dapo Akande, 'The Jurisdiction of the International Criminal Court over Nationals of Non-Parties: Legal Basis and Limits', *Journal of International Criminal Justice, 2003*, vol. 1, p. 626.

649 Jackson, 2016, p. 1062, see *supra* note 646.

650 ICC, OTP, Informal Expert Paper, 2003, para. 9, see *supra* note 508.

651 Fausto Pocar, 'The Proliferation of International Criminal Courts and Tribunals: A Necessity in the Current International Community', *Journal of International Criminal Justice*, 2004, vol. 2, p. 308.

652 Sliedregt, 2014, p. 1145, see *supra* note 90.

653 Marieke Wierda and Anthony Triolo, 'Resources', in Luc Reydams and Jan Wouters and Cedric Ryngaret (eds.), *International Prosecutors*, Oxford, Oxford University Press, 2012, p. 135.

criminal tribunals and therefore to dispense justice expeditiously, in a cost- effective manner and with a direct impact on the population amongst which crimes had been perpetrated."[654] In addition, hybrid models may lead to pluralizing international criminal justice, and thereby to a horizontal expansion of the judicial narrative.[655] This is also the common destination of the complementarity principle. Therefore, when there is a hybrid court, there is no reason for the Court's intervention. However, at the ICC era, there could be a systematic relationship between hybrid courts and the ICC. It is asserted that the future of the international criminal justice system will be at the hands of hybrid courts.[656]

This prediction warns of marginalization of the Court. However, the ICC is still able to preserve its unique role in the international criminal justice system by assuming a monitoring and managing role. The Court can assume two functions here. Firstly, if the hybrid courts are able and willing to deal with all cases, the Court will monitor their actions. Secondly, in the case of inability or unwillingness, the Court can step in to prosecute the bigger fish based on a division of labor. Indeed, in this scenario, the States are replaced with the hybrid courts in their relationship with the Court and the complementarity rule. Opening a preliminary examination on situations of crisis enables the Court to adopt such roles, even in the case of hybrid courts. The presence of the ICC is also beneficial for hybrid and regional courts. For instance, the deferral of the ICC to regional tribunals might enhance their own legitimacy.[657]

The Special Criminal Court for the Central African Republic will be an experiment concerning the relationship between the Court and hybrid tribunals. Dealing with the protracted conflict in the CAR, on April 22, 2015, the Central African Republic's transitional parliament voted to adopt a law to create a Special Criminal Court to investigate and prosecute war crimes and crimes against humanity that have been committed in the CAR since 2003.[658] It is the first time that a hybrid tribunal has concurrent jurisdiction with the ICC. The law sets out a framework for the relationship between different jurisdictional levels. Article 37 states that the ICC has priority jurisdiction over the Special Criminal Court when the ICC Prosecutor "is seized of a case entering concurrently in the jurisdiction of the ICC and the Special Criminal

654 SCSL, Report on the SCSL Submitted by the Independent Expert Antonio Cassese, 12 December 2006, para. 293.

655 Drumbl, 2011, p. 226, see *supra* note 525.

656 For instance, Abulhak says "there is an assumption that in the years to come, the ICC, will become a solitary judicial island dealing with IHL cases at the international level… but the possibility that the era of hybrids is behind us should be of concern… because post-conflict societies, usually lack necessary resources to purse such projects" (Tarik Abdulhak, 'Complementarity of Procedures: How to Avoid Reinventing the Wheel', in Carsten Stahn and Mohamed M. El Zeidy (eds.), *The International Criminal Court and Complementarity: From Theory to Practice*, Cambridge University Press, 2011, p. 956).

657 Jackson, 2016, p. 1069, see *supra* note 646.

658 International Federation for Human Rights, New Special Criminal Court: A Key Step Toward Justice, 24 April 2015, available at: www.fidh.org/en/region/Africa/central-african-republic/new-special-criminal-court-a-key-step-toward-justice.

Court."[659] It was mentioned that the Prosecutor, to select their situations and cases, is in need of dialogue with the states concerned. Hybrid courts are a suitable form within which such a dialogue and cooperation occur. In the context of the CAR, the Court can make an agreement with the local government, based on the division of labor to select situations.

As to non-State organized groups, this is a different story. In each conflict, there is a chance that an armed group takes control over a territory and assumes judicial tasks. Common Article 3 of the Geneva Conventions that is addressed to each Party to the conflict, prohibits the passing of sentences without a regular and constituted court and without "affording all the judicial guarantees which are recognized as indispensable by civilized peoples". It implies that Common Article 3 recognizes that there is the possibility of armed groups carrying out criminal proceedings. The Taliban in Afghanistan or ISIS in Iraq and Syria are clear examples of this phenomenon. However, Kleffner argues that Article 17 rejects the applicability of the proceedings carried out by non-State groups. He argues that the term 'State' referred to in Article 17 excludes those investigations and prosecutions carried out by non-State actors.[660] In this scenario, if proceedings carried out by non-State entities comply with the statutory requirement, one can argue that ICC intervention would not serve the interests of justice.[661] Therefore, the proceedings carried out by non-State actors do not make a case or situation inadmissible before the Court.

3.2.3.1. Arguments Supporting Establishing the Inaction Test

There are some arguments in favor of the inaction test. The Appeals Chamber, in its judgment in the Katanga case, put forward a literal argument in favor of the inactivity test. Article 17(1)(a) refers to 'carrying out the investigation or prosecution'. According to the Appeals Chamber, using the definite article 'the' instead of the indefinite 'a' "emphasizes that the reference is made to an investigation or prosecution that is actually ongoing. Similarly, in Article 17(1)(b), unwillingness and inability refer to the decision of a State, after investigation, not to prosecute the person concerned."[662] Such an inference can be drawn from Paragraph 2 of Article 17 as well. The Paragraph refers to the phrases, 'the proceedings were or are being undertaken', 'an unjustified delay in the proceedings', and 'the proceedings were not or are not being conducted independently'. All these clauses imply the existence of proceedings in advance. Indeed, Article 17

---

659 Valérie Arnould, 'The Uncertain Promise of Hybrid Justice in the Central African Republic', Africa Policy Brief, September 2015, available at: www.egmontinstitute.be/wp-content/uploads/2015/09/APB14.pdf, last accessed at 9 May 2017.

660 Kleffner, 2008, p. 109, see *supra* note 41.

661 Jann K. Kleffner, 'The Law and Policy of Complementarity in Relation to Criminal Proceedings Carried Out by Non-State', in Carsten Stahn and Mohamed M. El Zeidy (eds.), *The International Criminal Court and Complementarity: From Theory to Practice*, Cambridge University Press, 2011, p. 719.

662 ICC, Appeals Chamber, Katanga case, 25 September 2009, para. 76, see *supra* note 495.

"contemplates that at least initiate steps are taken such as establishing an investigative unit securing the site and collecting evidence."[663]

Given the implication embodied in Article 17, the Appeals Chamber concludes that "the initial questions to ask are (1) whether there are ongoing investigations or prosecutions, or (2) whether there have been investigations in the past, and the State having jurisdiction has decided not to prosecute the person concerned."[664] Therefore, "it is only when the answers to these questions are in the affirmative that one has to look to the second halves of sub-paragraphs (a) and (b) and to examine the question of unwillingness and inability."[665] In the Appeals Chamber's words, taking a different starting point means to "put the cart before the horse."[666] In addition to the literal reading of Article 17, a logical reading of Article 17 proves the precedence of the proceedings over the inability or unwillingness test. Robinson argues that the unwillingness and inability tests are exceptions, because Article 17 says 'unless'. Therefore, "where its predicate condition is not satisfied, there would be no role the exception could play, because the test in the heading has failed with or without exception."[667] The Appeals Chamber in the Simone Gbagbo case reaffirms that "in case of inaction, the question of unwillingness or inability does not arise."[668]

Article 17 deals with the scenarios of unwillingness and inability, but there is no explicit reference to the notion of inaction. Therefore, the literal interpretation of Article 17 needs an extra argument to bring the inactivity test into effect. Given this necessity, the Appeals Chamber refers to the major purpose of the Court, namely, ending impunity. According to the Appeals Chamber, if the Court's intervention is limited to the scenarios of unwillingness and inability, "the Court would be unable to exercise its jurisdiction over a case as long as the State is theoretically willing and able to investigate and to prosecute the case, even though that State has no intention of doing so. Thus, a potentially large number of cases would not be prosecuted by domestic jurisdictions or by the International Criminal Court."[669] This is the case in particular because "the Court cannot force a State to act in relation to a particular case, and cannot assume that declaring a case inadmissible would result in an inactive State opening investigation."[670] Indeed, if inactivity does not authorize the Court to step in, a gap through which perpetrators could evade punishment will emerge, because states had abstained from doing anything.[671] This scenario leads to a safe haven for

663 Kleffner, 2008, p. 104, see *supra* note 41.
664 ICC, Appeals Chamber, Katanga case, 25 September 2009, para. 78, see *supra* note 495.
665 Ibid.
666 Ibid.
667 Robinson, 2011, p. 465, see *supra* note 496.
668 ICC, Appeals Chamber, Simone Gbagbo case, 27 May 2015, para. 30, see *supra* note 605.
669 ICC, Appeals Chamber, Katanga case, 25 September 2009, para. 79, see *supra* note 495.
670 Ben Batros, 'The Evolution of the ICC Jurisprudence on Admissibility', in Carsten Stahn and Mohamed M. El Zeidy (eds.), *The International Criminal Court and Complementarity: From Theory to Practice*, Cambridge University Press, 2011.
671 Kleffner, 2008, p. 105, see *supra* note 41.

international culprits, where they can continue the commission of crimes without fear of justice. However, the Court has been established to prevent atrocities go unpunished.

Inadmissibility of a case requires that "at least one State with jurisdiction over the case is investigating, prosecuting or trying that case, or has done so."[672] In the Katanga case, the Defense had argued that the DRC was able to prosecute the accused, and therefore, the case would be inadmissible. However, based on this test, the Appeals Chamber confirmed that the case was admissible, since the DRC had confirmed that there were no investigations into allegations against the Appellant. For that reason alone, the Appeals Chamber considered that Article 17(1)(a) does not present a bar to his prosecution before the Court.[673]

Robinson, who was among the drafters of Article 17 of the Rome Statute, rejects any confusion around Article 17, because he believes that "the text of Article 17 expressly provides not a one-step test but a two-steps test."[674] Robinson mentions that in drafting negotiations, the delegations required that a State must actually conduct an investigation or prosecution to forestall ICC admissibility. He refers to an early proposal made by Canada which would thereby have allowed a declaration of inadmissibility if there was simply a reasonable prospect of national investigation, but it was rejected.[675]

3.2.3.2. Proofs of Being Active

3.2.3.2.1. Features of Active National Proceedings

Inactivity results in admissibility, whereas activity when displaying willingness and ability to genuinely investigate leads to inadmissibility. However, being active requires some qualifications. The domestic proceedings are considered active when they are concrete. The PTC II, in its decision on the admissibility challenge made in the Kony case, asserts that "this assessment cannot be undertaken on the basis of hypothetical national proceedings that may or may not take place in the future: it must be based on the concrete facts as they exist at the time."[676] Mere promise and statements do not suffice, but evidence of concrete actions are required. For instance, when Libya had submitted that it intended to take the statements of two individuals to show that its domestic jurisdiction was active, the PTC requested more information from the Libyan government to determine if it was just intention or something more. According to the Chamber it should have known "(i) whether these testimonies have been taken; and, if so, (ii) on what date; (iii) whether they were taken by the national investigating team; and (iv) whether written statements have been prepared."[677]

---

672 ICC, PTC I, Lubanga case, 10 February 2006, para. 30, see *supra* note 45.

673 ICC, Appeals Chamber, Katanga case, 25 September 2009, para. 80, see *supra* note 495.

674 Robinson, 2011, p. 462, see *supra* note 496.

675 Ibid., p. 469.

676 ICC, PTC II, Kony case, 10 March 2009, paras. 49–52, see *supra* note 220.

677 ICC, PCT I, Gaddafi case, Decision Requesting Further Submissions on Issues Related to the Admissibility of the Case Against Saif Al-Islam Gaddafi, 7 December 2012, para. 15.

Another straightforward example is Kenya's challenge against the admissibility of those cases, which had been presented before the Court. The Kenyan Government argued that it was undertaking judicial reforms that would enable it to conduct national criminal proceedings for all crimes arising from the post-election violence.[678] Judge Ekaterina, in her chapter, asserts that "It was evident that Kenya's understanding of the test was that mere preparation to initiate an investigation or prosecution would be sufficient."[679] However, such a perception is not consistent with the statutory test to assess the complementarity requirement. Therefore, the Chamber held that judicial reform actions and promises of future investigative activities, instead of ongoing investigations, do not satisfy the admissibility challenge requirement.[680]

Apart from being concrete, the domestic proceedings should be progressive. The evidence introduced by the State concerned should prove that the domestic proceedings are taking place at the time of making a decision on the admissibility challenge.[681] It does not suffice to show that the domestic jurisdiction had been activated at a period of time in the past. The Appeals Chamber of the Court states that "the admissibility of a case must be determined on the basis of the facts as they exist at the time of the proceedings concerning the admissibility challenge."[682] The Chamber argues that "the admissibility of a case under Article 17(1)(a), (b) and (c) of the Statute depends primarily on the investigative and prosecutorial activities of States having jurisdiction. These activities may change over time. Thus, a case that was originally admissible may be rendered inadmissible by a change of circumstances in the concerned States and vice versa."[683] In the ICC PTC's words, the evidence presented in support for the Admissibility Challenge must demonstrate that the domestic authorities are taking 'progressive' investigative steps.[684] Kai Ambos refers to two kinds of inaction, namely a prior inaction and a posteriori inaction.[685] The former impedes the initiation of proceedings at the outset, but the latter terminates the proceedings after some initial investigate steps. Both of these inactions may make a situation or case admissible before the Court.

---

678 ICC, Ruto case, Application on Behalf of the Government of Kenya Challenging the Admissibility, 31 March 2011, paras 2,5,12,47–66 and 67–99.

679 Ekaterina Trendafilova, 'Africa and International Criminal Court: A Judge's Perspective', in Gerhard Werle, Moritz Vombaum (eds.), Africa *and the International Criminal Court*, 2013, TMC Asser Press, p. 23.

680 ICC, PTC II, Ruto case, 30 May 2011, paras. 64–70, see *supra* note 253.

681 ICC, PTC I, Simone Gbagbo case, 11 December 2014, para. 35, see *supra* note 554. And, ICC, Appeals Chamber, Katanga case, 25 September 2009, para. 80, see *supra* note 495.

682 ICC, Appeals Chamber, Kenyatta and Hussein Ali case, Decision on the 'Filing of Updated Investigation Report by the Government of Kenya in the Appeal against the Pre-Trial Chamber's Decision on Admissibility', 28 July 2011, para. 9.

683 Ibid., And, ICC, Appeals Chamber, Ruto and Arap Sang, Decision on the 'Filing of Updated Investigation Report by the Government of Kenya in the Appeal against the Pre-Trial Chamber's Decision on Admissibility', 28 July 2011, para. 10.

684 ICC, PTC I, Gaddafi case, 31 May 2013, para. 73, see *supra* note 561. And, ICC, PTC I, Al-Senussi case, 11 October 2013, para. 66, see *supra* note 544.

685 Ambos, 2011, p. 1086, see *supra* note 370.

A clear instance here is the situation in Georgia. In this situation, the Prosecutor opened the preliminary examination in August 2008. From then until 2015, according to the Prosecutor's report, the national investigations were ongoing and progressive in both Georgian and Russia. However, in March 2015, the Government of Georgia informed the OTP that the national proceedings in relation to the potential cases had been suspended. Based on this development, and "with no foreseeable resumption apparent, and no other investigations in relation to such conduct underway in other states, the Office assessed that the potential case identified in its Request would be admissible, due to State inaction."[686]

Here, "the mere preparedness to take such steps or the investigation of other suspects is not sufficient."[687] Such activities do not make a case inadmissible before the Court if they do not continue to the next step. The case of Simone Gbagbo in the Côte d'Ivoire situation is a good example here. In February 2012, the PTC III issued a warrant of arrest against Simone Gbagbo for her criminal responsibility for four counts of crimes against humanity, namely: murder; rape and other sexual violence; persecution; and other inhuman acts, allegedly committed in the context of post-electoral violence in the territory of Côte d'Ivoire in 2010 and 2011.[688] In March 2012, the Registrar of the Court notified Code d'Ivoire of the arrest warrant and requested the arrest and surrender of Ms Gbagbo to the Court.[689] On 30 September 2013, Côte d'Ivoire challenged the admissibility of the case against Simone Gbagbo by arguing that, in 2012, domestic proceedings had been instituted against the accused based on allegations similar to those made in the case before the Court.[690] In addition, Côte d'Ivoire expressed its willingness and ability to try Gbagbo for those crimes.[691] On 11 December 2014, PTC I rejected Côte d'Ivoire's challenge, and concluded that Côte d'Ivoire's domestic authorities were not "taking tangible, concrete and progressive investigative steps into Gbagbo's criminal responsibility."[692] PTC held that "for a State to discharge its burden of proof that there is currently no situation of inaction at the national level, it needs to substantiate that an investigation or prosecution is in progress at this moment."[693] The Judges in the PTC declared the Simone Gbagbo case admissible before the Court upon taking into account the domestic proceedings against the accused. In assessing the domestic proceedings to determine whether they cover the same conduct, PTC based its findings on the alleged conduct underlying the crimes and considered their legal characterization as an added indicator of the actual subject matter of the domestic proceedings.[694]

---

686 ICC, OTP, Report on Preliminary Examination Activities (2015), para. 255.
687 ICC, Appeals Chamber, Kenyatta and Hussein Ali case, 28 July 2011, para. 40, see *supra* note 682.
688 ICC, PTC, Simone Gbagbo case, Warrant of Arrest for Simone Gbagbo, 29 February 2012.
689 ICC, Appeals Chamber, Simone Gbagbo case, 27 May 2015, para. 5, see *supra* note 605.
690 Ibid., para. 7.
691 Ibid.
692 ICC, PTC I, Simone Gbagbo case, 11 December 2014, para. 36, see *supra* note 554.
693 Ibid., para. 35.
694 Ibid., para. 49.

PTC noted that three sets of proceedings, running in parallel, were open against Ms Gbagbo in Côte d'Ivoire.[695] The first set of proceedings had targeted Gbagbo for economic crimes. In this regard, the PTC states that "the conduct alleged against Gbagbo in these proceedings is clearly of a different nature to that giving rise to her criminal responsibility as alleged in the case before the Court."[696] The second set of proceedings instituted against Gbagbo concerned alleged crimes against the State.[697] The Chamber concluded that these proceedings "do not cover the same conduct that is alleged in the case before the Court."[698] The third set of proceedings concerned crimes against individuals.[699] Regarding this category, the PTC concluded that "these are crimes of the same nature as those alleged in the case before the Court."[700] Nonetheless, the Judges found that the documentation available did not "demonstrate that concrete, tangible and progressive investigative steps are being undertaken."[701] Therefore, the case was declared admissible before the Court. In December 2014, Côte d'Ivoire appealed the PTC's decision. Côte d'Ivoire alleged that, *inter alia*, the PTC had erred in applying rigorous criteria for the determination of the existence of an investigation or prosecution in Côte d'Ivoire.[702]

On 27 May 2015, the Appeals Chamber delivered its judgment, and confirmed the PTC's decision.[703] The Appeals Chamber argued that "the presumption in favor of domestic jurisdictions only applies where it has been shown that there are (or have been) investigations and/or prosecutions at the national level."[704] In addition, the Appeals Chamber recalled that "the question is not merely a question of investigation in the abstract, but is whether the same case is being investigated by both the Court and a national jurisdiction."[705] Taking into account the domestic proceedings against Ms Gbagbo in Côte d'Ivoire, the Appeals Chamber stated that it was reasonable for the PTC to find the economic crimes to be of a different nature.[706] As regards crimes against the State, the Judges in the Appeals Chamber confirmed the finding of the PTC that this conduct was not "the same as that alleged before the Court."[707] As to the crimes against individuals, the Ivorian government tried to demonstrate that its domestic system was active. To demonstrate that the domestic proceedings were ongoing regarding the case at hand, the Ivorian government provided the Court with, *inter alia*, a piece of evidence showing that the civil party had applied to participate

695 Ibid., para. 46.
696 Ibid., para. 47.
697 Ibid., para. 48.
698 Ibid., para. 49.
699 Ibid., para. 50.
700 Ibid.
701 Ibid., para. 78.
702 See: ICC, Appeals Chamber, Simone Gbagbo case, 27 May 2015, para. 48, see *supra* note 605.
703 Ibid., para. 141.
704 Ibid., para. 2.
705 Ibid., para. 31.
706 Ibid., para. 99.
707 Ibid., para. 100.

in the proceedings against Gbagbo. However, the Court dismissed the applicability of such evidence. According to the PTC, "it appears that the investigative activities undertaken by the domestic authorities are not tangible, concrete and progressive, but, on the contrary, sparse and disparate."[708] Later, the Appeals Chamber added that "Côte d'Ivoire does not explain how such desire relates to the question of whether domestic authorities are investigating the same case as that before the Court."[709] The Judges in the Appeals Chamber clarified that the expression 'the case is being investigated', appearing in Article 17, must be understood as "requiring the taking of steps directed at ascertaining whether the person is responsible for the alleged conduct."[710] Indeed, the important issue is the State's activities rather than the initiatives of other parties to a case. The latter does not necessarily result in the former. The Ivorian authorities claimed that "this information is significant in light of Côte d'Ivoire's procedural rules allowing victims to report an offence to the judicial authorities."[711] However, as mentioned, domestic proceedings should be concrete and progressive. What matters is that the potential capacity of the domestic legal system leads to concrete activities. In the words of the Court, the government needs tangible proof "to demonstrate that it is actually investigating."[712] In light of the foregoing, the Appeals Chamber found that "it was not unreasonable for the PTC to conclude that the investigative steps, in view of their number rand frequency, were spare and disparate."[713]

At the time of the admissibility challenge, Gbagbo was in custody in Côte d'Ivoire. However, merely being in custody is not a sufficient indication of being active. From this point of view, Rastan advocates the Court's decision to declare the Lubanga case admissible while the accused had already been in custody in the DRC. Rastan asserts that, contrary to the widespread perception about the Lubanga case, "the suggestion that the DRC justice system appeared capable does not mirror the reality portrayed in numerous reports."[714] Therefore, Rastan sees the Lubanga case as an instance of inactivity that justified the Court's intervention. Ultimately, Rastan sets a guiding rule by saying that the mere fact that a person is in custody in the custodial State does not demonstrate that an actual investigation has been undertaken; but "the Court will need to examine whether any specific investigative acts have been conducted or are planned."[715]

3.2.3.2.2. Relevant Evidence to Prove Domestic Activity

If a State claims that it is dealing with the same case that has been selected by the Court, it needs to provide the Court with 'evidence' proving that its domestic proceedings

708 ICC, PTC I, Simone Gbagbo case, 11 December 2014, para. 65, see *supra* note 554.
709 ICC, Appeals Chamber, Simone Gbagbo case, 27 May 2015, para. 118, see *supra* note 605.
710 Ibid., para. 28.
711 Ibid., para. 115.
712 ICC, Appeals Chamber, Kenya situation, 30 August 2011, para. 80, see *supra* note 225.
713 ICC, Appeals Chamber, Simone Gbagbo case, 27 May 2015, para. 131, see *supra* note 605.
714 Rastan, 2011, footnote 76, see *supra* note 17.
715 Ibid., p. 448.

are ongoing. This rule is widely accepted by the Court's Chambers that "a State that challenges the admissibility of a case bears the burden of proof to show that the case is inadmissible."[716] In the words of the Appeals Chamber, "the principle of complementarity expresses a preference for national investigations and prosecutions but does not relieve a State, in general, from substantiating all requirements set forth by the law when seeking to successfully challenge the admissibility of a case."[717] This is because the evidentiary principle is that whomever makes a claim should prove their claim.

In this context, evidence means "all material capable of proving that an investigation is ongoing and that appropriate measures are being envisaged to carry out the proceedings."[718] The Statute does not set out a standard of proof for the purpose of determining the admissibility of a case. However, the Court itself has set some guidelines. In the admissibility assessment, the Court is not called to determine whether such evidence is enough to establish the criminal responsibility of the accused but, instead, whether the State is taking steps to investigate.[719] It means that the evidentiary threshold of the admissibility assessment is lower than the threshold of the judgment of criminality. Kleffner states that the evidentiary threshold, in this context, is akin to the *prima facie* test.[720] *Prima facie* evidence is "sufficient to establish a fact in the absence of any evidence to the contrary but is not conclusive."[721] Such evidence should have "a sufficient degree of specificity and probative value that demonstrates that it is indeed investigating the case. It is not sufficient merely to assert that investigations are ongoing."[722] Here, the provided evidence should be sufficiently clear. If a State is unable to present evidence of specific and probative qualification, "it would be unreasonable to suggest that the Court should accept that an investigation, capable of rendering a case inadmissible before the Court, is underway."[723]

Lack of clarity in the evidence provided by the Ivorian authorities, in challenging admissibility of Ms Gbagbo's case, resulted in declaring the case admissible before the Court. In that case, the PTC found that "the information available to [it] on the scope of the national proceedings against [Ms] Gbagbo is also unclear with respect to the crimes that are allegedly being pursued."[724] According to the Chamber, the challenging State "must be able to show the contours or parameters of that investigation in order to determine the subject-matter of the national investigation."[725] However, from the

---

716 ICC, Appeals Chamber, Kenya situation, 30 August 2011, para. 62, see *supra* note 225. And, ICC, PTC I, Gaddafi case, 7 December 2012, para. 9, see *supra* note 677. And, Pre-Trial Chamber I, Transcript of Hearing, 10 October 2012, p. 64 line 18 and p. 65, line 1.

717 ICC, Appeals Chamber, Al-Senussi case, 24 July 2014, para. 159, see *supra* note 107.

718 ICC, PTC I, Gaddafi case, 7 December 2012, para. 10, see *supra* note 677.

719 ICC, PTC I, Gaddafi case, 31 May 2013, para. 122, see *supra* note 561.

720 Kleffner, 2008, p. 209, see *supra* note 41.

721 Ibid., footnote 257.

722 ICC, Appeals Chamber, Kenya situation, 30 August 2011, para. 61, see *supra* note 225.

723 ICC, Appeals Chamber, Gaddafi case, 21 May 2014, para. 84, see *supra* note 558.

724 ICC, PTC I, Simone Gbagbo case, 11 December 2014, para. 75, see *supra* note 554.

725 Ibid., para. 76.

other side, the Court should avoid adopting a rigid and tough approach to establish the evaluative framework within which the complementarity rule is examined. Judge Ušacka states that "the drafters of the Statute agreed to establish a high threshold when they drafted the legal and factual requirements for unwillingness and inability in paragraphs 2 and 3 of Article 17. The Court should not circumvent this threshold created by unwillingness or inability by requiring a State to prove e.g. the existence of a full-fledged investigation or prosecution of a case in order to establish that there is no situation of inactivity. It is important to adhere to the spirit of the Statute when giving such interpretations."[726] Indeed, there should be equality between the Prosecutor and the States as to the evidentiary threshold in the context of an inactivity statement. To prove the inactivity status, the Prosecutor must show that, *prima facie*, the domestic jurisdictions are dormant. To prove the opposite, the States should show that their jurisdiction is activated on a *prima facie* base as well.

The evidence of such features cannot be defined in an exclusive matter. Each case requires its relevant evidence. The PTC in the Gaddafi case referred to some evidence as examples. According to the Chamber, "depending on the circumstances, directions, orders and decisions issued by authorities in charge of the investigation as well as internal reports, updates, notifications or submissions contained in the file arising from the Libyan investigation of the case" are pieces of valuable evidence, "to the extent that they demonstrate that Libyan authorities are taking concrete and progressive steps to ascertain whether Mr Gaddafi is responsible."[727] The Appeals Chamber in the situation of Kenya mentions some alternative instances. According to the Appeals Chamber, "interviewing witnesses or suspects, collecting documentary evidence, or carrying out forensic analyses" are sufficient evidence proving that a case is being investigated in the meaning of Article 17.[728] In the admissibility challenge decision as to the Al-Senussi case, the PTC added some other guidelines. The Chamber observes that "the appropriateness of the investigative measures, the amount and type of resources allocated to the investigation, as well as the scope of the investigative powers of the persons in charge of the investigation" are significant to the question of whether or not there is a situation of 'inactivity' at the national level.[729]

3.2.3.3. Admissibility of Self-Referrals in light of the Inaction Test

Self-referrals pose the question of admissibility. To exercise the Court's jurisdiction over a situation, such a situation should be admissible. A situation is admissible if the Prosecutor finds that the States are not able or not willing to deal with it. A self-referral may be understood as a waiver of the complementarity rule in favor of the Court. It means that the referring State voluntarily relinquishes its right to exercise

---

726 ICC, Appeals Chamber, Ruto case, Dissenting Opinion of Judge Anita Ušacka, 20 September 2011, para. 27.

727 ICC, PTC I, Gaddafi case, 7 December 2012, para. 11, see *supra* note 677.

728 ICC, Appeals Chamber, Kenya situation, 30 August 2011, para. 40, see *supra* note 225.

729 ICC, PTC I, Al-Senussi case, 11 October 2013, para. 210, see *supra* note 544.

jurisdiction.[730] However, the complementarity assessment has a bearing upon the Court. It is an obligation upon the Prosecutor to assure that the Court intervenes complementarily. A self-referral does not waive the Court's obligation to assess the complementarity. The complementarity principle is not merely based on considerations of State sovereignty, but also on considerations of appropriateness and pragmatism.[731] Article 17 of the Rome Statute declares a situation admissible due to inability or unwillingness of States. Initially, a self-referral was seen by the Court as an instance of unwillingness or inability. PTC I, in its decision on the arrest warrant application against Lubango, asserted that the referral letter sent by the president of the DRC was proof that the DRC was indeed unable to investigate the crimes.[732] Later, the Trial Chamber of the Court in the Katanga case considered a self-referral as a kind of unwillingness. The Chamber maintained that a form of unwillingness under Article 17 is "the case of a State, which may not want to protect an individual, but, for a variety of reasons, may not wish to exercise its jurisdiction over him or her."[733] The Chamber stated this second form of unwillingness "aims to see the person brought to justice, but not before national courts."[734] Later, this interpretation was replaced by the idea that inaction is an independent factor in assessing the complementarity requirement. When a State is inactive at the domestic level, there is no need to find out whether it has been because of its unwillingness or its inability.

Some argue that self-referrals are in contradiction with the states' obligation to investigate and prosecute international crimes. The preamble of the Statute recognizes that "it is the duty of every State to exercise its criminal jurisdiction over those responsible for international crimes." The complementarity principle rests on the premises of the primary responsibility of States in prosecuting the core crimes. The complementarity rule has been seen as a catalyst for states to encourage them to investigate the ICC-identified crimes.[735] Indeed, the Court intends to encourage and persuade the States to take action. From this perspective, welcoming self-referrals appears questionable. Nouwen asserts that the ICC has diminished the notion of responsibility to investigate and prosecute domestically by adopting a policy to invite states to refer situations.[736] She labels this contradiction as a 'catalyzing effect paradox'. She asserts that this paradox happens because the ICC is most keen to exercise its jurisdiction in those cases where complementarity has the greatest chances of catalyzing genuine domestic proceedings, especially in the case of self-referrals.[737] Although this argument has merit, it is not compelling.

---

730 Kleffner, 2008, p. 214, see *supra* note 41.

731 Stigen, 2008, p. 248, see *supra* note 96.

732 ICC, PTC I, Lubanga case, 10 February 2006, para. 35, see *supra* note 45.

733 ICC, Trial Chamber II in Katanga considered inaction as a form of unwillingness. See: ICC, Trial Chamber II, Reasons for the Oral Decision on the Motion Challenging the Admissibility of the Case (Article 19 of the Statute), 16 June 2009, para. 77.

734 Ibid.

735 Kleffner, 2008, p. 216, see *supra* note 41.

736 Nouwen, 2013, p. 407, see *supra* note 226.

737 Ibid., p. 408.

Regarding the States' duty to prosecute, the Court provides a different understanding of the States' obligation to prosecute. The Court's Appeals Chamber acknowledges that States have a duty to exercise their criminal jurisdiction over international crimes, but stresses that "the sovereign decision of a State to relinquish its jurisdiction in favor of the Court may well be seen as complying with the 'duty to exercise [its] criminal jurisdiction', as envisaged in the sixth paragraph of the preamble."[738] Indeed, one can say that the classical rule of 'prosecute or extradite' has been given a new meaning at the ICC era. The scope of this rule has been developed to 'prosecute or extradite or surrender'. Consistent with such a viewpoint, the Appeals Chamber in the Katanga case added that the surrendering of a suspect that has already been in the custody of the referring State should not be considered as a decision not to prosecute, but it is a decision to bring the suspect to prosecution at the international level.[739]

In those situations, where the referring State is able to conduct proceedings but prefers to have justice delivered through the ICC, the Court should activate its functioning through positive complementarity activities. Indeed, a mere referral is not *carte blanche* for the Court. If the positive complementarity fails to activate the national jurisdiction, then the Court can declare a situation admissible due to unwillingness of the referring state. Nonetheless, in many situations self-referral is a result of inability of the referring state. Van der Wilt has examined most self-referrals in the history of the Court up to and including 2015, namely those situations referred by Uganda, the DRC, the CAR and Mali. He admits that "they all share an air of helplessness."[740] He insists that these claims should not come to us as a surprise, because they reflect reality.[741] In addition, even if a State is able to take action, but it prefers the Court's intervention to benefit from the Court's presence, it means that it is not willing to prosecute and investigate. In other words, inactivity ultimately refers to inability or unwillingness as predicated by the Rome Statute.

Rejecting self-referrals results in impunity. The Appeals Chamber in the case of Katanga's admissibility challenge rejects the idea that the general prohibition of a relinquishment of jurisdiction in favor of the Court may foster compliance by States with the duty to exercise criminal jurisdiction. The Chamber argued that "under the Rome Statute, the Court does not have the power to order States to open investigations or prosecutions domestically. It is purely speculative to assume that a State that has refrained from opening an investigation into a particular case or from prosecuting a suspect would do so, just because the International Criminal Court has ruled that the case is inadmissible."[742] As the Chamber clarifies, there is no guarantee that a State fulfills its responsibility to prosecute the ICC-identified crimes in the absence

738 ICC, Appeals Chamber, Katanga case, 25 September 2009, para. 85, see *supra* note 495.

739 Ibid., para. 82.

740 Harmen van der Wilt, 'Self-Referrals As an Indication of the Inability of States to Cope with Non-State Actors', in Carsten Stahn (eds.), *The Law and Practice of the International Criminal Court*, Oxford University Press, 2014, p. 212.

741 Ibid., p. 213.

742 ICC, Appeals Chamber, Katanga case, 25 September 2009, para. 86, see *supra* note 495.

of the Court's intervention. On the contrary, as El Zeidy says, if the ICC rejected self-referrals, there is a great possibility that the situation would not be dealt with and it leads to denial of justice.[743] Therefore, the Court's intervention does not put obstacles in the way of States to take the initiative, because there is no prospect for their intervention.

3.3. BURDEN OF PROOF IN THE COMPLEMENTARITY ASSESSMENT

The burden of proof in the complementarity assessment has not been dealt with in the Rome Statute and other legal texts of the Court. This issue, like many other matters, has been left for judicial interpretation.[744] Some scholars insist that all cases and situations are admissible before the ICC, unless there is a bar to admissibility in the form of the proceedings stipulated in Article 17.[745] Robinson argues that Article 17 enumerates the conditions of inadmissibility, therefore, "it is inadmissibility, not admissibility, which must be proven under the design of the Statute."[746] Schabas adopts this approach to Article 17, and asserts that "there is a presumption of admissibility unless one of the conditions set out in Article 17 is present."[747] Indeed, these scholars, by reading Article 17 in a literal sense, state that the admissibility is the principle and inadmissibility is the exception. If this is the case, it means that States should prove that a situation or a case is inadmissible before the Court.

To declare a case inadmissible before the Court, two requirements should be met. First, there should be concrete proceedings in progress at the domestic level. Secondly, those proceedings should be genuine. Each limb of the complementarity rule, namely activity and genuineness, needs proof. When there is a presumption in favor of admissibility of a case or situation, it means that if a State disagrees, it needs to challenge the admissibility of the given situation or case under Article 18 or Article 19 of the Rome Statute. In the Kenya situation, the Appeal Chamber rejected Kenya's argument that there should be leeway in the exercise of discretion in the application of the principle of complementarity. The Chamber argued that unless there is a jurisdiction conflict between a State and the Court, the case is admissible. According to the Appeals Chamber, "although Article 17(1)(a) to (c) of the Statute does indeed favor national jurisdictions, it does so only to the extent that there actually are, or have been, investigations and/or prosecutions at the national level."[748]

---

743 El Zeidy, 2008, p. 222, see *supra* note 522.

744 ICC, OTP, Informal Expert Paper, 2003, para. 53, see *supra* note 508.

745 Stahn, 2008, p. 105, see *supra* note 486.

746 Robinson, 2011, p. 464, see *supra* note 496.

747 Schabas, 2010, p. 193, see *supra* note 20.

748 ICC, Appeals Chamber, Kenya situation, 30 August 2011, para. 43, see *supra* note 225. And, ICC, Appeals Chamber, Ruto case, Dissenting Opinion of Judge Anita Ušacka, 20 September 2011, para. 44. And, ICC, Appeals Chamber, Simone Gbagbo case, 27 May 2015, para. 58, see *supra* note 605.

However, it does not mean that the Prosecutor is free from proving their allegations. In the Al-Senussi case, the Defense had raised allegations against the ability of the Libyan government, but those claims were uncertain. Therefore, the Chamber dismissed the Libyan government from disproving those allegations, while the burden of proof was on the government's shoulders. The Chamber argued that "the burden of proof that lies with Libya cannot be interpreted as an obligation to disprove any possible 'doubts' raised by the opposing participants in the admissibility proceedings."[749] The PTC, in its decision, insisted that "although Libya carries the burden of proof, any factual allegation raised by any party or participant must be sufficiently substantiated in order to be considered properly raised."[750] In this regard, the Prosecutor states that the PTC's decision "reflects the correct approach whereby the party advancing an argument needs to substantiate his or her submissions with supporting evidence."[751] This rule is applied to the Prosecutor too.

The Prosecutor has to substantiate their claim of inability of the State concerned. Article 17 obliges the Court to determine a case inadmissible where the domestic proceedings are in progress unless they lack genuineness. The Prosecutor's obligation under Article 17 has a necessary implication. To discharge their task to declare a case inadmissible, if the conditions are met, the Prosecutor shall explore and examine the situation in question to determine whether the statutory conditions of inadmissibility exist. Indeed, one can ask how the Prosecutor is able to be satisfied that a case does not need to be declared inadmissible without examination and searching. There is a philosophical difficulty in proving a negative and non-existence. To prove inactivity, the Prosecutor should demonstrate that they have already sufficiently explored possibilities of domestic action. The Prosecutor's task may be satisfied by demonstrating the reasonable steps taken to determine whether any national investigation or prosecution was undertaken. For instance, prior to the Article 18 process, "the OTP might refer to its contacts with relevant governments and other efforts to identify whether national proceedings were underway. After the Article 18 process, where the OTP has notified all States Parties and all States that would normally exercise jurisdiction over the crimes concerned, and has not received any notification from States, this fact alone should be sufficient to establish *prima facie* the absence of national proceedings."[752]

The second limb of the complementarity rule is the genuineness of the national proceedings. When it is proved that the domestic proceedings are ongoing, or have already been in place, the burden of proof is on the Prosecutor to substantiate those proceedings that are not genuine. Here, there is a presumption in favor of genuineness of the national proceedings. The ICC Informal Expert Paper, by referring to the situation in which the national proceedings are in progress, asserts that "in such circumstances, the case will be inadmissible, unless the exceptions in those provisions are established."[753]

749 ICC, PTC I, Al-Senussi case, 11 October 2013, para. 239, see *supra* note 544.
750 Ibid., para. 208.
751 ICC, Appeals Chamber, Al-Senussi case, 24 July 2014, para. 160, see *supra* note 107.
752 ICC, OTP, Informal Expert Paper, 2003, para. 57, see *supra* note 508.
753 Ibid., para. 19.

The experts provide more arguments. First, "the term 'unless' suggests a distinct issue, one that logically must fall on the party arguing for admissibility." Secondly, they assert that "this conclusion is further bolstered by a policy of giving the benefit of the doubt to States exercising jurisdiction and assuming that they are acting in good faith. In addition, it is an evidentiary principle that a party alleging bad faith generally carries the burden."[754] Many Chambers have confirmed this presumption. For instance, the PTC I, in the Gaddafi case, asserts that "a case is presumed to be inadmissible if it is being investigated or prosecuted by a State which has jurisdiction over it, 'unless' such judicial activity is not genuine."[755] The Chamber puts the burden of proof on the Prosecutor. It invokes the principle of '*onus probandi actori incumbit*', accordingly, "the burden of proof rests with the party making an allegation, namely, it is for the party alleging that State judicial action is not 'genuine' to provide supporting evidence."[756] However, if the Prosecutor manages to substantiate that the domestic proceedings are not genuine and a State challenges this finding, it is the task of the challenging entity to prove that it is genuinely dealing with the case at hand. According to PTC in the Gaddafi case, "the inadmissibility of the case is premised on both limbs of Article 17(l) (a) of the Statute and the challenging State is required to substantiate all aspects of its allegations to the extent required by the concrete circumstances of the case."[757] Later, the Appeals Chamber repeated this conviction by saying that "in respect of Article 17(1) (a) of the Statute that what a State challenging admissibility needs to prove is that it is conducting a genuine investigation or prosecution – which requires proof of both limbs of the provision."[758]

3.4. GENUINENESS REQUIREMENT FOR THE DOMESTIC PROCEEDINGS

Article 17(1) reads that a case is inadmissible if it is being investigated or has been investigated by a State, unless the State is or was unwilling or unable 'genuinely' to carry out an investigation or prosecution. The adverb 'genuinely' may refer to unwillingness or inability, thereby describing the quality of the unwillingness or inability. In this interpretation, the concentration is put on the proof of inability and unwillingness. This approach makes the Prosecutor's assessment tougher. The burden of proof in declaring a State unwilling or unable is upon the Prosecutor. However, it is possible that the adverb 'genuinely' refers to investigation or prosecution. In this scenario, the term 'genuinely' relates to the phrase 'to carry out the investigation or prosecution'.[759]

754 Ibid., para. 54.

755 ICC, Gaddafi case, Application on Behalf of the Government of Libya Pursuant to Article 19 of the ICC Statute, 1 May 2012, para. 92.

756 Ibid.

757 ICC, PTC I, Gaddafi case, 31 May 2013, para. 52, see *supra* note 561.

758 ICC, Appeals Chamber, Al-Senussi case, 24 July 2014, para. 166, see *supra* note 107.

759 Kleffner, 2008, p. 115, see *supra* note 41.

This interpretation sounds stronger. The drafters of the Rome Statute intended to mean the quality of the domestic proceedings. The domestic criminal proceedings should be genuine to keep a situation or case inadmissible before the Court. The proceedings are genuine if they aim to deliver justice and bring the culprits to justice, as enshrined in Paragraph 2 of Article 17. The proceedings in this context include all stages, including the sentencing phase. Therefore, the assessment of genuineness of the proceedings includes the matter of sentencing.[760] However, the genuineness assessment should be based "on procedural and institutional factors, not the substantive outcome."[761] It means that what is important is genuineness of the proceedings and process, even if the national proceedings result in the acquittal of the accused.

The complementarity rule seeks genuine proceedings either with punishment or without it at the end. However, an acquittal should be genuine to make a case inadmissible. The Simone Gbagbo case is an example here. Despite the fact that she was wanted by the ICC, the Côte d'Ivoire tried the accused on its own. At the end, a local court acquitted the former first lady Simone Gbagbo of crimes against humanity and war crimes charges linked to her role in the 2011 civil war.[762] Such an acquittal should be assessed by the Prosecutor to see if it is genuine. It should be noted that the Prosecutor's monitoring over the national proceedings should continue until the end of the proceedings and it includes pronouncing sentences if applicable. It is imaginable that a State conducts the proceedings in an acceptable way, and it convicts the accused at the end, but after the conviction, it intentionally fails to carry out the sentence or grants the convicted person with a pardon to preserve the legal appearance of its sham proceedings. Ambos asserts that a pardon as a post-conviction measure can hardly constitute a ground for admissibility, since "it will be difficult to demonstrate that it was taken to shield the person concerned from criminal responsibility."[763] However, even if this fact is difficult to prove it is still imaginable.

The complementarity rule is a two-pronged test. The first limb is quantitative. It requires that the domestic proceedings be ongoing and make progress. The second component is qualitative. It requires that the ongoing domestic proceedings meet a degree of quality that is described by Article 17 as genuineness. In other words, the genuineness in Article 17 is a qualifier. It is a qualifier because it restricts "the class of national proceedings that require deference from the ICC. Without such a qualifier, any national proceeding would preclude ICC action, even if the national proceeding were fraudulent or hopelessly inadequate."[764] Therefore, the mere existence of proceedings in the national sphere is not enough. Maybe, the State is willing to investigate and

[760] ICC, OTP, Statement by Mr. Stewart Deputy Prosecutor of the International Criminal Court, Transitional Justice in Colombia and the Role of the ICC, 13 May 2015, p. 9.

[761] ICC, OTP, Informal Expert Paper, 2003, para. 46, see *supra* note 508.

[762] The Guardian, Ivory Coast's Former First Lady Simone Gbagbo Acquitted of War Crimes, 28 March 2017, available at: www.theguardian.com/world/2017/mar/28/ivory-coast-simone-gbagbo-acquitted-war-crimes-humanity, last accessed at 9 May 2017.

[763] Ambos, 2011, p. 1087, see *supra* note 370.

[764] ICC, OTP, Informal Expert Paper, 2003, para. 21, see *supra* note 508.

prosecute but in a non-genuine way. In Cryer's words, this notion that warrants the Court's assessment "reduces the opportunity for cheating (non-prosecution, or sham/shielding trials, or delays or proceedings inconsistent with an intention to bring the person to justice), and provides a monitoring mechanism by which such cheating may be discovered."[765] The concern about the quality of the domestic proceedings was reflected in Rule 9 of the Rules of Procedure and Evidence of the ICTY, which explicitly permits the Tribunal to assert its primacy "where it appears to the Prosecutor that in any such investigations or criminal proceedings instituted at the ICCs of any State... there is a lack of impartiality or independence, or the investigations or proceedings are designed to shield the accused from international criminal responsibility." Given this status, the impunity notion enshrined in the Rome Statute should be read in light of genuineness. Impunity is ended only when genuine proceedings are in progress. It is so because only genuine proceedings can bring culprits to justice.[766]

The genuineness test empowers the Court to monitor national affairs. For this reason and to keep a balance between monitoring power of the Court and the security and sovereignty of States, the drafters selected genuineness as the least objectionable term. It was so because genuineness is considered sufficiently objective. Genuineness is close to 'in good faith' or 'not in a false manner' (with respect to willingness) and effectively (with respect to inability).[767] However, those two similar objectives were rejected because they were considered too subjective or ambiguous.[768] Instead, the word 'genuinely' was inserted in article 35 (preparatory committee 1996–8) as it was regarded as reflecting a more objective connotation.[769] Genuineness in prosecution and investigation of the ICC-identified crimes refers to willingness and ability of a national legal system to bring the perpetrators of the core crimes to justice. Realizing this goal requires some prerequisites and conditions. Proceedings are considered genuine if these prerequisites are in place. For instance, an available law that make prosecution of the ICC-identified crimes possible is a prerequisite in fighting impunity. If a State lacks such a legal necessity, it shows that its proceedings are not genuine. In other words, they are not aimed at bringing the culprits to justice.

It is worth saying that the Court's scrutiny of the quality of the domestic proceedings have been an impressive achievement and welcome development in the history of the international criminal justice system. As Cryer asserts, "with the creation of the system of oversight and inter-relationship of international and national jurisdictions, we can speak of a regime of international criminal law enforcement, one which not only provides a set of norms and expected behaviors but also sets up a system designed to identify and rectify instances of cheating."[770] In addition, Rastan, by referring to the Court's strong supervisory powers over national proceedings and creation of

765 Cryer, 2005, p. 165, see *supra* note 96.
766 Stigen, 2008, p. 215, see *supra* note 96.
767 Nouwen, 2013, p. 62, see *supra* note 226.
768 El Zeidy, 2011, p. 130, see *supra* note 19. And, Holmes, 2002, p. 674, see *supra* note 488.
769 Kleffner, 2008, p. 85, see *supra* note 41.
770 Cryer, 2005, p. 148, see *supra* note 96.

powerful incentives to promote domestic compliance, asserts that "the entry into force of the Rome Statute is about more than the establishment of a new court: it creates a global compliance system for the enforcement of international criminal law."[771] This development brings the domestic proceedings, which have been considered as a matter of absolute sovereignty, under supervision of the Court. It proves that the traditional understanding of sovereignty has changed. The sovereign states have agreed to put a part of their sovereignty under the scrutiny of the Court.

The Court's monitoring of genuineness of the national proceedings has some features. Firstly, it is not general monitoring and assessment. The Court's assessment of the national proceedings is situation- and case-specific. The Court has not been established as a supervisory body or appellate court to evaluate national judicial decisions as a whole. It is something that was explicitly mentioned by the International Law Commission in the process of establishing the ICC. According to the Report of the *Ad hoc* Committee, "it was stressed that the standards set by the [International Law] Commission were not intended to establish a hierarchy between the International Criminal Court and national courts, or to allow the International Criminal Court to pass judgment on the operation of national courts in general."[772] On the contrary, the Court's power to scrutinize domestic proceedings is highly limited to specific cases presented before the Court. The case-based assessment has a result: an assessment of the State's overall justice system is not necessary.[773] The Prosecutor, in a report on the Libya situation to the UNSC, refers to the fact that "the Office will not evaluate the Libyan judicial system as a whole."[774] The OTP Policy Paper on preliminary Examinations refers to this limitation on the admissibility assessment too.[775] Monitoring and evaluating the domestic proceedings as to specific cases should be conducted merely in view of the admissibility assessment. Such an assessment does not involve reviewing the rights of the accused.[776] From such a perspective, the suggestion of working as a human rights Court has been widely rejected.

However, being case-specific does not mean that the Court is barred from adopting a contextual assessment of the domestic proceedings with respect to specific cases. On the contrary, such an approach is, to some degree, inevitable and would be of help to assess the admissibility of specific cases. Some scholars in informal papers suggest that inferences can be drawn from general context. For instance, "where a system is shown to be independent, impartial and meeting standards of genuineness, this may contribute

771 Rastan, 2010, p. 132, see *supra* note 131.

772 Report on the Ad hoc Committee on the Establishment of the International Criminal Court, 6 September 1995., para. 43.

773 Nouwen, 2013, p. 74, see *supra* note 226.

774 ICC, OTP, Prosecutor Statement to the United Nations Security Council on the situation in the Libyan Arab Jamahiriya, pursuant to UNSCR 1970 (2011), 16 May 2012, para. 7.

775 ICC, OTP, Policy Paper on preliminary Examinations, para. 46: "an admissibility determination is not a judgment or reflection on the national justice system as a whole. If an otherwise functioning judiciary is not investigating or prosecuting the relevant case(s), the determining factor is the absence of relevant proceedings."

776 Mégret, 2011, p. 372, see *supra* note 153.

to an inference of genuineness in the particular case. Conversely, where a system is shown to be plagued with political interference, scripted trials, and unwillingness to pursue certain groups of offenders or offences, this may contribute to an inference of a lack of genuineness in the particular case."[777] It is, in particular, the case in the situational phase when the Court should assess the likelihood that a potential situation will be addressed by national institutions. As the scholars in their informal paper assert, in this context, statistical analyses and the history of the national proceedings may be of relevance in early stages.[778]

Secondly, the Court's scrutiny of the domestic proceedings is based on interaction with States. Interaction and supervision establish complementarity as a mechanism through which the Court can engage States.[779] The 'scrutiny' function of the Court constitutes a context in which the positive complementarity activities can be activated. Stahn states the Court may take on a "proactive role in the supervision of investigations and prosecutions and enter into communication and cooperation with States in the exercise of its classical complementarity powers."[780] The Court should adopt a friendly and dialectic approach when it monitors national proceedings. It should be recalled that the Court is intended to complement national jurisdictions, and as such it requires cooperation instead of competition. Therefore, when the Prosecutor determines that the conditions of admissibility of a case are met, it should initially consult with the relevant State and inquire about the State's status.

Thirdly, the Court's monitoring of national proceedings, in view of the admissibility assessment, is an ongoing process. The Prosecutor, in his first report to the UNSC on Sudan, explained that the complementarity assessment is an ongoing process.[781] Irrespective of the decision rendered by the Court about the admissibility of a case, its monitoring continues. It implies that the complementarity test may be revisited several times before the commencement of the trial.[782] If it declares a case admissible, such a decision may be challenged under Article 19. Likewise, if it declares a case inadmissible, it continues its supervision to assure the continuation of an inadmissibility status. Indeed, a deferral does not give the State *carte blanche* to proceed in a genuine manner thereafter.[783] Therefore, in accordance to Article 18(3), a deferral is "open to review by the Prosecutor six months after the date of deferral or at any time when there has been

---

777 ICC, OTP, Informal Expert Paper, 2003, para. 35, see *supra* note 508.

778 Ibid., para. 43. The Court sometimes refer to such contextual information. For instance, the PTC in the Al-Senussi case states that "submissions of a general nature indicating significant defects of Libya's national judicial system may be relevant as 'contextual information', information of this kind can be considered only to the extent that such systemic difficulties have a bearing on domestic proceedings against Mr Al-Senussi, such that it would warrant a finding of one (ICC, PTC I, Al-Senussi case, 11 October 2013, para. 245, see *supra* note 544).

779 Kleffner, 2008, p. 328, see *supra* note 41.

780 Stahn, 2008, p. 104, see *supra* note 486.

781 ICC, OTP, First Report of the Prosecutor of the ICC to the Security Council pursuant to UNSC 1593 (2005), 29 June 2005, P. 4.

782 Ambos, 2011, p. 1080, see *supra* note 370.

783 Stigen, 2008, p. 523, see *supra* note 96.

a significant change of circumstances based on the State's unwillingness or inability genuinely to carry out the investigation." This feature of the Court's scrutiny function contributes to the catalyst effect of the complementarity rule.

3.5. SITUATION OF STATE'S UNWILLINGNESS

It is evident that some degree of subjective review of national practice will be unavoidable, in particular in terms of determination of whether a state's activities constitute a genuine unwillingness to investigate.[784] Willingness and unwillingness is a matter of intention arising from the hidden mind. Article 17(1)(a) reads that the Court shall declare a case inadmissible if the case is being investigated or prosecuted by a State, unless the State is unwilling or unable to carry out the investigation or prosecution genuinely. Unwillingness and inability tests are disjunctive. It means the case is admissible to the ICC if either test is satisfied. If a State is unwilling to conduct genuine proceedings, it does not bar the Court from intervention, even though the State has done some judicial activities in reality. In this scenario, those domestic proceedings can be called 'sham proceedings'. A determination of unwillingness involves an assessment of a state's intention.[785] States lack any mind to have an intention. Therefore, "any 'will' or 'intention' of a State will be the will or intention of individuals representing the state, with which the State can be identified."[786] Intention is not a concrete phenomenon, and its proof is not straightforward. An intention may be recognized through indicators. Actions and concrete indicators are mirrors of hidden intentions. An assessment of unwillingness involves a search for indicia of a purpose of shielding the person from criminal responsibility or a lack of intent to bring the person to justice.[787] In determining unwillingness, Paragraph 2 of Article 17 introduces three indicators, namely shielding from criminal responsibility, delay in proceedings, and lack of impartiality and independence. These factors are exhaustive, however, they can be applied in the alternative.[788] They are exhaustive, because they are exceptions.[789] Being an exception requires narrow interpretation. Given the three factors referred to in Article 17, the Appeals Chamber asserts that for a case to be admissible it must be shown that "the proceedings were or are being conducted in a manner which, in the circumstances, is inconsistent with an intent to bring the person concerned to justice."[790]

To determine whether a State is willing, its willingness is assessed specifically with respect to a case or situation. Such an assessment is neither done in the abstract nor

784 Drumbl, 2011, p. 206, see *supra* note 525.
785 Nouwen, 2013, p. 63, see *supra* note 226.
786 Stigen, 2008, p. 252, see *supra* note 96.
787 ICC, OTP, Informal Expert Paper, 2003, para. 47, see *supra* note 508.
788 Ambos, 2011, p. 1089, see *supra* note 370. And, Nouwen, 2013, p. 69, see *supra* note 226. And, Stigen, 2008, p. 314, see *supra* note 96.
789 El Zeidy, 2008, p. 168, see *supra* note 19.
790 ICC, Appeals Chamber, Al-Senussi case, 24 July 2014, para. 1, see *supra* note 107.

regarding the domestic legal system as a whole. The complementarity assessment does not deal with this question if a state, in general, is willing to combat international crimes, but it tries to find an answer for the question of whether the State is willing to investigate or prosecute the case at hand. It implies that divergence in willingness is imaginable. A State may be willing to launch the fight against international crimes in a selective manner. National authorities "may be eager to investigate crimes by rebel groups but be reticent with respect to government forces."[791] In this scenario, those cases which have been faced with the unwillingness of the State will be admissible before the Court.

3.5.1. Due Process Framework in Determining Unwillingness

The chapeau of Paragraph 2 of Article 17 frames a clause that requires interpretation. According to Paragraph 2, "in order to determine unwillingness in a particular case, the Court shall consider, having regard to the principles of due process recognized by international law whether one or more of the following exist." Due process regulates the conduct of legal proceedings in a way that safeguards the position of the individual charged.[792] For this reason, the OTP suggests that principles of due process may be assessed in light of the provision of Article 67 that deals with the rights of the accused.[793] Due process pays considerable attention to the rights of the accused. By reading Paragraph 2, a question arises: is a case admissible under Article 17 if the Court determines that the State asserting jurisdiction over it will not provide the defendant with due process?

The interpretative approach to due process is of great importance. If this clause is interpreted in a broad and liberal way, it provides the Court with broader authorities to monitor the national legal systems. Indeed, if the due process is interpreted as an independent criterion, it empowers the Prosecutor to assess the national legal systems from the perspective of human rights. In this scenario, if the domestic system does not keep up with the international human rights standards, the Court can declare a case admissible based on unwillingness of the domestic system.[794] The judgment of the Appeals Chamber of the Court, in the context of the Al-Senussi's challenge, observes that, at first sight, the text and chapeau of Article 17 could potentially be read to support the position arguing that "a State is unwilling genuinely to carry out the investigation or prosecution if it does not respect the fair trial rights of the suspect."[795]

---

791 ICC, OTP, Informal Expert Paper, 2003, para. 45, see *supra* note 508.

792 Kleffner, 2008, p. 129, see *supra* note 41.

793 ICC, OTP, Policy Paper on Preliminary Examinations, para. 55.

794 It should be noted that some scholars in the Informal Expert Paper have argued that the lack of due process at the domestic proceedings leads to inability instead of unwillingness. According to the paper, the Court should take into account a State's "legal regime of due process standards, rights of accused, [and] procedures' when determining whether it is able to investigate and prosecute" (see: ICC, OTP, Informal Expert Paper, 2003, p. 28, see *supra* note 508).

795 ICC, Appeals Chamber, Al-Senussi case, 24 July 2014, para. 213, see *supra* note 107.

The second approach to the due process clause is a narrow one. According to the recent interpretation, the due process clause constitutes an interpretive framework within which the three factors mentioned in Paragraph 2 should be read. From this angle, in this scenario, due process is not an independent factor besides other indicators of unwillingness, but itself limits the scope of other factors. In other words, the chapeau and its subparagraphs are conjunctive. It means that shielding, unjustified delay, and impartiality and independence of the proceedings should be understood in light of the principle of due process recognized by international law. It implies that the assessment of quality of justice requires that procedural as well as substantive due process rights should be taken into account.[796]

There are two arguments in favor of this interpretation: textual and contextual. From a textual perspective, the due process clause is a subordinate clause. Grammatically speaking, "subordinate clauses depend on independent clauses for their meaning– which means that the chapeau is not separate from the three subparagraphs, but simply explains how the Court should determine whether one or more of the paragraphs are satisfied."[797] From a contextual perspective, the contexts in which the Court has been established should be taken into account. The Court is a criminal tribunal with mandates to deal with crimes. It is not a court of human rights.[798] The ICC is tasked to prosecute individuals, but not to supervise States compliance with their international human rights obligation.[799] The Appeals Chamber, in its judgment on the admissibility of the Al-Senussi case, states that if a case could be admissible merely because domestic proceedings do not fully respect the due process rights of a suspect, it "would necessarily involve the Court passing judgment generally on the internal functioning of the domestic legal systems of States in relation to individual guarantees of due process."[800] However, the Chambers insists that "had this been the intention behind Article 17, the Appeals Chamber would have expected this to have been included expressly in the text of the provision."[801] Judge Ušacka, in her dissenting opinion, insists it would have been doubtful that the Statute was adopted if such a mandate had been given to the Court.[802] The mandates of the Court are independent from other institutions. The Court is not a mechanism to remedy general human rights violations at domestic criminal proceedings.[803] It is a criminal court to put an end to the culture of impunity of the perpetrators of the ICC-identified crimes.

---

796 El Zeidy, 2008, p. 169, see *supra* note 19.

797 Heller, 2006, p. 262, see *supra* note 566.

798 Carsten Stahn, 'Sentencing Horror or Sentencing Heuristic? A Reply to Heller's Sentence-Based Theory of Complementarity', in William A. Schabas, Yvonne McDermott and Niamh Hayes (eds.), *The Ashgate Research Companion to International Criminal Law: critical perspectives*, Ashgate, 2013, p. 365.

799 Nouwen, 2013, p. 68, see *supra* note 226. And, Mégret, 2011, p. 385, see *supra* note 153.

800 ICC, Appeals Chamber, Al-Senussi case, 24 July 2014, para. 219, see *supra* note 107.

801 Ibid.

802 ICC, Appeals Chamber, Separate Opinion of Judge Anita Ušacka, Al-Senussi case, 24 July 2014, para. 10.

803 Stahn, 2011, p. 247, see *supra* note 297.

The Appeals Chamber, in its judgment on the Defense's challenge against the admissibility of the Al-Senussi case, clarifies that Article 17(2) "as a whole defines the circumstances in which a State is unwilling genuinely to carry out the investigation and/or prosecution."[804] The Appeals Chamber, in response to the Defense, stated that "admissibility proceedings are not primarily a mechanism to complain about human rights violations."[805] Some years earlier, in the context of the Katanga case, the Appeals Chamber had made the same assertion: "a challenge to admissibility under Article 19(2)(a) of the Statute is not the mechanism under which to raise alleged violations of the rights of the accused in the course of the prosecutorial process. It is a limited procedure that triggers the relevant Chamber's powers to determine the admissibility of the case under Article 17 of the Statute."[806]

However, in the Al-Senussi case the Appeals Chamber acknowledged that "violations of human rights may, in specific and limited circumstances, play a role in the determination as to whether a case is inadmissible."[807] The Chamber explained that the concept of being 'unwilling' to genuinely investigate or prosecute is "primarily concerned with a situation in which proceedings are conducted in a manner which would lead to a suspect evading justice as a result of a State not being willing genuinely to investigate or prosecute."[808] Therefore, the primary reason for the inclusion of the trio of factors in Article 17(2) is not for "the purpose of guaranteeing the fair trial rights of the suspect generally."[809] Nevertheless, it does not mean that "the Court must turn a blind eye to clear and conclusive evidence demonstrating that the national proceedings completely lack fairness."[810] As the Appeals Chamber affirmed, "there may be circumstances, depending on the facts of the individual case, whereby violations of the rights of the suspect are so egregious that the proceedings can no longer be regarded as being capable of providing any genuine form of justice to the suspect so that they should be deemed, in those circumstances, to be inconsistent with an intent to bring the person to justice."[811] In the case against Al-Senussi, the Defense had claimed that Al-Senussi lacked access to the Defense, and therefore they were not able to give instructions to the accused. Although it could be a violation of the rights of the accused, the Appeals Chamber argued that such a violation did not pertain to the issue of admissibility. According to the Chamber, "the Defense does not explain how the fact that Mr Al-Senussi was unable to give instructions to the Defense representing him at this Court would lead per se to a finding that Libya is unwilling or unable genuinely to investigate and prosecute Mr Al-Senussi in Libya."[812] The Appeals Chamber, in its

804 ICC, Appeals Chamber, Al-Senussi case, 24 July 2014, para. 216, see *supra* note 107.
805 Ibid., para. 169.
806 ICC, Appeals Chamber, Katanga case, 25 September 2009, para. 113, see *supra* note 495.
807 ICC, Appeals Chamber, Al-Senussi case, 24 July 2014, para. 169, see *supra* note 107.
808 Ibid., para. 218.
809 Ibid.
810 Ibid., para. 229.
811 Ibid., para. 3.
812 Ibid., para. 179.

judgment, recognized that the accused had a right of access to a lawyer also in the early stages of the proceedings, but the Chamber insisted that "in the context of admissibility proceedings, the Court is not primarily called upon to decide whether at domestic proceedings certain requirements of human rights law or domestic law are being violated. Rather, what is at issue is whether the State is willing genuinely to investigate or prosecute."[813]

Later, Al-Senussi, with eight others, including Gaddafi, were tried and sentenced to death over crimes linked to the 2011 revolution.[814] However, the convictions were opposed by many, who argued that the trial was not fair and it represented a miscarriage of justice.[815] In February 2017, the UN Support Mission in Libya, in cooperation with the Office of the United Nations High Commissioner for Human Rights, issued a report on the conduct of this trial. The report concludes that the trial fell short of international fair trial standards.[816] In May 2017, the Court's Prosecutor, in her report to the UNSC, referred to these reports and recalled the Appeals Chamber decision that due process violations should be egregious to make a case admissible before the Court.[817] Given these facts, the Prosecutor announced that she would examine the report to determine whether "new facts have arisen which negate the basis on which the PTC found Mr Al-Senussi's case inadmissible before the Court."[818]

Now, it can be better understood why an Italian proposal was rejected during the drafting process of the Rome Statute. At the time, Italy proposed a definition of unwillingness that would have specifically made the absence of national due process a ground for admissibility: "In deciding on issues of admissibility under this article, the Court shall consider whether… (ii) the said investigations or proceedings have been or are impartial or independent, or were or are designed to shield the accused from international criminal responsibility, or were or are conducted with full respect for the fundamental rights of the accused."[819] However, this approach was dismissed.

Here, the question of applicability of the 'abuse of process' doctrine arises. According to this doctrine, a court of law has authority to stop a judicial proceeding, "at the outset and less frequently in the process, by declining jurisdiction in a judicial cause, where to do otherwise would be odious to the administration of justice."[820] Delay in bringing the accused to justice, breaking the promises to the accused regarding his prosecution

813 ICC, Appeals Chamber, Al-Senussi case, 24 July 2014, para. 190, see *supra* note 107.
814 BBC, Libya Trial: Gaddafi son sentenced to death over war crimes, 28 July 2015, available at: www.bbc.com/news/world-africa-33688391.
815 For instance, see: BBC, Libya death sentences cast long shadow over rule of law, 12 August 2015, available at: www.bbc.com/news/world-africa-33855860.
816 UN, United Nations Support Mission in Libya and Office of the United Nations High Commissioner for Human Rights, Report on the Trial of 37 Former Members of the Gadhafi Regime, 21 February 2017, available at: www.ohchr.org/Documents/Countries/LY/Trial37FormerMembersQadhafiRegime_EN.pdf.
817 ICC, OTP, Statement of ICC Prosecutor to the UNSC on the Situation in Libya, 9 May 2017, available at: www.icc-cpi.int//Pages/item.aspx?name=170509-otp-stat-lib.
818 Ibid.
819 Draft Proposal by Italy, UN Doc. A/AC.249/1997/WG.3/IP.4, 5 August 1997.
820 ICC, Appeals Chamber, Lubanga case, 14 December 2006, para. 27, see *supra* note 8.

and bringing the accused to justice by illegal means are instances of the abuse of process.[821] In 2006, the Appeals Chamber, in one of its decisions in the Lubanga case, posed the question of whether this doctrine is applicable under the Statute as part of the applicable law. In response, the Chamber asserted that the possibility of the applicability of due process should be explored under the admissibility requirement, because in the legal system of the Court, "admissibility is the only ground envisaged by the Statute for which the Court may validly refrain from assuming or exercising jurisdiction in any given case."[822]

Given this framework, the Appeals Chamber rejected the applicability of the abuses of process doctrine because it "is not listed as a ground for relinquishing jurisdiction in Article 17 of the Statute."[823] The Appeals Chamber argued that such an absence is effective because the factors enshrined in Article 17 are exhaustive. Therefore, "no room is left for recourse to the second or third source of law to determine the presence or absence of a rule governing a given subject."[824] Indeed, in the eyes of the Chamber, if Article 17 was not exhaustive, abuse of process would find its place as an applicable principle of law under either sub-paragraphs (b) or (c) of paragraph 1 of Article 21 of the Statute, but Article 17 has been formed in an exhaustive manner. It implies that the Rome Statute's silence about other probable factors carries a denial of unmentioned elements. Based on this interpretation, the Appeals Chamber concludes that "the Statute does not provide for stay of proceedings for abuse of process as such."[825] Here, the doctrine '*male captus bene detentus*' comes up too. According to this rule, 'wrongly captured' may lead to 'properly detained'. Traditionally, under this rule, judges cannot look at how the suspect is brought before the jurisdiction of the State of the current prosecuting court. Indeed, it forces judges to adhere to the non-inquiry rule and a restricted notion of a fair trial.[826]

However, following the human rights revolution, this traditional understanding assumed a change in light of human rights law. The new reading of the rule results in the abuse of process doctrine, which means, "courts in principle have jurisdiction but will use their discretion not to exercise that jurisdiction if the *male captus* is so serious that to continue exercising jurisdiction would constitutes an abuse of the court's process."[827] Therefore, the courts should assess the events, which happened to the accused before his appearance before the court. However, the question is that of which remedy should be provided if the *male captus* occurs. Is staying the proceedings a suitable remedy or not? Paulussen, in his book, has addressed this issue in detail. He states that "the fact that one is dealing with suspects of international crimes cannot in any way be used

821 Ibid., para. 28.
822 Ibid., para. 34.
823 Ibid.
824 Ibid.
825 Ibid., para. 35.
826 Christophe Paulussen, *Male Captus Bene Detentus? Surrendering Suspects to the International Criminal Court*, Intersentia, 2010, p. 1022.
827 Ibid., p. 2013.

as an excuse to violate human rights."[828] According to him, nowadays tribunals have stressed the importance of human rights, due process and fair proceedings and have not limited these concepts to the courtroom.[829] Paulussen concludes that when the *male captus* occurs, appropriate remedies must be granted. However, in granting these remedies, "one must avoid paving the way for absurd consequences which are counter to the concept of justice: through a strict application of the remedy of release in the case of an unlawful arrest. In such a case it better to keep a suspect in custody and to grant appropriate and real remedies instead, taking account the seriousness of *the male captus*."[830] Paulussen states that "the public and international community of the victims, will not grasp how a suspect of genocide can be released because he has not been promptly informed of the reasons for his arrest, especially if that person is not re-arrested and subsequently flees."[831] Therefore, to apply this law, the context in which they are going to be applied should be taken into account. It was mentioned that there is a distinction between international context and national sphere. It is not reasonable to transform all ruling principals at the domestic level into the international sphere without paying attention to the contextual differences. What is a remedy at the national level may be considered unsuitable in the international phase. At the ICC legal system, for instance, a reduction in sentence could be an option.

3.5.2. Shielding from Justice

The first indicator of unwillingness of a State to conduct their national proceedings genuinely is shielding the person concerned from criminal responsibility for ICC crimes. Some authors believe that shielding from criminal responsibility is widely broad, and other criteria mentioned in paragraph 2 of Article 17 can be put under its umbrella.[832] Indeed, those situations in which there is no intent to bring the accused to justice are instances of shielding from criminal responsibility. From this angle, the term 'justice' in other sub-paragraphs should be understood as criminal justice.

Shielding the accused from criminal responsibility is highly related to intentions. It is an assessment of a state of mind. In Article 17, shielding from criminal responsibility is the most subjective grounds of unwillingness.[833] It is evident that the hidden intent of an abstract entity like a State cannot be read. However, such an intention can be demonstrated through concrete actions and circumstances. The Policy Paper on preliminary Examinations lists a large number of indicators proving the intended shielding, such as manifestly insufficient steps in the investigation or prosecution; deviations from established practices and procedures; ignoring evidence

828 Ibid., p. 1027.
829 Ibid., p. 634.
830 Ibid., p. 1027.
831 Ibid., p. 1021.
832 El Zeidy, 2008, p. 170, see *supra* note 19. And, Holmes, 2002, p. 675, see *supra* note 488. And, Kleffner, 2008, p. 159, see *supra* note 41.
833 Nouwen, 2013, p. 63, see *supra* note 226.

or giving it insufficient weight; intimidation of victims, witnesses or judicial personnel; irreconcilability of findings with evidence tendered; manifest inadequacies in charging and modes of liability in relation to the gravity of the alleged conduct and the purported role of the accused; mistaken judicial findings arising from mistaken identification, failures of disclosure, manipulated or coerced statements, and/or undue admission or non- admission of evidence; lack of resources allocated to the proceedings at hand as compared with overall capacities; and refusal to provide information or to cooperate with the ICC.[834]

In conducting an inquiry into the state of States' minds, the contextual or circumstantial evidence plays a prominent role. For this reason, the record and practices of the national proceedings in the past can be a factor. This standard requires a comparison between the current practice and what has been typical by taking into account the domestic legal system and its practices. For instance, if the sanction determined by the domestic jurisdiction lacks proportionality with its typical sentencing regime, it can uncover an intention of shielding. Shielding from criminal responsibility should be understood in light of the principles of due process. Punishment without proportionality is inconsistent with a fair trial. Kleffner asserts that in this scenario the decision must be specifically directed at shielding.[835] This consideration does not contradict Article 80 of the Rome Statute that insists that domestic penalties are not affected by the penalties referred to in the Statute. The foregoing proportionality is examined within the domestic legal framework of the State concerned.

'Shielding' means shielding from criminal responsibility. What is important here is the responsibility and accountability, regardless of its result. If due process warrants acquittal of the accused, such an acquittal is not an instance of shielding from criminal responsibility. In this regard, the question of amnesties arises. Whatever shields the accused from criminal responsibility falls within the scope of part (a) of Paragraph 2. The reason behind shielding does not matter. Even if shielding occurs in good faith, for instance to maintain peace, it does not change the case. In other words, "the purpose of shielding need not necessarily result from breaches of international law by and to the bad faith on behalf of a state."[836]

Again, shielding from criminal responsibility in Article 17 is open to two interpretations. One can say that the reason and intent behind shielding does not matter. In this scenario, amnesties, even if they serve valuable goals like peace, would fall within the notion of shielding. However, from a different angle, one can read shielding as a matter of carrying bad faith in its nature. Indeed, shielding refers to unwillingness arising from bad faith. Although the second reading sounds fine, it seems that, under Article 17, amnesties cannot be offered to make a case inadmissible. Article 17(1) deals with the complementarity rule. The rule refers to the conflict of jurisdictions. In other words, it is a matter of criminal law in nature. Therefore, non-

---

834 ICC, OTP, Policy Paper on Preliminary Examinations, para. 51.

835 Kleffner, 2008, p. 135, see *supra* note 41.

836 Ibid., p. 137.

judicial actions are manifestly outside of its scope. However, the issue of amnesties and the dilemma between peace and justice can be taken into account under the 'interests of justice' requirement.

3.5.3. *Unjustified Delay in Delivering Justice*

The second proof of unwillingness is an unjustified delay at the domestic proceedings, if such a delay is inconsistent with the intent to bring the person concerned to justice. Under this scenario, the domestic proceedings commence, but they do not continue to the end due to an unjustified delay. Unjustified delay makes a case admissible before the Court only if another cumulative requirement is fulfilled, namely inconsistency with the intent to bring the person concerned to justice is fulfilled. Therefore, four conditions should be met: 1. The proceedings have already been commenced; 2. There is a delay in the proceedings; 3. The delay is unjustified; and 4. The unjustified delay is not consistent with the intent to deliver justice.

Initially, in the preparation process, the notion of 'undue delay' was introduced. However, it was criticized as being too low as a threshold for unwillingness. Hence, it was resolved by replacing the first draft with the term 'unjustified delay'. The replaced adjective has an implication in favor of the domestic proceedings. It "provides the Sate with the opportunity to explain the reason for the delay before the Court makes a determination on admissibility."[837] The delay under Article 17 should be unjustified. It means there is a possibility of justified delay. Therefore, the State concerned has the opportunity to justify the delay in its proceedings.

To determine if a delay is justified or unjustified, the principles of due process are helpful. These principles direct the Court to follow the jurisprudence of human rights tribunals. 'To be tried without undue delay' or 'a hearing within a reasonable time' is one of the accused's rights enshrined in the human rights instruments.[838] A study of the jurisprudence of human rights organs shows that "there is no one- size-fits-all answer as to when too long time has elapsed in a national criminal proceeding."[839] Therefore, what constitutes an unjustified delay depends on the circumstances. It implies that to determine a delay without justification in the proceedings, the delay should not be "translated into a fixed number of years, months or years."[840] In the Al-Senussi case, the Defense alleged that the domestic proceedings as to Al-Senussi in Libya were taking place with unjustified delay. The PTC asserted that "any such unjustified delay must be made not against an abstract ideal of 'justice', but against the specific circumstances surrounding the investigation concerned."[841] In the specific circumstances at hand, the

837 El Zeidy, 2008, p. 181, see *supra* note 19.

838 For instance, Article 14 (3)(c) International Covenant on Civil and Political Rights. And, Article 6(1) of the European Convention on Human Rights.

839 Stigen, 2008, p. 292, see *supra* note 96.

840 ICTR, Trial Chamber III, Decision on Defense Motion for Stay of Proceedings, Rwamakuba case, 03 June 2005, para. 26.

841 ICC, PTC I, Al-Senussi case, 11 October 2013, para. 223, see *supra* note 544.

Chamber concluded that "a period of less than 18 months between the commencement of the investigation in relation to Mr Al-Senussi and the referral of the case against him to the Accusation Chamber cannot be considered to constitute an unjustified delay inconsistent with an intent to bring Mr Al-Senussi to justice."[842]

To determine the time span that constitutes an unjustified delay, the normal length of national proceedings may be taken into account as an important factor.[843] Therefore, proceedings which exceed the usual national practice and which are not convincingly explained may constitute an unjustified delay.[844] However, it should be borne in mind that prosecuting international crimes is more complex than prosecuting ordinary crimes. Therefore, such complexity should be taken into account. One justification for delay in the proceedings, as mentioned by the Inter-American Court of Human Rights, is the complexity of the case at hand.[845] It is evident that if a case is complex, it takes a longer time to gather evidence. This complexity intensifies in the case of war-torn societies. In the Simone Gbagbo case, for instance, Côte d'Ivoire pointed out that the State had recently emerged from a conflict and lacked the considerable material and human resources required to investigate Gbagbo.[846] However, the Appeals Chamber dismissed this statement by saying that Côte d'Ivoire had merely explained difficulties, without explaining the relevance of these submissions to the PTC's analysis of admissibility.[847] However, as Judge Ušacka, in her dissenting opinion on the Gaddafi case, had pointed out stringent standards impose "unnecessarily high requirements on States with a legal and judicial system in transition and would unduly burden their transitional justice efforts", while "States that do not have such difficulties more easily meet these high standards."[848] Justice requires these differences to be taken into account.

3.5.4. *Impartiality and Independence of the Domestic Proceedings*

Lack of impartiality or independence in the domestic proceedings makes a case admissible before the Court. This test has a retroactive effect. It means that the terminated proceedings will be assessed in connection with the impartiality and independence standards. These dual standards are effective in the complementarity assessment if they are inconsistent with the intent to bring the person concerned to justice. Indeed, impartiality and independence tests, like the unjustified delay standard, ultimately refer to shielding the accused from criminal responsibility. Therefore, the impartiality or independence tests do not allow the Court to monitor upholding human rights status at the domestic sphere.

---

842 Ibid., para. 229.

843 Christoph Safferling, *International Criminal Procedure*, Oxford University Press, 2012, p. 103.

844 Holmes, 2002, p. 676, see *supra* note 488.

845 Inter-American Court of Human Rights, Genie-Lacayo V Nicaragua case, 29 January 1997, para. 77.

846 ICC, Appeals Chamber, Simone Gbagbo case, 27 May 2015, para. 120, see *supra* note 605.

847 Ibid., para. 122.

848 ICC, Appeals Chamber, Gaddafi case, Separate Opinion of Judge Anita Ušacka, 21 May 2014. para. 62.

Independence means that the judicial body, in making its decisions, is not ordered or directed by external actors and factors. The Appeals Chamber of the Court defines independence as "being independent of the executive and the legislature, as well as of the parties to the proceedings."[849] Impartiality refers to the personal relationship between the judicial systems and the culprits. According to the Appeals Chamber, "in respect of impartiality, the personal or subjective impartiality of a judge is presumed unless the contrary is shown; yet consideration also needs to be given as to whether objective reasonable doubts as to impartiality arise."[850] If the judicial system lacks impartiality, it can easily lead to shielding the accused from justice. Impartiality, in the assessment of the genuineness of the domestic proceedings, plays a more important role in particular when the State organs and members are accused of involvement in the crimes. However, it should be borne in mind that "impartiality does not mean that we must necessarily prosecute all groups in a given situation. Impartiality means that we will objectively apply the same criteria for all."[851] The intention of not bringing the accused to justice should be determined by taking into account the surrounding circumstances. The OTP's Policy Paper on Preliminary Examinations refers to some indicators of impartiality, such as "connections between the suspected perpetrators and competent authorities responsible for investigation, prosecution or adjudication of the crimes as well as public statements, awards, sanctions, promotions or demotions, deployments, dismissals or reprisals in relation to investigative, prosecutorial or judicial personnel concerned."[852]

3.6. SITUATION OF A STATE'S INABILITY

The second instance that affects the genuineness of national proceedings is inability. If the local State is unable to genuinely conduct the proceedings in connection with the same case before the Court, the case will be admissible even if the State concerned is willing to deal with the case at the domestic level.

The inability assessment is more straightforward than unwillingness. Firstly, it is more objective than its counterpart. It is because inability is a fact-driven notion.[853] Secondly, the due process principles do not play a role here. In the context of the unwillingness assessment, the Rome Statute sets an evaluative framework, namely the due process principles. This standard is absent with respect to examination of inability. However, there is another evaluative framework, namely, the national legal system of the State concerned. The PTC of the Court in the Gaddafi case asserts that the ability of a State "must be assessed in the context of the relevant national system and procedures.

849 ICC, Appeals Chamber, Al-Senussi case, 24 July 2014, para. 250, see *supra* note 107.
850 Ibid.
851 ICC, OTP, Prosecutor's Statement at the Informal Meeting of Legal Advisors of Ministers of Foreign Affairs, 24 October 2005, p. 6.
852 ICC, OTP, Policy Paper on Preliminary Examinations, para. 54.
853 Holmes, 2002, p. 677, see *supra* note 488.

In other words, the Chamber must assess whether the Libyan authorities are capable of investigating or prosecuting Mr Gaddafi in accordance with the substantive and procedural law applicable in Libya."[854]

Inability, like unwillingness, has an object. The object of inability is in carrying out the proceedings. Being unable to conduct proceedings is a general concept that embraces many instances. Paragraph 3 of Article 17 refers to some instances, such as inability to obtain the accused or necessary evidence, but it immediately rejects the idea of exhaustiveness of these situations by saying that "otherwise unable to carry out its proceedings." As El Zeidy notes, this clause was added during the work of the Preparatory Committee "to serve as a catch-all clause for all sorts of situations that might arise in the course of the domestic process."[855] The State's inability should result from specific causes. Under Article 17, the causes of inability are total collapse, substantial collapse or unavailability of the national judicial system. Therefore, the Court should consider both the causes (collapse) and the consequences (not able to carry out).[856] The Appeals Chamber, in one of its judgments, states: "to make a finding of inability under Article 17(3) of the Statute, the Court must be satisfied that there is both a 'total or substantial collapse or unavailability' of the national judicial system and that, as a result, the State is unable to obtain the accused or the necessary evidence and testimony or otherwise unable to carry out its proceedings."[857]

3.6.1. The situation of Collapse of National Judicial System

The first cause of inability is substantial collapse and the second one is total collapse. The status of collapse in the meaning of Article 17 refers to the collapse of the domestic judicial system rather than all State institutions and authorities.[858] The object of collapse is material capacities. It carries connotations such as the lack of judicial infrastructure as well as a lack of trained personnel.[859] The Appeals Chamber of the Court has listed some indicators relevant to the determination of inability, such as the scope, methodology and resources of investigation, progress in the judicial proceedings, seeking for international assistance, the serious security situation, the absence of protection programmes for witnesses and the lack of control over certain detention facilities.[860] The collapse test lies in contrast with unavailability, whose object is law

854 ICC, PTC I, Gaddafi case, 31 May 2013, para. 200, see *supra* note 561.
855 El Zeidy, 2008, p. 224, see *supra* note 552.
856 Nouwen, 2013, p. 64, see *supra* note 226.
857 ICC, Appeals Chamber, Al-Senussi case, 24 July 2014, para. 265, see *supra* note 107.
858 Kleffner, 2008, p. 154, see *supra* note 41.
859 El Zeidy, 2008, p. 226, see *supra* note 552.
860 ICC, Appeals Chamber, Al-Senussi case, 24 July 2014, para. 138, see *supra* note 107. In addition, the Office of the Prosecutor in its Policy Paper on preliminary Examinations asserts that in conducting its evaluation, "the Office may consider, *inter alia*, the ability of the competent authorities to exercise their judicial powers in the territory concerned; the absence of conditions of security for witnesses, investigators, prosecutors and judges or the lack of adequate protection systems; the absence of the required legislative framework to prosecute the same conduct or forms of responsibility; the lack of

and legal capacities. Total collapse may be equated with inaction.[861] However, it is a posterior inaction, because, in the scenario of inability, the national proceedings precede inability. The situation of inaction is a deliberate choice, but inability is out of the state's hands.

In the preparatory process, the term 'partial collapse' was replaced with 'substantial' collapse. It should be seen as an attempt to reduce the elements of subjectivity.[862] The 'substantial' adjective lies between total and partial. The partial test refers to the size of collapse, in particular in terms of the geographical scope of collapse. If the partial collapse were intended, the inability of the State would be proved if the State's effective control fails in some part.[863] However, this approach was rejected, because it is imaginable that a State is able to remedy the situation by "shifting resources or transferring the trial to other intact venues."[864] Therefore, the 'substantial' adjective was selected. A collapse is substantial if "it is of such intensity that it affects a significant part of domestic justice system."[865] Such intensity can be determined in light of consequences, such as an inability to arrest the suspects. These considerations are of great importance in assessing the ability of the national systems in those societies affected by war.

Inability to put suspects under arrest is an obstacle to carrying out the proceedings. The referral of the situation in Uganda was exclusively justified based on the inability of Uganda to apprehend the suspects. The letter of referral of situation of Uganda, dated 16 December 2003 expressed: "there was no doubt that Ugandan courts have the capacity to give captured LRA leaders a fair and impartial trial", but "it cannot succeed in arresting the members of the LRA leadership and others most responsible."[866] In February 2007, the Ugandan Minister of Internal Affairs asserted in the Parliament that "the very reason why we took the case to ICC was because we tried to catch Kony and Otti and other leaders but we could not catch them. So, we said, who has the powers that can reach them and we found that ICC had those powers. So, we went to them vey deliberately."[867] However, it should be noted that the Court itself lacks any enforcement or police force to apprehend the culprits. The ICC's history also shows this institution has not been entirely successful in implementing its arrest warrants. The main value of the Court's intervention here is issuing a warrant that could be implemented in all States Parties' territories. Therefore, the inability to arrest under Article 17 should be construed narrowly. If such an inability does not arise from the situation of collapse, it is not reasonable to impose such a burden upon the Court to step in to assist States

adequate resources for effective investigations and prosecutions; as well as violations of fundamental rights of the accused" (ICC, OTP, Policy Paper on Preliminary Examinations, para. 57).

861 Ambos, 2011, p. 1092, see *supra* note 370.

862 El Zeidy, 2008, p. 236, see *supra* note 552.

863 Ambos, 2011, p. 1093, see *supra* note 370.

864 Stigen, 2008, p. 316, see *supra* note 96. And, Holmes, 2002, p. 677, see *supra* note 488.

865 El Zeidy, 2008, p. 226, see *supra* note 552.

866 Nouwen, 2013, p. 121, see *supra* note 226.

867 Ibid., p. 175.

in apprehending suspects. In such a scenario, when this obstacle is removed by the arresting of suspects the admissibility of the case before the Court is challengeable, unless otherwise the State is still unable to conduct the proceedings.

When a State suffers from substantial or total collapse, its ability to apprehend the suspects or/and to collect the evidence will be lost. These consequences result in the inability of the State to conduct the proceedings in a genuine manner. The situation of Libya was a case-study for the Court to examine the inability tests in detail. When Libya challenged the admissibility of the case of Saif-Islam Gaddafi before the Court, the accused had been in detention controlled by Zintan militia outside of the central government's control. The PTC, given this fact, found that Libya is unable to conduct the proceedings due to inability to take the accused under its control. Under the inability test, lack of access to the accused- either he is at large or others have already captured him- leads to inability. According to PTC, although the central government had deployed all efforts to obtain Mr Gaddafi's transfer, no concrete progress to this effect was shown. Due to this fact, and because the Chamber was not persuaded that this problem may be resolved in the near future, the Court recognized the inability of Libya.[868]

As to ability in evidence gathering, one of the main indications of being capable of conducting the proceedings is the ability to take testimonies. In the situation of Libya, the PTC, by mentioning that the Libyan government did not have control over certain detention centers, stated that Libya would not be able to guarantee that all of the witnesses would testify.[869] According to the Chamber, "lack of full control over certain detention facilities has a direct bearing on the investigation against Mr Gaddafi."[870] Apart from access to the witnesses, the status of insecurity may result in inability of a State to take evidence and testimonies. It should be mentioned that "not simply any 'security challenge' would amount to the unavailability or a total or substantial collapse of the national judicial system rendering a State unable."[871] However, if the situation of insecurity leads to a level affecting the continuation of proceedings, it should be taken into account as a factor making the States unable. An unstable security situation may be an obstacle to the Court's investigation and prosecution too. For instance, in the Libya situation, the Prosecutor claimed that "instability currently precludes the Office

868 ICC, PTC I, Gaddafi case, 31 May 2013, para. 201, see *supra* note 561. In the case of Al-Senussi, the same PTC noted that "the Chamber is of the view that the issue of whether the Al-Hadba prison is under the control of Libya is relevant to the Chamber's consideration of Libya's ability to obtain Mr Al-Senussi and to carry out its proceedings against him, within the meaning of Article 17(3) of the Statute" (ICC, PTC I, Al-Senussi case, 11 October 2013, para. 263, see *supra* note 544).

869 ICC, PTC I, Gaddafi case, 31 May 2013, para. 209, see *supra* note 561.

870 Ibid., para. 210. In the case of Al-Senussi this assertion was repeated: "the Chamber is of the view that, depending on all the relevant circumstances, the lack of control over detention facilities where relevant witnesses may be located may be a relevant factor to take into account when determining the State's ability to collect the 'necessary evidence and testimony' to carry out the proceedings within the meaning of Article 17(3) of the Statute" (ICC, PTC I, Al-Senussi case, 11 October 2013, para. 267, see *supra* note 544).

871 ICC, PTC I, Al-Senussi case, 11 October 2013, para. 261, see *supra* note 544.

from conducting investigations within Libyan territory in relation to both existing and possible new cases."[872] It is imaginable that when there is insecurity, the witnesses avoid giving testimony because they are concerned about the consequences of their actions. In the Chamber's words, "in the context of a potentially precarious security situation across the country, witnesses may be afraid of coming forward or may be eliminated, ultimately causing prejudice to the domestic proceedings."[873] In addition, insecurity may cause inability in other forms. The threats or violence against judicial authorities can prevent the judges from continuing with the proceedings. In this scenario, the national proceedings stop due to inability of the states in the sense of Article 17. That is why the existence of a witness protection program at the domestic level is important for the Court. Such a program aims at protecting the witnesses and those persons who will be subject to risk due to testimonies of witnesses. Victims and witnesses of some special crimes need more protection. For instance, as to the gender-based and sexual crimes, "the failure to provide gender-sensitive witness protection could also be considered a sign of inability."[874] However, it is worth saying that the protection program is relevant as far as it impacts the ability of the states to conduct the proceedings. Therefore, where such a program is absent but the evidence can be collected, such a deficiency does not matter. This was the case as to the Al-Senussi case. The PTC insisted that, in comparison with the Gaddafi case, some aspects like the absence of effective witness protection program or the lack of control over detention centers did not have the same impact on the investigation of Al-Senussi, because Libya managed to collect the evidence through other means.[875] The Chamber justified the different conclusions in both cases by mentioning that Libya was able to submit substantially more evidence in the Al-Senussi case than in the case of Gaddafi.[876] It was contrary to those who believed that the Court was affected by some big powers to avoid prosecuting Al-Senussi, due to his information that would be embracing to some powers.[877]

Although the national measures to improve the security situation are of relevance to its assessment, these progressions should have resulted in concrete progress at the time of challenge. In the Gaddafi case, the PTC noted that, although the relevance of specific submissions related to progress made, "multiple challenges remain and that Libya

---

872 ICC, OTP, Twelfth Report of the Prosecutor of the International Criminal Court to the United Nations Security Council pursuant to UNSCR 1970 (2011), November 2016, para. 13.

873 ICC, PTC I, Al-Senussi case, 11 October 2013, para. 283, see *supra* note 544.

874 Louise Chappell and Rosemary Grey and Emily Waller, 'The Gender Justice Shadow of Complementarity: Lessons from the International Criminal Court's Preliminary Examinations in Guinea and Colombia', *The International Journal of Transitional Justice,* 2013, vol. 7, p. 464.

875 ICC, PTC I, Al-Senussi case, 11 October 2013, para. 297–308, see *supra* note 544.

876 ICC, Appeals Chamber, Al-Senussi case, 24 July 2014, para. 96, see *supra* note 107. In addition, The Appeals Chamber in its judgment insists that "a mere difference in conclusion in two cases does not in itself demonstrate unreasonableness in respect of the present appeal. In any event, the conclusion in the present case can be distinguished from that in the Gaddafi case" (para. 279). The Chamber states that "the main distinguishing factor between the two cases is the fact that the central authorities were unable to obtain Mr Gaddafi" (para. 203).

877 See: Robert Cryer, 'The ICC and its Relationship to Non-States Parties', in Carsten Stahn (ed.*), The Law And Practice of the International Criminal Court,* Oxford University Press, 2015, p. 274.

continues to face substantial difficulties in exercising its judicial powers fully across the entire territory."[878] Therefore, the Chamber concluded that the Libyan national system cannot yet be applied in full in areas or aspects relevant to the case.

3.6.2. *Situation of Unavailability of the National Judicial System*

The third scenario that makes a State unable to conduct the proceedings genuinely is unavailability. Unavailability is not a straightforward notion, and embraces a spectrum of objects.[879] Unavailability is something different from the collapse situation. It is necessary to clearly determine the scope of unavailability, because it is an exception to inadmissibility of cases, and therefore requires a narrow interpretation. Judge Song, in his dissenting opinion in the Gaddafi case, provides a definition for the term 'unavailability'. According to him, the correct interpretation of the term, "in context, and in light of the object and purpose of the Statute, is that the national judicial system is incapable of being used, which incorporates the notion of being inaccessible, in the circumstances of a particular case."[880] Unavailability refers to the normative obstacles, contrary to the collapse test, which refers to practical impediments. A contextual interpretation can be put forward to enhance this definition. The Rome Statute uses the term 'availability' in Article 88. According to this provision, States Parties "shall ensure that there are procedures available under their national law for all of the forms of cooperation which are specified under [Part 9 of the Statute]." It is submitted that "this requires not only that relevant legislation exists, but also that there are no impediments to its application, and that it is capable of producing adequate results."[881] Therefore, Article 88 of the Rome Statute suggests that unavailability connotes the normative aspects in Article 17 as well. In spite of the above-mentioned issue, the history of the Court shows some situations in which the unavailability has been used in a broader sense. For instance, the PTC in the Gaddafi case categorized the inability of the Libyan government under the title of 'unavailability', while such inability was a result of some practical restrictions. In the words of the Chamber "although the authorities for the administration of justice may exist and function in Libya, a number of legal and factual issues result in the unavailability of the national judicial system for the purpose of the case against Mr Gaddafi."[882]

By limiting unavailability to the normative incompetence, the argument of Uganda, in its referring letter, would be questionable. Uganda, in its referring letter, had said that

878 ICC, PTC I, Gaddafi case, 31 May 2013, para. 205, see *supra* note 561.

879 For instance, Stigen suggests that four factors may lead to a judicial system's classification as 'unavailable': i) inadequate legal provisions; ii) legal obstacles to the use of the system; iii) factual obstacles to the use of the system; and iv) the system's incapability of producing the desired result (see: Stigen, 2008, p. 318, see *supra* note 96).

880 ICC, Appeals Chamber, Gaddafi case, Separate Opinion of Judge Sang-Hyun Song, 21 May 2014, para. 25.

881 Stigen, 2008, p. 317, see *supra* note 96.

882 ICC, PTC I, Gaddafi case, 31 May 2013, para. 215, see *supra* note 561.

"inability in this instance does not in any way imply the total or substantial collapse of the national judicial system within the purview of Article 17(3), but merely the 'unavailability' of the system, because Uganda is unable to obtain the accused since those most responsible are either sheltered in the Sudan or in remote regions of Uganda for limited time periods."[883] However, if the judicial system of a State functions and its national law is available to proceed with the proceedings, the inability of the State to arrest the suspects at large is not inability in the meaning of Article 17(3).

3.6.2.1. Normativity of Unavailability Test

In the preparatory process, it was insisted that the unavailability concept should be clearly defined.[884] Unavailability of the domestic judicial system refers to the legal incompetency of such a system. If there is a legal barrier in way of the proceedings that have already commenced, it makes the State concerned unable to conduct the proceedings genuinely. Such unavailability is meant in connection with a specific case. The admissibility criteria pertain "ultimately to the handling of individual cases and not to the general activities of judicial systems."[885] Therefore, it is imaginable that States with a working criminal system can be found unable. Mégret sees the normative nature of unavailability scenario as a form of 'willed inability' and a failure that was planned in advance.[886] Indeed, the inability in the forms of unavailability embraces some degree of unwillingness in itself.

Unavailability includes both deficiencies in procedural and substantive law. As to procedural law, an example is difficulty in proving some crimes. It is in particular the case with respect to sexual violence and gender-based crimes. Difficult or discriminatory requirements for corroboration in relation to rape are a procedural rule that has been established within some legal systems. For instance, in some criminal legal systems, rape is proven if four men give testimonies in an accurate way and in detail.[887] In these systems, the rape victim's statement and report is not considered convincing evidence. Such unavailability of an effective evidence system may make a State unable to conduct proceedings.

As to substantive law, if national law has not criminalized a behavior consisting of ICC-identified crimes, the judicial system of the State concerned is unavailable in the meaning of Article 17. Therefore, to avoid the Court's intervention, "incorporation of the Rome Statute crimes into domestic law is necessarily, but only to the extent that existing domestic law does not cover all the conduct."[888] Although incorporation of the ICC-identified

---

883 Nouwen, 2013, p. 121, see *supra* note 226.

884 UN, Press Release, Preparatory Committee on International Criminal Court Continues Considering Complementarity between National and International Jurisdictions, 2 April 1996, accessible at: www.un.org/press/en/1996/19960402.12773.html.

885 Stigen, 2008, p. 324, see *supra* note 96.

886 Mégret, 2011, p. 380, see *supra* note 153.

887 This is the case, for instance, as to the Islamic Shari Law.

888 Nouwen, 2013, p. 41, see *supra* note 226.

crimes is not obligatory, it has some advantages that make it desirable. For instance, "an international label might draw greater attention to atrocity crimes among governments, the press and the general public."[889] In addition, qualification of international crimes conveys an impression that the underlying acts are a matter of the international community rather than solely a matter of domestic interests.[890] It also has some legal implications. For instance, a distinguishing feature of international crimes is the duty imposed upon states to ensure their prosecution.[891] In addition, statutes of limitations and blanket amnesties do not apply to core crimes. The absence of international titles from domestic criminal law might deprive some national jurisdiction of such advantages.

As discussed, under the thematic prosecution doctrine, the Prosecutor tends to select those crimes that are often under-prosecuted. It implies that national legal systems have widely ignored these crimes. This unavailability may result in the inability of states to genuinely address such crimes. Gender-based and sexual crimes are among the top priorities of the Prosecutor. So, in most of the choices made by the Prosecutor sexual crimes exist. It requires States to have a suitable legal system that is available to deal with such crimes. As to sexual crimes, the lack of substantive law may lead to unavailability. The concept of rape is a good example here. The ICC Elements of Crimes define rape in quite a broad sense. Accordingly, rape means penetration of any part of the body of victims with a sexual organ or of the anus or vagina with any object or non-sexual organs. However, "national penal codes often define rape in terms of vaginal penetration only, thereby excluding male and female victims who were raped otherwise."[892] Such a gap may result in the unavailability of the domestic legal system in prosecuting sexual crimes. Due to these wide differences, Susana Sacouto and Katherine Cleary suggest that, in the preliminary examination stage, the ICC Prosecutor should "examine a state's laws, procedures, and policies governing the investigation and prosecution of sexual violence and gender-based crimes, even where the State seems capable and willing to try other crimes."[893] As Inder states, the absence of relevant or effective legislation preventing violence against women can "conspire to create a State of unwillingness and inability to genuinely prosecute gender-based crimes."[894]

3.6.2.2. Legal Characterization: Ordinary Crimes or International Crimes

In examination of the availability of legal systems, an important question is whether the legal characterization of crimes plays a role in the admissibility assessment of

---

889 Stahn, 2013, p. 360, see *supra* note 1720.

890 Kleffner, 2008, p. 53, see *supra* note 41.

891 William A. Schabas, *Unimaginable Atrocities: Justice, Politics and Rights at the War Crimes Tribunals,* Oxford University Press, 2012, p. 40.

892 Chappell and Grey and Waller, 2013, p. 463, see *supra* note 874.

893 Sacouto and Cleary, 2009, p. 344, see *supra* note 365.

894 Women's Initiatives for Gender Justice, Gender Report Card on the International Criminal Court, November 2010, p. 42, available at: /www.iccwomen.org/news/docs/GRC10-WEB-11-10-v4_Final-version-Dec.pdf.

cases. In other words, if the legal characterizations enshrined in the Rome Statute are absent from the national law, does it make a case admissible before the Court? The Rome Statute gives an answer different from those replies provided by its counterparts in the *ad hoc* tribunals. The Statutes of the *ad hoc* tribunals explicitly reject the credibility of prosecution under the category of ordinary crimes.[895] In addition, the UNSC Resolution 827(1993) stated "all states shall take any measures necessary under their domestic law to implement the provision of the present Resolution and the Statute, including the obligations of states to comply with request for assistance or orders by a trial chamber under Article 29 of the Statute."[896] In the context of the Rule 11*bis* deferrals, the ICTR case law emphasizes the importance of the sameness between the characterization of international crimes and crimes at the domestic level. The ICTR chamber, in its decision on the Prosecutor's request for referral to the Netherlands, stated that "the tribunal only has authority to refer cases where the State will charge and convict only for those international crimes listed in its Statute as opposed to ordinary crimes such as homicide."[897] Another instance was the Bagaragaza case that was the subject of a request for deferral to states. The first request, initiated by the prosecutor, sought to remove the case to Norway. The Trial Chamber held that Norway did not have a comparable law under which to try the accused and the Appeals Chamber upheld the decision.[898] Indeed, according to the ICTR judges, Norway would only proceed on charges of murder rather than genocide. There were some arguments in favor of such a rigid attitude to the national legal systems. It was widely submitted that international crimes have some original features, in particular their massiveness. Nonetheless, ordinary crimes are incapable of representing these features well.[899]

At the ICC, denying the applicability of ordinary crimes has changed. The Rome Statute has adopted a more flexible approach to the national legal systems. The Statute obliges the states to adapt their national legislations with respect to merely two issues. First, facilitating cooperation with the Court[900], and secondly to criminalize offences

---

895 Article 10 (2)(a) of the ICTY Statute and Article 9(2)(a) of the ICTR Statute read: "A person who has been tried by a national court for acts constituting serious violations of international humanitarian law may be subsequently tried by the International Tribunal only if: (a) the act for which he or she was tried was characterized as an ordinary crime."

896 Paragraph 4.

897 ICTR, Trial Chamber III, Decision on Prosecutor's Request for Referral of the Indictment to the Kingdom of the Netherlands, 13 April 2007, para. 11.

898 ICTR, Trial Chamber III, Decision on the Prosecution Motion for Referral to the Kingdom of Norway, 12 May 2006, paras. 16–18.

899 At a panel meeting on complementarity that was organized by the CICC, it was felt that prosecuting core crimes such as murder or rape, rather than their international equivalents, is not desirable, since ordinary crimes do not represent the scope, scale and gravity of the conduct (See: Morten Bergsmo, Olymbia Bekou and Annika Jones, 'Complementarity after Kampala: Capacity Building and the ICC's Legal Tools', in Morten Bergsmo (ed.), *Active Complementarity: Legal Information Transfer*, Torkel Opshal Academic Epublisher, 2011, p. 12).

900 Article 88: "States Parties shall ensure that there are procedures available under their national law for all of the forms of cooperation which are specified under this Part."

against the ICC administration of justice.[901] The Rome Statute is to some extent non-self-executing, and does not lend itself to direct application at domestic courts.[902] It implies that the States have to enact the implementing legislation if they intend to cooperate and cooperate with the Court. Without effective national legislation, complementarity is simply a dead letter.[903] It is a principle enshrined in Article 27 of the Vienna Convention on the treaties that provides "a party may not invoke the provisions of its internal law as justification for its failure to perform a treaty." Article 70(4) of the Rome Statute, however, does not impose any obligation upon States as to the complementarity rule. In the ICTY Chamber's words, "the Statute of the ICC leaves the characterization of the crimes open to national courts."[904] PTC I, in its decision on the admissibility of the Gaddafi case, notes that "the assessment of domestic proceedings should focus on the alleged conduct and not its legal characterization."[905] The Chamber set a standard: "a domestic investigation or prosecution for 'ordinary crimes', to the extent that the case covers the same conduct, shall be considered sufficient."[906] Based on this standard, the Chamber concluded that Libya's lack of legislation criminalizing crimes against humanity does not render the case admissible before the Court.

In the case of Al-Senussi, the defendant was accused of 'persecution' before the Court. The Libyan criminal law lacks such a title, but if a crime targets people because of belonging to a specific group, it will be an aggravating factor, which is taken into account in sentencing under articles 27 and 28 of the Libyan Criminal Code. Given this fact, the Appeals Chamber of the Court acknowledged that "there is no requirement in the Statute for a crime to be prosecuted as an international crime domestically."[907] Therefore, the Chamber concluded that "the conduct underlying the crime of persecution is sufficiently covered in the Libyan proceedings so that the conduct being investigated is substantially the same as that alleged before the Court" and thereby reaffirmed the inadmissibility of the case before the Court.[908] In the words of the Appeals Chamber, "what is required is that the crimes prosecuted at the domestic level cover 'substantially the same conduct' as those charged by the Court…[I]t is the alleged conduct, as opposed to its legal characterization, that matters."[909] Later, in the Simone Gbagbo case, the domestic proceedings were ongoing. However, the Court was of the opinion that it covered different conduct. To uphold this conclusion, the Appeals Chamber stated "the PTC considered both the factual description and legal characterization of the allegations, in order to determine whether the conduct covered

---

901 Article 70 (4)(a): "Each State Party shall extend its criminal laws penalizing offences against the integrity of its own investigative or judicial process to offences against the administration of justice referred to in this article, committed on its territory, or by one of its nationals."

902 Ryngaert, 2011, p. 865, see *supra* note 483.

903 Hall, 2011, p. 1025, see *supra* note 24.

904 ICTY, Judgment, Amir Kubura case, 15 March 2006, para. 257.

905 ICC, PTC I, Gaddafi case, 31 May 2013, para. 85, see *supra* note 561.

906 Ibid., para. 88.

907 ICC, Appeals Chamber, Al-Senussi case, 24 July 2014, para. 115, see *supra* note 107.

908 Ibid., para. 122.

909 Ibid., para. 119.

by the purported domestic proceedings in Côte d'Ivoire was irrelevant to the Court's proceedings."[910] Indeed, the Chamber did not limit itself to the legal characteristics, but it took into account the substance. Heller argues that rejecting the international crime requirement and permitting States to prosecute ordinary crimes nearly fully maximizes the likelihood of prosecution and conviction, because the complexity of international crimes discourage the State to take the initiative.[911] As Rastan states, the Court is not a standard-setting body. So, "the Statute grants states broad discretion in how they wish to penalize and repress ICC crimes. That is why the admissibility test is not strict adherence to any formal set of codes contained in the Statute."[912]

The States should bring the perpetrators of ICC-identified crimes to justice. Names do not play a significant role here. It suffices that the charges at the national level are sufficiently the same to the charges within the ICC. Here, the nature is assessed rather than the legal characterization. Therefore, "investigating and prosecuting crimes under the ICC's jurisdiction as ordinary crimes is acceptable under the complementarity principle as long as the provisions render the State able genuinely to bring the perpetrator to justice."[913] It has been correctly asserted that "it seems a waste of resources for international courts to step in when national systems are active, even if the charges in a particular indictment are not international in nature."[914] The assessment of the complementarity rule is conduct-oriented. The conduct has a generic sense. Such generality does not require sameness in the legal characteristics. Such similarity is desirable but not legally necessary.

However, the national prosecution, irrespective of the characterization of crimes, should represent the nature of ICC-identified crimes. The national proceedings should deal, substantially, with the same conduct. The ICC-identified crimes are inherently wide-reaching and large. Such enormity should be enshrined in the national prosecution. It is not enough if the domestic jurisdiction merely addresses some incidental crimes. It is something that is referred to by Rastan, "while a case for the purpose of admissibility should related to the same person, it need not require symmetry in the legal qualification unless it can be shown that such characterization would deprive the alleged offense of its essential features."[915] Indeed, the national jurisdiction should indicate and show that the international crimes are prosecuted domestically. Nonetheless, it is believed that in most cases, "judging individuals for ordinary domestic crimes will be the equivalent of denying a crucial contextual and systematic aspect to their acts. Revealing a partial unwillingness to try them."[916] For this reason, incorporating the ICC-identified crimes in the national law is beneficiary.

---

910 ICC, Appeals Chamber, Simone Gbagbo case, 27 May 2015, para. 71, see *supra* note 605.
911 Heller, 2016, p. 646, see *supra* note 634.
912 Rastan, 2011, p. 449, see *supra* note 17.
913 Stigen, 2008, p. 321, see *supra* note 96.
914 Schabas, 2012, p. 43, see *supra* note 891.
915 Rastan, 2011, p. 452, see *supra* note 17.
916 Mégret, 2011, p. 384, see *supra* note 153.

The ICC will function as a model court developing international criminal law.[917] The ICC is an international law maker in the context of criminal matters. The law, policy, and practices of the Court may be followed by all states. Moreno-Ocampo refers to the impact of the ICC cases and rulings as a shadow of the law.[918] The shadow of the ICC's law is worldwide. The Court has no intention to change national jurisdictions. Instead, the states themselves adapt their domestic legal systems. It is widely accepted that the complementarity principle creates harmonization in the national criminal justice systems as to the ICC-identified crimes. In Nouwen's words, complementarity pulls, to some extent, towards international harmonization.[919] States seek to incorporate the ICC legal system into their national legal system in order to enable themselves to prosecute the ICC-identified crimes. The Resolution adopted by the Organization of African Union during the 31st Ordinary Session African Commission on Human Rights calls upon "States that have ratified the Rome Statute to rapidly incorporate it into their domestic legislation in order to be able to implement the principle of complementarity with their national courts."[920] States try to preempt the Court's intervention. During the Statute drafting process, it was assumed that states would not want to relinquish jurisdiction under complementarity, therefore they would reinforce their domestic ability to prosecute international crimes.[921] Nonetheless, it is a choice for States. If they decide not to intervene, the ICC is not powerful enough to force them to do something.

The most visible impact of the complementarity scheme has been considered to be its effect on domestic legislation.[922] Without sufficiency in the legislative capacity, states are not able to combat international crimes. Having legislation in place is the first step and priority in ending impunity and constitutes a means of materializing the application of complementarity.[923] In the words of the UNSG, "Efforts must be made to implement the full architecture of the Rome Statute, inducing Rules of Procedure and Evidence, Elements of Crimes, witness assistance and reparation and gender advisors."[924] States see the legislative implementation as a safeguard against ICC intervention.[925] Generally speaking, a gap in domestic law may increase the need for international intervention.[926] The Uruguayan explanatory memorandum, accompanying the draft ICC implementation law, states that "it is not possible to exercise the principle of complementarity if the crimes within the jurisdiction of the

917 Stigen, 2008, p. 14, see *supra* note 96.

918 Moreno-Ocampo, 2011, p. 21, see *supra* note 1.

919 Sarah Nouwen, 'Complementarity in Uganda: Domestic Diversity or International Imposition?', in Carsten Stahn and Mohamed M. El Zeidy (eds.), *The International Criminal Court and Complementarity: From Theory to Practice*, Cambridge University Press, 2011, p. 1150.

920 Resolution on the Ratification of the Statute of the International Criminal Court by OAU Member States, May 2002, available at: www.achpr.org/sessions/31st/resolutions/59/.

921 Mégret, 2011, p. 365, see *supra* note 153.

922 Stahn, 2008, p. 100, see *supra* note 486.

923 Bergsmo, Bekou and Jones, 2011, p. 12, see *supra* note 899.

924 UN, Report of the UN Secretary-General, The Rule of Law and Transitional Justice in Conflict and Post-Conflict Societies, 11 October 2011, para. 23.

925 Kleffner, 2008, p. 337, see *supra* note 41.

926 Bergsmo, Bekou and Jones, 2011, p. 1059, see *supra* note 899.

Court do not constitute at the same time, punishable conducts within the scope of the jurisdiction of national judges."[927]

4. AVAILABILITY OF SITUATIONS

The body of literature on the ICC situation and case selection has largely focused on the admissibility issue. Gravity and complementarity have been matters for considerable debate inside and outside of the Court. Various admissibility challenges have enriched the jurisprudence of the Court. Considerable efforts have been devoted to developing and clarifying the admissibility requirement in order to organize the situation and case selection at the ICC. The Prosecutor of the Court and its Judges, in addition to scholars and commentators have developed and interpreted the process and criteria of the situation and case selection to enhance consistency, transparency and coherency at the ICC's selectivity. In spite of all these efforts aiming to legalize and legitimize the Prosecutor's selections, what finally shapes the Court's choices is not a legal consideration. Both situation and case selection consists of two functions: selection and prioritization. The admissibility requirement under Article 17 is a statutory threshold for both selection and prioritization. A situation should be sufficiently grave and should not be investigated at the domestic level to be declared admissible before the Court. However, because of the selectivity of the Court, situations are prioritized based on their gravity. In conducting an investigation, prioritization should be given to the situation that has more gravity in comparison with other grave situations. However, being admissible under Article 17 is not a sufficient condition to initiate an investigation. In addition to being admissible, a situation should be available to warrant an investigation. Availability is a major factor in prioritizing situations and cases.

Paragraph 51 of OTP Policy Paper on Case Selection and Prioritization suggests 'operational factors' as a major consideration that should be taken into account in the case prioritization, "to ensure that the Office focuses on cases in which it appears that it can conduct an effective and successful investigation leading to a prosecution reasonable prospect of conviction."[928] The Policy Paper introduces four categories of operational factors: a) the quantity and quality of evidence already in the possession of the Office; b) international cooperation and judicial assistance to support the Office's activities; c) the Office's capacity to effectively conduct the necessary investigations within a reasonable period of time, including the security situation in the area where the Office is planning to operate or where persons cooperating with the Office reside; and d) the potential to secure the appearance of suspects before the Court, either by arrest, surrender or pursuant to a summons.[929] These various factors "stand in no

[927] See: Kleffner, 2008, p. 335, see *supra* note 41.

[928] ICC, OTP, Policy Paper on Case Selection and Prioritization, para. 51.

[929] Ibid.

hierarchical order to each other. The specific weight to be given to each individual criterion will depend on the circumstances of each case."[930]

The Policy Paper brings to light that what, at the end, activates the Court's jurisdiction over a case are operational factors. Introducing these non-legal factors should be seen as a welcome development. Operational factors refer to practical limitations and restrictions of the Court. By recognizing the outside reality, the Court will be able to manage its authorities and obligations in a more reasonable way, in addition to expectation management. Operational factors make cases in sequence based on their availability. Prioritizing based on operational factors is not a substantive and value-oriented task. Here, the Prosecutor prioritizes a case that has a bright prospect of success in trial. A case that more likely reaches a conviction, in the eyes of the Prosecutor, should be given priority over a case without such a prospect, even if the latter has more gravity than the former in terms of its nature or scale. This consideration offers a new vision and perspective to the prosecutorial discretion. In addition to the admissibility of a case or situation, availability also matters. One example showing the effects of operational factors is the DRC situation. In this situation, the Court initially targeted Ituri, while there were reports of the commission of serious crimes having been committed in the provinces of Ituri, North and South Kivu. Focusing on Ituri was seen as a strategic decision arising from better security conditions for conducting an investigation in Ituri thanks to the presence of UN peacekeepers in the region.[931] In other words, the Ituri crisis was more available.

Incorporating the operational and practical factors in the situation and case selection sounds not to be just, but it is inevitable. The Prosecutor is mainly dependent on the State's cooperation to further her investigations. As the former Prosecutor of the Court has said, "the ICC is independent and interdependent at the same time."[932] Even if the Court is prepared to initiate an investigation into a situation, it is not able to reach its goal without State cooperation. Bosco, in his remarkable book, describes that the first Prosecutor of the Court, from the outset, had adopted a policy to not confront the powerful states across the world in order to benefit from their support and cooperation, in order to fulfill the Court's mandates that resulted in "an exceptionally cautious court that even skeptical major powers can tolerate and to a degree support."[933] The Court's history indicates that the absence of State's cooperation leads to the Prosecutor's failure to further her cases. For instance, the Prosecutor lacked Kenya's cooperation to obtain the relevant evidence. Eventually, such non-cooperation enforced the Prosecutor to withdraw all charges in all cases within the Kenyan situation due to the lack of

---

930 Ibid., para. 52.

931 Payam Akhavan, 'Are International Criminal Tribunals a Disincentive to Peace?: Reconciling Judicial Romanticism with Political Realism', *Human Rights Quarterly*, 2009, vol. 31, p. 631.

932 ICC, OTP, Moreno-Ocampo's Statement Made at the Ceremony for the Solemn Undertaking of the Chief Prosecutor of the ICC, June 16 2003.

933 Bosco, 2014, p. 20, see *supra* note 391.

evidence.[934] Another example is the Darfur situation. Owing to the absence of practical support, the Prosecutor has not managed to deliver justice yet.[935] Priority should be given to those situations that enjoy a greater prospect of success. If the Prosecutor initiates an investigation but fails to conduct it, such a consequence hurts the credibility of the Court. A court that is famous for its failures loses its deterrent effect over time, and its voice is not heard anymore.

Availability has not been referred to in the Rome Statute. However, the Prosecutor has established this notion based on her interpretation of Article 54 of the Rome Statute that specifies the Duties and powers of the Prosecutor with respect to investigations. According to Paragraph 1 (b) of Article 54, the Prosecutor shall "take appropriate measures to ensure the effective investigation and prosecution of crimes within the jurisdiction of the Court." The opening part of this paragraph obliges the Prosecutor to ensure the effectiveness of her investigations and prosecutions. The Court should preserve its reputation by conducting efficient and effective investigations and prosecutions. It should not hurt its legitimacy by representing a failed and fragile Court. To reach such a goal, a case or situation should be available, taking into account operational factors that are needed for conducting an investigation or situation. The Court functions selectively and in an exemplary manner, but it has to function first.

However, it does not mean that the Prosecutor should succumb to the political interests of the states. If State cooperation is seen as the only factor to select a situation or case, the result will be a selective justice without justification. It is obvious that States prefer to direct the Court in a way that does not hurt their interests. Therefore, it may result in intentional non-cooperation in order to defeat the Prosecutor. In addition, the operational considerations may motivate culprits to hold power to make the investigation of the Court difficult, and consequently, to terminate a case due to unavailability. To avoid such a consequence, the insistence should be put on preliminary examinations instead of the investigations. Operational factors, including State cooperation, are factors that should be taken into account regarding initiating of an investigation. Those factors, however, do not affect opening a preliminary examination. Upon conducting the preliminary examination, if the Prosecutor determines that the priority should not be given to the situation in which the chance of success is low, the Prosecutor may avoid initiating an investigation, but they must proceed with the preliminary examination activities. During this preliminary phase, the Prosecutor has

[934] On 5 April 2016, the Trial Chamber V of the ICC by majority decided to terminate the case against William Ruto and Arap Sang. Already, on 13 March 2015, the Trial Chamber had terminated the proceedings against Kenyatta.

[935] The need for State cooperation is not limited to the ICC. In the ICTY, there are some instances showing that the Prosecutor of the ICTY had to not continue with a case due to non-availability of evidence because to non-cooperation of other actors. For instance, as to the case of NATO air campaign, Den Ponte curtailed her investigation. She had said that "I quickly concluded that it was impossible to investigate NATO, because NATO and its member States would not cooperate with us. They would not provide us access to the files and documents" (Carle Del Ponte, *Madame Prosecutor: Confrontations with Humanity's Worst Criminals and the Culture of Impunity: A Memoir*, Other Press, 2009, page 60).

an opportunity to explain that non-investigation is a result of non-cooperation. They can follow public diplomacy and outreach activities to preserve the legitimacy of the Court, and to promote and encourage States to cooperate with the Court. The Situation Selection Document and the Case Selection Document are useful tools here.

The Case Selection Document lists all selected cases for investigation and prosecution among the provisional case hypotheses, and it "will also be used to prioritize cases."[936] Although this Document has been suggested by the Prosecutor in view of the case selection, this mechanism could be used in the situational phase too. Indeed, besides the Case Selection Document, a Situation Selection Document should be designed by the Prosecutor. The content of the Document is dynamic, and "will be reviewed and updated accordingly."[937] Whatever is included in the Document necessarily has passed the gravity threshold as the admissibility rule. In the Document, however, the cases are organized in sequence and order. The case with top priority will be prosecuted first. The number of cases that could be given priority is determined taking into account 'the basic size', that determines the number of cases and situations that should be dealt with by the Prosecutor in a period of time. Therefore, the Situation and Case Selection Documents "will also inform decisions on the appropriate number of cases to be pursued within any given situation, whether to proceed with further cases, or whether to end its involvement in a situation."[938]

In the latest Strategic Plan, the OTP has insisted that an essential shift in strategy of the Office has been made to improve the quality and efficiency of the Office's work, namely, prioritizing quality of work over quantity by focusing resources on fewer cases.[939] The Office mentions that this strategy, besides the wide limitations of the Court, lead to an undesirable result: "some necessary investigations have had to be postponed", and consequently, "this has impacted on the Office's ability to react to ongoing crimes; negatively influenced the perception of the Office."[940] It has forced the Prosecutor to design and propose the 'basic size' to prevent an overreach of the Office and to make the Office more predictable, however, the Prosecutor admits that "even with the proposed basic size, the Office will still need to priorities amongst its cases."[941] By drawing the Case Selection Document, the expressive function of the Court is fulfilled too. It meets, largely, the expectations by showing that the Court has done something. The first Prosecutor of the Court in 2006 adopted a policy known as

936 ICC, OTP, Policy Paper on Case Selection and Prioritization, para. 11.

937 Ibid., para. 10.

938 Ibid., para. 12.

939 ICC, OTP, Strategic Plan (2016–2018), para. 1.

940 Ibid., para. 5. In addition, the Strategic Plan insists that "notwithstanding these resource increases, the Office still faces a gap between needs and means. The Office rightly prioritizes quality over quantity of work. However, faced with resource constraints, the Office has had to make difficult decisions by not starting certain investigations or placing others on hold. This has damaged the Office's ability to respond to evolving situations (e.g. Libya, Darfur, Mali), and impacted negatively in terms of perception (e.g. delay in investigating both sides in Côte d'Ivoire)" (para. 44).

941 Ibid., para. 7.

the 'sequenced approach to selection', "whereby cases inside the situation are selected according to their gravity."[942] This sequence approach, instead of a simultaneous one, has some side effects because it may hurt the impartiality of prosecutions. However, through the Case Selection Document the Prosecutor can cope with this problem. The Document can show all those cases that are awaiting prosecution. Such an approach secures the impartiality of the Court. To realize such a goal requires that the Document will be publicized. Nonetheless, the Case Selection Policy Paper explicitly expresses the confidentiality of the Document.[943] With such a feature, the Case Selection or the Situation Selection Document is unable to serve the expressive mandates of the Court.

It should be noted that prioritization is a dynamic process. In the Prosecutor's word, "Prioritization governs the process by which cases that meet selection criteria are rolled-out over time."[944] If circumstances surrounding a case change, its priority in the Case selection document therefore changes. Hence, the Office "shall continuously re-evaluate, based on the same criteria, whether it can continue to conduct the necessary investigations leading to a prosecution with a reasonable prospect of conviction."[945] If it appears to the Office at any given point in time that the Office is not able to continue with a situation or case that has already been prioritized, "the Office may decide to deprioritize and postpone the investigation of that case until conditions have improved." In addition, the Office may reconsider "such a decision if the circumstances have changed favorably, including the extent to which the Office has been able to overcome any operational obstacle(s) to conducting an effective investigation."[946] Indeed, deprioritization is another side of the prioritization coin. However, the mechanism of deprioritization needs more clarification. For instance, it is not clear that if the Court issues an arrest warrant against a suspect, and later it is known that the Court is unable to arrest the wanted person, the Prosecutor will have to deprioritize the selected case.[947]

This Chapter shows that taking into account the reality is an indispensable factor in the ICC situation selection regime. There are some statutory and legal factors that direct the Prosecutor in selecting a situation or case, but these legal factors do not have the final say. Practical and operational factors and considerations substantially affect the Prosecutor's choices. It per se shows that the expectations about the ICC should live up to realities surrounding this institution.

942 ICC, OTP, Statement of the Prosecutor of the International Criminal Court, Mr. Moreno-Ocampo to the UN Security Council pursuant to UNSCR 1593 (2005), 14 June 2006, p. 2.

943 ICC, OTP, Policy Paper on Case Selection and Prioritization, para. 15.

944 Ibid., para. 48.

945 Ibid., para. 53.

946 Ibid.

947 See: Mohamamd Hadi Zakerhossein, Comments on the ICC OTP'S Draft Policy Paper on case Selection and Prioritization, 29 March 2016, available at: justicehub.org/article/comments-icc-otps-draft-policy-paper-case-selection-and-prioritisation.

CHAPTER III
INTERESTS OF JUSTICE

Upon declaring a situation admissible and available for conducting an effective investigation, the Prosecutor approaches the end of the preliminary examination. However, it is not yet the end of the road of the situation selection. The last criterion that should be taken into account before the Prosecutor decides to select a situation is the interests of justice presumption. Article 53(1)(c) of the Rome Statute obliges the Prosecutor to consider whether "taking into account the gravity of the crime and the interests of victims, there are nonetheless substantial reasons to believe that an investigation would not serve the interests of justice." Introducing the interests of justice notion provides the Prosecutor with "an enormous scope for what amounts to a highly discretionary determination."[948] The Prosecutorial discretion is not limited to select a specific situation, but it includes her discretion to reject other situations. Therefore, the judgment of the ICC as legitimate and credible depends also on the lack of its Prosecutor's discretion to initiate an investigation.[949] The interests of justice presumption under Article 53 has some remarkable features that make this concept unique in the situation selection process. The Prosecutor of the Court holds that the issue of the interests of justice represents "one of the most complex aspects of the treaty."[950] The current chapter closes the substantive part of studying the situation selection by shedding light on the meaning and effects of the interests of justice concept in the Rome Statute. The interests of justice presumption is, however, applicable to the case selection process too. A case is selected for prosecution if its selection does not have any countervailing effects on the interests of justice.

In this Chapter, the interest of justice presumption as a factor that plays a prominent role in the situation selection regime will be discussed to provide a better understanding of this notion.

---

948 Schabas, p. 660, see *supra* note 20.

949 Stigen, 2008, p. 412, see *supra* note 96.

950 ICC, OTP, Policy Paper on the Interests of Justice, 2007, p2.

1. EXCEPTIONALITY OF THE INTERESTS OF JUSTICE REQUIREMENT

The OTP has designed four phases in the preliminary examination.[951] Phase 1, according to the OTP Policy Paper on preliminary Examinations, aims at preventing those situations which are manifestly outside of the Court's jurisdiction to be examined. Phase 2 entails assessing the jurisdiction of the Court. Phase 3 examines the admissibility requirement. The last phase deals with the statutory requirement of the interests of justice. When a situation reaches the threshold of Phase 4, it implies that the given situation has already crossed the high threshold of other strict and special requirements, namely jurisdiction, admissibility and availability. The ICC is highly selective. The limited recourses of the Court can mobilize only a few investigations and prosecutions. These limitations have resulted in setting up many conditions that should be observed when the Prosecutor selects a situation for investigation in order to secure the best possible choice. Until Phase 4, the Prosecutor examines a situation to determine if there is a reasonable basis to initiate an investigation. By then, there is a presumption against conducting an investigation and prosecution. Indeed, at the ICC doing an investigation is the exception, not the rule.[952] All the statutory requirements should be met if an investigation is going to be started. The Court, as a last resort mechanism, intervenes only in the exceptional circumstances. The jurisdictional parameters enshrined in the Rome Statute ban many potential situations and cases from arriving at the ICC's agenda. Jurisdiction, however, is merely a starting point. Even if a situation falls within the jurisdiction of the Court, there is the admissibility requirement that should be met. When a situation is declared admissible, it means that such a situation is sufficiently grave. The gravity of a situation is something extra to the inherent gravity of the ICC-identified crimes that are committed in the context of the given situation. The gravity as the admissibility rule uncovers the exceptionality of circumstances that warrant the Court's intervention. It leads to establishing a strong presumption in favor of initiating an investigation where the threshold of sufficient gravity is met.[953] In addition to the gravity test, the complementarity rule directs the Prosecutor to determine whether there is no genuine action at the domestic level. Otherwise, the Prosecutor has to defer to the national jurisdictions that are able and willing to deal with a situation. In addition, before Phase 4, the Prosecutor shall determine whether the given situation is available, too. Availability means that the practical and operational features, that are usually absent, are in place to facilitate conducting an effective investigation or prosecution.

In spite of satisfying all these rigid conditions, a grave situation under the jurisdiction of the Court and available for taking further steps may still fail to be investigated. If the selection of a situation does not serve the interests of justice, the

951 ICC, OTP, Policy Paper on preliminary Examination.

952 Schabas, 2010, p. 661, see *supra* note 20.

953 ICC, OTP, Policy Paper on the Interests of Justice, p. 5.

Prosecutor is banned from initiating an investigation. In the context of Phase 4, a new presumption in favor of investigation and prosecution is established. When the statutory conditions to initiate an investigation are not met yet, the rule is non-investigation. This presumption requires the Prosecutor to conduct a preliminary examination to assure that there is a reasonable basis to begin an investigation. Nonetheless, when the criteria enshrined in Article 53 have been met, in the normal course of event, the Prosecutor should conduct an investigation. However, in the exceptional circumstances a situation, which would otherwise qualify for selection by the OTP, may not be pursued, because the Prosecutor finds that it does not serve the interests of justice.[954] Indeed, the interests of justice notion is an exception that nullifies those exceptional circumstances that warrant the Court's intervention. In other words, the interests of justice test is a countervailing requirement.[955] It nullifies the appropriateness and the necessity of the Court's investigation and prosecution. This concept may pause the Court's operation at the last minute.

Another sign of the exceptionality of the interests of justice presumption is its relevant evidentiary threshold. The preliminary examination is conducted on the reasonable basis standard. However, the lack of the interests of justice presumption should be determined based on the substantial reasons test. The procedure law of the Court has established various evidentiary thresholds regarding different stages at the ICC. Each stage has a different standard of proof because of its own function and features. In the preliminary examination, the standard of proof is low, because it is a preliminary stage. The scale and scope of the available information in this phase is narrow, thus, it warrants a low evidentiary threshold. However, even in the preliminary examination stage, reasonableness differs from substantiality. In the Rome Statute, the 'substantial reasons' notion has not been defined, but the case law has provided a definition in another occasion. 'Substantiality' is required when the Prosecutor examines whether there are substantial grounds to believe that the person committed the crime charged in the confirmation of charges hearing (Article 61 of the Rome Statute). The evidentiary standard applicable at this stage of proceedings has been defined in the jurisprudence of the Court. According to the Judges, in the confirmation hearing, the Prosecutor needs to offer "concrete and tangible proof demonstrating a clear line of reasoning underpinning [her] specific allegations" in order to provide sufficient grounds.[956]

In addition, the Appeals Chamber of the Court has clarified that in the confirmation hearing, PTCs may evaluate ambiguities, inconsistencies and contradictions in the evidence or doubts as to the credibility of evidence to avoid "risk of cases proceeding to trial although the evidence is so riddled with ambiguities, inconsistencies,

954 Ibid., p. 1.

955 Ibid., p. 2.

956 ICC, PTC I, Al-Mahdi case, Decision on the Confirmation of Charges Against Ahmad Al Faqi Al Mahdi, 24 March 2016, para. 18. And, ICC, PTC II, Decision on the Confirmation of Charges Against Dominic Ongwen, 23 March 2016, para. 17.

contradictions or doubts as to credibility."[957] Therefore, substantiality requires not only a reasonable probability (reasonableness), but there should be reasons enhancing the chosen probability. In other words, the substantiality test requires that a reasonable probability be enhanced and supported by concrete and tangible proof, in addition to being protected from contradictory reasons. Indeed, the selected probability should outweigh its rivals. Such an interpretation can be used to determine the definition of the substantial reasons in the interests of justice requirement, too. Here, the necessity of non-prosecution should be reasonable. However, it is a necessary condition, but not a sufficient one. The probability that an investigation does not serve the interests of justice should be reasonable, but there should be supporting reasons in place. Here, a degree of objectivity is needed. The interests of victims and justice should be subject to concrete and tangible threats and risks by the Court's intervention. Here, an objective assessment is necessary, and a mere speculation is not sufficient.

The interests of justice concept is an exception in exceptions. It declares per se the importance of those interests and values that can stop the Court's intervention. Only something extremely crucial can barricade the way of the Court to go further. Such an affair should be more valuable than the value of prosecution. To determine what can have such a countervailing effect on the Court's proceedings, a narrow approach should be adopted that is consistent with the exceptionality of the interests of justice. This feature directs to lives of victims and their physical and mental safety and well-being whose value may outweigh the prosecution's value.

2. DISTINCTION FROM THE ADMISSIBILITY REQUIREMENT

When the Prosecutor examines the interests of justice requirement, it implies that the admissibility of the given situation has already been evaluated. The interests of justice condition needs to be considered where "positive determinations have been made on both jurisdiction and admissibility."[958] Therefore, there is no need to duplicate the examination of those criteria that have been satisfied. In the preliminary examination, each phase has a dividing line with other stages. Nonetheless, in the literature some traces of confusion between the interests of justice and the admissibility requirement are visible. Some believe that the interests of justice presumption aims at providing the Prosecutor with some leeway in situations where "a relevant State opts to employ non-prosecutorial responses to mass violence such as truth commissions."[959] Nevertheless, it seems that such a view has not emanated from a correct point. The question under

957 ICC, Appeals Chamber, Mbarushimana case, Judgment on the Appeal of the Prosecutor Against the Decision of Pre-Trial Chamber I of 16 December 2011 Entitled Decision on the Confirmation of Charges, 30 May 2012, para. 46.

958 ICC, OTP, Policy Paper on the Interests of Justice, p. 2.

959 De Guzman, 2008, p. 1412, see *supra* note 274.

Article 53 does not revolve around a comparison between prosecution at the ICC and alternative mechanisms at the domestic level to see which one serves better the interests of victims and justice. Rather, the question is whether prosecution at the ICC serves the interests of justice due to the adverse effects it may have on victims' interests. The Rome Statute does not accept non-criminal mechanisms as an alternative to the Court's intervention under the complementarity rule.

Modern international criminal law has witnessed two major responses to mass atrocities: criminal and alternative mechanisms, such as truth commissions or traditional mechanisms such as the Rwandan Gacaca courts.[960] Establishing the ICC has been grounded on the idea that justice has priority over the alternative or traditional mechanisms. The preamble of the Rome Statute defines the ending impunity as one of the constituent objectives of the Court. It makes clear that the drafters have expressed a strong preference for prosecution.[961] By ratifying the Statute, States Parties to the Court have accepted the precedence of prosecution enshrined in the Rome Statute. At the ICC system, however, alternative mechanisms are accepted but as complementary measures. At the ICC, retributive justice and restorative justice "ultimately have similar goals and can benefit from each other."[962] The coordination and cooperation between the ICC and alternative mechanisms could lead to a division of labor. Mechanisms such as truth commissions may investigate crimes committed by subordinates while the ICC should investigate crimes committed by leaders.[963] Moreover, regarding the interests of justice requirement, alternative mechanisms may play a role. As will be discussed, if the interests of victims require the Prosecutor not to initiate an investigation, at least, an alternative mechanism should be in place in order to avoid an absolute impunity.

The gravity is another pillar of the admissibility requirement, which is assessed in Phase 3 of the preliminary examination. However, some confuse the interests of justice concept for the gravity requirement. For instance, Wouters states that the Prosecutor has to reexamine the criterion of gravity of the crime in light of the interests of justice.[964] Nevertheless, this interpretation makes the interests of justice concept redundant. The interests of justice notion has an independent meaning and function. The gravity as the admissibility rule is a factor to select a situation for investigation, whereas the interests of justice test is a factor to rebuff a situation.

In addition, some writers have defined a task for the interests of justice requirement, while it is not consistent with the constituent objective of this notion. There is no way to evade from considering the operational factors and practical considerations at the

960 See: Anne-Marie de Brouwer and Ruvebana, 'The Legacy of the Gacaca Courts in Rwanda: Survivors' Views', *International Criminal Law Review*, 2013, vol. 13, 937–976.

961 Elizabeth B. Ludwin King, 'Does Justice Always Require Prosecution? The International Criminal Court and Transitional Justice Measures', *The George Washington International Law Review*, 2013, vol. 45, p. 106.

962 Thomas Hethe Clark, 'The Prosecutor of the International Criminal Court, Amnesties and the Interests of Justice: Striking a Delicate Balance', *Washington University Global Studies Law Review*, 2005, vol. 4, p. 407.

963 Safferling, 2012, p. 98, see *supra* note 843.

964 Wouter, Verhoeven and Demeyere, 2008, p. 297, see *supra* note 374.

ICC's operation. Since this category of factors is not explicitly referred to by the Rome Statute, some have categorized them under the interests of justice requirement, in order to enable the Prosecutor to give considerations to those factors.[965] In this sense, the interests of justice notion is called 'relative gravity', in contrast with the 'legal gravity' under Article 17.[966] However, it does not sound like a good way to fill the gap in the Rome Statute about the operational factors in the situation selection process. The interests of justice concept has its specific functions. Operational factors are a matter of admissibility that plays a role in the situation prioritization process. As mentioned, the Prosecutor has accepted the applicability of operational factors in the case selection process. The prospect of an effective prosecution is a ground on which the applicability of operational factors work. A situation and case should be both admissible and available. For initiating an investigation, the interests of justice are taken into account after examining operational factors. Operational factors have no determinate space in the procedure and structure of the Court, but the Prosecutor has correctly put them in the admissibility phase. When a situation is not available, there is no need to examine the interests of justice requirements, since such a situation falls out of the priorities of the Prosecutor to initiate an investigation. If there is no chance for investigation, there is no need to explore a countervailing factor. The interests of justice presumption surfaces when a situation or case is available for doing an investigation or prosecution. If a situation is not available, there is no need to see if the Court's intervention may result in adverse effects. It should be borne in mind that the interests of justice notion acts as a last resort matter.

3. NECESSITY OF EXAMINATION

In selecting a situation, the Prosecutor shall prove that a situation falls within the ICC's jurisdiction and is admissible. The existence of these requirements needs proof. By contrast, the Prosecutor does not need to prove that conducting an investigation into the given situation serves the interests of justice. Generally speaking, prosecuting the most serious crimes of concern to the international community serves the interests of justice, and this is the presumption on which criminal tribunals are grounded. Paragraph C of Article 53(1) of the Rome Statute uses the term 'nonetheless'. It shows that the interests of justice notion is an exception to a rule. Logically, the existence of exceptions needs to be proved, not their inexistence. The Prosecutor is exempted from demonstrating that the Court's investigation or prosecution serve the interests of justice. Nonetheless, despite the fact that this rule is exceptionable, the Prosecutor must explore the possibility of the existence of an exception. It resembles the dual functions of the Prosecutor in collecting the evidence. At the ICC, the accused enjoys a

965 Kai Ambos, The Colombian Peace Process and the Principle of Complementarity of the International Criminal Court: An Inductive, Situation-based Approach, Springer, 2010, p. 51.
966 De Guzman, 2008, p. 1413, see *supra* note 274.

strong presumption of innocence.[967] However, the Prosecutor is obliged to "investigate incriminating and exonerating circumstances equally" simultaneously.[968] It is similar to the Prosecutor's statutory obligation to inspect the circumstances showing that an investigation does not serve justice, while there is a presumption in favor of conducting such an investigation.

The Rome Statute acknowledges that in some exceptional circumstances, the Court's intervention might not serve the interests of justice. In these circumstances, the interests of justice presumption has a countervailing effect. It means that if an investigation does not serve the interests of justice, the Prosecutor shall refrain from pursuing the given situation. It is ultra vires if the Prosecutor continues, while the interests of justice are in danger. To avoid this situation, the Prosecutor shall explore all exceptions to assure that her initiative is without adverse effects on the interests of justice. Therefore, the Rome Statute obliges the Prosecutor to examine the interests of justice presumption to determine whether exceptionally there are substantial reasons pressing her not to initiate an investigation. For this reason, in the case of communications, when PTCs are asked by the Prosecutor to issue an authorization for an investigation, the Judges should be satisfied that the Prosecutor has adequately examined the potentials that may make her believe that the investigation does not serve the interests of justice.

The jurisprudence of the Court shows that the PTCs' Judges have departed from their initial tendency not to delve into the interests of justice presumption. In both situations in Kenya and Côte d'Ivoire, the judges did not examine the interests of justice provision seriously, but in the situation in Georgia a new approach was adopted. Initially, in the situations in Kenya and Côte d'Ivoire, where the first Prosecutor had applied to the Chambers for an authorization to initiate an investigation, the Prosecutor's application did not elaborate how he had determined that there were not substantial reasons to believe that the interests of justice was not in danger. The Prosecutor had firstly stated that "Prosecutor is not required to establish that an investigation is in the interests of justice, but rather, whether there are specific circumstances which provide substantial reasons to believe it is not in the interests of justice to do so at that time."[969] Based on this understanding, the Prosecutor had just mentioned that "based on the available information, the Prosecutor has no reason to believe that the opening of an investigation into the situation would not be in the interests of justice."[970] The PTCs did not delve into the issue neither. They insisted that the judicial overview is exercised only when the Prosecutor decides that an investigation would not be in the interests of justice.[971] They went further and added that "the Prosecutor does not have to

---

967 Article 66 (1) of the Rome Statute: "everyone shall be presumed innocent until proved guilty before the Court in accordance with the applicable law."

968 Article 54.1(a) of the Rome Statute.

969 ICC, PTC III, Situation in Côte d'Ivoire, 3 October 2011, para. 59, see *supra* note 3.

970 ICC, PTC II, Kenya situation, 31 March 2010, para. 61, see *supra* note 33. And, ICC, PTC III, Situation in Côte d'Ivoire, 3 October 2011, para. 60, see *supra* note 3.

971 ICC, PTC II, Kenya situation, 31 March 2010, para. 63, see *supra* note 33. And, ICC, PTC III, Situation in Côte d'Ivoire, 3 October 2011, para. 207, see *supra* note 3.

present reasons or supporting material in this respect."[972] Indeed, there was a common understanding between the Prosecutor and the Judges about the dormant nature of the interests of justice presumption. The then Prosecutor had not provided the Chambers with materials showing that he had assessed the interests of justice requirement, and the Chambers did not ask him to provide more information, since the issue of the interests of justice was not awakened by the Prosecutor.

Later, in the situation in Georgia, the new Prosecutor of the Court made a change and offered more insight into the process of considering the interests of justice presumption. In her application for an authorization to initiate an investigation into the situation in Georgia, the Prosecutor referred to the views of victims who had supported the Prosecutor's investigation. The Prosecutor stated that the victims had manifested "their interests in seeing justice done in various ways."[973] The Prosecutor then explained how she had sought to ascertain victims' interests "through direct consultations with organizations representing victims in Georgia as well as through an examination of communications and publicly available information."[974] One indicator of the victims' demand for an investigation, in the eyes of the Prosecutor, was the large amount of communications.[975] In addition, the Prosecutor put insistence on the role of the civil society. According to the Prosecutor's Request, "Georgian human rights organizations representing victims have in consultations with, communications to the Prosecution and public reports repeatedly stressed the desire of victims who have survived the August 2008 conflict to restore justice."[976]

Given communications from the victims, in addition to the consultations with organizations representing victims or knowledgeable of the interests of victims, the Prosecution stated she had not received "views that the interests of justice would not be served by an investigation into the situation in Georgia."[977] In assessing the Prosecutor's application, the PTC I gave considerations to the victims' interests and stated "taking into account the representations of victims, received under Article 15(3) of the Statute, which overwhelmingly speak in favor of the opening of an investigation, the Chamber considers that there are indeed no substantial reasons to believe that an investigation would not serve the interests of justice."[978] However, it should be noted that the Prosecutor needs to adopt effective and various measures to ensure the generality of the interests of justice assessment. The Prosecutor needs to use those sources that are impartial and neutral about prosecution or non-prosecution to be able to represent the victims' needs and views well. Generally speaking, the international

972 ICC, PTC II, Kenya situation, 31 March 2010, para. 63, see *supra* note 33. And, ICC, PTC III, Situation in Côte d'Ivoire, 3 October 2011, para. 207, see *supra* note 3.
973 ICC, OTP, Georgia situation, Request for Authorization of an Investigation Pursuant to Article 15, 13 October 2015, para. 338.
974 Ibid.
975 Ibid., para. 340.
976 Ibid., para. 341.
977 Ibid., para. 343.
978 ICC, PTC I, Georgia situation, 27 January 2016, para. 58, see *supra* note 330.

human rights NGOs tend to stick to criminal justice instead of peace. This requires the Prosecutor to hear other voices by extending her sources. Local NGOs or missions could be an option.

4. A CONCEPT WITHOUT DEFINITION

The interests of justice concept is left without definition and clarification in the Rome Statute. It is understandable that a concept such as the interests of justice with considerable effects but without a clue provokes challenges and divergences. However, the silence in the Rome Statute regarding the interests of justice notion is intentional. The founders of the ICC deliberately decided to leave the interests of justice notion open to the ensuing interpretations. There were some reasons persuading the drafters of the Statute not to delve into the notion of the interests of justice. Firstly, it was a pragmatic choice to pave the way to concluding the Rome Statute. The interests of justice concept and the issues arising from it were quite challenging from the outset. It provoked hot debates in the preparatory process. There would not have been a prospect for arrival at an agreement and consensus if the drafters had decided to elaborate the concept. From one side, some believed in the absoluteness of criminal justice, and did not agree with any exception. On the other, some advocated the necessity of exceptions for the Court's intervention if the interests of justice would require so. For instance, the United States circulated a 'non-paper' using the truth commissions as a model for allowing the prosecutor to defer to an amnesty. However, the proposal, motivated strong opposition from NGOs and did not appeal the States' delegations.[979] It became evident that arrival at an agreement on the opposite ends of the spectrum was not feasible. Therefore, the drafters decided to find a compromise.

Arrival at compromises was a tactic that was widely deployed by the Court's founders in order to make the conclusion of the Statute possible. At the Rome Conference, it was a cost that needed to be paid to obtain more benefits. It is in particular the case regarding the interests of justice notion. The term 'interests of justice' has been used in different parts of the Rome Statute. Schabas asserts that the expression is used where there is "the need for discretion and the inability of legal texts to codify answers for difficult issues."[980] The interests of justice concept as a barrier of prosecution was recognized, but its meaning and conditions remained indeterminate. The drafters did not shoulder the responsibility for defining the term, but put it on the shoulder of the Court in the future. The ambiguity surrounding some notions such as the interests of justice in the Rome Statute has been constructive. It constituted the Court by making it possible to be agreed on, and it also constitutes and develops international criminal law by giving space to the judicial interpretation to respond questions. International criminal law is

979 Enneth A. Rodman, 'Is Peace in the Interests of Justice? The Case for Broad Prosecutorial Discretion at the International Criminal Court', *Leiden Journal of International Law*, 2009, vol. 22, p. 103.

980 Schabas, 2010, p. 663, see *supra* note 20.

fed by tribunals' jurisprudence. The Courts play a prominent role in the development of this field due to its permanency and expressive and educational functions. The interests of justice notion in the Rome Statute provokes the endless debate of the dilemma between peace and justice among scholars too, and the Court's jurisprudence in this regard can direct the relevant debate to a more certain standpoint.

The silence in law about the interests of justice concept, however, was not merely caused by the variance in beliefs among the different delegations in the Rome Conference. Another reason that justified the openness of the interests of justice concept is the plurality in its understanding and its context-oriented feature. It seems that there is no single answer for the question of peace or justice. The issue does not have a one-fits-all resolution. Indeed, as Mnookin suggests, managing the tension between peace and justice does not require a categorical either/or choice of one value to the exclusion of the other.[981] It left the ICC open to criticism if it would adhere to a narrow, Western punitive conception.[982] The interests of justice was not defined precisely, because it should not be defined. The Court needs to adopt a case-by-case approach to determine whether or not its intervention is in favor of justice. A mechanical analysis of a problem as complex and varying as peace and justice is not workable.[983] The Rome Statute has recognized that in some occasions the Court's intervention might not serve the interests of justice, but it does not define and determine those occasions and circumstances. It is because these occasions differs from situation to situation. As a result, it was impossible to predict the "individual choices that the Prosecutor might make in the interests of justice."[984] At the backdrop of the silence in the Rome Statute, the Prosecutor of the Court issued a Policy Paper on the Interests of Justice in 2007. This Policy will be discussed.

5. A VICTIM-ORIENTED NOTION

Article 53 of the Rome Statute does not clarify the meaning of the interests of justice concept. Justice does not have a single or typical meaning. Criminal prosecution represents a major part of justice, but not the whole of this multifaceted notion. It is a concept that bears a wide range of definitions. Justice means different things to different people.[985] A broad understanding of the term 'justice' in Article 53 will allow a broader range of factors to be considered.[986]

---

981 Robert H. Mnookin, 'Rethinking the Tension between Peace and Justice: The International Criminal Prosecutor as Diplomat', *Harvard Negotiation Law Review*, 2013, vol. 18, p. 149.

982 Tim Allen, Trial Justice: the ICC and the Lord's Resistance Army, Zed Books, 2006, p. 177.

983 Mahnoush Arsanjani, 'The International Criminal Court and National Amnesty Laws', *Proceedings of the Annual Meeting*, 1999, vol. 93, p. 66.

984 Schabas, 2011, p. 182, see *supra* note 170.

985 Schabas, 2012, p. 87, see *supra* note 891. And, Ludwin King, 2013, p. 105, see *supra* note 961. And, Janine Natalya Clark, 'Peace, Justice and the International Criminal Court: Limitations and Possibilities', *Journal of International Criminal Justice*, 2011, vol. 9, p. 523.

986 Stigen, 2008, p. 353, see *supra* note 96.

Although the interests of justice expression in Article 53 has not been defined by the Rome Statute, its meaning can be deduced from the indicators existing in the article. Reading these indicators gives a clue of the connotation of the interests of justice presumption. Article 53(1)(c) refers to two factors that influence the interests of justice, namely the gravity of crime and the interests of victims. Understanding the factors in Article 53 shall be guided by the objects and purposes of the Statute.[987] Indeed, in construing the interests of justice concept a teleological approach is needed. Given the fact that the ICC is a mainly a court to serve the interests of victims, the interpretation of the interests of justice and all its components should serve the victim-friendly objectives of the Court.

The 'gravity of crime' in Article 53(1)(c) differs from the 'gravity of a case' in Article 17 of the Statute. The difference in the wording denotes the difference in the meaning. The gravity of a 'case' is broader than the gravity of 'crime'. A case is composed of, *inter alia,* one or more crimes. If the gravity of crime referred to the gravity requirement as the admissibility rule, it would make Article 53(1)(c) redundant because the gravity of a case is examined under the admissibility requirement. Therefore, there is no need to duplicate its examination in the interests of justice requirement's assessment.

The gravity of crime in Article 53 is not an independent factor. The assessment of the gravity of crime may lead to two different results. If crimes are really serious and grave, the Prosecutor should investigate them. The seriousness of crimes is encouraging for prosecution, rather than discouraging it. This is meaningless if it is said that if a crime is too serious, its prosecution does not serve the interests of justice. On the contrary, the prosecution at the ICC is directed to target the most serious international crimes. The more serious a crime is, more priority is given to its prosecution. Therefore, this understanding of the gravity of crime is not intended by Article 53.

Another probability is that the gravity of crimes is not serious. If this is the case, one may state that prosecuting non-serious crimes does not serve the interests of justice at the ICC. Although this belief is sound, this interpretation of the gravity of a crime in the interests of justice notion is not convincing. The crime gravity as a filtering factor in the situation and case selection process is assessed when the admissibility requirement is examined. Less serious crimes are deprioritized in the situation selection process. Such crimes do not reach the interests of justice phase. Therefore, the gravity in the context of the interests of justice notion should have a different and independent meaning from the gravity as the admissibility threshold. How can the seriousness of crimes warrant the stay of investigations and prosecutions?

The gravity of crime in Article 53 lacks an independent connotation. This feature should be understood in light of another factor referred to in the article, namely the interests of victims. Adding the interests of victims to the gravity of crime indicates that there is a relationship between them. The gravity of crimes is a component that affects the interests of victims. Here, the interests of victims are the main general factor that

---

987 ICC, OTP, Policy Paper on the Interests of Justice, p. 1.

plays a determinative role in the interests of justice presumption. From this perspective, the gravity of crime refers to the scale of impacts of ongoing crimes on the victims. For this purpose, the gravity of crimes should be taken into account to assess the interests of victims. This directs the Prosecutor to give considerations to the seriousness and gravity of crimes and their adverse impact on the victims if the Court's intervention is a cause for the continuation of crimes. Indeed, the interests of justice concept in Article 53 predicts an exceptional situation in which the Court's investigation or prosecution can intensify the crimes that are being committed with grave devastating impacts on the affected victims. It is a hypothetical situation that is probable to occur. If it happens, the Prosecutor needs to suspend its activities for the sake of victims. However, because the interests of justice standard operates exceptionally, its prerequisites should be interpreted narrowly and strictly. It implies that there should be a proof of casual relationship between the Prosecutor's intervention and the adverse effects on the victims. Therefore, the consequences of the Prosecutor's action are not examined by mere speculation and in the abstract, but need an objective and fact-driven assessment. For instance, the rebel should have shown their real readiness for stopping the atrocities and have referred to the threat of the ICC prosecution as an actual obstacle in the way of peace.

Putting the interest of victims at the heart of the interests of justice means that justice in Article 53 is associated with the victims and is for victims. Article 53 uncovers the meaning of justice at the ICC. Justice is done when it is in conformity with the interests of victims. The interests of justice notion under Article 53 enhances the role and voice of the victims at the ICC. It provides tremendous opportunity for the Court to serve the interests of victims. Investigations and prosecutions as the criminal aspects of justice should be conducted for victims. Article 53 demonstrates that the ultimate goal of the Court is to serve the victims. The interests of justice concept establishes a normative framework within which the Court should seek justice: No action should hurt victims. Prosecuting crimes is in the victims' interest, but if it hurts other interests of victims, it should be ceased. The interests of justice notion in the Rome Statute is a victim-oriented notion. Until Phase 4 in the preliminary examination, only one interest of the victims' interests is sought by the Prosecutor, namely the right to justice. The right to justice represents the narrow meaning of justice, i.e. criminal justice. Victims need criminal justice. The Prosecutor of the Court, for instance, has grounded her decision to initiate an investigation into a situation on the victims' demands. However, criminal justice is neither the only interest of victims nor the only dimension of justice. The victims of the core crimes have a large number of needs that may precede and outweigh criminal justice. They need security, well-being, peace and truth. Justice is a right, as life is a right, but the latter is more valuable than the former. Security must always be a primary concern.[988] A prosecution that is blind to the interests of victims does not serve the interests of justice in the Rome Statute. The purist of justice as an absolute and non-negotiable value may jeopardize other important goals. Victims

[988] Stigen, 2008, p. 444, see *supra* note 96.

demand justice, but not at any price.[989] Therefore, the enforcement of criminal justice should not be required when, for instance, it would cause the deaths of thousands.[990] The Court's jurisprudence has not dealt with a concrete case yet regarding the interests of justice notion. However, the situation in Syria could be an example here. In the context of the current crisis in Syria, the dilemma between peace and justice has emerged. If, for instance, the State forces commit ICC-identified crimes but they do not surrender if they see that they would face justice in The Hague, prosecution must not hamper the peace. First peace and safety, next justice. The safety of victims is a matter of great concern in the Rome Statute. The drafters of the Statute endeavored to provide the victims with adequate protection. Article 68 sets a general obligation upon the Court to "take appropriate measures to protect the safety, physical and psychological well-being, dignity and privacy of victims." When the protection of the victims at the micro level is of cardinal importance, how one can accept that the Rome Statute would permit the Prosecutor to be indifference to the safety of the victims at the macro level by conducting investigation and prosecution? The interests of justice presumption has been predicted to protect the interests of victims even at the macro level.

The interests of justice presumption and its countervailing effect is applicable to the case selection too. The expression 'interests of justice' was first proposed regarding cases. In the drafting process, the UK proposed that the Prosecutor should be granted wide discretion to decide not to investigate if, for instance, the offender was very old or very ill.[991] As the minds of drafters were not familiar with the situation notion, they planted their domestic products in the field of the ICC. Domestic legal matters were case-oriented. However, the emergence of the situation notion at the ICC architecture established a conceptual framework that led to the new normative rules.

In the case phase, the number of factors that should be taken into account is more. The factors referred to in Article 53(2)(C) are illustrative, rather than exclusive.[992] The Rome Statute obliges the Prosecutor to take into account some factors, 'including' the age of the accused and the interests of victims if she decides to initiate a prosecution. In the situational phase, when there is no actual case and the accused is not determined yet, the factors evolve around the interests of victims. In the case phase, by contrast, the actual accused is known. Here, the interests of victims still play an important role, but the circumstances surrounding the accused are added to the factors that should be taken into account. Justice is a comprehensive notion embracing the interests of a wide range of actors, including victim and accused. Nevertheless, it should be noted that in taking into account the interests of the accused, the context in which the ICC operates should be given considerations. The accused's rights have grown in the context of domestic and national jurisdictions. Planting the accused's rights in the field of the international criminal justice system without paying attention

989 Ibid., p. 366.
990 Ibid., p. 359.
991 Schabas, 2010, p. 663, see *supra* note 20.
992 Stigen, 2008, p. 353, see *supra* note 96.

to their different contexts is questionable. The rights of the accused should be observed, but at the ICC the victims' rights prevail. Prosecuting very old criminals at the domestic level may be seen unnecessary for justice, but in international criminal law due weight should not be attached to this factor, unless extremely exceptional circumstances warrant so.[993] The Thirith case in the Extraordinary Chambers at the ICCs of Cambodia (ECCC) is an example. She was accused of a large number of crimes, such as crimes against humanity. However, the ECCC found her unfit to stand trial, in particular, because she suffered from Alzheimer's.[994] The circumstances of the accused could be considered in the sentencing phase, but to initiate a case, a highly narrow approach to their countervailing effects on prosecution should be adopted. The victims have an interest in seeing justice done.[995] Steps should be taken to reach justice as much as possible. If punishment is not fair, a trial or pre-trial activity should be conducted.

6. A CONTEXT FOR THE APPLICABILITY OF THE INTERESTS OF JUSTICE: JUSTICE OR PEACE

In practice, the interests of justice notion has not been applied by the ICC, because it has not been officially tabled before the Court.[996] In theory, however, a context in which the interests of justice notion in the Rome Statute may be arisen is the dilemma between peace and justice. Indeed, the prime and characteristic example that may not serve justice in the sense of Article 53 is a situation in which peace considerations surface. Article 53 might be read broadly enough to permit the Prosecutor to defer an investigation or prosecution that might obstruct peace.[997] In some occasions, a conflict between peace and the Court's investigation and prosecution crops up. The conflict represents the well-known dilemma between peace and justice. The dilemma has provoked hot debates since the establishment of the ICC. This long-running debate has intensified and will continue as the possibility of national leaders being brought to trial is more likely nowadays, since insulation from prosecution is no longer a certainty for former Heads of State.[998] Leaders do not surrender to justice easily if they commit crimes. This fact triggers the peace-oriented demands, because when there is no prospect for justice, obtaining peace is desirable.

The Court is a criminal tribunal, and prosecution and criminal investigation are intrinsic for its functioning. The ICC has been established to put an end to impunity of perpetrators of the international crimes. This objective is essentially realized by criminal measures. However, the criminal approach of the Court to conflicts may

---

993 Ibid. p. 367.

994 See: www.eccc.gov.kh/en/indicted-person/ieng-thirith-former-accused.

995 ICC, OTP, Policy Paper on the Interests of Justice, p. 5.

996 Stahn, 2015, p. 229, see *supra* note 616.

997 Mnookin, 2013, p. 152, see *supra* note 981.

998 HRW, Selling Justice Short: Why Accountability Matters for Peace, 2009, p1.

contradict peace processes. If it happens, Article 53 offers a way to resolve the conflict. Peace is not explicitly mentioned as a factor that can affect the interests of justice, but it can be embedded in the interests of victims. Peace per se does not contradict justice. However, the central thesis in the dilemma between peace and justice is that peace is contradictory, because it might include amnesties. Peace could be obtained without offering an amnesty, however, what is common regarding the atrocities is reaching peace through amnesties. Indeed, the original conflict occurs between amnesties and criminal justice.[999] As will be seen, supporters of amnesties argue that those bearing the greatest responsibility for atrocities do not lay down their arms if they see that they will not face criminal charges.[1000] If they do not surrender, the conflict most likely will continue, and it intensifies the misery of victims. This research focuses on the relationship between peace and justice when the former involves amnesties that contradict the latter.

In the Rome Statute, there is no inherent conflict between peace and justice. If peace serves the interests of victims, then it will be in the interests of justice in its broad sense. The authority of the UNSC to refer a situation to the ICC under Chapter VII of the UN Charter signals the message that justice and peace can work in tandem. UNSC referrals prove that justice may serve peace. Similarly, the interests of justice notion shows that peace may serve justice too. Justice has a broader meaning under Article 53.[1001] If peace saves the lives of victims, it serves the interests of justice from the angle of the Rome Statute. The dilemma between peace and justice represents a narrow interpretation of justice and a specific understanding of peace. Nonetheless, it seems that the Rome Statute has embraced a wide interpretation and victim-oriented understanding of justice that can be compromised on peace.

Debates about the dilemma between peace and justice are still fierce and lively. The Prosecutor describes this topic as "the point where many of the philosophical and operational challenges in the pursuit of international criminal justice coincide", while "there is no clear guidance on what the content of the idea is."[1002] Some promote the primacy of justice and others campaign giving space to peace. The current chapter seeks to provide a brief description of different approaches to the dilemma between peace and justice to understand the Rome Statute's attitude to the issue in question.

---

999 It should be noted that amnesties might be granted in different forms, such as de jure amnesties, de facto amnesties (when the issue of accountability is not referred to and remains silence) and even in some situations, negotiators grant official positions in order to persuade the rebels to lay down their arms, like the situation in Afghanistan (See: HRW, 2009, see *supra* note 998. And Jack Snyder and Leslie Vinjamuri, 'Trials and Errors: Principle and Pragmatism in Strategies of International Justice', *International Security*, 2003, vol. 28, p. 36).

1000 HRW, 2009, p. 2, see *supra* note 998.

1001 Darryl Robinson, 'Serving the Interests of Justice: Amnesties, Truth Commissions and the International Criminal Court', *European Journal of International Law*, 2003, vol. 14, p. 488.

1002 ICC, OTP, Policy Paper on the Interests of Justice, p. 2.

6.1. JUSTICE SUPPORTERS

Justice supporters are those who believe that in the dilemma between peace and justice, justice should be given priority. In addition to the academic advocators, some UN organs and international NGOs are among the faithful supporters of the primacy of justice over peace. Justice supporters put forward some arguments to enhance their assertion. Vriezen by studying the UN organs' approaches to the issue of amnesty concludes that the UN position on amnesties in theory is that amnesty laws for international crimes are rejected.[1003] However, she admits that in practice the UN is willing to adapt its policy when confronted with a situation in which "amnesty may do more good for the human rights situation than would impunity."[1004] They have adopted a deontological and dogmatic approach to criminal justice. They argue that there is a legal and moral obligation to prosecute international crimes. From a Kantian perspective, the international community has a moral obligation to prosecute perpetrators of international crimes, and victims have a moral right to see that their perpetrators are prosecuted.[1005] From a legal perspective, it has been argued that although "any State has the sovereign right to grant amnesty to rebels", if "the conduct of the participants in the armed conflict is alleged to amount to international crime", States could not legally declare an amnesty for crimes under international law that are the subject of universal jurisdiction.[1006] Some believe that prosecuting serious international crimes is a duty pursuant to customary international law.[1007] Indeed, it has been considered as a rule that violations of *jus cogens* crimes should always be subject to prosecution.[1008] The UN Set of Principles for the Protection and Promotion of Human Rights through Action to Combat Impunity indicate that States have a duty to investigate serious crimes under international law, and to take measures to ensure that those suspected of criminal responsibility "are prosecuted, tried and duly

1003 Vera Vriezen, *Amnesty Justified? The Need for a Case By Case Approach in the Interests of Human Rights*, Wolf Legal Publishers, 2011, p.176, For instance, Article 18 of the Declaration on the Protection of All Persons From Enforced Disappearances, adopted by the UN General Assembly in 1992, explicitly rejects amnesty law or similar measures that might have the effect of exempting the perpetrators from criminal sanctions.

1004 For instance, the UNSC in the situations of Haiti (1993), Croatia (1996) and Sierra Leone (2000) approved of amnesty measures. See: Ibid. pp. 140–9.

1005 Joris van Wijk, 'Should We Ever Say Never? Arguments against Granting Amnesty Tested', in Rianne Letschert, Roelof Haveman, Anne-Marie de Brouwer and Antony Pemberton, *Victimological Approaches to International Crimes: Africa, Intersentia,* 2011 p. 292.

1006 SCSL, Appeals Chamber, Kallon and Kamara case, Decision on Challenge to Jurisdiction: LOMÉ Accord Amnesty, 13 March 2014, para. 20.

1007 HRW, *The Meaning of the Interests of Justice in Article 53 of the Rome Statute, 2005 p.* 3. Robinson states that some crimes are under treaty-based obligation to be prosecuted, including, genocide, torture and Genève convention of 1949 and are reinforced by equivalent customary international law obligations. With respect to other crimes, there is no treaty based obligation: how, there are convincing reason to suggest that under current or emerging customary international law there is a duty to bring to justice (See: Robinson, 2003, p. 491, see *supra* note 1001).

1008 Bassiouni, 2013, p. 957, see *supra* note 255.

punished."[1009] From this perspective, amnesties are illegitimate because they contradict the obligation to combat international crimes. Given such an obligation, the HRW proposes a strict construction of the term 'interests of justice' in Article 53 of the Rome Statute.[1010] The organization has adopted an absolute approach to the primacy of justice. Any of the ICC investigation "could be seen as inherently disruptive of any ongoing peace process", but the HRW insists that political stabilization should not be allowed to dictate the ultimate fate of ICC prosecutions, because it "would undermine the objectives of the Rome Statute."[1011] From such a perceptive, it is asserted that the price of temporarily increased tension might be justified to reach a long-term peace.[1012]

In addition, a teleological argument is invoked here. Non-occurrence of crimes is a goal that is sought by peace supporters. However, justice advocators argue that the crime prevention is not realized through peace. Amnesties diminish the prospect for justice and encourage others to materialize their criminal minds. Moreover, justice supporters cast doubt that peace could be an alternative to justice. The justice advocators have coined the slogan 'no peace without justice'.[1013] They believe that justice is an essential component of a stable peace.[1014] Lasting peace is not obtained without justice. They assert that it is justice that leads to peace. It has been argued that international prosecution of criminals who had seized the power resulted in their marginalization, and it in turn facilitates stability and peace.[1015] For instance, the HRW refers to the cases of Charles Taylor and Karadzic and Mladic as proof of the efficiency of justice in the stability and peace process. In Bosnia, for instance, the indictment of Radovan Karadzic prevented his participation in the peace talks leading to the Dayton negotiations.[1016]

'Cognitivism theory' has a role in the justice supporters' reasoning. The theory of cognitivism as a knowledge-based approach states that change in principle beliefs and normative ideas can trigger changes in behavior.[1017] From this perspective, advocators of accountability believe that trials send a strong signal to would-be perpetrators of atrocities that they will be held individually accountable for their actions, and thereby strengthening the rule of law.[1018] From this perspective, the perpetrators of the

---

1009 UN Social and Economic Council, Updated Set of Principles for the Protection and Promotion of Human Rights through Action to Combat Impunity, 2005.

1010 HRW, 2005, p. 1, see *supra* note 1007.

1011 Ibid., p. 5.

1012 Stigen, 2008, p. 386, see *supra* note 96.

1013 For the first time 'No Peace Without Justice' emerged with an Italian NGO established in 1993 and adopted this name for itself.

1014 ICC, OTP, Policy Paper on the Interests of Justice, p. 8.

1015 HRW, 2009, p. 4, see *supra* note 998.

1016 Ibid.

1017 Andreas Hasenclever, Peter Mayer and Volker Rittberger, *Theories of International Regimes*, Cambridge University Press, 2004, p. 143. There are many instances, which indicate the impact of new ideas on the course of international politics. For instance, the abolition of colonialism was a fruit of international change of ideas about legitimacy criteria and emergence of the fundamental norm and right to self-determination.

1018 Snyder and Vinjamuri, 2003, p. 17, see *supra* note 999.

atrocious crimes are considered rational actors who take into account the consequences of their actions and decisions. The HRW warns that the impact of justice is too often undervalued in resolving a conflict.[1019] The awareness of those conducts constituting criminal behavior at the ICC is increasing as a result of the ICC's prosecutions. This may result in behavioral changes simply out of fear of prosecution. For example, in the CAR, a rebel commander demobilized his child soldiers after learning about the ICC's prosecution of Congolese rebel leader Lubanga on charges of recruitment of child soldiers, claiming he had not known using child soldiers was a crime.[1020] Weerdesteijn addresses the question of the rationality of dictators in order to find an effective way in stopping them from perpetrating crimes. She divides dictators into two categories. Some dictators take into account a benefit-cost analysis in their decision-making process, like Milošević. On the contrary, others make their decisions ideologically, regardless of the consequences of those decisions, like Pol Pot.[1021] Weerdesteijn argues that for those perpetrators who are instrumentally rational measures such as sanctions, military intervention or criminal prosecution may have preventive effects. However, those leaders who are devote to the ideology are less responsive to pressure from outside of their country.[1022] It should be given consideration that even those perpetrators who justify their atrocities by the ideology, the prospect of prosecution could be effective. The Court has expressive mandates. It is intended to deliver the message that such norms are absolute and should not be violated. The expressive function of justice here may change behaviors following altering beliefs.

Although the foregoing arguments have some merits, they are unable to arrive at an absolute conclusion about the dilemma between peace and justice. Each reason has a margin that is open to exceptions. For instance, there are some instances of the successful peace deals where there is no report of crimes after the conclusion of a peace agreement and granting amnesties. El Salvador and Mozambique have been referred to as two situations in which amnesties have been highly effective in curbing abuses when implemented in a credible way.[1023] Van Wijk by assessing Mozambique, Angola and Uganda concludes that the assumed negative effects cannot be found.[1024] He argues that the three country studies illustrate that the pragmatic arguments against amnesties are not always valid.[1025] Interestingly, the HRW that adopts a fierce approach to peace acknowledges that "there is not one formula that is suitable to all situations", and refers to a well-known counter-example, namely Mozambique, where the country has remained without any justice.[1026] Moreover, it should be recalled that even justice

1019 HRW, 2009, p. 3, see *supra* note 998.

1020 Ibid., p. 7.

1021 Maartje Weerdesteijn, *The Rationality of Dictators: Towards a More Effective Implementation of the Responsibility to Protect, Intersentia,* 2016, p. 370.

1022 Ibid., p. 374.

1023 Snyder and Vinjamuri, 2003, p. 6, see *supra* note 999.

1024 Van Wijk, 2011, p. 314, see *supra* note 1005.

1025 Ibid.

1026 HRW, 2009, p. 7, see *supra* note 998.

alone lacks immediate deterrent effect. There are some situations in where the criminal justice intervention did not result in deterrence. For instance, the Srebrenica genocide occurred only two years after the 1993 UN Resolution creating the ICTY.[1027] Conflicts in Kosovo (1998–1999) and the Former Yugoslav Republic of Macedonia (2001) are other instances in which the intervention of the international criminal justice system failed to prevent crimes. As it is evident, there is no common pattern for relationship between peace and justice. Each situation has its own story. There are some instances where peace deals work well, while at the same time, there are some other instances where peace did not last for a long time, and failed to prevent the continuance of crimes. This thesis is not going to add one or more instances to one of the sides of the debate. The weight of empirical issues should be understood in light of the relativity and flexibility surrounding the issue of the interests of justice. If no side of arguments is prevailing, a plural approach is necessary to be adopted. It is something that is enshrined in Article 53. At the ICC legal system, criminal justice is the primary choice, but peace still has a chance to be chosen by the Court. However, for this purpose, a case-by-case approach must be adopted.

Even from a moral perspective, the absoluteness of a criminal approach is not fair. Justice supporters should provide an answer to the question of a situation in which the pursuit of justice may increase the violence. The problem of deontological attitudes is their absoluteness and blindness. They demand criminal justice in an absolute way without any exception, and they are blind to the consequences of such a demand. Justice supporters are indeed in favor of retributivism. The Kantian 'an island society about to disband' is a good example showing the content of retributivism. According to this exemplary situation, if someone commits a murder he is deserved to be punished even if he is the last person of a society.

As to the cognitivist effects of criminal justice, there is no disagreement with the expressive function of punishment and criminal law. The ICC insistence on the prosecution gradually leads to a change in behavior. However, as mentioned, the shortcoming of this viewpoint is its absoluteness. As far as there is a matter of priority and primacy, there is no animosity. However, if justice seekers insist that justice is unexceptional then some doubts arise. At the ICC, both prosecution and non-prosecution in the exceptional circumstances have expressive functions. They both show that the Court is intended to serve the interests of victims.

6.2. PEACE SUPPORTERS

Contrary to those justice-seekers who adopt an absolute approach to the primacy of prosecution, for peace supporters the value of criminal justice is relative. They argue from different angles. From a pragmatic perspective, there is an interaction between peace and justice. These two notions are two sides of one coin. If the lasting peace needs

[1027] Snyder and Vinjamuri, 2003, p. 20, see *supra* note 999.

justice, there is no justice without peace neither. Criminal justice can be administrated if there is stability. Giving priority to peace does not challenge the value of criminal justice, but it considers peace as a prerequisite for justice. Here, the question is not whether we must prioritize criminal justice or non-prosecution measures, but the question is whether we must pursue justice even in the exceptional circumstances where there is no prospect for justice due to the lack of peace and security. This thinking adopts a realistic approach to the conflict resolution. As Rodman says, international criminal law can build on the capability and willingness of political actors, but it cannot help settle a conflict without them.[1028] International trials tend to contribute to the ending of abuses only when spoiler groups are weak[1029], and if prior political and military efforts are in place.[1030] For instance, the ICTR was mainly accomplished in the context of the military victory of the Tutsi-led Rwanda Patriotic Front armed forces.[1031] This feature might appear less legitimate, but remains very real.[1032] If justice has sufficient power to be administered, there is no space for amnesties. However, the question of peace or justice arises when there is no immediate chance for the success of justice. The success in administering justice is not a result of justice itself, but it succeeds if it is backed by power and political pressures. Indeed, even justice is highly associated with political considerations. In the absence of a decisive victory, a formal amnesty might be a necessary step in the process of consolidating peace and the rule of law.[1033] No peace without justice does not represents the whole of truth. It denies the necessity of peace while justice depends on peace. Denial of political considerations in the purist of justice is an empty slogan.

The distinction between negative peace and positive peace, proposed by Galtung, may shed some light on the stance of peace supporters. Negative peace is the state of no war and violence.[1034] Positive peace is something more than the inexistence of war. It refers to the circumstances after war, when the rule of law prevails and the roots of violence and war are cut. Positive peace requires criminal justice because it is one of the consequences of the rule of law. Impunity is a symptom and sign of lawlessness. Peace needs justice, since violence is not switched off "like a tap by the mere agreement of a peace accord" and an agreement to put down the arms does not guarantee a real peace.[1035] However, to reach the positive peace we need negative peace first. Justice, the rule of law, democracy and other social values are not preserved and respected in times of war. By contrast in some occasions, demanding those values may result in the rise in casualties. The interests of justice notion, from this perspective, enables the Prosecutor

1028 Rodman, 2009, p. 108, see *supra* note 979.

1029 Snyder and Vinjamuri, 2003, p. 19, see *supra* note 999.

1030 Leslie Vinjamuri, 'The ICC and the Politics of Peace and Justice', in Carsten Stahn (ed.),*The Law and Practice of the International Criminal Court*, Oxford University Press, 2015, p. 23.

1031 Snyder and Vinjamuri, 2003, p. 24, see *supra* note 999.

1032 Stigen, 2008, p. 376, see *supra* note 96.

1033 Snyder and Vinjamuri, 2003, p. 18, see *supra* note 999.

1034 Baljit Singh Grewal, John Galtung, *Positive and Negative Peace*, 2003, accessible at: www.activeforpeace.org/no/fred/Positive_Negative_Peace.pdf.

1035 Clark, 2011, p. 542, see *supra* note 985.

to hold back from criminal proceedings when prosecution might "prolong an armed conflict or dissuade a tyrant from stepping down."[1036]

In addition to the fact that justice depends on politics, peace supporters advance moral arguments in favor of the precedence of peace. Peace should be given priority if it meets the immediate needs of the victims better. This victimological perspective does not consider criminal justice as an ultimate goal, but it sees justice as a tool; a tool that is intended to serve the interests of victims. Justice is desirable thanks to its beneficial effects for the victims. It implies that criminal justice is commendable as long as it serves the victims. In the dilemma between peace and justice, if justice hurts victims, peace should lead. Here, a consequentialist morality is adopted. The value of peace and justice are examined in light of their consequences. The question is whether the Prosecutor of the Court should take into account the possibility that her actions might jeopardize ongoing peacemaking efforts; efforts that have harmed reduction results. Justice should not be assessed without its consequences; it is senseless.[1037] Criminal justice should be sought with responsibility. It is a shift from a duty-based to a result-based approach.[1038] If the delivery of justice results in adverse consequences, it loses its legitimacy. Punishment is a tool, not a goal itself. If punishment has reverse effects, it should not be delivered.

If criminal justice worsens a conflict and hurts the peace process, it is not moral to insist on it. A justice that results in casualties is unjust. It is a vicious morality that closes its eyes on the fatal consequences of its demands. If the centrality of criminal justice is put on anything but the victims, it uses the victims as a tool. From such a perspective, it has been recommended that in the midst of a war, the priority must be placed on ending the war as soon as possible, instead of prosecution.[1039] Article 6 of Protocol II Additional to the Geneva Conventions encourages authorities to grant the 'broadest' possible amnesty at the end of hostilities in international armed conflicts.[1040] The main objective of the paragraph is to create conditions for reconciliation in a divided state.[1041] The provision aims to promote an end to the conflict by discouraging combatants from fighting to the death.[1042] At the ICC legal system, such considerations fall within the scope of the 'interests of justice' criterion.[1043]

1036 Rodman, 2009, p. 104, see *supra* note 979.

1037 Stigen, 2008, p. 358, see *supra* note 96. And, Rodman, 2009, p. 121, see *supra* note 979.

1038 Vinjamuri, 2015, p. 15, see *supra* note 1030.

1039 Mnookin, 2013, p. 170, see *supra* note 981.

1040 "At the end of hostilities, the authorities in power shall endeavor to grant the broadest possible amnesty to persons who have participated in the armed conflict, or those deprived of their liberty for reasons related to the armed conflict, whether they are interned or detained."

1041 Arsanjani, 1999, p. 65, see *supra* note 983.

1042 William A. Schabas, 'A Synergistic Relationship: The Sierra Leone Truth and Reconciliation Commission and the Special Court for Sierra Leone', in William A. Schabas, Shane Darcy (eds.), *Truth Commissions and Courts: The Tension Between Criminal Justice and the Search for Truth*, Springer, 2004, p. 167.

1043 Stigen, 2008, p. 380, see *supra* note 96.

It is not fair if conflict resolutions are drafted without giving considerations to the local and affected communities. Justice is primarily for victims, not for politicians, human rights activists and scholars who see and understand justice from the lens of books. Sitting at the desk in offices and libraries and drafting resolutions for conflicts are not effective. It is neither moral if it leads to harmful consequences. International criminal justice seeks a global justice, but this universality should not deny the local interests. *Fiat justitia ruat cælum* (let justice be done though the heavens fall) is a dangerous understanding of justice. If such an approach to justice at the domestic level is justifiable, it is not acceptable in the international criminal justice system, where there are unimaginable atrocities with mass victimization. The legal theories should not be tried at the price of the lives of victims.

Moreover, insisting on criminal prosecutions without taking into account the consequences acts against its own objectives because it risks causing more atrocities, while the criminal justice is claimed to prevent atrocities. Ignoring the reality can provoke humanitarian backsliding (Sudan), stall peace talks (Uganda), and intensify violence (Libya).[1044] The situation in Sudan is a clarifying example here. Upon the issuance of an arrest warrant against Al-Bashir, the Sudanese president ordered the expulsion of 10 international aid organizations such as Oxfam.[1045] This reaction triggered the alert of worsening the humanitarian crisis in Sudan. In the Gravity Chapter, it was discussed that the Prosecutor takes into account the impact of crimes to determine the gravity of a situation or a case. Attacks on peacekeepers at the ICC case law have been an instance that is declared sufficiently grave by arguing that the suspension of peacekeeping operations has wide adverse effects on the local people who benefit from the peacekeepers. The same argument is applicable in the interests of justice presumption. If prosecuting has wide and objective devastating effects on victims and affected society, it should be stopped. It is a clear inconsistency if the Prosecutor takes into account the impacts of crimes on victims, but she does not give considerations to the impact of her own actions. Peace seekers suggest a do-no-harm rationale. A doctrine that suggests that the standard for pursuing justice during conflict should be that such an intervention will not impede the prospect for achieving peace.[1046] It may result in sequencing of justice. There is a linier relationship between peace and justice, if the former serves the fundamental interests of victims.

6.3. THE PROSECUTOR STATUS QUO

The Rome Statute gives a tiny space to peace and amnesties. The Rome Statute accepts the possibility of the priority of peace, though in the exceptional circumstances.

1044 Vinjamuri, 2015, p. 27, see *supra* note 1030.

1045 The Guardian, Sudanese President Expels Aid Agencies, 5 March 2009, available at: www.theguardian.com/world/2009/mar/05/sudan-aid-agencies-expelled.

1046 Vinjamuri, 2015, p. 21, see *supra* note 1030.

Article 53(1)(c) recognizes that investigation and prosecution may fail to be commenced because of the interests of victims. In a nutshell, the ICC has not closed its doors on peace and amnesties, but it opens its doors for these considerations so hard. The UNSC's power under Article 16 of the Statute is a venue to give space to peace, but not the only one.

The OTP Policy Paper on the Interests of Justice sets out 'the Office of the Prosecutor's understanding' of the concept of the interests of justice.[1047] The Rome Statute has put some obligations on the Prosecutor's shoulders. To fulfill her statutory obligations, the Prosecutor has considerable degree of discretion. The prosecutorial discretion includes her right to interpret those relevant concepts that have been left undefined in the Rome Statute. The Prosecutor exercises her authorities based on her understanding. However, understanding has a dynamic nature, and is open for a change. That is why the Policy Paper insists that the understanding of the interests of justice notion is "subject to revision based on experience."[1048] In addition, the Prosecutor's understanding may alter "in the light of legal determinations by the Chambers of the Court."[1049] The Prosecutor's decision not to initiate an investigation due to the lack of interests of justice is reviewed by a PTC. If the Chamber's view differs from the Prosecutor's, the Prosecutor's understanding should be adapted to the judges' understanding who have the final word. In addition, the Policy Paper insists that the interests of justice presumption needs to be tackled on a case-by-case basis that depends on "the facts and circumstances of the case or situation."[1050] Therefore, it is admitted that the Paper offers "only limited clarification in the abstract."[1051] As mentioned, the interests of justice presumption has no one-size-fits-all answer.

Regarding the dilemma between peace and justice, the Paper emphasizes the distinction between 'interests of justice' and 'interests of peace'. It adds that the Prosecutor is responsible to administer justice, while the interests of peace falls "within the mandate of institutions other than the Office of the Prosecutor."[1052] It has been asserted that in the Rome Statute there is a division of labor between the Prosecutor and the UNSC. It is the latter that is responsible for taking into account the interests of peace by exercising its power under Article 16 of the Rome Statute.[1053] In the ideal circumstances, such a division may work. Nevertheless, in the normal course of events

---

1047 ICC, OTP, Policy Paper on the Interests of Justice, para. 1.

1048 Ibid.

1049 Ibid.

1050 Ibid.

1051 Ibid.

1052 ICC, OTP, Policy Paper on the Interests of Justice, 2007, para. 1. In the October 2012 speech in Pretoria, South Africa, Prosecutor Bensouda stated: "I should stress here that the 'interests of justice' [of Article 53] must not be confused with the interests of peace and security, which falls within the man- date of other institutions, notably the UN Security Council and the African Union. The Court and the Office of the Prosecutor itself are not involved in political considerations. We have to respect our legal limits. The prospect of peace negotiations is therefore not a factor that forms part of the Office's determination on the interests of justice" (Mnookin, 2013, p. 149, see *supra* note 981).

1053 HRW, 2005, p. 2, see *supra* note 1007.

it is not clear that the Security Council will fulfill its designated responsibility when there is a conflict.[1054] The UNSC is not reliable due to its political composition. It is imaginable that the Council does not take the action when it is necessary. Article 16 has not been exercised yet. In addition, Article 16 is a matter of States' will, rather than the victims' needs and views. It makes a concern similar to what resulted in forming *proprio motu* power of the Prosecutor. The drafters were concerned that due to prevailing political considerations, no referral would be made by States Parties or the UNSC. It persuaded them to authorize the Prosecutor of the Court to take the initiative independently. Such a necessity is not limited to initiating an investigation, but it exists when the interests of victims require the suspension of a prosecution. Therefore, the interests of justice mechanism could be used to avoid starting an investigation that in the exceptional circumstances may affect the interests of victims adversely.

Apart from the foregoing consideration, the distinction between peace and justice in the Policy Paper sounds simplistic. What matters here, from a human trial perspective, is not peace as an ultimate value, but the interests of victims. The Prosecutor is not responsible for peace, but she is responsible to protect and respect the interests of victims. It means that the Prosecutor is not obliged to constitute peace, but she has not allowed destroying it either, if her actions have negative consequences for victims. Protecting victims falls within the Prosecutor's mandate.

Reality proves the interaction between peace and justice. It is difficult to deny such a mutual relationship. For this reason, and despite making a distinction between peace and justice, the Policy Paper at the end acknowledges that there is a legal and statutory space for peace and amnesties in the Rome Statute if they serve the interest of victims. The Paper is hesitant to accept the peace considerations by saying that it will not "speculate on abstract scenarios", but it endorses that "a decision not to proceed on the basis of the interests of justice should be understood as a course of last resort."[1055] It is a last resort, but anyway it is a legal and legitimate resort.

The spirit of the interests of justice presumption is that the interests and needs of victims should be taken into account in the situation selection process. The interests of victims should not be determined on a top-down approach. Victims can express their own interests. Therefore, the Prosecutor emphasizes on a direct contact through dialogue with the victims themselves as well as representatives of local communities to ascertain their views.[1056] For this purpose, the OTP sends missions to the situation countries in order to contact with the victims. In the context of mass atrocities, there are a large number of victims. It is most probable that there is disagreement among victims. Methodologically speaking, the Prosecutor needs to use reliable empirical measures to collect all views of victims as much as possible. First, the importance of outreach activities and education should be insisted. To have genuine views of victims, the Court should increase the knowledge and awareness of the Court, its limitations and

1054 Rodman, 2009, p. 120, see *supra* note 979.
1055 ICC, OTP, Policy Paper on the Interests of Justice, p. 9.
1056 Ibid. p. 6.

abilities, in order to manage expectations. Second, discrimination should be avoided. The views of victims irrespective of their content should be taken into account. To realize it, the Prosecutor is committed to hearing all voices through different mediums such as respected intermediaries and representatives and "those who may be able to provide a comprehensive overview of a complex situation", including local leaders and NGOs.[1057] From this perspective, the viewpoint of the HRW can be criticized. HRW has asserted that "while victims may have many different interests related to an ICC prosecution and/or investigation, only those that relate to achieving justice are relevant for the purposes of Article 53."[1058] It is a clear example of using victims as a tool. HRW advises the Prosecutor to be receptive to hearing the views of victims, but it emphasized that those views are not all necessarily relevant to a determination under Article 53.[1059] Indeed, the HRW advocates a show hearing without any effect on the Prosecutor's decision. The victims' voices are heard, in the eyes of the HRW, as long as their voices coordinate the findings and understating of the Prosecutor and supporters of her decision to investigate or prosecute. As soon as there is a disagreement, those voices lose their value and validity. It is evident that such an approach is not consistent with the interests of victims.

It should be noted that the interests of victims in Article 53 differs slightly from the preference of victims. The Rome Statute does not request the Prosecutor to hear the voices of the victims to see if the majority is in favor of prosecution. Criminal justice is the rule at the ICC and it is not subject to election and poll. In Article 53, the interests of victims should be assessed in an objective manner rather than subjective. Apart from collecting the victims' views, the Prosecutor should take into account the tangible evidence that show that the presence of the Court hampers stopping atrocities. As mentioned, the interests of justice are adversely affected if the victims are hurt. To examine and understand the loss that is experienced by the victims, the Prosecutor should hear the victims as the coordinator evidence. Some argue that the Court should take into account victim wishes with respect to whether a local alternative justice mechanisms should be employed.[1060] However, the interests of justice do not give a space to desirability and preference, but it gives considerations to the real harm. The victims should be heard to make a judgment if the Prosecutor's intervention makes them subject to real danger and risk. Alternative or traditional justice mechanisms are a matter of complementarity. As discussed, the Court functions as a criminal court. It is imaginable that in some cases the domestic systems prefer alternative responses to crimes. A margin of freedom is preserved for them. The division of labor between the ICC and national systems could be an option here. The Court focuses on the senior perpetrators and the national proceedings deal with other culprits. However, as

---

1057 Ibid.

1058 HRW, 2005, p. 6, see *supra* note 1007.

1059 Ibid., p. 7.

1060 Gregory Gordon, 'Complementarity and Alternative Forms of Justice: A New test for ICC Admissibility', in Carsten Stahn and Mohamed M. El Zeidy (eds.), *The International Criminal Court and Complementarity: From Theory to Practice*, Cambridge University Press, 2011, p. 794.

mentioned, the interests of justice is an exception to prosecution at the ICC only if the prosecution adversely affects the interests of victims.

6.4. PRELIMINARY EXAMINATION AS A PLATFORM FOR A PLURAL APPROACH

Both justice and peace matter as long as they serve the interests of victims. In the normal course of events, primary is with justice. Delivering criminal justice at the ICC is not a matter of preference, but it is an obligation. The international criminal justice system assumes criminal functions. At the ICC, criminal justice is the rule. For this reason, non-prosecution mechanisms are called alternative because they do not follow the dominant retributive paradigm of ensuring accountability.[1061] However, sometimes the interests of victims warrant non-action of the Court. Here, the success in serving the interests of victims requires some compromises with criminal justice.[1062] Justice supporters insist exclusively on criminal justice. However, peace is also a value that needs to be balanced against the importance of prosecution rather than simply discarded. For this reason, in South Africa, for instance, justice in the sense of criminal trials was traded for peace, because it was not possible to have both.[1063] Nonetheless, in the architecture of the Court there is a capacity to preserve the primacy of justice more, even if there is a need to give space to peace. Indeed, the structure of the Court has been created by taking into account all of its unique features, abilities and limitations. Given these features, preliminary examination as a unique stage at the ICC's structure should be seen as the most effective mechanism to reduce the side effects of the Court's limits. Preliminary examination could be seen as a solution in the context of the dilemma between peace and justice too. Justice supporters insist on criminal justice and see peace as a non-acceptable alternative. Nevertheless, at the ICC legal system, if the Prosecutor does not open an investigation, and stays in the preliminary examination for the interests of victims, it does not mean that there has been nothing done for justice. The Rome Statute does not prescribe an absolute impunity.

At the ICC, the preliminary examination forms a part of criminal justice delivered by the Court. The value of preliminary examination in delivering justice should not be ignored. By opening a preliminary examination, the Prosecutor shows that the Court's jurisdiction has been activated to deliver justice. Conducting a preliminary examination has many expressive mandates. By determining that one or more crimes within the jurisdiction of the Court are committed, the ICC recognizes the victimhood of victims, and contributes to the establishment of the truth. It per se creates a great

---

1061 Valiñas Marta, 'Interpreting Complementarity and Interests of Justice in the Presence of Restorative-Based Alternative Forms of Justice', in Carsten Stahn and Larissa Van den Herik (eds.) *Future Perspectives on International Criminal Justice*, Asser Press, 2010, p. 268.

1062 Rodman, 2009, p. 119, see *supra* note 979.

1063 Clark, 2011, p. 539, see *supra* note 985.

barricade in the way of denying atrocities. These benefits are sought in criminal justice too.

In addition, when the interests of justice presumption bars the Prosecutor from conducting an investigation, the acquiescence of the Court may hurt its reputation and result in misjudgment of the Court. In addition, it might reinforce the culture of impunity. Preliminary examination is a proper mechanism to lower these undesirable consequences. By examining the admissibility requirement and determining the gravity of a situation, the Prosecutor, as suggested by this thesis, shall draft and publish a situation selection Document. The Document lists all situations under the Court's jurisdiction that are admissible. However, those situations are listed on the basis of their availability by taking into account the ability of the Court to deal with them. Therefore, the Document could manage expectations. It shows that the Court has taken the initiative and has heard the voice of voiceless victims. Moreover, it indicates the limitation of the Court and the obstacles in exercising the Court's jurisdiction. When the Prosecutor decides to give priority to peace efforts, she can put the given situation in the Situation Selection Document, at least at the end of the list. It should be insisted that making a peace deal under the interests of justice notion should be conducted in good faith. It means that if amnesties are given to facilitate peace, amnesties should remain valid as long as the perpetrators stick to peace. Vriezen argues that "trust is both a consequence and a condition of the rule of law", therefore instituting proceedings after granting an amnesty violates this trust that may lead to the return of conflict.[1064] Keeping a preliminary examination open in such a situation is an opportunity for monitoring the commitment to peace after concluding a peace deal. HRW has stated that "at the very least, peace agreements should not foreclose the possibility of justice at a later date."[1065] This statement should be understood in the way mentioned above. Otherwise, false amnesties could hamper the way of peace in the future.

Some argue that de jure or de facto amnesties on some occasions have been contributing factors to the ongoing commission of crimes after peace agreements were signed.[1066] The break-up of the ceasefire provided in Abidjan, Côte d'Ivoire, concluded in 1998 less than two months after its conclusion is an example.[1067] Such a concern is reduced by conducting a preliminary examination. The Prosecutor may surrender to a peace deal, but decisions arising from the preliminary examination are preliminary and are subject to a change in the future. The interests of justice may operate and bar conducting an investigation, but it does not lead to a carte blanche. In addition, the Prosecutor has the power to monitor the peace process to see how it goes. If peace remains only on paper and without concrete effects, then the Prosecutor can proceed.

1064 Vriezen, 2011, p. 248, see *supra* note 1003.
1065 HRW, 2009, p. 8, see *supra* note 998.
1066 Ibid., p. 57.
1067 Ibid., p. 58.

6.5. PEACE AS A TOOL FOR JUSTICE

As mentioned, in some exceptional circumstances, it is necessary, but a necessary evil, that justice raises a flag of surrender. The evacuation of justice, however, could foster the culture of impunity. Therefore, a compromise should be worked out by the Prosecutor in order to avoid the adverse effects of such evacuation as much as possible. As mentioned, the preliminary examination structurally has some capacities in this regard. However, it is the authority and art of the Prosecutor that should be exercised to activate those capacities. In respect of both justice and peace, the Court has potential.[1068] It is up to the Prosecutor to manage how it activates these potentials. Justice has some instrumental purposes for peace because it has effects on peace negotiations.[1069] The Prosecutor should benefit from these potentials. Although the Rome Statute allows the Prosecutor not to initiate an investigation or prosecution, it is against the purposes of the Statute if such permission is understood as an absolute non-action. The Prosecutor, even in the case of the precedence of peace, should seek accountability. The Policy Paper on the Interests of Justice highlights that considerations of "guaranteeing lasting respect for international justice" are touchstones.[1070] When peace should be given priority for the sake of victims, the Prosecutor has the capacity to insert some traces of accountability into a peace process. The peace process is a win-win game. The prosecutor has to grant key concessions, but she can manage to win some concessions, too. Indeed, the Prosecutor's authority under Article 53 should be seen as a 'last-resort bargaining tool'.[1071] It should be understood as part of her responsibility to fight impunity. Prosecution is ideal for defeating impunity. However, when prosecution is not feasible, the Prosecutor should select alternative measures of accountability. Insisting on justice "does not necessarily mean an end to peace talks."[1072] It is true, but if it is accepted that accountability and justice may be pursued in various ways. Accountability is not a matter of all or nothing. A compromise is feasible.

The Prosecutor in the Policy Paper indicates that "with the entry into force of the Rome Statute, a new legal framework has emerged and this framework necessarily impacts conflict management efforts."[1073] It is defiantly a correct description of the ICC era. The establishment of the ICC has added an accountability perspective to the world order. Therefore, as the Prosecutor asserts "any political or security initiative must be compatible with the new legal framework insofar as it involves parties bound by the Rome Statute."[1074] However, it is a coin with two sides. One side is that the international community should consider justice. On the other, the Prosecutor needs to take into account peace as well. When amnesties are inevitable, the Prosecutor as an

1068 Clark, 2011, p. 522, see *supra* note 985.
1069 Vinjamuri, 2015, p. 14, see *supra* note 1030.
1070 ICC, OTP, Policy Paper on the Interests of Justice, 2007 p. 4.
1071 Hethe Clark, 2005, p. 409, see *supra* note 962.
1072 HRW, 2009, p. 3, see *supra* note 998.
1073 ICC, OTP, Policy Paper on the Interests of Justice, p. 4.
1074 Ibid.

important actor in the world should be active and pursue justice and peace together. The Prosecutor is not the only actor in the international sphere. The Prosecutor should take into account the effects of her decisions on other global efforts who seek serving the victims. Indeed, the Prosecutor should operate in co-ordination with, rather than in opposition to, international efforts to address conflicts.[1075] Therefore, when the interests of victims warrant non-prosecution, the Prosecutor should direct the peace process towards the minimum accountability. When there is a possibility of having peace and justice together, it is not reasonable to leave one of them. At the ICC era, the Prosecutor to assume a diplomatic role to ensure accountability.[1076] Mnookin argues that the Prosecutor instead of ignoring the tension between the pursuit of peace and the pursuit of justice must "diplomatically manage this tension."[1077] The prospect for investigation and prosecution should be used by the Prosecutor as a leverage in the peace process to improve the alternative accountability. In a nutshell, the Prosecutor of the ICC should be a party to the peace negotiations in the situation countries.

As mentioned, when prosecution is not available, an alternative should be applicable. Blanket amnesties are widely rejected as a response to the core crimes.[1078] The Inter-American Court of Human Rights has held that Peru's blanket amnesty laws, "designed to eliminate responsibility are inadmissible, because they are intended to prevent the investigation and punishment of those responsible for serious human rights violations."[1079] Moreover, the experience of Sierra Leone shows that blanket amnesties may end in a culture of impunity in which brutal acts continue.[1080] Therefore, amnesties should be subject to the alternative forms of accountability, if they are necessary. These alternatives can fulfil the expressive mandates of the Court to some degree. At least, their existence signals a message. Truth commissions or the traditional forms of justice are tabled here. The Prosecutor may drop investigation and prosecution in exchange for a truth commission and other forms of traditional justice. If it is not possible to obtain 100 percentage of justice, it does not exempt the Prosecutor from attempting to obtain 10 percent of it. The OTP Policy Paper in itself fully endorses 'the complementary role' that can be played by truth seeking, reparation programs, institutional reform and traditional justice mechanisms in the pursuit of a 'broader justice'.[1081] Alternative mechanisms play prominent roles here, in particular, regarding recording the history and preserving the truth. The ICC is not able to deal with all cases. It concerns particular events and cannot comprehensively capture what occurred during an entire conflict.[1082] In addition, because of the phenomenon of the mass victimization at the ICC operations, the Court is not able to hear all victims. On the contrary, truth

1075 Rodman, 2009, p. 121, see *supra* note 979.
1076 Ibid.
1077 Mnookin, 2013, p. 145, see *supra* note 981.
1078 Robinson, 2003 vol. 14, p. 484, see *supra* note 1001.
1079 Inter-American Court, Barrios Altos Case, Judgment, 14 March 2001, paras. 41–44.
1080 Robinson, 2003 vol. 14, p. 496, see *supra* note 1001.
1081 ICC, OTP, Policy Paper on the Interests of Justice, p. 8.
1082 Ludwin King, 2013, p. 92, see *supra* note 961.

commissions, for instance, can supplement the Court as a valuable means to give a voice to victims.[1083] Moreover, truth commissions have been seen better mechanisms for rehabilitation of offenders. From this perspective, restorative mechanisms might contribute more to the offender's reintegration as it might provide some basis for better understanding the misdeeds.[1084] Therefore, alternative mechanisms have various benefits that can be used as an alternative as an exception.

If criminal justice gives space to alternative mechanisms, traditional justice should be adopted so that it can deal with war crimes, if they want to be credible.[1085] To stop the Court's intervention, a State needs to demonstrate that an alternative or traditional mechanism is more than just a way of protecting the guilty from prosecution.[1086] What here is important is the 'quality' of the amnesty program that should be carefully examined by the Prosecutor.[1087] The Prosecutor can preserve the quality of amnesties. For instance, the Prosecutor must explore the reasons why an amnesty was chosen instead of prosecutions.[1088] To assume such a quality, it has been suggested that a peace deal including amnesties should be concluded under international scrutiny and agreement, then "it can likely be presumed that the amnesty was not given illegitimately."[1089] The South African model is an example of exercising an alternative mechanism. In South Africa, a blanket amnesty was rejected.[1090] The Promotion of National Unity and Reconciliation Act (1995) of South Africa established The Truth and Reconciliation Commission (TRC) and tasked it with a mandate to establish and complete the causes, nature and extent of gross human rights violations committed under apartheid from March 1960 to December 1993. The TRC was comprised of the Human Rights Violation Committee tasked with assessing the account of victims. The Amnesty Committee had to evaluate amnesty applications, and the Reparation and Rehabilitation Committee was tasked with formulating a reparation policy.[1091] The TRC has been seen as crucial in breaking the tyranny of silence.[1092] Mato Oput developed by Acholi people of northern Uganda is another example. This tradition involved the guilty acknowledging responsibility, and asking for forgiveness and paying compensation and being reconciled with the victims' family through sharing the bitter drink.[1093]

1083 Robinson, 2003, p. 484, see *supra* note 1001. And, Declan Roche, Truth Commission Amnesties and the International Criminal Court, *British Journal Criminology*, 2005 p. 574.

1084 Stigen, 2008, p. 438, see *supra* note 96.

1085 Nouwen, 2013, p. 154, see *supra* note 226.

1086 Roche, 2005, p. 569, see *supra* note 1083.

1087 Hethe Clark, 2005, p. 409, see *supra* note 962.

1088 Stigen, 2008, p. 451, see *supra* note 96.

1089 Hethe Clark, 2005, p. 410, see *supra* note 962.

1090 HRW, 2009, p. 8, see *supra* note 998.

1091 Robert Peacock, 'The South African Truth and Reconciliation Commission: Challenges in Contributing to Reconciliation', in Rianne Letschert, Roelof Haveman, Anne-Marie de Brouwer and Antony Pemberton, *Victimological Approaches to International Crimes: Africa*, Intersentia, 2011, pp. 318–319.

1092 Ibid., p. 321.

1093 Gordon, 2011, p. 763, see *supra* note 1060.

7. DECISION NOT TO INITIATE AN INVESTIGATION

If the Prosecutor decides not to initiate an investigation due to the lack of the interests of justice requirement, she has to inform the PTC, which has been seized of the given situation. Here, the Prosecutor's decision is an exception to her general obligation to investigate a situation. Therefore, it should be under judicial review in order to ensure that the Prosecutor does not evade her statutory obligations. Upon conducting the preliminary examination, the Prosecutor may initiate an investigation, if there is a reasonable basis for this purpose. However, it is probable that the Prosecutor terminates the preliminary examination if a case or situation falls outside of the Court's jurisdiction or if they are not admissible. The other probability is that the Prosecutor keeps the preliminary examination open, but puts the given situation or case in the Situation/Case Selection Document awaiting an investigation or a prosecution when the relevant operational factors become available. However, the fate of the preliminary examination in the case of the lack of interests of justice is not determinate. It seems that the lack of the interests of justice presumption is similar to the status of unavailability, due to its temporary nature. In this scenario, the given situation falls within the ICC's jurisdiction, while it is admissible and available, too. However, because of the exceptional circumstances, the Prosecutor decides not to continue to preserve the interests of victims. Yet the exceptional circumstances are temporary. They are obstacles that might be lifted in the future. The Prosecutor may keep the situation open in order to monitor the peace process to see if the suspension is still necessary. Amnesty, like a contract, is valid to the extent that the parties to the contract comply with its terms.[1094] Therefore, the Prosecutor may refuse to initiate an investigation or prosecution, but it does not mean that she has to terminate the situation or case in question. On the contrary, the Prosecutor should continue monitoring the circumstances to see if the exceptional obstacles are lifted for opening an investigation. Timing is a powerful tool at the disposal of the Prosecutor to manage the tension between peace and justice.[1095] The cautious wait-and-see approach is applicable to the assessment of both complementarity and the interests of justice presumption. Contrary to the mantra 'justice delayed is justice denied', the most promising way to promote justice may be to postpone it.[1096] Here, the openness of the preliminary examination helps the efficiency of the peace agreements too. Indeed, the Prosecutor serves implementing a peace deal by monitoring it.

The other issue that should be given consideration is that the interests of justice presumption under Article 53 is examined before the beginning of an investigation or prosecution. It means that in the case phase, the Prosecutor before applying for an arrest warrant against the accused should make a decision about the interests of

1094 Arsanjani, 1999, p. 67, see *supra* note 983.

1095 Mnookin, 2013, p. 159, see *supra* note 981. And, Rodman, 2009, p. 122, see *supra* note 979. And, HRW, 2005, p. 2, see *supra* note 1007.

1096 Vinjamuri, 2015, p. 29, see *supra* note 1030.

justice presumption. Therefore, if the peace or justice dilemma comes up after issuing a warrant, legally speaking, there is no space for taking into account the interests of justice presumption. From this perspective, the situation in Uganda can be studied. In the context of the situation in Uganda, the conflict between peace and justice occurred. The debates did not result in a determination by the Court, because the peace process did not reach its end. However, it made a context in which lively debates happened. Many recommended the Prosecutor to exercise his power under Article 53 against the issued arrest warrants to facilitate the peace with the LRA. At the local level, some traditional and religious leaders opposed the Court's intervention.[1097] For instance, Father Carlos Rodriguez, a Spanish priest in Northern Uganda, stated the arrest "would practically close once and for all the path to peaceful negotiations as a means to end this long war."[1098] In addition, some local NGOs in Uganda, unlike the international NGOs, disagreed with the Court's warrants. Save the Children in Uganda, for instance, published a public statement in February 2004, expressing concern for the security of children abducted by the LRA if the investigation is carried out during continuing armed conflict.[1099] The OTP itself insisted that the ICC warrants against the top leadership of the LRA could not be subject to negotiations.[1100] The situation in Uganda was referred by the Ugandan government to the ICC in 2004. However, the peace process led to crisis in marriage between the Court and Uganda that ended in the failure of peace negotiations.[1101] Upon the unsuccessful end of the peace negotiations, the disagreements continued. Some blamed the ICC, whose intervention allegedly undermined the peace prospect. Kenneth insists that Kony would not sign a peace agreement that would leave him vulnerable to trial either in Kampala or The Hague, unless his forces had been so weakened.[1102] On the contrary, others insisted on the positive effects of the Court in Uganda and on the peace process itself. For instance, Nouwen states that the ICC arrest warrants helped to put the issue of accountability firmly on the Juba negotiating table.[1103] Moreover, some observers believe that the ICC warrants motivated the LRA leadership to negotiate for peace in the first place.[1104] In addition, HRW argues that the warrants isolated the LRA from some of its support base, in particular Sudan; after the referral was announced, Sudan agreed to a protocol allowing Ugandan armed forces to attack LRA camps in southern Sudan, and in October 2005 the government of Sudan signed a memorandum of understanding with the Court agreeing to cooperate with arrest warrants issued against LRA

1097 Allen, 2006, p. 132, see *supra* note 982.
1098 Ibid., p. 85.
1099 Coalition to Stop the Use of Child Soldiers, CRC Country Briefing, June 2005, available at: www.crin.org/en/docs/resources/treaties/crc.40/Uganda_CSUCS_report_update.pdf.
1100 Moreno-Ocampo, 2011), p. 28, see *supra* note 1.
1101 Nouwen, 2013, p. 140, see *supra* note 226.
1102 Rodman, 2009, p. 114, see *supra* note 979.
1103 Nouwen, 2013, p. 162, see *supra* note 226.
1104 Eric S. Fish, Peace 'Through Complementarity: Solving the Ex Post Problem in International Criminal Court Prosecutions', *The Yale Law Journal*, 2010, Vol. 119 p. 1713.

commanders.[1105] Also, the ICC's shadow had some catalyzing effects on local justice practices in Uganda.[1106] The Uganda's International Crime Division (ICD) is an example here. The ICD was established by a legal notice that Uganda's chief justice issued in May 2011. The ICD is mandated to try genocide, crimes against humanity, and war crimes as well as terrorism, human trafficking, piracy, and any other international crime defined in Uganda's 2010 International Criminal Court Act, 1964 Geneva Conventions, or any other criminal law.[1107]

Nevertheless, in these debates something has been ignored: Article 53 is not applicable to the stage after warrants are issued. The interests of justice mechanism barricades the way of opening an investigation or prosecution. It does not have effect when an investigation or prosecution is already in place. For this reason, some have recommended to amend the Rome Statute in order to provide a greater opportunity for peace negotiations, taking into account the inability of the Prosecutor to suspend a case after the indictment stage that undermined the peace negotiations in Juba between the LRA and the Ugandan government.[1108]

Nonetheless, it does not mean that the Prosecutor is disarmed if such a scenario happens. Withdrawal of charges could be an option here. In the Kenyatta case, the Prosecutor of the Court had to withdraw the charges against the president of Kenya. In December 2014, the Trial Chamber V (b) issued a decision in which it directed the Prosecutor either to withdraw the charges in the case or to indicate that the evidentiary base had improved to a degree, which would justify proceeding to trial.[1109] On 5 December 2014, the Prosecutor filed a notice stating that she withdraws the charges against Kenyatta, without prejudice to the possibility of bringing new charges later on the same or similar factual circumstances should it obtain sufficient evidence to do so.[1110] The charges were withdrawn because under ordinary circumstances where there is insufficient evidence, the charges would be withdrawn.[1111] In the Kenyatta case, the Prosecutor believed that the non-cooperation of Kenya was the main reason leading to the insufficiency of the evidence. Likewise, upon the issuance of an arrest warrant, if the Prosecutor determines that the interests of justice require the suspension of the issued warrant, she can withdraw the charges against the accused in order to nullify the issued arrest warrant. In this scenario, as was the case in the Kenyatta case, the withdrawal is without prejudice to the possibility of bringing new charges against the accused "at a

1105 HRW, 2009, p. 31, see *supra* note 998.

1106 Nouwen, 2013, p. 158, see *supra* note 226.

1107 For more information about the ICD see: HRW, Justice for Serious Crimes before National Courts: Uganda's International Crimes Division, January 2012, available at: www.hrw.org/sites/default/files/reports/uganda0112ForUpload_0.pdf.

1108 Fish, 2010, pp.1704–5, see *supra* note 1104.

1109 ICC, Trial Chamber V(b), Kenyatta case, Decision on Prosecution's Application for a Further Adjournment, 3 December 2014.

1110 ICC, Trial Chamber V(b), Kenyatta case, Notice of Withdrawal of the Charges against Uhuru Muigai Kenyatta, 5 December 2014.

1111 ICC, Trial Chamber V(b), Kenyatta case, 3 December 2014, para. 21, see *supra* note 1109.

later date, based on the same or similar factual circumstances, should [the Prosecution] obtain sufficient evidence to support such a course of action."[1112]

8. A MISSING MONITORING SYSTEM

The interests of justice presumption is a factor that should be taken into account regarding both communications and referrals.[1113] Under the Rome Statute, in the case of communications, if the Prosecutor decides not to initiate an investigation solely because investigating would not serve the interests of justice, her decision should be confirmed by the PTC. As to referrals, such a decision is challengeable as well according to Article 53(3)(b).

If the Prosecutor decides to initiate an investigation, there is no need for proving the interests of justice. However, as mentioned, the Prosecutor is obliged to explore the potential countervailing circumstances that may persuade her not to initiate an investigation if the interests of justice require so. In the case of communications, the PTC has an opportunity to assess the Prosecutor's efforts to find out if she must not initiate an investigation. However, as to referrals, even such minimum scrutiny is absent. The Prosecutor does not need to get an authorization from Judges to initiate an investigation into a referred situation. Her determination about the jurisdiction and the admissibility of a given situation is challengeable under Article 18 or Article 19 of the Statute. However, the interests of justice test is immune from challenges thanks to the presumption favoring its existence. This is the same story as to the case phase. When the Prosecutor intends to apply for a warrant, only the Prosecutor's decision not to prosecute because of the interests of justice considerations is challengeable. Otherwise, regardless of the trigger that has activated the relevant situation, the Prosecutor's determination that there is no reason to stop proceedings due to the lack of the interests of justice is not challengeable.

In February 2009, before the PTC of the Court issued two arrest warrants against Al-Bashir, some Sudanese organizations filed an application to the PTC I, seizing the situation in Darfur, under Rule 103 of the Rules of Procedure and Evidence. The applicants had requested that no arrest warrant would be issued by the PTC on grounds that, *inter alia,* it would have grave implications for the peace building process in Sudan and therefore it would not serve the interests of justice.[1114] Without addressing the substance of the request, the Chamber highlighted that Rule 103 of the Rule of Procedure and Evidence requires an applicant to secure the leave of the competent

---

1112 ICC, Trial Chamber V(b), Kenyatta case, 5 December 2014, para. 3, see *supra* note 1110.

1113 In the case of referrals for instance, the Mali Situation Article 53 Report states "based on its assessment of the situation, including through its missions to Mali of August and October 2012, there are no substantial reasons to believe that the opening of an investigation would not serve the interests of justice" (para. 172).

1114 ICC, PTC I, Darfur Situation, 4 February 2009, para. 3, see *supra* note 278.

Chamber prior to submitting any observation.[1115] For this purpose, as provided for in the consistent case law of the Court, the first and foremost factor for leave to be granted is the relevance of the application to an issue that is actually before the competent Chamber.[1116] However, in the given case, the Chamber concluded that this first requirement was not met because the matters to which the applicants had referred were unrelated to any issue before the Chamber.[1117] In the view of the Chamber, "the Statute does not entrust the Chamber with the power to review the Prosecution's assessment that the initiation of a case against a given individual through the issuance of an arrest warrant or a summons to appear would not be detrimental to the interests of justice."[1118] The Chamber emphasized that "it was the States Parties' express will that the power to, and responsibility for, carry out such assessment, lies with the Prosecution."[1119]

The Chamber correctly grounded its decision in the text of the Rome Statute; however, it shows a gap in the Rome Statute. The interests of justice notion is a mechanism to suspend the Court's intervention. When the Prosecutor initiates an investigation into a situation, it implies that the investigation serves the interest of victims and justice. Such a determination falls within the Prosecutorial discretion. However, since such a discretion may be exercised in a wrong way, the Prosecutor's determination should be brought under the judicial review. The interests of justice presumption is examined by taking into account the victims' interests. It is imaginable that the Prosecutor does not pay sufficient attention to the needs and interests of victims. The Prosecutor has interest in prosecution and investigation. Such a preference may affect her determination. Therefore, the Prosecutor's decision to initiate an investigation should be challengeable by the victims. If the Court is going to act as a court having the victims at its heart of attention, the interests of victims should be guaranteed at maximum. Assigning the final word about the interests of victims to the Prosecutor does not sound like a fair way to secure the maintenance of the victims' interests. As Groenhuijsen has stated, the OTP is not so willing to consider the role of the victims in the Rome Statute.[1120] It creates the risk of marginalization of the victims' needs and views in the Prosecutor's determinations. Therefore, a check-and-balance mechanism should be established. The founders of the ICC endeavored to make a prosecutor who is responsive and responsible for her decisions when they are against the interests of States. However, such a consideration was not given to the interests of victims, while the interests of victims should be given priority.

The ICC has been established to serve the interests of victims rather than the interest of States. The main interest common among the States that is respected and pursued by

1115 Ibid., para. 6.
1116 Ibid., para. 8.
1117 Ibid., para. 30.
1118 Ibid., para. 22.
1119 Ibid., para. 30.
1120 Marc S. Groenhuijsen, 'Victims' Rights and the International Criminal Court: The Model of the Rome Statute and its Operation', in W. J. M. Genugten, M. P. Scharf and S. E. Radin (eds.), *Criminal Jurisdiction 100 Years after the 1907 Hague Peace Conference*, T.M.C. Asser Press, 2009.

the Court is the interest in respecting and protecting the victims of the most serious international crimes. From such a perspective, it is a reasonable expectation that the victims be able to bring the Prosecutor's decision under judicial scrutiny, when they see that the Prosecutor's discretion might not serve their interest. The Rome Statute has accepted that exceptionally the Court's intervention might not serve the interests of justice. Such an idea has its own implications that should be observed. The Statute intends to prevent the Court's intervention in some circumstances when it hurts the victims. Such a harmful result should be effectively prevented. Judicial review assures the effectiveness and efficiency of such prevention. When there is an obligation that should be fulfilled, logically speaking, there should be a monitoring mechanism. The Rome Statute should be open to those interpretations that expand the scope of judicial scrutiny. In the case of referrals, a mechanism like the authorization mechanism that is in place regarding the communications should be established. When all situations should undergo a preliminary examination, the relevant Prosecutor's decision and determination should undergo a judicial scrutiny in the same way. The Rome Statute was written by taking into account the interest of States seriously. Now, it is time to read the Statute by considering victims.

PART FOUR

SITUATION SELECTION IN LIGHT OF EXPRESSIVISM

CHAPTER I
CONCEPTUALIZATION OF EXPRESSIVISM IN THE CONTEXT OF THE ICC

The ICC operates on a selective basis. The Court is not able to handle all situations and cases under its jurisdiction. More importantly, it is not intended to deal with all those situations and cases, because it is only a last resort mechanism, rather than a replacement to national jurisdictions. Combating international crimes is first an obligation upon States. In addition to its inability, the complementarity principle directs the Court to be hesitant to deal with all situations and cases. The permanency of the Court increases its excessive workload, and makes this organization more selective. Selectivity is a built-in feature of the Court that should be taken into account if someone wants to comprehend the Court well. All objectives, functions, mandates and structures of the Court should be understood in light of its selectivity. Selectivity is, indeed, a conceptual framework with normative implications. The Court was established on the backdrop of this major feature that may hurt its legitimacy and reputation. Therefore, the Court needs to operate under a theory that corresponds to its selectivity. Theories explain why a judicial system should be in place, given its abilities and inabilities. Given the arguments that will be put forward by this research, expressivism sounds like such a theory that fits the Court's selectivity. It gives expressive mandates to the Court.

The Court has been empowered with tools necessary to fulfil its expressive mandates, and to reduce the adverse effects of its selectivity. For instance, the concept of situation emerged to preserve the impartiality of the Court. The Court is not able to prosecute all cases, but it is not allowed to concentrate on the crimes committed by one side to a conflict. Therefore, the exercise of the Court's jurisdiction is situation-oriented. The preliminary examination is another crucial tool at the Court's disposal that helps this organization to decrease its selectivity and restrictions. Preliminary examination is a mechanism that expands the activities and authorities of the Court. In the case phase, the Prosecutor could address only one or a few actual cases, whereas she is able to deal with a more general context in the situational stage. The ICC Preliminary examination is a *sui generis* stage in the international criminal justice system. The original function of conducting the preliminary examination is to make a determination whether there is a reasonable basis to initiate an investigation into a situation. It may imply that the preliminary examination is only an intermediary tool for serving cases. However, the functions and benefits of this preliminary stage go beyond such a mandate. The preliminary examination assumes independent ends. The Court, as this thesis promotes, operates under the theory of expressivism, and the preliminary examination is an effective structure for the expressive mandates of the Court.

Upon descripting the situation selection process and criteria in the preceding Parts, the latest Part of this research studies the situation selection regime from the lens of expressivism. Expressivism is a normative and evaluative framework that has been adopted by this research to analyze the situation selection regime at the ICC. Adopting expressivism has the capacity to lessen the side effects of selectivity that are harmful for the Court's legitimacy.

In the 'General Introduction' part, the expressivism theory was defined. Expressivism determines the main function of the situation selection regime. According to this theory, the ICC selects a situation or a case to convey a message. Indeed, the Court selection regime is an instrument for projecting and promoting what the Court is intended to endorse. These messages are intended to address two main groups, namely victims and States. Victims and the affected communities are the local audiences of the ICC expressive mandates, and States are the global recipients. As to victims, the Court intends to serve their interests by recognizing their victimhood and giving voice to them, in addition to creating space for repairing their suffering partially and in a symbolic and expressive way. Victims are at the heart of the Court's attention, and they are the major audiences of the Court's expressive mandates. The Court needs to serve the victim's interests in an expressive manner, because the Court's selectivity does not allow the Court to meet all demands and needs of the victims. Apart from the victims, States are the wider audiences of the Court's expressive functions. The ICC by its exemplary and complementary intervention intends to encourage and to push States to take the initiative.

1. EXPRESSIVISM AND ITS BENEFICIAL EFFECTS ON VICTIMS

Victims have a unique status in the Court's functioning, and the Court serves their interests, *inter alia,* through expressive measures. The ICC needs to adopt and integrate a 'victim perspective' into its entire works and all aspects of its operations. Integrating a victim perspective at all stages of the Court's works means that the Court should take into account needs, views and interests of victims at all areas of its works. This perspective requires the Court to follow and stick to two rules regarding victims: harm reduction and no harm. The Court should struggle to reduce suffering of victims. In addition, all functions and areas of the Court's operations and works should be regulated by no harm principle. It means that nothing at the Court should hurt victims or increase their suffering. The recent rule was discussed in the interests of justice presumption Chapter. Moreover, a victim perspective requires the Court to adopt a victim-responsive approach. It means that the Court should have interaction and consultation with victims through, in particular, outreach activities. Considering the Court from this perspective promotes the idea that the ICC should be seen as an instrument for serving the interests of victims rather than the interest of States. The ICC is first and foremost an international organization. However, it has been established by States to facilitate fulfilling their responsibility to protect victims. Founding States of the Court should be seen from the perspective of 'sovereignty as responsibility' rather than 'sovereignty as power'.[1] The Court intends to create the greatest good and happiness for the greatest number of the major beneficiaries of its functioning, namely victims. The Court intends to deliver justice, and the principal beneficiaries of the ICC's justice are victims.

1.1. THE EMERGENCE OF THE VICTIMS' RIGHTS IN THE ICC

Criminal law was initially private. At the time, revenge played a key role in shaping justice. Over time, however, criminal law shifted to the public sphere. During this period, crimes were not considered merely as harm inflicted on individuals, but they were considered as actions against the public order as well. Indeed, a public aspect was added to the phenomenon of crime, and States became responsible to combat crimes. This transformation reduced the role of victims. At the national level, "victims used to be the forgotten party for a long time."[2] Upon the revolution of human rights, the public aspect of crimes remained intact. However, more attention was paid to the accused and his rights. It was a welcome development, but this movement ignored the victims' rights. Victims bore the brunt of the crimes involved.[3] The marginal role of the victims paved the way for the emergence of the victims' rights movement. The movement promoted the view that crime should be regarded as an infringement of the individual's rights.[4]

From such a perspective, victims should be at the heart of the attention in criminal law. The victims' rights activists call for a balancing of rights between victims and the accused. It has even been argued that victims should have greater rights within national criminal justice systems, because they are directly affected by criminal processes.[5] In such a context, the restorative justice emerged. This sort of justice focuses on the needs

---

1 See: Maartje Weerdesteijn, *The Rationality of Dictators: Towards a More Effective Implementation of the Responsibility to Protect*, Intersentia, 2016.

2 Marc S. Groenhuijsen and Anne-Marie de Brouwer, 'Participation of Victims: Commentary', in André Klip and Göran Sluiter (eds.) *Annotated Leading Cases of International Criminal Tribunals: the International Criminal Court* (2005–2007), Intersentia, 2010, p. 273.

3 Antony Pemberton and Rianne M. Letschert and Anne-Marie de Brouwer, 'Coherence in International Criminal Justice: A Victimological Perspective', *International Criminal Law Review*, 2015, vol. 15, p. 340.

4 Anne-Marie de Brouwer and Marc S. Groenhuijsen, 'The Role of Victims in International Criminal Proceedings', in Sergey Vasiliev and Göran Sluiter (Eds.), *International Criminal Procedure: Towards a Coherent Body of Law*, Cameron May, 2009, p. 151.

5 Brianne McGonigle Leyh, *Procedural Justice: Victim Participation in International Criminal Procedure*, Intersentia, 2011, p. 6.

of the affected people in the response to crimes.[6] Restorative justice has witnessed two main approaches: process-oriented and result-centered. In the process-oriented approach, the focus is on the inter-personal communications among the parties to a crime. This kind of restorative justice advocates for non-criminal proceedings with the victim-centered approaches.[7] It is generally conceived as a process that involves bringing together victims and offenders to seek collaboratively to heal the harm caused by the offence.[8] The outcome-oriented approach pays attention to a restorative and reparative solution. This reading of justice puts its stress on harm suffered by victims rather than crime.[9] However, the process leading to such an outcome could be still criminal and coercive.

The victims' rights movement has been productive in the international sphere, too. The creation of an international forum protecting the victims' rights has furthered the individualization of international criminal justice.[10] Individuals have become subjects of international law, besides States. They assume both responsibilities and rights, and they can be either victims or perpetrators of crimes. The first product of the victims' rights movement in the international sphere was the 1985 UN Declaration of Basic Principles of Justice for Victims of Crime and Abuse of Power. Article 6 of this Declaration reads "the responsiveness of judicial and administrative processes to the needs of victims should be facilitated by: Allowing the voices and concerns of victims to be presented and considered at appropriate stages of the proceedings where their personal interests are affected, without prejudice to the accused."[11]

In the context of the international criminal justice system, the establishment of the ICC marked a striking paradigm shift regarding the role of victims. The Court has been intended to serve the interests of victims. The architecture and structure of the Court have been designed in conformity to such a purpose. Enhancing the role of victims at the ICC and giving them a voice in the proceedings arises from the fact that justice sought by the Court is not only punitive, but it is restorative, too.[12] Serving the interests of victims would be a goal of the Court, separate and distinct from punishing wrongdoers.[13] Victims had been noticeably missed from the international criminal justice campaign. Before the ICTY and ICTR, victims of international crimes were seen

6 Margaret M. De Guzman, 'An Expressive Rationale for the Thematic Prosecution of Sex Crimes', in Morten Bergsmo (ed.), *Thematic Prosecution of International Sex Crimes*, Torkel Opsahl Academic EPublisher, 2012, p. 28.

7 McGonigle Leyh, 2011, p. 46, see *supra* note 5.

8 De Guzman, 2011, p. 526, see *supra* note 6.

9 McGonigle Leyh, 2011, p. 493, see *supra* note 5.

10 Luc Reydams and Jed Odermatt, 'Mandates', in Luc Reydams and Jan Wouters and Cedric Ryngaert (eds.), *International Prosecutors*, Oxford University Press, 2012, p. 109. And, De Brouwer and Groenhuijsen, 2009, p. 151, see *supra* note 78.

11 UN General Assembly, Declaration of Basic Principles of Justice for Victims of Crime and Abuse of Power, 29 November 1985.

12 "Recognized that the ICC has not only a punitive but also a restorative function" (ICC, ASP, Court's Revised Strategy in Relation to Victims, 5 November 2012, p. 2.).

13 War Crime Research Office, *Victim Participation before the International Criminal Court*, American University, 2007, p. 1.

only as witnesses. They were called to testify before tribunals in order to contribute to further a case.[14] However, the independence and autonomy of victims were not recognized. Victims had a role in delivering justice, but in a passive way. The ad-hoc tribunals initially failed to see victims as victims. The approaches adopted by the *ad hoc* tribunals were based on the idea that the tribunals primarily were established to punish perpetrators of war crimes.[15]

It is believed that the ICC's regime for victims can, in part, be traced back to the dissatisfaction over the *ad hoc* tribunal system.[16] Once, an ICTY judge had complained that victims were reduced to instrumentalised witnesses.[17] Another judge advised that the tribunal "must work harder to communicate with the peoples of the former Yugoslavia", who "often have little idea of what the [ICTY] is doing, except from what they learn via distorted news coverage and state-controlled propaganda."[18] As to the ICTR, the statement of Carla Del Ponte, the then Prosecutor of the ICTR, addressed to the UNSC in 2000, is remarkable when she said "nor should we forget the role of victims in the justice process. The voices of survivors and relatives of those killed are not sufficiently heard. Victims have almost no rights to participate in the trial process, despite the widespread acceptance nowadays that victims should be allowed to do so."[19]

To fill such a gap, the NGOs and some civil-law-oriented countries advocated the participation of victims in the ICC proceedings.[20] These efforts resulted in a system in which the victims are still able to attend the Court as a witness, but an independent status as victim is added. The dual status of victims, however, is under the Court's control.[21] In the ICC system, three types of victims' rights are recognized:

---

14 De Brouwer and Groenhuijsen, 2009, p. 149, see *supra* note 4.

15 Ibid.

16 Christine Van den Wyngaert Hon, 'Victims before International Criminal Courts: Some Views and Concerns of an ICC Trial Judge', *Case Western Reserve Journal of International Law*, 2011, vol. 44, p. 476. And, War Crime Research Office, 2007, p. 2, see *supra* note 13.

17 See: Claude Jorda and Jérôme de Hemptinne, 'The Status and Role of the Victim', in Antonio Cassese (ed), *the Rome Statute of the International Criminal Court: A Commentary*, Oxford University Press, 2002, p. 1387.

18 Statement by Ms. Gabrielle Kirk McDonald, President of the International Criminal Tribunal for the Former Yugoslavia to the United Nations General Assembly, 1999, available at: www.icty.org/en/press/address-united-nations-general-assembly-judge-gabrielle-kirk-mcdonald-president-international.

19 ICTY, Press Release, Address to the Security Council by Carla del Ponte, Prosecutor of the International Criminal Tribunal for the former Yugoslavia and Rwanda, 24 November 2000, available at: www.icty.org/en/press/address-security-council-carla-del-ponte-prosecutor-international-criminal-tribunals-former, last accessed at 5 April 2017.

20 Salvatore Zappala, 'The Rights of Victims v. the Rights of the Accused', *Journal of International Criminal Justice*, 2010, vol. 8, p. 159.

21 When the Trial Chamber considers an application by victims who have this dual status, it will establish whether the participation by a victim who is also a witness may adversely affect the rights of the defense at a particular stage in the case. The Trial Chamber will take into consideration the modalities of participation by victims with dual status, the need for their participation and the rights of the accused to a fair and expeditious trial (See: ICC, Trial Chamber I, Lubanga case, Decision on Victims Participation, 18 January 2008, para. 134).

participation, protection, and reparation.[22] The OTP's Policy Paper on Victims Participation insists that "under the Rome Statute, victims are actors of international justice rather than its passive subjects. Their participation is a statutory right, not a privilege bestowed on a case-by-case basis."[23] The ICC has made a great change in the international community's approach to victims. Such a change, however, is rooted in the 1985 United Nations Declaration of Basic Principles of Justice for Victims of Crime and Abuse of Power.[24] The Declaration affirms "the necessity of adopting national and international measures in order to secure the universal and effective recognition of, and respect for, the rights of victims of crime and of abuse of power."[25]

The Court's approach to victims is one of those measures taken by the international community. The ICC was created as a tool to preserve victims' interests. Serving the victims is an end that has facilitated empowering the Court with necessary functions and powers for this purpose. Even some hail the Court as a 'victims' court'.[26] The criminal venture is not an end in itself, but a means to deliver justice for the victims.[27] Victims of international crimes have the right to justice at the international level.[28] This right implies that international courts should afford victims a greater role in the criminal process.[29] Victims should be "the main beneficiaries of justice."[30] Therefore, the victims' rights constitute a cornerstone of the Rome Statute system.[31] In the architecture of the ICC, victims participate in the process of proceedings. The participation of victims in the proceedings has been called a 'Copernican revolution' in international criminal procedure.[32]

The expansion of the procedural status of victims in the ICC was the product of restorative justice.[33] The Court has incorporated some restorative features in its

22 De Brouwer and Groenhuijsen, 2009, p. 155, see *supra* note 4.

23 ICC, OTP, Policy paper on Victims' Participation, 12 April 2010, p. 1. And, Judge René Blattman States "victims' participation is not a concession of the Bench, but rather a right accorded to victims by the Statute" (ICC, Trial Chamber I, Lubanga case, Separate and Dissenting Opinion of Judge René Blattman to Decision on victim's participation, 18 January 2008, para. 13).

24 Van den Wyngaert Hon, 2011, p. 478, see *supra* note 16. And, War Crime Research Office, 2007, p. 2, see *supra* note 13.

25 Paragraph 1.

26 Human Rights Center University of California, The Victims' Court? A Study of 622 Victim Participants at the International Criminal Court, 2015, p. 1.

27 Athanasios Chouliaras, 'The Victimological Concern as the Driving Force in the Quest for Justice for State-Sponsored International Crimes', in Rianne Letschert and Roelof Haveman, Anne-Marie de Brouwer and Antony Pemberton, *Victimological Approaches to International Crimes: Africa*, Intersentia, 2011, p. 63.

28 Valentina Spiga, 'No Redress without Justice: Victims and International Criminal Law', *Journal of International Criminal Justice*, 2012, vol. 10, p. 1380.

29 McGonigle Leyh, 2011, p. 494, see *supra* note 5.

30 ICC, ASP, The Impact of the Rome Statute System on Victims and Affected Communities, Annex V(a), 2010, para. 17.

31 ICC, ASP, Resolution on Victims and Affected Communities, Reparation and Trust Fund for Victims, 27 November 2013.

32 Spiga, 2012, p. 1379, see *supra* note 28.

33 Sergey Vasiliev, 'Victim Participation Revisited: What the ICC is Learning About Itself', in Carsten Stahn (ed), *The Law and Practice of the International Criminal Court*, Oxford University Press, 2015, p. 1194.

outcome-oriented sense in its system. In particular, it has resulted in reparation ordered by the court.[34] Restorative justice is grounded on the idea that "participation and reparation play an important role in achieving justice for victims."[35] However, it does not mean that the Court seeks private justice. ICC crimes are public wrongs. In this sense, these crimes should be publicly investigated, prosecuted, condemned and punished, because "perpetrators should be called to account by the polity as a whole, not just by the individual victim."[36] The ICC deals with international crimes whose impact is intra-national. These crimes are of concern to the international community as a whole. The Court's intervention through coercive measures and punishment is an indicator that these crimes matter to the international community. Punishment expresses the public feature of these crimes. Although the ICC may aim at achieving restorative goals, the process is not necessarily restorative.[37] The practice of international human rights supervisory bodies indicates that prosecution of the international criminals is increasingly considered to be an integral part of the remedy owed to victims.[38] For this reason, it has been Stated that rather than a restorative justice institution, the ICC should be more described as victim-friendly.[39]

1.2. COURT'S MESSAGES FOR VICTIMS

One of the OTP's strategies is "to ensure that victims are able to fully exercise their right to participate in ICC proceedings, in a manner that is sensitive to their rights and interests."[40] In addition, the OTP has adopted a strategical principle "to systematically address the interests of victims in the work of the Office, seeking their views at an early stage, before an investigation is launched, and continuing to assess their interests on an on-going basis."[41] Based on this strategy, the OTP has grounded a policy to promote "direct interaction with victims and victims' associations at all stages of its activities and on an ongoing basis from the preliminary examination."[42] The right-based approach to victims has been adopted as the Court's strategy to empower victims as vital actors in the justice process rather than a passive recipient of services and magnanimity.[43]

---

34 Ibid., p. 1136.

35 ICC, ASP, Report of the Court on the Strategy in relation to Victims, 10 November 2009, para. 3.

36 Stanford Encyclopedia of Philosophy, Theories of Criminal Law, 14 October 2002, available at: https://plato.stanford.edu/entries/criminal-law, Last accessed at 5 April 2017.

37 McGonigle Leyh, 2011, p. 499, see *supra* note 5.

38 Spiga, 2012, p. 1377, see *supra* note 28.

39 Vasiliev, 2015, p. 1194, see *supra* note 33.

40 ICC, OTP, Policy Paper on Victims' Participation, p. 3.

41 The Prosecutorial Strategy is based on four fundamental principles: i) positive complementarity; ii) focused investigations and prosecutions; iii) addressing the interests of victims; and iv) maximizing the impact of the Office's work (See: ICC, OTP, Prosecutorial Strategy (2009-2012), 1 February 2010, para. 22).

42 ICC, OTP, Policy Paper on Victims' Participation, p. 1.

43 ICC, ASP, Court's Revised Strategy in relation to Victims, 5 November 2012, para. 6.

In the ICC, victims are right-holders whose rights' protection is one the Court's aim. The victims' concerns and views have an independent value and function, independent from other actors within the Court. The PTC refers to the independence of victims and insists that "such independence should be preserved, including *vis-à-vis* the Prosecutor, so that victims can present their interests."[44] It per se enhances the dignity and autonomy of the victims at the ICC.

The victims' participation in the proceedings results in the acknowledgment of victimhood. The presence of the victims in the criminal proceedings delivers the message that they have not been denied or ignored. Formal recognition of victimization is the most important feature of participating in the international criminal justice system.[45] The perpetrators of the core crimes tend to hide and deny their unimaginable atrocities to protect themselves from the potential prosecutions in the future. The official denial of past horrors treats the victims as if they were negligible.[46] Such an experience of being morally insignificant leads to a second wound of silence.[47] Victims remain silent, because they think their voices are not valuable to be heard by society. The opposite of denial is acknowledgement. The ICC attempts to recognize the victimhood of the affected people in order to prevent the denial of atrocities.

Knowledge or factual truth needs acknowledgment because certain truths may already be known, but they have often previously been officially denied.[48] An official acknowledgment blocks the way of denial. Engagement in the proceedings is a major pillar in the acknowledgment of crimes that shapes collective memory for the construction of a shared identity.[49] The victims' participatory right at the ICC is an effective mechanism for the engagement in the proceedings. Victims of international crimes are objects of the perpetrators' actions through the process of us-them thinking. In this context, victims are excluded from the perpetrator's moral community.[50] It is a salient feature of international crimes that victims are rarely perceived as victims at the time of the commission of crimes.[51] Dehumanization of victims results in social death.[52] This concept reflects the processes by which victims of international crimes

44 ICC, PTC I, Situation in the DRC, Decision on the Applications for Participation in the Proceedings of VPRS 1, VPRS 2, VPRS 3, VPRS 4, VPRS 5 and VPRS 6, 17 January 2006, para. 51.

45 Marc S. Groenhuisen and Antony Pemberton, 'Genocide, Crimes against Humanity and War Crimes: A Victimological Perspective on International Criminal Justice', in Rianne Letschert and Roelof Haveman and Anne-Marie de Brouwer and Antony Pemberton, *Victimological Approaches to International Crimes: Africa*, Intersentia, 2011, p. 33.

46 Frank Haldemann, 'Drawing the Line: Amnesty, Truth Commissions and Collective Denial', in Rianne Letschert and Roelof Haveman, Anne-Marie de Brouwer and Antony Pemberton, *Victimological Approaches to International Crimes: Africa,* Intersentia, 2011, p. 265.

47 Ibid., p. 268.

48 Paul Gready, The Era of Transitional Justice: The Aftermath of the Truth and Reconciliation Commission in South Africa and Beyond, Routledge, 2011, p. 20.

49 Chouliaras, 2011, p. 64, see *supra* note 27.

50 Groenhuisen and Pemberton, 2011, p. 2, see *supra* note 45.

51 Pemberton and Letschert and de Brouwer, 2015, p. 335, see *supra* note 3.

52 James Waller, *Becoming Evil: How Ordinary People Commit Genocide and Mass Killings,* Oxford University Press, 2002, p. 237.

become mere objects in the eyes of perpetrators.[53] As a result of such a process, victims of atrocities disappear from the public domain.[54]

The denial of dignity and autonomy of victims pave the way of repressing them. Given this fact, the ICC is intended to restore the victims' destroyed dignity by giving them a voice. Participation in the proceedings is a procedural right that reflects the value of the victims in the group.[55] Committing international crimes is facilitated through blaming victims. In the eyes of perpetrators, victims are suffering due to their own shortcomings.[56] In contrast with this conviction, the Court intends to show that blames should be put on the shoulders of the offenders, instead of victims. The ICC seeks justice for the victims in a manner that involves re-humanizing them.[57] In this re-humanization process, the victims become socially visible. Denying crimes serves to render victims invisible in society. Therefore, the remedy required to redress this injustice should result in the visibility of victims.[58] Attendance at the Court for expressing views and needs makes the victims visible.

2. EXPRESSIVISM FOSTERS THE POSITIVE COMPLEMENTARITY

The second main addressee of the Court's expressive mandates are States. Regarding States, the Court has a 'norm projection' function.[59] The Court's intervention is intended to show that there are some norms that should be protected by States. It is primarily the responsibility of States to combat the violation of these norms. The Court exercises its jurisdiction on the complementarity principle. Only in the case of the lack of genuine proceedings at the domestic level, the Court can initiate an investigation. Authorizing the Prosecutor to assess the national proceedings in order to evaluate the complementarity requirement as a part of the preliminary examination endows the Prosecutor with monitoring powers. Monitoring national jurisdictions in light of the positive approach to the complementarity principle that seeks to activate the national jurisdictions is a gradual, and probably slow, process. The preliminary examination has no time limit in the ICC legal system. Such an openness is consistent and necessary for the mandates of the preliminary examination.

53 Pemberton and Letschert and de Brouwer, 2015, p. 351, see *supra* note 3.

54 Haldemann, 2011, p. 270, see *supra* note 46.

55 Jo-Anne Wemmers, 'Victims' Need for Justice: Individual versus Collective Justice', in Rienne Letschert and Roelof Haveman, Anne-Marie de Brouwer and Antony Pemberton, *Victimological Approaches to International Crimes: Africa,* Intersentia, 2011, p. 149.

56 Groenhuisen and Pemberton, 2011, p. 30, see *supra* note 45.

57 Ibid., p. 31.

58 Haldemann, 2011, p. 272, see *supra* note 46.

59 David Luban, 'Fairness to Rightness: Jurisdiction, Legality and the Legitimacy of International Criminal Law', in A. Besson and John Tasioulas (eds.), *The Philosophy of International Law,* Oxford University Press, 2010, p. 576.

In addition, the Court advocates the positive approach to complementarity. This policy is enhanced by this educational function of the Court. The responsibility for prosecuting international crimes is primarily on the shoulder of States. The Court shall encourage and facilitate national jurisdictions. The Court's intervention has an encouraging and demanding effect in this regard. The Court should be considered successful when no case reaches the Court, thanks to the prompt intervention of the domestic jurisdictions. The Court's influence on the national systems is of great importance in serving the interests of victims. National criminal justice systems can provide justice to a larger number of victims.[60] Taking into account this fact, the ICC shall attempt to activate the national jurisdictions through its expressive activities.

Complementarity has two dimensions. Many scholars have referred to these two aspects in different words. Nouwen describes these two aspects as complementarity being the big idea and complementarity as the admissibility rule.[61] Elsewhere, she referred to these two different approaches to complementarity as anti-impunity and catalyst effect approaches.[62] The former Prosecutor of the Court defines these dimensions as the admissibility test and positive complementarity.[63] Some label these two dimensions as the legal dimension or complementarity *stricto sensu* and the policy dimension of complementarity.[64] Kleffner divides complementarity into two types: complementarity as a legal principle and complementarity as legal rule.[65] Some experts have referred to these dual approaches to complementarity as partnership and vigilance.[66] Rastan names the different faces of complementarity as an admissibility principle and a burden-sharing principle.[67] The OTP, in its Strategic Plan for 2009–2012, labeled these aspects as positive complementarity and the admissibility test. According to the Strategic Plan, "the Principle of complementarity has two dimensions: i) the admissibility test, i.e. how to assess the existence of national proceedings and their genuineness, which is a judicial issue; and ii) the positive complementarity concept, i.e. a proactive policy of cooperation aimed at

---

60 The Redress Trust, Victim Participation in Criminal Law Proceedings: Survey of Domestic Practice for Application to International Crimes Prosecutions, September 2015, p. 71.

61 Ibid., p. 13.

62 Ibid., p. 107.

63 Luis Moreno-Ocampo, 'A Positive Approach to Complementarity: The Impact of the Office of the Prosecutor', in Carsten Stahn and Mohamed M. El Zeidy (eds.), *The International Criminal Court and Complementarity: From Theory to Practice,* Cambridge University Press, 2011, p. 23.

64 Patrícia Pinto Soares, 'Positive Complementarity and the Law Enforcement Network: Drawing Lessons from the Ad Hoc Tribunals' Completion Strategy', *Israel Law Review*, 2013, vol. 46. pp. 319–321.

65 Jann K. Kleffner, *Complementarity in the Rome Statute and National Criminal Jurisdiction,* Oxford University Press, 2008, p. 100.

66 ICC, OTP, Informal Expert Paper: The Principle of Complementarity in Practice, 2003, para. 3.

67 Rod Rastan, 'Complementarity: Contest or Collaboration?', in Morten Bergsmo (ed.), *Complementarity and the Exercise of Universal Jurisdiction for Core International* Crimes, Torkel Opsahl Academic EPublisher 2010, p. 83.

promoting national proceedings."[68] Stahn calls these forms the classic and positive complementarity.[69]

2.1. DEFINITION OF POSITIVE COMPLEMENTARITY

In the Kampala Conference, the Bureau Report on Stocktaking offered a definition for the positive complementarity. According to the Bureau, this notion "refers to all activities/actions whereby national jurisdictions are strengthened and enabled to conduct genuine national investigations and trials of crimes included in the Rome Statute, without involving the Court in capacity building."[70] The positive complementarity is not explicitly mentioned in the Rome Statute. This idea became relevant to the literature from one of the well-known statements made by the first Prosecutor of the Court. Moreno-Ocampo asserted that "a truly effective international justice system would be a system where no case reaches the Court as States assume their primary responsibility to investigate."[71] Elsewhere, he suggested a different evaluative test in assessing the Court's success. According to him, "the absence of trials before this court, as a consequence of the regular functioning of national institutions, would be a major success."[72] Schabas rejects Moreno-Ocampo's idea. He argues this idea is not "really a very compelling message for States Parties, who were investing large sums of money in the institution and who expected to see trials and convictions."[73] Nonetheless, trial and pure judicial functions are not the only functions of the Court. Some extra-judicial activities lie in the functions of the Court. The idea of a court without a case has been accepted by many authors. Stahn summarizes the idea of writers of 'the Complementarity from Theory to Practice' in these words: "international justice is no longer measured by institutional performance, but is judged by its actual ability to solve problems: whether and to what extent it is able to make domestic jurisdiction work."[74]

The complementarity principle organizes the relationship between States and the Court. Such a relationship was initially based on competition. Complementarity was merely understood as a conflict resolving method for the concurrent jurisdictions.

68 ICC, OTP, Strategic Plan (2009–2012), para. 16.

69 Carsten Stahn, 'Taking Complementarity Seriously: On the Sense and Sensibility of 'Classical', 'Positive' and 'Negative' Complementarity', in Carsten Stahn and Mohamed M. El Zeidy (eds.), *The International Criminal Court and Complementarity: From Theory to Practice*, Cambridge University Press, 2011, p. 251.

70 ICC, ASP, Report of the Bureau on Stocktaking (Complementarity): Taking Stock of the Principle of Complementarity: Bridging the Impunity Gap, 25 March 2010, para. 16.

71 Moreno-Ocampo, 2011, p. 24, see *supra* note 63.

72 Statement made by Mr. Moreno-Ocampo, Ceremony for the Solemn Undertaking of the Chief Prosecutor, 16 June 2003, available at: www.iccnow.org/documents/MorenoOcampo16June03.pdf.

73 William A. Schabas, *An Introduction to International Criminal Court*, Cambridge University Press, 2011, p. 156.

74 Carsten Stahn and Mohamed M. El Zeidy (eds.), *The International Criminal Court and Complementarity: From Theory to Practice*, Cambridge University Press, 2011, p. 5.

Concurrency in jurisdictions requires rules of priority in some cases.[75] Under the complementarity principle, the Court was seen as a rival for the national jurisdictions. Over time, this reading was changed. As a policy matter, the positive complementarity replaced the competition with cooperation.[76] Positive complementary does not see the national jurisdictions as the rivals that should be defeated. By contrast, they are the Court's partners in reaching a common destination.

The Rome Statute contemplates an institution that may never be employed, if States fulfill their obligation by exercising jurisdiction over core crimes.[77] Those objectives are not realized by the Court's inaction. By contrast, this destination may be reached only if the Court is proactive. Positive complementarity is a program of action.[78] In light of the Court's limited resources, it could only contribute to international justice if most States exercised their obligations to investigate crimes.[79] Yet, the ICC is not meant to be a passive institution.[80] Article 54 1(b) of the Rome Statute provides that the Prosecutor shall "take appropriate measures to ensure the effective investigation and prosecution of crimes within the jurisdiction of the Court." The article is worded in a general style, and is not limited to prosecutions before the Court. Stahn asserts that this provision is a positive basis for managerial use of authority.[81] Under this article, the Prosecutor is obliged to enhance effective investigations and prosecutions across the world. It is the responsibility of the Court to pave the way for States to discharge their responsibilities as well. Moreno-Ocampo has referred to this responsibility of the Court by saying that "the first task of the Prosecutor's office [is to] make its best effort to help national jurisdictions fulfill their mission."[82] In Stahn's words, the positive complementarity is the "enabling side of the complementarity principle."[83] There are many practical and political obstacles for States to administer justice. Reduction of these costs could have been a consequence of implementation of the policy of positive complementarity.[84] From this perspective, the positive complementarity could be

75 Göran Sluiter, Hakan Friman and Suzannah Linton (eds.), *International Criminal Procedure: Principles and Rules,* Oxford University Press, 2013, p. 117.

76 Stahn, 2011, p. 261, see *supra* note 69.

77 John T. Holmes, 'Complementarity: National Courts versus the ICC', in Antonio Cassese, Paola Gaeta and John R.W.D. Jones (eds.), *The Rome Statute of the International Criminal Court: A Commentary,* Vol(I), Oxford University Press, 2002, p. 667.

78 Sarah M.H. Nouwen, Complementarity in the Line of Fire: the Catalyzing Effect of the ICC in Uganda and Sudan, Cambridge University Press, 2013, p. 20.

79 Christopher Hall, 'Positive Complementarity in Action', in Carsten Stahn and Mohamed M. El Zeidy (eds.), *The International Criminal Court and Complementarity: From Theory to Practice,* Cambridge University Press, 2011, p. 1017. However, Hall adds that Passive complementarity is a bit misnomer, because Prosecutor will be active in assessing whether States have been fulfilling their complementarity obligations.

80 Ibid., p. 1014.

81 Stahn, 2011, p. 265, see *supra* note 69.

82 ICC, OTP, Moreno-Ocampo' Statement to the Assembly of States Parties to the Rome Statute of the International Criminal Court, 22 April 2003.

83 Stahn, 2011, p. 235, see *supra* note 69.

84 Nouwen, 2013, p. 378, see *supra* note 78.

called 'constructive complementarity'.[85] It constructs a new global system and order. The core element of this system is the idea of shared responsibility. For this reason, Stahn asserts the ICC "is not purely a court of last resort, a final arbiter over the admissibility assessment, but a guardian of accountability."[86] One of the ICC judges states that "the overall goal of the Statute to combat impunity can also be achieved by the Court through means of active cooperation with the domestic authorities."[87]

Ending impunity is feasible through positive complementarity. The positive complementarity activities inspire and encourage domestic justice systems.[88] The Court is not able to combat all crimes on its own. It needs participation of other actors. The impunity gap "is a real prospect as many national systems do not have the capacity to process international crimes committed by subordinates, where their leaders are being tried before the Court. The long term solution is clearly to develop national legal systems."[89] The Court should attempt to put an end to the culture of impunity through burden-sharing with States. In the words of Ryngaert, "the positive complementarity means that the Court and the State cooperate with a view to bringing international criminals to justice."[90] Here, the Court assumes a managerial role thereby directing the national jurisdictions towards a way designated at the Court's discretion. States function under the supervision of the Court. It is a major development because "one of the problems related to the prosecution of international crimes was the absence of a system of oversight."[91]

2.2. MATERIALIZING POSITIVE COMPLEMENTARITY

The positive complementarity activities are various. These potential activities have been addressed sufficiently. Since this dimension is undefined, it has been

85 Some define the positive of complementarity in the scope of the complementarity rule or in other words in the context of jurisdiction. Here, the positive complementarity corresponds with the negative complementarity. Negative complementarity means that unless a State is unwilling/unable, the Court has no jurisdiction. Positive complementarity means the unwillingness/inability criteria apply only if there is a conflict between the Court and a national jurisdiction (See: Silvana Arbia, 'Proactive Complementarity: A Registrar's Perspective and Plans', in Carsten Stahn and Mohamed M. El Zeidy (eds.), *The International Criminal Court and Complementarity: From Theory to Practice*. Cambridge University Press, 2011, p. 54).

86 Stahn, 2011, p. 239, see *supra* note 69.

87 ICC, Appeals Chamber, Gaddafi case, Separate Opinion of Judge Anita Ušacka, 21 May 2014, para. 65.

88 William W. Burke-White and Scott Kaplan, 'Shaping the Contours of Domestic Justice: The International Criminal Court and an Admissibility Challenge in the Uganda Situation', in Carsten Stahn and Göran Sluiter (eds.), *The Emerging Practice of the International Criminal Court*, Martinus Nijhoff Publishers, 2009, p. 113. And, Rastan, 2010, p. 83, see *supra* note 141. And, Nouwen, 2013, p. 8, see *supra* note 78.

89 Arbia, 2011, p. 56, see *supra* note 85.

90 Cedric Ryngaert, 'Horizontal Complementarity', in Carsten Stahn and Mohamed M. El Zeidy (eds.), *The International Criminal Court and Complementarity: From Theory to Practice*, Cambridge University Press, 2011, p. 865.

91 Robert Cryer, *Prosecuting International Crimes: Selectivity and the International Criminal Law Regime*, Cambridge University Press, 2005, p. 148.

too underdeveloped to have its effects in practice.[92] In this regard, two different approaches can be adopted: expansive and narrow. The former demands the Court assist the states in conducting domestic proceedings, but the latter is limited to merely encouraging states to investigate domestically.[93]

2.2.1. Encouragement

Encouragement is the point of departure for the Court's attitude to States under positive complementarity. Encouragement should be provided to both national jurisdictions and other actors in the international sphere. Encouraging national actions and promoting anti-impunity initiatives could be general, for example in public statements, or specific, for example in private bilateral meetings.[94] The first Prosecutor of the Court admits that positive complementarity "will encourage national proceedings wherever possible."[95] It is the OTP policy to encourage "genuine national proceedings where possible."[96]

Encouragement means communicating with States. The Court as a whole must interact with national authorities to encourage domestic activities such as the adoption of implementing legislation.[97] To reach this destination requires diplomacy. The OTP functions in two distinct contexts. In the internal plane, it is a legal organ of the Court, but in the external context it assumes some diplomatic roles. As soon as the dormant jurisdiction of the Court is awoken, the Prosecutor should materialize positive complementarity. By opening the preliminary examination, the main stage for exercising positive complementarity commences. Moreno-Ocampo maintains that the preliminary examination phase "offers the most promising and the first opportunity for the OTP to serve as a catalyst for the initiation of national proceedings."[98]

Encouraging is not limited to States. In the international criminal justice system, the Court is not alone. In addition to States, non-State actors in this field play a prominent role. The Prosecutor of the Court states that "the ICC alone cannot win the fight against impunity."[99] The Court is highly dependent on cooperation from other actors. Even NGOs and civil society can provide the Court with great cooperation, and the Court needs to have a connection with them. For instance, the Court suffers from the time

---

92 Nouwen, 2013, p. 110, see *supra* note 78.

93 Ibid., p. 378.

94 ICC, OTP, Informal Expert Paper: The Principle of Complementarity in Practice, 2003, para. 7.

95 ICC, OTP, Statement of the Prosecutor Luis Moreno-Ocampo to Diplomatic Corps The Hague, Netherlands 12 February 2004.

96 ICC, OTP, Paper on Some Policy Issues before the Office of the Prosecutor, September 2003, p. 5.

97 Stahn, 2011, p. 248, see *supra* note 69. It should be noted that the ASP is of the view that this action should primarily be a task of the ASP Secretariat. (See, ICC, ASP, Compilation on implementing legislation, 1 June 2010).

98 Moreno-Ocampo, 2011, p. 25, see *supra* note 63.

99 ICC, OTP, Prosecutor Lecture, The International Criminal Court – Current Challenges and Future Prospects, 16 December 2013, p. 5, available at: www.dfa.ie/media/dfa/alldfawebsitemedia/ourrolesandpolicies/ourwork/iccprosecutorvisitsireland/Lecture-delivered-by-Prosecutor-of-ICC-at-RIA-in-Dublin-on-16-December-2013.pdf).

gap between the occurrence of crimes and the moment when it starts an investigation. It endangers the existing evidence in the field. To overcome such a problem, the OTP has adopted a strategy to cooperate with NGOs and other first responders in the scene of the crimes. According to this strategy, "the office has begun to discuss with then NGO community how first responders could support the office in its work and what support could be expected from the office."[100] Positive complementarity requires a communicative and cooperative relationship with NGOs to maximize their capacities in fighting international crimes.

2.2.2. Reverse Cooperation

The relationship between the Court and States is mutual. It is a two-way road. Not only States cooperate with the Court, but the Court also assists States in prosecuting ICC crimes. The statutory base for such an up-down cooperation is Article 93(10). According to Paragraph (a) of this article, "the Court may, upon request, cooperate with and provide assistance to a State Party conducting an investigation into or trial in respect of conduct which constitutes a crime within the jurisdiction of the Court or which constitutes a serious crime under the national law of the requesting State." This article demonstrates that the ICC and domestic jurisdictions are not competing, but mutually reinforcing each other. However, it has been said that this article does not provide for the Court *proprio motu* authority to supply States with information.[101] To provide States with cooperation needs a request to be made by a state. This kind of cooperation is called 'reverse cooperation'. Gioia refers to the main features of reverse cooperation as "1. It is meant to happen on request of a state; 2. The Court may provide cooperation, so it is not under an obligation; 3. It is envisaged mainly taking place in the context of evidentiary matters; 4. Both Chamber and Prosecutor can be addressees of a request; and 5. It can also be lent to the benefit of non-member States."[102]

The assistance provided by the Court can be categorized in two ways, namely informative assistance and capacity building. The Court can provide States with information in order to pave the way of the prosecution and investigation at the domestic level. In certain situations, it is advisable to "assist a State genuinely willing to investigate and prosecute by providing it with the information gathered by the Office from different public sources."[103] The OTP may provide States with information it has received from public resources. In the words of Moreno-Ocampo, "it is a proactive use of OTP information to help Sates to fulfill their obligations. To achieve a common responsibility."[104] Article 93(1)(b)(i) refers to some instances of the information-

---

100 ICC, OTP, Strategic Plan (2016–2018), para. 25.

101 Nouwen, 2013, p. 99, see *supra* note 78.

102 Federica Gioia, 'Complementarity and Reverse Cooperation', in Carsten Stahn and Mohamed M. El Zeidy (eds.), *The International Criminal Court and Complementarity: From Theory to Practice*, Cambridge University Press, 2011, pp. 811–12.

103 ICC, OTP, Paper on Some Policy Issues before the Office of the Prosecutor, September 2003, p. 5.

104 Moreno-Ocampo, 2011, p. 24, see *supra* note 63.

oriented assistance such as transmission of statements, documents or other types of evidence obtained in the course of an investigation or a trial conducted by the Court.

To provide information in an effective way, the OTP has established the Law Enforcement Network (LEN). This system has been established for "the exchange of information, the coordination of activities and the development of common standards."[105] It is a network thereby which States can obtain the information necessary for the national prosecutions. "Specialized organizations, such as INTERPOL and EUROPOL, are seen as potential participants in the network."[106] Based on the LEN, the ICC plays as a network actor. However, this mechanism does not meet all needs. For this reason, the OTP in its strategic plan for 2016–2018, suggests setting up some mechanisms like 'open source crimes database' that provides "investigators and prosecutors with easily accessible data on potential crimes, witnesses and perpetrators."[107]

The second type of assistance that might be provided by the Court is capacity building. This kind of assistance embraces a wide range of activities such as "training of police, investigators and prosecutors, capacity building with regard to protection of witnesses and victims, forensic expertise, training of judges and training of defense counsel, security for and independence of officials."[108] Training would advance the overall objective of building a network of States able to carry out effective prosecutions.[109] As Moreno-Ocampo insists, the OTP "contributes to the efforts of situation countries to build expertise and capacities by calling their experts and lawyers to participate in investigative activities."[110]

In providing States with assistance, the financial considerations should be taken into account. The OTP suffers from budgetary limits. Some argue that the restricted budget of the Court must be directed towards criminal proceedings rather than capacity construction.[111] According to this group, it is for other actors to provide technical assistance to states.[112] The Strategic Plan adopted by the OTP in 2016 emphasizes that capacity building "might be further strengthened through the creation of a globally available training and technical support capacity."[113] Stahn also argues that the positive complementarity measures and activities are discretionary, because the

---

105 ICC, OTP, Strategic Plan (2012 – 2015), p. 29.

106 Soares, 2013, p. 336, see *supra* note 64.

107 ICC, OTP, Strategic Plan (2016–2018), para. 96.

108 ICC, ASP, Report of the Bureau on Stocktaking (Complementarity): Taking Stock of the Principle of Complementarity: Bridging the Impunity Gap, 18 March 20120, para. 17(2).

109 ICC, OTP, Informal Expert Paper, 2003, para. 12, see *supra* note 94.

110 Moreno-Ocampo, 2011, p. 27, see *supra* note 63.

111 Morten Bergsmo and Olympia Bekou and Annika Jones, 'Complementarity and the Construction of National Ability', in Carsten Stahn and Mohamed M. El Zeidy (eds.), The International Criminal Court and Complementarity: From Theory to Practice, Cambridge University Press, 2011, p. 1063.

112 Paul F. Seils, 'Making Complementarity Work: Maximizing the Limited Role of the Prosecutor', in Carsten Stahn and Mohamed M. El Zeidy (eds.), *The International Criminal Court and Complementarity: From Theory to Practice,* Cambridge University Press, 2011, p. 1013. And, Moreno-Ocampo, 2011, p. 25, see *supra* note 63.

113 ICC, OTP, Strategic Plan (2016–2018), para. 96.

Court has limited capacity and must balance its own responsibilities against domestic priorities.[114] At the Kampala Conference, the delegations had a major concern, namely, to prevent the imposition of financial burden upon the Court under the name of positive complementarity. In one of the Conference reports, it was maintained that it is not envisaged that the positive complementarity activities "would entail additional resources for the Court, nor should the Court become a development organization or an implementing agency."[115] However, it was insisted that "the relevant organs of the Court could, within the limits of their respective mandates, also act as a catalyst for assistance, helping to bridge the divide between donors and potential partner countries."[116]

Although the budget is a major factor in exercising the Court's policies, insisting on a free positive complementarity rests on a misperception of the premises. The budget of the Court should not be meant to be used merely for conducting prosecutions. The Court is empowered with financial resources in order to realize its mandates. In budgeting and allocating the budget it should be taken into account that whatever is consistent with the objectives of the Court can have some funds. The positive complementarity activities fall within the Court's objective. As some of the experts have mentioned, "the commitment of resources and energy into these activities is expected to prove a sound and effective investment, by reducing the need for intensive investigations and prosecutions by the ICC."[117] The Court is mandated to enhance a global system of criminal justice through both judicial activities and positive complementarity actions. Both mandates need financial resources.

114 Stahn, 2011, p. 268, see *supra* note 69.

115 ICC, ASP, Report of the Bureau on Stocktaking (Complementarity): Taking Stock of the Principle of Complementarity: Bridging the Impunity Gap, 18 March 2010, para. 42.

116 Ibid., para. 45.

117 ICC, OTP, Informal Expert Paper, 2003, para. 5, see *supra* note 94.

CHAPTER II

IMPLICATIONS OF EXPRESSIVISM ON THE SITUATION SELECTION

As discussed, the expressive functions of the Court has two main audiences, States and victims. Adopting expressivism as the normative framework within which the situation selection at the ICC should be framed and shaped has some implications in relation to both victims and States.

1. SELECTION OF A SITUATION FOR CONDUCTING PRELIMINARY EXAMINATION AS A PLATFORM TO SERVE VICTIMS

As mentioned, the ICC is unable to address needs of all victims, and to hear voices of all affected people, and to cover all kinds of victimhood. The Court has to select relatively few situations for investigation and an even smaller number of cases for prosecution. Such selectivity is, however, justified by expressivism. The Court takes action in an exemplary and expressive way. This criminal institution is intended to create, project and promote some norms at the international level, and to keep the victims' hope to see justice alive. Therefore, the Court is not intended to operate in a far-reaching and inclusive manner. Nonetheless, the Court has adopted some mechanisms to enhance the scope of its expressive initiatives in order to reach a larger number of victims. In this regard, the most meaningful mechanism that serves the expressive mandates of the Court is preliminary examination. Preliminary examination is unique for the Court. This procedural stage has been designed to serve the specific goals of the Court, given its selectivity. International crimes are committed in the context of mass atrocities, mass victimization, and mass perpetrators. However, the preliminary examination phase is capable to broaden the scope of the Court's intervention.

The Court's action is limited neither to few cases, nor to investigation and prosecution. This is a major difference between the Court and other criminal tribunals at the domestic level that should be taken into account in the understanding of the Court. The procedure and architecture of the Court have been constructed based on the special features and needs of the Court. In the preliminary examination, the Prosecutor of the Court enjoys flexibility. Many legal and practical restrictions in the investigation and prosecution phases are absent from the preliminary examination. The Prosecutor can easily start a preliminary examination. Only those situations that are manifestly outside of the jurisdiction of the Court remain behind the closed doors of the Court. However, there is no assessment of admissibility and other statutory criteria to open a preliminary examination. Under the Rome Statute, the Prosecutor has an absolute power for this purpose. Her decision to open a preliminary examination is not reviewed by the Chambers. Merely opening a preliminary examination assumes expressive mandates. It expresses that the international community takes the initiative; it signals out that they do not remain unnoticed the atrocities. In late 2016, the Court faced a temporary legitimacy crisis: a wave of withdrawals from the Rome Statute surged, and three African States declared their intention to terminate their membership in the Court. They justified their decision by claiming that the Court exclusively targets the African countries and ignores other situations in other parts of the world. This perception might not be accurate, since it does not consider the whole architecture of the Court.

By 2017, the Prosecutor has initiated investigations into 10 situations; 9 of them were African.[118] Yet, there is a large number of non-African situations under preliminary examination that involved, *inter alia*, crimes allegedly committed by powerful States.[119] Nevertheless, this part of the Court's structure has been mainly overlooked by the Court's critics. The Prosecutor's reaction to a crisis is not limited to initiating an investigation. Conducting a preliminary examination is also at the Prosecutor's disposal. Preliminary examination, as the situation selection process, can assume a function to manage the expectations in light of the theory of expressivism. Selectivity fits the Court if an expressive mandate is determined for its functions. Indeed, the Court addresses only a handful of situations, thereby delivering a message. Preliminary examination serves the expressive mandate of the Court by delivering messages that the international community is not indifferent to the perpetration of unimaginable atrocities and is responsive to victims of core crimes.

During the preliminary examination, the Prosecutor is able to take a wide range of actions. Major positive effects of listening to victims can be largely obtained in the preliminary examination. By the assistance of the intermediary organizations, the OTP can develop a constructive relationship with victims. Communication activities play a prominent role in this regard that should be brought to the center of the OTP's activities. The Prosecutor of the Court does not resemble an ordinary prosecutor at the domestic criminal systems. She is the Prosecutor of a unique judicial system with unique authorities and responsibilities. Therefore, she should not be limited to criminal investigation and prosecution tasks. There are many major obstacles in the road to

---

118 These situations are as follows: Congo, Uganda, Libya, Sudan, Central African Republic I and II, Mali, Côte d'Ivoire and Kenya.

119 These situations include Iraq (the crimes committed allegedly by the UK troops), Afghanistan (the crimes committed allegedly by the US forces), Ukraine (the crimes committed allegedly by Russia) and Palestine (the crimes committed by Israel) (See: ICC, OTP, Report on Preliminary Examinations Activities (2016)).

criminal justice. By opening the preliminary examination, the Court is capable to do some minimal acts in favor of victims.

Based on preliminary examinations, the Prosecutor issues the Article 53 Reports explaining the preliminary examination process. In the reports, the Prosecutor firstly deals with the issue of jurisdiction. The Prosecutor's declaration that the Court has jurisdiction over a situation has expressive values. It is a kind of acknowledgment of the victimhood that prevents the denial of atrocities. In the assessment of both jurisdiction (in particular to find out the scale of crimes and their nature) and the admissibility requirement and in particular its gravity component, the Prosecutor addresses the victims. She hears the views and needs of the victims. Even when there are exceptional circumstances that persuade the Prosecutor not to initiate an investigation given the interests of justice, the execution of a preliminary examination assumes expressive mandates. It signals out that the crimes are committed, they are grave and deserve to be investigated, however, taking into account victims' interests, timing is not suitable for an investigation.

From the expressivist perspective, in the ICC, the expressive value of the preliminary examination is no less than prosecution and trial. Expressivism tries to show the condemnation of crimes. Such a condemnation is not obtained exclusively by punishment. In Hanna's words, we express our seriousness with a number of extra-punitive elements of the criminal justice systems, such as the degree of investigative efforts.[120] It does not mean that punishment is not desirable for the expressivist. By contrast, sentences have major expressive mandates. However, other parts of the Court have expressive mandates too. Duff provides a compelling example here. He maintains that "suppose that a defendant dies shortly after conviction, or for some other reason cannot be punished: justice has still been done by his trial, since he has been held to account."[121] From such a perspective, even the mere issuance of an arrest warrant by the Court is important. Even if there is no practical advantage of the issuance of such warrants, "the ICC can merely deliver symbolic justice by stigmatizing the accused."[122] There is a long and tough way ahead of the Court to investigate a situation. Only a handful of situations manage to pass the high threshold of investigation.

If the Court is limited to these small situations, its influence will considerably decrease. Due to the criminal nature of investigations and prosecutions, it is not recommendable to loosen the legal tights and borders of these stages in order to broaden the scale of the Court's activities. However, the preliminary examination phase seems to be able to make up for such a shortcoming. The Prosecutor has been empowered to wider opportunities and possibilities in the preliminary examination. Besides legal criteria,

---

120 Nathan Hanna, 'Say What? A Critique of Expressive Retributivism', *Law and Philosophy*, 2008, vol. 27, pp. 138–139.

121 Antony Duff, 'Authority and Responsibility in International Criminal Law', in Samantha Besson and John Tasioulas (ed.), *The Philosophy of International Law*, Oxford University Press, 2010, p. 598.

122 Payam Akhavan, 'International Criminal Justice in the Era of Failed States: The ICC and the Self-Referral Debate', in Carsten Stahn and Mohamed M. El Zeidy (eds.), *The International Criminal Court and Complementarity: From Theory to Practice*, Cambridge University Press, 2011, p. 302.

operational factors are major obstacles in the way of investigation. For this reason, a 'situation selection document', similar to the 'Case Selection Document' that has been introduced by the Prosecutor in relation to the case phase should be adopted to show all situations that fall within the jurisdiction of the Court that have the potentiality to warrant an investigation. This mechanism is a list encompassing all situations that are ranked based on their priority and gravity. However, such a plan should be public and accessible. Determination and establishment of the Court's jurisdiction in a situation imply that ICC crimes have been committed, even if such a situation does not lead to an investigation due to lack of the admissibility requirement or priority.

A significant consequence of the preliminary examination for victims is that by opening the preliminary examination, the Trust Fund for Victims (TFV) is able to support the victims within a situation without a need for trial and conviction. The Court's investigation and prosecution are slow and frustrating for victims. Reparation and concrete support lie among the first demands of the victims. Preliminary examination gives the victims a chance to see justice in the reparation form. The Rome Statute has predicted an independent entity, which is mandated to address the reparation. The Trust Fund for Victims was established in September 2002 by decision of the ASP "for the benefit of victims of crimes within the jurisdiction of the Court, and of the families of such victims."[123] This entity is meant to fulfil the Court's reparative mandates. Victims of international crimes may claim reparation for the harm suffered. The UN General Assembly has adopted Resolution 60/147, which points out that victims are entitled to the following forms of reparation: restitution, compensation, rehabilitation, satisfaction, and guarantees of non-repetition.[124]

Article 75 of the Rome Statute states "the Court may make an order directly against a convicted person specifying appropriate reparation to, or in respect of, victims, including restitution, compensation, and rehabilitation." The importance of the reparation regime at the ICC is such that "the success of the Court is, to some extent, linked to the success of its reparation regime."[125] It is mainly because of the fact that the victims are often dissatisfied with classical retributive justice.[126] They need something more than punishment and that is why Rule 97(1) of the Rules of Procedure and Evidence provides that "taking into account the scope and extent of any damage, loss or injury, the Court may award reparation." Reparation could be granted in two ways: individual and collective if in the either case the victims suffered personal harm.[127] However, reparation on an individualized basis does not appear

---

123 Article 79 (1) of the Rome Statute.

124 UN, General Assembly, Basic Principles and Guidelines on the Right to a Remedy and Reparation for Victims of Gross Violations of International Human Rights Law and Serious Violations of International Humanitarian Law, 16 December 2005.

125 ICC, PTC I, Lubanga case, Decision concerning Pre-Trial Chamber I's Decision of 10 February 2006 and the Incorporation of Documents into the Record of the Case against Mr Thomas Lubanga Dyilo, 27 February 2006, para. 136.

126 Wemmers, 2011, p. 151, see *supra* note 55.

127 ICC, Trial Chamber I, Lubanga case, Decision Establishing the Principles and Procedures to be Applied to Reparation, 7 August 2012, para. 217.

to be very practical.[128] The large number of victims hampers the Court to repair the entirety of individual loss and harm. Nonetheless, the Trial Chamber II in the Katanga case awarded the victims individual reparation in the form of symbolic compensation of USD 250 per victim. The Chamber stressed that this symbolic amount, while not intended to compensate for the entirety of the harm, does provide meaningful relief to victims for the harm they have suffered.[129] Collective reparation has more symbolic value, and thus are more consistent with the expressive mandates of the Court. They cover a larger number of victims. Rule 98(3) of the Rules of Procedure and Evidence provides a trial chamber with a right to order an award for collective reparation against a convicted person "where the number of victims and the scope, forms and modalities of reparation make a collective award more appropriate." This kind of reparation will be a macro-level approach that focuses on the needs of society as a whole.[130] In the case of collective reparation, the TFV is responsible to manage them.

TFV has two main functions. First, the TFV provides assistance to victims of a specific case allowed by the judicial process. In this regard, the TFV seizes of an order for reparation where it would determine whether a particular individual was eligible to receive an award and to determine the nature and size of the reparation to be awarded.[131] For instance, the Trial Chamber dealing with the Lubanga case endorsed the suggestion made by the Trust Fund that "a community-based approach, using the [Trust Fund]'s voluntary contributions, would be more beneficial and have greater utility than individual awards, given the limited funds available and the fact that this approach does not require costly and resource-intensive verification procedures."[132]

Second, it assists victims of the broader situations before the ICC, regardless of whether the harm they suffered stems from particular crimes charged by the Prosecutor in a specific case.[133] For the purpose of the latter, the resources used are "other than those collected from awards for reparation, fines and forfeitures" that are mainly provided by donations.[134] In helping the victims, the TFV takes into account the victims' needs and harm suffered. For example, the AVSI Foundation in northern Uganda has been established by the TFV targeting victims mostly at the individual level through physical rehabilitation.[135] In the DRC, the outbreak of child soldiering has encouraged the TFV to take some actions in favor of children, for instance, by

128 Marc S. Groenhuijsen, 'Victims' Rights and the International Criminal Court: The Model of the Rome Statute and its Operation', in W. J. M. Genugten and M. P. Scharf and S. E. Radin (eds.), *Criminal jurisdiction 100 Years after the 1907 Hague Peace Conference*, T.M.C. Asser Press, 2009, p. 307.

129 ICC, Press Release, Katanga case: ICC Trial Chamber II awards victims individual and collective reparation, 24 March 2017, available at: www.icc-cpi.int/Pages/item.aspx?name=pr1288, last accessed at 7 April 2017.

130 Wemmers, 2011, p. 148, see *supra* note 55.

131 ICC, Appeals Chamber, Lubanga case, Judgment on the Appeals Against the Decision Establishing the Principles and Procedures to be Applied to Reparation, 3 March 2015, para. 147 (d).

132 ICC, Trial Chamber I, Lubanga case, 7 August 2012, para. 217, see *supra* note 127.

133 ICC, The Trust Fund for Victim, Learning from the TFV'S Second Mandate: From Implementing Rehabilitation Assistance to Reparation, 2010, p. 47.

134 Ibid.

135 Ibid., p. 5.

providing them with a kit containing most of the supplies needed for his or her livelihood rehabilitation activity of choice.[136]

In spite of all of these institutional measures, the success of the Court in serving the interests of victims depends on the attitude on the part of the authorities operating the system.[137] There is a gap between the law in books and the law in action. Groenhuijsen has concerns about the adverse effects of the hostile attitude of some organs of the Court towards the victims. He, for instance, refers to the first period of the ICC activities, when the OTP did everything to marginalize the role of victims.[138] Groenhuijsen correctly points to a common problem in approaching to the ICC and in the understanding of this *sui generis* organization at the international level. As he mentions, specifically about the victims, "the prosecutors and judges at the ICC are all lawyers with a lifetime of trial experience behind them. It looks very likely that their views on the proper role of the victims during proceedings have taken shape in the formative years of their careers and can hardly be affected by a couple of afternoons of training by the Victims and Witnesses Unit employees at the ICC."[139]

The ICC as an international court differs from the typical criminal tribunals at the domestic level. To understand the Court, a suitable perspective marking the distinctions and differences should be taken. Many expectations about the Court arise because the Court is wrongly understood as a normal court like other criminal tribunals. The ICC should refrain from trumpeting up high expectations, but it should acknowledge its limitations, and communicate to victims what it can and cannot offer.[140] Given this facts, the Prosecutor should be more responsive to communications received by her office. The fate of most communications is unknown because there is not necessarily a public response and there is no possibility to review the Prosecutor's decision not to initiate an investigation or even not to open a preliminary examination. At very least, the Prosecutor can publicize the communications received by her office without prejudicing the confidentiality of their senders.

2. LENIENT COMPLEMENTARITY ASSESSMENT

Shaping the situation selection at the ICC by taking into account the expressive mandate of the Court has some implications in relation to States. As mentioned, complementarity is a notion consisting of two dimensions, namely, the complementarity principle and the complementarity rule. There is an interaction between these aspects of the complementarity notion. Complementarity intends to put an end to impunity, while the Court remains a last resort in the direct battle against impunity. Being a complementary

136 Ibid., p. 13.
137 Groenhuijsen, 2009, p. 400, see *supra* note 128.
138 Ibid., p. 309.
139 Ibid.
140 Pemberton and Letschert and de Brouwer, 2015, p. 366, see *supra* note 3.

court leads to the idea of positive complementarity. No functions, however, should be ignored in favor of others. The ASP, in its report to the first review conference of the ICC in 2010, referred to this point by noting that "actions under positive complementarity must not be misused to avoid justice."[141]

It is meaningless if the complementarity principle is accepted but its effects on the complementarity rule are put aside. The relationship between the complementarity principle and the complementarity rule resembles the relationship between the spirit and the text of law. The text should be read and understood in light of its spirit and context. Article 17 of the Rome Statute as the statutory framework of the complementarity rule explicitly refers to the complementarity principle as the normative framework governing the complementarity rule. The positive complementarity activities are an integral part of the complementarity system or complementarity as a whole. Positive complementarity should be given space before exercising the complementary jurisdiction of the Court over a specific situation or case. The Prosecutor of the Court should try to activate the national legal systems by encouraging and assisting them. At least, the Prosecutor should give States a chance to discharge their responsibility to combat international crimes. If these initiatives fail, then the Prosecutor could pave the way for the Court's intervention. Indeed, the process of the Court's intervention is as follows: encouragement, cooperation, and finally, action. Moreno-Ocampo refers to elements of the sophisticated approach of the Statute to national proceedings as "dialogue (who is doing what) cooperation (we can help you if you need) and independent decisions to intervene (we shall do it if you don't)."[142] Such an approach may change the orthodoxy of the top-down perspective governing international criminal justice. To rethink justice from a bottom-up perspective is one of the most pressing challenges of the next few decades.[143] The preliminary examination is the main stage within which the positive complementarity could be conducted. The Court should avoid expedition in the preliminary examination.[144] The direct intervention of the Court is not the ultimate and desirable goal or function of the Court. By contrast, the Court should do its best to make a change in the national sphere. It needs dialogue, interaction and cooperation, all of which need time. Moreover, the Court should be positive and open to measures that may activate domestic jurisdiction. Declaring a case admissible is not an advantage for the Court. As mentioned, the Court's success should be assessed by taking into account its preliminary examination activities too.

---

141 ICC, ASP, Report of the Bureau on Stocktaking: Complementarity, 18 March 2010, para. 25.

142 Moreno-Ocampo, 2011, p. 22, see *supra* note 57.

143 Stahn and El Zeidy, 2011, p. 17, see *supra* note 74.

144 Two staff of the ICC OTP in a joint article explain why the preliminary examination is a time consuming process. For instance, they say that if the policy is not to open investigations when the prospect of the States', initiative are bright, it takes time since in this scenario the Court gives the State concerned more time. (See: Fabricio Guariglia and Emeric Rogier, 'The Selection of Situations and Cases by the OTP of the ICC', in Carsten Stahn (ed.), *The Law and Practice of the International Criminal Court,* Oxford University Press, 2015, pp. 355–356).

Here, the decision of PTC II on the Kenya's admissibility challenge can be brought under question. On 8 March 2011, PTC II, by majority, decided to summon three Kenyan suspects to appear before the Court, namely Ruto, Kosgey and Arap Sang. Some days later, the Government of Kenya, pursuant to Article 19 of the Statute, challenged the admissibility of the cases against the three persons for whom summons to appear had been issued. In April 2011, Kenya filed more than 900 pages containing materials relevant to its challenge, and in addition filed a request for cooperation and assistance under Article 93(10) of the Statute. This provision is the statutory base for reverse cooperation. According to Paragraph 10 (a), "the Court may, upon request, cooperate with and provide assistance to a State Party conducting an investigation into or trial in respect of conduct which constitutes a crime within the jurisdiction of the Court or which constitutes a serious crime under the national law of the requesting State." In June 2011, the Chamber issued its decision on Kenya's request and thereby rejected the first cooperation request. It did not terminate Kenya's attempt to appeal to the Court's cooperation. In September 2011, Kenya filed the second cooperation request. However, this request was rejected too. PTC III, in denying the request of Kenya, argued that the Court is under no obligation to automatically grant a cooperation request submitted by a State, due to "the usage of the verb 'may' in Article 93(10)(a) of the Statute."[145] Upon the first request, PTC issued its decision on the admissibility challenge made by the government of Kenya on 30 May 2011. In its decision, the Chamber took into account the cooperation request. However, the Chamber denied the relevance of such a request on the issue of admissibility. The Chamber stated that "the request for assistance has no linkage with the issue of admissibility, which is regulated under part II of the Statute. *Ergo*, a determination on the inadmissibility of a case pursuant to Article 17 of the Statute does not depend on granting or denying a request for assistance under Article 93(10) of the Statute. This conclusion finds support in the fact that a State may exercise its national jurisdiction by way of investigating or prosecuting, irrespective of and independent from any investigative activities of the Prosecutor."[146]

In addition, the Chamber asserted that the Article 19 regime is independent from the request under Article 93(10), and "there is no indication whatsoever in the Statute that the application of articles 17 and 19 are subject to granting a request for assistance under Article 93(10) of the Statute."[147] It is evident that the Chamber has adopted a purely literal approach to the issue of admissibility and the relevant statutory provisions. The interpretation of the Chamber appears to be consistent with the text of the Rome Statute, but it is inconsistent with its spirit. The complementarity rule should be understood and read in light of the complementarity principle, and it requires the Court to adopt a positive approach to complementarity. When a State has intent

145 ICC, PTC III, Decision on the Second Request for Assistance Submitted on Behalf of the Government of the Republic of Kenya Pursuant to Article 93(10) of the Statute and Rule 194 of the Rules of Procedure and Evidence, 12 July 2012, para. 17.

146 ICC, PTC II, Ruto case, Decision on the Application by the Government of Kenya Challenging the Admissibility of the Case Pursuant to Article 19(2)(b) of the Statute, 30 May 2011, para. 34.

147 Ibid., para. 35.

to exercise its jurisdiction, the Court should be willing to assist the State concerned. It is consistent with being a court as the last resort. However, it is possible that a request for assistance is a sham request in order to evade justice by making delays in the proceedings. If it is so, it could be assessed under the scenario of unwillingness referred to in Article 17. Here, the Court can conditionally declare a case inadmissible, provided the State proceeds with the case at hand within a timeframe determined by the Court upon receipt of the requested information. Therefore, there could be a reasonable compromise between the different considerations. The mainstream reading of the text of the Rome Statute does not support this interpretation. However, the spirit of the Statute and reading its text from a teleological perspective can give space to positive complementarity. The Rome Statute needs amendments to adapt positive complementarity in a more effective way.

The Prosecutor should activate the Court's jurisdiction over a situation or case gradually and step by step. Without an exercise of positive complementarity, the Prosecutor should prevent activating the Court's jurisdiction. Here, and as a conclusion, the suggestion of Stahn can be put forward. He suggests some techniques that "allow the Court to give sufficient space to domestic investigations and prosecutions, while retaining checks and balances inherent in the complementary regime."[148] Firstly, He advocates flexibility towards domestic jurisdiction to investigate and build cases after the filing of an admissibility challenge. Stahn asserts that, at present, states face a 'race against time' in admissibility proceedings.[149] However, the States should be given reasonable time to investigate and build the case after the notice of an admissibility challenge, and prior to a final decision on admissibility.[150] Judge Ušacka, in her dissenting opinion about the admissibility challenge raised by Kenya, refers to the tendency among the Court to prefer expedition in the national proceedings. However, she disagreed with such rough insistence. She asserts that

> "The PTC's prevailing consideration was that the proceedings had to be conducted expeditiously. However, the PTC did not explain why this was the case or why the efficacy of proceedings before the Court was at stake. Neither Article 19 of the Statute nor rule 58 of the Rules of Procedure and Evidence specifically use the term 'expeditious'. The criminal proceedings before the PTC were, at the time of the admissibility proceedings, at a very early stage. The suspects were not in detention as the PTC had issued summonses to appear. Nor can it be said that the suspects' right to be tried without undue delay (Article 67(1)(c) of the Statute) would have been compromised by a decision of the PTC to slightly prolong the admissibility proceedings. Finally, as there was no ongoing conflict in Kenya, the impact of the admissibility proceedings on the investigation of the Prosecutor, which is according to Article 19(7) of the Statute suspended during such proceedings, was probably limited. Therefore, it must be concluded that expeditiousness was unduly emphasized in the PTC's

148 Carsten Stahn, 'Admissibility Challenges before the ICC: From Quasi-Primacy to Qualified Deference', in Carsten Stahn (ed.), *The Law And Practice of the International Criminal Court,* Oxford University Press, 2015, p. 258.

149 Ibid., p. 255.

150 Ibid., p. 254.

exercise of discretion and given too much weight, especially in comparison to the Appellant's sovereign right to investigate and prosecute the case itself."[151]

In this regard, Heller's proposition can be put forward. Heller, by proposing a radical complementarity, argues that "as long as a State is making a genuine effort to bring a suspect to justice, the ICC should find his or her case inadmissible regardless of the prosecutorial strategy the State pursues, regardless of the conduct the State investigates."[152] For this purpose, he suggests relaxing 'the same person' requirement to permit 'pyramidal' investigative strategies.[153] Pyramidal prosecutorial strategy is a strategy to build up a case gradually by targeting the low-level perpetrators first and then pursuing the higher-level ones. Del Potne notes that "building a case against the most senior persons responsible may involve a series of cases which would up the ladder, prosecuting lower-level perpetrators in the collection of evidence against the higher-level perpetrators, or in obtaining the substantive cooperation of insiders."[154] As mentioned, this policy is followed by the ICC OTP too. Such a strategy could be helpful for domestic prosecutions. Therefore, Heller recommends that the Court not find a State inactive "with regard to high-level suspects targeted by the OTP simply because the State is pursuing a pyramidal strategy."[155] A delay in prosecuting could be justified. If it is not the case, the Court should declare a case admissible. However, it seems that the Court is hesitant to accept such a flexible approach. In the Ruto case, the Kenyan government invoked the foregoing 'bottom up' approach and argued that it could not be considered inactive because it had opened formal investigation against the wanted persons by "building on the investigation and prosecution of lower level perpetrators."[156] However, this argument was rejected by both the PTC and the Appeals Chamber.[157] It shows that the Judges are not ready to make a change in understanding the complementarity principle yet. However, there is no legal barrier in shifting the current approach in a permanent institution like the ICC. The Court is dynamic to remain effectively permanent.

Secondly, as Stahn suggests, to avoid the side effects of such flexibility, more intense monitoring after deference to the national jurisdiction is necessary. This attitude seeks

---

151 ICC, Appeals Chamber, Ruto case, Dissenting Opinion of Judge Anita Ušacka, 20 September 2011, para. 29.

152 Kevin Jon Heller, 'Radical Complementarity', *Journal of International Criminal Justice,* 2016, vol. 14, p. 640.

153 Ibid., p. 664.

154 Carla Del Ponte, 'Investigation and Prosecution of Large-Scale Crimes at the International Level: The Experience of the ICTY', Journal of International Criminal Justice, 2006, vol. 4, p. 543.

155 Heller, 2016, p. 643, see *supra* note 152.

156 ICC, Ruto case, Application on Behalf of the Government of Kenya Challenging the Admissibility, 31 March 2011, para. 71.

157 ICC, PTC II, Ruto case, Decision on the Application by the Government of Kenya Challenging the Admissibility of the Case Pursuant to Article 19(2)(b) of the Statute, 30 May 2011, para. 58. And, ICC, Appeals Chamber, Kenya situation, Judgment on the Appeal of the Republic of Kenya Against the Decision of Pre-Trial Chamber II of 30 May 2011 Entitled Decision on the Application by the Government of Kenya Challenging the Admissibility of the Case Pursuant to Article 19(2)(b) of the Statute, 30 August 2011, para. 83.

"to minimize the risks associated with deference, i.e. to ensure that a case does not fall off the radar screen after an admissibility challenge."[158] Giving opportunity to States does not affect the interest of others, including victims. Apart from strict monitoring to find if the Court's intervention is warranted, the Court can start victim-friendly activities by protecting and supporting victims.

Thirdly, the 'inconditional admissibility' could be a practical proposition in order to make a compromise between the complementarity principle and the complementarity rule. Such a technique is suitable "in cases in which doubt remains in relation to the feasibility of final deference to a domestic jurisdiction."[159] Here, the Prosecutor can set up a deadline for the State challenging the admissibility of the case to activate its jurisdiction over the same case before the Court. Such an approach was already mentioned by the Libyan government in its challenge against the admissibility of the Al-Senussi case. In that case, Libya requested the PTC to declare the case against Mr Al-Senussi inadmissible before the Court or, in the alternative, "to consider implementing a positive approach to complementarity by declaring the case inadmissible subject to the fulfillment of express conditions or other ongoing obligations."[160] Seils advocates giving time to States in order to develop their proceedings, but he believes that the only legal avenue open to the Prosecutor to stop proceedings before the Court for this purpose is to invoke the 'interests of justice' provision in Article 53.[161] Nonetheless, the interests of justice notion does not deal with the state-oriented issues. This notion is intended to serve the interest of victims. The Prosecutor has discretion to be able to declare a case inadmissible conditionally. There is no provision in the Rome Statute to prevent her from such an authority.

Although Stahn suggests these methods in the context of the admissibility challenges, they are not limited to such a context. Indeed, these techniques can be applied in the context of the situational phase, when there is no challenge against admissibility yet. During preliminary examination, when the Court faces inactivity of the states, it should begin its reaction with positive complementarity activities, i.e. by encouraging states to take the initiative. For this purpose, the Prosecutor can use the above-mentioned techniques, namely flexibility, monitoring and conditional approval. The preliminary examination is a stage for monitoring and assessment. This stage has not been designed for expeditious decisions. The Prosecutor should be in constant contact and dialogue with the states. It is a place where the Court has an opportunity to exercise the greatest impact on national legal systems.[162] In contrast with other judicial functions of the Prosecutor, the preliminary examination is mostly based on non-judicial actions such as diplomacy and negotiations.

---

158 Stahn, 2015, p. 255, see *supra* note 148.

159 Ibid., p. 254.

160 ICC, Al-Senussi case, Application on Behalf of the Government of Libya Pursuant to Article 19 of the ICC Statute, 1 May 2012, para. 206.

161 Paul Seils, 'Putting Complementarity in Place', in Carsten Stahn (ed.), *The Law And Practice of the International Criminal Court*, Oxford University Press, 2015, p. 314.

162 Ibid., p. 309.

CONCLUSION

This book 'Situation Selection at the International Criminal Court (Law, Policy, Practice)' aimed to clarify and rationalize the process in which a situation is selected at the ICC, and to explain the criteria that are applied in selecting a situation. The ICC law, the prosecutorial policies and the practice of the Court in this regard were studied in detail. In addition, a normative and evaluative framework was established, namely the expressivism theory, through which the ICC law, policies and practices as to the situation selection regime were justified and evaluated.

This ending section of this study summarizes the main results from this research and identifies some significant recommendations for the Court.

1. 'SITUATION' AS A CONCEPT WITH AN AMBIGUOUS DEFINITION

The 'situation' notion should be defined precisely, and the identification stage should be recognized and designed within the ICC's architecture. The borders of the preliminary examination and its objects should be defined precisely in order to enhance the quality of its functioning.

Part One of this research was tasked to address a conceptual question: what does a situation mean in the Rome Statute? Situation is a unique notion at the ICC legal system. This is the point of departure for the Court's functioning. The Court activates its jurisdiction over a situation. The situational phase precedes the case stage at the ICC. In spite of its importance, the situation notion has not been defined by the Rome Statute. A situation in the sense of the Rome Statute consists of two elements, namely the contextual element and jurisdictional parameters. The contextual component is the factual aspect of a situation that refers to a concrete crisis. Although the contextual element of a situation is not a legal concept, the contextual elements of the ICC-identified crimes are of assistance in determining a situational context. An internal or international armed conflict, or a campaign of systematic or widespread attacks against civilian populations may constitute a crisis that is the central component of the situation notion. A crisis may stem from various reasons, such as electoral competitions, war on natural resources or ideological and political tensions. A crisis is a critical distinguishing factor that contributes to separating a situation from other situations. In determining a situation, a concrete crisis is defined in terms of jurisdictional parameters referred to in the Rome Statute.

More than one decade after the establishment of the ICC, it seems that there is no clear perception of the situation notion yet. This research has referred to some instances that uncover the misunderstanding of the situation concept. It seems that there is no end for such a misperception. In May 2017, the Prosecutor of the Court, in addressing the UNSC on the situation in Libya, stated that her office would consider crimes against migrants in Libya. This ambition shows that the Prosecutor has confused the notion of situation with the territory concept. Referring to a situation is not equal to referring to a territory. The UNSC has referred to the ICC a specific situation related to Libya, not the territory of this country. There should be a nexus between ensuing incidents and the initial crisis if they are going to be dealt with under one situation.[163] The Judges of PTC III, in authorizing the Prosecutor to initiate an investigation into the situation of Côte d'Ivoire, had adopted a correct approach. They initially authorized the Prosecutor to investigate the post-election violence that had been ongoing since 2010.[164] Later, by obtaining more information, they extended the temporal jurisdiction to 2002 by identifying a nexus between crimes committed between 2002 and 2010 and the foregoing post-election violence.[165] According to the Appeals Chamber, crimes in Cote d'Ivoire were committed in a single situation "in which an ongoing crisis involving a prolonged political dispute and power-struggle culminated in the events in relation to which the Chamber earlier authorized an investigation".[166]

Moreover, it should be recalled that the Court's functioning is situation-oriented because the generality of situations has two major advantages for the Court. First, by preventing the Prosecutor to conduct one-sided prosecutions or investigations, the impartiality of the Court is preserved. This feature of the situation concept has a normative aspect. It means that the Prosecutor has to activate the Court's jurisdiction over a situation in the sense of the Rome Statute. A non-inclusive and partial situation is not a situation in this sense and it can not constitute an object for opening a preliminary examination. From such a perspective, accepting UNSC referrals as to the situations in Libya and Darfur could be criticized. The referring Resolutions exclude nationals of non-member States from the Court's jurisdiction. Secondly, given the inability of the Court to prosecute all cases, by incorporating the notion of situation into the Court's legal system, the Court finds an opportunity to deal with a situation instead of few cases. A situation to some extent represents all cases arising from the context of the situation and a situation-oriented intervention can help the Court to further its expressive mandates.

163 Mohammad Hadi Zakerhossein, Crimes Against Migrants in Libya Manifestly Outside of the Prosecutor's Jurisdiction, 22 May 2017, available at: https://justicehub.org/article/zakerhossein-crimes-against-migrants-libya-manifestly-fall-outside-icc-prosecutors.

164 ICC, PTC III, Decision Pursuant to Article 15 of the Rome Statute on the Authorization of an Investigation in the Situation in the Republic of Côte d'lvoire, 3 October 2011.

165 ICC, PTC III, Decision on the Prosecution's Provision of Further Information Regarding Potentially Relevant Crimes Committed between 2002 and 2010, 22 February 2012.

166 Ibid., para. 36.

2. IDENTIFICATION STAGE: THE MISSING PHASE AT THE ICC ARCHITECTURE

Part Two of this book dealt with the situation selection process at the ICC. The current layout of the situation selection process has three stages, namely trigger mechanism, preliminary examination and determination stage. However, this layout needs amendment. Chapter II of Part Two discussed the shortcomings of the existing layout. The commencement of the preliminary examination stage should be determined precisely. The ISIS situation in Iraq and Syria that was dealt with the Prosecutor and was discussed in this book shows that there is a missing stage between the trigger mechanism and the preliminary examination.

According to the OTP Policy Paper on preliminary Examinations there are four phases in the preliminary examination stage. However, there is again a contradiction. While Phase One of the process is considered as a part of the structure of the preliminary examination, the OTP Policy Paper says that the preliminary examination of a given situation commences formally in Phase Two. This layout, however, is not logical. An independent stage should be recognized that bridges the trigger mechanism to the preliminary examination stage. In this distinct phase, the validity of the referring entity or the identity of communicators should be identified (this could be the case in the Palestine situation). In addition, if a situation is manifestly outside of the Court's jurisdiction, it should not reach the preliminary examination by determining it during this stage. However, such a jurisdictional assessment is very lenient, and it does not include the admissibility assessment. Moreover, if a referral does not refer a situation in the Rome Statute sense, it is during this stage that the Prosecutor shall request amendments and adaptations to the referral in question.

3. SELECTING A SITUATION FOR HIGHLIGHTING A FORGOTTEN CRIMINAL THEME

Part Three of this book described and analyzed the situation selection criteria at the ICC. According to the Rome Statute, in selecting a situation three factors should be taken into account, namely jurisdiction, admissibility and the interests of justice presumption. The admissibility requirement consists of two elements, gravity and complementarity. The gravity factor that should be assessed prior to the complementarity assessment is a selective factor in selecting and prioritizing a situation.

The gravity requirement has not been defined by the Rome Statute. However, the Court's Prosecutor has expressed her own interpretation of this statutory requirement. According to the Prosecutor, the gravity of a situation or a case is determined by considering four factors, namely the scale, manner, impact or nature of crimes. In prioritizing a situation over other situations, the scale of crimes within a situation is the primary factor. The number of casualties is an objective standard that can be used in a comparative manner to determine the degree of gravity of a situation. However, it is not the only factor that has been introduced by the Prosecutor. There are other options. One of them is the nature of crimes. At first sight, the recent factor might refer to a hierarchy between the ICC-identified crimes in which some criminal acts could be considered graver than others. However, the nature of crimes has a different function in selecting a situation. This factor directs to the 'thematic prosecution' doctrine. Thematic prosecution orients cases on the criminal themes. In other words, a case is selected on the strength of the charge(s) it includes. Thematic prosecution is in itself based on the theory of expressivism. Expressivism facilitates norm-setting and norm projection at the ICC. Based on this mandate, thematic prosecution guides the Prosecutor to prioritize a specific criminal theme and a specific category of crimes in order to promote prosecution of those crimes. Such prioritization is justifiable because those themes are generally under-prosecuted, and do not trigger the judicial initiative at the national level. Indeed, these themes of criminality are surrounded by a thick culture of impunity that needs the Court's intervention to be shattered. There is no prospect of accountability for the commission of these crimes because they are not considered serious domestically, and their victims are not heard. Gender-based crimes and sexual crimes are a perfect example here. These sorts of crimes have been historically tolerated. In addition to gender-based crimes, the OTP has devoted attention to two other criminal themes: child soldering (Lubanga case) and crimes against cultural property (Al-Mahdi case).

Thematic prosecution does not mean that other crimes are not serious, but that if the Court has to prioritize a category of crimes and victims over others, a voice should be given to those victims who are mainly voiceless and are not even seen and hence remain absent from prosecutorial proceedings at both the international and national level.

4. COMPLEMENTARITY AS RULE AND COMPLEMENTARITY AS PRINCIPLE

Chapter II of Part Three was tasked to describe and analyze the admissibility requirement. The concept of complementarity has two dimensions. The first aspect is legal, which is enshrined in Article 17 of the Rome Statute. Contrary to the *ad hoc* tribunals, the primary in prosecuting the ICC-identified crimes is with States. In the case of concurrent jurisdictions, the Court's jurisdiction is negated as long as a State is genuinely active. Complementarity as a rule aims at preserving the Court's status as a last resort. At the same time, it furthers ending impunity by giving the Court a monitoring authority that enables this institution to intervene in the case of States' inaction or lack of a genuine action. Complementarity in this sense is a component of the admissibility requirement. A situation is admissible before the Court, only if there is no alternative at the domestic level. However, the complementarity assessment is conducted in light of another aspect of complementarity that is teleological.

Complementarity as a principle draws a wider picture of the international criminal justice system. In this system, the ICC as the only permanent institution has an important role that is mainly managerial. The ICC has been established to complete efforts of other actors, States and non-States, in ending impunity and protecting victims. The ICC is not intended to replace other actors acting at the domestic and international level. The Court's inabilities make this institution dependent on the others' contributions. The Court's main mandates are expressive. The ICC's presence, monitoring and exceptional interventions take place to deliver a message, namely, that other actors should take action. Indeed, the Court mainly functions as a trigger mechanism. In the ICC-era, the Court has a central role in triggering and activating States and other organizations to take their responsibilities in combating international crimes. Under the principle of complementarity, the Court's success should not be assessed by taking into account the number of prosecutions before the Court. On the contrary, the effectiveness of the Court should be mainly assessed in light of its efficiency in managing the international criminal justice system and in activating other actors within this system.

Understanding the complementarity rule as a mechanism that facilitates the complementary role of the ICC in the broad system of international criminal justice requires some flexibility in assessing the national jurisdictions to determine whether they are genuinely dealing with ICC crimes. Under the Rome Statute, a case should be admissible before the Court to pave the way of investigating a situation. In the situational phase, in the absence of concrete cases, potential cases are objects for a complementarity assessment. A case consists of two components: person and conduct. There are two approaches in defining the notion of conduct, namely narrow and broad. The narrow approach defines the conduct concept strictly, and in a way that requires the sameness between the conduct that is prosecuted by the Court and what is before national jurisdictions. Such a mirroring revolves around the notion of incidents. An incident-oriented prosecution requires the sameness in victims, locations and times of the commission of the crimes.

The broad approach does not put its insistence on incidents. This approach is premised on the idea that States should address those contexts and situations of crises that are dealt with by the ICC. In this interpretation, incidents are important but it is not always necessary that States prosecute the same incidents that are wanted by the Court. In the case of difference between what is wanted by the ICC and what is prosecuted by a State, the Court should adopt a dialectic approach to find out the reasons behind the State's decision not to prosecute cases that are given priority by the Court. As the Court may have to prioritize a case over other cases based on operational factors, it is also imaginable that States have to deprioritize a graver case because of their operational considerations and inabilities. The ICC should not consider States as rivals. It is the Court that has the final word in the complementarity assessment, but it should do it with good faith and in consistency with the soul of the complementarity principle. The Court's intervention should not be seen as positive progress that, as a result, should be pushed. By contrast, the ICC should give an opportunity to States to take action. It is a part of expressive mandates of the Court. Opening a preliminary examination and being flexible to States in the complementarity assessment protects the victims' interests too. The Prosecutor should adopt a dialectic and positive approach to States for giving them space and opportunity to take action on their own. The Court should remain the 'last resort' prosecuting body, but should step in as the first promoter and manager of delivering justice.

5. NO HARM TO VICTIMS PRINCIPLE

The Court should integrate a victims' perspective into all of its aspects and areas of works and operations. The victims' perspective means that the Court should take into account the needs, views and interests of victims in its functioning at all stages. Such a perspective requires that the Court protects victims from harm and prevents hurting victims by own means. Harm reduction and no harm are those two principles that the Court shall stick to. Giving a voice to victims and adopting reparative measures are two actions that can reduce the victims' suffering and trauma.

If conducting an investigation or a prosecution does not serve the interests of justice, the Prosecutor shall refrain from pursuing the situation or case in question. Contrary to other statutory criteria, the Prosecutor does not need to prove that conducting an investigation serves the interests of justice. It is a presumption based on which the Court operates as a criminal institution. Nonetheless, the Prosecutor shall examine all circumstances to determine whether there are substantial reasons to believe that the Court's intervention does not serve the interests of justice. Discharging this obligation, however, is now free from judicial review- that is a shortcoming at the ICC. Abstaining from an investigation that contradicts the interests of justice is an obligation, and some degree of judicial supervision is needed to ensure that such an obligation is fulfilled.

The 'interests of justice' requirement, in practice, has not been at the center of the Court's jurisprudence. It has been a dead provision. This sits in contrast to the theoretical interests of justice notion, which has a cardinal role in discovering the Court' goal. The concept of the 'interests of justice' represents and projects the importance of the victims' interests at the ICC. Criminal prosecution should be avoided if the interests of victims require it. It shows that the ultimate value at the ICC that should be taken into account in delivering criminal justice is the interests of victims. The interests of justice presumption states that the Court should reduce the victims' suffering, and should refrain from whatever hurts victims. Prosecuting the ICC-identified crimes are both a moral and legal obligation, but it is not an absolute task. Prosecution should not be done at the cost of the interests or lives of victims.

In the literature, the interests of justice presumption is discussed in the context of the dilemma between peace and justice. This dilemma should be resolved case-by-case. However, in the extreme exceptional circumstances, namely, if justice contradicts reaching a peace deal that requires granting amnesties to the perpetrators of atrocities, the priority should be given to peace if it puts an end to misery and suffering of victims by terminating a conflict. In such exceptional circumstances, however, the Prosecutor of the Court should assume an active role in making a peace deal and in monitoring its implementation afterwards. The division between peace and justice is not straightforward. These two notions have interaction.

6. A NEED FOR EXTENDING JUDICIAL REVIEW OF THE PROSECUTOR'S DECISIONS

In the last Chapter of Part Two it was discussed that the current judicial scrutiny system at the ICC is chiefly state-oriented. It means that this system has been shaped to resolve the States' concerns about creating a dominant Prosecutor. Upon conducting a preliminary examination, the Prosecutor shall determine whether there is a reasonable basis to initiate an investigation. As long as the Prosecutor's decision whether or not to initiate an investigation into a situation affects the interests of States, her decision can be challenged by States and is reviewable by the Court's Judges. If the Prosecutor decides to initiate an investigation in the case of the UNSC's referrals, States, members or non-members, have a right to challenge the Prosecutor's decision as to the admissibility of the situation in question.

In the case of referrals, if the Prosecutor decides not to initiate an investigation, the referring State can bring her decision under the judicial review. The situation of the Registered Vessels of Comoros is an example here. Even if the Prosecutor determines that a situation should not be investigated, taking into account the interests of justice requirement, her decision could be checked by the Court's Judges even in the absence of a State's challenge. In addition, empowering the Prosecutor of the Court with authority independent of a States' will has been compromised with a strong judicial review system. In the case of communications, the Prosecutor's decision to initiate an investigation into a situation is not effective unless it is supported by a judicial authorization. Here, the judicial authorizations substitutes for the State's will. The situations in Kenya, Cote d'Ivoire and Georgia underwent a judicial review before reaching the investigation stage.

Nonetheless, if a situation has nothing to do with State's interests, the judicial review diminishes. If the Prosecutor receives a large number of communications, but she decides not to open a preliminary examination or not to initiate an investigation, there is no way to challenge such a negative decision. Situations in Iraq (2006) and ISIS (2015) are two examples here. Moreover, in the case of referrals, if the Prosecutor decides to initiate an investigation, while there are reasons that the 'interests of justice' requirement which links with the interests of victims require inaction on the part of the Prosecutor, there is no way for victims to challenge the decision. This issue surfaced in the situation in Uganda when the peace efforts were in danger in light of the Court's intervention.

Indeed, the judicial review system at the ICC suffers from wide shortcomings. Such a system has not been primarily established to serve the interests of victims. It is necessary to extend and amend the current system reflected in the core legal texts of the ICC in order to integrate the victims' interests. Opening a preliminary examination has some expressive functions for victims. It is the Prosecutor's responsibility, rather than her authority, to open a preliminary examination if the prerequisites in this regard are met. Likewise, it is her responsibility to avoid opening a full investigation if such an action does not serve the interests of the victims. Fulfilling these obligation requires judicial scrutiny.

Until that moment, all interpretations that are consistent with a broad and inclusive judicial review system are welcome. For instance, the authority of the Court's Judges to *proprio motu* review the Prosecutor's decision not to initiate an investigation, because of the interests of justice, has been worded in a general sense in the Rome Statute. Therefore, it should be interpreted broadly to embrace both referrals and communications.

7. AN EXPRESSIVE SITUATION SELECTION

Chapter III of Part Two studies the preliminary examination stage as it is. The main phase in which the situation selection is processed is the preliminary examination stage. Preliminary examination operates like a factory. It receives an input (a situation), and upon processing this input produces an output (the Prosecutor's decision whether or not to initiate an investigation). Preliminary examination is a process in which the Prosecutor examines a situation to determine whether the statutory requirements to initiate an investigation are met. If a situation falls within the ICC's jurisdiction and is declared admissible, the Prosecutor initiates an investigation, unless the interests of justice presumption requires differently. This process is information-driven and conducted on the 'reasonableness' evidentiary threshold. It implies that findings arising from this stage are preliminary and not necessarily binding in the ensuing stages.

Part Four, following describing and analyzing the current function of the preliminary examination, introduces an expressive function for the Court that is consistent with the victim-friendly feature of the ICC. The ICC's inabilities outweigh its abilities. The Court's limitations and restrictions make this institution widely selective. The Court is not able to prosecute all crimes within its jurisdiction. In addition to its inability, the ICC is not intended to function as the panacea. Under the complementarity principle, the Court only complements functions of other actors in the international criminal justice system. For such a selective institution whose selectivity has a normative aspect, a theory is required that is able to justify this feature of the Court. In this regard, expressivism can be offered. Expressivism allows the Court to function in an exemplary and selective manner. A theory creates an evaluative framework within which the Court's effectiveness and success should be assessed. It is expressivism that preserves the effectiveness of the Court even by taking into account the fact that the Court only deals with a handful of crimes under its jurisdiction.

A majority of the situations brought to the Prosecutor's attention do not reach the investigation stage. There are many legal and practical obstacles in the way of initiating an investigation. This fact can hurt the effectiveness and legitimacy of the Court. A costly institution that is unable to do something with a large number of crises would lose its efficiency, and, consequently, its legitimacy. In this context, the preliminary examination helps the Court with reducing its selectivity side effects. The ICC is a criminal tribunal but not a classical or ordinary one. The ICC has its unique legal system and functions. Comparing the Court with ordinary courts at the domestic level is an incorrect comparison. The ICC's effectiveness is largely evaluated in light of its success in dealing with the situation of crisis. However, its reaction to a situation of crisis is not limited to classical tools of criminal courts, including investigation and prosecution. Preliminary examination is an unprecedented tool at the ICC's disposal that enables this institution to realize its objectives, in spite of its selectivity. Opening and conducting a preliminary examination has expressive functions. Regarding States, the preliminary examination is a context in which the positive complementarity activities should be carried out. Priority in prosecution is for States. The Court shall give States sufficient space and opportunity to activate their jurisdiction over a specific situation. The complementarity assessment in the preliminary examination stage should not be conducted strictly. The Court's intervention in a situation by opening a preliminary examination delivers a message that encourages and persuades States to take action. There is no deadline for conducting a preliminary examination as long as there is a prospect for facilitating States to take action.

In addition, at the ICC, the needs and interests of victims are at the heart of the Court's functioning. Reading the preliminary examination from such a perspective expands the capacities of this pre-investigative stage. Selectivity deprives many victims from access to justice. However, conducting the preliminary examination creates wider spaces for victims to step in and to be heard. In the preliminary examination, the victimhood and the commission of crimes could be recognized. Recognition and acknowledgement of victimhood at the ICC effectivity block the denial of crimes in the future. Moreover, the ICC Trust Fund for Victims at can begin its reparative programs during a preliminary examination, and even before forming a case.

Preliminary examination is not the ultimate destination at the ICC, but it is a bridge that should be passed. However, since passing this stage is slow and difficult in practice, entering this stage and conducting it have many benefits that should not be underestimated. The history of the Court shows that the preliminary examination activities are much more available than its ability to investigate and prosecute. So, when this stage can provide the greatest number of victims with the greatest happiness, the insistence should be put on this fruitful stage.

8. IMPLICATIONS OF DESIGNING AN EXPRESSIVE SITUATION SELECTION REGIME

Integrating expressivism in the situation selection regime produces some implications.

a) In evaluating the effectiveness of the Court, its success in activating and triggering other actors in international criminal justice system should be taken into account, including States, organizations, media and 'lawfare' activities. A marked shift needs to occur in the understanding of the preliminary examination stage. Given the ICC's expressive mandates and functions, more attention should be paid to preliminary examination. The Court is successful if it has a successfully completed preliminary examination.
b) There should not be a demand for expediting a preliminary examination. The preliminary examination has not only an accessary and bridging function, but it could be regarded as an end in itself in some circumstances. The Court should heavily and wisely invest in the preliminary examination to realize its objectives. The Rome Statute has not set any timeframe for conducting the preliminary examination stage. This absence and silence should be regarded as an agreement with focusing on the preliminary examination activities. From such a perspective, the long duration that has been devoted to conducting the preliminary examination in the situation in Colombia should not be seen as a shortcoming in the OTP's activities. The OTP opened a preliminary examination into the situation in Colombia in 2004 and by 2017 the Prosecutor was still monitoring the national activities in order to complete its complementarity assessment.
c) Outreach activities should be at the center of the Court's functioning, and should stimulate sizeable and heavy investments. The Court has expressive mandates, and expressing and delivering its educational messages need outreach activities. As a court that has the interests of victims at the heart of its attention, the ICC needs interactions, communication and consultation with victims. All these activities should be done through outreach activities. Here, the idea of the Situation Selection Document comes up. The Prosecutor needs to set up a Situation Selection Document and publicize it. The Document would list all situations that meet the sufficient gravity requirement. It means that all situations that are selected by the Court are announced and known. Then, the Prosecutor deals with the complementarity issue, and starts positive complementarity activities to facilitate domestic actions. Such an interaction with States takes time. However, the status of the situation and the Prosecutor's activities and the relevant challenges and achievements are public. Even if the Prosecutor furthers a situation due to inaction of States, the interests of justice may require inaction of the Prosecutor. In such exceptional circumstances, the Document explains the reasons behind the Prosecutor's decision not to act. Finally, even if operational factors bar the Prosecutor from initiating a full investigation,

the Document clarifies the problems and delivers the message that as soon as the obstacles are resolved, an investigation will be initiated.

d) The Prosecutor should show tolerance and leniency in opening preliminary examinations. Preliminary examination is an integrated part of the Court's reaction to unimaginable atrocities. It is imaginable that a situation is selected without a prospect of immediate investigation, just to activate the preliminary examination activities. In opening a preliminary examination, what matters is that the Court has jurisdiction, regardless of its narrowness or broadness. As soon as there is a statutory basis for the Court to step in, the Court should follow it. All interpretations and understandings that facilitate opening a preliminary examination should be welcomed, such as personal jurisdiction. The ICC lacks universal jurisdiction. As an international organization, its jurisdiction has been shaped based on delegated jurisdictions. States that are Parties to the Rome Statute delegate their own jurisdiction over their territories and nationals to the Court. Therefore, the Court's jurisdiction is primarily limited to territories and nationals of States Parties. There is only one exception, namely, when the UNSC refers a situation. A UNSC's referral can extend the Court's jurisdiction over territories and nationals of non-member States. Exercising jurisdiction based on territorial jurisdiction has some advantages for the Court. Having access to the territory on which the ICC-identified crimes are committed facilitates a more effective prosecution by providing the Court with wider access to evidence, victims and perpetrators. In the absence of territorial jurisdiction, exercising personal jurisdiction leaves less room for the Court's intervention. However, it does not mean that the Prosecutor shall refrain from taking action based on personal jurisdiction. In the Rome Statute, personal jurisdiction is as valid as territorial jurisdiction. These two kinds of jurisdictions are alternative. Priority is for territorial jurisdiction, but personal jurisdiction is still a sufficient substitute.

The Rome Statute obliges the Prosecutor to intervene when the Court has only personal jurisdiction. Nonetheless, the Prosecutor in the ISIS situation provided an incorrect interpretation. She did not open a preliminary examination by arguing that there would be only national jurisdiction, and it would provide her office with a narrow jurisdictional basis. This interpretation clearly contradicts the Rome Statute and its constituent objectives. The Court aims at ending impunity in an expressive manner. When a territorial State has evaded justice by avoiding joining the Court, but there is a narrow path for piercing into the situation of crisis through national jurisdiction, the Court should use this opportunity. The ICC should welcome all opportunities enabling it to give a voice to voiceless victims, and to project a crisis and thereby attract the attention of the international community and other actors in the international criminal justice system. The Court functions selectively and the Court's selectivity is enshrined in various areas, including a situation where the Court has only personal jurisdiction.

9. TO CONCLUDE

After more than one decade from the Court's birthday, it is time to assess the Court through the lens of a posterior knowledge, i.e. based on the Court's experience in reality. The Court was founded on the basis of ambitions and over-high aspirations and expectations. The objective reality demonstrates that the Court is unable to achieve its ambitions. Great and high expectations were shaped but the Court has not lived up to them, because they were unrealistic. If the international community intends to support the ICC it needs to manage the expectations. We need to adopt a quite realistic and fairly down-to-earth approach to the Court and it requires lessening and reducing our expectations. Expressivism draws a Court with realistic, however modest, abilities that can satisfy the expectations that have been created based on its expressive functions. Expressivism is a pretty modest and rather humble understanding of the Court, Yet it at least have much to do with reality. Inflating the Court with desirous and wishful mandates and goals is only building a giant without limbs that loses its reputation and legitimacy. It is time for the Court's proponents to promote a Court that has humble objectives but is able to realize them. In the Introductory Chapter, it was mentioned that the ICC has been criticized for its selection policy. Paying more attention to the preliminary examination by adopting expressivism could resolve the misunderstandings of the Court that produce criticism.

BIBLIOGRAPHY

Abdulhak T., 'Complementarity of Procedures: How to Avoid Reinventing the Wheel', in Carsten Stahn and Mohamed M. El Zeidy (eds.), *The International Criminal Court and Complementarity: From Theory to Practice*, Cambridge University Press, 2011.

Abtahi H., *Crimes against Humanity and the Armed Conflict Nexus: From Nuremberg to the ICC*, 4 December 2013, available at https://ssrn.com/abstract=2363608.

Akande D. and Shah S., 'Immunities of State Officials, International Crimes and Foreign Domestic Courts', *European Journal of International Law*, 2011, vol. 21.

Akande D., 'The Jurisdiction of the International Criminal Court over Nationals of Non-Parties: Legal Basis and Limits', *Journal of International Criminal Justice*, 2003, vol. 1.

Akande D., 'The Legal Nature of Security Council Referrals to the ICC and its Impact on Al Bashir's Immunities', *Journal of International Criminal Justice*, 2009, vol. 7.

Akande D., *An International Court of Justice Advisory Opinion on the ICC Head of State Immunity Issue*, 31 March 2016, available at: www.ejiltalk.org/an-international-court-of-justice-advisory-opinion-on-the-icc-head-of-state-immunity-issue/#more-14178.

Akande D., *ICC Issues Detailed Decision on Bashir's Immunity But Gets the Law Wrong*, 15 December 2011, available at: www.ejiltalk.org/icc-issues-detailed-decision-on-bashir's-immunity-at-long-last-but-gets-the-law-wrong/).

Akhavan P., 'Are International Criminal Tribunals a Disincentive to Peace?: Reconciling Judicial Romanticism with Political Realism', *Human Rights Quarterly*, 2009, vol. 31.

Akhavan P., 'International Criminal Justice in the Era of Failed States: The ICC and the Self-Referral Debate', in Carsten Stahn and Mohamed M. El Zeidy (eds.), *The International Criminal Court and Complementarity: From Theory to Practice,* Cambridge University Press, 2011.

Akhavan P., 'Justice in The Hague, Peace in the Former Yugoslavia? A Commentary on the United Nations War Crimes Tribunal', Human *Rights Quarterly*, 1998, vol. 20.

Alai C. and Mue N., 'Complementarity and the Impact of the Rome Statute and the International Criminal Court in Kenya', in Carsten Stahn and Mohamed M. El Zeidy (eds.), *The International Criminal Court and Complementarity: From Theory to Practice*, Cambridge University Press, 2011.

Allen T., Trial Justice: the ICC and the Lord's Resistance Army, Zed Books, 2006.

Altman D., 'The Landscape of Silence: Sexual Violence Against Men in War', *Culture, Health and Sexuality*, 2016, vol. 18.

Amann D.A., 'Group Mentality, Expressivism and Genocide', *International Criminal Law Review*, 2002, vol. 2.

Ambos K. and Stegmiller I., 'Prosecuting International Crimes at the International Criminal Court: Is There a Coherent and Comprehensive Prosecution Strategy?', *Crime Law Social Change*, 2013, vol. 59.

Ambos K., 'The Colombian Peace Process (Law 975 of 2005) and the ICC's Principle of Complementarity', in Carsten Stahn and Mohamed M. El Zeidy (eds.), *The International Criminal Court and Complementarity: From Theory to Practice*, Cambridge University Press, 2011.

Ambos K., 'Thematic Investigations and Prosecution of International Sex Crimes: Some Critical Comments from a Theoretical and Comparative Perspective', in Morten Bergsmo (ed.), *Thematic Prosecution of International Sex Crimes*, Torkel Opsahl Academic EPublisher, 2012.

Ambos K., The Colombian Peace Process and the Principle of Complementarity of the International Criminal Court: An Inductive, Situation-based Approach, Springer, 2010.

Amerasinghe C.F., Principles of the Institutional Law of International Organization, Cambridge University Press, 2005.

Annan K.A., *We the People, United Nations,* 2000, available at: www.un.org/en/events/pastevents/pdfs/We_The_Peoples.pdf.

Antonio M., 'Article 14', in Otto Triffterer (ed.), *Commentary on the Rome Statute of the International Criminal Court*, C.H. Beck. Hart. Nomos, 2008.

Arbia S., 'Proactive Complementarity: A Registrar's Perspective and Plans', in Carsten Stahn and Mohamed M. El Zeidy (eds.), *The International Criminal Court and Complementarity: From Theory to Practice*, Cambridge University Press, 2011.

Arbour J.L., 'The Need for an Independent and Effective Prosecutor in the Permanent International Criminal Court', *Windsor Yearbook of Access to Justice*, 1999, vol. 17.

Arnould V., 'The Uncertain Promise of Hybrid Justice in the Central African Republic', *Africa Policy Brief*, September 2015.

Arsanjani M., 'The International Criminal Court and National Amnesty Laws', *Proceedings of the Annual Meeting,* 1999, vol. 93.

Arsanjani M.H. and Reisman W.M., 'The Law-in-Action of the International Criminal Court', *The American Journal of International Law*, 2005, vol. 55.

Bantekas I., 'The Need to Amend Article 12 of the ICC Statute: Remedying the Effects of Multilateral Treaties upon Third Parties', *New Criminal Law Review*, 2009, vol. 12.

Bassiouni M. C., *Introduction to International Criminal Law*, Martinus Nijhoff Publishers, 2013.

Batros B., 'The Evolution of the ICC Jurisprudence on Admissibility', in Carsten Stahn and Mohamed M. El Zeidy (eds.), *The International Criminal Court and Complementarity: From Theory to Practice*, Cambridge University Press, 2011.

Bekker P.H.F., The Legal Position of Intergovernmental Organizations: A Functional Necessity Analysis of Their Legal Status and Immunities, Brill, 1994.

Bergsmo M. and Kruger P., 'Article 53', in Otto Triffterer (ed.), *Commentary on the Rome Statute of the International Criminal Court*, C.H. Beck. Hart. Nomos, 2008.

Bergsmo M. and Ling C.W., 'Towards Rational Thematic Prosecution and the Challenge of International Sex Crimes', in Morten Bergsmo (ed.), *Thematic Prosecution of International Sex Crimes*, Torkel Opsahl Academic EPublisher, 2012.

Bergsmo M. and Pejic J., 'Article 15', in Otto Triffterer (ed.), *Commentary on the Rome Statute of the International Criminal Court*, C.H. Beck. Hart. Nomos, 2008.

Bergsmo M., Bekou O. and Jones A., 'Complementarity after Kampala: Capacity Building and the ICC's Legal Tools', in Morten Bergsmo (ed.), *Active Complementarity: Legal Information Transfer*, Torkel Opshal Academic Epublisher, 2011.

Bergsmo M., Bekou O. and Jones A., 'Complementarity and the Construction of National Ability', in Carsten Stahn and Mohamed M. El Zeidy (eds.), *The International Criminal Court and Complementarity: From Theory to Practice*, Cambridge University Press, 2011.

Boas G., Bischoff J. L. and Reid N. L., International Criminal Law Practitioner Library Volume II: Elements of Crimes under International Law, Cambridge University Press, 2009.

Bosch O., 'A Legislative Evolution: UNSC Resolution 1540 Revisited', in Vesselin Popovski and Trudy Fraser (eds.), *The Security Council as Global Legislator*, Routledge, 2014.

Bourgon S., 'Jurisdiction Ratione Personae', in Antonio Cassese, Paola Gaeta and John R.W.D. Jones (eds.), *The Rome Statute of the International Criminal Court: A Commentary*, Oxford University Press, 2002.

Bowett D.W., 'Jurisdiction: Changing Patterns of Authority over Activities and Resources', *British Yearbook of International Law*, 1982, vol. 53.

Brierly J., 'The Nature of War Crimes', in James Leslie Brierly, Hersch Lauterpacht and Claud Humphrey Meredith Waldock, *The Basis of Obligation in International Law and Other Papers*, Clarendon Press, 1958.

Burke M.J. and Weiss T.G., 'The Security Council and Ad Hoc Tribunals: Law and Politics; Peace and Justice', in Vesselin Popovski and Trudy Fraser (eds.), *The Security Council as Global Legislator*, Routledge, 2014.

Burke R., 'UN Military Peacekeeper Complicity in Sexual Abuse: The ICC or a Tri-Hybrid Court', in Morten Bergsmo (ed.), *Thematic Prosecution of International Sex Crimes*, Torkel Opsahl Academic EPublisher, 2012.

Burke-White W.W. and Kaplan S., 'Shaping the Contours of Domestic Justice: The International Criminal Court and an Admissibility Challenge in the Uganda Situation', in Carsten Stahn and Göran Sluiter (eds.), *The Emerging Practice of the International Criminal Court*, Martinus Nijhoff Publishers, 2009.

Buss D., 'Performing Legal Order: Some Feminist Thoughts on International Criminal Law', *International Criminal Law Review*, 2011, vol. 11.

Byron C., War Crimes and Crimes Against Humanity in the Rome Statute of the International Criminal Court, Manchester University Press, 2009.

Caban P., 'Preliminary Examinations by the Office of the Prosecutor of the International Criminal Court', *Czech Yearbook of Public and Private International Law*, 2011, vol. 2.

Calvo-Goller N.K., *The Trial Proceedings of the International Criminal Court*, Martinus Nijhoff Publishers, 2006.

Cassese A., 'Is the ICC Still Having Teething Problems?', *Journal of International Criminal Justice*, 2006, vol. 4.

Cassese A., 'On the Current Trends towards Criminal Prosecution and Punishment of Breaches of International Humanitarian Law', *European Journal of International Law*, 1998, vol. 9.

Cassese A., *International Criminal Law*, Oxford University Press, 2008.

Chappell L., Grey R. and Waller E., 'The Gender Justice Shadow of Complementarity: Lessons from the International Criminal Court's Preliminary Examinations in Guinea and Colombia', *The International Journal of Transitional Justice*, 2013, vol. 7.

Chehtman A., 'Jurisdiction', in Markus D. Dubber and Tatjana Hornle (eds.), *The Oxford Handbook of Criminal Law*, Oxford University Press, 2014.

Chouliaras A., The Victimological Concern as the Driving Force in the Quest for Justice for State-Sponsored International Crimes, in Rianne Letschert, Roelof Haveman, Anne-Marie

de Brouwer and Antony Pemberton, *Victimological Approaches to International Crimes: Africa*, Intersentia, 2011.
Clark J.N., 'Peace, Justice and the International Criminal Court: Limitations and Possibilities', *Journal of International Criminal Justice,* 2011, vol. 9.
Clark R.S., 'Complementarity and the Crime of Aggression', in Carsten Stahn and Mohamed M. El Zeidy (eds.), *The International Criminal Court and Complementarity: From Theory to Practice*, Cambridge University Press, 2011.
Clark T.H., 'The Prosecutor of the International Criminal Court, Amnesties and the Interests of Justice: Striking a Delicate Balance', *Washington University Global Studies Law Review,* 2005, vol. 4.
Combs N.A., 'Evidence', in William A. Schabas and Nadia Bernaz, *Routledge Handbook of International Criminal Law,* Routledge, 2011.
Condorelli L. and Villapando S., 'Referral and Deferral by the Security Council', in Antonio Cassese, Paola Gaeta and John R.W.D. Jones (eds.), *The Rome Statute of the International Criminal Court: A Commentary,* Vol(I), Oxford University Press, 2002.
Corrina H., 'The U.N. Security Council's Referral of the Crimes in Darfur to the International Criminal Court in Light of U.S. Opposition to the Court: Implications for the International Criminal Court's Functions and Status', *Berkeley Journal of International Law,* 2006, vol. 24.
Coté L., 'Independence and Impartiality', in Luc Reydams, Jan Wouters and Cedric Ryngaert (eds.), *International Prosecutors,* Oxford University Press, 2012.
Council of Europe, European Committee on Crime Problems, 'Extraterritorial Criminal Jurisdiction', *Criminal Law Forum,* 1999, vol. 3.
Cronin-Furman K. and Taub A., 'Lions and Tigers and Deterrence. Oh My: Evaluating Expectations of International Criminal Justice', in William A. Schabas, Yvonne McDermott and Niamh Hayes (eds.), *The Ashgate Research Companion to International Criminal Law: Critical Perspectives,* Ashgate, 2013.
Cryer R., 'The ICC and its Relationship to Non-States Parties', in Carsten Stahn (ed.), *The Law And Practice of the International Criminal Court,* Oxford University Press, 2015.
Cryer R., Friman H., Robinson D. and Wilmshurst E., *An Introduction to International Criminal Law and Procedure,* Cambridge University Press, 2014.
Cryer R., Prosecuting International Crimes: Selectivity and the International Criminal Law Regime, Cambridge University Press, 2005.
Daqun L., 'Has Non-Immunity for Heads of State Become a Rule of Customary International Law?', in Morten Bergsmo and Lung Yan (eds.), *State Sovereignty and International Criminal Law,* Torkel Opsahl Academic EPublisher, 2012.
De Brouwer A. and Groenhuijsen M.S., 'The Role of Victims in International Criminal Proceedings', in Sergey Vasiliev and Göran Sluiter (eds.), *International Criminal Procedure: Towards a Coherent Body of Law,* Cameron May, 2009.
De Brouwer A., 'The Importance of Understanding Sexual Violence in Conflict for Investigation and Prosecution Purposes', *Cornell International Law Journal,* 2015, vol. 48.
De Brouwer, A. and Ruvebana E., 'The Legacy of the Gacaca Courts in Rwanda: Survivors' Views', *International Criminal Law Review,* 2013, vol. 13.
De Guzman M. M., 'Gravity and the Legitimacy of the International Criminal Court', *Fordham International Law Journal,* 2008, vol. 32.
De Guzman M. M., 'How Serious are International Crimes? The Gravity Problem in International Criminal Law', *Columbia Journal of Transnational Law,* 2012, vol. 51.

De Guzman M.M., 'An Expressive Rationale for the Thematic Prosecution of Sex Crimes', in Morten Bergsmo (ed.), *Thematic Prosecution of International Sex Crimes*, Torkel Opsahl Academic EPublisher, 2012.

De Guzman M.M., 'Choosing to Prosecute at the International Criminal Court', *Michigan Journal of International Law*, 2012, vol. 33.

De Guzman M.M., 'Giving Priority to Sex Crime Prosecutions: The Philosophical Foundations of a Feminist Agenda', *International Criminal Law Review*, 2011, vol. 11.

De Hert P. and Holvoet M., 'Article 15: Prosecutor', in Paul de Hert, Jean Flamme and Mathias Holvoet (et al.) (eds.), *Code of International Criminal Law and Procedure, Annotated*, Larcier, 2013.

De Vlaming F., 'Selection of Defendants', in Luc Reydams, Jan Wouters and Cedric Ryngaret (eds.), *International Prosecutors*, Oxford University Press, 2012.

Del Ponte C., 'Investigation and Prosecution of Large-Scale Crimes at the International Level: The Experience of the ICTY', *Journal of International Criminal Justice*, 2006, vol. 4.

Del Ponte C., *Madame Prosecutor: Confrontations with Humanity's Worst Criminals and the Culture of Impunity: A Memoir*, Other Press, 2009.

Dixon R., 'Article 7 (1)', in Otto Triffterer (ed.), *Commentary on the Rome Statute of the International Criminal Court*, C.H. Beck. Hart. Nomos, 2008.

Dong J., 'Prosecutorial Discretion at the International Criminal Court: A Comparative Study', *Journal of Politics and Law*, 2009, vol. 2.

Dormann K., 'Paragraph 2 (a)', in Otto Triffterer (ed.), *Commentary on the Rome Statute of the International Criminal Court*, C.H. Beck. Hart. Nomos, 2008.

Drumbl M.A., 'Policy Through Complementarity: The Atrocity Trial as Justice', in Carsten Stahn and Mohamed M. El Zeidy (eds.), *The International Criminal Court and Complementarity: From Theory to Practice*, Cambridge University Press, 2011.

Du Plessis and Pete S., 'Who Guards the Guards', *African Security Review*, 2004, vol. 13.

Du Plessis M., Implications of the AU Decision to Give the African Court Jurisdiction over International Crimes, Institute for Security Studies Paper, 2012.

Duff A., 'Authority and Responsibility in International Criminal Law', in Samantha Besson and John Tasioulas (ed.), *The Philosophy of International Law*, Oxford University Press, 2010.

Dutton Y., Rules, Politics and the International Criminal Court: Committing to the Court, Routledge, 2013.

Dworkin R., *Taking Rights Seriously*, Harvard University Press, 1977.

El Zeidy M. M., 'Origin and Genesis of Complementarity', in Carsten Stahn and Mohamed M. El Zeidy (eds.), *The International Criminal Court and Complementarity: From Theory to Practice*, Cambridge University Press, 2011.

El Zeidy M. M., 'The Gravity Threshold under the Statute of the International Criminal Court', *Criminal Law Forum*, 2008, vol. 19.

El Zeidy M. M., The Principle of Complementarity in International Criminal Law: Origin, Development and Practice, Martinus Nijhoff Publishers, 2008.

Engle K., 'Feminism and Its (Dis)contents: Criminalizing Wartime Rape in Bosnia and Herzegovina', *The American Journal of International Law*, 2005, vol. 99.

Fish E.S., 'Peace Through Complementarity: Solving the Ex Post Problem in International Criminal Court Prosecutions', *The Yale Law Journal*, 2010, Vol. 119.

Fouladvand S., Complementarity and Cultural Sensitivity: Decision-Making by the ICC Prosecutor in relation to the Situation in the Darfur Region in Sudan and the Democratic Republic of the Congo, the Degree of Doctor of Philosophy, University of Sussex, 2012.

Freehills H.S., *The Competence-Competence Doctrine and the Enforcement of Arbitral Awards*, January 2011, available at: www.lexology.com/library/detail.aspx?g=70303764-71b7-4352-babb-6c8c8d399190.

Gaeta P., 'Genocide', in William A. Schabas and Nadia Bernaz, *Routledge Handbook of International Criminal Law*, Routledge, 2011.

Gioia F., 'Complementarity and Reverse Cooperation', in Carsten Stahn and Mohamed M. El Zeidy (eds.), *The International Criminal Court and Complementarity: From Theory to Practice*, Cambridge University Press, 2011.

Goldstone R. J., 'International Crimes Against Women: Prosecuting Rape as a War Crime', *Case Western Reserve Journal of International Law*, 2002, vol. 34.

Gordon G., 'Complementarity and Alternative Forms of Justice: A New Test for ICC Admissibility', in Carsten Stahn and Mohamed M. El Zeidy (eds.), *The International Criminal Court and Complementarity: From Theory to Practice*, Cambridge University Press, 2011.

Gready P., The Era of Transitional Justice: The Aftermath of the Truth and Reconciliation Commission in South Africa and Beyond, Routledge, 2011.

Greenawalt A., 'Justice without Politics: Prosecutorial Discretion and the International Criminal Court', *New York University Journal of International Law and Politics*, 2007, vol. 39.

Greijer S., 'Thematic Prosecutions for Crimes Against Children', in Morten Bergsmo (ed.), *Thematic Prosecution of International Sex Crimes*, Torkel Opsahl Academic EPublisher, 2012.

Grewal B.S. and Galtungl J., *Positive and Negative Peace*, 2003, accessible at: www.activeforpeace.org/no/fred/Positive_Negative_Peace.pdf.

Groenhuijsen M.S. and De Brouwer A., 'Participation of Victims: Commentary', in André Klip and Göran Sluiter (eds.) *Annotated Leading Cases of International Criminal Tribunals: the International Criminal Court* (2005–2007), Intersentia, 2010.

Groenhuijsen M.S., 'Victims' Rights and the International Criminal Court: The Model of the Rome Statute and its Operation', in W.J.M. Genugten, M.P. Scharf and S.E. Radin (eds.), *Criminal Jurisdiction 100 Years after the 1907 Hague Peace Conference*, T.M.C. Asser Press, 2009.

Groenhuisen M.S. and Pemberton A., 'Genocide, Crimes Against Humanity and War Crimes: A Victomological Perspective on International Criminal Justice', in Rianne Letschert and Roelof Haveman, Anne-Marie de Brouwer and Antony Pemberton, (eds.), *Victimological Approaches to International Crimes: Africa*, Intersentia, 2011.

Gross O. and Aolain F., Law in Times of Crisis: Emergency Powers in Theory and Practice, Cambridge University Press, 2006.

Grotius H., The Rights of War and Peace, Including the Law of Nature and of Nations, M. Walter Dunne, 1901.

Guariglia F. and Rogier E., 'The Selection of Situations and Cases by the OTP of the ICC', in Carsten Stahn (ed.), *The Law and Practice of the International Criminal Court,* Oxford University Press, 2015.

Guariglia F., 'The Selection of Cases by the Office of the Prosecutor of the International Criminal Court', in Carsten Stahn and Göran Sluiter, *The Emerging Practice Of The International Criminal Court*, Martinus Nijhoff Publishers, 2009.

Guariglia F., 'Those Most Responsible versus International Sex Crimes: Competing Prosecution Themes?', in Morten Bergsmo (ed.), *Thematic Prosecution of International Sex Crimes*, Torkel Opsahl Academic EPublisher, 2012.

Haldemann F., 'Drawing the Line: Amnesty, Truth Commissions and Collective Denial', in Rianne Letschert and Roelof Haveman, Anne-Marie de Brouwer and Antony Pemberton, *Victimological Approaches to International Crimes: Africa,* Intersentia, 2011.

Hall C., 'Positive Complementarity in Action', in Carsten Stahn and Mohamed M. El Zeidy (eds.), *The International Criminal Court and Complementarity: From Theory to Practice,* Cambridge University Press, 2011.

Hampton J., The Moral Education Theory of Punishment, *Philosophy and Public Affairs,* 1984, vol. 13.

Hanna N., 'Say What? A Critique of Expressive Retributivism', *Law and Philosophy,* 2008, vol. 27.

Harvard Law School's Research, 'Draft Convention on Jurisdiction with Respect to Crime', *American Journal of International Law,* 1935, vol. 29.

Hasenclever A., Mayer P. and Rittberger V., *Theories of International Regimes,* Cambridge University Press, 2004.

Hegel G. W., The Elements of the Philosophy of Right, 1820.

Heller K. J., 'A Sentence-Based Theory of Complementarity', in William A. Schabas, Yvonne McDermott and Niamh Hayes (eds.), *The Ashgate Research Companion to ICL: Critical Perspectives*, Ashgate, 2013.

Heller K. J., 'Radical Complementarity', *Journal of International Criminal Justice,* 2016, vol. 14.

Heller K. J., 'Situational Gravity under the Rome Statute', in Carsten Stahn and Larissa van den Herik (eds.), *Future Perspectives on International Criminal Justice,* T.M.C. Asser Press, 2010.

Heller K. J., 'The Shadow Side of Complementarity: The Effect of Article 17 of the Rome Statute on National Due Process', *Criminal Law Forum,* 2006, vol. 17.

Hilaire M., *United Nations Law and the Security Council,* Ashgate Publishing limited, 2005.

Holmes J. T., 'Complementarity: National Courts versus the ICC', in Antonio Cassese, Paola Gaeta and John R.W.D. Jones (eds.), *The Rome Statute of the International Criminal Court: A Commentary,* Vol(I), Oxford University Press, 2002.

Holmes J. T., 'The Principle of Complementarity', in Roy S. Lee (ed.), *The International Criminal Court: The Making of the Rome Statute,* 1999.

Human Right Watch, The Meaning of the Interests of Justice in Article 53 of the Rome Statute, 2005.

Human Rights Center University of California, The Victims' Court? A Study of 622 Victim Participants at the International Criminal Court, 2015.

Human Rights Watch, Ituri: Covered in Blood Ethnically Targeted Violence in Northeastern Democratic Republic of Congo, 2003.

Human Rights Watch, Justice for Serious Crimes before National Courts: Uganda's International Crimes Division, January 2012.

Human Rights Watch, Selling Justice Short: Why Accountability Matters for Peace, 2009.

Human Rights Watch, Yemen: No Accountability for War Crimes, January 2017.

ICC, The Trust Fund for Victim, Learning from the TFV'S Second Mandate: From Implementing Rehabilitation Assistance to Reparation, 2010.

ICTY, 20 Years of the ICTY: Anniversary Event and Legacy Conference Proceedings, Grafika Saran, 2014.

International Federation for Human Rights, *Mali: The Hearing of Al Mahdi before the ICC is a Victory,* 30 September 2015.

International Federation for Human Rights, *New Special Criminal Court: A Key Step Toward Justice,* 24 April 2015.

Jackson M., 'Regional Complementarity', *Journal of International Criminal Justice,* 2016, vol. 14.

Jacobs D., 'A Shifting Scale of Power: Who Is in Charge of the Charges at the International Criminal Court And the Uses of Regulation 55', William A. Schabas, Niamh Hayes and Yvonne McDermott (eds.), *The Ashgate Research Companion to International Criminal Law: Critical Perspectives*, Ashgate, 2013.

Jorda C. and De Hemptinne J., 'The Status and Role of the Victim', in Antonio Cassese (ed), *the Rome Statute of the International Criminal Court: A Commentary,* Oxford University Press, 2002.

Kaleck W., Double Standards: International Criminal Law and the West, Torkel Opsahl Academic Publisher, 2015.

Kaul H., 'Preconditions to the Exercise of Jurisdiction', in Antonio Cassese, Paola Gaeta and John R.W.D. Jones (eds.), *The Rome Statute of the International Criminal Court: A Commentary,* Oxford University Press, 2002.

Keohane, R.O., After Hegemony: Cooperation and Discord in the World Political Economy, 1984.

Kim Y.S., The ICC: A Commentary of the Rome Statute, Wisdom House, 2003.

Kip C. and Bair J.P. (eds.), *International Due Process and Fair Trial Manual,* ABA Center for Human Rights, 2014.

Kirsch P. and Robinson D., 'Referral by States Parties', in Antonio Cassese, Paola Gaeta and John R.W.D. Jones (eds.), *The Rome Statute of the International Criminal Court: A Commentary,* Oxford University Press, 2002.

Kiyani A.G., 'Al Bashir and the ICC: The Problem of Head of State Immunity', *Chinese Journal of International Law,* 2013, vol. 12.

Klabbers J., An Introduction to International Institutional Law, Cambridge University Press, 2002.

Kleffner J.K., 'The Law and Policy of Complementarity in Relation to Criminal Proceedings Carried Out by Non-State', in Carsten Stahn and Mohamed M. El Zeidy (eds.), *The International Criminal Court and Complementarity: From Theory to Practice,* Cambridge University Press, 2011.

Kleffner J.K., Complementarity in the Rome Statute and National Criminal Jurisdiction, Oxford University Press, 2008.

Kreb C., 'The Crime of Genocide and Contextual Elements: A Comment on the ICC Pre-Trial Chamber's Decision in the Al Bashir Case', *Journal of International Criminal Justice,* 2009, vol. 7.

Kress C., 'The Procedural Law of the International Criminal Court in Outline: Anatomy of a Unique Compromise', *Journal of International Criminal Justice,* 2003, vol. 1.

Laving L., The Reliability of Open Source Evidence in the International Criminal Court, Master thesis, Lund University, 2014.

Leyh G., Procedural Justice: Victim Participation in International Criminal Procedure, Intersentia, 2011.

Luban D., 'Fairness to Rightness: Jurisdiction, Legality and the Legitimacy of International Criminal Law', in A. Besson and John Tasioulas (eds.), *The Philosophy of International Law,* Oxford University Press, 2010.

Ludwin King E., 'Does Justice Always Require Prosecution? The International Criminal Court and Transitional Justice Measures', *The George Washington International Law Review,* 2013, vol. 45.

Lulu Z., 'Brief Analysis of a Few Controversial Issues in Contemporary International Criminal Law', in Morten Bergsmo and Lung Yan (eds.), *State Sovereignty and International Criminal Law*, Torkel Opsahl Academic EPublisher, 2012.

MacPherson B., Authority of the Security Council to Exempt Peacekeepers from International Criminal Court Proceedings, *ASIL Insight*, July 2002.

Mahony C., 'Prioritising International Sex Crimes before the Special Court for Sierra Leone: One More Instrument of Political Manipulation?', in Morten Bergsmo (ed.), *Thematic Prosecution of International Sex Crimes*, Torkel Opsahl Academic EPublisher, 2012.

Margueritte T., 'International Criminal Law and Human Rights', in William A. Schabas and Nadia Bernaz, *Routledge Handbook of International Criminal Law*, Routledge, 2011.

Mariner J., UN Peacekeepers who Rape and Abuse are Criminals – so Treat Them as Such, August 2015.

Marler M.K., 'The International Criminal Court: Assessing the Jurisdictional Loopholes in the Rome Statute', *Duke Law Journal*, 1999, vol. 49.

Marta V., 'Interpreting Complementarity and Interests of Justice in the Presence of Restorative-Based Alternative Forms of Justice', in Carsten Stahn and Larissa Van den Herik (eds.) *Future Perspectives on International Criminal Justice*, Asser Press, 2010.

McDonald G.K. and Swaak-Goldman (eds.), Substantive and Procedural Aspects of International Criminal Law: The Experience of International and National Courts: Commentary, Brill, 2000.

Mégret F., 'Too Much of a Good Thing? Implementation and the Uses of Complementarity', in Carsten Stahn and Mohamed M. El Zeidy (eds.), *The International Criminal Court and Complementarity: From Theory to Practice*, Cambridge University Press, 2011.

Meron T., 'From Nuremberg to The Hague', *Military Law Review*, 1995, vol. 149.

Merryman J.H., The Civil Law Tradition: An Introduction to the Legal System of Western Europe and Latin America, Stanford University Press, 1969.

Mnookin R.H., 'Rethking the Tension between Peace and Justice: The International Criminal Prosecutor as Diplomat', *Harvard Negotiation Law Review*, 2013, vol. 18.

Moreno-Ocampo L., 'A Positive Approach to Complementarity: The Impact of the Office of the Prosecutor', in Carsten Stahn and Mohamed M. El Zeidy (eds.), *The International Criminal Court and Complementarity: From Theory to Practice*, Cambridge University Press, 2011.

Müller A. and Stegmiller I., 'Self-Referrals on Trial from Panacea to Patient', *Journal of International Criminal Justice*, 2010, vol. 8.

Nouwen S., 'Complementarity in Uganda: Domestic Diversity or International Imposition?', in Carsten Stahn and Mohamed M. El Zeidy (eds.), *The International Criminal Court and Complementarity: From Theory to Practice*, Cambridge University Press, 2011.

Nouwen S., Complementarity in the Line of Fire: the Catalyzing Effect of the ICC in Uganda and Sudan, Cambridge University Press, 2013.

Nsereko D.N., 'Article 18', in Otto Triffterer and Kai Ambos, *The Rome Statute of the International Criminal Court: A Commentary*, TC.H Beck. Hart. Nomos, 2016.

Nyawo J., Selective Enforcement and International Criminal Law, Intersentia, 2017.

Ohlin J.D., 'Peace, Security and Prosecutorial Discretion', in Carsten Stahn and Göran Sluiter, *The Emerging Practice of the International Criminal Court*, Martinus Nijhoff, 2009.

Okoth J., 'Africa, the United Nations Security Council and the International Criminal Court: the Question of Deferrals', in Gerhard Werle and Moritz Vombaum (eds.), *Africa, the UN Security Council and the International Criminal Court: The Question of Deferrals in Africa and the International Criminal Court*, TMC Asser Press, 2013.

Olásolo H. and Rojo E.C., 'The Application of the Principle of Complementarity to the Decision of Where to Open an Investigation: The Admissibility of Situations', in Carsten Stahn and Mohamed M. El Zeidy (eds.), *The International Criminal Court and Complementarity: From Theory to Practice*, Cambridge University Press, 2011.

Olásolo H., 'The Role of the International Criminal Court in Preventing Atrocity Crimes', in Héctor Olásolo, *Essays on International Criminal Justice*, Hart Publishing LTD, 2012.

Olásolo H., The Triggering Procedure of the International Criminal Court, Martinus Nijhoff Publishers, 2005.

Paulussen C., *Male Captus Bene Detentus? Surrendering Suspects to the International Criminal Court*, Intersentia, 2010.

Peacock R., 'The South African Truth and Reconciliation Commission: Challenges in Contributing to Reconciliation', in Rianne Letschert, Roelof Haveman, Anne-Marie de Brouwer and Antony Pemberton, *Victimological Approaches to International Crimes: Africa*, Intersentia, 2011.

Peake J., 'A Spectrum of International Criminal Procedure: Shifting Patterns of Power Distribution International Courts and Tribunals', *Pace International Law Review*, 2014, vol. 26.

Pemberton A. and Letschert R.M. and De Brouwer A., Coherence in International Criminal Justice: A Victimological Perspective, *International Criminal Law Review*, 2015, vol. 15.

Pocar F., 'The Proliferation of International Criminal Courts and Tribunals: A Necessity in the Current International Community', *Journal of International Criminal Justice*, 2004, vol. 2.

Politi M., 'Reflections on Complementarity at the Rome Conference and Beyond', in Carsten Stahn and Mohamed M. El Zeidy (eds.), *The International Criminal Court and Complementarity: From Theory to Practice*, Cambridge University Press, 2011.

Popovski V., 'The Legislative Role of the Security Council's Thematic Resolutions', in Vesselin Popovski and Trudy Fraser (eds.), *The Security Council as Global Legislator*, Routledge, 2014.

Popovski V., 'The Security Council and the International Criminal Court', in Vesselin Popovski and Trudy Fraser (eds.), *The Security Council as Global Legislator*, Routledge, 2014.

Quenivet N., 'The Security Council as Global Executive but not Global Legislator: the case of Child Soldiers', in Vesselin Popovski and Trudy Fraser (eds.), *The Security Council as Global Legislator*, Routledge, 2014.

Ramsden M. and Chung C., 'Reasonable Grounds to Believe: An Unreasonably Unclear Evidentiary Threshold at the ICC Statute', *Journal of International Criminal Justice*, 2015, vol. 13.

Rastan R., 'Complementarity: Contest or Collaboration?', in Morten Bergsmo (ed.), *Complementarity and the Exercise of Universal Jurisdiction for Core International* Crimes, Torkel Opsahl Academic EPublisher 2010.

Rastan R., 'Jurisdiction', in Carsten Stahn (ed.), *The Law and Practice of the International Criminal Court*, Oxford University Press, 2015.

Rastan R., 'Situations and Case: Defining the Parameters', in Carsten Stahn and Mohamed M. El Zeidy (eds.), *The International Criminal Court and Complementarity: From Theory to Practice*, Cambridge University Press, 2011.

Rastan R., 'The Jurisdictional Scope of Situations before the International Criminal Court', *Criminal Law Forum*, 2012, vol. 23.

Reydams L. and Odermatt J., 'Mandates', in Luc Reydams and Jan Wouters and Cedric Ryngaret (eds.), *International Prosecutors*, Oxford University Press, 2012.

Robinson D., 'Serving the Interests of Justice: Amnesties, Truth Commissions and the International Criminal Court', *European Journal of International Law*, 2003, vol. 14.

Robinson D., 'Territorial State Referrals and Reflections on ICL Discourse', *Journal of International Criminal Justice*, 2011, vol. 9.

Robinson D., 'The Inaction Controversy: Neglected Words and New Opportunities', in Carsten Stahn and Mohamed M. El Zeidy (eds.), *The International Criminal Court and Complementarity: From Theory to Practice*, Cambridge University Press, 2011.

Roche D., 'Truth Commission Amnesties and the International Criminal Court', *British Journal Criminology*, 2005.

Rodman E.A., 'Is Peace in the Interests of Justice? The Case for Broad Prosecutorial Discretion at the International Criminal Court', *Leiden Journal of International Law*, 2009, vol. 22.

Ryngaert C., 'Horizontal Complementarity', in Carsten Stahn and Mohamed M. El Zeidy (eds.), *The International Criminal Court and Complementarity: From Theory to Practice*, Cambridge University Press, 2011.

Ryngaert C., *Jurisdiction in International Criminal Law*, Oxford University Press, 2008.

Sacouto S. and Cleary K., 'The Importance of Effective Investigation of Sexual Violence and Gender-Based Crimes at the International Criminal Court', *Journal of Gender Social Policy and the Law*, 2009, vol. 17.

Safferling C., *International Criminal Procedure*, Oxford University Press, 2012.

Sarooshi D., International Organizations and Their Exercise of Sovereign Powers, Oxford University Press, 2005.

Schabas W. A., *Rwanda Tribunal Symposium and Victors Justice*, 16 August 2009.

Schabas W.A. and El Zeidy M.M., 'Article 17', in Otto Triffterer and Ambos (eds), *The Rome Statute of the International Criminal Court: A Commentary*, C.H. Beck. Hart. Nomos, 2016.

Schabas W.A., 'A Synergistic Relationship: The Sierra Leone Truth and Reconciliation Commission and the Special Court for Sierra Leone', in William A. Schabas, Shane Darcy (eds.), *Truth Commissions and Courts: The Tension between Criminal Justice and the Search for Truth*, Springer, 2004.

Schabas W.A., 'International Criminal Tribunals: A Review of 2007', *Journal of International Human Rights*, 2008, vol. 6.

Schabas W.A., 'Prosecutorial Discretion and Gravity', in Carsten Stahn and Göran Sluiter (eds.), *The Emerging Practice of the International Criminal Law*, Martinus Nijhoff Publishers, 2005.

Schabas W.A., 'The Rise and Fall of Complementarity', in Carsten Stahn and Mohamed M. El Zeidy (eds.), *The International Criminal Court and Complementarity: From Theory to Practice*, Cambridge University Press, 2011.

Schabas W.A., 'The Short of Arm of International Criminal Law', in William A. Schabas and Yvonne McDermott and Niamh Hayes (eds.), *The Ashgate Research Companion to International Criminal Law: critical perspectives*, Ashgate, 2013.

Schabas W.A., 'Victor's Justice: Selecting Situations at the International Criminal Court', *Marshall Law Review*, 2010.

Schabas W.A., *An Introduction to International Criminal Court*, Cambridge University Press, 2011.

Schabas W.A., *Obama, Medvedev and Hu Jintao may be Prosecuted by International Criminal Court, Pre-Trial Chamber Concludes*, 15 December 2011, available at: http://humanrightsdoctorate.blogspot.nl/2011/12/obama-medvedev-and-hu-jintao-may-be.html.

Schabas W.A., The International Criminal Court: A Commentary on the Rome Statute, Oxford University Press, 2010.

Schabas W.A., Unimaginable Atrocities: Justice, Politics and Rights at the War Crimes Tribunals, Oxford University Press, 2012.

Schabas W.A., War crimes and Human Rights Essays on the Death Penalty, Justice and Accountability, Cameron May, 2008.

Schaefer B.D. and Groves S., *The Motivation for the Referral of Libya to the ICC: Political Pressure or Justice?*, 4 March 2011, available at www.heritage.org/africa/report/the-motivation-the-referral-libya-the-icc-political-pressure-or-justice.

Seider N., Jurisdiction over Peacekeeping Forces Before and After the Establishment off the International Criminal Court and the Impacts off Security Council Resolution 1422 and So-Called Article 98 Agreements, Thesis of Masters of Law, University of Cape Town.

Seils P., 'Putting Complementarity in Place', in Carsten Stahn (ed.), *The Law And Practice of the International Criminal Court,* Oxford University Press, 2015.

Seils P.F., 'Making Complementarity Work: Maximizing the Limited Role of the Prosecutor', in Carsten Stahn and Mohamed M. El Zeidy (eds.), *The International Criminal Court and Complementarity: From Theory to Practice,* Cambridge University Press, 2011.

Seils P.F., 'The Selection and Prioritization of Cases by the Office of the Prosecutor of the International Criminal Court', in Morten Bergsmo (ed.), *Criteria for Prioritizing and Selecting Core International Crimes Cases*, Torkel Opsahl Academic EPublisher, 2010.

Sellars K., 'Imperfect Justice at Nuremberg and Tokyo', *European Journal for International Law,* 2011.

Shany Y., 'In Defense of Functional Interpretation of Article 12(3)', in Chantal Meloni and Gianni Tognoni (eds.), *Is There a Court for Gaza? A Test Bench for International,* Asser Press, 2012.

Shoamanesh S.S. and Dutertre G., *The ICC and Cultural Property: Reinforced Legal Enforcement of the Protection of Cultural Property in Armed Conflict,* 22 June 2016, available at: www.international-criminal-justice-today.org/arguendo/the-icc-and-cultural-property/.

Sivakumaran S., 'Sexual Violence Against Men in Armed Conflict', *The European Journal of International Law,* 2007, vol. 18.

Sloane R., *The Expressive Capacity of International Punishmen*t, Columbia Public Law and Legal Theory Working Paper, 2006.

Sluiter G. and Friman H. and Linton S., *International Criminal Procedure: Principles and Rules,* Oxford University Press, 2013.

Sluiter G., International Criminal Adjudication and the Collection of Evidence: Obligations of States, Intersentia, 2002.

Smeulers A. and Weerdesteijn M. and Hola B., 'The Selection of Situations by the ICC: An Empirically Based Evaluation of the OTP's Performance', *International Criminal Law Review,* 2015, vol. 15.

Snyder J. and Vinjamuri L., 'Trials and Errors: Principle and Pragmatism in Strategies of International Justice', *International Security,* 2003, vol. 28.

Soares P.P., 'Positive Complementarity and the Law Enforcement Network: Drawing Lessons from the Ad Hoc Tribunals' Completion Strategy', *Israel Law Review,* 2013, vol. 46.

Spiga V., 'No Redress without Justice: Victims and International Criminal Law', *Journal of International Criminal Justice,* 2012, vol. 10.

Stahn C. and El Zeidy M.M. (eds.), The International Criminal Court and Complementarity: From Theory to Practice, Cambridge University Press, 2011.

Stahn C., 'Admissibility Challenges before the ICC: From Quasi-Primacy to Qualified Deference', in Carsten Stahn (ed.), *The Law And Practice of the International Criminal Court,* Oxford University Press, 2015.

Stahn C., 'Complementarity: A Tale of Two Notions', *Criminal Law Forum*, 2008, vol. 19.

Stahn C., 'Introduction', in Carsten Stahn and Mohamed M. El Zeidy (eds.), *The International Criminal Court and Complementarity: From Theory to Practice,* Cambridge University Press, 2011.

Stahn C., 'Judicial Review of Prosecutorial Discretion: 5 Years on', in Carsten. Stahn and Göran Sluiter, *The Emerging Practice of the International Criminal Court*, Martinus Nijhoff, 2009.

Stahn C., 'Sentencing Horror or Sentencing Heuristic? A Reply to Heller's Sentence-Based Theory of Complementarity', in William A. Schabas, Yvonne McDermott and Niamh Hayes (eds.), *The Ashgate Research Companion to International Criminal Law: critical perspectives,* Ashgate, 2013.

Stahn C., 'Taking Complementarity Seriously: On the Sense and Sensibility of 'Classical', 'Positive' and 'Negative' Complementarity', in Carsten Stahn and Mohamed M. El Zeidy (eds.), *The International Criminal Court and Complementarity: From Theory to Practice,* Cambridge University Press, 2011.

Stahn C., 'The Ambiguities of Security Council Resolution (1422)', *European Journal of International Law,* 2003, vol. 14.

Stahn C., *Why the ICC Should Be Cautious to Use the Islamic State to Get out of Africa: Part 2,* 3 December 2014, available at: www.ejiltalk.org/why-the-icc-should-be-cautious-to-use-the-islamic-State-to-get-out-of-africa-part-2.

Stegmiller I., 'Interpretative Gravity under the ICC Statute: Identifying Common Gravity Criteria', in Carsten Stahn and Mohamed M. El Zeidy (eds.), *The International Criminal Court and Complementarity: From Theory to Practice*, Cambridge University Press, 2011.

Stigen J.M., 'The Admissibility Procedures', in Carsten Stahn and Mohamed M. El Zeidy (eds.), *The International Criminal Court and Complementarity: From Theory to Practice,* Cambridge University Press, 2011.

Stigen Jo M., The Relationship Between the International Criminal Court and National Jurisdictions: the Principle of Complementarity, Brill Nijhoff, 2008.

Sunstein C.R., 'On the Expressive Function of Law', *University Of Pennsylvania Law Review,* 1996, vol. 144.

Tallgren I., 'The Sensibility and Sense of International Criminal Law', *European Journal of International Law,* 2002, vol. 13.

The Redress Trust, Victim Participation in Criminal Law Proceedings: Survey of Domestic Practice for Application to International Crimes Prosecutions, September 2015.

Trendafilova E., 'Africa and International Criminal Court: A Judge's Perspective', in Gerhard Werle, Moritz Vombaum (eds.), *Africa and the International Criminal Court*, 2013, TMC Asser Press.

Turner J., 'Accountability of International Prosecutors', in Carsten Stahn (ed.*), The Law and Practice of the International Criminal Court*, Oxford University Press, 2015.

Turone G., 'Powers and Duties of the Prosecutor', in Antonio Cassese, Paola Gaeta and John R.W.D. Jones (eds), *The Rome Statute of the International Criminal Court: A Commentary*, Oxford University Press, 2002.

Vagias M., The Territorial Jurisdiction of the International Criminal Court, Cambridge University Press, 2014.

Valdez-Arroyo F.M., 'Prospect for Thematic Prosecution of International Sex Crimes in Latin America', in Morten Bergsmo (ed.), *Thematic Prosecution of International Sex Crimes*, Torkel Opsahl Academic EPublisher, 2012.

Van den Wyngaert Hon C., 'Victims before International Criminal Courts: Some Views and Concerns of an ICC Trial Judge', *Case Western Reserve Journal of International Law*, 2011, vol. 44.

Van der Wilt H., 'Self-Referrals As an Indication of the Inability of States to Cope with Non-State Actors', in Carsten Stahn (eds.*), The Law and Practice of the International Criminal Court*, Oxford University Press, 2014.

Van der Wilt H., 'States' Obligations to Investigate and Prosecute Perpetrators of International Crimes: The Perspective of the European Court of Human Rights', in Carsten Stahn and Mohamed M. El Zeidy (eds.), *The International Criminal Court and Complementarity: From Theory to Practice*, Cambridge University Press, 2011.

Van Sliedregt E., 'International Criminal Law', in Markus D. Dubber and Tatjana Hornle (eds.), *The Oxford Handbook of Criminal Law*, Oxford University Press, 2014.

Van Wijk, 'Should We Ever Say Never? Arguments against Granting Amnesty Tested', in Rianne Letschert, Roelof Haveman and Anne-Marie de Brouwer and Antony Pemberton, *Victimological Approaches to International Crimes: Africa, Intersentia*, 2011.

Vasiliev S., 'Victim Participation Revisited: What the ICC is Learning About Itself', in Carsten Stahn (ed), *The Law and Practice of the International Criminal Court*, Oxford University Press, 2015.

Ventura M.J., 'The Reasonable Basis to Proceed Threshold in the Kenya and Côte d'Ivoire *Proprio Motu* Investigation Decisions: The International Criminal Court's Lowest Evidentiary Standard?', *The Law and Practice of International Courts and Tribunals*, 2013, vol. 12.

Verhoeven S. and Demeyere B., 'The International Criminal Court's office of the Prosecutor: Navigating between Independence and Accountability?', in Doria and Gasser and Bassiouni (eds), *The Legal Regime of the International Criminal Court*, Martinus Nijhoff Publisher, 2009.

Vinck P. and Pham P.N., 'Outreach Evaluation: The International Criminal Court in the Central African Republic', *International Journal of Transitional Justice*, 2010, vol. 4.

Vinjamuri L., 'The ICC and the Politics of Peace and Justice', in Carsten Stahn (ed.*),The Law and Practice of the International Criminal Court*, Oxford University Press, 2015.

Vriezen V., Amnesty Justified? The Need for a Case By Case Approach in the Interests of Human Rights, Wolf Legal Publishers, 2011.

Waller J., Becoming Evil: How Ordinary People Commit Genocide and Mass Killings, Oxford University Press, 2002.

War Crime Research Office, Victim Participation before the International Criminal Court, American University, 2007.

Weerdesteijn M., The Rationality of Dictators: Towards a More Effective Implementation of the Responsibility to Protect, Intersentia, 2016.

Wemmers J., 'Victims' Need for Justice: Individual versus Collective Justice', in Rienne Letschert and Roelof Haveman, Anne-Marie de Brouwer and Antony Pemberton, *Victimological Approaches to International Crimes: Africa,* Intersentia, 2011.

Wendt A., 'The State As Person in International Theory', *Review of International Studies,* 2004, vol. 30.

White N.D., *The Law of International Organizations,* Manchester University Press, 2005.

Wierda M. and Triolo A., 'Resources', in Luc Reydams and Jan Wouters and Cedric Ryngaret (eds.), *International Prosecutors*, Oxford, Oxford University Press, 2012.

Williams S.A. and Schabas W.A., 'Article 12', in Otto Triffterer (ed.), *Commentary on the Rome Statute of the International Criminal Court*, C.H. Beck. Hart. Nomos, 2008.

Williams S.A. and Schabas W.A., 'Article 17', in Otto Triffterer (ed.), *Commentary on the Rome Statute of the International Criminal Court*, 2008.

Williams S.A., 'Article 11', in Otto Triffterer (ed.), *Commentary on the Rome Statute of the International Criminal Court*, C.H. Beck. Hart. Nomos, 2008.

Wippman D., 'Atrocities, Deterrence and the Limits of International Justice', *Fordham International law Journal* 1999, vol. 23.

Women's Initiatives for Gender Justice, *Gender Report Card on the International Criminal Court,* November 2010.

Wouters J. and Verhoeven S. and Demeyere B., 'The International Criminal Court's Office of the Prosecutor: Navigating between Independence and Accountability?', *International Criminal Law Review,* 2008, vol. 8.

Yee L., 'The International Criminal Court and the Security Council: Article 13(b) and 16', in Roy S. Lee, *The International Criminal Court: Making of the Rome Statut*e, Kluwer Law International, 1999.

Zakerhossein M.H., 'To Bury a Situation Alive: A Critical Reading of the ICC Prosecutor's Statement on the ISIS Situation', *International Criminal Law Review, 2016,* vol. 16.

Zakerhossein M.H., *Comments on the ICC OTP's Draft Policy Paper on Case Selection and Prioritization,* JusticeHub, 29 March 2016, available at: https://justicehub.org/article/comments-icc-otps-draft-policy-paper-case-selection-and-prioritisation.

Zamani G., Law of International Organizations: Personality, Responsibility, Immunity, The SD Institute of Law Research and Study, 2009.

Zappala S., 'The Rights of Victims v. the Rights of the Accused', *Journal of International Criminal Justice*, 2010, vol. 8

Zimmermann A., 'Palestine and the International Criminal Court Quo Vadis?', *Journal of International Criminal Justice,* 2013, vol. 11

ICC CASE TABLES

Abu Garda case, Decision on the 34 Applications for Participation at the Pre-Trial Stage of the Case, 25 September 2009.

Abu Garda case, Summary of the Prosecutor's Application under Article 58, 20 November 2008.

Ahmad Harun case, Trial Chamber I, Warrant of Arrest for Ahmad Harun, 16 April 2007.

Al Bashir case, Appeals chamber, Judgment on the Appeal of the Prosecutor against the Decision on the Prosecution's Application for a Warrant of Arrest against Omar Hassan Ahmad Al Bashir, 3 February 2010.

Al Bashir case, OTP, Prosecution Application for a Warrant of Arrest, 14 July 2008.

Al Bashir case, OTP, Prosecution Document in Support of Appeal against the Decision on the Prosecution's Application for a Warrant of Arrest against Omar Hassan Ahmad Al Bashir, 6 July 2009.

Al Bashir case, OTP, Prosecution's Urgent Request for an Order Clarifying whether Article 97 Consultations with South Africa Have Concluded and that South Africa is Under an Obligation to Immediately Arrest and Surrender Omar Al Bashir, 13 June 2015.

Al Bashir case, PTC I, Corrigendum to the Decision Pursuant to Article 87(7) of the Rome Statute on the Failure by the Republic of Malawi to Comply with the Cooperation Requests Issued by the Court with Respect to the Arrest and Surrender of Omar Hassan Ahmad Al Bashir, 12 December 2011.

Al Bashir case, PTC I, Decision on the Prosecution's Application for a Warrant of Arrest against Omar Hassan Ahmad Al Bashir, 4 March 2009.

Al Bashir case, PTC I, Second Decision on the Prosecution's Application for a Warrant of Arrest, 12 July 2010.

Al Bashir case, PTC II, Decision on the Cooperation of the Democratic Republic of the Congo Regarding Omar Al Bashir's Arrest and Surrender to the Court, 9 April 2014.

Al Bashir case, PTC II, Al Bashir case, Decision on the Cooperation of the Republic of Chad Regarding Abdel Raheem Muhammad Hussein's Arrest and Surrender to the Court, 13 November 2013.

Al Bashir case, PTC II, Decision Following the Prosecutor's Request for an Order Further Clarifying that the Republic of South Africa is under the Obligation to Immediately Arrest and Surrender Omar Al Bashir, 13 June 2015.

Al Bashir case, PTC II, Decision on the Cooperation of the Federal Republic of Nigeria Regarding Omar Al-Bashir's Arrest and Surrender to the Court, 5 September 2013.

Al Bashir case, PTC II, Decision on the Non-Compliance by the Republic of Uganda with the Request to Arrest and Surrender Omar Al-Bashir to the Court and Referring the Matter to the United Nations Security Council and the Assembly of States Parties to the Rome Statute, 11 July 2016.

Al Bashir case, PTC II, Decision on the Non-Compliance by the Republic of Djibouti with the Request to Arrest and Surrender Omar Al-Bashir to the Court and Referring the Matter to the United Nations Security Council and the Assembly of the States Parties to the Rome Statute, 11 July 2016.

Al Bashir case, The Observations Submitted by the Democratic Republic of the Congo pursuant to the Decision Requesting Observations on Omar Al-Bashir's visit to the Democratic Republic of Congo' dated 3 March 2014.

Al-Mahdi case, ICC, Trial Chamber VIII, Decision on Victim Participation at Trial and on Common Legal Representation of Victims', 8 June 2016.

Al-Mahdi case, PTC I, Decision on the Confirmation of Charges against Ahmad Al Faqi Al Mahdi, 24 March 2016.

Al-Mahdi case, Trial Chamber VIII, Judgment and Sentence, 27 September 2016.

Al-Senussi case, Application on behalf of the Government of Libya Pursuant to Article 19 of the ICC Statute, 1 May 2012.

Al-Senussi case, ICC, Appeals Chamber, Judgment on the Appeal of Mr Abdullah Al-Senussi against the decision of Pre-Trial Chamber I of 11 October 2013 Entitled Decision on the admissibility of the case against Abdullah Al-Senussi, 24 July 2014.

Al-Senussi case, PTC I, Decision on the Admissibility of the Case against Abdullah Al-Senussi, 11 October 2013.

Al-Tuhamy case, PTC, Al-Tuhamy case, Warrant of Arrest for Al-Tuhamy Mohamed Khaled with under seal and ex parte Annex, 18 April 2013.

Bemba case, ICC, PTC II, Bemba case, Decision Pursuant to Article 61(7)(a) and (b) of the Rome Statute on the Charges of the Prosecutor against Jean-Pierre Bemba Gombo,15 June 2009.

Bemba case, ICC, PTC III, Warrant of Arrest for Jean-Pierre Bemba Gombo Replacing the Warrant of Arrest Issued on 23 May 2008, 10 June 2008.

Bemba case, PTC III, Decision on the Prosecutor's Application for a Warrant of Arrest against Jean-Pierre Bemba Gombo, 10 June 2008.

Bemba case, PTC III, Fourth Decision on Victims' Participation, 12 December 2008.

Bemba case, Trial Chamber III, Decision on 772 Applications by Victims to Participate in the Proceedings, 18 November 2010.

Gaddafi case, Appeals Chamber, Judgment on the Appeal of Libya Against the Decision of Pre-Trial Chamber I of 31 May 2013 Entitled Decision on the Admissibility of the Case Against Saif Al-Islam Gaddafi, 21 May 2014.

Gaddafi case, Appeals Chamber, Separate Opinion of Judge Anita Ušacka, 21 May 2014.

Gaddafi case, Appeals Chamber, Separate Opinion of Judge Sang-Hyun Song, 21 May 2014.

Gaddafi case, ICC, PTC I, Decision on the Admissibility of the Case against Saif-Al-Islam Gaddafi, 31 May 2013.

Gaddafi case, PCT I, Decision Requesting Further Submissions on Issues Related to the Admissibility of the Case against Saif Al-Islam Gaddafi, 7 December 2012.

Gaddafi case, PTC I, Decision on the Prosecutor's Application Pursuant to Article 58 as to Muammar Mohammed Abu Minyar Gaddafi, Saif Al-Islam Gaddafi and Abdullah Al-Senussi, 27 June 2011.

Gaddafi case, PTC I, Decision Requesting Further Submissions on Issues Related to the Admissibility of the Case Against Saif Al-Islam Gaddafi, 7 December 2012.

Gaddafi case, PTC I, Warrant of Arrest for Saif Al-Islam Gaddafi, 27 June 2011.

Gaddafi case, Separate Opinion of Judge Anita Ušacka, Judgment on the Appeal of Libya Against the Decision of Pre-Trial Chamber I of 31 May 2013 Entitled 'Decision on the Admissibility of the Case Against Saif Al-Islam Gaddafi', 24 July 2014.

Georgia Situation, OTP, Corrected Version of Request for Authorization of an Investigation Pursuant to Article 15, 17 November 2015.

Georgia situation, OTP, Request for Authorization of an Investigation Pursuant to Article 15, 13 October 2015.

Georgia situation, PTC I, Decision on the Prosecutor's Request for Authorization of an Investigation, 27 January 2016.

Georgia situation, Registry, Report on the Victims' Representations Received Pursuant to Article 15(3) of the Rome Statute, 4 December 2015.

Harun and Kushayb case, ICC, PTC I, Decision on the Prosecutor's Application under Article 58(7), 27 April 2007.

Katanga and Chui case, Decision on the Set of Procedural Rights Attached to Procedural Status of Victim at the Pre-Trial Stage of the Case, 13 May 2008.

Katanga and Chui case, PTC II, Reasons for the Oral Decision on the Motion Challenging the Admissibility of the Case (Article 19 of the Statute), 16 June 2009.

Katanga and Chui case, Trial Chamber II, Grounds for the Decision on the 345 Applications for Participation in the Proceedings Submitted by Victims, 23 September 2009.

Katanga case, Appeals Chamber, Judgment on the Appeal of Mr. Germain Katanga against the Oral Decision of Trial Chamber II of 12 June 2009 on the Admissibility of the Case, 25 September 2009.

Katanga case, Defense, Motion Challenging the Admissibility of the Case by Defense of Germain Katanga Pursuant to Article 19 (2) of the Statute, 11 March 2009.

Katanga case, OTP, Prosecution Response to Motion Challenging the Admissibility of the the Case by the Defense of Germain Katanga, Pursuant to Article 19(2)(a), 30 March 2009.

Katanga case, OTP, Prosecution's Response to Document in Support of Appeal of the Defense for Germain Katanga against the Decision of the Trial Chamber *'Motifs de la décision oral relative à l'exception d'irrecevabilité de l'affaire'*, 31 July 2009.

Katanga case, PTC I, Decision on the Confirmation of Charges, 30 September 2008.

Katanga case, PTC I, Decision on the Evidence and Information Provided by the Prosecution for the Issuance of a Warrant of Arrest for Germain Katanga, 6 July 2007.

Katanga case, PTC I, Urgent Warrant of Arrest for Germain Katanga, 2 July 2007.

Kenyatta and Hussein Ali case, Appeals Chamber, Decision on the Filing of Updated Investigation Report by the Government of Kenya in the Appeal against the Pre-Trial Chamber's Decision on Admissibility, 28 July 2011.

Kenyatta case, Decision on the Prosecutor's Application for Summonses to Appear for Francis Kirimi Muthaura, Uhuru Muigai Kenyatta and Mohammed Hussein Ali, 8 March 2011.

Kenyatta case, PTC II, Decision on Victims' Participation at the Confirmation of Charges Hearing and in the Related Proceedings, 26 August 2011.

Kenyatta case, PTC II, Decision on the Prosecutor's Application for Summonses to Appear for Francis Kirimi Muthaura, Uhuru Muigai Kenyatta and Mohammed Hussein Ali, 8 March 2011.

Kenyatta case, Trial Chamber V(b), Decision on Defense Request for Conditional Excusal from Continuous Presence at Trial, 18 October 2013.

Kenyatta case, Trial Chamber V(b), Decision on Prosecution's Application for a Further Adjournment, 3 December 2014.

Kenyatta case, Trial Chamber V(b), Notice of Withdrawal of the Charges against Uhuru Muigai Kenyatta, 5 December 2014.

Kony case, Appeals Chamber, Judgment on the Appeal of the Defense against the Decision on the Admissibility of the Case under Article 19 (1) of the Statute of 10 March 2009, 16 September 2009.

Kony case, Appeals Chamber, Refiled Document in Support of Defense Appeal against Decision on the Admissibility of the Case under Article 19(1) of the Statute dated 10 March 2009, 15 April 2009.

Kony case, PTC II, Decision Initiating Proceedings under Article 19, Requesting Observations and Appointing Counsel for the Defense, 21 October 2008.

Kony case, PTC II, Decision on the Admissibility of the Case under Article 19(1) of the Statute, 10 March 2009.

Kony case, PTC II, Warrant of Arrest for Joseph Kony issued on 8th July 2005 as amended on 27 September 2005, 13 October 2005.

Kony case, Trial Chamber II, Warrant of Arrest for Kony Issued on 8 July 2005 as Amended on 27 September 2005.

Kushayb case, OTP, Prosecutor's Application under Article 58(7), 27 February 2007.

Laurant Gbagbo, Pre-Trial Chamber I, Decision on Victims' Participation and Victims' Common Legal Representation at the Confirmation of Charges Hearing and in the Related Proceedings, 4 June 2012.

Laurent Gbagbo Case, Appeals Chamber, Judgment on the Appeal of Mr Laurent Koudou Gbagbo Against the Decision of Pre-Trial Chamber I on Jurisdiction and Stay of the Proceedings, 12 December 2012.

Laurent Gbagbo case, PTC I, Decision Adjourning the Hearing on the Confirmation of Charges Pursuant to Article 61(7)(c)(i) of the Rome Statute, 3 June 2013.

Laurent Gbagbo case, PTC I, Decision on the confirmation of charges against Laurent Gbagbo, 12 June 2014.

Laurent Gbagbo case, PTC I, Decision on the Corrigendum of the Challenge to the Jurisdiction of the Interactional Criminal Court on the basis of Articles 12(3), 19(2), 21(3), 55 and 59 of the Rome Statute Filed by the Defense for President Gbagbo, 15 August 2012.

Laurent Gbagbo case, PTC III, Decision on the Prosecutor's Application Pursuant to Article 58 for a Warrant of Arrest against Laurent Koudou Gbagbo, 30 November 2011.

Libya situation, Gaddafi case, Application on Behalf of the Government of Libya Pursuant to Article 19 of the ICC Statute, 1 May 2012.

Libya situation, OTP, Prosecution Response to Application on Behalf of the Government of Libya Pursuant to Article 19 of the ICC Statute, 5 June 2012.

Libya situation, OTP, Prosecution's Response to Application on Behalf of the Government of Libya relating to Abdullah Al-Senussi Pursuant to Article 19 of the ICC Statute, 3 May 2013.

Libya Situation, OTP, the Prosecution Response to Application on Behalf of the Government of Libya Pursuant to Article 19 of the ICC Statute, June 2012.

Lubanga case, Appeals Chamber, Judgment on the Appeal of Mr. Thomas Lubanga Dyilo Against the Decision on the Defense Challenge to the Court's Jurisdiction Pursuant to Article 19 (2)(a) of the Statute of 3 October 2006, 14 December 2006.

Lubanga case, Appeals Chamber, Judgment on the Appeals Against the Decision Establishing the Principles and Procedures to be Applied to Reparation, 3 March 2015.

Lubanga case, Appeals Chamber, Judgment on the Prosecutor's Appeal Against the Decision of Pre-Trial Chamber I Entitled Decision on the Prosecutor's Application for Warrants of Arrest, Article 58, 13 July 2006.

Lubanga case, Appeals Chamber, The Appeals of The Prosecutor and The Defense against Trial Chamber I's Decision on Victims' Participation of 18 January 2008, 11 July 2008.
Lubanga case, ICC, PTC I, Decision of the Confirmation of Charges, 29 January 2007.
Lubanga case, ICC, PTC I, Decision on the Prosecutor's Application under Article 58, 10 February 2006.
Lubanga case, ICC, Trial Chamber I, Judgment Pursuant to Article 74 of the Statute, 14 March 2012.
Lubanga case, PTC I, Decision on the Application for Participation in the Proceedings of VPRS1, VPRS2, VPRS 3, VPRS4, VPRS5, VPRS6, 19 January 2006.
Lubanga case, PTC I, Decision concerning Pre-Trial Chamber I's Decision of 10 February 2006 and the Incorporation of Documents into the Record of the Case against Mr Thomas Lubanga Dyilo, 27 February 2006.
Lubanga case, Trial Chamber I, Decision Establishing the Principles and Procedures to be Applied to Reparation, 7 August 2012.
Lubanga case, Trial Chamber I, Separate and Dissenting Opinion of Judge René Blattman to Decision on victim's participation, 18 January 2008.
Lubanga case, the Appeals Chamber, Decision of the Appeals Chamber on the Joint Application of Victims a/0001/06 to a/0003/06 and a/0105/06 concerning the Directions and Decision of the Appeals Chamber of 2 February 2007, 13 June 2007.
Lubanga case, Trial Chamber I, Decision on Victims Participation, 18 January 2008.
Lukwiya case, PTC II, Warrant of Arrest for Raska Lukwiya, 8 July 2005.
Mbarushimana case, Appeals Chamber, Judgment on the Appeal of the Prosecutor Against the Decision of Pre-Trial Chamber I of 16 December 2011 Entitled Decision on the Confirmation of Charges, 30 May 2012.
Mbarushimana case, ICC, PTC I, Decision on the Defense Challenge to the Jurisdiction of the Court, 26 October 2011.
Mbarushimana case, ICC, PTC I, Decision on the Confirmation of Charges, 16 December 2011.
Muhammad Hussein case, PTC I, Decision on the Prosecutor's Application under Article 58 relating to Abdel Raheem Muhammad Hussein, 1 March 2012.
Muthaura case, ICC, PTC II, Decision on the Application by the Government of Kenya Challenging the Admissibility of the Case Pursuant to Article 19(2)(b) of the Statute, 20 May 2011.
Ntaganda case, Appeals Chamber, Judgment
on the appeal of Mr. Bosco Ntaganda Against the Decision on the Defense's Challenge to the Court's Jurisdiction in Respect of Counts 6 and 9, 22 March 2016.
Ntaganda case, Appeals Chamber, Judgment on the Prosecutor's Appeal Against the Decision of Pre-Trial Chamber I Entitled 'Decision on the Prosecutor's Application for Warrants of Arrest', 13 July 2006.
Ntaganda case, Application on Behalf of Mr Ntaganda Challenging the Court's Jurisdiction in Respect of Counts 6 and 9 of the Document Containing the Charges, 1 September 2015.
Ntaganda case, PTC II, Decision on the Prosecutor's Application under Article 58 to Issue an Arrest Warrant against Ntaganda, 13 July 2012.
Ntaganda case, Reply on Behalf of Mr Ntaganda to Prosecution Response to the Application on Behalf of Mr Ntaganda Challenging the Court's Jurisdiction in Respect of Counts 6 and 9 of the Documents Containing the Charges, 24 September 2015,

Ntaganda case, Trial Chamber VI, Decision on the Request by the Legal Representative of the Victims of the Attacks for Leave to Present Evidence and Victims' Views and Concerns, 15 February 2017.

Ntaganda case, Trial Chamber VI, Decision on Victims' Participation in Trial Proceedings, 6 February 2015.

Ntaganda case, Trial Chamber, Second Decision on the Defense's Challenge to the Jurisdiction of the Court in Respect of Counts 6 and 9, 4 January 2017.

Ongwen case, ICC, PTC II, Decision on the Confirmation of Charges Against Dominic Ongwen, 23 March 2016.

Ongwen case, PTC II, Decision Establishing Principles on the Victims' Application Process, 4 March 2015.

Ruto case, Appeals Chamber, Dissenting Opinion of Judge Anita Ušacka, 20 September 2011.

Ruto case, Appeals Chamber, Decision on the Filing of Updated Investigation Report by the Government of Kenya in the Appeal against the Pre-Trial Chamber's Decision on Admissibility, 28 July 2011.

Ruto case, Appeals Chamber, Dissenting Opinion of Judge Anita Ušacka, 20 September 2011.

Ruto case, Application on Behalf of the Government of Kenya Challenging the Admissibility, 31 March 2011.

Ruto case, PTC II, Decision on the Application by the Government of Kenya Challenging the Admissibility of the Case Pursuant to Article 19(2)(b) of the Statute, 30 May 2011.

Ruto case, PTC II, Decision on the Confirmation of Charges Pursuant to Article 61(7)(a) and (b) of the Rome Statute, 23 January 2012.

Simone Gbagbo case, Appeals Chamber, Judgment on the Appeal of Côte d'Ivoire Against the Decision of Pre-Trial Chamber I of 11 December 2014 Entitled Decision on Côte d'Ivoire's Challenge to the Admissibility of the Case against Simone Gbagbo, 27 May 2015.

Simone Gbagbo case, PTC I, Decision on Côte d'Ivoire's Challenge to the Admissibility of the Case against Simone Gbagbo, 11 December 2014.

Simone Gbagbo case, PTC III, Decision on the Prosecutor's Application Pursuant to Article 58 for a Warrant of Arrest against Simone Gbagbo, 2 March 2012.

Simone Gbagbo case, PTC, Warrant of Arrest for Simone Gbagbo, 29 February 2012.

Situation in CAR I, PTC I, Decision Requesting Information on the Status of the Preliminary Examination of the Situation in the Central African Republic, 30 November 2006.

Situation in Côte d'Ivoire, ICC, PTC III, Decision Pursuant to Article 15 of the Rome Statute on the Authorization of an Investigation into the Situation in the Republic of Côte d'Ivoire, 3 October 2011.

Situation in Côte d'Ivoire, OTP, Request for Authorization of an Investigation Pursuant to Article 15, 23 June 2011.

Situation in Côte d'Ivoire, PTC II, Order to the Victims Participation and Reparation Section Concerning Victims' Representations Pursuant to Article 15(3) of the Statute, 6 July 2011.

Situation in Côte d'Ivoire, PTC III, Decision on the Prosecution's Provision of Further Information Regarding Potentially Relevant Crimes Committed Between 2002 and 2010, 22 February 2012.

Situation in Darfur, Appeals Chamber, Judgment on Victim Participation in the Investigation Stage of the Proceedings in the Appeal of the OPCD Against the Decision of Pre-Trial Chamber I of 3 December 2007 and in the Appeals of the OPCD and the Prosecutor Against the Decision of Pre-Trial Chamber I of 6 December 2007, 2 February 2009.

Situation in Darfur, OTP, Public Redacted Version of the Prosecutor's Application under Article 58, 14 July 2008.
Situation in Darfur, PTC II, Decision on the Prosecutor's Request for a Finding of Non-Compliance against the Republic of the Sudan, 9 March 2015.
Situation in Darfur, PTC I, Decision on Application under Rule 103, 4 February 2009.
Situation in Egypt, PTC II, Decision Assigning the Request for Review of the Prosecution's decision of 23 April 2014 not to Open a Preliminary Examination concerning Alleged Crimes Committed in the Arab Republic of Egypt and the Registrar's decision of 25 April 2014,12 September 2014.
Situation in Egypt, Re-filing before the President of the Pre-Trial Division of the Request for Review of the Prosecutor's Decision of 23 April 2014 not to Open a Preliminary Examination Concerning Alleged Crimes Committed in the Arab Republic of Egypt and the Registrar's Decision of 25 April 2014, 1 September 2014.
Situation in Egypt, Request for Review of the Prosecutor's Decision of 23 April 2014 not to Open a Preliminary Examination Concerning Alleged Crimes Committed in the Arab Republic of Egypt and the Registrar's Decision of 25 April 2014, 23 May 2014.
Situation in Kenya, Appeals Chamber, Judgment on the Appeal of the Republic of Kenya Against the Decision of Pre-Trial Chamber II of 30 May 2011 Entitled Decision on the Application by the Government of Kenya Challenging the Admissibility of the Case Pursuant to Article 19(2)(b) of the Statute, 30 August 2011.
Situation in Kenya, Decision on a Request for Leave to Appeal, 11 February 2011.
Situation in Kenya, OTP, Request for Authorization of an Investigation Pursuant to Article 15, 26 November 2009.
Situation in Kenya, PTC II, Decision Pursuant to Article 15 of the Rome Statute on the Authorization of an Investigation into the Situation in the Republic of Kenya, 31 March 2010.
Situation in Kenya, PTC II, Order to the Victims Participation and Reparation Section Concerning Victims' Representations Pursuant to Article 15(3) of the Statute, 10 December 2009.
Situation in Kenya, Registrar, Corrigendum to the Report on Victims' Representations and Annexes 1 and 5, 29 March 2010.
Situation in Kenya, Reply on Behalf of the Government of Kenya to the Responses of the Prosecutor, Defense and OPCV to the Government's Application Pursuant to Article 19 of the Rome Statute, 13 May 2011.
Situation in Kenya, Trial Chamber III, Decision on the Second Request for Assistance Submitted on Behalf of the Government of the Republic of Kenya Pursuant to Article 93(10) of the Statute and Rule 194 of the Rules of Procedure and Evidence, 12 July 2012.
Situation in the CAR I, OTP, Prosecution's Report Pursuant to Pre-Trial Chamber Ill's 30 November 2006 Decision Requesting Information on the Status of the Preliminary Examination of the Situation in the Central African Republic, 15 December 2006.
Situation in the DRC, ICC, Appeals Chamber, Judgment on Victim Participation in the Investigation Stage of the Proceedings in the Appeal of the OPCD Against the Decision of Pre-Trial Chamber I of 7 December 2007 and in the Appeals of the OPCD and the Prosecutor Against the Decision of Pre-Trial Chamber I of 24 December 2007, 19 December 2008.

Situation in the DRC, ICC, PTC I, Decision on the Applications for Participation in the Proceedings of VPRS 1, VPRS 2, VPRS 3, VPRS 4, VPRS 5 and VPRS 6, 17 January 2006.

Situation in the DRC, ICC, PTC I, Decision Requesting Clarification on the Prosecutor's Application under Article 58, 6 September 2010.

Situation in the DRC, Judge Pikis Separate and Partly Dissenting Opinion, Judgment on the Prosecutor's Appeal Against the Decision of Pre-Trial Chamber I Entitled Decision on the Prosecutor's Application for Warrants of Arrest, Article 58, 13 July 2006.

Situation in the DRC, Presidency, Decision Assigning the Situation in the Congo to Pre-Trial Chamber I, 5 July 2004.

Situation in the DRC, Request Submitted pursuant to Rule 103(1) of the Rules of Procedure and Evidence for Leave to Participate as Amicus Curiae with Confidential Annex 2, 10 November 2006.

Situation in Uganda, ICC, Presidency, Decision Assigning the Situation in Uganda to Pre-Trial Chamber II, 5 July 2004, Annexed Letter.

Situation in Uganda, PTC II, Decision on Victims' Applications for Participation a/0010/06, a/0064/06 to a/0070/06, a/0081/06 to a/0104/06 and a/0111/06 to a/0127/06, 10 August 2007.

Situation on Registered Vessel of the Comoros, Appeals Chamber, Decision on the Admissibility of the Prosecutor's Appeal Against the Decision on the Request of the Union of the Comoros to Review the Prosecutor's Decision not to Initiate an Investigation, 6 November 2015.

Situation on Registered Vessel of the Comoros, PTC I, Partly Dissenting Opinion of Judge Peter Kovacs, 16 July 2015.

Situation on Registered Vessel on the Comoros, ICC, Referral under Articles 14 and 12(2)(a) of the Rome Statute Arising from the 31 May 2010 Gaza Freedom Flotilla Situation, 14 May 2013.

Situation on Registered Vessels of Comoros, Application for Review Pursuant to Article 53(3)(a) of the Prosecutor's Decision of 6 November 2014 not to Initiate an Investigation in the Situation, 29 January 2015.

Situation on Registered Vessels of the Union of the Comoros, Appeals Chamber, Judgment on the Prosecutor's Application for Extraordinary Review of Pre-Trial Chamber I's 31 March 2006 Decision Denying Leave to Appeal, 13 July 2006.

Situation on Registered Vessels of the Union of the Comoros, PTC I, Decision on the Request of the Union of the Comoros to review the Prosecutor's Decision not to Initiate an Investigation, 16 July 2015.

Sylvestre Mudacumura case, PTC II, Decision on the Prosecutor's Application under Article 58, 13 July 2012.

OTP DOCUMENTS

OTP, Annex to the Paper on Some Policy Issues before the Office of the Prosecutor: Referrals and Communications, 2003.

OTP, Background Situation in the Central African Republic, 22 May 2007.

OTP, First Report of the Prosecutor of the ICC to the UN Security Council Pursuant to UNSCR 1970 (2011), 4 May 2011.

OTP, First Report of the Prosecutor of the International Criminal Court, Mr. Moreno-Ocampo, to the Security Council, 29 June 2005.

OTP, Paper on Some Policy Issues before the Office of the Prosecutor, September 2003.

OTP, Policy Paper on Case Selection and Prioritization, 15 September 2016.

OTP, Policy Paper on Children, November 2016.

OTP, Policy Paper on Preliminary Examinations, 2 November 2013.

OTP, Policy Paper on Sexual and Gender-Based Crimes, June 2014.

OTP, Policy paper on Victims' Participation, 12 April 2010.

OTP, Prosecutorial Strategy (2009-2012), 1 February 2010.

OTP, Report of the Prosecutor of the ICC, Mr. Moreno-Ocampo to the Second Assembly of States Parties to the Rome Statute of the International Criminal Court, 8 September 2003.

OTP, Report on the Activities Performed During the First Three Years (June 2003-June 2006).

OTP, Report on the Preliminary Examination Activities (2013).

OTP, Report on the Preliminary Examination Activities (2014).

OTP, Report on the Preliminary Examination Activities (2015).

OTP, Report on the Preliminary Examination Activities (2016).

OTP, Response to Communications Received concerning Iraq, 9 February 2006.

OTP, Response to Communications Received concerning Venezuela, 9 February 2006.

OTP, Situation in Columbia, Interim Report, November 2012.

OTP, Situation in Mali, Article 53(1) Report. 16 January 2013.

OTP, Situation in the CAR II, Article 53(1) Report, 24 September 2014.

OTP, Situation on Registered Vessels of Comoros, Greece and Cambodia: Article 53(1) Report, 6 November 2014.

OTP, Statement of the Prosecutor of the International Criminal Court, Fatou Bensouda, on Concluding the Preliminary Examination of the Situation Referred by the Union of Comoros.

OTP, Statement of the Prosecutor of the International Criminal Court on the Alleged Crimes Committed by ISIS, 8 April 2015.

OTP, Strategic Plan (2016–2018), July 2015.

OTP, Strategic Plan (June 2012–2015), 11 October 2013.

OTP, Twelfth Report of the Prosecutor of the International Criminal Court to the United Nations Security Council pursuant to UNSCR 1970 (2011), November 2016.

ABOUT THE AUTHOR

Mohammad Hadi Zakerhossein holds a master in criminal law from Tehran University. He conducted his PhD research at Tilburg University and published, inter alia, in renowned international journals, including the International Criminal Law Review.

School of Human Rights Research Series

The School of Human Rights Research is a joint effort by human rights researchers in the Netherlands. Its central research theme is the nature and meaning of international standards in the field of human rights, their application and promotion in the national legal order, their interplay with national standards, and the international supervision of such application. The School of Human Rights Research Series only includes English titles that contribute to a better understanding of the different aspects of human rights.

For previous volumes in the series, please visit http://shr.intersentia.com.

Published titles within the Series:

69. Stefanie Jansen-Wilhelm, *Accepting Assistance in the Aftermath of Disasters* ISBN 978-1-78068-329-4
70. Helen Beckmann-Hamzei, *The Child in ICC Proceedings* ISBN 978-1-78068-339-3
71. Karel De Meester, *The Investigation Phase in International Criminal Procedure: In Search of Common Rules* ISBN 978-17-806-8305-8
72. Nelleke Koffeman, *Morally Sensitive Issues and Cross-Border Movement in the EU* ISBN 978-1-78068-349-2
73. Roland Moerland, *The Killing of Death* ISBN 978-1-78068-351-5
74. Andrea Broderick, *The Long and Winding Road to Disability Equality and Inclusion* ISBN 978-1-78068-358-4
75. Christina Peristeridou, *The Principle of Legality in European Criminal Law* ISBN 978-1-78068-357-7
76. Emilie Kuijtk, *Humanitarian Assistance and State Sovereignty in International Law* ISBN 978-1-78068-366-9
77. Lize R. Glas *The Theory, Potential and Practice of Procedural Dialogue in the European Convention on Human Rights System* ISBN 978-1-78068-375-1
78. Paulien de Morree, *Rights and Wrongs under the ECHR* ISBN 978-1-78068-418-5
79. Malu Beijer, *The Limits of Fundamental Rights Protection by the EU* ISBN 978-1-78068-455-0
80. Marie Elske Gispen, *Human Rights and Drug Control* ISBN 978-1-78068-454-3
81. Bart van der Sloot, *Privacy as Virtue: Moving Beyond the Individual in the Age of Big Data* ISBN 978-1-78068-505-2

www.ingramcontent.com/pod-product-compliance
Ingram Content Group UK Ltd.
Pitfield, Milton Keynes, MK11 3LW, UK
UKHW051919100926
8556IPUK00021B/1252

9 781780 686189